When the Old Left Was Young

WHEN THE OLD LEFT WAS YOUNG

Student Radicals and America's First Mass Student Movement, 1929–1941

ROBERT COHEN

New York   Oxford
OXFORD UNIVERSITY PRESS

Oxford University Press

Oxford   New York
Athens   Auckland   Bangkok   Bogota   Bombay
Buenos Aires   Calcutta   Cape Town   Dar es Salaam
Delhi   Florence   Hong Kong   Istanbul   Karachi
Kuala Lumpur   Madras   Madrid   Melbourne
Mexico City   Nairobi   Paris   Singapore
Taipei   Tokyo   Toronto

and associated companies in
Berlin   Ibadan

Copyright © 1993 by Robert Cohen

Published by Oxford University Press, Inc.,
198 Madison Avenue, New York, New York 10016

First issued as an Oxford University Press paperback, 1997

Oxford is a registered trademark of Oxford University Press

Library of Congress Cataloging-in-Publication Data
Cohen, Robert.
When the old left was young:
student radicals and America's first mass student protest movement,
1929–1941 / Robert Cohen.
p.   cm.   Includes bibliographical references and index.
ISBN 0-19-506099-7
ISBN 0-19-511136-2 (pbk.)
1. Student movements—United States—History—20th century.
2. College students—United States—Political activity—History—20th century.
3. Depressions—1929—United States—History.
I. Title.
LA229.C62   1993   378.1'981—dc20   92-22733

9 8 7 6 5 4 3 2 1

Printed in the United States of America
on acid-free paper

To my parents,
Marvin and Shirley Cohen
and to the memory of my grandparents,
Ben and Rose Cohen,
Irving and Florence Balas

Acknowledgments

This study began as a dissertation in the UC Berkeley history department. I owe a great debt to my dissertation chair, Diane Shaver Clemens, for her encouragement, advice, and willingness to share her knowledge of international relations during the Age of Roosevelt. Diane's commitment to her students, to her scholarship, and to a more democratic university have been inspirational. Her friendship and guidance made my dissertation work more enjoyable than I would have thought possible. Leon Litwack offered helpful criticism, which convinced me to broaden the scope of the study. I am also grateful to Leon for emphasizing the literary possibilities of historical writing and insisting that historians write for the public rather than just for the academy or themselves. Michael Rogin's comments on several drafts of this study were invaluable, as was his encouragement to look at the Old Left critically but empathetically. My understanding of the American Left also has been enhanced by discussions with Candace Falk and Richard Boyden. I am indebted to Candace for providing me with the opportunity to work on the Emma Goldman Papers Project while completing this study. Goldman's brilliant writings on the Spanish Civil War influenced my own thinking, as did her radical critique of Stalinism. My thanks to James Kettner for being so generous with his time and advice.

My interest in the political history of the American university originated in an undergraduate seminar at SUNY Buffalo taught by Jesse Lemisch. Jesse's pioneering scholarship in this area served as a model for my own work, and I am grateful for his friendship, support, and for his criticism of parts of the manuscript. My thanks go as well to another of my former teachers at Buffalo, Philip Altbach in the School of Education, whose publications have helped make the study of American student politics an exciting field. Athan Theoharis of Marquette University opened up a valuable source for this study by encouraging me to obtain the FBI documents on the student movement.

The Berkeley campus itself is a great teacher about student politics. I learned much about the dynamics of student protest from my former colleagues on the *Daily Californian*—including David Pickell, Will Miner, Colleen Lye, Leigh Anne Jones, and Drew Digby—and from a whole generation of fellow activists in the Association of Graduate Student Employees, Berkeley's divestment movement, and the Graduate Assembly.

This study could not have been completed without the resources of many archives and libraries and the assistance of their staffs. I am especially grateful to Elizabeth Denier and the rest of the staff at the FDR Library in Hyde Park, New York, for promptly processing the Joseph P. Lash Papers, and making accessible this rich collection of documents on the American student movement of the 1930s. My thanks to the archivists at the Swarthmore College Peace Collection, the Tamiment Institute Library at NYU, the New York Public Library and its Schomburg Center for Research in Black Culture, the YWCA National Board Archives in New York, the American Civil Liberties Union Archives at Princeton University, and the National Archives in Washington, D.C. I am also indebted to the Carlson Library at the University of Toledo and the Tamiment Institute Library at NYU for allowing me to use microfilmed copies of Duke University's collection of the Socialist Party of America Papers.

Since American college campuses constituted the student movement's base, constituency and political environment, I found it necessary to undertake extensive research on individual campuses. This research was greatly expedited by the talented archivists and fine archival collections of many campuses. I owe a special debt to City College of New York archivist Barbara Dunlap for her help in tracking down materials on that campus's student protesters and administration. J. R. K. Kantor and his successor as University of California archivist, William Roberts, as well as other staff members at the Bancroft Library, were of great assistance in uncovering sources on UC Berkeley and UCLA. My thanks to the archival staffs at Barnard College, Brooklyn College, Columbia University's Columbiana Collection and Low Library, the Regenstein Special Collections Department of the University of Chicago, Emory University, Fisk University, Harvard University, Howard University, Hunter College, the University of Michigan and its Labadie Collection, the State University of New York at Buffalo, Oberlin College, the Ohio Historical Society, the Southern Historical Collection at the University of North Carolina, Chapel Hill, the University of Texas, the University of Toledo, UCLA, Vassar College, the University of Virginia, the University of Wisconsin, and the Wisconsin Historical Society. The libraries of Dartmouth College, the University of Illinois, the University of Kansas, the University of Kentucky, Marshall University, and Ohio State University were generous in lending me their student publications. My thanks to the interlibrary loan departments at UC Berkeley's Doe Library and the University of Toledo's Carlson Library for obliging me in what I am sure seemed an unending stream of requests for student and radical publications from across the United States.

I was very fortunate that former activists and leaders from the student movement allowed me to interview them. Their memories offered an important supplement to the written record. Celeste Strack Kaplan, Monroe Sweetland, the late F. Palmer Weber, and the late Larry Rogin not only took time to talk with me, but also assisted me in contacting other movement veterans. I am grateful to the following Depression era alumni for sharing with me their memories of the student movement: Riva Stocker Aaron, Dorothy Burnham, Joseph Clark, Kenneth B. Clark, Homer Coke, Richard Criley, Hal Draper, Theodore Draper, Judah Drob, Mary Felton Drob, Ishmael Flory, Elizabeth Pope Franklin, Marge Frantz, Emanuel Geltman, Serril Gerber, Harold Goldstein, Max Gordon, Gil Green, Robert Hall, Albert Herling, John Herling, Esther Cooper Jackson, James E. Jackson, the late Joseph P. Lash, Toni Locke, Leonard Lurie, Harry Magdoff, William Mandel, Henry May, the late Jack McMichael, the late William Parry, Paul Porter, Harry Ring, Shura Kamenir Saul, Morris Schappes, Judith Solomon, Nathan Solomon, Lil Sweetland, George Watt, the late James Wechsler, Vivian Weinstein, Max Weiss, Leon Wofsy, and Molly Yard. Toni Locke, Henry May, and Max Gordon were generous in providing me with documents from their student activist days. My knowledge of the movement was also enhanced by discussions at the American Student Union's 50th anniversary reunion, held in Long Beach, California, and organized with great skill by Leo Rifkin.

The initial research for this study was made possible by funding from UC Berkeley's Humanities Research Fellowship and the History department's Eugene McCormac and Max Farrand Fellowships. My final research trips were funded by grants from the University of Toledo and the Toledo Humanities Institute. Georgian College in Orillia, Ontario, generously made available an office in which to begin revising the manuscript. My thanks to Richard Allen, Tiffany Patterson, Michael Kay, Frederico and Pura Arcos, Lorin Cary, Carol Menning, William Hoover, Roger Ray, Michael Meranze, Mary Odem, and Janice Hughes for their friendship and support. I hope that Gary and Wanda Davis know how much I appreciate all their help over the years and their role in making my southern California research trips so pleasurable. Thanks to all my friends, relatives and friends of friends who housed me during my low budget research trips through the Midwest and South and to the East Coast. I am grateful to Judith Preissle, Guy Larkins and the University of Georgia's department of Social Science Education for providing a congenial environment in which to complete this work.

I am indebted to Vivian McLaughlin for skillful copy-editing of the typescript. My thanks to Sheldon Meyer for his patience and understanding, which enabled me to delay the completion of the manuscript until I had made use of essential sources recently released in the Lash Papers. Elizabeth Bryan, Joan Stroer, and David Pickell provided valuable assistance with the final proofreading.

Many Americans of my generation learned their first lessons about the Great Depression not from history books, but from their parents. I grew up with my father's stories of the hard times he and his brothers endured as children in a Brooklyn ghetto during the 1930s. I want to thank him for sharing those stories and sparking my interest in Depression America. My thanks to my mother and my sister Myra for encouraging me to complete this study, and to the first student rebels I ever met, my sister Judith and my brother Steven. Final revisions of this book were made at Jack and Pat Hyman's cottage off of Lake Couchiching, and I thank them for both that idyllic Canadian refuge and their love and support.

The historian to whom I owe the most is my wife, Rebecca Hyman. Ever since our days as Berkeley graduate students, Rebecca has encouraged me in this study and helped me retain my enthusiasm for both historical scholarship and more important things. Her intellectual comradeship and love have made all the difference. And to Daniel Langston, the youngest rebel in our family, thanks for coming along at just the right moment.

Athens, Georgia
December 1992   R. C.

Contents

Introduction

> It was a time when frats, like the football team, were losing their glamor. . . . Instead my generation thirsted for another kind of action, and we took great pleasure in the sit-down strikes that burst loose in Flint and Detroit. . . . We saw a new world coming every third morning. . . . When I think of the library I think of the sound of a stump speaker on the lawn outside because so many times I looked up from what I was reading to try to hear what issue they were debating now. The place was full of speeches, meetings and leaflets. It was jumping with issues.
>
> Playwright Arthur Miller, Michigan '38, "The University of Michigan," *Holiday Magazine* (December 1953), 70.

The student rebels of the Depression era rank among the most effective radical organizers in the history of American student politics. They built a large and influential student protest movement, organized America's first national student strikes, and shaped political discourse on campus for the better part of a decade. No college generation before them and only the New Left insurgents of the 1960s after them ever had as much impact on student politics in twentieth-century America.

The American student movement of the 1930s emerged as students groped for solutions to the double barreled crisis which confronted their generation: the Great Depression and the growing rift in international relations that ultimately led to World War II. In contrast to the mass youth movements of Nazi Germany and Fascist Italy, the American student movement did not exploit the crises of the Depression decade to appeal to the worst instincts of the young. National chauvinism, racism, and militarism—hallmarks of these European movements of the Right—were anathema to the leftist organizers who launched and led the American student movement. Student activists in the United States used the crisis atmosphere of their time for much more humane ends, fanning their classmates' egalitarian idealism and revulsion for war and fascism. The American student movement proved attractive to many young men and women because, as political scientist and former 1930s student activist John P. Roche recalled, it offered them the opportunity to transform the

United States from "a nation sunk in poverty and depression, racked by racial and religious discrimination and seemingly on 'The Road to War' . . . to a society governed by the principles of economic and political justice and human equality, living in a peaceful world."[1]

No protest movement in Depression America was more unexpected than the student movement, nor more symbolic of the transformation from the reactionary politics of the 1920s to the progressive politics of the 1930s. In the decade preceding the Great Depression, college students had represented one of America's most staunchly Republican constituencies. Student culture in that prosperous decade had been elitist and WASP-dominated; its championship of selfish materialism calls to mind the YUPPIE culture of the Reagan era, with its "Don't Trust Anyone Under $30,000" mentality. The student movement of the 1930s—led by a diverse coalition of communists, socialists, liberals, pacifists, and Trotskyists—worked along with the Depression itself to challenge the bourgeois collegiate culture inherited from the 1920s. The movement encouraged students to identify with the working class rather than the upper class, to value racial and ethnic diversity instead of exclusivity, and to work for progressive social change. This activism helped to ensure that by 1936 Republican dominance of national student politics had gone the way of the raccoon coat and the other relics of the 1920s campus world.

Along with the labor movement and other progressive insurgencies of Depression America, the student movement contributed to the formation of a national consensus on behalf of a more activist and humane federal government and a more caring society. The student movement helped introduce and popularize the idea that poverty should not force any Americans to drop out of school, and that Washington should ensure this by providing direct federal aid to students. Often the movement's vision for governmental assistance to the underprivileged went well beyond the New Deal, as when the students called for federal dollars to aid *all* needy youths—rather than the small percentage actually receiving aid from New Deal agencies. Nonetheless, the generous idealism which motivated such demands attracted Eleanor Roosevelt, the New Deal's most forceful advocate for youth, and led her to befriend and cooperate with the movement's leaders. Mrs. Roosevelt sensed that whether these young activists attacked the New Deal for doing too little for youth or rallied to save the New Deal youth programs from right wing budget-cutters, the students were kindred spirits because they shared her desire for an unprecedented federal effort to rescue the Depression's young victims.

Unlike the other movements for social change in Depression America, the student movement devoted as much attention to foreign policy as to domestic issues. Students grappled with isolationism more intensively and visibly than any other group in Depression America, knowing that their generation would be called to fight the next war. The movement's largest national demonstrations were anti-war and anti-fascist strikes aimed at staving off world war. Some of the movement's most dedicated activists not only marched for this cause, but died for it on the battlefields of Spain; fighting valiantly but futilely to stop the spread of fascism before it engulfed all of Europe.

Although international crises drew their attention overseas, the student rebels of the Depression generation also devoted considerable energy to battling for change in their own backyard: within the college gates. Recognizing that suppression of student dissent could jeopardize the entire student movement, these activists sought to advance the cause of free speech on campus. Scholars examining the history of academic freedom in this era have tended to focus upon the faculty.[2] But, in fact, students waged the largest and most effective struggles for political liberty on campus in Depression America.

The student movement championed a concept of student political rights which was much more expansive and modern than that held by many university administrators during the early 1930s. College presidents and deans clung to *(in loco parentis)* disciplinary traditions inherited from the nineteenth century, which gave them veto power over student political expression. They claimed the authority to gag student rebels, much as parents had the authority to silence rowdy children. Student activists rejected this collegiate oversight, insisting that they were not errant children, but rather citizens with First Amendment rights. The students' position was decades ahead of its time, and would not be adopted by the Supreme Court until 1969, when it ruled (in *Tinker v. Des Moines Independent Community School District*) that students do not "shed . . . their constitutional rights . . . at the school house gates."[3] The chasm between student radicalism and administration paternalism concerning student political rights led to a series of campus free speech fights during the early 1930s. Movement organizers risked suspension, expulsion, and arrest to secure free speech rights which students today take for granted.

The conflict over free speech on college campuses in Depression America also contained a hidden history, one of political surveillance, which archival research and documents obtained under the Freedom of Information Act have only recently begun to uncover. Though the student protests of the Depression era were almost always non-violent and lawful, anti-radical administrators, nonetheless, turned over to the Federal Bureau of Investigation information on their activist students, resulting in the opening of FBI files on literally thousands of these students. The complicity of college presidents and deans with the FBI in this trampling of student civil liberty compromised the very ideal of the university as a center of free intellectual discourse and pursuit of truth. The student radical who engaged too publicly in such discourse might very well end up with an FBI file, courtesy of her or his local college administrator. This informing also represented a violation of the trust which was supposed to exist between students and college officials—as administrators gave the FBI *confidential* data regarding the political affiliations, activities, and ideas of student activists. Indeed, unlike the physician, lawyer, or psychiatrist, the college administrator of the Depression era seemed to lack a strong professional ethic regarding confidentiality, at least with regard to the records of radical students.[4]

The FBI's spying on the student movement was, of course, connected to allegations that the student movement was communist-dominated. Though other leftist and liberal groups had a significant impact on the movement, no group played a larger or more decisive role in the student movement's leadership than the communists. Many of the most influential national officers in Depression America's two largest student movement organizations—the American Student Union and the American Youth Congress—were either in or close to the Communist Party or Young Communist League. Communists achieved a degree of influence in American student politics far superior to their meager impact on the larger national polity. Not even in the labor movement, where communists had an impressive presence during the 1930s, could communist influence compare with what it was in the student movement.

Historians of American Communism have been locked in a bitter debate about the character of communist-led movements. Theodore Draper and other traditional anti-communist historians judge such movements harshly, focusing on their flaws, particularly the Russia-centered mind-set of the communists who led these movements. A newer school of historians, led by Maurice Isserman, takes issue with Draper. These anti-anti-communist historians stress the strengths of communist-led movements in the U.S. and argue that communists succeeded in building mass movements because they were more responsive to American political realities than to Comintern dictation.[5]

During the student movement's early stages, communist behavior in the movement had some of the characteristics suggested in Isserman's work on the Communist Party; it was innovative, self-directed, and centered on American political realities. But in the final and self-destructive stage of the movement, these qualities vanished and communist student leaders acted in as Russia-centered and dogmatic a manner as Draper might predict. The shift came because the Nazi-Soviet Pact and the new imperatives of Soviet foreign policy forced communist students to chose between their loyalty to Stalin and their loyalty to the anti-fascist movement they had helped to build on American campuses; they opted for Stalin, and in so doing destroyed the student movement.

The student movement's history is clearly too complex to be captured by either one-sided indictments or defenses of the communist past. Communists had great strengths as political organizers and worked tirelessly to convert American campuses from bastions of elitism and apathy to centers of egalitarianism and activism. But these radicals also had grave weaknesses—the worst of which was their eagerness to defend the indefensible when it came to Stalin and his cruelties. This is what Eleanor Roosevelt biographer and former American Student Union leader Joseph

P. Lash meant when, in looking back upon the student movement, he acknowledged: "We were fearless paladins of truth when it came to the world outside the left; we were little better than apologists when it came to the left itself." [6]

As democratic as the student movement was in its demands for a more egalitarian America, internally the movement suffered from some quite undemocratic tendencies. The communists, and at times their socialist and Trotskyist counterparts, displayed a penchant for vanguardism, disingenuousness, and secrecy in the way they wielded power in the student movement's leading organizations. Such deficiencies were especially common among the communists, since they were the most numerous and powerful of the student movement's leaders, as well as the most insensitive to questions concerning democratic process. The communists also refused to be open about the links between their political positions—particularly those on foreign policy—and Soviet policy. In some cases, communists, including several national leaders of the movement, concealed their Party ties even from fellow activists and allies of the movement.

To set the historical record straight, I have tried to be as open about these flaws in the movement as I have been about the movement's more positive accomplishments. This has not been easy, because the task of writing an open and honest history of communist-led movements involves some troubling ethical problems. The most vexing of these problems concerns the conflicting claims of individual privacy and historical accuracy. If a movement leader was secretly a communist, should the historian preserve or end that secrecy? This question is complicated by the fact that during the Cold War era certain individuals were persecuted for real or imagined communist affiliations. But with the Cold War over and the threat of anti-communist political persecution as much in the past as the Berlin Wall, there is no longer a risk that the historian's candor will lead to any such persecution. Thus where it has been essential to the movement's history, I have indicated the affiliations of movement leaders—even those that chose not to disclose them—during the Depression era.

The student movement of the Depression era should be remembered, however, as more than a history of the communists who helped lead it. The majority of rank and filers who joined the movement's organizations and marched in its demonstrations were not communists. And since their presence, as much as anything the communists did, made the student movement so significant a force in American life, this must be their history too. In a very critical sense, these non-communist rank and filers were even more important than the communists who helped lead the movement. There could be a viable student movement only so long as the movement's leftist leaders responded to the crises of their decade in a manner which non-communists regarded as logical and appealing. When these leaders lost touch with the movement's non-communist majority—as they did following the Nazi-Soviet Pact—the communists became as powerless as generals without an army, and like old soldiers they (and the movement) soon faded away.

At its peak in the late 1930s, the student movement's demonstrations involved hundreds of thousands of students annually—by some estimates, almost half of America's entire undergraduate population. The size of this movement makes it impossible to provide a detailed account of student political campaigns on all of the nation's college campuses. When portraying such a movement, it is necessary to be selective. But while selective, I have not been arbitrary. The student movement had major battlegrounds, events, and ideals that its participants recognized, so that in setting the narrative I have sought to be faithful to the movement's own sense of itself—particularly with regard to the order and importance of events.

The student movement's history has been neglected by political historians of the Great Depression. Taken together, in fact, three of the best and most widely read political histories of the United States during the Depression decade (including Arthur Schlesinger Jr.'s multi-volume *Age of Roosevelt*) devote less than a page to this era's student movement. In the half-century that has passed since the death of the student movement, historians have published only two slim monographs and a handful of articles and chapters about that movement.[7]

Having traveled across the country researching a student movement that even many archivists and historians had never heard of, I naturally pondered the reasons for this historical amnesia. Was it a legacy of McCarthyism? By working to make pariahs out of communists and ex-communists, Senator Joseph McCarthy and other congressional red probers did make it difficult for historians to write a full or fair-minded history of communist-led movements. This is almost certainly why the only significant account of the student movement published by a historian during the 1950s was a single chapter in a volume of the strongly anti-communist Fund for the Republic series on communist influence in American life, which belittled and castigated the student movement at every turn.[8] But by far the greatest harm that McCarthyism did to the historical record was to prod former leaders of the student movement—in fear of political persecution—to destroy some of the movement's main organizational files and correspondence.[9]

Damaging as it was, however, McCarthyism was not alone responsible for the historians' neglect of the student movement. After all, McCarthyism eventually collapsed, and consequently movement veterans could feel increasingly free to discuss their days as student activists. In fact, over the past few decades it has been these movement veterans—through their memoirs—rather than professional historians who have written the most about the Depression era student movement. Unfortunately, the pattern of neglect by historians continued.[10]

This neglect seems to be connected to the obvious fact that the Depression era campus insurgency was a movement of the young. Historians, as a middle-aged group, tend not—outside of those working on the era of the 1960s—to take youths seriously enough to study their ideas or the history of student politics. Few history departments have anyone specializing in the history of youth and student politics. Historians sometimes act as if only presidents, senators and other "adults" can make political history. I recall only too well job interviews with fellow historians who seemed to think my topic a strange outgrowth of the Berkeley political atmosphere in which I wrote my dissertation. "What kind of history is that?" "What does that have to do with political history?" The tone of such queries, as much as the words themselves, gave more than a hint of bias against historical studies of youth and student protest.

Such responses and the historiographical neglect of the student movement seem more understandable when we consider the way Americans remember the 1930s. The first images which come to mind from that decade are not student protests, but rather breadlines and Hoovervilles wrought by the Great Depression. Next come the images of a self-assured Franklin Roosevelt attempting to end the economic crisis through his New Deal programs. We also remember the 1930s as a decade in which a dizzying array of protest movements—including the union organizing drives and sit-down strikes, the Townsend, Share Our Wealth, and unemployed movements, the Farm-Labor insurgency, the Commonwealth Federation, and the End Poverty in California campaign—arose and agitated to change America. With all of these adult-led movements surging, FDR governing, and the Communist Party itself growing, youth and student rebellion could not always be at center stage. This contrasted with the New Left student movement of the 1960s, which was born in the spotlight. The New Left did not have to compete for attention, since it emerged at a time when the adult Left—hobbled by the Cold War and McCarthyism—and the labor movement—weakened by bureaucratization and corruption—were only shadows of their former selves. Given how much other significant protest activity and political change existed in Depression America, the 1930s could never be seen, as the 1960s sometimes are, as a decade dominated by youth protest. It is little wonder, then, that the Depression era student movement has received so little historical attention.

I hope this study will encourage historians and the public to rediscover this lost generation of student rebels. These young activists questioned the inequities and irrationalities of American capitalism at a time when such questioning was sorely needed. Their ambitious agenda for social change at times seemed unrealistic to more moderate leaders, such as President Roosevelt—who admonished them not to "seek or expect Utopia overnight."[11] But FDR proved no more successful than the students in devising steps to end the Depression or prevent war. Moreover, whatever its failures in fulfilling its agenda, the student movement made a profound difference to the college generation it served. "There is no question," recalled historian Henry May, who was a student activist at Berkeley and Harvard in the 1930s,

> that the movement broadened our education. Everything that was happening—in Spain and Ethiopia and Detroit, in American politics, in literature and the arts—was important and relevant. Each of us was a responsible citizen of the world, with the duty of making up his mind, joining with others, taking action. Each person's decisions and actions would make a difference . . . in changing the world. This was more than a theory, it was a faith and a way of life. Even those who could never quite believe it all still remember its powerful attraction.[12]

This extraordinary sense of engagement, this "thirst to have a hand in the shaping of history"[13] enabled the Depression generation to build America's first mass student movement. And it distinguished these compassionate student activists from the politically apathetic and self-interested youths who dominated American campus life during most of this century.

Quotations are rendered as they appeared in the original documents, with a minimum of editorial insertions. To preserve the tone and style of the students' political discourse, I have avoided using the term "sic" where minor spelling or grammatical errors occur. I include (bracketed) corrective or explanatory material with the quotations only when this is absolutely necessary to make quotations comprehensible.

When the Old Left
Was Young

Chapter 1

Dancing on the Edge
of a Volcano

Though we graduate students expected the revolution very soon and planned to encourage it, we did not expect any help from the Berkeley undergraduates. Not that they would oppose—they would simply, as usual, be unaware that anything was happening. A singular accomplishment of American higher education, as one reflects on it, was the creation of a vast network of universities, public and private, which . . . caused no one any political embarrassment of any kind. In other countries they created trouble from time to time, but not here. A control system which subtly suggested that whatever the students most wanted to do—i.e., devote themselves to football, basketball, fraternities, college tradition, rallies, hell raising, a sentimental concern for the old alma mater and imaginative inebriation—was what they should do was basic to this peace. The alumni rightly applauded this control system and so, to an alarming extent, did the faculty. An occasional non-political riot was condoned and even admired; some deeper instinct suggested that it was a surrogate for something worse.

Economist John Kenneth Galbraith, memoir of Berkeley during the early Depression years. *There Was Light: Autobiography of a University, Berkeley, 1868–1968*, Irving Stone, ed. (New York, 1970), 28.

Herbert Hoover's America was a dismal place in 1931. The president had failed to end or even mitigate the economic crisis, which began with the stock market crash of 1929. Unemployment had spiraled out of control; the number of jobless Americans had soared from 429,000 in 1929 to more than nine million in 1931. The Hoover White House had undermined its credibility in 1929 and 1930 by erroneously predicting economic recovery. But by late summer 1931 even some of the president's closest congressional allies were glumly admitting that the end of the Depression was not in sight. Breadlines and shanty-towns—dubbed "Hoovervilles" to mock the impotent president—had spread across the nation, grim testimony to the hunger and homelessness wrought by the Great Depression. Municipalities and private charities could not keep pace with the need of millions of unemployed Americans for economic assistance. Relief workers, local officials, and liberals on Capitol Hill in August 1931 called for a special session of Congress to legislate aid for the unemployed; they warned that without federal relief dollars, the coming winter would bring widespread starvation.[1]

That same month, as their elders in Washington fretted over how to ready themselves for another year of Depression, students at the University of California at Berkeley also began to prepare for the coming year. But for Berkeley students that preparation did not include discussions of hunger, poverty, or other Depression-related problems. As the fall 1931 semester began, fraternities and football, sororities and parties, were the talk of the campus. In its opening editorial of the semester, the *Daily Californian,* Berkeley's student newspaper, gave advice to new students, making it sound as if their most serious problems would be chosing the proper Greek house and deciding whether to participate "in sports, in dramatics or publications." The editor also informed the freshmen that they were "fortunate to have a classmate in [football] coach Bill Ingram . . . [who will] bring back another 'Golden Era' for California athletics." Though focusing primarily on these apolitical concerns, the editorial did turn to the economy long enough to make the naive assertion that "the class of 1935 . . . is fortunate to be starting out in a year which promises prosperity . . . ."[2] In predicting prosperity, the editor closed his eyes not merely to the pessimistic national economic reports, but also to local developments. Only the previous day, San Francisco Mayor Angelo Rossi had sent an open letter to the White House suggesting that economic conditions would continue to deteriorate in the Bay Area. Rossi informed President Hoover that only federal aid could get San Francisco through the next winter because the city was overwhelmed by the task of feeding the swelling ranks of jobless San Franciscans.[3]

The upbeat and apolitical thinking of students on the Berkeley campus was not the least bit unusual for American undergraduates in the early Depression era. Most American college students seemed remarkably unconcerned about the national economic crisis during the first two years of the Great Depression. No student protests were held to demand work or relief for the unemployed. No anti-Hoover movement emerged on campus during these years, despite President Herbert Hoover's inept handling of the economy and his refusal to provide sufficient federal dollars to feed the hungry. Most college student newspapers slighted Depression-related news; they reported about fraternities and football much more avidly and often than they did about growing breadlines and Hoovervilles.[4]

The traditional social events of the nation's predominantly middle-class undergraduate population proceeded in 1929, 1930, and 1931 almost as if the Depression did not exist. This was especially true for the sorority and fraternity houses, whose activities generally set the tone for undergraduate life. Their social calendars suggest that at a time when the poor went hungry, the middle class went dancing. Though the Depression had slowed down the economy, it had yet to depress the party scene on campus. During a single weekend in October 1931, twenty-five Greek houses at the University of Wisconsin held parties; a similar level of party activity could be found on many campuses.[5]

Student parties during the early Depression years were every bit as lavish as their counterparts in the prosperous 1920s. At the University of Michigan, for example, the Pan-Hellenic Ball in November 1931 drew "more than 300 couples [who] danced to the music of Gene Austin and his Victor recording artists," a band which appeared weekly on a national NBC radio show. "Striking black and white programs in the form of miniature leather picture frames were distributed to the guests." In true high society style, the ball featured a "grand march" of the couples and a coterie of chaperones, including the president of the University and the dean of students. A less formal but equally lavish affair was thrown by a sorority at the University of Wisconsin in 1930; this party featured a fashion revue in which guests saw "dainty, gaily covered gowns . . . back-glittering rhinestones and twinkling slippers."[6] Such gala events were the collegiate norm.

Even in their rallies and riots, undergraduates revealed how far removed their world was from that of impoverished Americans. In 1930, the same year when the unemployed held hunger marches in dozens of cities, the biggest rallies on the nation's college campuses had nothing to do with the Depression. Political rallies and political violence were almost completely alien to undergraduates. The goals of collegiate rallies and riots ranged from cheering athletic heroes and razzing competing undergraduate groups to celebrating after exams. These gatherings all had one thing in common: they were totally apolitical events.

Harvard produced the largest student riot in the nation in 1930. This apolitical disturbance, which occurred on May 7, involved some 1500 undergraduates, and was so violent that it made the front page of the *New York Times*. The occasion for the violence was the conclusion of exam week. At 11:45 p.m. a student appeared outside a dormitory and sounded taps on a bugle, which served as a signal for a wild display of "high spirits." Students began hurling light bulbs out of their dormitory windows; then, over a thousand collegians poured out of the dormitories—some clad in pajamas, others half-dressed. A dozen policemen arrived, but they could not restore order, so the riot squad was called in. Firemen also appeared on the scene after students pulled a fire alarm. The students greeted them with bottles, fruit, and other missiles. The battle continued for over an hour and ended with one student arrested and two hospitalized.[7]

This same semester, Harvard's boisterous students provoked the nation's largest mass arrest of undergraduates during the early 1930s. Police jailed more than 200 Harvard students in a riot which followed a Harvard hockey team victory in February 1930. Major apolitical riots in this period resulted in the arrest of students on other campuses. There were 156 such arrests at the University of Pennsylvania, 150 at Albion College in Michigan, 46 at the City College of New York, 12 at Yale, and 7 at the University of Wisconsin.[8]

Student violence during the first two years of the Great Depression sometimes promoted class consciousness, but not the type of class consciousness about which Karl Marx wrote. This violence was between different *academic* classes: freshmen against sophomores, juniors against seniors. Moreover, this type of conflict represented an annual collegiate ritual on many campuses (which should not be surprising considering that this was an age when the youth culture of the campuses often required freshmen to wear beanies). Columbia students, for instance, became riotous during the college's Freshman Class Banquet, held in a posh restaurant at Hastings-on-Hudson in April 1930. More than a hundred Columbia freshmen had just finished the banquet's second course when several dozen sophomores invaded the restaurant and assaulted them. A wild melée ensued, with fists flying, furniture overturning, and glass shattering. Only the arrival of state troopers prevented the complete destruction of the restaurant. Outraged that they had chosen his restaurant as the site for their freshman-sophomore riot, the proprietor filed lawsuits demanding over $50,000 in damages from the students.[9]

Such disturbances not only reflected the sophomoric character of undergraduate culture, but also attested that where students were prone to excess, it was excess in pursuit of trivial collegiate rivalries. Where students were willing to defy the law, it was a defiance almost always barren of political meaning or thought. Though the riots occurred in the early 1930s, these events were the product of a much older pattern of juvenile undergraduate behavior. The disturbances were part of a male-dominated tradition of collegiate rowdiness, which had been a hallmark of collegiate life for generations. As one education reporter explained in 1931, student riots often erupted "at a particular time and place because they have always occurred at a particular time and place. They are traditional. The class of 1933 must riot because the classes of 1923, 1903, and 1893 did the same thing."[10]

Of all the extracurricular activities which preoccupied undergraduates none was more prominent than intercollegiate football. At coeducational and men's colleges, these athletic contests were the occasions for the year's largest and most celebrated gatherings of undergraduates. The huge crowds at the stadiums on Saturdays, which on many campuses included tens of thousands of students and alumni, were only one component of collegiate footballmania. Rallies, parties, yell leader contests, bonfires, and other ritualized expressions of support gave football a pervasive presence on campus—so much so that critics called the sport "King Football." And since the football season coincided with the beginning of the academic year, it helped introduce students to one another in an apolitical atmosphere; it siphoned off energy that might otherwise have gone into more serious (perhaps even political) activities.[11]

The frenetic campus activity that accompanied big college football rivalries almost defies belief. At the University of Kansas in November 1930, for instance, students planned an entire day of "rallies, speeches and general demonstrations . . . to arouse pep for the annual Missouri-Kansas game." School mascot "Dock Yak" was set "to come to the University and do his bit toward instilling pep in the student body by dispensing his potent sugar-coated pills." The Kansas student government thought these activities so important that its leaders asked the chancellor of the University to cancel classes for the day—a request he turned down. In the past, Kansas's exuberant day of football rallies had ended in damage to property and disruption of class sessions. This time the pre-game festivities mocked Depression America's homeless: the title students chose for this day of fun and athletic "boosterism" was "Hobo Day." Treating the hobo as a quaint and comical figure, rather than as a somber symbol of the economic crisis, the Hobo Day events on campus featured a contest for which "everyone is expected to come on the hill dressed in a costume fitting in with his idea of what the well-dressed hobo should wear." "Prizes" were to "be awarded for the best dressed hobo and hoboette."[12]

The apolitical character of undergraduate life from 1929 through 1931 had it critics on campus. A few liberal, radical, and intellectual students bemoaned the provincialism of their classmates. But no matter how trenchant these criticisms, the national student body paid them little heed. A case in point was the experience of Edward R. Murrow, the most prominent student critic of collegiate political apathy at the start of the 1930s. Murrow, who in these early Depression years served as the president of the National Student Federation (NSF)—America's association of college student governments—came into office chiding undergraduates for focusing so much of their time on "fraternities, football and fun." He hoped that during his presidency the NSF could awaken student interest in national and international problems. Toward this end, Murrow initiated a variety of NSF activities, including a radio news show, *University on the Air* on the Columbia Broadcasting System (CBS), aimed at a student audience.[13]

Although Murrow's broadcasts were historic because they began his connection with CBS and helped launch his stellar journalistic career, neither they nor any other NSF activity in the Hoover era had much national impact on undergraduates. The campuses remained politically inert. Murrow left office as he had entered it, criticizing the political ignorance of American undergraduates. His parting address to the national NSF convention at Toledo in December 1931 again took collegians to task for "their greatest sins . . . . : campus consciousness, political apathy, and smug complacency."[14]

If the apolitical character of undergraduates in the United States irritated such reform-minded Americans as Murrow, it absolutely astonished radical Europeans. Viewing American undergraduates in an international context, Harold Laski, a leftist British scholar, expressed shock at their unfamiliarity with American politics. After lecturing at Harvard, Yale, and the universities of Minnesota and North Carolina in 1931, Laski pronounced the American college student an "almost non-political animal [who] talks of American politics as though they were the remote affairs of a distant planet." Laski was so struck by this apolitical collegiate mind-set that he published a magazine article: "The Political Indifference of the American Undergraduate." He found that European college students were far superior to their American counterparts in both their understanding of politics and involvement in important political events.

> Everyone knows how great a part the student played in the emancipation of Russia and Spain. The contribution of the universities to the political life of England and France has been outstanding. . . . To the European observer few things are more startling than the contrast in this respect with America. . . . The idea that citizenship involves on his [the American student's] part an active interest in [political] affairs simply does not . . . occur to him.[15]

Laski observed that business rather than politics interested undergraduates. Political service seemed relatively unattractive to students because in their eyes politicians were corrupt, and an honest political career "rarely offers the spectacular career of industry." They thought that businessmen rather than politicians would shape American society. Laski concluded that the American undergraduate of 1931 "lacks a sense of the positive state because the predominance of the business man has given him no notion of its possibilities."[16]

There was nothing new about either Laski's discussion of the pro-business orientation of undergraduates or Murrow's complaints about collegiate political apathy. Though Murrow and Laski made their observations about undergraduates in 1931, these closely paralleled the criticisms of American students articulated by liberals and radicals in the 1920s. Laski's discussion of student adulation for capitalists was similar to Paul Blanshard's finding in 1926 that undergraduates "too often regard college as a back door to big business." Blanshard, an organizer for the League for Industrial Democracy (LID), a socialist-led educational organization, toured the nation's campuses repeatedly during the 1920s, but despaired of ever making an impact on undergraduates so long as "the diluted culture of salesmanship dominates undergraduate life." Norman Thomas, a colleague of Blanshard in the LID, shared his pessimism about the student political conscience. Thomas concluded in 1923 that most students were too avaricious to concern themselves with the flaws in the capitalist system. He found the undergraduate definition of success similar to that of the Chamber of Commerce. "The supreme god over all for most of our students is success measured by the usual standard of the credit rating one possesses and the kind of automobile one drives or in which one is driven."[17]

Much like Murrow in the early 1930s, Thomas during the 1920s was appalled that undergraduates preferred football, fraternities, and parties to serious political thought. Thomas blamed these student rituals for the intellectual shallowness and social conformity of undergraduates. He condemned the tendency of "fraternity houses to turn out a standardized product," which left students thinking, acting, and even dressing alike. Driving this point home, Thomas in 1923 told the story of a

> father who looked vainly for his son at Yale. Finally he went home in despair and telegraphed President Hadley: "Send home my son at once." The President replied: "Which is he?" To which the answer came: "Any one will do. They all look alike."[18]

The reason for the continuity in these complaints about undergraduates is that American students had changed remarkably little either politically or economically since the 1920s. The prevalent undergraduate style of life and thought from 1929 until 1932 was shaped less by the Great Depression than by both the values of 1920s America, and the collegiate traditions inherited from that prosperous and politically conservative decade. During the opening years of the Depression, collegians continued to behave as if the prosperity of the 1920s had never ended. The economic crisis had yet to shatter the optimistic spirit, insularity, and materialism of the dominant college student culture.

This puzzling indifference to the Depression is linked to both the class background of collegians and the type of youth culture this generated on campus. College students came largely from the middle class and, unlike working class Americans, could usually afford to ignore the Depression in its early stages. Their families had emerged from the 1920s with savings and other assets, which they could draw upon to keep the economic crisis temporarily from their doors.[19] Though these middle-class Americans could not permanently escape the Depression, their economic crisis was delayed during the time it took their financial resources to dwindle. For the majority of middle-class college youths, the Depression began after—some two years after—the Depression devastated blue-collar America. This is why from 1929 through 1931 collegians barely took notice of the economic crisis.

This collegiate behavior was a far cry from that of millions of unemployed Americans, thrown into crisis and despair by the Great Depression; it suggests that in the first stages the Depression was not a national crisis shared by those on both ends of the social scale. The sense of crisis and the growing blight of poverty did not affect all social classes equally or simultaneously from 1929 through 1931. America, as always, consti-

tuted a stratified society, but now the key division existed between those
who could and those who could not afford to ignore the Depression. And
since the majority of collegians in 1931 fell into the former category, the
apolitical undergraduate culture they inherited from the prosperous 1920s
could continue to dominate student life on most campuses.[20]

College enrollment figures reflected the ability of the middle class to
shelter its youth from the economic crisis during the early Depression
years. Between 1929 and 1930 American undergraduate enrollments increased 4.4 percent, from 1,053,955 to 1,100,737. This upward trend accelerated in the next academic year, when enrollments rose by 4.9 percent. In order to handle this growing student population, college and
university staff expanded, reaching record highs in 1930 and 1931. At a
time when factories, banks, and farms were closing down, higher education remained a growth industry.[21]

The student population was one of the last groups in society stung
by the unemployment crisis because a majority of undergraduates did not
work their way through school. At the dawn of the Great Depression 77
percent of the women and 54 percent of the men attending college paid
none of their college expenses—instead, their parents paid the bill.[22] It
was these non-working students who had the most time to engage in campus activities, and at the private and most of the public colleges and universities they set the tone of student life.

The survey data collected by sociologist Robert Angell at the University of Michigan between 1929 and 1931 suggests just how economically
buffered this leisured undergraduate majority was from the Depression.
Angell found that 73.7 percent of the non-working students at Michigan
had either a stable or rising income. These students were doubly fortunate because while their incomes held or improved, prices fell, due to the
deflationary impact of the slumping economy. Consequently, they could
obtain bargain prices for many goods and services. This meant that, in
Angell's words, their "standard of living went up, since the main items
. . . [they purchased] all show increased consumption."[23]

Their relatively affluent backgrounds and their location amidst one
of the nation's few growth industries encouraged undergraduates to un-
derestimate the seriousness of the economic crisis. Even a calamity as grave
as the stock market crash attracted little attention or concern among undergraduates. Students tended to assume that the crash—as regrettable as
it might be—would not hurt them personally; they would be able to continue living the comfortable middle-class life. Capturing this nonchalant
collegiate spirit, the editor of Vassar's student newspaper wrote on
Thanksgiving 1929,

> The holiday was set aside by our forefathers as a day when they
> could take a long rest and think about their blessings. . . . We have our
> blessings too, though they may be that Dad didn't put all his substance

on the stock market; that new fur coats are pretty nice; and that dancing at the Ritz is a comfort . . .[24]

In the months following the crash, students also saw no need to become alarmed because they thought President Hoover would prevent Wall Street's misfortune from producing a lasting economic slump. On those rare occasions when the student press commented on the economic crisis, it tended to praise "the President's zest for action and progress," and to claim that thanks to Hoover "the backbone of the crisis is now broken." This faith in Hoover was consistent with the Republican assumptions and pro-business orientation that undergraduates had held throughout the 1920s. During that decade collegians—even though not active in political campaigns—polled more strongly in favor of conservative and pro-business Republicans than did the general electorate.[25]

The dominant student attitude toward the economy during the early Depression years had an elitist cast, bordering on arrogance. Undergraduates tended to assume that they were the future leaders of society, whose skills and education assured them promising careers in any economic climate. Such attitudes derived from the exclusive nature of American higher education. Despite the growth of college enrollments between 1900 and 1931, the undergraduate population remained small relative both to its age group and the rest of society. In 1931, the peak year of undergraduate enrollment during the first third of the twentieth century, only 12 percent of all college age youth were able to enroll in institutions of higher education.[26] With a college education conferring such clear elite status, it was natural for students to consider themselves too high on the social scale to have any worries about unemployment. James Wechsler, a Columbia alumnus, recalled that this attitude was widespread among his classmates who entered college in 1931. "We felt we were lucky to be there because according to legend, a college degree would give us a big advantage over our contemporaries in the ultimate pursuit of [career goals and economic] success."[27]

This undergraduate overconfidence received considerable reinforcement from the older generation. In December 1930, more than a year after the stock market crash, a leading college employment officer was still telling students and the press that the "ambitious and capable" college graduate "ought not consider the present business depression . . . a great obstacle" to obtaining a well paying job.[28] Advising college graduates in an article published during the 1930 commencement season, Bruce Barton, the advertising industry pioneer, stressed that they would have no trouble finding employment. In fact, Barton was concerned that graduates might spoil themselves by "taking too good a job at first," rather than working their way up to the top. Citing Barton and echoing his sentiments, Barnard College's student newspaper, the *Bulletin,* gave advice to the graduates of 1930, assuring them of their pick of jobs. Ignoring the possibility that the Depression could hurt them, the *Bulletin* suggested that after graduating college women should

> try to get dad . . . to let you on your own for a year. . . . Knock about for a year. Get a job and give it up and get another. . . . When the migration is over, then get another degree or take a life job or marry. You will begin to be equipped for life. . . . Your stock in any market will go up immediately.[29]

Not all college students, however, were so fortunate as the Barnard editor's words might suggest. A significant minority of undergraduates could not look to "dad" for financial support. Some 20 percent of the male and 11 percent of the female undergraduates in the United States received no parental economic support and were entirely self-supporting during their college years. And an even larger minority was partially self-supporting, so that 46 percent of the men and 23 percent of the women undergraduates were employed during their college years. Soon after the Depression began, this working minority began to experience difficulties securing the part-time jobs they had traditionally relied upon. At Columbia University, for example, students who needed employment to help finance their education had fallen into "dire straits" by fall 1931, according to the college administration. Jobs for these Columbia students had declined by 75 percent since 1930.[30]

The problems of these working students were largely ignored by the affluent campus majority from 1929 through 1931. The dominant undergraduate culture proved as blind to the hardships the Depression had brought on to campus as it had been to the poverty spreading in society at large. Such blindness was apparently facilitated by the relatively small proportion of collegians who lacked basic necessities such as food and clothing. At Michigan, for instance, Angell found that of the 85 working students adversely affected by the Depression in 1931, only three had cut their diet "to the extent of impairing their health."[31] Students in such desperate circumstances were likely to drop out of college, which only added to the tendency of the affluent majority to be insulated from the plight of needy youths. And their plight was too serious a matter to be addressed by student social institutions, which seemed capable of little more than boosting the traditional juvenile campus rituals: rushing, hazing, proms, homecomings, football, interclass rivalries, and riots.

This juvenile mind-set and the middle-class atmosphere on campus made the early Depression years especially difficult for low income students—adding a psychological burden to students already hard pressed with economic problems. Thrust into this culture of affluence and classmates still bent on acting as if the Depression did not exist, working students could easily end up feeling alienated. As one midwestern student observed in 1930, "Being in narrow financial straits and seeing other students who have plenty of money, automobiles and such things drive many a student worker to ruin a good disposition."[32]

For low income students it was sometimes easier to accept the collegiate majority's affluence, than its indifference to campus poverty. They felt that there was no excuse for neglecting the suffering of one's class-mates—and this neglect left some of the less privileged students bitter. Film critic Pauline Kael, who as a student encountered great financial difficulty working her way through college during the Great Depression, re-called that such insensitivity was especially strong among the campus's social elite in the Greek houses. Even three decades later, when Kael spoke to Studs Terkel about her college years, she remained angry about this insensitivity.

> There were kids who didn't have a place to sleep, huddling under bridges on the campus. I had a scholarship, but there were times when I didn't have food. The meals were often three candy bars. . . . There was an embarrassment at college where a lot of the kids were well-heeled. I still have a resentment against the fraternity boys and the sorority girls with their cashmere sweaters and the pearls. Even now, when I lecture at colleges, I have this feeling about those terribly overdressed kids. It wasn't a hatred because I wanted these things, but because they didn't understand what was going on. . . . The rich kids . . . didn't give a damn.[33]

Though there were an insufficient number of indigent students to produce campus breadlines or other highly visible symbols of distress, the plight of these students could have become a campus issue in 1930 or 1931 had the dominant undergraduate culture not been so snobbishly bourgeois. The traditional attitude of the affluent student majority was that if you could not afford college, you did not belong there. And in its early stages the Depression had not altered this way of thinking. Indeed, on many campuses, particularly the more exclusive private colleges, stu-dents from prosperous families continued to display patronizing or hos-tile attitudes toward economically disadvantaged collegians. At Harvard, students who lacked the funds to live in dormitories were disparaged as "meatballs." Journalist Theodore White recalled that few of his more wealthy Harvard classmates in the 1930s—who were appropriately known as "white men"—would have anything to do with him since he was a "Jew-ish meatball."[34]

Such attitudes were by no means confined to Harvard. On almost all campuses the competitive social atmosphere promoted by the fraternity-sorority system taught students to value affluence and a leisured lifestyle, and to look down upon—and reject from membership in their clubs and social activities—students who could not afford that lifestyle. This was even true at less exclusive public institutions, such as the University of Kansas. In the fall of 1930, the editor of that university's student newspaper com-plained that the collegiate culture which prevailed on the Lawrence campus was out of step with the national image of Kansas as "a democratic western state." He charged that student life at Kansas was "snobbish" and fostered "some of the most rigid social distinctions of any institution in the country." At Kansas those students in the highest campus "caste," the better Greek houses, would rarely associate with non-Greeks, who by definition "do not rate." The fraternity or sorority member who dated outside this "caste" was seen as "virtually a social failure."[35]

Student concern about dating was not limited, however, to questions about who was dating whom. The issue of how much regulatory authority the colleges had over student dating also aroused interest among undergraduates. In fact, it was not the Depression, but dating regulations which provoked America's most militant student protest in 1930. This protest erupted at Montana State College in Bozeman, where students went on strike against regulations that required them to terminate their dates in time for an 11 p.m. dormitory curfew. Similarly, University of Wyoming President A.G. Crane provoked a student strike in 1931 by undertaking a "crusade against college lovemaking." According to student affidavits, Crane sparked the walkout when he "made a round of parked cars during an intermission of a university dance Friday night, opened the machine [car] doors, and made remarks concerning the morals of the couples found petting."[36]

These protests—and similar, though less militant anti-paternalist protests—on other campuses suggest where American student priorities lay during the early Depression years. Undergraduates who could not be bothered with economic or political issues lost their apathy quickly when it came to defending their social lives from adult supervision.[37] It was on these lifestyle issues that the dominant student culture showed its only liberal tendencies—advocating that collegians should be able to dance, drink, and date free from the overbearing moral policing of college officials.[38]

These tendencies toward social permissiveness again attest that undergraduates in 1930 and 1931 were heirs of the student culture of the 1920s. The only national rebellion on the campuses in the 1920s had been on lifestyle issues. Jazz Age collegians pioneered a freer sexual and social life, portrayed in F. Scott Fitzgerald's novels and symbolized in the daring dress and socializing of the flappers. The irony had been that these same students whose attacks on cultural puritanism shocked their parents in the 1920s, nonetheless shared their conservative Republican political values.[39] Conforming to this pattern, collegians in 1930 and 1931 who were too politically coventional even to conceive of revolting against Herbert Hoover, dropped their conservative demeanor when confronted with threats to their social life.

Even in this cultural sphere, however, the undergraduates of the early Depression years—though supportive of the permissive attitudes toward drinking and dating handed down from the 1920s—were hardly a rebellious lot. Culturally the undergraduates of 1930 and 1931 were a postrevolutionary generation: they were the beneficiaries of a cultural revolt already fought and largely won by their predecessors in the Jazz era. Though willing to oppose administrators who tried to turn the clock back on their social life, students such as those who did strike at Montana and Wyoming, were sporadically defending old gains, not pioneering new forms of social and sexual rebellion.

By the late 1920s and early 1930s, the new forms of student cultural rebellion that had appeared on the campuses a half-decade earlier had now grown old. For instance, the risqué flapper dresses of the coeds and the baggy trousers of the male students, which symbolized the "collegiate semi-bohemianism" of the 1920s had become passé. However, what replaced them were not more rebellious clothes, but rather more conventional ones. At the women's colleges dressing became increasingly formal. "The disappearence of the flapper" had, as the *New York Times* observed, been followed in the late 1920s by the "advent of the lady." And for men on many campuses, especially in the eastern colleges, the trend was toward the "utmost conservatism in dress." A liberal Ivy League critic complained in 1931 that the "Yale or Princeton student who wishes to make a mark dresses like a young banker on the Exchange—smartly, expensively, unostentatiously. He jumps into black suits and stiff collars at the slightest provocation." Among undergraduates, "insurgency is outmoded," and had been so since "about 1928," the *Times* concluded. "They are now painfully conformist."[40]

With even cultural rebelliousness a fading memory on campus and political apathy ascendant, the American student body of 1931 seemed to have almost no radical potential. This left some less conventional students, such as William Harlan Hale, in a gloomy mood. Hale had spent his college years at Yale editing a liberal literary magazine, aimed at rousing student interest in political issues and cultural criticism. As his graduation approached in the spring of 1931, Hale confessed that the magazine had failed in its purpose because at Yale, as at other colleges, the average undergraduate was a "collared conservative." That year, in his *New Republic* article pessimistically entitled "A Dirge for College Liberalism," Hale portrayed the college rebel as an endangered species, and predicted that the future held out the "prospects of a continuing inertia" on campus.[41] Hale's article, however, had not even mentioned the Depression. Since the economic crisis had yet to hit Hale and most of his classmates, the retiring liberal editor failed to foresee its potential for awakening the spirit of revolt on campus. Events would soon prove his eulogy for collegiate insurgency quite premature.

II

The Depression finally began to overwhelm the collegiate middle class in 1932. This was the first peacetime year in twentieth-century America when college enrollments fell, slipping by more than 4 percent. It had taken three years of the worst economic crisis in American history to bring college enrollments down. The fact that the Depression's impact on campus had been so delayed was, in the words of a 1932 *New York Times* report, a testament to "the intense faith . . . of the American people in higher education. . . . The college has been the last institution in the country to show in the number of its clientele the effects of the Depression." The 1932 enrollment drop demonstrated that the middle class was losing its ability to shelter its youth from the economic crisis. Although funds and faith in higher education had initially insulated the American campus from that crisis, by 1932 not even the middle class could keep the Great Depression off campus. And in the coming year this negative trend would show no sign of abating. In 1933 enrollments again declined by more than 4 percent; thus within this two-year period some 80,000 youths who ordinarily would have attended college were, because of the Depression, unable to do so.[42]

The drop in enrollments which began in 1932 contributed to a fiscal crisis among American colleges and universities; it denied these institutions the income traditionally received from tuition and other student fees. This year also brought a substantial cut in state funding of higher education and an unprecedented drop in private financial contributions. Some colleges reported that in the 1932–33 academic year their gift income had fallen by as much as 80 percent.[43]

This poor economic news led to the most severe retrenchment since the rise of the American university. College administrators eliminated educational programs, slashed building and maintenance expenditures, increased student fees, and reduced both the number and salaries of faculty. According to the American Association of University Professors (AAUP), 1932 was economically the worst year in history for faculty: 77 out of the 125 colleges and universities polled by the AAUP reported a decline in faculty salaries.[44]

Reports from campuses throughout the United States indicated that the 1932–33 academic year was emerging as the worst economic period that undergraduates had ever faced. According to a survey taken in October 1932, 76 out of 77 colleges and universities confronted "the most urgent need in . . . [their] history for scholarships, loans, deferred tuition payments and opportunities for earning during term time." While the wealthiest institutions, such as Harvard, had the funds to meet this unprecedented demand for student aid, many colleges and universities discovered that the reduction in their own income left them unable to assist this growing army of needy students—and without such aid, tens of thousands of students were forced to drop out.[45]

With the economic crisis overtaking the American collegiate world in 1932, the mood on campus began to change. Though the juvenile escapades and athletic ballyhoo did not cease, they were losing support; the collegiate culture was gradually becoming eroded by the Depression. "Officials of institutions from Boston to Berkeley estimated that the chief effect of the Depression had been to modulate the carefree joy of campus life and to focus the attention of students on books and blackboards," according to a *New York Times* survey in the fall of 1932. "The student of 1932, many of the replies indicated, has sold the flashy roadster and is buying second-hand books, and more than ever before is asking for . . . low priced dormitory rooms, and a chance to work his way." Faculty members found their students becoming more serious, concerned about social and political questions, eager for answers about why the Depression had begun and how it could be ended.[46]

Another sign of the changing mood on campus in 1932 came with a shift in collegiate attitudes toward low income students. Collegiate snobbery and indifference to the problems of working students did not vanish overnight. Indeed, they never disappeared completely. But as the Depression deepened in 1932 and launched an era of retrenchment on campus, these old attitudes were challenged. As students awakened to the seriousness of the Depression off campus, they began to face its effects on campus. Student complaints and exposés about the problems of working and unemployed undergraduates surfaced with increasingly frequency, as did criticism of classmates who had ignored or contributed to the exploitation of working students.

Letters, articles, and editorials began to appear in the undergraduate press that sympathized with low income students and documented their increasing hardships. Typifying this new concern about campus poverty, the University of Michigan campus daily in the winter of 1932 published a story showing that "dozens of students who are carrying a full load of school work . . . may be found rooming together in some attic at a dollar and a half a week, living on milk and crackers and occasionally a can of beans." The article revealed that for such students clothing was almost as big a problem as food; they could not afford new clothes, and in some cases were going through their entire college careers in the tattered garments they had worn daily since high school.[47]

These reports revealed that because low income students so desperately needed work in order to stay in school, they were ripe for exploitation by employers. From many campus communities came complaints about a steadily worsening work environment, in which student employees were overworked and underpaid. Students who did domestic work in private homes and those who labored in rooming houses were terribly exploited, complained an irate undergraduate, who wrote to the campus daily at the University of Wisconsin in 1932. His letter told of housewives using the Depression as a pretext for firing their full-time maids—who earned room and board plus $5 to $8 per week—and hiring in their place unsalaried students, who were required to do all the work formerly done by the maid in exchange for "only a mattress and meals." This student also reported that local boarding houses hired undergraduates to tend the furnaces and maintenance work, but paid them no wages. All the student workers received for their labor was "the privilege of sleeping in an ill-lighted, cold basement room." He concluded that students needed a labor union to "remedy this condition which amounts to nothing more nor less than slavery."[48]

The campus press began to recount the grievances of many other types of student employees, including restaurant workers. Students complained that campus area restaurants gave them less than thirty cents' worth of food for an hour of hard labor. Meals given to student workers were charged at retail value rather than wholesale prices. In the worst of these restaurants, students found that their hourly labor earned them only "hash-house meals worth five or six cents," and food that was either going bad or already spoiled.[49]

Among the most prominent targets of this new criticism were the fraternity and sorority houses. They were accused of being among the most exploitative employers—underpaying low income students who worked in their kitchens, a practice held to be especially egregious since this victimized their own classmates. At UC Berkeley, for instance, a student angrily wrote that

> the various refined clubs, fraternities and sororities . . . regard the needy students as so many free laborers. It has been the experience of the writer that in most cases an hour or even longer period of "stepping on it" in dishwashing and other delicate jobs brings nothing more than a plate full of hash or some hamburgers. Many students put up with it, ruin their digestion with yesterday's leftovers, and suffer in general simply because there is no way out.[50]

A similar report from the University of Michigan chided the "enlightened girls and boys of the sororities and fraternities" for paying their student dishwashers the equivalent of ten cents an hour. "Nowhere, except in the exploited cotton belt of the South are such low wages paid."[51]

Along with this growing willingness to acknowledge the crisis in the part-time job market came an equally significant change in student attitudes toward their career prospects. As the Depression worsened in late 1931 and early 1932, the arrogant undergraduate notion that the college-educated were too elite a group to have their careers ruined by the slumping economy began to be questioned. Student anxieties about their career prospects soared as employment figures in the business world and the professions grew more dismal. Compounding these worries was the increasing acknowledgment by campus employment offices that graduates now faced an unprecedented job crisis. Students began publicly to discuss their fear that this constricted job market might be a permanent problem rather than a temporary aberration.[52]

The Depression was striking too close to home to be ignored by collegians and, as a result, a sense of vulnerability appeared in undergraduate culture. Students came to recognize that they could become victims of the economic crisis because they had witnessed the losses of the middle class and well educated in their midst. These included: faculty who either lost salaries or jobs; classmates who either dropped out or worked poorly paying jobs to continue in school; graduates whose college degrees had proven useless in the depressed job market; and parents whose savings had been exhausted and careers disrupted by the Depression.

As the Depression entered its third year, undergraduates started to discuss a prospect that in the 1920s would have been unthinkable: that college graduates would face downward rather than upward social mobility, and experience poverty rather than prosperity. The image of the college graduate standing in a soup line found its way into student discourse, reflecting the fact that on campus overconfidence was giving way to anxiety concerning the future of college-trained youth. This could be seen, for instance, in a Thanksgiving editorial written by Reed Harris, editor of Columbia's student newspaper, which stressed that a college degree was no shield against the economic crisis. Harris mocked President Hoover's call for Americans to pick "out everything possible to be thankful for"; choosing instead to visit those too poor to afford Thanksgiving turkey— New Yorkers standing on a soup line.

> Here shivering miserably . . . waiting patiently for the long line in which they were standing to move that they acquire their meagre portion of free soup, we found graduates of the class of 1931, and others of classes not much older. Wearily these men, we discovered, had been dragging themselves from office to office in search of a job regardless of its nature. . . . Yet these men a short time ago left college filled with ambition of a type so high that only a newly graduated and somewhat naive senior, whose sheepskin was still damp with the ink of many signatures, could conceive of them. One can scarcely believe that these bedraggled, ambitionless and prematurely aged individuals are the men who less than a year ago . . . pursued rather carefree existences at various centers of learning. . . . What a sad grey the original white collars of the great middle class have attained.[53]

The realism and pessimism reflected in Harris's editorial became widespread among undergraduates as the Depression continued because not only were student attitudes shifting, the student population itself was changing. The students who had entered college before the Depression were graduating. By fall 1932, the freshmen/women, sophomores, and juniors were all classes that had entered college after the economic crisis began—making this the first year in which members of the Depression generation outnumbered those who started college before the Depression. By the following fall there would no longer be an undergraduate class that had entered college before the Depression. This meant that the college population was becoming progressively more distant from the prosperous campus world of the 1920s. This generational change helped to foster a sense that the apolitical, insular, "rah-rah" collegiate culture inherited from the 1920s was outdated and fast becoming irrelevant to the needs of college youth in Depression America.

With a new student generation emerging and the economic crisis shaking both middle-class youths and their colleges in 1932, students started to question the traditional undergraduate notion that college years should be a fun-filled retreat from the real world. The old collegiate rituals which had been the heart of the apolitical student lifestyle inherited from the 1920s came under scrutiny as never before. Symptomatic of this new, serious spirit was the debate that erupted at Vassar College—the oldest and most elite women's college in the United States—over the junior prom in 1932.

Vassar proms were an old and expensive tradition, costing thousands of dollars for the luxurious hall rental, the band, taxis, flowers, gowns. A vocal group of students, including the editors of the college's newspaper, the *Vassar Miscellany News*, advocated the cancellation of the prom because they thought it self-indulgent to engage in expensive partying at a time when so much of the surrounding community had been impoverished by the Depression. These students argued that there was no justification for Vassar

> to flaunt its extravagance in the face of a community which has learned the meaning of starvation. . . . It is manifestly unessential to our well-being that we expose ourselves annually to the delights of Prom . . . . Have we any right to go on fulfilling Hollywood's picture of the Vassar girl when it involves a greater expense than we have been willing to devote to organizations which are striving to alleviate the misery of every Main Street?[54]

Vassar, they argued, had already fallen behind other campuses in recognizing the need to cease the traditional frivolity in this period of grave economic crisis. "Yale realized the necessity," wrote the editor of the *Vassar Miscellany News*, "and eliminated its Derby Day celebrations; Williams has given up its fall house parties. If we dispense with our Proms we shall not have the glory of innovators, but if we do not we shall deserve the ultimate criticism of blindness and egotism."[55]

Criticism of the prom grew stronger and persisted for over a month at Vassar. The *Vassar Miscellany News* ran four editorials attacking the insensitivity of those who had organized this party. In the face of these attacks, prom organizers moved toward a compromise: they would cut the price of prom tickets by one-third and donate fifty cents from each ticket to aid the unemployed in the Poughkeepsie community. But this was denounced as mere tokenism by the prom's critics. "To spend the couple of thousand dollars that will be spent in all on this pleasant ritual," the Vassar newspaper editorialized,

> and then with a philanthropic smirk give some seventy-five dollars to relieve starving and homeless people—this seems to us worse than jeering

openly . . . . For some reason or other we believe that the profound needs of human beings for food, clothes, home, security, peace of mind, are more important than the need of a lot of well-fed young bourgeoises for a Junior Prom.[56]

Critics of the prom at Vassar understood that they reflected a new "school of thought flourishing in this particular world debacle"—that promoted an ideal of social responsibility which would have been alien to collegians in the less troubled world of the 1920s. According to the *Vassar Miscellany News*

> The theme-song of the school is "make the younger generation aware of the unhappy world, the community of which they are a part," shatter the prejudices they inherit from their upper middle class relatives; shatter the eat-drink-and be-merry-ness with which they pursue pleasure, at proms, on weekends; make them see that they are dancing on the edge of a volcano; make them feel the next war, the twelve million unemployed, the race conflicts, the undernourished children . . . destroy their complacency, make them challenge the status quo . . .[57]

Although the Vassar prom was not canceled in 1932, the severe criticism surrounding it suggested that the party was over for the old apolitical student culture, which had created and championed proms and all of the other insulating rituals of undergraduate life. No longer would such rituals and the carefree lifestyle they symbolized go unchallenged on campus. The Depression, having at last caught up with the college world in 1932, set the stage for the politicization of American student culture: a process that would involve questioning not merely proms but profits, not just the inequities on campus but the inequality of the capitalist system itself. And the lead role in shaping this new collegiate world would be played by a type of political activist who in the previous decade had not the slightest influence on undergraduate life—students in communist and socialist organizations.

Chapter 2

Cafeteria Commies

> Daniel, a tall young man . . . wore his curly hair long. Steel-rimmed spectacles and a full mustache, brown like his hair, made him look if not older than he was then more self-possessed and opinionated. Let's face it, he looked cool, deliberately cool. In fact nothing about his appearance was accidental. If he'd lived in the nineteen thirties and came on this way he would be a young commie. A cafeteria commie.
>
> E.L. Doctorow, *The Book of Daniel* (New York, 1971), 4.

Leadership in the collegiate transition from political apathy to activism came from the Left and initially it came with a New York accent. Almost all of Depression America's early eruptions of student protest—including the student expedition to Harlan County, the Columbia free speech strike, and the City Colleges' anti-tuition movement during the 1932 spring semester—either occurred on or were launched from campuses in New York City. Though consisting of only a small minority of the student body in New York, the city's campus radicals were the best organized, most politically ambitious and militant student activists in the nation. New York's emergence as the center of the student revolt of the early 1930s was largely the work of the National Student League (NSL), the New York-based radical organization responsible for orchestrating the first political protests by collegians during the Depression decade. The birth of the NSL in December 1931 marked the organizational beginning of student activism in the Depression era. Coming at a time when nationally militant political protest did not yet exist on campus, the NSL's founding in New York attested that the city's student activists were ahead of their time and of the rest of American undergraduates on the road to mass protest.

The role that New York's campuses played in igniting the student movement was facilitated by the city's unique political climate. New York was the capital city of American radicalism during the Depression decade.

Here the Communist Party, which during this decade became America's largest radical organization, had its national headquarters and strongest following. The city was also a stronghold for the Socialist Party, which had considerable influence in metropolitan area labor unions. The radical intelligentsia too made New York its home and used the city as a base for publishing the nation's most important leftist magazines and journals. Evoking the intense radicalism and heated ideological debate in New York during the Depression, Lionel Abel recalled that intellectually the city's leftists "went to Russia and spent most of the decade there . . . . New York became the most interesting part of the Soviet Union . . . the one part of that country in which the struggle between Stalin and Trotsky could be openly expressed. And was! And how!"[1] The dynamism of the radical movement in New York spilled over on to the city's campuses.

On Manhattan's Upper West Side the campus intellectual milieu was a student radical's delight. Within a twenty block radius of the Columbia campus lived the greatest assemblage of academic progressives and radicals in Depression America. The faculties of Columbia University and Teachers College boasted some of the nation's most famous liberal and Left-leaning professors, including John Dewey, George Counts, Franz Boas, and Rexford Tugwell. Less intellectually prominent, but more active in campus politics were the young radical instructors and graduate students who had been attracted to Columbia by its eminent faculty and liberal reputation. Several of these young radical academics, including Donald Henderson and Addison Cutler, had especially close links to undergraduate leftists. Henderson, in fact, would serve as the NSL's first executive secretary.[2]

Also in the Columbia neighborhood was Union Theological Seminary, home to two of America's most renowned religious radicals, Reinhold Niebuhr and Harry Ward. Niebuhr had presided over a Commission of Christian Associations in 1931 that generated great controversy in Protestant circles by advocating a socialist America. He and Ward inspired a whole generation of radical young theologians, who as college chaplains would help make the campus YMCAs and YWCAs active in the struggle for peace and social justice.[3]

A few subway stops away from Union Theological Seminary and Columbia was the uptown campus of the City College of New York (CCNY), which produced student radical leaders at about the rate that Notre Dame churned out college football stars. The initial impetus leading to the birth of the NSL came from the CCNY campus. CCNY's prominence in the early stages of the student movement derived from sources quite different from Columbia's. CCNY lacked Columbia's cast of eminent liberal and Left-leaning faculty, who might attract bright undergraduate radicals. Indeed with the exception of the philosopher Morris Raphael Cohen, the CCNY faculty was virtually barren of distinguished liberal scholars. The advent of a vibrant student Left at CCNY, in fact, had nothing to do with the faculty. CCNY bred student radicalism because of the explosive interaction between the Depression, the working class culture of the student body, the larger radical milieu of New York, and the repressive policies of an intolerant campus administration.[4]

New York was one of the few cities in Depression America that ran a tuition-free municipal college system. CCNY, Hunter College for women, and Brooklyn College together constituted the nation's largest free city college system. Because they were tuition-free, these colleges attracted a student population quite different from that of most colleges. Where the average college was predominantly middle class, the student body at New York's municipal colleges had a much higher percentage of students from low income families.[5]

Because these New York city college students often came from families with virtually no savings, when the economy crashed, their parents could not shelter them from the consequences. They were stung by the Depression much sooner than most American collegians. Indeed, while nationally the middle-class student body was relatively unaffected by the Depression until 1932, the overwhelmingly working-class student body in New York's municipal colleges had already been badly hurt by the Depression in early 1931. At the city colleges, students had difficulty paying for even such basic necessities as textbooks, lunch, and transportation. Symptomatic of the hard times which beset city college students soon after the Depression began, was an incident economist Harry Magdoff witnessed as a CCNY undergraduate.

> Jobs were unavailable. But then there was a sign up on the bulletin board . . . "Jobs available—Part-time for Chemical Engineering Students." Gee, everybody was envious . . . . It turned out it was to shovel snow. There was a heavy snowfall in New York. They knew that if they announced snow shoveling jobs they'd have a thousand guys applying. So that by limiting it to chemical engineering they were able to cope with the thing.[6]

This relative economic deprivation had political consequences. The personal anxieties and political questioning that the economic crisis unleashed nationally on campus in 1932 had already progressed much further in these depressed City College campuses.

The unique ethnic and political background of the student body in New York's city colleges helped make their campuses fertile ground for leftist organizers—so much so that Hunter and Brooklyn College radicals would be only slightly less prominent than their CCNY counterparts in founding the NSL. These municipal college students came overwhelmingly from the city's ghettoes, which were enclaves of East European Jewish immigrants. Within these ghettoes was a powerful minority tradition of radical politics and working-class organization. Though radicals never constituted a majority within these ghetto communities, their voices dominated some of the city's leading Yiddish cultural institutions, including the Jewish press. This radical tradition was an inheritance of the socialist bund and the days of resistance to the Czar; it was also the outcome of Jewish concentration in the garment industry's work force and in their socialist-led labor unions.[7]

The ghetto world, so different from mainstream America, was one in which leftists were not seen as pariahs. Radical activists were tolerated, and their views attracted a respectful hearing in an immigrant community that had grown accustomed to such politics in Europe. It was easy to grow up in New York's ghettoes without experiencing the type of hostility toward radicalism common in much of America. Indeed, if one's parents and friends were involved in the ghetto's radical circles, anti-capitalist thought could seem normal rather than deviant. Literary critic Alfred Kazin, raised in a Brooklyn ghetto during this era, recalled that for him " 'Socialism' was a way of life since everyone . . . I knew in New York was a Socialist, more or less . . . . I was a Socialist as so many Americans were 'Christians'; I had always lived in a Socialist atmosphere." [8]

Exposed to radicalism before they ever set foot on a college campus, some of the student activists who came out of these ghetto communities began radical organizing at an early age: during their adolescent and high school years. This would be an added source of strength for the student movement on New York's campuses in the early 1930s because it meant that the student Left's leaders included political veterans. Among the NSL's founders, Joseph Clark, Max Gordon, and Max Weiss had this type of organizing experience. In their pre-college days, Clark, Gordon, and Weiss had been active in the Young Communist League (YCL), the Communist Party's youth organization. Through the YCL they developed skills as political pamphleteers, speakers, and strike organizers. Moreover, YCL members (and their counterparts in the Young People's Socialist League, the Socialist Party's youth group) were active in several New York high schools during the early 1930s, so that by the time such radical activists as Clark and Gordon arrived at college, they were already accustomed to the task of politically recruiting classmates in a school setting.[9]

The seriousness and political sophistication of students with this type of Party background was extraordinary. This could be seen, for instance, at New Utrecht High School in Brooklyn, one of the city's more politically active schools. Here in 1930 Joseph Clark exhibited some of the same leadership qualities that he would display as a college radical organizer the following year. At New Utrecht, Clark helped establish a History Club. While most youths their age struggled through basic civics courses and knew little about Marxism, Clark and his fellow History Club members were analyzing the radical issues of the day and holding debates on them between communist and socialist students.[10]

These young leftists were often better informed about radical issues than were their high school teachers. At New Utrecht the students' knowledge and militance frightened some instructors. So in 1930 school authorities tried to close down the History Club, and when they did, Clark and his fellow radicals responded not as chastened school children but as defiant militants. The students protested vigorously and tried to show that the assault on their club was an example of the type of political suppression that characterized the entire capitalist system. History Club member George Watt, who later became a national leader of the student movement, recalled the defense of their club as

> a very dramatic moment when right in this little school you had almost a replica, a reenactment of what was going on in the larger society. . . . I remember walking into the Club and there was Joe Clark . . . pointing his finger at the faculty advisor . . . who had just ordered the Club's suspension. [Joe began] shouting at him "You have taught us the lesson of state power and its oppression" . . . . And around the room were thirty members of the service squad, like that was the police power right in the classroom. So that for young minds like ours that left a very, very strong imprint.[11]

As they would do later at the college level, Clark and his YCL comrades at New Utrecht sought to use immediate economic issues as a vehicle for politicizing their classmates. The issue they focused upon at New Utrecht was a milk price increase in the cafeteria. The school's predominantly working-class student body had been hurt by the Depression and had difficulty affording this price increase. So, when the YCL organized a milk boycott, the student response was overwhelming. The protests prodded the school administration to stop the price increase. Outside observers were astounded that such an effective protest could be organized by such young students. The New York *Daily News* was so impressed by the militance that before long it dubbed New Utrecht "the cradle of the American revolution."[12]

There was an unmistakable precociousness to these students who engaged in political activism so early in their lives. They were confident that the Left held the keys both to history and political organization, and that as part of the Left they—despite their youth—could lead effective political actions. Such confidence was evident in George Watt's attitude toward the milk protest at New Utrecht. Though prior to the milk boycott Watt "hadn't any experience in this kind of organization," his lack of political experience did not faze him in the least. Watt was certain that he could help lead the boycott to victory because he would follow the advice in Communist Party leader William Z. Foster's *Strike Strategy*. This was, Watt recalled,

> a manual on how you organized a strike; how you set up committees, rank and file committees; how you get community support; how you neutralize certain sectors and direct your main fire against the main target. It was a very useful little pamphlet which I applied almost literally in almost every instance to the student organization. And it worked. It worked very well.[13]

While students with Clark's and Watt's organizing experience played an important role in the early NSL, they did not constitute a majority within the League's founding group. Among the ghetto-raised students who participated in creating the NSL, it was more common to find youths who had been Left-leaning, but not members of socialist or communist groups in their pre-college years. Though not politically active in high school, such NSL founders as Harry Magdoff, Adam Lapin, and Joseph Starobin had—in a slightly less obvious way than those already in leftist youth organizations—been groomed for collegiate radicalism by the working-class immigrant milieu of their ghetto communities. Such students came from households which (though not affiliated with a radical party) tended to be strongly pro-union, broadly sympathetic to the Left and to the struggles radicals were waging against reactionaries in Europe. Of his political background and that of most of the City College NSLers, Harry Magdoff recalled that it was common to find

> a father who had been a union member, had been in strikes for years. Kids had suffered . . . . An environment in which the class problems— unemployment, seasonal unemployment, negotiations, problems of the union [were pervasive]. They were the children of workers and even small business people who had lived through . . . hard times in the garment trades. So it's not like they were middle class kids from Long Island . . . and they're not red diaper babies [children of Communist Party members]. But there is a tradition of another sort. I mean, I knew about unions. I knew there was a Russian revolution . . . . One of my earliest childhood memories is being on the elevated train and people swarming around with red things . . . flowing dresses and so on, singing songs and carrying whiskey bottles. This was the Lower East Side . . . . I was four years old. And what was it [they were celebrating]? The czar was overthrown! . . . These were experiences that were very important—living in a ghetto situation with alot of Russians.[14]

The cultural institutions of their Jewish ghetto communities provided Magdoff and other City College activists with an added impetus for radical politics. Along with fellow NSL founders Adam Lapin and Joseph Starobin, Magdoff attended the Sholom Aleichem schools as a youngster. Although not designed to promote radicalism, these secular Yiddish schools put students in touch with European literature—some of which was on the Left and served as a powerful inducement to radical thought. The Yiddish press, with its radical political discourse and reviews of leftist books, which students like Magdoff read avidly, helped to reinforce this Left cultural experience.[15]

The link between exposure to Yiddish culture and radicalization was, of course, not automatic or universal. In fact, the vast majority of Yiddish speaking New Yorkers were not radical. What the Yiddish cultural milieu did, however, was provide a path toward radical thought and the European Left which was less available in middle America. Thus, it increased the possibility of radicalization, particularly since this cosmopolitan atmosphere was rendered all the more politically charged by the Depression,[16]

These New York students fluent in Yiddish, who had been raised amidst ghettoes as Russian as they were American, were in but not quite yet of America; they were, as Irving Howe has put it, "still in some deep sense part of Europe."[17] The political implications of living in the United States while still thinking at least partially in European terms could be quite radical because it facilitated a certain critical detachment from the American social order, and an awareness of alternative systems of political thought and organization. Having grown up as children of European immigrants, the young radicals who emerged from these ghetto communities understood the European radical tradition and sensed that Americans could benefit from it. For Magdoff this European sensibility led to the conviction that something was radically wrong with American undergraduate life. Even while attending high school, in the days just prior to the advent of the student movement he would help build, Magdoff looked toward a European alternative to American collegiate provincialism. As a writer for his high school student newspaper, Magdoff told his classmates:

> Look, the students of Hungary, they're concerned with the real issues of the people. They're rioting; they're closing the universities . . . . Look at the American students with their fur coats and with parties, and getting drunk . . . . We're going to be different. This isn't the way students should be. They should be concerned.[18]

As a CCNY student in 1931, Magdoff sought to translate this vision into reality by working to build a radical student movement. His first step in this work was as a founder of *Frontiers,* a radical magazine at CCNY. This was published by the communist-leaning CCNY undergraduate group which Magdoff helped lead, the Social Problems Club. Even at this early point in the Depression CCNY was already a campus with an unusually vocal core of leftist students, which in addition to the Social Problems Club, included a socialist-led student organization, the Student Forum, as well as a sprinkling of Trotskyists, Lovestoneites, and anarchists. The campus also had a distinctive dissident tradition in that while most of the American student body had been politically quiescent in the 1920s, CCNY students had waged a very stormy and successful battle against compulsory ROTC. Memories of that struggle lingered. For CCNY's small core of leftists, the campus remained a hotbed of political debate, that raged in the alcoves of the school cafeteria—a critical meeting place that served as a center of intellectual life at this commuter college.[19]

To this dissident tradition *Frontiers* added a sensitivity to the new political possibilities created by the Depression. The magazine's first issue, in February 1931, reflected how—in contrast to the nation's middle-class undergraduate population—CCNY's more blue-collar student body had already been hard hit by the Depression. *Frontiers* reported that among CCNY students, "Parents, relatives, friends are unemployed . . . and plans of a successful professional career begin to seem chimerical." Such conditions at CCNY gave these young radicals an unusual insight into the forces that would soon shape a new and more politically aware college generation nationally. *Frontiers* prophetically predicted that the Depression would shatter "the aloofness and unconcern . . . towards the political and social events of the world" that had been the "customary attitude of college students."[20]

Adult influence on these CCNY radicals remained indirect and derived from the *Frontiers* group's desire to emulate the work of the communist wing of the city's intelligentsia. The CCNY students who founded *Frontiers* were seeking to bring to their classmates the type of iconoclastic Marxist journalism the *New Masses* brought to the adult Left. Indeed, when the student editors of *Frontiers* needed cartoons and photos to illustrate their stories, they took the subway down to the *New Masses* office, where they were allowed to recycle old graphics from the magazine. The student writers for *Frontiers* echoed the *New Masses* and the Communist Party in their adoration of the Soviet Union and in their concern that a hostile capitalist world was preparing for war against the U.S.S.R.[21]

It was on this last issue, war preparations, that *Frontiers* ignited a conflict with the CCNY administration—a conflict that set in motion the events leading to the NSL's formation. In its first editorial, *Frontiers* reopened the controversy over military training by calling for its abolition at CCNY. *Frontiers* editorialized that even if its courses were voluntary, the military science department had no place in an institution of higher learning because of "the central danger of Mili. Sci.—its function as the agency for the dissemination of jingoist, imperialist propaganda."[22]

This radical stance proved intolerable to Frederick C. Robinson, CCNY's president. Robinson was an acerbic, bespectacled little man, who, to several generations of CCNY students, seemed the living embodiment of political intolerance and academic pomposity.[23] Robinson loathed radicalism and thought students too immature to be granted political autonomy on campus. In Robinson's view, undergraduates were "beset with the storm and stress of adolescence" and subject to political impulses which "spring from inexperience and undue emotion." If allowed to run free, students driven by such impulses could "bring discredit upon themselves and their college." So Robinson concluded it was up to him to police the political life of undergraduates at college, just as parents police the personal conduct of their children at home. It was, Robinson said, the job of the college administration to censor student publications so that they did not "overstep . . . the grounds of decent journalism . . . become the cat's-paws of outside agitators and embroil the college in matters foreign to the purpose of its foundation."[24]

In line with this thinking, Robinson, infuriated by the anti-ROTC editorial, moved to suppress the first issue of *Frontiers* in February 1931. Under Robinson's orders, college officials broke into the locker where most of the copies of the magazine were stored and confiscated them. Claiming that the publication had been issued without proper authorization, Robinson revoked the charter of its publisher, the CCNY Social Problems Club, and suspended its president, Max Weiss. When Club members published a leaflet protesting Robinson's actions, he suspended ten of them.[25]

In response to the suppression of *Frontiers,* CCNY activists worked to build a citywide anti-censorship coalition. This effort yielded letters of support for the suspended students and *Frontiers* from campuses throughout New York City. Facing this pressure and a strike threat, the college's trustees agreed to review the case. The trustees, in a face-saving statement, expressed full confidence in Robinson, but then proceeded to authorize publication of *Frontiers* and reinstated ten of the eleven students that the CCNY president had suspended.[26]

The citywide campaign against Robinson's censorship brought CCNY's communist and communist-leaning students into closer contact with their counterparts on the city's other campuses. Their victory over Robinson enabled these hundred or so students to see the advantages of a coordinated citywide coalition of collegiate radicals. Moreover, it convinced them to create a permanent coalition by founding the New York Intercollegiate Student Council, an organization composed of eleven small, Left-oriented student groups from seven campuses in the metropolitan area.[27]

Though the Council was formed initially for the defensive purpose of protecting free speech for collegiate leftists, its organizers soon developed broader ambitions. They hoped that the Depression would enable them to take the offensive and build a strong leftist movement on the city's campuses. Toward this end, the Council reorganized in the fall of 1931 as the New York Student League (NYSL). The League established a lively political magazine, the *Student Review,* as a vehicle for building a community of radical student activists throughout New York. Bolstered by their local success and the positive response to the magazine, the NYSL shifted its organization and focus beyond New York. During the 1931 Christmas vacation, the NYSL changed its name to the National Student League and dedicated itself to the goal of radicalizing American college students.[28]

If judged by the number of students involved, the NSL's formation and first convention were hardly impressive events. At the League's first convention in March 1932 only twenty-five colleges and universities were represented—and these were primarily East Coast schools.[29] This gathering, like the NSL's founding in 1931 attracted little attention nationally on campuses; it was all but ignored by the student press, which was still predominantly apolitical. But despite these humble beginnings, the NSL would soon have a significant impact on campuses and change the face of American student politics. The NSL pioneered a new approach to radical student organizing, which would liberate the American student Left from its decade-long isolation and political impotence.

The mere fact of the NSL's creation was an unprecedented event for the campus Left; it marked the first time in the history of American student radicalism that no single organization monopolized Left organizing on campus. Prior to the NSL's birth, only one national leftist organization existed on campuses. This was the educational organization founded by Upton Sinclair in 1905, which was led primarily by socialists—though it was not officially affiliated with the Socialist Party. Sinclair's organization was originally known as the Intercollegiate Socialist Society (ISS); it was renamed the League For Industrial Democracy (LID) in 1921, and through that decade was led by adult socialists Harry Laidler and Norman Thomas.[30] The socialists' monopoly on campus radical organizing had an unhealthy effect on the student Left and contributed to its weakness in the 1920s. The NSL's founding in 1931 introduced a competitive element in the student Left, which helped prod the LID out of the doldrums into which it had fallen during the 1920s.

The LID had proven so politically ineffective in the 1920s that by the time the Depression began the American student Left was barely alive. Campus radicalism had just gone through ten of its leanest years since the rise of the American university. In 1929 the LID's student membership was miniscule—slightly more than 1000 out of a national undergraduate population of over a million—and the organization had little impact or visibility on campus.[31] LID leaders blamed their failure to attract students in the 1920s on the conservative national mood. But some of the responsibility for their poor political track record rested with the LID itself. LID national leaders frequently behaved more like teachers than political organizers. In line with the LID's motto of "education for a new social order," LID leaders placed so much emphasis on education that they seemed unable to engage in agitation on campus. LID leaders would spend months arranging academic lectures about radical principles, but little time showing collegians how to act on those principles. Despite all the energy and funds the LID devoted to publishing political pamphlets, these tracts displayed the same imbalance. A student learned much from LID literature about what was wrong with the steel industry, or why unionization and industrial democracy were worthy goals, but nothing about how to convert dissatisfaction about these issues into active political protest. None of the LID pamphlets during the 1920s were devoted to campus politics or the problems of building a student movement.[32]

Even the term "student movement" remained alien to the education-minded LID during the 1920s; it was not used in the LID's lectures, pamphlets, or newsletters. The LID was unable to look beyond the lecture hall toward the building of an aggressive student movement, fighting to restructure the university or society. Though committed to socialistic ideals, the LID's view of students in the university context was not essentially radical. The LID accepted the conventional academic notion that student days should be devoted solely to study. Instead of working to replace this conventional notion with a radical new image of the student as political activist, the LID had focused on providing the literature and lectures necessary to make one's pensive undergraduate years include exposure to socialist thought—reflecting an academic rather than an activist orientation.

The LID's failure to focus on the essentials of student organizing developed because the League was not strictly or primarily a student organization. Though the LID did have an intercollegiate council, during the 1920s this council had functioned only sporadically, and it was not the students on this council but the adult leaders of the LID—prominent Socialist Party and Left-liberal figures—who dominated the LID's national leadership. These leaders, men and women in their thirties and forties, were as concerned with building non-student LID chapters in the community as they were with increasing campus LID membership. The LID's most prominent national officers, including Norman Thomas, Paul Blanshard, and Harry Laidler were simply too old to think in student terms; they failed to see the need to use campus problems as a bridge to larger political issues.[33]

Since Thomas, Laidler, and most of the national LID cadre were not students, they could not picture themselves as leaders of a student movement. As published authors several decades senior to their college audiences, touring LID lecturers fell naturally into a role roughly equivalent to that of visiting professors—only these LID "professors" analyzed major social issues from a socialist perspective. F.O. Matthiessen, a student at Yale when he first heard Norman Thomas speak, was struck by the LID leader's academic style:

> His views were very different from those of our Yale professors, but he was still a kind of professor all the same. . . . Thomas never served to do much more than educate some middle class intellectuals. He was never able, like [Eugene V.] Debs, to command a real mass movement.[34]

In adhering to a scholastic approach to student politics, the LID's national leadership was perpetuating the tradition inherited from the early days of the Intercollegiate Socialist Society (ISS). Throughout the Progressive Era, the ISS had been entirely academic in its campus work; its avowed purpose was "promoting an intelligent interest in socialism among college men and women . . . through the formation of study clubs in the colleges and universities." The ISS did not engage in active political campaigns, but was "purely a discussion, a study organization."[35] And when the ISS renamed itself the LID in 1921, this strategy did not change. In fact, the top leaders of the LID throughout the 1920s, Harry Laidler and Norman Thomas, were ISS veterans brought up amidst a student political world in which socialist ideas were studied and discussed, but rarely acted upon.

Memories of the ISS experience also limited the militancy of the League for Industrial Democracy during the 1920s because they lowered the national leadership's expectations concerning the potential political strength of the campus Left. Both Thomas and Laidler had lived through the anti-radical hysteria of wartime and post-World War I America, which brought the ISS and much of the American Left to the brink of collapse. These LID leaders had been so scarred by the Red Scare and so accustomed to censorship, speaker bans, and general political repression on American campuses that they could not envision a complete reversal of the collegiate political order. Consequently, they could not foresee a future where the campuses—for the first time in American history—would become the base for a mass student protest movement.[36]

The excessively scholastic character of the LID found expression at the campus as well as at the national level. Throughout 1920s the dominant form of LID campus organization was the study (or discussion) group. At Yale, for instance, the LID affiliate's criteria for membership in the 1920s was more akin to a Phi Beta Kappa chapter than to an organization of political activists. Indeed, Yale LID leaders took pride in the fact that admission to their little chapter was not automatic, but had to be earned. One of these Yale LID officers reported that the chapter

> which now includes thirty-five members is exclusive; it admits only those to membership who show a keen interest in its work. It excludes those who are indifferent. A student meets us on the campus. He wants to be admitted to the Club. We ask whether he reads the newspapers, the *Nation*, the *New Republic*, the *Freeman*; whether he cares about the issues the Club is discussing. If he answers "Yes" he is admitted. If the answer is "No" he is refused.[37]

This same brand of introverted academic radicalism set the tone for the Cornell LID chapter during the 1920s, leading one disenchanted member to complain that the organization was being scorned as too "high brow" by most students; it was "a mere debating society, attracting radical students, but rather ineffective in reaching the outsider."[38]

If the student Left was to become a real force on campus in the 1930s, it would have to change its organizing strategy and create a more effective approach than the study group program of the old LID. The NSL's founders recognized this need for change; they pioneered tactics that were less academic than those which had been used so unsuccessfully by the LID during the 1920s. The NSL had no patience with ivory tower radicalism; the organization rejected the notion that the college radical's duty was solely to study or discuss radicalism. Instead, the League called for students to become activists in the struggle for egalitarian change both on and off campus. Indeed, at the core of the NSL's founding program in December 1931 was a call to immediate action on a set of ambitious yet practical political demands.[39]

NSL leaders perceived that the surest route to politicizing undergraduates was to engage them in struggles relating to political, social, and economic issues of concern to the student community. The NSL program emphasized the importance of mobilizing students around campus based issues: thirteen of the eighteen points in the program concerned collegiate issues. Here the NSL committed itself to rallying students on behalf of academic freedom, unemployment insurance for idle graduates, a free student-run employment agency, state aid to needy collegians (funded by taxes on the rich), increased appropriations for public education. The program also called for the ending of: college military training, racial and sexual discrimination on campus, exorbitant educational fees and textbook prices, compulsory campus religious services, faculty interference in extracurricular activities, and censorship of student publications. The NSL demanded complete political autonomy for student groups and freedom for students to "affiliate with such outside organizations as they choose."[40]

The NSL's extensive agenda for action on campus-related issues represented a significant breakthrough for the American student Left; it provided a vehicle for going beyond the study group mentality inherited from the LID of the 1920s and working to mobilize undergraduates for concrete political goals. The NSL helped give the student Left a sense of identity which it had lacked in previous decades. The League introduced the novel idea that campus conditions could provide student radicals with important issues around which to organize a mass, activist, and autonomous student movement as opposed to merely performing educational work or serving as an auxiliary of an adult organization like the LID. In fact, beginning with the NSL's original platform in 1931, entitled "For a National Student Movement," the term "student movement" became central to the campus Left, and with that term came the notion that such a movement could play an important role in strengthening American radicalism. NSL leaders prided themselves on having founded the most militant group of student activists in the nation and "the only independent organization of students, led by students, committed to a program of activity based on immediate student concerns."[41]

The NSL's birth marked a new departure in campus politics not only because the group pioneered an innovative approach to student organizing, but also because the NSL's founders included communists. This was a surprising development which broke with a tradition of communist inactivity on campus. The Communist Party and its youth organization, the Young Workers League (later renamed the Young Communist League) had viewed college students in the 1920s as an unreliable bourgeois element whose privileged economic position located them "in the camp of reaction." Even undergraduates who openly embraced radicalism were suspect, a Young Workers League leader explained in 1923, because "they bring with them . . . the prejudices, the mental restrictions of their former middle class environment. A young worker in the League is worth more than two students."[42] This narrow proletarian orientation meant that communist youth organizers forfeited control of the "bourgeois" college Left to the LID during the 1920s. The YCL's structure in the 1920s reflected this same bias; it had branches in factories and working class communities, but not on college campuses.[43]

The Depression did not initially change the way that adult leaders of the American Communist Party thought about college students. These leaders adhered to the ultra-radical Third Period dogma, set by the Comintern, which stressed the imminence of proletarian upheaval and revolution. In line with this proletarian orientation, the Communist Party hierarchy remained obsessed with blue-collar organizing and in 1931, the year of the NSL's birth, demonstrated no interest in mobilizing "bourgeois" college youth.[44]

Unlike these adults, however, communist students saw new opportunities on the horizon for radical student organizing. To exploit these new opportunities, they joined with their classmates, a larger group of communist sympathizers from City, Columbia, Brooklyn, and Hunter Colleges, in founding the NSL. These young leftists understood, from the type of first-hand observation available only to students, that the Depression had the potential to politicize the colleges, rendering obsolete the Communist Party's traditional indifference to student organizing. A new generation of radicals was emerging in the United States, bringing with it an interest in student politics and a sensitivity to campus realities that had been absent from the Communist Party in the past.[45]

The involvement of young communists in founding the NSL marked a substantial break with the proletarian orientation of not only the CPUSA, but also the international communist hierarchy. This point was driven home to NSL founder Joseph Clark at the Amsterdam Anti-war Congress a year after the creation of the League. Here Clark, a communist student, was so struck by the negative attitude of Young Communist International (YCI) leaders towards student organizing that he launched into a heated debate with one of these leaders, a German communist, over the importance of building student movements.[46] Clark attacked the still popular communist notion that radicals should focus all of their attention on workers and factories. He challenged the German communist leader's contention that radical organizing would yield nothing in bourgeois educational institutions. Clark stressed the importance of creating "student movements having a life of their own, issues of their own." In response, the doctrinaire German communist, according to Clark, "finally became a little exasperated with me and asked 'Du bist Student oder Kommunist?' [Are you a student or a Communist?] And at that time I had sufficient independence of mind to say 'Ich bin Student und Kommunist.' [I am a student and a Communist.] In other words, that I saw no contradiction in that."[47]

Clark's words and the advent of the NSL itself are reminders that all communists did not think alike. At a time when the adult leaders of the American CP and the YCI were still largely indifferent to student organizing, Clark and other YCLers in the NSL were enthusiastic student organizers—confident that a major radical movement could be built on

American college campuses. And somewhere in between the indifference of the adult CP and the enthusiasm of the NSLers stood the leadership of the American YCL during the early 1930s. YCL leaders still gave priority to organizing working-class youth, and in the NSL's early days, they focused much more on factories than on campuses. Indeed, the national reports of YCL leaders in 1931 and early 1932 do not even mention college youth. But at the same time, the YCL leadership approved of the involvement of student YCLers in the NSL and helped provide the embryonic NSL with some of the contacts it needed to form an intercampus organizational network. The national YCL leadership, in other words, was sympathetic and cooperative with the NSL, but did not yet see college campuses as a central arena for the radicalization of youth.[48]

As a communist-influenced organization, the NSL was unusual in that its birth was was not dictated from above—by the CP or national YCL leaders—but rather evolved from below, out of the agitation of communist rank and filers and communist sympathizers in the wake of the CCNY free speech fight. NSL founder Harry Magdoff, who was not a YCLer when he helped establish the NSL, underscored this point, recalling that the NSL's creation "wasn't a plot" of the Communist Party or YCL leadership.

> It was just the other way around. It was a movement that developed and generated excitement. We decided on the NSL . . . . We the guys at City College and the other [campuses]. We corresponded with each other. We had very exciting meetings in the citywide Student League. We corresponded through the *Student Review*. We were moving. We wanted a student movement.[49]

Echoing Magdoff, NSL founder Max Gordon, a YCL member at the time of the NSL's birth, stressed that the YCLers active in founding the NSL were not under orders to do so from either the CP or the YCL. He and his fellow Communist students "operated on their own," in their student organizing because the YCL at this point was "not predominantly interested in the student movement; it was predominantly interested in the young workers' movement."[50]

The NSL's early autonomy was also evident in the League's finances. It began its life financially independent and received no economic assistance from either the YCL or CP. For its economic survival the League relied upon dues from its members and subscriptions to its magazine, which in an era of Depression kept the NSL chronically poor. Harry Magdoff recalled that because of this lack of funds he, as editor of the NSL's national magazine, was constantly facing "the problem of getting out a magazine and not having money to pay for it. And the printer refusing to do it. [I was] trying to raise money to pay the bill for three or four months." Being poor was so trying, Magdoff joked, that "Goddamn it, if the Party would give some help it would have been welcome . . . ."[51]

Although the NSL was born as a joint venture of communist sympathizers and YCLers, the latter quickly assumed a dominant role in the student organization. YCLers brought with them the manipulative political style which they had learned in the communist movement. Thus in NSL chapters, key policy decisions were increasingly shaped in advance via caucuses (called "fractions") of communist members, particularly in the YCL strongholds. Since YCLers constituted the only group operating in this coordinated fashion within the NSL, their voice was often the decisive one. On some campuses YCL hegemony grew so complete that it led to almost comical situations. This was the case at Hunter College, where according to Joseph Clark, only one of the NSL activists

> was not a member of the YCL. And after a while the YCL members came over to this one person and said "look this is a little absurd if we have to have a separate meeting beforehand to decide what's going to happen. Why don't you just join [the YCL] and we'll at least eliminate one meeting?"[52]

Hunter's case was unusual, however, in that on most campuses YCLers constituted a minority within the NSL chapters. No matter how big or small the YCL group on campus, because it was an open secret that YCL factions were making NSL decisions, activists sometimes decided that in order to have a hand in policy making they would join the YCL. This was, for instance, a major impetus for George Watt's decision to join the YCL. In Brooklyn College's NSL chapter, Watt recalled,

> most of the people were not in the YCL . . . . The YCL had a . . . caucus operating as an organized faction within the NSL. And I used to come to [NSL] meetings and decisions would already be made, and I'd be confronted with people already having their minds made up about what they were going to do, what action they were going to take and so on. So that you felt that if you weren't in . . . [the YCL] you weren't where the action was . . . . That certainly may have drawn people [into the YCL] . . . . People don't want to be outside the action . . . . [It was] another factor that I feel I must honestly say also led me to join the YCL.[53]

The growing YCL dominance in the NSL was not, however, simply the result of caucusing or sly political maneuvering; it also represented the outcome of the ideological affinity between NSLers who were and those who were not YCL members. The non-YCLers in the NSL were often as pro-Soviet and anti-capitalist as the communists. The positions the YCL desired were often no different than those the unaffiliated students in the NSL would have supported anyway. Had this not been the case, the YCL's flagrantly undemocratic practice of pre-arranging NSL positions in communist caucuses might have become an issue in the League: a consensus over policy prevented any controversy over process. The ideological affinity between YCLers and unaffiliated radicals in the NSL was so strong, in fact, that non-YCLers could serve in important positions in the student organization without ever being pressured into taking a political position by the communists. This was the case, for instance, with several of the editors of the NSL's national magazine, who were given free rein to write as they pleased, despite the fact that they were not YCLers.[54] The political proximity between the two groups was such that often the most active students who entered the NSL unaffiliated eventually gravitated toward YCL membership.

Though YCL influence over the NSL seems to suggest that the Student League was a typical communist front organization, the NSL was in one very important respect distinct from most communist fronts: it initially ran with little direction from CP or YCL headquarters. The NSL was, as former NSL activist Theodore Draper put it, "on a longer leash than any other communist organization." This existed because the NSL had emerged at a time when the national leadership of the the CP and YCL—preoccupied with mobilizing workers—showed little interest in student organizing. During the first critical year of the NSL's life, neither the Party nor the YCL leadership cared enough about the campuses to devise strategies or goals for the young communists in the NSL. Since the Party elite had not developed positions on student organizing, the communists in the NSL freely invented their own strategies for building the student movement. This gave the NSL a freewheeling quality which was unusual for an organization in which communists were prominent.[55]

This degree of autonomy from the CP/YCL leadership had a salutary effect on the NSL. Because the NSL was not the creation of the Party elite, it did not inherit a full dose of the extreme sectarianism which so limited the CP's effectiveness during the early Depression years. And it was during this time when CP and YCL leaders, in accord with the Third Period line, continuously spewed forth divisive attacks upon even fellow leftists, denouncing Socialist Party leaders as class enemies and "social fascists."[56] Led by and for students, the NSL was able to formulate policies that were based more on campus realities than Comintern dogma. The NSL's effectiveness was facilitated by this, since it meant that the student organization's tactics came not from party bureaucrats but from youths who understood the campus political environment in which they were organizing.

II

In the semester following its birth the NSL would become a magnet for some of Depression America's most rebellious college students. Part of the attraction the League held for these campus rebels was that the NSL captured their radical disillusionment with both capitalism and mainstream politics in America. That disillusionment was rooted in the

Depression itself—the way that the crisis was not only impoverishing millions of Americans, but also closing the door of economic opportunity to an entire generation of college youth fated to, as the NSL put it, face a job market blighted by a "staggering" unemployment rate. To these students the American economic system appeared callous and irrational. Articulating this student outrage, an early NSL editorial charged that

> the years which have been spent in universities preparing for useful careers, were, for society and for students, only wasted years. The energy, the hope, the labor of youth, these things which could be society's most valuable asset, were thrown into discard like an obsolete machine. A social order which involves this waste and this conflict is sick. . . . "Go to the breadlines," it says, . . . "and in your hunger and misery, let your trained intelligence contemplate the wretchedness of idle bodies and unemployed minds."[57]

Although the NSL's platform was not explicitly communist, the organization was born with what one NSL activist aptly called a "revolutionary temperament."[58] The NSL was certain that not only the economy, but the political structure was in decay. What was needed was a "new social order," more rational, resilient, and democratic than capitalism. There would, in the NSL's view, be an extended period of class conflict before this new socialistic order could be attained: A struggle emerged which pitted workers and their battle for a new and more egalitarian America against the ruling class, determined to preserve its privileges under the bankrupt capitalist system. And according to the NSL, students could, if properly directed by the Left, assume a progressive role in this class struggle. "In spite of having been trained in the habits and the service of the ruling class," college students, because of the Depression, would soon be unemployable. Therefore their "broader interests lie with" the proletariat, the "class which is striving to build a new social order."[59]

The NSL did not call outright for a Soviet America, but the League's rosy pronouncements about Stalinist Russia leave little doubt that in envisioning a more just and Depression-free social order the League leaned heavily on the Soviet model. NSL leaders believed that all the inefficiency and poverty which burdened Depression America could at once be eliminated if the nation followed the example set by the Soviet Union. When NSL leaders looked at the U.S.S.R., they saw a socialist utopia. This naive idealism was reflected in point five of the NSL program, which specified that upon the American

> student movement . . . devolves the historic obligation of popularizing the achievements of the Soviet Union. Because the Soviet Union is the only country in the world which has been able to avoid crises and to eliminate unemployment and mass poverty, because planned economy as exemplified in the Five Year Plan is raising the standard of living of its population, the Soviet Union stands out as an inspiration and guide to us

in other parts of the world who are witnessing the social and economic evils which accompany Capitalism.[60]

The NSL's pro-Soviet position and its link to the communist movement had a definite appeal to some students angered by the Depression and the breakdown of capitalism. The CP possessed great prestige with many of these young radicals because of its leadership in labor and unemployment struggles and its ideological and political ties to the Soviet Union. This was, it must be recalled, the pre-Moscow trials era, when the Soviet revolution still enjoyed great prestige in radical and progressive circles—where the Soviet Union continued to be viewed as the world's one worker-run, depression-proof nation.[61]

An equally important part of the brand of radicalism espoused by the NSL was scorn for liberalism. Born when Herbert Hoover was still in the White House—and the New Deal had not as yet arisen to resuscitate liberalism—the NSL regarded liberalism as terminally ill. Liberals seemed to be as lost as Hoover in groping for a solution to the economic crisis.[62] For the rebellious undergraduate of 1932, the rudderless state of liberalism seemed a marked contrast with the NSL and its Marxist analysis. At a time when liberals were confused about causes of and solutions to the economic crisis, the NSL was supremely confident, claiming in fact to have all the answers about what caused the Depression (capitalism), how to end the economic crisis (move toward socialism), and how students could expedite that change (build an anti-capitalist student movement). As the Hoover years drew to a close amidst anxiety and confusion, such certitude appeared a great asset, and it helped attract students into the NSL. This was true for James Wechsler who, in explaining how he and several friends ended up joining the NSL, recalled during the last year of the Hoover era

> the absence of clear, affirmative plausible alternatives to Marxism, the hesitancy of scholars and statesmen in the face of the Marxist critique. It was not merely what the Communists said that enthralled us; it was what other men failed to say. The self-assurance of the Communists proved contagious; the liberal loss of nerve repelled us.[63]

While the NSL's radicalism made the organization extremely attractive to the nation's most rebellious students, it also prevented the League from becoming a mass membership organization. A student body raised on Republicanism and capitalism was—even amidst a Depression which was moving it leftward—hardly likely to enroll in a pro-Soviet student group. The NSL's strength, then, would not be in its membership figures, which remained small, but rather in its ability to serve as a political spark plug igniting protests by, hundreds, thousands, and finally more than a hundred thousand students—most of whom were not NSL members.[64] The NSL, in the leftist lingo of the time, served as a vanguard organization which (along with a reinvigorated campus LID) set the stage for America's first mass student movement.

The NSL's effectiveness as a vanguard organization derived from the League's ability to orchestrate political campaigns around issues that attracted mainstream students. And thus resulted the crowning irony of the NSL's political life: Despite the fact that NSLers scorned American liberalism, they knew how to appeal to students with liberal values and did so with great skill and effect. Though NSLers, as radicals, bemoaned the piece-meal reforms championed by liberal leaders in the past, these same NSLers, as realistic student organizers, were masters at championing their own list of reforms which aroused strong campus support.

Despite their own leftwing predilections, NSLers were pragmatic rather than dogmatic when it came to relating to mainstream students; so much so that during the early 1930s they became the most effective student organizers on behalf of many ostensibly liberal causes, including academic freedom and state aid to education. He and his fellow NSL leaders championed such causes, Joseph Clark explained, because they

> knew that to build a [student] movement you had to proceed on issues with which a wide group of people would be in agreement, and we utilized these very well. . . . We had a vision that the Communists would have to get out of the complete circle of isolation and sectarianism in which they were immersed during the period when the NSL was formed.[65]

The NSL was a paradoxical amalgam of ideological staleness, political insight and tactical innovation. When NSLers discussed the Soviet Union, their thought was thoroughly derivative, echoing *Daily Worker* propaganda. But when it came to the problems of organizing American students, NSLers thought for themselves and thought imaginatively. They predicted early and accurately that the Depression was going to shake the collegiate middle class out of its traditional political apathy. They were the first radicals in twentieth century America to recognize the political potential of the campuses. In addition, they understood that if student activists ran their own political organizations "formed for the purpose of developing a *student* movement on the basis of conditions and problems facing the students," they could ignite mass protest.[66] They were also the organizers who began translating this vision of insurgent campuses into political reality, by initiating a series of dramatic student protests during the 1932 spring semester.

Chapter 3

Springtime of Revolt

We have been immensely heartened by the recent appearance of a new student spirit on campus. Critics of the American undergraduate who have deplored his herd-mindedness, his conservatism, his preoccupation with parties, athletics and career-hunting, his . . . indifference to public affairs, have witnessed with pleasant surprise the emergence of large numbers of students interesting themselves actively, intelligently, practically, passionately in the political, social and economic problems of these critical days. The most dramatic expressions of the new student spirit have been the student Kentucky expedition and the Columbia Free-speech strike. . . . The new student movement . . . . is a vital new force in American life . . . .

Newton Arvin	Max Eastman
Sherwood Anderson	Waldo Frank
Roger Baldwin	Michael Gold
Malcolm Cowley	Oakley Johnson
H.W.L. Dana	Scott Nearing
John Dos Passos	Mark Van Doren
Theodore Dreiser	

"An Appeal," *Student Review* (October 1932), 21.

Tune: Coming Round the Mountain

Oh, we'll bring the Constitution when we come.
Oh, we'll bring the Constitution when we come.
Oh, we'll bring the Constitution
Now is *that* a revolution.
Oh, we'll bring the Constitution when we come.
Oh, to Hell with the Constitution when you come.
Oh, to Hell with the Constitution when you come.
Oh, to Hell with the Constitution
We must guard our institutions
For you're just a bunch of Rooshians
When you come.

"Songs Composed by Kentucky Student Delegation,"
Student Review (May 1932), 21.

T he spring of 1932 marked the dawn of a new age in American student politics. Shaken by the Depression, collegians began to discard their traditional political apathy. Even college debating teams were affected, choosing as their leading topic that spring "social planning of industry," and arguing over whether the "Stuart Chase plan," the "Charles Beard plan," or the Socialist plan offered the best way out of the economic crisis.[1] And college students were doing more than talking about politics; they were starting to become involved in political actions, signaling a major change on campus. Where for the past decade political activism had been a rarity among college youth, beginning in 1932 such activism became increasingly common. The campuses were entering an era of protest: from the spring of 1932 until the end of the Depression decade not a semester would pass without some significant expression of political protest by American undergraduates.

The shift toward activism became evident during a series of political protests led by the NSL in the spring semester of 1932. These initial political actions involved only a minority of students, most of whom were from just one region of the country—the Northeast. But these protests were the start of something big; they gave life to a dissident tradition, which by the mid-1930s would yield the first mass student protest movement in American history. The student political actions of the spring of 1932 did not focus upon a single issue. Instead, there were a diversity of concerns, ranging from the exploitation of workers off campus to free speech and economic problems on campus. Though the issues around which students mobilized were diverse, all of this activism was characterized by a common spirit: a desire to prove that undergraduates cared about the problems of Depression America and were organizing to address those problems. This was a conscious revolt against the apolitical collegiate lifestyle inherited from the 1920s, which because of the Depression had begun to seem anachronistic; it was an attempt to replace that lifestyle with a more adult-like and political undergraduate tradition that would be more appropriate to a generation and a society troubled by hard times.[2]

The spring revolt was also significant because in it Columbia students were as prominent, and at times more prominent, than their counterparts from New York's municipal colleges. This represented a change from the past year, the NSL's formative period, during which CCNY was the key campus in the radical student movement. In contrast with CCNY, Columbia was a relatively affluent institution and the radicals on Morningside Heights did not come from low income backgrounds. The Columbia Left was also not so heavily Jewish as the CCNY, Brooklyn, and Hunter College Left. In fact, the key NSL leaders at Columbia during this early period were WASPs—and in this respect too, Columbia was more typical of the American student population than were New York's city colleges. Columbia was, of course, too much of an elite university, whose faculty was too liberal and location in New York too distinctive to ever be considered a truly typical American university. But the prominence of Columbia students in several of the collegiate political actions of the spring of 1932 at least suggested the potential of the NSL to reach beyond low income youth, thus attracting students from the type of middle-class backgrounds it would have to mobilize if it was to ignite a mass movement on the nation's campuses.[3]

The first student political action to attract national attention in Depression America was the student expedition to Kentucky's coal region in March 1932. Organized from New York by the NSL, a small group of students volunteered to travel south to bring food and clothing to the striking coal miners in Harlan and Bell counties. The students also planned to investigate charges that Kentucky police and vigilantes, paid by the coal companies, were brutalizing the strikers. The NSL launched the expedition in the hope of not only providing humanitarian aid to the miners, but also of raising the political consciousness of undergraduates. NSL leaders thought that by exposing students to capitalism at its worst—the poverty and bloody class conflict of the Kentucky coal region—they could radicalize them. Through this expedition the NSL sought to demonstrate that students, despite their youth and political inexperience, could act effectively on behalf of those victimized by the Depression.[4]

Kentucky's coal miners needed whatever assistance they could get from the students; they had been hard hit by the Depression. With the price of coal plummeting, mine operators had cut production, so that miners could work only three days a week. The combination of poor hours and low wages left the miners with weekly paychecks of only four to five dollars. Making matters worse, the coal operators paid the miners in scrip, forcing their employees to buy at company stores, where their pay was usually worth no more than 50 or 60 cents on the dollar. By February 1931 this bleak situation had become intolerable, as the companies imposed an additional 10 per cent wage cut—provoking 11,000 miners to strike. "We starve while we work; we might as well strike while we starve," explained one striking miner.[5]

The coal operators in Kentucky, who in the words of labor historian Bert Cochran "ran the enclosed communities like rapacious feudal barons," controlled the local police and criminal justice system and were able to mobilize them against the strikers. The coal operators used deputies and their own armed men to assault the miners. One of these violent attacks, in May 1931, wrought a half hour of machine gun fire and at least four deaths. This violence and the immense political power of the coal operators intimidated the United Mine Workers (UMW), whose leaders abandoned the seemingly hopeless strike. When the UMW walked away from the Kentucky struggle, the communist-led National Miners Union stepped in and worked to organize the coal strike.[6]

Though more defiant than the UMW, the National Miners Union fared no better than its predecessor in battling the formidable coal operators, who continued to control the region with an iron fist. But if the communists could not match the power of the coal companies in Kentucky, they could and did hurt the companies' image nationally by publicizing both the poverty of the miners and the brutal repression of their strike. A key component of this campaign, which influenced the students and helped lead to their Kentucky expedition, was its mobilization of some of the nation's leading writers on behalf of the miners.[7]

Alarmed by the violence in Kentucky, novelists Theodore Dreiser and Waldo Frank headed a small delegation of writers, which in November 1931 and February 1932 traveled to Kentucky to investigate the miners' strike. Their visits to the coal region helped draw attention to the miners' plight. But the hostile reception accorded to Dreiser's group by Kentucky police and coal company thugs showed that attempts to assist the miners could be dangerous. Two members of the delegation, including Waldo Frank, were beaten bloody by local deputies. Kentucky officials also sought to indict the entire delegation under the criminal syndicalism laws.[8]

NSL leaders praised the writers' delegation for publicizing the harsh treatment of the miners in Kentucky and "test[ing] freedom of speech, and assembly in that region." NSLers credited that delegation with exposing "the reign of terror prosecuted against the trade union activities of coal miners."[9] Soon after the writers returned from Kentucky, the NSL published a passionate article by novelist and delegation member John Dos Passos, depicting the strikers as an oppressed and impoverished group, valiantly struggling against the tyranny of the coal operators. Here Dos Passos told of a union meeting held in a

> low frame [church] hall . . . packed with miners and their wives; all faces were out of early American history. Stepping into the hall was going back a hundred years. . . . These were the gaunt faces, the slow elaborations of talk and courtesy, of the frontiersmen who voted for Jefferson and Jackson, and whose turns of speech were formed on the oratory of Patrick Henry. I never felt the actuality of the American revolution so intensely as sitting in that church, listening to the mountaineers with their old time phrases getting up on their feet and explaining why the time to fight for freedom had come again.[10]

The writers' expedition to Kentucky had its most immediate campus impact in New York City. The expedition had been organized by Dreiser out of his West 57th Street studio; and the harassment of these New York based writers in Kentucky for simply bringing to light conditions in the coal region struck close to home, angering faculty as well as students in the city. On March 3, 1932 professors from almost every college and university in the New York City area joined with over 150 other educators in publishing a petition protesting the violations of civil liberties in Harlan and Bell Counties. This protest drew praise from the student press in New York.[11]

Among New York's small core of student activists, the Dreiser expedition to Kentucky generated a wave of sympathy for the miners and a desire to do something on their behalf. One of the students so affected was Columbia NSL leader Robert Hall. A native Mississippian, Hall had come to Columbia hoping to attain the skills necessary to help transform the South politically and economically. He was convinced that unless there was a revolution in labor and race relations and a thorough modernization of the southern farm economy, the South would remain a backward and impoverished region. These concerns led Hall to major in agricultural economics at Columbia and to become an active communist. Hall's contacts with the communist movement in New York generated the idea of organizing a student expedition to the Kentucky coal region. The idea emerged during a discussion between Hall and a woman active in the communist-dominated International Workers' Order (IWO). Hall recalls that after he voiced his concern about the miners, the IWO organizer "asked if I would lead a student delegation to Harlan, Kentucky [because] there was hunger in those mountains." Hall quickly seized upon the idea, and other NSL leaders were equally enthusiastic.[12]

The NSL's announcement that it would be organizing a student expedition to the coal fields provoked an angry response from Kentucky law enforcement officials. They saw the student trip as essentially a repetition of the Dreiser delegation, which in their view was simply a group of Yankee radicals that had come to stir up trouble. Bell County Prosecutor Walter B. Smith warned "these rattle-brained college students . . . to stay out of southeastern Kentucky." Harlan Sheriff John Henry Blair threatened that if the students coming to Kentucky did not "watch their step," he would "file them along with the other exhibits in the Harlan and Pineville jails . . ."[13] Students had good reason to take these threats seriously, since the Kentucky police had recently beaten and indicted members of the writers' delegation. Even as students went among their college faculty seeking donations for the Kentucky trip, they were reminded of the dangers. Sympathetic professors agreed to help fund the expedition, but expressed fear that in Kentucky their students might face violence and death.[14]

Neither the warnings of belligerent Kentucky deputies nor the assaults on previous delegations intimidated the NSL. The threats by Kentucky officials actually created campus support for the expedition because they suggested that these officials had something to hide, making the delegation's aim of investigating conditions in the coal fields seem all the more critical. These threats and the condescending tone of the statements the Kentuckians made in denouncing the delegation angered students, including the editor of the *Columbia Spectator*. Responding to the Bell County Prosecutor's crack that "college students are lollipops," the *Spectator* denounced the "flophouse tactics" of this "alleged stool of the mineowners," and wished the expedition

> the best of luck in this praiseworthy attempt to feed a few hundred American citizens who, in accordance with the most noble precepts of

our fair country, are being slowly starved to death in order that the mine owners of Harlan county might rest their fastidious buttocks on upholstered chairs.[15]

The threats and potential danger associated with the upcoming Harlan trip came as no surprise to the NSL activists who organized the expedition. They thought of American capitalism as an oppressive class system held together by violence, and they saw the threats as one more sign that fascistic employers would stop at nothing in their drive to thwart unionization. For some of the young radicals this element of danger gave the Harlan trip a special romantic appeal; it meant standing on the front lines of the American class struggle beside courageous workers battling some of the nation's cruelest capitalists. This would be an opportunity for student leftists to prove that their militancy equalled and even surpassed that of their adult counterparts. In this defiant spirit one student radical confided to a comrade just prior to leaving for Harlan that "one hundred and fifty students will not be as easily cowed as [the] eight or ten writers [in the Dreiser delegation]; and I don't think we'll sublimate abrogation of our constitutional privileges . . ." Another of the student radicals, worried about the zeal of fellow activists going to Harlan, told a friend that he hoped to see him after the Kentucky trip, "though in light of X's romanticism I may not be alive next Friday."[16]

Contrary to the expectations of this worried student, however, NSL leaders did not allow revolutionary romanticism to cloud their political judgement. The trip's organizers adopted an undogmatic and sober tone as they prepared for the expedition. The NSLers avoided confrontational rhetoric; they portrayed the expedition as an investigatory and relief mission, rather than as a fighting brigade about to enter the trenches of class warfare. Conscious that ultra-radical posturing might scare off the very students they were hoping to politicize, NSLers went out of their way to demonstrate that their primary interest in Harlan was humanitarian aid rather than revolutionary martyrdom.

In this spirit NSL leader Robert Hall, when in the process of organizing the delegation, warned his fellow students that in order to avoid antagonizing the Kentucky police, they should not dress down in the Left-proletarian fashion of the day. Hall advised that "no one should wear leather jackets, which [would mark them] as left wingers . . . 'the mark of the beast.' "[17] Members of the delegation heeded Hall's advice, so that when the American public viewed the Associated Press photographs of the first Kentucky-bound busload of students, which departed from New York City on March 23, 1932, they saw a very respectable looking group of collegians clad in suits and skirts.[18] This same pragmatic approach would prevail throughout the Kentucky trip, during which, as one delegation member recalled, "all words which might impute communism to us were taboo."[19]

The eighty-student delegation which set out to visit Harlan was small, but it was, nonetheless, ten times the size of the writers' delegation and the biggest effort yet to bring direct aid to the striking miners. The composition of the student delegation suggested, however, that the NSL had yet to mobilize much support beyond its home base in New York City. The majority of delegation members were from the New York campuses, including Columbia, City College, Hunter College, Brooklyn College, Union Theological Seminary, and New York University. Nonetheless, the presence of student delegates from the University of Tennessee, the University of Wisconsin, Harvard and Smith Colleges, and the selection of Kentucky as the sight for the NSL's first major action showed that the League's ambitions extended far beyond New York.[20]

In their attempt to expand the student movement's base, the NSL sought to transcend ideological as well as geographical boundaries. Despite the NSL's pro-communist orientation, the League organized the Harlan delegation on a non-sectarian basis. Expedition organizers welcomed into the delegation unaffiliated students, and even socialists—this at a time when the Communist Party adhered to the Comintern's Third Period line, which dictated that communists shun the socialists and condemn them as "social fascists." The NSL's unifying approach led a number of socialists to join the delegation, and they were impressed by the absence of sectarian rancor during the expedition. Underscoring the spirit of unity on the Kentucky trip, one of the socialist delegation members, after describing the positive interaction between socialists and communists on the expedition, observed:

> I have never seen a finer or more intelligent set of Communists than those with whom we traveled. Not only our songs harmonized, but they even listened sympathetically to X's plea for a united proletarian movement that would utilize socialist tactics where the class struggle was not sharp enough or effective to stress.[21]

The delegation was not, however, composed solely of radicals. Its members also included more moderate students, whose political experience had been confined to discussions in liberal study groups and volunteer work in local settlement houses. These moderates and liberals came to the expedition, in the words of delegation leader Robert Hall, with "a rather indefinite interest in labor problems and a somewhat vague liberal sympathy with the working class."[22]

Though to an objective observer the eighty-student delegation might seem unimposing, to Kentucky mine operators and their allies, eighty students too many were coming to the coal region; they saw to it that the students were harassed even before the delegation reached Kentucky. At Knoxville, Tennessee, where the students stayed overnight prior to entering Kentucky, a number of hotels refused them accommodations. Detectives tailed the delegation. The following day, as the first busload of students and the two miners serving as their guides approached the Cumberland Gap—still in Tennessee—a group of cars, packed with angry people who shouted and made menacing gestures at the students, followed and surrounded the bus. As the delegation crossed into Kentucky, it found a hostile crowd milling near the state line. Several men stepped forward from the crowd, demanding that the bus pull over, and since one of them pointed a revolver at the bus driver, he quickly complied.[23]

Threats shot out from the crowd. Despite the students' protests, deputies seized the two miners who had been serving as guides for the delegation. As the police evicted these miners, the crowd chanted: "We want them." When NSL leader Robert Hall stepped out of the bus to speak for the student delegation, there were calls for a lynching. Hall attempted to calm the Kentuckians by assuring them that the students had come to the coal region on a peaceful and legal mission, "to make an impartial investigation of the coal fields. Charges of violations of constitutional rights, of violence and lawlessness have been made. We have come to see for ourselves whether these charges are true." Even as Hall spoke, however, a deputy pulled out his revolver and threatened to "put a bullet" between the NSL leader's eyes.[24]

County prosecutor Walter B. Smith took the lead in confronting the students. Smith made a speech denouncing the collegians as "Yankees, aliens and agitators." He insisted that irrespective of the students' "specious claims to liberty," they had no right to conduct any type of investigation in Kentucky. Smith demanded that the delegation leave the state immediately. But the students stood their ground; they refused to turn back. Armed guards escorted the students to the courthouse in Middlesboro, where they were to be held for questioning.[25]

When the students arrived at Middlesboro another angry crowd awaited them. Any illusions the students may have held about Kentucky justice were shattered by the kangaroo court which ensued. County prosecutor Smith's questioning was saturated with anti-Semitic, anti-communist, and xenophobic images. He depicted the delegation as an un-American group, composed of Russian-born Jewish communists. In a typical round of questioning, which drew much laughter from the Kentucky courtroom crowd, Smith ordered Arthur Goldschmidt, a Columbia undergraduate, to identify himself, and then asked, "How do you spell that J-E-W-O-L-D-S-C-H-M-I-D-T?"[26]

Before the questioning could go much further, however, Hall—perhaps because of his experience as an NSL leader and his poise as an older student and native southerner—had the presence of mind to object to the whole procedure. He demanded to know whether the students were under arrest. Informed that they were under investigation, but not yet arrested, Hall told the court "In that case I protest. You have no legal right to subject us to an investigation. If we are not under arrest, you cannot question us. We will refuse to answer." When Smith threatened to throw him into jail if he did not cooperate, Hall replied "I would rather rot in jail than forfeit a single one of my constitutional rights." Following Hall's lead, the rest of the delegation refused to answer Smith's questions.[27]

Smith interpreted this defiance as final proof that the students were "aliens come into our midst to spread . . . propaganda." He ordered the delegation to leave Kentucky and announced that he and his deputies would escort the students to the state line. Before the students could leave the courtroom, however, they were again denounced and threatened. The chief attorney for Bell County's coal operators, standing next to the judge and claiming to speak for him, shouted:

> These people are here to investigate us. But we can tell them that before we allow interference with our sacred institutions, the . . . Tennessee River . . . will run red with blood. We don't want them to come here with a bowl of soup and a hunk of Sovietism to feed our people.

The courthouse crowd responded to this tirade with chants of "Amen brother!"[28]

Surrounded by armed vigilantes, police and a large, hostile crowd, the students who had come to Kentucky on the first bus had no choice but to leave the state. During this forced exodus, Kentucky law enforcement officials moved from threats to actual physical abuse of the students. This violence erupted on the bus after Smith told student delegation members he possessed a letter proving their visit was the result of a communist plot. When the students asked Smith to show them the letter, he gave it to Elinor Curtis, a Columbia graduate student. Curtis, who thought the letter fraudulent, began taking notes about it, which alarmed Smith. Smith demanded that Curtis return the letter immediately, and when she refused, a deputy intervened and began to twist her arm violently. Another student tried to come to her aid. But the deputy charged at him and punched him in the jaw, forcing the stunned undergraduate to strike his head against the luggage rack.[29]

The second busload of students arrived in Kentucky one day later; it fared no better than the first. This group tried to elude the police by taking a back route to Bell County. Smith soon caught up with this second bus, however, when it ran out of gas on a steep mountain road. Fresh from their heated encounter with the first group of students, Smith and his deputies were angry and aggressive.

When Joe Leboit, a leader of this student delegation, attempted to prevent the police from boarding the bus by demanding to see a search warrant, the deputies declared that they did not need a warrant. Leboit protested that if the police boarded the bus, they would be violating the students' constitutional rights. "You have no constitutional rights," Smith replied. "Why, aren't we in the United States?" asked Leboit. "No," Smith responded, "You're in Kentucky." "Well then," said Leboit, "We demand our constitutional rights under the constitution of Kentucky." "There is no constitution in Kentucky," Smith said. "I'm the constitution, I'm the highest court of authority. I am the law." The deputies then pushed Leboit aside, boarded the bus and forced the students to drive out of the state. [30]

Deputies roughed up several students on this second delegation's trip back from Kentucky. These assaults were even more lawless than the violent incident on the first bus because they occurred on Tennessee soil, where the Kentucky police had no legal authority. The assault began after the bus crossed into Tennessee, when Leboit demanded that Smith and his deputies leave the bus, since it was no longer in their jurisdiction. Smith ordered Leboit to be silent and move to the back of the bus, but Leboit refused. The deputies responded by jumping Leboit and beating him bloody. A scuffle ensued in which the police literally kicked two students off the bus, injured a woman student, and hit a fourth delegation member in the head with a revolver.[31]

After its ejection from Kentucky and final departure from the police in Tennessee, the student delegation regrouped, determined to continue its pro-labor mission. Though recognizing that Kentucky law enforcement officials had made it impossible for them to bring direct material aid to the miners, the students attempted to assist the miners politically. The assault on the students had been picked up by the wire services and made national news. The delegation sought to use the publicity generated by their confrontation with Kentucky police to call attention to the plight of the striking miners. Claiming that their delegation had been victimized by the same "reign of terror" used to suppress the strikers in the coal region, the students sent representatives to the Governors of Kentucky and Tennessee, demanding an investigation of police brutality and violations of miners' and students' constitutional rights. Leaders of the student delegation carried these same demands to Washington; they requested that the Justice Department provide federal protection for a new student investigation of conditions in the coal region, and urged Congressional action on behalf of the miners. The students even brought these demands directly to the Hoover White House.[32]

Despite this flurry of protest activity, the students failed to convince state government officials or the Hoover Administration to aid the miners and investigate police brutality in Kentucky. Governor Ruby Laffoon of Kentucky told the student delegates he had no authority to redress their grievances. The Governor of Tennessee proved even less cooperative, terming the student delegates "uninvited guests," and warning them to avoid communism. Hoover Administration officials showed no concern about the lawlessness the students had encountered in Kentucky and Tennessee. The Justice Department announced that the conflict in the coal region was "a matter to be handled by the states." When the students attempted to take their case to President Hoover, they got no further than "the secretary of the secretary of the secretary of Mr. Hoover."[33]

While unable to move the Hoover Administration or its counterparts at the state level, the students managed to build support on Capitol Hill for the striking miners. The students helped provide liberal Senators with the political ammunition they needed to battle successfully for a congressional investigation of the coal strike. Delegation members met with the Senate Committee on Manufactures and offered evidence of misconduct by the Kentucky police. The students presented the Committee with .45 caliber bullets, which Kentucky deputies gave them with the warning that if the delegation sought to return with federal protection "this is what we would do to a United States deputy marshal who attempted to open up the highways through Kentucky."[34]

The harassment of the student delegation in Kentucky generated considerable public criticism of the coal operators and their allies. The coal companies came out of the incident looking reckless and brutal because their allies and agents had assaulted innocent youths. Articulating this rising public anger about conditions in the coal region, the *New York Herald Tribune* condemned county prosecutor Smith's mistreatment of the student delegation. The *Tribune* accused Smith of employing "primitive methods of legal violence," "gun rule," and "perversion of law." The *Tribune* condemned Smith's belligerent speeches to the students as examples of "narrow minded and fearful ignorance," and expressed concern for the rights of striking miners who lived within his jurisdiction.[35]

The disruption of the Harlan expedition by Kentucky police angered students and drew over 3,000 telegrams and letters of protest nationwide.[36] This support came from places where the NSL had never penetrated before, including the traditionally conservative schools of the South. Among the student bodies sending telegrams protesting the mistreatment of the delegation were those from Kentucky, Arkansas, Texas, Virginia, and North Carolina.[37] Even some students who prior to the Harlan trip had thought "that reports from the Kentucky and Tennessee [of exploitation and brutalization of the miners] were gross exaggerations hatched by overzealous radicals" became convinced—because of the mistreatment of the student delegation—"that most reports from those mining sections are badly understated."[38] The disruption of the expedition sparked student demonstrations in Chicago, outside the home of Samuel Insull, a utilities magnate who owned mines in Kentucky, and in Philadelphia by the offices of a J.P. Morgan affiliate and miner owner.[39]

The Harlan trip stirred up the student Left, inspiring the still small, but increasingly militant campus radical groups to undertake a series of pro-labor actions. Following the example set by this first NSL-led delegation, two midwestern student expeditions to the Illinois coal belt were launched in the spring of 1932. Both of these expeditions met with the same kind of police intervention which the students had encountered in Kentucky. The largest expedition, organized out of the University of Chicago, attracted 150 students and teachers; it was turned back in the Illinois coal region by a shot gun wielding sheriff. Boldest of all were the five Arkansas students from Commonwealth Labor College, who went to Kentucky in April 1932, seeking to carry on the investigatory and relief mission of the first student delegation. A band of armed vigilantes assaulted these students in Kentucky before they could reach the miners.[40]

II

For the NSL, the Harlan trip and the subsequent student publicity campaign on behalf of the miners served as both political baptism and confidence builder. These activists saw the expedition as a sign that students were coming of age politically; it showed that college youth could organize meaningful and serious political actions with national impact. NSLers boasted that the student delegation to Harlan represented a "historic vanguard" because it marked the first great break away from the apolitical, juvenile collegiate past—the world of fraternities and football—and the initial step toward converting the campuses into centers of political thought and action: "For the first time American students have come out of their shell and realized themselves as a social force."[41]

NSLers came away from the Kentucky trip feeling that the expedition had borne out both the League's leftist critique of capitalism and agitational approach to student organizing. In the official NSL account of the expedition, "Kentucky Makes Radicals," Robert Hall argued that by exposing delegation members to "the fascist regime in the coal fields," the NSL radicalized even the most moderate among them, teaching them more about the oppressive side of American capitalism than they could ever learn in their classes or discussion groups. Hall pointed out that some of the student delegation members had come to the expedition out of organizations that "were no more than liberal discussion clubs." According to Hall, at the beginning of the Kentucky trip, these liberal delegates had little in common with the radicals on the expedition. But by the end of the trip, all of the delegation members, angered by the assault upon them, spoke with one voice, uniting behind a radical statement condemning the police "terrorism" to which they and the miners were subjected.[42]

Although as radicals, NSL leaders naturally trumpeted the anti-capitalist implications of their experience in Kentucky, they also emphasized the constitutional issues at stake in the coal region. The NSLers were practical enough to recognize that mainstream students not yet ready to condemn capitalism were receptive to protests against brazen violations of civil liberties. Consequently, during and after the Kentucky trip these activists worked successfully, in the words of NSL founder Joseph Clark, "to make civil liberties and . . . the repression of civil rights and liberties an issue, and the basis for the development of their own organization."[43] Delegation leader Robert Hall took this same pragmatic approach with him when he appeared before the Senate Committee on Manufactures, during the congressional investigation of conditions in the coal region, which the student expedition had helped initiate. Hall avoided revolutionary hyperbole; instead he chose to detail the vigilanteism and police brutality which he and his fellow students had observed in Kentucky. Hall argued that in light of these abuses the federal government should step in to protect the rights of the miners.[44]

Even the NSL's main competitor on campus, the student LID, was impressed by the Kentucky expedition and the way that the NSL organized it. Upon returning to New York, student LID leader Joseph P. Lash, a delegation member and one of the students assaulted by the deputies, published an article praising the expedition.[45] A half century later, Lash looked back upon the Kentucky trip as "an important part of my life . . . . It was an eye opener," which showed him that "civil liberties had no meaning" in the coal region and that the miners "had no one to appeal to." Lash had been impressed as well by the political backbone NSLers had demonstrated in leading busloads of students down to a strike area so violent as Harlan. "The Communists were willing to take chances and do work where work had to be done." Noting that the "Communists were on their best behavior" during the Kentucky trip, Lash was struck by how well they got along with the socialist students. Indeed, in Lash's view, the student expedition to Kentucky was a successful pioneering venture into the type of coalition politics which would only later be adopted by adult communists (during the Popular Front era, which began in 1935). According to Lash, the

> Harlan expedition [demonstrated] that the Socialist and Communist students . . . and non-affiliated students could work together, and this was a way to fight what we considered fascism. And it had a unifying effect, particularly upon the two college organizations, the NSL and the student LID. And I was certainly one of those people who was affected by it.[46]

It was not merely student delegation members who were impressed with their Kentucky trip. Skeptical adult observers too conceded that the students conducted their work for the miners with surprising skill and intelligence. The editor of the *Nation* admitted that initially he was critical of the proposed student expedition to the coal region because he had thought collegians too young, immature, and naive to mount a serious political action. But after watching the students in action, the *Nation* editor was impressed with the political savvy the delegates displayed in rebounding from their assault in the coal region, and using the publicity it had attracted to focus national attention on the plight of the miners. In his eyes, these college youths had proven themselves more effective in aiding the miners than their adult counterparts, including the Dreiser delegation. The *Nation* editorial concluded that the student delegation "contributed more to the Kentucky fire than any of the numerous previous expeditions have."[47] And the conduct of the student delegation members even impressed their adversaries, including the editor of the *Middlesboro*

Daily News, an anti-union newspaper in Harlan County, who, though hostile to the students, "could not help but admire their courage."[48]

The expedition was, of course, far from a complete success. The students had been prevented from bringing material relief to the miners. The Senate hearings and publicity that the student delegation had helped generate for the miners were essentially moral victories: the hunger and harsh realities of the coal region remained. Nonetheless, the Harlan trip signaled the emergence of a new and more productive era for the student Left. Though the delegation could not end the suffering of the miners, its presence in Kentucky suggested that at least this generation—unlike the self-absorbed students of the past decade—cared enough to try. Those buses to Kentucky took students away from not only their campuses, but from a long history of collegiate political inertia. And if their moral victory in Kentucky looked large to the students, this was because it seemed to tower over any previous achievement of America's politically apathetic student body. Harlan also proved that student activists could transcend the sectarianism which had weakened the adult Left and the scholasticism which had traditionally dulled the campus Left. In showing that student radicals could do more than talk—and had indeed risked their own safety in order to assist the miners—the Harlan expedition suggested that the student Left of the 1930s would be more militant and action oriented than its academic predecessors.

III

The Harlan expedition proved to be only the start of a very busy spring semester for the NSL. Less than a week after confronting suppression in Kentucky, the NSL mobilized against another restriction of student political expression—at Columbia University. Here President Nicholas Murray Butler's administration caused an uproar on April 1, 1932 by expelling Reed Harris, the muckraking editor of the *Columbia Spectator,* the college's student newspaper. The free speech fight led by the NSL on Harris' behalf would be the stormiest campus protest yet seen in Depression America; it culminated in the first political strike by college students during the 1930s.

While the NSL would play the key role in leading the Columbia censorship battle, the story of this controversy begins not with the League but with Reed Harris himself. There was nothing in Harris' background that anticipated his emergence as a college rebel. Born to an affluent family, Harris began his educational career in a conservative manner, winning the DAR prize for a history essay and spending a summer at a Citizens Military Training Camp. Harris then attended the Staunton Military Academy in Virginia, where he was a classmate of Barry Goldwater. Upon arriving at Columbia, Harris became involved in traditional campus extracurricular activities, playing football on the freshman team and joining a fraternity. The following year he even joined the Vigilance Committee, the sophomore group which hazed freshman. Yet by his senior year, Harris was writing editorials more fiery and radical than the editor of any other major college daily.[49]

Harris' radicalization occurred during his tenure as editor of the *Spectator*. Elevated to the editorship in a year when the economy was deteriorating rapidly, Harris found himself moved by "the spirit of inquiry, the spirit of questioning . . . . It was a college education in a time of depression, a time when there was great ferment in the world . . .[which] did cause us to question some of the existing standards of the times."[50] And questioning was what Harris did at the *Spectator*, exposing the elitism of college fraternities, the corruption in the Columbia administration, the suffering on the city's breadlines, the political bankruptcy of the Hoover administration, and the greed of anti-union employers.[51]

What made Harris so special was that he combined a radical sensibility and a gift for polemical writing. Harris had a biting wit, and his editorials went right for the jugular. In his first editorial controversy, Harris called upon the Columbia Athletic Association to open its financial records for inspection. Harris accused the Association of misusing student money and charged that the university had forsaken its educational mission by commercializing the football program, which he termed "a semi-professional racket."[52] As a consequence of these editorials, Harris was besieged by "football players, who threatened to beat us up, and alumni who intimated that we should retire."[53]

The muckraking style that characterized Harris' writing was something new for the *Spectator*. This was one of the reasons why his editorials so infuriated administrators, alumni, and student partisans of traditional college culture. They had simply never before encountered an undergraduate editor like him. Prior to Harris' editorship, the Columbia student newspaper reflected the values of the dominant student culture; it had been generally apolitical, insular, and tinged with Ivy League elitism. Until Harris, the *Spectator*'s editors had, in the words of James Wechsler, who would himself later follow in Harris' footsteps as editor-in-chief,

> always behaved in the best tradition of American college journalism: unhesitant pandering to the Administration, only intermittent and usually uninformed comment on affairs outside the realm of the University, devout catering to the institutions made sacred by Trustees, Alumni and their subordinates.[54]

Harris wanted to bring the student press closer to the standards of professional journalism. He believed that student journalists should be serious, critical, and above all free to "say what we think regardless of the consequences."[55] His concept of student journalism clashed with that of more traditional students, alumni, and administrators. They thought the student newspaper should function as a booster rather than critic of the school. They wanted a paper that would show deference to the campus administration and reverence for alma mater. This is what the Secretary of Columbia's Alumni Association meant when—after bemoaning Harris' negative commentary on the Columbia athletics program—he complained that "the editor of the *Spectator* is too serious. He should be more collegiate."[56] The metropolitan press, however, recognized a kindred spirit in Harris and sided with him rather than with his detractors in this dispute. The New York *World Telegram,* for instance, responded to the Alumni Association official's charge that Harris was insufficiently collegiate by arguing that collegiatism was equivalent to a type of mindlessness, which all intelligent journalists should avoid: "It is not collegiate to think. That is why American colleges and universities are glorified nurseries. It is only collegiate to be rah, rah boys."[57]

Harris grew even more controversial as the Depression deepened. Though the *Spectator* editor was neither a communist nor an NSL member, he endorsed the NSL's efforts to raise political awareness on campus and to assist the victims of the Great Depression. He urged students to drop their self-absorption and begin confronting the major problems troubling Depression America. Under Harris' editorship, the *Spectator* applauded the NSL-sponsored expedition to Harlan County in March 1932. He dispatched a *Spectator* reporter to travel with the delegation and published articles detailing conditions in the coal region. When Kentucky police disrupted the expedition, Harris editorialized against the "bigotry and intolerance" of the Kentucky legal establishment.[58]

By the middle of the spring semester the Columbia administration could no longer tolerate Harris. On March 31, Hebert Hawkes, Columbia's Dean of Students called Harris to his office. In this meeting the dean raised strong objections to the *Spectator*'s recent series criticizing the management of Columbia's dining halls. The articles had charged Columbia management with profiteering, exploiting student waiters, and serving poor food. Hawkes demanded that Harris offer proof for these charges within twenty-four hours.[59]

If Dean Hawkes thought Harris would defer to the administration's authority, he was mistaken. Having spent his term as *Spectator* editor trying to promote serious journalism, Harris naturally responded to Hawkes' demand by invoking the ethics of professional journalism. Harris sent a letter to Dean Hawkes summarizing the *Spectator*'s findings concerning the dining halls, but he refused to divulge the names of the individuals who had served as sources for the dining hall articles. Harris claimed that as a journalist he had a right to protect the confidentiality of his sources. He believed that in this case the *Spectator* had a special obligation to maintain this confidentiality, because the dining hall employees who spoke to the newspaper feared they would lose their jobs if the administration learned their identities.[60]

Harris not only refused to name his sources or comply with Hawkes' demand for "proof" of the dining hall charges, he also criticized the paternal condescension the dean had displayed in making this demand. Harris opened his letter to Hawkes by arguing that the dean rather than the *Spectator* had departed from the standard of civility which the Columbia administration claimed it was upholding:

> I want to protest against the manner in which I was "demanded" to produce an explanation [for the dining hall exposé]. You have repeatedly said to me that my mode of presentation in my editorial column has been unmannerly. Surely the dictatorial tone you adopted yesterday was not an example for me to follow in changing the tone of that column. In spite of the fact that we have had, almost constantly, major differences of opinion, I believe that I have acted in a gentlemanly manner while in your office during my term as editor of Spectator. That you should have adopted a tone suited only to a sargeant in the Marine Corps surprises me.[61]

Dean Hawkes refused to recognize the editor's right to protect his sources. He responded to Harris' letter on April 1 by informing Harris that he had been expelled and must appear before the Committee on Instruction for a hearing. Hawkes justified the expulsion (in a prepared statement which was soon released to the press) on the grounds that "material published in the Spectator during the last few days is a climax to a long series of discourtesies, innuendoes and misrepresentations which have appeared in this paper during the current academic year and calls for disciplinary action."[62]

Hawkes' press statement contradicted his initial explanation to Harris about the cause of his expulsion. The dean proved unable to get his story straight about whether the expulsion had been provoked solely by the dining hall exposé, or rather by Harris' persistent muckraking and radical editorials over the course of the entire year. Actually the dining hall information was not new; it had originally appeared in the newspaper in 1931, before Harris became editor. This fact, along with the inconsistent statements by Hawkes and other Columbia administrators fueled speculation that the dining hall exposé had been merely a pretext used by campus officials anxious to gag an iconoclastic editor—who had become too critical of the university and too sympathetic to the new student activism promoted by the NSL. The expulsion order was widely viewed as a case of administration anti-radicalism, a blatant example of intolerance toward dissent, on a level not seen at the relatively liberal Columbia campus since the repression which had accompanied World War I and the red scare.[63]

The expulsion order outraged Harris. He immediately issued a public statement denouncing the Columbia administration for violating his free speech rights and denying him a fair hearing. Harris charged that the expulsion order proved that the Columbia administration was suffering from "regimented, hypocritical thinking," which made a mockery of its own liberal pretensions:

> One of the first things which is impressed upon any Columbia student is that the University is a center of liberalism. After being sentenced before trial yesterday by Dean Hawkes and then given a mock hearing at which it was revealed that Dr. Butler sanctioned the action, I am completely disillusioned concerning the liberalism of Columbia. The freedom of expression when it runs contrary to the administrative policy of the university is non-existent. The fine public utterances of Dr. Butler are seldom carried out.[64]

The charge of hypocrisy was more than merely a rhetorical device on Harris' part. The expelled editor was genuinely shocked that Columbia, home of one of America's most liberal faculties, would stoop to censoring a student newspaper. Harris was equally shocked by the illiberal manner in which he was expelled, without even a semblance of due process. What Harris had overlooked here was that academic liberals rarely applied their principles of toleration to undergraduates. Because of the paternalistic way that they viewed youth and undergraduates, the same administrators who endorsed intellectual freedom for the faculty could easily justify suppressing those freedoms for undergraduates.

Although Columbia's President Nicholas Murray Butler presided over a liberal faculty on Morningside Heights, his brand of liberalism was shallow when it came to student rights. During the 1930s President Butler became one of America's leading proponents of the view that undergraduates, unlike the faculty, had no right to academic freedom. Butler argued that as far as the status of undergraduates was concerned academic freedom "has no meaning whatever. It relates solely to the freedom of thought and inquiry and teaching on the part of accomplished scholars."[65] Since undergraduates were not "accomplished scholars" their speech could, in Butler's eyes, never be covered by the exclusively professorial right to academic freedom.

Butler's view of college students was similar to that of most American college administrators of his era. They tended to view undergraduates paternally, as immature teenagers who needed guidance enroute to adulthood. Since such college administrators did not see students as full-fledged adults, they saw no reason to grant students the rights or political autonomy of adults. On many campuses these assumptions resulted in non-students—administrators, faculty or alumni—having veto power over undergraduate political institutions.

For students, being subject to this paternalistic oversight meant living with restrictions on their political freedom. If a student organization during the early 1930s wanted to hold a meeting or bring an outside speaker to campus this often had to be cleared with a college administrator or faculty adviser. This veto system often barred controversial speakers and issues from campus. Some campuses had bylaws against using the college grounds for partisan political activity, and these were invoked to ban any brand of political organizing that might be distasteful to campus admin-

istrators. College officials employed this same type of control over the
student press. And such control, as one critic wrote in 1932, effectively
limited freedom of the press on campus.

> Some forty percent of the college [student] publications in the United
> States suffer under a system in which each editor is supervised in his
> activities by a "faculty advisor" whose real function is that of a censor. By
> this means, much of the criticism prepared against the administration is
> deleted before the publication reaches the press.[66]

Students who failed to comply with the decisions of their political
overseers could expect a political fate similar to Harris'—facing expulsion
or other disciplinary action as punishment for their insubordination. In
fact, the same academic year in which Harris was expelled, eight other
students were dismissed from their editorships or expelled from college
because of their refusal to adhere to administration editorial restrictions,
and twelve others left their posts under apparent administration pressure.[67] This censorship, as Reed Harris pointed out in 1932, had the effect of intimidating students and discouraging them from airing critical,
unconventional political views. "In the treatment meted out to college editors," Harris wrote

> we have a key to the apparent immaturity of American students. They
> are kept that way by the men who watch their every move. As soon as an
> undergraduate editor begins to wake up and speak in criticism of things
> as they are, he is bound, gagged and, if convenient, tossed into the world
> outside the university, perhaps for fear lest he demoralize the more timid
> students by whom his writing is read.[68]

College administrators had not only the political power, but the legal
right to exert disciplinary authority over undergraduates. The Courts
consistently enforced the traditional *in loco parentis* doctrine, ruling that
the college administrator and "teacher stands in place of the parent—*in
loco parentis*—with the same power to control and punish."[69] Throughout
the first third of the twentieth century, state and federal judges, citing
this paternalistic legal doctrine, backed even the most arbitrary disciplin-
ing of undergraduates by college administrators. In one of the most famous of these cases, the New York Court of Appeals upheld the expulsion of a Syracuse University undergraduate even though the University's
only justification for dismissing her was its vague statement that she was
not a "typical Syracuse girl."[70] The Court ruled that administrators could
expel anyone they thought was detracting from the moral or intellectual
well being of the school, and they were not obligated to reveal the reason
for the expulsion. State Courts in Pennsylvania and Florida further restricted student political rights by ruling that colleges could expel students
without even holding a hearing. Federal and state courts also ruled that

the college did not have to present students with the evidence used to expel them, nor did they have to give students an opportunity to defend themselves.[71]

By enforcing the *in loco parentis* doctrine and granting administrators almost absolute legal authority over their students, the Courts provided these university officials with a virtual license to police and censor undergraduate political expression. Administrators knew they could trample the civil liberties of students without any legal repercussions. When Columbia University expelled a student for making anti-war speeches during World War I, the Courts upheld the expulsion. Albany College won a similar decision in 1921, when it expelled a student because of his socialistic political opinions. Even the United States Supreme Court unanimously ruled in favor of restricting student political freedom, when it upheld the right of land grant colleges in the 1930s to expel students who refused to take mandatory courses in military training.[72]

The censorship conflict at Columbia involved far more, then, than a dispute over a few articles; it represented a clash between partisans of two ways of thinking about college students and their political rights. On the one side was the Columbia administration, asserting its right to treat students as immature youths, who could be censored and disciplined at the pleasure of college officials. On the other side was Reed Harris, who had rejected the infantilization inherent in the the *in loco parentis* doctrine, insisting that as a student journalist he was not a senseless child who could be spanked, but a citizen and editor with rights that must be respected.

Standing alongside Harris was the NSL, which from the day of its birth had recognized that it would be impossible to build a mass student movement on campus unless undergraduates enjoyed free speech rights. This is why in its founding platform the NSL in December 1931 pledged to "prosecute an unending fight for academic freedom; to the end that neither instructors nor students shall be gagged in classrooms and out, and that they may not suffer discipline for their political beliefs." In this same document the NSL had demanded complete autonomy for both the student press and all other student political institutions:

> College publications must not be subject to censorship by administration, faculty bodies and trustees, and officers of publications must not be disciplined for political or economic views expressed. Student clubs must be beyond faculty or administration censorship and must be permitted to affiliate with such outside organizations as they choose.[73]

At Columbia in 1932 the NSL made good on these pledges to battle for student free speech rights. The League's support for Harris was evident from almost the moment of his expulsion. The NSL, and its Columbia chapter, the Social Problems Club, mobilized the pro-Harris students with great speed and skill. On the day of the expulsion order, the NSL issued a statement denouncing the Columbia administration for its "un-

warranted interference with freedom of study and freedom of the press."
Though the expulsion had been announced on Friday, and student organizing is difficult on the weekend, by Sunday the NSL was already convening a citywide protest meeting on Harris' behalf. This meeting, held
in a downtown theater, drew over 1000 students (from campuses
throughout New York City), to that point the largest undergraduate political rally of the decade. At this meeting, strategy was discussed, a statement from Harris read, and the NSL declared that it had "accepted leadership of the fight to reinstate Reed Harris." The NSL also announced
that it would hold a mass protest meeting at Columbia the following day.[74]

With the NSL at the helm, the anti-expulsion protests at Columbia
got off to a roaring start on Monday, April 4. The planned mass meeting
drew over 2000 students and culminated in the crowd's overwhelming
support of a one day student strike—called by the NSL—scheduled for
April 6. The protesters also sent a delegation to Dean Hawkes, which
criticized him for censoring the student press and asked that Harris be
reinstated. But the dean would not relent; he argued that the expulsion
involved "not a question of censorship, but one of courtesy . . . . Harris
never found a basis for the evils he criticized."[75]

Hawkes' arguments did not persuade the delegation, nor were they
satisfactory to Harris' former colleagues on the student newspaper. The
Spectator protested the expulsion by leaving its regular editorial space blank
and running a black rule on the masthead where Harris' name had formerly appeared. On the front page appeared an editorial praising Harris
as a man of conscience "who detested mediocrity . . . . Columbia College
was too small to hold him." The *Spectator* concluded that the rise of censorship at Columbia had left the university's liberal reputation in shambles.[76]

Student support of Harris was not confined to the Columbia campus.
The NSL organized delegations from other metropolitan campuses to aid
in the picketing for the Columbia strike. Editorials in favor of Harris appeared in many college newspapers. Forty student newspaper editors nationwide signed a petition protesting the expulsion on the grounds that
"the right to free expression of beliefs . . . is not one to be tampered
with."[77] Off campus, Harris attracted the support of newspapers sensitive
to the censorship issue, and the American Civil Liberties Union, which
agreed to provide Harris with counsel.[78]

Not all Columbia students, however, sympathized with Harris. The
expelled editor's earlier criticism of football and fraternities had alienated
partisans of the traditional collegiate culture, who were quite happy to see
Harris censored. The fraternity-dominated Student Board of Represena-
tives (Columbia's elected student government) greeted Harris' expulsion
by passing a resolution expressing "complete confidence in the fair-
mindedness and sound judgement of Dean Herbert E. Hawkes in his recent disciplinary action."[79] A small group of Harris opponents formed an

ad hoc organization, the Spartans, seeking to undermine the drive to reinstate the expelled editor.

During the first pro-Harris mass meeting, Spartans heckled and threw apples at the speakers. In response, the rally organizers invited the hecklers to speak. One of the Spartans, Shelly Wood of the Crew team, accepted this offer, but could think of nothing more to say to the crowd than "Well you called me yellow. Here I am." A second Spartan got up and shouted "Everyone knows that these things [in the dining hall] were going on but Harris had no right to bring them up." James Wechsler, who was present at the rally, recalled that the inarticulateness of these Harris foes "inevitably strengthened the belief of the Harris legions that witlessness was arrayed with oppression on the other side of the campus barricades."[80] The Spartans could not slow the groundswell of support for Harris which was emerging on the Columbia campus.

When Columbia students came to campus on April 6, they encountered their classmates picketing, carrying "free speech" banners and urging them to join the one day strike in protest against the expulsion. The picketers distributed NSL strike leaflets which praised Harris' "militant editorial policy," and listed three demands: "1. The reinstatement of Reed Harris; 2. An investigation of the John Jay dining room by a student committee; 3. An investigation of charges of professionalism in athletics to be made by a student committee."[81] Student support for the strike was overwhelming. Over 75 percent of the student body boycotted classes, and most of these students joined the campus rally demanding Harris' reinstatement.[82]

Emotions ran high on the day of the strike. Harris supporters were out in force defending him and the new critical sensibility he represented. In opposition were the athletes and fraternity men, who embodied the values of the traditional collegiate lifestyle inherited from 1920s; their most cherished goal was the promotion of school spirit. Since they deemed the Harris supporters guilty of undermining the good name of the college, the anti-Harris students responded by behaving the way traditional undergraduate leaders had customarily acted in the face of nonconformity on campus: hazing and physically assaulting strike leaders.

This violence began in the morning on the picket line when a varsity football player attacked one of the pro-Harris leafleters. Later, as several Harris partisans tried to use black crepe to gag the statue of alma mater—symbolizing the gagging of the expelled editor—several varsity athletes grabbed the crepe, tied the protester in it and punched him. Anti-Harris students showered eggs upon every speaker who criticized the Columbia administration, including a Protestant minister, who responded by denouncing the hecklers as "regular hired thugs." The athletes and fraternity men also ripped down pro-Harris banners of demonstrators from the architecture school and neighboring Barnard college, and in the process knocked one architecture student unconscious. In defending his involvement in these assaults, one strike opponent told the *New York Times* that "no 'gentleman' would have published what Harris did . . . but on questioning he conceded that 'gentlemen' occasionally threw eggs. He said he represented the 'administration' in throwing them."[83]

Aside from bruising a half dozen protesters, the anti-Harris rioters failed to hurt the Columbia strike. In fact, the assaults and the willingness of Harris supporters to withstand physical violence for the sake of free speech built sympathy for the strike both on and off campus. James Wechsler, who covered the story for the *Spectator,* recalled feeling a great surge of admiration for such protesters as Tim Westwood, a Columbia law student who, after having been beaten bloody by a gang of anti-Harris students, returned to the library steps to give an impassioned speech in defense of Harris and free speech. Westwood had, in Wechsler's eyes, offered "a conspicuous example of gallantry under fire . . . . He seemed the personification of the invincible cause of freedom, and I could only pity those who failed to appreciate the magnificence of the moment."[84] To outside observers, moreover, such as syndicated columnist Heywood Broun, the massive size of the strike when compared with the relatively small band of violent anti-Harris students only served to demonstrate that it was Harris rather than President Butler who had carried the day. Broun concluded that the Columbia administration

> has been placed in the ludicrous position of having none but athletes on its side . . . . For the first time in the history of American education football players were observed fighting to get into class. The whole affair may prove so epoch making that from now on the brawny boys will be ready to die for dear old calculus . . . . It seems to me that a college paper ought to be more than a bulletin in which to print the time and place of the next meeting of the French Society. The Spectator under Reed Harris was enlivened by a bold challenge to tradition both in campus life and beyond. The issue of free speech has been distinctly raised by the editor's expulsion . . . . Accordingly . . . I'm for Harris and dead against Butch Butler and his football favorites.[85]

In fomenting the Harris controversy the Columbia administration proved as politically inept as its violent student suppporters. When Dean Hawkes expelled Harris he apparently did not know—or think to check— that the *Spectator* editor was in the final week of his twelve-month term of office. At the time the dean informed Harris of his expulsion, the *Spectator* had just held its annual election in which the staff of the paper chose the new editor-in-chief. Harris had already written the final editorial of his term. Had the Columbia administration been more knowledgeable and cautious, then, it could have been rid of Harris' editorial voice without provoking a strike, by merely waiting a few days for his tenure at the *Spectator* to end.[86]

The Butler administration's failure to do its political homework and inquire into Harris' status on the *Spectator* was not simply an oversight; it was a reflection of the fact that in 1932, Hawkes and Butler still assumed that student politics had not changed since the 1920s. These administrators did not painstakingly search for the least provocative way to silence Harris because they did not understand that Columbia undergraduates could be provoked into mass protest on campus. They were so accustomed to dealing with a politically quiescent student body, as in the 1920s, that they saw neither the possibility of a strike nor the necessity of thinking ahead tactically about how to handle the Harris case without provoking a strike. Hawkes and Butler were simply out of touch with the new political mood on campus, the restlessness and uneasiness wrought by the Depression, and the readiness of the new breed of student activists to challenge what they saw as unjust actions by campus administrators.

Although shocked by the student strike, the Columbia administration initially tried to give the impression that it had been unaffected by the walkout. Dean Hawkes insisted that the protests would not change his mind, and that Harris would never be reinstated. But soon after the strike, the administration began to backpedal. The first concession came on April 9, when Columbia's Commons Committee announced that it would conduct an investigation into the management of the university's dining halls. This was a major break with the administration's earlier position that the *Spectator*'s criticism of the dining halls had been groundless.[87]

The final retreat of the Columbia administration came on April 20, 1932 when, after a series of meetings between university officials and Harris' attorney, Acting Dean Nicolas McKnight announced the reinstatement of the expelled editor. In exchange for this concession, Harris had apologized for the letter he had written chastizing Dean Hawkes. McKnight also announced that upon reinstatement, Harris had chosen to resign from the university—an act which was portrayed as voluntary but which was in fact part of the settlement between the two sides of the dispute.[88]

Harris owed his reinstatement to the political furor which the student protests had generated. President Butler was convinced that "the university's position was legally sound and would have been sustained by the courts." But the strike persuaded him that the political price for maintaining that position would be too high; it would lead to further protests and more negative press for Columbia. Thus the day after Harris' reinstatement was announced, Butler—in endorsing the out of court settlement—confided to the university's attorney that "the annoyance and misrepresentation which would follow upon widespread and sensational newspaper publicity would far outweigh any advantage to be gained by winning a court action."[89] John Godfrey Saxe, the university counsel, concurred in this judgement, pointing out in his reply to Butler that legal action against Harris was politically inadvisable because the case would drag on for months, "carrying continual aggravation " for the Columbia administration.[90]

Privately, several Columbia administrators voiced strong disapproval of the settlement. They felt the university had made too big a concession by agreeing to reinstate Harris. They also were dissatisfied with Harris' apology, which had recanted nothing from the controversial dining hall exposé. Indeed, the administration had given much ground; its original negotiating position with Harris' attorney had been that he would not be reinstated unless he submitted an apology to the university conceding "that the discipline which was administered to him had nothing whatever to do with the freedom of the press or the right of free speech."[91] But Harris had refused to make such a sweeping apology, forcing the administration to accept a much more limited note from him that mentioned only the letter to Hawkes. The failure of the university to obtain such a broad apology was a point of contention within the administration during the final vote on the Harris settlement, and it was mentioned by one administrator to justify his vote against the settlement.[92]

As the administration went public with its decision to reinstate Harris, face saving was the order of the day. Dean McKnight, trying to put the settlement in the most favorable possible light for the administration, portrayed the Harris case in a thoroughly disingenuous manner. Though the administration's initial refusal to reinstate Harris was now being reversed, McKnight denied that the decision to expel Harris had been wrong. McKnight told the press that "the university authorities fully supported Dean Hawkes in the action which he had taken as to Reed Harris and that the Reed Harris case did not come within the principle of free speech and freedom of the press . . ."[93] McKnight tried to make it appear as if Harris had been reinstated because he had apologized for his letter to Hawkes; the dean claimed that this letter had "precipitated the disciplinary action against Harris," when in fact the administration had previously maintained that the dining hall articles had provoked the expulsion.[94]

Although Harris' supporters cheered the reinstatement of the expelled editor, they criticized the university's refusal to acknowledge that free speech was at issue, or that the initial decision to discipline Harris had been wrong. As Roger Baldwin, director of the American Civil Liberties Union, explained: "The university's statement sustaining Dean Hawkes' expulsion of Harris when at the same time Harris is reinstated leaves us a little breathless. But face saving does not contribute to consistency." Mocking the adminstration, Norman Thomas told a crowd of Columbia students that he had never seen

> a more inconsistent peace treaty in my life—it backs Dean Hawkes and at the same time reinstates Harris . . . . The university ought to offer a course in how to write political platforms on which everybody can ride . . . . Whoever drew it up ought to go to Chicago to help the old parties write their platforms.[95]

The *Spectator* pronounced the university's statement "typical of the wavering and contradictory" methods used by the administration throughout the Harris case.[96]

The National Student League saw Harris' reinstatement as a "magnificent" victory for the student movement. In the NSL's view the administration's retreat demonstrated that students—if organized correctly—could stop political suppression on campus. By securing free speech for critics of the university, the NSL believed it was creating the political space necessary for a mass protest movement to arise on campus. The NSL interpreted the widespread student participation in the Harris protest as proof that the League's founding platform was correct in stressing that campus issues could serve as the key to politicizing undergraduates. In leading the Columbia struggle to a succesful conclusion, the NSL prided itself on having pioneered an innovative tactic, the student strike, consequently establishing a new tradition of protest. According to the NSL, the Columbia revolt showed

> that a new day had dawned in American student life. A new and almost anomalous tradition was to take its place beside the ivy-covered stories of the champion crew and the old college fence. Students had used the [strike] weapon of the working class in defense of a student right.[97]

The NSL was euphoric in the wake of the Columbia strike and with good reason. In full glare of national press attention, the League had organized the most effective student protest in recent memory. The NSL's success in its Columbia campaign was all the more impressive, given the small size of the Columbia NSL chapter. This skillful mobilization effort elicited a great deal of admiration for the NSL among students who had previously had little contact with the communist-led organization. Columbia alumnus James Wechsler recalled that

> for the large number of students who sympathized with Harris, this was a first glimpse of Communists in action and, as was to occur so often, they simply seemed to be the most dedicated and energetic champions of a great cause . . . . They resolutely took command of the proceedings and, since no college course had tutored us in such arts as the painting of picket signs, the Communists swiftly dominated the machinery of protest . . . . ; there could not have been more than thirty of them on the Columbia campus at the time. But they were tireless.[98]

As in the Kentucky expedition, the NSL at Columbia mobilized students around a civil liberties issue which had broad appeal. Once again the NSL, which could be very critical of the shortcomings of liberalism, nonetheless proved adept at honing its message in a way that stirred the student body's liberal conscience. It was the NSL rather than any liberal organization on campus which waved the liberal banner of free speech. Ironically, though in theory a communist-led organization like the NSL lacked the liberal's reverence for free speech rights (and communists would surely deny those rights to reactionaries), in practice the NSL had to fight against a prominent liberal university to preserve those very free speech rights to which liberalism was ostensibly wedded.[99]

The timidity of the faculty during the Reed Harris controversy further promoted the conclusion that the communist-led NSL had behaved more liberally than Columbia's liberals. In all of Columbia University only sixteen teachers would sign a pro-Harris petition, and of these, only one, Mark Van Doren, was a professor. Such eminent liberal faculty members as John Dewey refused to get involved in the controversy. The protesters saw this faculty apathy as the product of fear—professors not wanting to risk their jobs by siding with Harris and alientating the administration; they viewed this "widespread failure to respond [to the petition as] new proof that Columbia's liberalism was a fraud." The fact that the only faculty member to address the Columbia strikers was Donald Henderson, the young communist economics instructor, led students to ask "why there were so many non-practicing liberals" at the university.[100]

At Columbia, the NSL not only outshone the liberal faculty and administration in standing up for liberal principle, it outorganized the traditional undergraduate leaders who had dominated student life since the 1920s. In obtaining Harris' reinstatement, the NSL proved that the fraternity-athletic establishment could be challenged and defeated—even when allied with a powerful college administration. What the Kentucky trip did on the road, Columbia brought back to the campus: demonstrating that the old collegiate insularity and apathy could be broken down under the leadership of the student Left.

The Columbia strike spurred further radical organizing on campus because it showed that the student Left could win political victories and change the tone of student life. At Columbia this change was as large as the gulf between the pointless freshman-sophomore riot of 1930 and the determined political battle for free speech in 1932. The Reed Harris struggle provided a glimpse of what the new American student politics of the 1930s would look like: it was left of center, critical of university authority, and conducive to the emergence of large scale campus protest. This was a sight which energized the student Left, by suggesting that its hopes for politically transforming the campuses were not unrealistic. Indeed, with the Kentucky and Columbia campaigns under their belts, NSLers approached campus organizing with a great sense of confidence, aware that in less than a month they had led the two most effective student political actions of the decade.

IV

Within weeks of the Reed Harris protests the NSL was again involved in a political battle in New York City. This time the issue was economic and linked directly to the Depression: a student fee hike in the municipal colleges of New York. In the past the municipal colleges—Brooklyn College, Hunter College, and City College—had been tuition-free, charging only the most nominal educational fees. But the Depression caused a decline in tax revenues, which threw the city college system into a fiscal crisis. The New York City Board of Higher Education sought to resolve this crisis in May 1932 by imposing tuition and mandating the payment of new library, laboratory and diploma fees, scheduled to take effect in the coming fall semester. This announcement alarmed many students in the city college system, most of whom had already suffered because of the Depression; they feared that their inability to pay the proposed fees would force them to drop out of college.[101]

The NSL responded to the fee announcement by organizing the largest citywide protest yet seen on New York campuses. The NSL began by circulating a questionnaire on the student body's economic status, to document the hardships of many city college undergraduates and demonstrate that most would be unable to shoulder the new fees. The League then formed a Student Fee Committee to coordinate intercampus mobilization over the fees. The first rally was set for Brooklyn College, but the Faculty Committee on Student Affairs prohibited the students from demonstrating on campus. Consequently, the NSL moved the rally to Borough Hall in Brooklyn, where on May 18 approximately 1000 students turned out in protest against the proposed fees.[102]

At the CCNY uptown campus the following week, the NSL mobilized the most financially strapped students in the city college system: those attending CCNY's night school. These students attended college at night because they had to work full time jobs during the day to make ends meet. Some 3000 night school students rallied against the fee hikes at CCNY on May 23. Speakers at this rally, citing statistics from the NSL survey, argued that if the fees went into effect 74 percent of the evening students would be forced to drop out of college. The NSL charged that in deciding to impose the fees the Board of Higher Education had abandoned its educational mission and succumbed to the pressure of "bankers and real estate interests." A similar anti-fee rally at Hunter College the following day attracted 500 students.[103]

Unlike the Reed Harris strike, the NSL in the fee fight at the city colleges did not encounter organized student opposition. Linked by their tight budgets and their belief in low cost public higher education, the student bodies united in opposition to the fees. One sign of this unity was the overwhelming student support for the NSL's anti-fee petition, which in a few weeks time had over 5000 student signatures—and by the end of the semester more than 10,000 signatures. Student governments and newspapers from all the city colleges denounced the fees as a threat not only to individual students, but also to the character of the New York municipal college system, in which merit rather than money was the basis for admission:

The College, during the last eighty-five years has typified a pure educational democracy, students have gained admission on no other basis
than that of mental ability. Because of this fact, the College has maintained an enviable reputation. Because of this fact, the student body at
the College has been characterized by an intellectual vigor which we point
to with pride. The establishment of fees would seriously cripple that reputation. For it would mean the setting up of a new standard for admission. It would set up an artificial money barrier . . . . It would change
the character of the College, put it a step nearer to some of our country
club establishments.[104]

Recognizing that ultimate decision making power regarding the fees
rested with the city government rather than with college administrators,
the NSL took its protests to City Hall. A delegation of forty-five students
from Brooklyn, Hunter, and City Colleges attended a meeting of the New
York Board of Estimate on May 27, seeking to attain a hearing on the fee
hikes. When the delegation sought to get the Board's attention during the
meeting by marching down the room's central aisle, police halted them.
Later in the meeting, NSL leader Joseph Clark shouted "We, delegated
students of the three city colleges protest . . ." But before Clark could
finish, city officials interrupted and told the students that since they were
not on the agenda, they would not be allowed to speak.[105]

The NSL returned to City Hall with a larger student delegation on
June 10. Again the students were denied speaking rights. Police moved in
to the evict the crowd of about 200 students, which was seeking access to
the Board of Estimate meeting. Angered at the Board's rebuff, the students defied the police by hoisting their spokesman on their shoulders,
massing around him "in protection and put[ting] up a stiff resistance to
the police. Not until after they had begun to picket the hall with their
placards and special reserves had arrived and surrounded them, were they
dispersed."[106] Later the protesters defied the police once more by holding
a rally on the plaza outside City Hall, drawing over 600 students.[107]

Throughout the fee protests, the NSL stressed how regressive it was
for the municipal college system to force lower-class students, the group
least able to afford it, to bail the city out of its fiscal crisis. The NSL
suggested that the fairest way to raise the revenues for the city colleges
was by raising income taxes, inheritance taxes, and gift taxes on those in
the higher brackets. The NSL also argued that New York City's government, still dominated by Tammany Hall—New York's corrupt Democratic
political machine—should eliminate its waste and dishonesty and not expect students to subsidize City Hall's financial inefficiency.[108]

While city officials had turned a cold shoulder to the protesting students initially, City Hall ultimately proved unable to ignore the sustained
campaign against the fees. The Board of Higher Education announced
on June 13 that it would appoint a special subcommittee to consider the
demands for abolition of the fees. This subcommittee met over the summer and quietly eliminated the fees.[109]

Given the fact that the new fees had been announced so definitively in May and that city officials were at first unwilling even to offer the anti-fee activists a hearing, the elimination of the fees was a remarkable victory for the NSL. The League had shown that thousands of students could be mobilized in defense of low cost public higher education. This was a lesson which seems to have affected New York's politicians, who as a consequence of the protests recognized that fee hikes threatened to alienate both students and their parents—jeopardizing thousands of votes on election day. Consequently, a few months after the students had won the fee fight, both leading candidates in the upcoming New York mayoralty race began to compete over who could create the stronger declaration against any new fees in the city college system.[110]

New York was not the only place where the NSL orchestrated impressive student protests against fee hikes in spring 1932. Almost simultaneous with the anti-fee campaign in New York, a similar movement emerged in Detroit. In 1931 the City College of Detroit had imposed a $100 tuition fee, which burdened the college's predominantly low income student body. When in the spring of 1932, the College indicated that it would be doubling its tuition, student protests erupted. The NSL helped lead several demonstrations at City Hall, one of which drew more than a thousand students. These protests ended successfully, with the revocation of the new tuition increase.[111]

V

The college commencement season was not a happy time for the class of 1932, which was graduating into a world of mass unemployment and political uncertainty. College seniors were about to hit the job market at a time when placements of graduates from even the most elite institutions, such as Yale, were down by two thirds from the previous year. At Reed College unemployment of graduates, which had been 6 percent in 1930, was about to hit 25.6 percent in 1932. Nonetheless many commencement speakers pasted smiles on their faces and gave the traditional cheerleading orations, urging the graduates not to be discouraged by hard times.[112] But not even these purveyors of optimism and sunny platitudes could remove the pall the Depression had cast. Indeed, at several campuses the clichés of graduation oratory were discarded, and the Depression intruded into these cap and gown ceremonies. At Notre Dame, for instance, General Electric Chairman Owen D. Young urged that the president be granted almost dictatorial powers to cope with the economic crisis. Such speeches served only to remind graduates that the society which awaited them seemed on the verge of coming unhinged.[113]

About the only organization on campus that resonated with excitement during commencement 1932 was the NSL. Hard times for American capitalism had meant good times for the student Left. The NSL had

just completed a semester in which it enjoyed a string of political suc-
cesses; its leaders felt that history was moving in their direction. "A new
student has arisen," explained the NSL national magazine at the end of
the 1932 spring semester.

> The economic crisis has been an excellent teacher of new values. The
> new student is breaking thru the old, narrow- fitting academic bonds. His
> school-fed illusions are fading away. He is beginning to realize that his
> life as a student is inextricably bound up with the social system under
> which he lives. This is proven by the widespread response to the events
> in Kentucky, the Columbia strike, the fight against fees in the free col-
> leges of Detroit and New York City . . . . The new student is learning
> to battle for his rights as a social individual.[114]

Such optimism and confidence were understandable, coming as they
did from young radicals who had recently stood up to vigilantes and deputies in the South, preserved low cost education in two cities, and won a
major free speech fight against one of the nation's most eminent college
presidents. But two busloads of students, plus New York and Detroit add
up to only a small part of America and its student population. The "new
student" whose emergence the NSL was celebrating in 1932 had yet to be
mobilized for political action on a truly national basis. The task of putting
together such a mobilization, building a genuine mass protest movement
on campus would be the key challenge confronting the student Left in
the wake of this first springtime of revolt.

Chapter 4

The Making of a
Mass Movement

We will not support the U.S. government in any war it may conduct.

> Americanized version of the Oxford Pledge, administered
> during the student strikes against war in the United States.
> "Meaning of April 13," *Student Review* (Summer 1934), 4.

In seventeen we went to war,
In seventeen we went to war,
In seventeen we went to war,
Didn't know what we were fighting for.
Time to turn those guns the other way.

> Anti-war chant of radical student protesters in the U.S. during
> the mid-1930s. Leslie Fiedler, "In Every Generation:
> A Meditation on Two Holocausts," in *Testimony,*
> David Rosenberg, ed. (New York, 1989), 218.

Our geographical isolation makes political isolation seem practical. And
we have 1917 on our conscience. We went to war ostensibly to make
the world safe for democracy, only to make it safe for J.P. Morgan.
We don't want to be fooled again. Haunted by the past, terrified by
the present, many, including those who considered themselves the most
"revolutionary" have taken refuge in trying to keep America out of
war by trying to keep America out of the world [through] . . . support of the Oxford Pledge.

> Joseph P. Lash, "Footnote to the Oxford Pledge" [1938].

Franklin Delano Roosevelt so dominated the American political scene from the fall of 1932 through the end of the
Depression decade that historians refer to these years as the Age of Roo-

sevelt. He won the 1932 presidential race in one of the greatest landslides
in American history, trouncing Hoover—who the electorate blamed for
the Depression—by almost seven million votes. FDR then presided over
the extensive New Deal recovery, relief and reform programs, whose popularity helped keep him in the White House longer than any other president. But Roosevelt's great popularity with the general public did not
initially carry over onto college campuses. During most of his first term,
neither FDR nor his major programs captured the imagination of the
American student body. Roosevelt's presidential campaign in 1932 failed
to generate much excitement on campus, and from 1933 to 1935 the cause
that most inspired college youth was world peace rather than the New
Deal.

If the choice had been left to college students, the straw polls show,
Franklin Roosevelt would not have been elected president in 1932. FDR
ran far behind Hoover in the campus polls taken shortly before election
day. Only 31 percent of the collegians polled supported Roosevelt, while
49 percent endorsed Hoover. Roosevelt even did badly on campuses where
he had direct, personal connections. At Harvard, FDR's alma mater, the
Democratic candidate lost to Hoover by a margin of more than three to
one: 1211 students there voted for Hoover, while only 395 cast their bal-
lots for Roosevelt. Support for Roosevelt was also weak among undergraduates at Columbia University, despite the fact that several of his key
advisers, popularly known as the New Deal "brain trust," including Raymond Moley, Rexford Tugwell, and Adolph Berle, were Columbia professors. With almost two thirds of Columbia undergraduates voting, FDR
attracted only 221 votes, losing not only to Hoover, who drew 307 votes,
but also to Norman Thomas, the socialist candidate, who won 421 votes.
This enabled Columbia socialists to boast at the Norman Thomas rally at
Madison Square Garden that "Columbia Professors May Write Roosevelt's
Speeches But Columbia Students Vote For Thomas." Roosevelt even lost
in his own backyard, at Vassar College, a few miles from his home in
Hyde Park. Though FDR had served as a trustee at Vassar, he ran a
dismal third in the college's straw poll, attracting only 105 votes, to 563
for Hoover, and 208 for Thomas.[1]

Roosevelt's failure to compete effectively with Hoover for the student
vote may seem strange in light of the Democratic landslide off campus,
but it is somewhat less surprising in the context of collegiate political history. In polls taken throughout the 1920s, college students had voted more
solidly Republican than had the general electorate, reflecting their middle-
class roots. Critics complained that in 1932 undergraduates were simply
conforming to the old collegiate pattern of "voting exactly as their fathers
vote" because they accepted "as handed down to them the ideals of a
comfortable owning class." The Harvard Crimson echoed this analysis, explaining Hoover's victory there as a consequence of the fact that "students
at Harvard are on the whole of the conservative monied class."[2]

It was, however, not simply the collegiate Republican tradition or the class background of the student body which rendered undergraduates so unreceptive to FDR in 1932. Some of the responsibility for the weak Democratic showing on campus rested with Roosevelt himself. He failed to run the type of inspiring or intellectually coherent campaign which might have attracted an upsurge of students into the Democratic ranks. The Roosevelt campaign did not articulate clear solutions to the economic crisis; its political message was riddled with contradictions. For instance, the campaign implied that the federal government had to do more on behalf of the unemployed, but also called for a balanced budget. Roosevelt's supporters on campus even implied that Hoover was spending too much federal money, and that a Roosevelt administration would bring "an immediate and drastic reduction of governmental expenditures."[3]

Students were put off by Roosevelt's tendency to avoid specifics. A columnist for UC Berkeley's student newspaper complained that on the campaign trail FDR voiced his ideas "in a vague, general manner. There may be meat there but it is hidden under a cloud of gush vaguely referring to the 'common man.' "[4] The students' low estimation of Roosevelt was influenced by much of the intelligentsia, which found him intellectually shallow. This was a time when even astute political writers, such as Walter Lippmann, saw Roosevelt as merely "a pleasant man who, without any important qualifications for office, would very much like to be president." Indeed, in criticizing Roosevelt during this era, student editors, including those of the *Columbia Spectator,* cited Lippmann approvingly when they berated FDR as "the Artful Dodger, whose mastery of misty rhetoric is still unmatched."[5]

Roosevelt's failure to build a Democratic undergraduate majority in 1932 is all the more striking because it came at a time of declining Republican influence on campus. Though Hoover defeated FDR on campus, he was also the first Republican presidential candidate since the First World War who received a plurality rather than an overwhelming majority of the student vote. The 49 percent that Hoover attracted on campus represented a sharp decline from both the 58.6 percent of the student vote which fellow Republican Calvin Coolidge had won in 1924 and the two to one landslide which Hoover himself had over Al Smith on campus in 1928.[6] The Republicans had lost the sweeping campus majority that they had enjoyed throughout the 1920s because the Depression prodded increasing numbers of students to question the economic individualism and limited government ideals which had prevailed during more than a decade of Republican ascendance. A significant minority of students was shifting leftward. Had he been able to attract the students radicalized by the Depression, FDR would not have lost to Hoover in the national college straw poll. Roosevelt's problem was that he not only lost the moderate students to Hoover, but also lost the growing leftwing student vote to Norman Thomas.

A surprisingly large minority of undergraduates rejected both major party candidates in favor of Norman Thomas. The socialist candidate attracted 18 percent of the 57,000 students participating in the college straw polls. This student vote for Thomas suggested that socialistic thinking or at least disillusionment with the two-party system had advanced much further on campus than off. Thomas' support among undergraduates dwarfed the 2.2 percent vote he received from the general electorate.[7]

The campus campaign for Thomas was much better organized and nationally coordinated than those of the major party candidates. By election day 1932 there were Thomas For President Clubs on more than 150 campuses, and they were far more active than their Democratic or Republican counterparts. The major parties did not pay much attention to the campuses because only a few hundred thousand collegians were of voting age. Thomas, on the other hand, devoted considerable time to the campuses because his financially strapped campaign needed student volunteers. He did better on campus than off because within the college gates he had to compete with only the ideas and not the large campaign chests of the major parties.[8]

Thomas' cogent socialist analysis of the Depression, which he articulated with great eloquence, appealed to youths searching for solutions to the deepening economic crisis. For students shifting leftward, FDR's vague intimations of reform paled in comparison with Thomas' call for massive federal aid to the needy and radical restructuring of the economy. These students thought Roosevelt too timid and moderate for the task of rescuing Depression America's collapsing economic system. Their straw poll voting attested that FDR in 1932 was "unsuccessful in channeling the mixed idealism and unrest that rallied nationally behind Thomas' candidacy."[9]

This student enthusiasm for Thomas in 1932 was a testament to how much had changed on campus since the 1920s. Throughout that prosperous decade, Thomas had toured the campuses for the LID, but his lectures on socialist and labor topics elicited little response from a student body which was overwhelmingly conservative politically. The Depression had at last given Thomas a campus following, as students, shaken by the economic crisis, became more receptive to criticism of capitalism. And it was not only the students who were changing, but Thomas himself. In contrast to his academic-style lectures on campus in the 1920s, Thomas in 1932 was acting as a political crusader on the stump. He was no longer asking students simply to study socialism, but was rather urging them to become active in his campaign to change and save America in its hour of crisis. This was a new and dramatic message; it generated a level of excitement on campus which had eluded Thomas in the 1920s.[10]

Thomas' campus campaign benefited from the revitalization of the student LID. By the fall of 1932 the socialist-led student LID was a much more dynamic organization than it had been at the beginning of the Depression. Student LID leaders had become aware the previous spring that the NSL, a new upstart leftist group, had out-organized them. The NSL's effective political actions in Harlan, the Reed Harris strike, and the City College tuition fight had attracted national attention, while the student LID—despite its longer history—had lacked initiative, doing little more than supporting the protests launched by the NSL. But student LID leaders proved quick learners. As the 1932–33 academic year began, the campus LID had shed its academic orientation in favor of a much more activist approach to student organizing. Energized by the Depression itself and influenced by the example set by the NSL, the LID ceased merely pondering politics in discussion groups, and began involving students in political agitation. For LIDers this agitation began with assistance to Thomas; they transformed the skeletal LID network into an effective national college campaign for the socialist candidate.[11]

The student campaign for Thomas contrasted with those of the major parties in that it was more of a protest movement than an electoral race. Thomas student organizers were seeking to change not just presidents, but economic systems. They saw the campaign as a way of popularizing socialist ideas on campus, and they were passionate in this political crusade. Indeed, non-radical students were sometimes astonished by the energy and zeal of the Thomas forces. At the University of Michigan, for instance, the Socialist Club engaged in a bit of direct action which shocked and angered editors of the *Michigan Daily*. Thomas supporters marched on the the offices of that student newspaper, protesting its anti-Socialist bias and its refusal to cover a blatant case of ballot tampering. Though the paper denounced the protesters as "loud-talking, little thinking radicals," the march did prod the *Daily* to cover the ballot tampering story. The march demonstrated just how militant Thomas' supporters could be in their drive to be heard on campus.[12]

If the student LID aided the Thomas campaign, the Thomas campaign in turn invigorated the LID by boosting the morale of its organizers and raising their political expectations. Though the LID-led campaign for Thomas on campus attracted a minority of undergraduates, it was a larger and more geographically diverse minority than had ever before been organized on campus for an anti-capitalist cause. On a number of campuses the socialist candidate did more than run a respectable third: at places like Smith College, the universities of Cincinnati, Minnesota, and Vermont, Thomas took second to Hoover and at the University of North Carolina at Chapel Hill, Thomas came in second to Roosevelt. On campuses in New York and Colorado Thomas managed to come in first. No one had expected that in a nation so wedded to the two party system, college youth would break with that system and opt for a socialist candidate in such substantial numbers. At Chapel Hill the shocked editors of the *Daily Tar Heel* observed that on their campus there had been "an immense protest vote which exceeded the wildest expectation of campus socialists, [that] gave Norman Thomas a two to one majority over Herbert Hoover and sent him within sixty votes of Franklin Delano Roosevelt."[13]

The Thomas campaign did more, however, than build the student LID's confidence; it made the LID more visible on campus, attracting new recruits to the organization and demonstrating that it could politically organize students at least as well as its rival on the student Left, the NSL. The 1932 election virtually passed the NSL by because the League did not see electoral politics as a vehicle capable of bringing radical change to America. The NSL therefore did not seek to counter the Thomas campaign by making a major effort on behalf of the far less attractive communist candidate for president, William Z. Foster—who would draw less than one percent of the student vote. This NSL inaction and the LID's success in the campaign helped to restore the competitive balance on the student Left, enabling the LID to make up for the ground it had lost to the NSL the previous spring.[14]

The college campaign for Thomas further strengthened the student LID by involving members of the Young People's Socialist League (YPSL), the Socialist Party's official youth group, in campus organizing. In the past YPSLs had focused most of their attention on blue-collar youth, since they assumed that these were the most likely recruits to the socialist movement. But the substantial student vote for Thomas helped convince the YPSLs that they should become more active in working with the LID on campus because undergraduates seemed to be moving leftward. YPSLs tended to be more militant and well versed in radical theory and history than the average LID member; they became the leftwing of the campus LID. In the metropolitan areas where the YPSL presence was significant, particularly New York and Chicago, its involvement in the student movement and the LID made both more dynamic.[15]

Given the fact that their candidate finished in third place, it may seem strange that socialist students came away from the presidential race in an upbeat mood. But the student polls did demonstrate an undergraduate desire for change. Taken together, slightly more students voted for new political leadership—for the Democratic, Socialist and Communist presidential candidates—than voted for Hoover and the status quo. The straw poll returns were also encouraging for campus radicals because they showed the socialists to be the one party that gained substantial new student support in 1932, compared with previous collegiate presidential polls.[16] This suggested that the student Left was shedding its marginality and becoming a significant minority on campus. Unable to foresee the great upsurge in FDR's popularity on campus—and the achievements of his administration which would prove that his critics in the student body and the intelligentsia had underestimated him—socialist students thought the 18 percent student vote for Thomas was only the beginning of an era of growth for the Socialist Party on campus.[17]

If the straw poll returns were encouraging to the student Left, so was the campaign that yielded those returns. The Thomas campaign had been the first truly national student protest movement to emerge in Depression America; it convinced LIDers that the NSL's success in fostering student dissidence on individual campuses could be duplicated on a far grander scale. Of this optimism following the campaign, former LID leader Joseph P. Lash recalled that there were Thomas For President Clubs all over . . . . The rallies in the colleges had been so big . . . . And I think it was one of the factors that convinced the LID people that a mass student movement could be built that was very close to the Socialists. And I certainly shared that view.[18]

This surge of confidence would encourage Lash and other LID leaders to think big, enabling them, in alliance with their NSL rivals, to envision and begin building a national student movement against war.

II

During the spring semester of 1933 the big news off campus came out of Washington. The Roosevelt administration rushed to Capitol Hill seeking the enactment of the New Deal's ambitious recovery and relief programs. This legislation, including such major bills as the National Industrial Recovery Act and the Agricultural Adjustment Act, sailed through Congress in record time during the first hundred days of FDR's presidency. Students seemed impressed by the president's recognition of the need for quick action to deal with the economic crisis. Consequently, Roosevelt's unpopularity on campus diminished considerably soon after he entered the White House.[19] But undergraduates also recognized that the New Deal might well fail to end the Depression. The recovery programs were criticized from the Left as too timid and from the Right as too recklessly experimental. This uncertainty about Roosevelt's legislative initiative prevented the new president from either becoming a dominant figure on campus or inspiring any significant level of pro-New Deal activism among undergraduates. Indeed, the newsmakers who inspired the most activism and support on campus during the 1933 spring semester were not New Dealers in Washington, but pacifists across the Atlantic—at Oxford University.[20]

Students at Oxford University startled their elders and attracted international attention on February 9, 1933 when they took a radical pacifist stance. By a vote of 275 to 173 the Oxford Union, the University's debating society, adopted a motion "that this House will in no circumstance fight for its King and country." The vote was shocking because it came at England's most conservative and aristocratic university. The debating society that passed the resolution was important not just for Oxford, but for the entire British nation; it was a "miniature parliament," often referred to as the "training ground for British Prime Ministers," which according to the *New York Times* "probably has produced more Cabinet material than any similar institution on earth." Alumni and public officials could barely believe the news reports: the future leadership of the British Empire had embraced pacifism.[21]

The Oxford Pledge evoked a storm of criticism. Assuming that the students who took the pledge were cowards, an anonymous critic sent the

Oxford Union a box containing 275 white feathers—one for each pacifist vote. Thirty anti-pacifist students stormed into the Oxford Union's meeting hall, grabbed the Union's minute book and tore out the page recording the pacifist pledge. Observing that no one tried to interfere with these invaders, another student critic sneered that "although you may have been unwilling to fight for King and country, I think you might have fought for the society's minute book." The London *Times* denounced Oxford's pacifist pledge as a childish act. Conservative leader Winston Churchill derided the students who took the pledge as "callow, ill-tutored youths." Addressing a meeting of the Anti-Socialist and Anti-Communist Union, Churchill fumed that the Oxford Pledge "was a very disquieting and very disgusting symptom. One could almost feel the curl of contempt upon the lips of the manhood of Germany, Italy and France when they read the message sent out by Oxford University in the name of Young England." Oxford alumni immediately organized a movement to reverse the vote and expunge the pacifist pledge from the Union's minutes.[22]

This criticism had little impact on students either at Oxford or on Britain's other campuses. The effort to expunge the pacifist vote from the Oxford Union's records failed miserably. In one of its largest meetings in years, the Union, with almost one-fourth of the entire student body present, voted 750 to 138 against removing the pledge from its records. The Oxford Pledge then moved beyond Oxford. Students adopted the pledge at Manchester and Glasgow Universities in March. The pledge also won in votes at Leicester, Cambridge, and the University College in Wales, and it was reported to have strong support at the University of London.[23]

During the same semester in which the Oxford Pledge swept across British campuses, an Americanized version began to attract a large following among undergraduates in the United States. Student assemblies at Northwestern, Chicago, and Syracuse Universities and an anti-war conference of eight California campuses followed Oxford's lead, declaring their opposition to war service of any kind. There were active campaigns on behalf of the pledge and against military service at about ninety American colleges and universities during the spring semester. College newspapers in every region of the United States praised the Oxford Pledge and supported an effort by Brown University's strongly anti-war newspaper to initiate a national student poll on pacifism and military service. The poll of 22,627 students revealed that the Oxford Pledge had a higher approval rating than FDR had mustered during the election: 39 percent of the students polled endorsed an Oxford-style pacifist stance against participation in any war, and another 33 percent said they would not serve in the military unless the United States was invaded.[24]

The poll results, which came from 65 colleges and universities in 27 states suggested that this generation of American college students overwhelmingly opposed U.S. involvement in an overseas war. Seventy-two percent of the students polled had declared their unwillingness to fight in such a war.[25] This strong anti-war vote and the great interest in the Oxford Pledge during the spring semester of 1933 grew in part out of the anxieties students felt concerning the deteriorating state of international relations. In Asia, war was already waging, as the militaristic Japanese empire, after seizing Manchuria, approached the Great Wall and launched its first bloody assaults on China proper. Confronting League of Nations criticism of its Manchurian aggression, Japanese delegates stormed out of the League meeting in February, and Japan withdrew from this international organization the following month. In the West, war clouds loomed. The German Reichstag granted absolute power to Nazi leader Adolph Hitler in March 1933. Hitler immediately unleashed a wave of anti-Jewish and anti-communist violence, provoking international protests and fear that the Nazi state's foreign policies might soon become as bloody and brutal as its domestic policy. These depressing developments rendered many American students eager to express their desire to avoid war, and to stay out of the increasingly messy affairs of Europe and Asia.[26]

Although these bleak international events facilitated the anti-war vote on America's campuses, that vote was as much an expression of disillusionment with the First World War as it was a reaction to the international tensions of 1933. This disillusionment linked college students in Britain and America and made it possible for the Oxford Pledge to cross the Atlantic. In both countries students recalled that in the First World War youth had fought and died for lofty political goals that were not achieved and promises that were never kept. The anti-war pledge represented a means of saying that this generation had learned from its predecessors and would honor their memory by refusing to be lulled to the battlefield by flowery speeches and false slogans.

The similarity in British and American anti-war thought was evident not only in the students' common support of the anti-war pledge, but also in the rhetoric they used to justify it. Replying to critics of the pacifist pledge, Oxford Union President F.M. Hardie explained that the pacifist vote must not be interpreted as a

> slur cast on the memory of thoses who were killed fighting for their King and country between 1914 and 1918. The question for the Union was that of how, since a solemn pledge had been given to those men that they were fighting in a war to end war, that pledge could best be carried into effect. The Union decided . . . quite sincerely and quite seriously that the best method of ending war was individual resistance to any future war.[27]

Students in the United States echoed these sentiments and Americanized them by focusing on the broken promise made by President Woodrow Wilson as America entered the World War in 1917. Wilson had pledged that this would be "a war to make the world safe for democracy," but instead, as American anti-war students pointed out, "a war for democracy installed dictators all over Europe." The pacifist pledge had been brought

to America so that students could be mobilized "to prevent another repetition of the fatal mistake of 1917," explained the editor of the *Brown
Daily Herald,* one of the key sponsors the American campus agitation on
behalf of that pledge in 1933.[28]

The influence of the First World War on American student supporters of the Oxford Pledge was so strong that they seemed unable to give a
speech or make an argument about foreign affairs without referring to
that war and its "lessons." Student anti-war activists used these lessons
from the War as a guide to understanding international conflicts in the
1930s. They were convinced that "the literature of the World War . . .
[was] a textbook for the future."[29] And if the story of World War I was
indeed a textbook for understanding the future, the first chapter of that
book would have been devoted to economics.

Persuaded by revisionist histories of the First World War, students
believed that economic factors had served as the central precipitant of
United States entry into that war. They were convinced that despite President Woodrow Wilson's lofty rhetoric, the United States went to war in
1917 not "to make the world safe for democracy," but to protect the profit
margins of American capitalists. The United States had, in the view of
campus peace activists, sided with the British in 1917 because powerful
American banks were major creditors of England and France, giving the
U.S. "high economic stakes in the victory of the Allies . . . . Dividends
and profits, not German atrocities and the *Lusitania* . . . [were] the chief
causes of America's intervention."[30] Such conclusions were especially attractive to a generation of undergraduates whose careers had been threatened by a depression which it blamed on big business. Students saw this
economic lesson from 1917 as a guide for understanding not just that war
but all wars. Consequently, as James Shotwell, a leading historian on campus in 1933 observed, "The tendency to find in economics the chief if not
the sole cause of war has grown in the United States in recent years and
has almost become an axiom in the thinking of the younger generation."[31]

Another critical lesson which student anti-war organizers drew from
the revisionist accounts of the First World War concerned war guilt and
the need to be skeptical of wartime propaganda demonizing the enemy.
Under President Wilson, Americans had gone to war believing that sole
responsibility for the conflict rested with the aggressive Germans and their
allies, whose militarism had run amok, threatening the very survival of
the western democracies. Anti-war students believed that such one-sided
thinking had swayed Americans in 1917 because of "hysteria over the
Lusitania and other incidents, . . . [and] the diabolical propaganda of the
Allies, particularly the British who . . . had controlled most of the means
of world communications."[32] Due to this hysteria and propaganda the
true causes of the war were, according to student anti-war activists, ob-
scured in 1917 as

historians on both sides took a holiday for the duration of the war. With
the Armistice, they slowly began to unravel the tangle of events which
propaganda bureaus had declared were simple . . . . [Revisionist histo-
rians] like Harry Elmer Barnes and Sidney Fay started to explore the
background of conflict in an effort to weigh the claims of . . . "war
guilt". . . . The memoirs of statesmen . . . readily corroborated their
discoveries. The result, of course, was to explode the assertions of both
sides. Neither the Triple Alliance nor the Allied powers could be "blamed"
for precipitating war . . . . [The] conflict was the outgrowth of imperialist rivalries and their symptoms: nationalism, militarism.[33]

Convinced that history tends to repeat itself, student anti-war activists
took these lessons about economics, war guilt and the origins of World
War I and applied them to the turbulent international scene of the 1930s.
If big business and its lust for profits played a key role in pressuring
Wilson to enter World War I, the students had no doubt that these same
forces would—unless exposed and opposed—push Roosevelt into a new
war in the 1930s. If the politicians' and plutocrats' propaganda had misled the American people in 1917, causing them to hate Germany and
believe they were fighting to make the world safe for democracy, these
leaders would again use these tactics to drum up war fever. In short, the
lessons from World War I were not limited to 1917; they were, in the eyes
of student activists, universal. This was the premise which led student
anti-war leaders to conclude in 1933 that

in all great wars in the past men have become drunk upon slogans. They
have been asked to fight for Belgian babies, for a world made safe for
democracy, and for lilies across the field. Today, historians who have the
courage to tell the truth, have smashed through the sham and hypocrisy
of the shibboleths. They tell us wars are fought for steel and gold and
land. They show us how the professional yes-men of big business have
used blind patriotism in every war to cover the trail of private profits.[34]

To campus anti-war organizers in the 1930s, the First World War
held lessons concerning not only foreign policy, but also political democracy at home. They stressed that though America ostensibly went to war
in 1917 to safeguard freedom, the war instead brought an enormous wave
of intolerance which trampled American civil liberty for the duration of
the conflict. As they looked back on this wartime intolerance, anti-war
students in the 1930s "felt ashamed, ashamed for our fathers and uncles."
"We were," recalled journalist Eric Sevareid, a Depression era anti-war
activist at the University of Minnesota, "revolted by the stories of the mass
hysteria of 1917, the beating of German saloon keepers, the weird spy
hunts, the stoning of pacifists, the arrests of conscientious objectors."[35]
Students feared that such bigotry and repression would recur if the United
States became involved in another war.

Student peace activists also saw the First World War as a special warning for academia. In their eyes, the university had sacrificed its intellectual integrity and freedom for the sake of the war effort. "As enlightened scholars," explained Eric Sevareid, "we considered that the professors of 1917 had degraded themselves and their sacred function by inventing preposterous theories about the essential depravity of the German race, the worthlessness of their art and the hidden evil of their music." Nor had students forgotten that academic freedom had been a wartime casualty, as anti-war professors from 1917–1919 were fired and silenced at campuses across the United States. Unless the university learned from this experience, warned the *Columbia Spectator,* it would be doomed to relive the "tragedy and corruption which ran rampant on . . . campus in 1917, . . . [when] honesty was purged and . . . the University transformed into a lie-factory for the production of cannon fodder and propaganda." The students also rebuked academics for turning "their universities into an armed camp," allowing the military to establish the Student Army Training Corp—a wartime program which converted masses of students into soliders—whose curriculum was set by the War Department rather than the professoriate. Hoping to prevent a repetition of this militarization of the university, student anti-war organizers would call for the abolition of ROTC.[36]

The prominence of the First World War in the thinking of American students in 1933 and beyond was a natural outgrowth of their generational experience. These students were "the War babies grown up."[37] Born during the Great War, they had been brought up on the stories of that mammoth conflict—stories which emphasized the brutality of the battlefield and the shattered hopes for a just peace settlement in Versailles. The anti-war movies, novels, and histories of the time left this generation of students haunted by the bloodshed and futility of that war. The undergraduates of the 1930s grew up a time when, in the words of two campus anti-war leaders,

> reciting the horrors of the last war became almost a fad . . . , but a fad which left a deep imprint. Hardly had the last flag ceased waving when the revelation began. There were novels and moving pictures like *All Quiet on the Western Front, The Case of Sergeant Grischa* and *A Farewell to Arms.* They were as widely known as Babe Ruth. They were the favorites of young people in short pants. They established a mood among millions . . . [against] war [and] . . . military barbarism.[38]

Having been raised in a nation still reeling from the First World War, students understood how easy it was for diplomacy to give way to warfare. Indeed, few generations in American history have been so pessimistic about international relations as were college students during the Roosevelt era. In the early and mid-1930s students commonly spoke of the "coming war" and "omens of a Second World War," fearing that unless something drastic was done American involvement in a new world war would be inevitable.[39] In a popular anti-war tract, student movement leaders Joseph P. Lash and James Wechsler made clear the linkage between this sense of foreboding and their status as "war babies grown up":

> Our generation was born during the tumultuous years of the First World War. So reputable an authority as Lloyd's will assure us that we have an excellent chance of dying in the next. The odds are immense that we will not attain senility before war breaks out. This realization has incessantly surrounded the lives of our contemporaries. We live next door to the executioner's block, hearing all the preparatory noises. A boom in the funeral industry appears to be the most enduring contribution which we will render to society. Attuned to this outlook, we can derive only the minimum comfort that knowledge of the future affords. Whatever our ultimate misfortune, we are at least prepared for the worst . . . . We shall not be astonished by the arrival of war nor startled by its horrors. We shall experience only the shock which occurs when dread becomes reality.[40]

For a generation with this gloomy outlook on the prospects of war, the international conflicts of the early and mid-1930s loomed especially large. Since they had grown up expecting war, an event such as the rise of Hitler served only to heighten this sense of imminent hostilities. And as the words of Lash and Wechsler suggest, for students there was an immediacy to the war danger because they knew that it would be their generation whose lives would be lost in a new world war. To students, then, international conflict seemed not remote and distant, but a matter of life and death for their generation. This is why in 1933, a time when economic issues were primary for most of Depression America, peace emerged as the hottest issue among college students.

In giving the highest priority to international affairs, college students do not conform to the textbook image of America during the early 1930s as a place where people were so "absorbed in meeting the endless personal crises of the depression [that] they had little patience with admonitions to direct their attention abroad."[41] This is not to minimize the significance of the economic crisis, which, as we have seen, started the process whereby students became politicized in the 1930s. But because of their age and generational background students felt threatened by the deterioration of international relations and the prospects of a war—a war which they knew could be even more devastating to their lives than had the Depression itself. This was why, as Lash and Wechsler wrote, fear of war outweighed even concern about the Depression on campus:

> We are fully cognizant that there are many other problems confronting us. We could recite at some length the necessity for passage of. . . [legislation] to relieve the economic dilemma of young people. Granting the abundance of our ills, war wins the destruction contest without any

serious competition. We give away no government secrets when we state
that life is a prerequisite to decent living. If we can preserve an interlude
of peace, the hope of such social readjustment can remain open.[42]

The prevalence of this type of thinking among a generation of undergraduates awakened politically by the Depression, scarred emotionally by
the last war, and fearful of the coming war, made the campuses fertile
ground for the growth of a mass student peace movement.

III

The student Left recognized the great potential of the anti-war issue
on campus. Even before the Oxford Pledge Movement had emerged in
England, the NSL and student LID had begun to lay the basis for a national student anti-war movement. Both organizations had strong anti-war
planks in their platforms and had chapters that promoted anti-war sentiment on campus. But the most impressive of the student Left's early attempts to organize the campuses against war was the convening of the
Student Congress Against War, held in Chicago in December 1932. This
NSL-sponsored congress constituted the largest national meeting of student activists since the beginning of the Depression; it attracted 680 delegates from 89 colleges and universities in 30 states.[43]

Like the Oxford Movement itself, the initial impetus for the Chicago
Congress came from abroad; but in this case, the source was communist
rather than pacifist. In August 1932 the NSL had sent Joseph Clark to
attend the World Congress Against War, a communist-sponsored peace
gathering in Amsterdam. Henri Barbusse and novelist Sherwood Anderson, leaders of the Amsterdam Congress, then telegramed the NSL asking
that it organize a nationwide conference of American students "to carry
on a fight against war." Excited by the request and feeling that it linked
them to a worldwide anti-war movement, the NSL publicized its connection to the Amsterdam Congress. The NSL magazine proudly headlined
its article on the League's participation in the Congress "WE ARE IN-
TERNATIONAL!" Heeding the appeal from Amsterdam and confident
that student anti-war sentiment was strong, the NSL organized the Chicago Student Congress.[44]

Though the Amsterdam Congress had inspired the Student Congress
Against War, the manifesto produced at Amsterdam saddled the NSL
with a serious organizing problem. That manifesto, reflecting the sectarianism of the Comintern Third Period line, had condemned the Socialist
International and its failure to oppose the First World War. If this manifesto was to be the basis for organizing the Chicago Student Congress, it
could alienate the socialist-led LID, which in the wake of the Thomas
campaign was the largest student activist group in the United States. The
NSL sought to overcome this problem by involving socialist students in

the planning of the Chicago Congress. Although this did not eliminate the mistrust the Amsterdam Manifesto had fostered among socialist students, it reassured them enough that they agreed to send a delegation— with some of the student LID's top organizers—to the Chicago Congress.[45]

At the Chicago Student Congress Against War, the NSL leaders again faced a test as to whether they were sufficiently non-sectarian to work with their socialist rivals in building an anti-war movement. The key issue was a resolution that came to the floor, which would have put the Congress on record as endorsing the Committee For the Struggle Against War. This resolution offended the socialist delegates because the Committee was organized on the basis of the Amsterdam Manifesto, which included its attack on the Socialist International. In the face of these socialist objections, the NSL agreed to withdraw the controversial resolution. The NSL further promoted unity at the Chicago Congress by electing several socialist student leaders to the Congress' continuations committee. These actions led the student LID to conclude in its official account of the Congress that "in Chicago the most encouraging sign at the whole affair was the honest bid the Communists made for a united front."[46]

The NSL's efforts to cooperate with the socialists were consistent with the non-sectarian approach it had taken in organizing the Harlan delegation. But the expedition to Kentucky had occurred nine months earlier, when the YCL and the adult leadership of the Communist Party (CP) had paid little attention to the NSL and student organizing. By the time of the Chicago Student Congress, however, the national leadership of the CP and YCL had become more interested in the student movement. This new interest arose because the communist leadership had been impressed by the NSL-led student strikes and activism in New York the previous spring. So in Chicago the eyes of the CP and YCL leaders were on the NSL, and they were not pleased with what they saw: the NSL had been too accommodating to the socialists. NSL leader Harry Magdoff recalled that because he led the forces of cooperation with the socialists at Chicago, CP leader Earl Browder "was furious" with him. "It was a problem that they [the CP leadership] had with me because I tried very hard to bring together . . . the NSL clubs and LID."[47]

YCL leader Gil Green went a step further than Browder, using the pages of the communist *Daily Worker* to criticize the NSL publicly for cooperating with socialist student leaders in Chicago. But these complaints had little impact on the NSL, which understood that cooperation with the LID was essential to the success of both the Congress and the entire student movement. Despite Green's criticism, the NSL's official account of the Congress boasted that the meeting had established a "basis of united action of all students and groups represented at the Congress." The account also mentioned that the Socialists and LID were part of this united front.[48] As at Harlan and as it would throughout its life, the NSL in Chicago had shown that it was more willing than the CP or YCL hierarchy to work with its socialist rivals and engage in coalition politics.

The Chicago Congress revealed that though the NSL and LID delegates differed in their assessment of the Socialist International, they agreed on fundamental questions of war and peace. Both saw imperialist wars as the product of capitalism and the international rivalries bred by that system as one bourgeois nation battled another "for foreign markets and fields for investment." So at the Chicago Congress both NSL and LID activists promoted this anti-capitalist perspective, incorporating it into the Chicago platform, which pledged students to oppose capitalist imperialism.[49]

Actually the greatest conflict at Chicago was not between socialists and communists, but between the leftist and pacifist delegates. The pacifists were associated with groups such as the Fellowship of Reconciliation, the Committee Against Militarism in Education, and campus YM and YWCAs; they had become anti-war activists primarily because of their religious principles. These Christian students had initiated a small drill resister movement on campus, in which more than 100 pacifists at state universities refused to enroll in required military training courses in 1932. Unlike most of the socialist and communist student activists, who would support class warfare and anti-colonial wars, the pacifists objected to all forms of violence.[50]

The NSL had made a bid for unity with pacifist students by inviting them and pacifist leader Jane Addams to address the Congress. But Addams' pacifist speech at the Congress drew criticism from the Left. Addams had condemned all wars, whereas the leftists at the Congress opposed only imperialist wars. The radicals at the Congress angered the pacifists by cheering for J.B. Matthews, when he challenged Addams by declaring that he "was not opposed to a war that would end capitalism." The pacifist students at the Chicago meeting, showing their support of Addams, issued a minority report from the Congress stating that "We believe that war is not right, even if used in trying to reach a worthy goal."[51]

Despite this philisophical division and political tension, the Congress united behind an ambitious anti-war program. This unity was possible because even though the delegates had different views of class violence, all were opposed to both an American military build-up and a repetition of the type of international conflicts and interventionism which had led to the First World War. The program endorsed by the Chicago Congress called for a nationwide anti-war campaign on campus, pledging students to convene college peace meetings, disseminate information regarding the role played by their colleges and universities in the First World War, organize "a mass struggle and agitation for the abolition of ROTC," and mobilize their classmates for "anti-war demonstrations on all military holidays and against all military displays at commencement exercises, Charter Day exercises, etc."[52]

Enlisting so large and ideologically diverse a group of students on behalf of this common program was a considerable achievement. The Chicago meeting had been a stormy affair, in which the significant political differences between the pacifist, socialist, and communist delegates were expressed openly and honestly. But in the end, all three groups realized that a larger student anti-war movement could be built only if they found common ground to begin organizing that movement together. This led one student to term the "congress . . . a remarkable display. Every group sacrificed some slice of its dogma to make a united front possible." Chicago had been the most productive meeting yet of student activists in Depression America. And it would later be viewed by these activists as an historic founding convention, where "the guiding principles of the student movement against war were established . . . . If any single enterprise can be viewed as the origin of . . . [the] vast . . . [anti-war] awakening, such was the Chicago Congress."[53]

The Oxford Pledge movement made it easier to translate the Chicago agenda into action. Soon after the Chicago delegates returned to campus and began to plan anti-war action for the semester, the news of the pacifist pledge from England hit. This provided student activists with a vehicle for promoting their anti-war position on campus. In explaining why the Oxford Pledge proved so useful an organizing tool for the peace movement on campus, SLID* leader Joseph P. Lash recalled that administering the Pledge at anti-war conferences on campus

> was a good way of expressing your feeling about war, and it almost inevitably meant that you would get a headline in the press. And that would start controversy, and then you could write letters to the editor explaining your point of view and you could have debates in the student body. It was a way of keeping your program going.[54]

The pledge served not only as a rallying point for anti-war students; it also bolstered their morale by making them feel that they were participating in a "united international action of students in all countries . . . fight[ing] against the military preparations and war policies of their governments." In providing what NSL leader James Wechsler termed" a sense of international union," the Oxford Pledge encouraged students to hope that they—unlike previous generations of anti-war activists—might actually manage to influence international relations and prevent war. Wechsler was among those swayed by the surge of optimism that the pledge generated on campus: "The people of one country do not stop war; the peoples of all countries, aligned together against their common enemies may. The Oxford Pledge was a vivid prelude to what might be hoped for on an ever wider scale."[55]

*In 1933 the student section of the League for Industrial Democracy changed its name to the Student League for Industrial Democracy (SLID). On this change, see 361n.11.

The Oxford Pledge was incorporated so quickly into the anti-war organizing spearheaded by the NSL and SLID that an Americanized version
of the pledge became virtually synonymous with student protest against
war in the United States in 1933. Because the Oxford Pledge was an exciting means of voicing anti-war sentiment, it may seem quite natural that
student radical organizers adopted and promoted the pledge. But in one
important respect this solidarity with the Oxford movement was surprising: the Oxford Pledge originated as a pacifist statement, while the Marxist NSLers (and leftwing socialists in the SLID) were—as had been clear
in the debates in the Chicago Congress—critical of pacifism. It would have
been inconsistent for them to have adopted a pledge that made it sound
as if they were completely renouncing war. They overcame this problem
by changing the phrasing of the pledge as they popularized it in the United
States. Students taking this revised, Americanized version of the Oxford
Pledge were declaring their intention to "refuse to support the government of the United States in any war it may conduct." Since the Marxist
position maintained that the only type of war the American government
could wage would be an imperialist war, the NSLers and other leftist students felt they could support the pledge because it was a rejection not of
all war, but only imperialist war.[56]

In this response to the Oxford Pledge the student Left again displayed a degree of political flexibility which strengthened the student
movement. Recognizing an innovative protest tactic when they saw one,
these young radicals adapted the pledge instead of rejecting it. They were,
in effect, following their tactical good sense as pragmatic organizers, and
relying on a semantic technicality—the rephrasing of the Oxford Pledge—
to free them from the pledge's obvious pacifist implications. This flexibility almost got communist NSLers in trouble with the leadership of the CP
and YCL. As NSL founder Joseph Clark recalled, the communist hierarchy was initially uncomfortable with the NSL, an organization in which
young communists were so prominent, associating itself so closely with
Oxford's pacifist stance:

> There was considerable questioning and concern in the Party and
> the YCL when we endorsed the Oxford Pledge because . . . it might
> convey the impression that the Communists didn't support revolutionary
> war. But since what we were dealing with was [war waged by] the U.S.
> government, the YCL and the Party went along.[57]

Here, as at Chicago, the NSL had adopted tactics considered unorthodox
by the communist hierarchy, and in so doing enhanced its leadership position in the growing anti-war movement on campus.

The process of promoting the Oxford Pledge and working together
on other anti-war activities in 1933 led to closer cooperation between the
NSL and the student LID. There were still some tensions and bickering
between the two groups because of their loyalties to rival radical parties
and competition for student recruits. But both NSL and LID activists rec-

ognized that they thought alike on the anti-war issue—so much so that before the year was out there was talk of merging the two groups. The NSL formally proposed such a merger in December. Though the student LID turned down this proposal because its leaders feared the NSL's links to the Communist Party, the SLID pledged to continue engaging in joint anti-war actions with the NSL. The SLID immediately fulfilled this pledge, joining with the NSL in anti-ROTC protests.[58]

IV

The collaboration between the NSL and the student LID facilitated the growth of the student movement; it meant that the nation's most daring and experienced student political organizers were beginning to search together for ways to mobilize their classmates. This collaboration quickly yielded Depression America's most innovative and effective form of campus political protest: the National Student Strike Against War. This one hour walkout, originated and led jointly by the SLID and NSL beginning in 1934, represented the first attempt at a nationwide strike by college students.[59]

The national anti-war strike was more daring than any previous campaign of the student Left. The idea for such a strike evolved out of the political experience that the young radicals in the NSL and SLID had accumulated since 1932. The notion that a student strike could serve as a dramatic form of college protest derived from the successful student walkout these leftists had orchestrated during the Reed Harris controversy in 1932. The National Student Strike Against War made use as well of the most effective student protest tactic of 1933, the Oxford Pledge, which was scheduled to be administered to students during the strike rallies. Strike organizers also tapped into the student body's deep disillusionment with the First World War by setting the date of the walkout in April, on the anniversary of United States entry into that war. This date was selected as a symbolic way of showing that students remembered the lessons of the last war—"the Great Betrayal of 1917," in which Americans were lulled by democratic rhetoric into an imperialist war—and would therefore "refuse to fight in the next war."[60]

Though promoting the Oxford Pledge, the strike was, in effect, a means of going a step further than Oxford. Now instead of merely pledging not to fight, students would show how they would make good on the pledge. The strike would be a "dress rehearsal" for any future war crisis, a vehicle for mobilizing the young to turn down military service in the event of a new war. SLID leader Joseph Lash, who helped conceive the idea for the strike, traced the student walkout to a "really syndicalist conception . . . [that] was a reflection of the revolutionary ferment of the early 1930s." Student anti-war activists believed, according to Lash, that war could be prevented by "a universal strike . . . If when the capitalists sat down to declare war on one another, all of us young people who had to fight the war would say 'No, we won't go,' . . . that then there couldn't be any war."[61]

The first student strike against war, on April 13, 1934, drew some 25,000 students. Coordinating a national walkout constituted a new challenge, which neither the NSL nor the SLID was able to handle with great skill. Planning for the strike had begun late, and the strike action had not been well publicized outside the student Left's stronghold in New York. Consequently, this first anti-war walkout was primarily an East Coast affair: 15,000 out of the 25,000 striking students were from the campuses of New York City. Yet even though the walkout mobilized only a small minority of the nation's undergraduate population, strike organizers viewed it as a stunning success. The strike had been the largest political demonstration by college students in all of American history. Never before had there been a sight like this: simultaneous protests against war on more than a dozen campuses, including Harvard, Johns Hopkins, Syracuse, Columbia and Chicago universities, CCNY, Vassar, Hunter, and Brooklyn College. There were even reports of anti-war assemblies on several California campuses.[62]

Nor were strike organizers alone in viewing the walkout as a major event. The strike generated considerable press coverage. The media was impressed with both the size and seriousness of the protest. Education reporters, who for years had been covering juvenile student riots and pep rallies, were startled at the sight of students striking against war, hoisting a "thousand [political] banners": "Schools, not Battleships"; "Abolish the ROTC"; "Refuse to Cooperate in Any War the United States Government May Undertake." They noted that an important change had occurred. "The traditional apathy of American youth in political matters" was being replaced with a tradition similar to that of students in Europe and Latin America, "whose immemorial role has been of political agitation en bloc."[63] Strike organizers, who in the past had to labor hard to attract press attention for their local student protests were, as Joseph P. Lash recalled, "completely bowled over" by "the publicity that the anti-war strike got in 1934. When the *New York Times* gave it the lead column story and it became an event [discussed nationally] it was totally unexpected."[64]

The anti-war mood on campus grew even stronger in the semesters following the student strike against war. During this period the anti-war movement received a major boost from the Senate. In mid-April 1934, the Nye Committee began investigating the armaments industry and its profiteering during the First World War. By the end of the year the committee was probing the role that American banks played in promoting United States intervention into the World War. The evidence unearthed by Nye's committee led many Americans to conclude that the United States had entered the war in 1917 "to save the skins of American bankers who had bet too boldly on the outcome of the war and had two billions of dollars of loans to the Allies in jeopardy."[65] The Nye revelations provided legitimation for the student anti-war movement's contention that the First

World War and United States foreign policy were guided by selfish economic interests. This compounded student disillusionment with that war and added support for the anti-war movement as it sought to prevent the United States from again entering such a conflict.[66]

Strike organizers in 1935 benefited not only from the Nye revelations, but also from their experience in the 1934 walkout. Learning from their previous mistakes, student activists began publicizing the strike long before the April walkout. The NSL and SLID also focused on broadening the sponsorship of the anti-war strike, seeking to attract support from non-radical organizations, which could help carry the strike beyond the East Coast. This search for allies proved successful. In contrast to 1934, when the NSL and SLID were the only student organizations endorsing the strike, the 1935 walkout had an impressive list of sponsors, including the National Council of Methodist Youth, the Interseminary Movement, regional councils of the National Student Federation, YM and YWCA chapters, the Youth section of the American League Against War and Fascism, and many student governments and newspapers.[67]

With such diverse groups sponsoring the strike some tension was inevitable among the walkout's organizers. The biggest flare up occurred a little more than a month before the strike. SLID leader Joseph Lash became annoyed by the behavior of the American League Against War and Fascism, because this communist-led organization was unilaterally issuing press releases about the strike and acting as if it alone was responsible for the anti-war protest. Lash threatened to remove the organization's name from the strike call unless it became more cooperative. This threat struck some of the religious pacifists as "undemocratic," and led Rix Butler, president of the Interseminary Movement to warn Lash that unless he included the League in the strike call his own organization would pull out of the strike. Lash backed down, and the strike coalition held together so well that this internal bickering never became public. Despite such disputes, the strike organizing brought some of the strike leaders closer together by involving activists from rival organizations in a common cause. Even Lash, who was still not entirely comfortable working with communists, noted that he "had a very cordial time drafting the [strike] call . . . with [communist NSL leader] Joe Cohen."[68]

The walkout's broad sponsorship helped to make the second Student Strike Against War far larger than the first. The 1935 strike drew about 175,000 students. Unlike the previous walkout, this strike was not dominated by New York City campuses. While the mobilization rate in New York remained almost identical to what it had been the previous year, turnout for the strike in the rest of the nation skyrocketed from 10,000 in 1934 to close to 160,000 in 1935.[69]

There were large strikes in every region of the country. On the West Coast, Berkeley led the way with 4000 striking, followed by 3000 at Los Angeles Junior College, 1500 at Stanford, and 1000 at UCLA and Oregon. In the Midwest, the University of Chicago had the largest strike, with

3500 participants; Minnesota had 3000 and Milwaukee State 2500, Wisconsin 2000, Northwestern, Oberlin, Ohio State, Michigan, and DePauw all had more than 1000 participants. The strike even penetrated a few campuses in the traditionally conservative South, where Texas Christian, Texas, Florida State, North Carolina at Chapel Hill, and Virginia Universities had sizable strike rallies. The Northeast remained a movement stronghold, led by Brooklyn College with 6000 strikers, 3500 at CCNY and Columbia, 3000 at the University of Pennsylvania, 2500 at Temple, and the participation of the entire student body at Vassar. On many campuses the walkouts were the first student political demonstrations in the history of these colleges and universities. Students who had never even seen a protest march before were now marching themselves and chanting the Oxford Pledge.[70]

Though the dimensions of the second student strike were new, its message was not. The speakers at the strike rallies and peace assemblies in 1935, again held on the anniversary of United States entry into the First World War, offered the familiar refrain that the nation must not go to war as it had in 1917. Strikers from coast to coast recited the "lessons" taught by the First World War: profiteering breeds war; politicians use lofty rhetoric to obfuscate the true economic nature of war; instead of promoting democracy the World War paved the way for new dictatorships, fascism and Nazism abroad, and political repression at home. The student protesters saw themselves as "realists who have learned the lessons of the class of 1917, and will practice what has been learned."[71]

The students in both strikes understood—emotionally as well as intellectually—how the First World War affected them and their desire to avoid a future war. The strikes represented an act of mourning for the last generation called upon to fight in a catastrophic war and a declaration of the students' hope and determination to save their own generation from a similar fate. This emotional linkage was evident at Springfield College, where on the night before the 1935 strike, students planted white crosses to memorialize the war dead and remind their classmates of "the Great Betrayal of 1917." It was also visible at the Columbia strike rally. Here Roger Baldwin, who had spent a year in prison for opposing the First World War, urged students to organize more effectively against war than had his generation. Following Baldwin's speech

> taps were played in honor of those students who lost their lives in the World War with the "addition that we are determined not to die as they did." Mr Baldwin then led the meeting in the Oxford Pledge . . . [and] the meeting pledged itself not to support the government in any war it may undertake.[72]

V

As political organizers, the student anti-war activists of the mid-1930s enjoyed far more success than any previous generation of students. In both 1934 and 1935 they mobilized record numbers of students for anti-war protests, and in the coming year their peace rallies would draw about 500,000 students, almost half of the entire American undergraduate population. The student movement's influence, however, extended far beyond these annual walkouts. The anti-interventionism promoted by the movement quickly dominated student thought concerning foreign policy. Indeed, a 1935 *Literary Digest* poll of 65,000 collegians found that 81 percent opposed bearing arms in an overseas war—up nine points since 1933. The anti-war consensus grew so strong on campus that mainstream students sounded little different than radicals when addressing issues of war and peace. In 1935, for instance, the National Student Federation's moderate president personally informed President Roosevelt "that the youth of America is uniting in an effort to maintain American neutrality so that they will not be caught in the same swift stream that caught humanity in 1914."[73]

Though their skill at political organizing was impressive, the student anti-war activists of 1933–35 popularized a view of foreign affairs that was in important respects mechanistic, anachronistic, and inaccurate. These young activists thought that their knowledge of the First World War's "lessons" helped them understand the international conflicts of the 1930s. But, in fact, most of these lessons would prove profoundly misleading. The students never stopped to consider that the insights gleaned from that war might not be relevant to the new and different international situation that prevailed during the Depression decade. The cliché about generals always fighting the last war was applicable here to the campus peace movement. The student anti-war activists in 1933–35 still had their heads in 1917; and in this sense, as NSL leader Joseph Clark recalled, they "relived an era . . . which no longer existed."[74] Fascinated with the scandalous revelations concerning the origins of United States intervention in the First World War, the students read too much into them, acting as if conclusions concerning that war were applicable to all wars.

Probably the most misleading lesson that students in the 1930s learned from World War I concerned the connection between economics and war. The revisionist accounts of the war and the influence of Marxism and the Nye Committee investigation converted many students into economic determinists. Viewing the First World War as the product of economic imperialism, they assumed that if the international conflicts in their own era led to a new war, it would repeat the tragedy of 1917: accomplishing nothing other than "the transfer of mines, mills and trade routes from one set of capitalists to another. These things are not worth dying for."[75] Such simplistic economic postulates from the last war left students unable to comprehend the unique nature of the coming European war: a struggle not over capitalist spoils, but over whether all of the continent was to fall to Nazi totalitarianism.

In their economic determinism, the anti-war activists assumed that idealistic rhetoric urging United States interventionism was sheer propaganda—a facade for profiteers. Determined not to become "drunk on slogans," as Americans had been when Woodrow Wilson's lofty words lured them into the First World War, anti-war organizers dismissed talk of an anti-fascist war, arguing that "A War 'Against Fascism' in 1935 is the counterpart of the War 'For Democracy' in 1917."[76] In effect, the students' understanding of the First World War had left them so jaded that rather than critically assessing the new cries for interventionism in Europe, they simply and erroneously dismissed them all as 1917-style war propaganda.

If the lessons students drew from World War I led them to misread the nature of the growing conflict in Europe, they also fostered an inaccurate assessment of American foreign policy. The students greatly exaggerated America's jingoistic and expansionist tendencies during the early and mid-1930s. Everywhere the anti-war protesters turned they thought they saw signs of 1917-style militarization of America: from the growing (yet still relatively small) War Department budgets to the Civilian Conservations Corps—which they misconstrued as an agency for militarizing youth. Contrary to what the anti-war movement preached, the United States was not heading toward massive rearmament and war during the early and mid-1930s. America was moving in the opposite direction, retreating into one of the most isolationist phases in its history. It would take years of German, Italian, and Japanese aggression before America would be shocked out of its deep isolationist slumber. Given this isolationist hegemony, the student movement's rhetoric about the imminent danger of the United States being pushed into World War by American militarists and capitalists was simply wrong—and so was its conclusion that in 1935 as in 1917 "The Greatest Enemy [of peace] is At Home."[77]

The students were not alone in their tendency to view foreign policy through the distorted lenses of 1917. Throughout the mid-1930s, Congress, reflecting the growing isolationist mood of the nation, crafted neutrality legislation designed to prevent a recurrence of the type of naval conflicts that helped push America into the First World War. Just as the students had been naive in hoping to stop war by taking an oath against military service, Congress was equally naive in believing that if its neutrality laws prevented another *Lusitania* incident this could keep America out of war.[78] Both on campus and Capitol Hill a rigid and mechanistic application of the lessons of one war to another confused the two eras and promoted an unrealistic faith that unilateral anti-interventionism by the United States could preserve world peace.

The anti-war movement on America's campuses did not err in all of its foreign policy pronouncements. The students were correct in arguing that the inequitable terms of the Versailles peace settlement helped set the stage for the rise of Hitler. The student movement also picked up quite early on the evils of Nazism in Germany, militarism in Japan, and fascism in Italy. Student anti-war activists were among the first Americans in the Depression decade to voice their disdain for these tyrannies. In 1933 student protesters angrily confronted Nazi Germany's ambassador in Manhattan and a Japanese naval delegation in Berkeley. The following year students took their anti-Nazi protests aboard the German cruiser *Karlsruhe,* docked in Boston Harbor, and an anti-fascist riot rocked CCNY during the visit of a youth delegation from Mussolini's Italy.[79] But while ahead of most Americans in recognizing and protesting against the brutality of fascism, these anti-war activists underestimated the strength of fascism. Like most Americans in the early 1930s, they did not foresee that fascism would spread and ultimately engulf Europe. And even had the students been prophetic enough to have anticipated this trend, they were too haunted by World War I to think strategically about containing fascism. The same students who took these anti-fascist actions in Berkeley, Boston, and New York also took the Oxford oath pledging themselves to military inaction—a sad irony since nothing short of military force could have reversed the fascist tide in Europe during the 1930s. In fact, at the very moment when American students were taking a pacifist pledge, students in Nazi Germany were burning pacifist books.[80] As they struck for peace on those World War I anniversaries, marched against the Wilsonian slogans of 1917 and championed anti-interventionism, students in the United States remained captives of the past: opposing the wrong war at the wrong time.

Chapter 5

Spies, Suppression, and Free Speech on Campus

> We no longer believe in free speech. We believe in responsible speech.
>
> Dr. Frederick Woellner, UCLA professor of education,
> endorsing the suspension of five student leaders during
> the 1934 free speech fight at UCLA.
> Chester S. Williams, "This Academic Freedom," *Intercollegian and Far Horizons*, (December 1934), 92.

As the student movement spread across America from 1933 to 1935, it encountered strong opposition from college and university administrators. The anti-war demonstrations and strikes, the mass endorsement of the Oxford Pledge, and the rising influence of leftist-led student organizations outraged many of these administrators. This activism seemed so radical and sudden a departure from the political quiesence of the collegiate past that campus officials often found it intolerable. The initial impulse of many college deans and presidents was to try suppressing this student activism, in a manner quite similar to that previously seen on New York's campuses during the early days of the NSL. But just as repression had failed to kill New York's student movement in 1931–1932, it would also fail to stop the rapid growth of the movement nationally in the mid-1930s. This was due in large part to the determined free speech fights waged by student activists, who made campus political rights a top priority for their movement. Free speech became a "cause célèbre" on campus because, as former NSL leader Celeste Strack recalled, students found administration acts of suppression politically offensive and personally insulting:

> While the war and peace issue was becoming big, academic freedom was already a hot issue because no matter what you wanted to talk about

> you were up against the effort . . . [of] the administration not to give
> you the right to talk like grown up people about issues. . . . They . . .
> [would] treat us like children, and that was very deeply resented, [and]
> . . . this was a very important question.[1]

The disrespect of college administrators for student political rights
ran deeper, however, than even most movement activists could have
guessed; it led these campus officials to infringe upon student civil liberties not only publicly but also covertly. College and university administrators opposed to the student movement became involved in secretly feeding information on student protesters to the Federal Bureau of Investigation
(FBI), enabling the Bureau to open dossiers on many of these Depression
era campus activists. The number of students turned in to the FBI by
college officials cannot be traced with complete precision, since the FBI
has still refused to release much of the relevant documentation. But the
magnitude of this political surveillance is suggested by the fact that from
a single campus, the University of Chicago, the FBI had in its files "the
names of two thousand individuals" active in the student movement from
the mid-1930s through 1941. If Chicago was typical, the FBI must have
had information on tens of thousands of Depression America's student
activists.[2]

The FBI files on the student movement reveal that college and university administrators willingly, even eagerly, provided information to the
FBI on the political activity of individual students and leftist-led campus
groups. This was done apparently without a thought that such informing
violated student rights—that undergraduates should be free to engage in
lawful political activity without having their names end up in an FBI file.
The FBI documents suggest that this administration insensitivity to student rights rendered the task of campus political surveillance almost ef-
fortless for the Bureau. Campus administrators were so cooperative that
all the FBI had to do to was dispatch agents to meet with university and
college officials, and they would instantly provide the Bureau with all the
information they had on student activists.[3]

This informing was often done by high ranking campus officials, usually the deans or other administrators charged with policing undergraduate life. At the University of Pennsylvania both the dean of student affairs and the vice president of the university gave the FBI the names of
Penn's leading student activists; at Ohio State University, Montana State
University, Temple University, Purdue University, the universities of Illinois and Missouri, and Middlebury College, the dean of men provided
this information to the FBI. Other deans served as FBI informants at
DePauw University, the universities of Minnesota, Hawaii, and Washington, Yale, Oberlin, Wesleyan University and Wilson Teachers College. On
some campuses, such as George Washington University, Indiana State
Teachers College and the universities of Chicago, Michigan and Ohio,
staffers of the college dean's or university president's office worked with
the FBI—providing the Bureau with membership lists and other assis-

tance in identifying leading student protesters. At Earlham, the college president himself, William C. Dennis, informed on student protest leaders. This was also the case at Middlebury College and at the University of Michigan, whose president, Alexander Ruthven, told the FBI that the student radicals on his campus "were definitely troublemakers"; and volunteered to "furnish all available details" on their ongoing activities to the Bureau.[4]

University involvement in political surveillance was not confined, however, to this work with the FBI. Campus administrators did more than serve as informers on their students; they also sought to have the police and others serve as informers for the University, who would secretly report to them about the off campus radical activities of their students. The extent of such intelligence gathering is impossible to measure nationally, since University officials—apparently sensing that this political espionage would be controversial if word of it leaked to the public—left few written records of it. But on at least one campus, UC Berkeley, enough of the record survives to suggest that University officials energetically cultivated a wide array of informants to assemble political dossiers on their students.[5]

At Berkeley, the UC administration of President Robert G. Sproul began covertly gathering intelligence on Berkeley student radicals in July 1934 with the encouragement of Earl Warren, then the Alameda County District Attorney. That month Warren sent a letter to UC Provost Monroe Deutsch, suggesting that the university work with law enforcement officials "to organize and coordinate their activities in combatting disloyal acts of the radical groups." The intelligence network assembled by the Sproul administration included Bay Area law enforcement officials and superpatriotic groups. Provost Deutsch and President Sproul began assembling this network by dispatching the Berkeley campus police chief to solicit intelligence information on campus radicals from the Sheriff and District Attorney of Alameda County, the police chiefs of Berkeley, Oakland, Piedmont and Alameda, the District Attorney of Contra Costa County, the commanders of three American Legion posts, the commanding officer of the California National Guard, and several other public officials.[6]

The confidential letter that Provost Deutsch sent out to these law enforcement officials and superpatriot groups soliciting help in constructing UC's intelligence network attests to the Berkeley administration's political intolerance. Deutsch made it absolutely clear that the University of California was committed both to political surveillance of the Left and to purging radical activists from the Berkeley campus:

> Occasionally one hears a rumor or report with reference to alleged radical acts on the part of members of the University of California. We should deeply appreciate receiving any or all reports of this character which may come to you. . . . The University of California is anxious not to harbor . . . anyone who is encouraging the overthrow of our govern-

> ment by force. . . . I shall take the liberty of sending you in a very few
> days Captain Walter T. Lee, chief of our police force, and we would
> regard it as a favor if you would place in his hands all information of this
> character which has come to you or which may hereafter come to you.[7]

The University's intelligence network grew quickly. Within a month of its founding, the network included a new member, the Industrial Association (IA) of San Francisco. The IA had served some of San Francisco's largest corporations in their battle against organized labor by spying on trade union and radical activists. By August 1934, the UC administration was receiving and using IA intelligence reports on campus radicals. In a typical report, the IA gave President Sproul the name of one UC student who "is quite active as an agitator for the Communist Party and also has the reputation as being a very effective 'soap box' orator [with] . . . potential for the spreading of Communist Propaganda at the University." Provost Deutsch was so happy with the information UC's intelligence network generated that within a month of its founding he was recommending that President Sproul order "that similar activity be carried on with reference to other sections of the University, particularly the University of California at Los Angeles."[8]

By November 1934, UC's intelligence network had expanded to include law enforcement officials from as far away as Monterey. That month Harry Noland, the Monterey County District Attorney, began providing the University with information on radicals from his region who were attending UC Berkeley. Here Noland warned Sproul of Richard Criley, a student he accused of being "a full fledged radical and a known Communist." Sproul then ordered the campus police to assemble a dossier and "get some further information on Mr. Criley."[9]

UC officials used such intelligence information in their attempts to intimidate student activists. Provost Deutsch boasted of such activity in a letter to Sproul in November 1934. Deutsch told of how he confronted Berkeley student protest leader John Rockwell about his radical associations. Rockwell denied that he was affiliated with any leftwing group, and Deutsch, according to his own account,

> thought that I would let him know that I was not so gullible on that score,
> so I asked him "Did you come from Carmel?" He admitted that he did.
> Then I asked him, "Didn't you and [Richard] Criley belong to the same
> [radical] organization there?" It took him off his guard but he admitted
> it.[10]

After this encounter, Rockwell—shocked by Provost Deutsch's knowledge of his political background—charged that Deutsch had tried to frighten him out of campus political activity by using information obtained from the American Legion's blacklist. Rockwell, of course, was unaware of the fact that the University did not have to rely on the Legion's blacklist because of UC's wide intelligence network.[11]

Exactly how much intelligence information UC's intelligence network yielded is not clear, since most of the dossiers it produced have apparently been destroyed. But judging from the data that the Sproul administration gathered from just one member of its intelligence network—Political Science Professor David Barrows, who was also a General and Commander of the California National Guard—these dossiers must have been extensive. In August 1934, Barrows, upon Deutsch's request, provided the Sproul administration with data on 41 Berkeley student radicals, gathered by "G–2," the National Guard's intelligence unit. At this time Barrows also informed Deutsch that he had information on 20–25 other student radicals and several new graduate students, upon which he was awaiting confirmation.[12]

Though Barrows' surveillance correspondence was addressed to Provost Deutsch, there is no doubt that UC President Sproul was involved personally in this intelligence operation. In fact, Barrows began one of these letter to Deutsch by informing the Provost that

> I am enclosing thirteen cards on what is known about the activities of certain students in this University who are or were Communists. This morning I left twenty-eight cards of other students with President Sproul, who intended to glance them over. This makes a total of about forty students out of a somewhat larger number of whom I have had occasion to secure reports in view of their actual or probable Communist activities.[13]

Nothing in this correspondence suggests that Professor Barrows, a former president of the University of California, saw any ethical problem with circulating dossiers on students in his own university. Professor Barrows reasoned that it was proper for him to have obtained this information in his capacity as a National Guard general, because the Guard needed it to be prepared for any potential battle with students engaged in "seditious and violent activity." And he apparently thought the University could make good use of this information to deal with potential troublemakers.[14]

In their secret work spying and informing on student radicals, college administrators were guided by the same anti-radical impulse that led to their public attempts to suppress student protest and faculty radicalism in the 1930s. They defined Left activism as aberrant behavior and viewed radical expression as nothing but propaganda, a category of inflammatory and misleading speech which had no place in a university, whose mission was objective inquiry and the pursuit of truth. According to Chancellor E.A. Burnett of the University of Nebraska, political subjects could be discussed on campus only "so long as they are judicial and informative rather than in the interests of propagandists. We would not knowingly permit any speaker to occupy a university platform if he is engaged in an effort to destroy the present form of government by revolutionary methods."[15] The professor who engages in such "partisan propaganda," explained President Charles Wesley Flint of Syracuse University, "discredits his profession and his institution as guides for students and as leaders for the community."[16] Since it was the college president's duty to prevent the discrediting of his institution, he was obligated, in the words of President Sproul, to silence those engaged in "spreading the poison gas of . . . class . . . warfare. . . . No society will tolerate for long those among its own servants who give aid and comfort to enemies seeking its destruction."[17]

Such anti-radicalism served as an especially strong inducement for suppression of student protest because it was wedded to an equally strong paternalistic sensibility among campus administrators. The same brand of administration paternalism which had led to the Depression era's first student free speech fights, at Columbia and CCNY, contributed to most of the repressive actions campus officials took against anti-war organizers. These administrators felt no compunction about suppressing anti-war activism because they saw students as immature youths in need of discipline and guidance rather than as adults with constitutional rights. College administrators believed that students lacked intellectual maturity and were therefore ripe for exploitation and manipulation by cynical radical agitators. President L.D. Coffman of the University of Minnesota stressed this theme in his speech, "The Exploitation of Youth," delivered before the National Association of State Universities in 1935. To Coffman, the political naiveté of collegians made them

> easy prey of the social racketeer who tells them that America is not the fair land of hope and opportunity that it was pictured to be . . . . The very folly and inexperience of youth make them easy victims of those who would use them for some ulterior purpose; the more majestic, the more emotional the appeal, the easier it is to lead the [college] youth. . . .[18]

Since undergraduates were deemed too intellectually weak and politically naive to defend themselves from the manipulations of radical propagandists, these college officials thought it their duty to protect their young flock from the wolves of the Left.

This condescending anti-radicalism allowed college officials to disregard civil liberties considerations and seek the banishment of radical activism from campus. For them suppression of radicalism on campus was equated not with the authoritarianism of a harsh dictator, but the firm hand of a concerned parent—and in this case a parent shielding youths from dangerous subversives. Syracuse University's Chancellor Flint had this in mind when he pledged to drive off campus "any organization [that] is openly affiliated, or still more if it is covertly affiliated with . . . [off campus radical groups under the] militant lash of paid secretaries and . . . persistent and occasionally fanatical propagandists."[19] Similarly, Provost Ernest C. Moore of UCLA threatened that students who allied themselves with the anti-war movement would be punished for working "to destroy the University by handing it over to the Communists."[20] President

Alexander Ruthven of the University of Michigan echoed these anti-radical sentiments, warning in 1935 that students who joined in the "perversive [anti-war] activities of a few professional agitators" would be expelled.[21]

Not even the doctrine of academic freedom could protect political liberty on campus during the 1930s. Most college presidents interpreted academic freedom in such narrow terms that it served to diminish rather than preserve free speech rights in academia. In their view, academic freedom constituted not a general right to free speech on campus, but only the privilege of academics to do research in their specialized areas and to present the findings which grew out of that research. As President Flint of Syracuse University explained in 1935, the type of speech protected by academic freedom was quite limited; it covered only the

> freedom to speak under compulsion of thought that which is worthy of being said by one who is qualified to be heard . . . . In other words, they [academics] are free only to speak on subjects on which they have earned the right to be heard . . . . Academic freedom is not a blank check; it is limited by deposits to the teacher's credit, the degree of his scholarly attainments. It is not . . . the right to unlimited expression whether or not possessing anything worth expressing; not license to scatter about publicly half-baked theories, egotistical vagaries, or to vocalize loose thinking masquerading as liberal thinking.[22]

This limited academic freedom could not protect students because campus administrators held that it applied only to professional scholars and teachers, not to a group so immature as undergraduates.[23]

Since the only form of speech protected on campus was—as this narrow doctrine of academic freedom specified—the scholarly pronouncements of professors concerning research in their areas of specialization, the degree of political freedom was often lower inside academia than it was outside. While off campus, partisan political speech tended to be protected by the first amendment, on campus such speech was either barred or severely restricted, since it was considered unprofessional and incompatible with scholarly standards. Indeed, adherents of this view of academic freedom thought that in order to be a professional scholar one had to sacrifice a measure of one's free speech rights. According to President Robert Gordon Sproul of the University of California, "In practice university professors can never be quite so free in speech and action as many other men for they cannot enjoy the license of speaking without investigation."[24]

This willingness to restrict free speech rights on campus in the 1930s derived not merely from this vision of scholarly neutrality, but from a mistrust of free speech itself. Most campus officials were definitely not civil libertarians. They thought unlimited freedom of speech could lead to trouble, promoting licentiousness rather than liberty. Thus President James L. McConaughy of Wesleyan University contended that "freedom is a dangerous tool; if you give it in a dictatorship, the dictator is soon murdered; if you give it to a group of thoughtless citizens, chaos may result . . . . Complete freedom is possible only in a Utopia."[25]

Given their belief that unlimited liberty was such a "dangerous tool", many college presidents felt it their duty to protect their schools and society by working, in the words of President Sproul, to "combine liberty with order." Liberty had to be restricted when it clashed with the needs of either the school or society. This was, as Sproul put it, limited "freedom within the framework of public good." Sproul defended this ideal of moderated liberty on the grounds that it "rediscovers what the Greek thinkers knew so long ago—that the supreme principle of human association in a free society is moderation in all principles."[26]

Despite Sproul's rhetoric about moderation and liberty, there was nothing moderate about this doctrine; it enabled college administrators to justify suppressing any form of speech which they found distasteful. In the name of liberty, it entitled the college president to act as a petty dictator, who could wipe out free speech whenever he deemed this necessary for preserving either the good name of the college or the public good. On these grounds President McConaughy of Wesleyan sought to make political suppression sound virtuous:

> Wisdom dictates some curtailment of complete freedom for the teacher—at least until the Utopian day when all teachers are wise. In war time we can not allow public servants—and teachers are public servants—to threaten the government's overthrow by complete freedom of expression. In peace some judgment has to be imposed upon them from above. Wherever possible this curb should be local, not by legislation.[27]

With the college gates guarded by such intolerant administrators, it is not surprising that there were many reports of attempts to bar both student anti-war protests and other radical dissent from campuses. Incidents involving overt restrictions on students' free speech rights occurred on at least 53 campuses between 1933 and 1935. Many of these campuses witnessed repeated free speech violations. These incidents were by no means restricted to obscure or third rate colleges; they erupted at some of America's leading institutions of higher education, including Harvard, the Universities of Michigan and Wisconsin, Columbia, Johns Hopkins, the Massachusetts Institute of Technology, UCLA, UC Berkeley, and the City College of New York.[28]

In the worst cases, the efforts of college administrators to prevent undergraduates from being infected by radicalism resulted in physical disruption of student protests. Some of the most anti-radical administrators personally supervised these disruptions during the first two national student strikes against war. One of the more high spirited of these administrators, Roscoe C. Ingalls, the Director of Los Angeles Junior College, became so incensed by the anti-war strike in 1935 that he tried to drown out the peace demonstrators at his college by

> roaring into microphones of the campus public address system. Next Director . . . Ingalls stationed himself in front of the speakers, blew a tin whistle until he was red in the face. Unavailing, he advanced on the library with a burly "Red squad" of policemen. When the students swarmed around them, the flustered policemen swung nightsticks, knocked out two girl students. Finally Director Ingalls turned on the sprinkler system, cleared the campus in two minutes.[29]

Ingall's type of direct personal intervention at the site of an anti-war demonstration was, however, somewhat unusual for a college president. More often, campus administrators seeking the physical disruption of anti-war demonstrations did not themselves serve on the front lines; they fostered such disruptions by encouraging anti-radical students—either explicitly or implicitly—to harass the anti-war activists. On some campuses this administration encouragement was both blatant and public, as when the President of San Jose State Teachers College responded to the appearance of a radical leaflet by urging that patriotic students throw these leftists off campus. The college president announced:

> I hope every true citizen on this campus, every one who loves the United States of America as well as the college will assist in the eradication of this festering sore. Will all loyal groups, clubs, classes and societies act immediately. Make plans to get the necessary information. If you know members of the group, please feel quite free to take them to the edge of the campus and drop them off.[30]

A similar call to violence was heard at Michigan State University during the second student strike against war, when J.A. Hannah, the Secretary of the University, told the press that "the administration of the college will have no objection if other students toss these radicals in the river."[31] Students answered Hannah's call to action. They disrupted the campus anti-war meeting by tossing fruit at the rally speakers and then jumping onto the stage, grabbing five protest leaders and throwing them into a nearby river. Reverend Harold Marley, one of the victims of the assault, visibly shaken by this collegiate intolerance, said that during the attack "for the first time, I realized how Negroes must feel on the way to a solitary tree."[32]

On some campuses, college officials were more covert in their support of anti-radical violence. These campus officials avoided public endorsements of such violence, but worked behind the scenes to organize attacks. In 1934 Louis O'Brien, Berkeley's Assistant Dean of Undergraduates, called a private meeting in which he conferred with conservative students and helped organize a vigilante squad, made up primarily of fraternity members, to harass striking students.[33] An almost identical meeting occurred at the City College of New York—and in both cases these meetings led directly to anti-radical violence.[34] In other cases, campus administrators, though not playing a role in organizing violent assaults on anti-war activists, gave a green light to such attacks, by either praising or refusing to discipline the perpetrators of this violence. Physical assaults on student anti-war activists went unpunished at virtually every campus which witnessed such violence, including Harvard, Johns Hopkins, UCLA, UC Berkeley, Columbia, CCNY, MIT, Michigan State, and the universities of Chicago, Connecticut, Washington, and Wisconsin.[35]

While violence was the most dramatic form of suppression on campus, it was not the most common. College administrators from 1933 to 1935 usually sought to keep anti-war demonstrations off the college grounds without having to resort to brute force. This was attempted through the enforcement of campus political rules restricting the students' freedom of assembly, freedom of speech, and freedom of the press on campus. The most widely used forms of non-violent suppression of student radicalism and anti-war activism were, in rank order: 1. the banning of anti-war meetings and leftist speakers from the college grounds; 2. the expulsion or suspension of students for participating in anti-war actions; 3. the censorship of anti-war literature, including editorial copy from student newspapers; 4. the banning of radical student organizations.[36]

Judging by their formal power and legal authority, college administrators should have been able to smash the anti-war movement and banish its organizers from their campuses. On virtually all questions of disciplinary authority, the courts bent over backwards to favor administrators in this era of *in loco parentis*. The courts gave colleges and universities virtual carte blanche to discipline and even expel troublesome undergraduates and to do so without even a semblance of due process. By December 1934, moreover, there could be no doubt at all over whether the courts would back college administrators who used their disciplinary authority to attack anti-war dissenters on campus. That month the Supreme Court, in *Hamilton v. Regents of the University of California,* affirmed UCLA's expulsion of two student anti-war activists who had refused to enroll in mandatory military training courses. Such decisions attested that students usually had little hope of litigating successfully against politically repressive administrators.[37]

Fortunately for the student movement, however, there was often a large gap between the legal authority and the actual political power of college officials in the 1930s. University and college political battles were usually settled on campus rather than in the courts, much to the detriment of repressive administrators. Through free speech protests, indignant student bodies could hold college deans and presidents accountable for their acts of political suppression. While campus administrators hurt individual activists by subjecting them to suspensions, expulsions, and other disciplinary actions, these punitive acts proved ineffective in inhibiting student protest. Indeed, such attempts at suppression usually backfired politically because students often viewed censored movement activists as martyrs to the cause of free speech, and therefore rallied to the student movement's side. This trend was evident nationally, for at the very time (1933–1935) when attempts at political repression on campus were multiplying, student anti-war protest grew enormously, from a small insurgency in the East into a national movement. But to comprehend the actual workings and impact of political repression on campus, it is necessary to explore such repression at close range—and for this we turn to the two most ambitious attempts to suppress the student movement in this era: on the East Coast, CCNY, and on the West Coast, UCLA.

II

No college tried harder than the City College of New York to suppress student protest. CCNY's President Frederick B. Robinson and his subordinates violated student free speech rights more frequently than any other college administration in Depression America. From 1931 to 1934 Robinson's anti-radical campaign resulted in the expulsion of 43 CCNY students, the suspension of 38, and the hauling of hundreds of undergraduates before campus disciplinary boards, inquiring into their political associations, beliefs, and protest activity. In this same period, every student radical organization and publication was at one point or another banned from the CCNY campus. Robinson never learned that such repression only fueled student protest. Indeed, though many CCNY activists look back upon Robinson with scorn, they credit him with being one of their most effective organizing tools. Through his abuse of student political rights, CCNY's president inadvertently helped radicalize thousands of students and kept the campus in turmoil.[38]

The more repressive Robinson became, the more creative CCNY's student radicals became in mocking and resisting him. In fall 1932, Robinson fired Oakley Johnson, an English instructor at CCNY, apparently because of his communist affiliation and his support of the student Left. When students staged a rally in Johnson's defense, Robinson called the police on to campus, who clubbed and dispersed the demonstrators. This was the first time a college president had used the police against student protesters during the Depression decade. The confrontations over the Johnson firing were followed by a wave of suspensions, which provoked a student strike at CCNY in October 1932. Led by the NSL, the student protesters denounced CCNY's violations of academic freedom and announced their plan to hold a mock trial of President Robinson and CCNY night school director Paul Linehan for those violations. Despite threats from the college's trustees to punish participants in the trial, some 1400 students attended this event in New York's Central Opera House on the last weekend of October, 1932.[39]

The mock trial displayed political theater on a grand scale. The "defendants," Robinson and Linehan, were charged with "deliberate persecution" of student activists at CCNY, "intimidation of teachers at the College, and responsibility for the arrest of" peaceful student protesters. The trial was conducted, for the most part, as if it were occurring in a real courtroom, complete with a prosecutor, defense attorney, and judges dressed in black robes—all of whom were NSL activists. Twenty-eight witnesses testified, documenting the various acts of political censorship and suppression committed by the defendants. The trial ended after a summation by "prosecutor" Joseph Starobin, who described the conflict at CCNY as a "fight for intellectual freedom." The audience, acting as a jury, found Robinson and Linehan guilty and "sentenced" them to vacate their positions in the CCNY administration. Robinson was not amused. Though he had not attended the trial, Robinson had a stenographer record the proceedings, and then sent the record to the college's trustees—who suspended 19 organizers of the trial.[40]

Robinson went even further in his assault on student protesters during the following semester in response to an anti-ROTC demonstration. The controversy began when the administration announced its decision to cancel afternoon classes so that students could attend military exercises in a pre-Memorial Day ceremony. Student anti-war activists complained that it was wrong for CCNY, as "one of the world's largest cultural institutions . . . [to] suspend intellectual activity to pay homage to the war machine within its cloistered walls"; they derided this military event as "jingo day," and urged that students use that occasion to rally against war.[41]

The "jingo day" protest on May 29, 1933, began peacefully, when about 400 students assembled near campus to hold an anti-war rally. But the rally gathered in such close proximity to the ROTC cadets' line up for their march to CCNY's stadium for the ceremonies, that as the rally grew, the police moved in and ordered the protesters to disperse. Complying with the police order, the students regrouped a half block away. After a brief rally, the demonstrators, carrying anti-ROTC and anti-jingo day banners, brought their protest directly outside the ceremony site by picketing around the stadium.[42]

Again the police intervened, forbidding the students from picketing and ordering them to disband. The protesters began marching away, when one of them shouted "Let's go to the stadium. We were all invited." Responding spontaneously to this call to action, the students abandoned their picket line and sought to enter the stadium. Police and ushers, however, blocked the way, informing the students that they could not enter the stadium with their picket signs. But after discarding their signs, the protesters were again refused admission to the stadium. The protesters retreated to the campus where they met to discuss strategy and—angered by hecklers who disrupted the meeting by showering the speakers with eggs—decided that they had a right to go to their college's ceremonies, and so returned to the stadium.[43]

The protesters' second attempt to gain admission to the stadium resulted in a wild melee as they were again barred from the ceremony. According to the *New York Times* report

> more than 100 of the demonstrators marched past the iron gates [of the stadium] but they found their further progress blocked by an inner line of wooden doors. Some hand-to-hand fighting followed as the cadet officers, administration sympathizers and policemen pushed the pacifists outside the stadium.[44]

At this point President Robinson, accompanied by the ROTC commander and other guests, arrived at the stadium and became embroiled in a confrontation with the protesters. Robinson "raised his umbrella and lashed out suddenly, striking nearly a dozen of the . . . [protesters] about the head and shoulders." Several students responded by pinning Robinson's arms, in an effort to get the umbrella away from him and thereby stop the assault. Police intervened, pushed the students away, and escorted Robinson into the stadium.[45]

Robinson claimed that he struck the students because they were rushing toward him and threatening him and his guests. But neither the American Civil Liberties Union's investigation nor the testimony of students and bystanders support his claim. According to the ACLU, Robinson had not been threatened by the students. The ACLU reported that their "investigation of the occurrence at City College on May 29 revealed that President Robinson left the sidewalk where he was walking with his party and attacked the parading students in the street with an umbrella, and that he himself was responsible for the riot that followed."[46] Robinson apparently had become so infuriated by the sight of a throng of students near the stadium entrance and by their jeering of him that he wielded his umbrella against them.[47]

. Shocked and outraged by Robinson's attack and by the announcement that participants in the demonstration would be punished, CCNY student activists immediately began to voice their criticism of the administration. CCNY's socialist-led Student Forum published a "jingo day issue" of its newsletter, headlined "ROBINSON RUNS AMOK ON CAMPUS: MADDENED PRESIDENT ATTACKS STUDENTS."[48] Campus officials were in no mood for such criticism. They stopped students from distributing this newsletter and seized the entire edition of the publication. The administration also announced that 29 student activists, three major radical student organizations on campus, and the student newspaper were suspended pending the completion of the disciplinary hearings.[49]

Despite these new restrictions on their campus political rights, CCNY student activists continued to organize against both Robinson and the suspensions. Under the leadership of the NSL and the SLID, several large protest rallies were held off campus in the week following the jingo day incident. The culmination of these protests was an "umbrella parade," which featured an immense replica of the weapon Robinson had wielded against the demonstrators.[50] CCNY student activists were not alone, however, in their criticism of Robinson. The *New Republic* suggested that CCNY's embattled president should step down because "any college president who descends to fisticuffs with his undergraduates has destroyed his usefulness as a preceptor of youth now and forever."[51]

Robinson's strong-armed manner of dealing with student protesters fostered the growth of anti-radical violence and the disruption of anti-war meetings at CCNY. Conservative students, particularly the more intolerant members of the campus ROTC and athletic teams, seem to have concluded that if it was proper for their college president to assault anti-war protesters, it was also proper for them to mount such attacks. These anti-radical students attempted to disrupt almost every protest meeting held in the weeks following the jingo day incident, employing physical violence and organized heckling. In one such meeting, socialist leader Norman Thomas could not complete his speech because twenty-five of these hecklers used automobile horns and police sirens to drown him out.[52]

This harassment might not have occurred, however, were it not for the organizing of an ROTC officer on the CCNY faculty. Apparently emboldened by Robinson's assault, this faculty member worked to create violent opposition to the student Left. According to a *New York Times* report, anti-radical students were "acting on the suggestion of Major Herbert M. Holton, Associate Professor of Hygiene [at CCNY]," when they decided to form a vigilance committee which would use "controlled force" against the anti-war protesters. Holton had made this suggestion at a meeting attended by college athletes in CCNY's Varsity Club shortly after the jingo day incident.[53] Neither Holton nor the disruptive anti-radical students—who unlike the anti-war activists actually had infringed upon student free speech rights—were ever punished or even investigated at CCNY for their acts of harassment.

The disciplinary hearings which followed the jingo day incident were extremely one-sided. The faculty committee which conducted these hearings proved unwilling even to consider the possibility that the jingo day incident might have been precipitated by President Robinson. Nor was the committee interested in examining how the conflict was facilitated by the restrictive campus regulations against political protest, the police, and the decision to bar the protesters from the stadium. The whole idea that infringements on the rights of students—including police dispersion of the picketers outside the stadium, the assault on protesters trying to enter the stadium, and the umbrella attack itself—had contributed to the crisis, and therefore merited the committee's attention, was simply alien to these unsympathetic faculty. Thus, instead of investigating why such a violent clash had occurred and what policy changes could prevent a repetition of it, the committee merely sought to determine which anti-war activists had participated in the jingo day protest, what campus rules they had broken, and how they should be punished.

The assumption that the anti-war activists were totally at fault for the jingo day incident guided the disciplinary hearings from beginning to end. This assumption was articulated not only by the committee, but by Mark Eisner, the chair of the college's board of trustees, who virtually judged the protesters guilty even before the hearing had begun. Eisner set the tone for the entire investigation in his public statement the day after the jingo day clash. He concluded that anti-war protesters "were deliberately obstructing a college function, the annual cadet review. Students who are found guilty can expect that their college days at City College are over."[54]

The disciplinary hearings, which began on June 1 and ultimately took testimony from over 100 students, were themselves a testament to the severe limits on free speech which confronted thousands of undergraduates during the early 1930s. The administrators and faculty on this disciplinary committee—like many of their colleagues across the nation—worked from the illiberal premise that any political demonstration held to protest either an action of the college or a regular college event constituted an intolerable attempt to "interfere with a stated college function."[55] Such protests merited suppression even if they were non-violent and not literally disruptive of the "stated college function." Thus in the case of the jingo day protest, the fact that students demonstrated against the scheduled military exercise was enough to convict them, even though they made no attempt to stop the ceremonies or interfere with the speeches.

Throughout the hearings, student activists clashed with the faculty and administration on the question of student political rights. These primarily communist and socialist students tried repeatedly to convince the disciplinary committee that by outlawing demonstrations at college functions the administration infringed upon their right to assemble peacefully. The students challenged the committee's assumption that in holding such a demonstration on jingo day they had interfered with a college function. In a typical exchange during the disciplinary hearings, NSL activist Herman Benson argued this point with Dean Morton Gottschall. When the Dean contended that the anti-war activists were guilty of interfering with the military exercises, Benson replied:

> No that wasn't interference because that didn't prevent the carrying out of the ROTC function. Q.[Gottschall] What do you call it then, if not interference; what name would you give it? A. [Benson] I would call it expressing our disapproval of ROTC and trying to bring our idea across to those who may have been there. Q.[Gottschall] That was interfering certainly. A. [Benson] In what way did it prevent the carrying out of the ROTC exhibition?[56]

Though the disciplinary committee repeatedly reminded the testifying students that their demonstration had violated campus regulations, the students insisted that their free speech rights should take precedence over such regulations. As one student activist told the committee, "We believe we are citizens of the college . . . and that . . . as citizens of the college we believe we have the right to protest."[57] Julian Prager, one of the students who would be expelled for his role in the jingo day demonstration, testified that no matter what the campus regulations said, "I believe we have a right to express our opinions in whatever way we see fit without infringing upon anybody's rights."[58] Soon the students began to see, however, that because their definition of political liberty on campus was much broader than the administration's, free speech battles were inevitable. NSL leader Joseph Budish told the committee "that we have reached a point where we cannot see eye to eye with the administration and that if they use sufficient pressure to make these so-called liberal principles be abandoned we would have to fight it out and take the consequences."[59]

The disciplinary committee responded to these civil liberties arguments with paternalistic and bureaucratic clichés. Committee members stressed that it was the faculty and administration who made the rules and that students had no choice but to obey them, even if they disagreed with them. The committee viewed any violation of these rules as youthful insubordination which had to be punished. Throughout the hearings, the committee insisted that any student who fell short of absolute obedience to campus regulations had no place in the college. Just how far CCNY faculty and administrators took this ethic of obedience was made clear in an exchange between Dean Gottschall and NSL leader Adam Lapin during the hearings. "Q.[Gottschall] Suppose we passed a rule prohibiting the congregating of three students on the campus? A. [Lapin] Would you gentlemen expect such a rule to be obeyed if passed? Q.[Gottschall] If it passed, we'd expect it to be obeyed."[60]

This demand for absolute obedience was a manifestation of faculty and administration paternalism—their belief that students were immature youths under their charge who had to be guided into adulthood. The type of adults they saw themselves as molding were dignified and proper gentlemen. And gentlemen, of course, would be far too civil to engage in boisterous street demonstrations, such as that seen on jingo day. This theme, that the protesters had behaved in an uncivil and immature manner, unbecoming gentlemen was stressed continually by the disciplinary committee. "I do very seriously object to a man conducting himself as though he were a rowdy and not a gentleman; and I think those [jingo day demonstrations] were rowdy and not gentlemanly actions," explained one committee member.[61]

CCNY student activists denied that they had behaved in an uncivil manner. They argued that their disorderliness had been provoked by the ungentlemanly behavior of the police, the cadets, and the president who attacked them. The activists also accused the disciplinary committee of employing a double standard in their application of the standard of gentlemanly conduct—charging that it was applied to radicals but not to the conservative students who used force to break up student anti-war meetings. When Joseph Starobin, an NSL leader, told the disciplinary committee that it was unfair for the administration to punish radical activists, while not even questioning the athletes and cadets who engaged in anti-radical heckling and violence, Professor Mead's rebuttal seemed to confirm the existence of an administration double standard. Mead told Starobin:

> That is not pertinent at all. In the first place the so called [anti-radical] Vigilantes did whatever they did off the College Grounds. A. [Starobin] They started on the College grounds. Q. [Mead] I don't know who was responsible and I don't see that that has a bearing upon the situation. That was a different situation. I was talking about organized groups of the College definitely engaged in advancing propaganda. I don't approve of what they did, but they had not propaganda in mind and were only interested in breaking up a meeting.[62]

It was not just the college's dispensing of unequal punishment, but the disciplinary process itself which offended CCNY anti-war activists. They charged that the disciplinary committee had violated their due process rights by suspending all of the campus' radical organizations even before the disciplinary hearings had started. But the committee defended its disciplinary action on the grounds that it had "a legal right to suspend . . . [student clubs] at any time," and even went on to criticize students for publicly protesting the suspensions. In response to this criticism, one NSL activist told the committee: "I maintain that we have the right to protest suspensions of that nature—suspensions without investigation. . . . Raised in the American tradition, we realized we had the right to protest any action."[63] This concept of student political rights was, however, one that the committee could not accept and one that it argued against during the hearing. Thus a member of the committee lectured the protesting student that

> when the faculty reaches a decision, even though it be wrong, as a good citizen of the college you must abide by that decision until it is changed. A. [unnamed student activist] How can we go about protesting? [Faculty Committee member] When you start protesting to the outside world your conduct is unbecoming a college student.[64]

At the conclusion of the hearings, the committee expelled twenty-one jingo day protesters and suspended eight others for an entire semester. The committee revoked the charters of the campus' three leading radical organizations, claiming that they were responsible for a "deliberately planned attempt to interfere with a stated college function." The students were found guilty of violating college rules though their participation in an unauthorized meeting on campus. The student Left at CCNY denounced the expulsions as a sign that the college had been converted into a "seething cauldron of administrative despotism." But despite widespread student anger over the expulsions, there was little that could be done to mobilize CCNY against the decision because the academic year had drawn to a close.[65]

Though the jingo day expulsions served only to anger the student body and bred further anti-war protest at CCNY, the Robinson administration persisted in its repressive policies. The administration refused students permission to hold a meeting on campus during the first anti-war strike in April 1934. When about a thousand students defied this ban by rallying on campus, Dean Morton Gottschall—taking a cue from President Robinson's earlier anti-radical assault—intervened personally to try to break up the unauthorized meeting.

> Gottschall, making a one man sortie against the mob, attempted to stop the meeting single handed. He ripped banners out of the leaders' hands and tried to compel [the main speaker, Student Council representative] Edwin Alexander '37 to get down from the flagpole [which he was using as a podium].[66]

Police then rushed in and forcibly dispersed the rally. As a result of this rally ten students were disciplined.

Before the year ended, CCNY witnessed another round of expulsions. In fall 1934, twenty-one CCNY student activists were expelled, twelve placed on probation and four suspended as a consequence of an anti-fascist protest. The event which sparked this new disciplinary round was a reception given to a visiting delegation of Italian fascist students by President Robinson, who invited the delegation to campus despite the objections of the CCNY student government. Robinson decided that the fascist delegation would be honored with a special assembly in CCNY's Great Hall. The administration refused to grant student protesters permission for an anti-fascist demonstration by the entrance to the campus, which they had hoped to hold on the day of the delegation's visit to CCNY. To these CCNY student activists the administration seemed to be employing a blatant political double standard by honoring fascists in the college assembly hall, while banning anti-fascists from marching even outside the hall. The anger generated by this administration behavior set the stage for one of the stormiest meetings in the history of the City College of New York.[67]

The meeting, which occurred before a packed house of some 2000 students on October 9, 1934, began tensely, as students jeered President Robinson during his opening remarks. Robinson shouted back at the students, "Guttersnipes, your conduct is worse than that of guttersnipes."

After Robinson completed his speech, Professor Arbib Costa of CCNY's Italian department made a brief welcoming speech and then gave the floor to CCNY Student Council representative Edwin Alexander, who was supposed to extend the student body's greetings to the visiting delegation. Before giving Alexander the microphone, Professor Costa warned him not to mention fascism in his remarks and told him that to do so would be discourteous. But Alexander, an NSL activist, disregarded this warning and began his Great Hall address with the words "I do not intend to be discourteous to our guests. I merely wish to bring them anti-fascist greetings from the student body of City College to the tricked, enslaved student body of Italy . . ." Before Alexander could utter another syllable, Professor Costa "took him by the arm away from the microphone." Members of the Italian Club then surrounded and assaulted Alexander. A full scale riot followed when students from the audience jumped onto the stage to assist Alexander.[68]

The CCNY administration and faculty responded to this incident in the same partisan manner that characterized their handling of the jingo day affair. Alexander's assailants were never investigated or punished, but disciplinary proceedings began immediately against Alexander and the other anti-fascist protesters. Initially, twenty-six of the demonstrators were suspended, as was the CCNY student government. The administration charged that the protesters had disrupted a college function and abridged the free speech rights of the visiting Italian students. These CCNY officials never considered that banning the demonstration outside the hall and using physical force to stop Alexander's anti-fascist speech constituted grievous violations of the student body's free speech rights. The disciplinary hearings were as extensive as they were partisan. They were the most sweeping internal political investigation on any American campus during the Depression decade, and involved the questioning of more than 100 students.[69]

Unlike the jingo day controversy, the Great Hall riot occurred at a good time of the year for the protesters—right in the middle of the semester. Working closely together throughout the disciplinary hearings, the NSL and SLID mobilized thousands of CCNY undergraduates in protest against the suspensions. These activists drew a crowd of over 1500 students in their mock trial of President Robinson, which indicted him for supporting fascism and violating academic freedom. The students held an "Oust Robinson" week, designed to build popular support for the president's dismissal; they organized demonstrations at City Hall and outside Robinson's home, in which 18 students were arrested. When, despite these protests, twenty-one of the suspended students were expelled, the protesters called for a strike. Over 2000 students, many of them sporting "I am a Guttersnipe" buttons, then boycotted classes in an effective and angry two-hour strike, which ended with the students burning Robinson and Mussolini in effigy.[70]

Though the protests failed to win the students' reinstatement, they succeeded in mobilizing liberal public opinion against President Robinson. Several of New York City's major liberal daily newspapers sharply criticized Robinson's behavior. The *New York Post* called upon the college to fire Robinson and replace him with "an abler and more liberal man." Most importantly, the Great Hall incident and the protests that followed helped turn a significant portion of CCNY alumni against Robinson. This shift was made clear in the address that Felix Frankfurter, then a Harvard Law Professor and one of CCNY's most eminent alumni, made at the college's annual alumni dinner soon after "Oust Robinson Week." Frankfurter told the Alumni Association:

> A state of irritability among the students at the College is hardly the proof of a wise administration. The authorities of the College assume excessive responsibility for the actions of students outside of college rooms and buildings. There is much confusion of power and responsibility in regard to discipline at the College. The real rulers of the world are undiscoverable, but there are too many rulers discoverable at City College. It is unworthy of you men to be afraid of the questioning of youth. If we cannot stand up to their questions I think we should be slightly suspicious of the solidness of our foundations.[71]

The CCNY Alumni magazine expressed similar sentiments, and there began an energetic alumni campaign against Robinson, which within a few years would bring an end to his stormy tenure as the president of CCNY.[72]

Robinson's removal from the CCNY presidency represented a major victory for the campus Left; it suggested that sustained protest on behalf of free speech could succeed against even the most repressive college administrator. The students' triumph over Robinson was, however, a testament not only to their organizing ability but also to Robinson's self-destructive tactics. In retrospect, it seems almost unbelievable that Robinson failed to recognize that his heavy handedness was inciting rather than reducing student protest. But what must be borne in mind here is that Robinson's behavior was guided by ideological rather than tactical considerations. As a committed foe of radicalism, Robinson felt it his duty to take a tough, unambiguous stand against leftist influence on the student body, regardless of the consequences.[73]

Robinson's anti-radical stance was also shaped by his paternalistic sensibility. He saw himself as a stern parent would in the face of youthful insubordination. Consequently, Robinson behaved as if protesting students were naughty children in need of discipline rather than citizens whose rights he was violating. Even in his private correspondence, Robinson clung to this understanding of his job, explaining to his son during a student strike at CCNY that "I suppose we shall have to spank a few more [students] just to let them know that students cannot determine whether they will or will not attend college."[74] It is little wonder, then, that Robinson came as close as he could to adminstering such a spanking—with his umbrella on jingo day—and that he would lose his job rather than soften his stance toward the student movement at CCNY.

III

Despite the turmoil it provoked, Robinson's hard line position against the student Left elicited applause from the nation's more conservative college administrators. One of these administrators, Ernest C. Moore, the vice president and provost of the University of California at Los Angeles was so impressed by CCNY's anti-radical policies that in 1934 he wrote President Robinson, expressing admiration for

> the qualities of backbone of which you and the administrative part of the College of the City of New York are possessed. Only the most thoroughgoing determination could have enabled you to do the splendid bit of housecleaning that you have done. It has cheered and encouraged us all. We as well as you have been bedeviled for years by the National Student League . . . . We hope that the [anti-radical disciplinary] action . . . will clear up the difficulties.[75]

At the time that he wrote this letter, Moore was already emulating the CCNY administration by attempting to do his own anti-radical "housecleaning"—suspending five students who he accused of aiding the efforts of "the National Student League to destroy the university."[76]

Moore's "housecleaning" at UCLA provoked the largest campus free speech protests on the West Coast during the 1930s. The UCLA suspensions were in part the product of friction between Moore and undergraduates, who demanded a student-controlled open forum at which political issues could be discussed on campus. Moore vehemently opposed this demand, claiming that it violated the political neutrality of the university. In early October 1934, Moore ordered the student council and its president, John Burnside, to stop agitating for the open forum. But Burnside refused to obey the Provost's order, and continued working with both the student council other student activists on behalf of the open forum. It was when they were in the process of organizing a student referendum on the open forum idea that Moore suspended Burnside and four other student leaders, charging that they were working to convert UCLA into "a hotbed of Communism."[77]

Of the five students suspended only one, NSL leader Celeste Strack, was a communist. Two of the other students, Sid Zsagri and Tom Lambert, had been active in Upton Sinclair's campaign for governor of California—a campaign which, despite its socialistic tone, had been opposed by the Communist Party. The other two suspended students, Mendel Lieberman and John Burnside, had no radical ties whatsoever, and all of the students with the exception of Strack were prominent leaders of main-stream student organizations at UCLA. Moore's charge that the four non-communists, whose only real offense had been supporting an open forum as a vehicle for insuring free speech on campus, were promoting communism was wild and unsubstantiated, as was his claim that they and Strack sought "to destroy" UCLA.[78]

The suspensions and wild charges reflected the panic which had seized Moore as a consequence of the rising tide of radicalism on the West Coast in 1934. Badly shaken by outbreak of the San Francisco general strike, Moore fretted in his diary that "it may be the beginning of Revolution. It ought to be put down definitely for a general strike is civil war—a form of defiance which does not belong in a civilized society."[79] Moore expressed similar anxieties about Upton Sinclair's gubernatorial candidacy, which he termed "a menace to California." The Provost's hostility to Sinclair contributed to his opposition to an open forum at UCLA, for the students had expressed a desire to use such a forum to learn about Sinclair's ideas and the issues in the gubernatorial race. This suggests that Moore, a member of Los Angeles' Republican Party central committee, had partisan motivations for opposing the forum—quite ironic given his public assertions that he forbade the open forum in order to preserve the campus' political neutrality.[80]

The threat Moore perceived from the Left in 1934 put him into a combative frame of mind, which shaped his interaction with UCLA student activists. He believed that the communists were conspiring to subvert public higher educational institutions. Moore confided to UC President Robert Sproul in May 1934,

> I have, as you know, been brooding over what the communists are trying to do to us here in the United States . . . . The method by which a persistent effort is being made to undermine and destroy the public school system, by making it impossible for the tax-paying public to support it, is . . . diabolically effective . . . . The result is that our tax-paying people . . . will not any longer pay taxes to support institutions for the training of young people who are devoting themselves to the overthrow of our government.[81]

This communist plot against the schools was, Moore told Sproul, a sign that "the class war is on," and that responsible educators must begin to "make battle plans" on ways to help defeat the reds in this war.[82]

Provost Moore's anti-radical battle plan included working closely with the police against the student Left. In August 1934, Moore met with H.C. Griswold of the California State Police. Griswold confirmed Moore's fears of communist subversion in the schools. The police officer warned Moore that the

> Communists . . . have orders . . . to center their efforts in the U.S. on these two universities [UCLA and UC Berkeley] . . . . Chief [of the

State Police] Mr. Harish told him recently that they propose to do two things 1) To make a crusade for sex freedom. Convincing the young people that they should live together without marrying if they want to and quite freely. 2) To make heavy war against compulsory military training.[83]

Moore accepted unquestioningly this melodramatic warning (it was only accurate about Left opposition to ROTC, which was already a matter of public record), and immediately passed the information along to President Sproul, urging an administration counterattack. Over the course of the 1934–35 academic year, the Los Angeles police department repeatedly provided Provost Moore with intelligence information about UCLA student radicals. Moore secretly initiated this intelligence work through a confidential letter to the Los Angeles police chief in September 1934. In at least one case, Moore gave the police the name of a student activist that he wanted placed under police survelliance and arrested.[84]

Well before the suspensions controversy, Moore made public his hostility to the student Left. From the beginning of the 1934 academic year, the provost emphasized that radical activity would not be tolerated at UCLA. Moore became personally involved in breaking up the meetings of student activists. In a mid-October diary entry, Moore describes one such intervention. On that day he saw NSL leader Celeste Strack "haranguing a group of boys in front of the library . . . . I went out to them and said you cannot hold a communist meeting here Miss Strack." Moore then called Strack into his office and told the NSL leader—who recently had been pressured into leaving the University of Southern California because of her anti-war organizing—that he knew she had caused "plenty of trouble [at USC] last year. I want to tell you that you cannot do . . . [that] here." Several days later, when Strack came to Moore's office to protest his political restrictions, the provost told Strack that he "did not want to see her, that I already told her all that I had to tell her." Strack responded by calling Moore a "coward for not allowing the students to conduct an . . . [open] forum." Moore rebuked the NSL leader, "asked her to leave the office and told her she was a traitor."[85]

Moore was so anxious to drive radicalism off the UCLA campus that he worked to pass the word among the student body that specific members of their class were engaged in illicit radical activity. According to Roberta Monks, a member of the undergraduate Scholarship and Activities Board, when she approached Provost Moore in October 1934 with a request for a study hall, "Dr. Moore burst forth with the startling assertion that Mr. [Mendel] Lieberman (the chairman of the board) was a communist because—so far as I could make out—he wanted an open forum." Moore then described Lieberman as part of a NSL-communist plot "to burn down the buildings, pillage—all sorts of horrible things." But neither Monks nor her classmates were swayed by Moore's tirade. In a letter to Moore's superior, UC systemwide President Robert Gordon Sproul, Monk confided that on the day of this meeting with Moore she was "most glad to make my departure [from the provost's office]," and that when she later told the board of Moore's depiction of Lieberman as a " 'dangerous subversive' it was met with laughter."[86]

Though by October 1934 undergraduates at UCLA had grown accustomed to Moore's anti-radical rhetoric, the suspensions nonetheless came as a shock to much of the student body. By singling out for punishment some of the campus' most prominent mainstream student leaders, Moore demonstrated to students (in a way mere radical rhetoric could not) that their civil liberties were not secure at UCLA. The provost's accusations against the suspended students seemed extreme—nothing less than conspiracy to destroy the school. Many UCLA undergraduates sensed immediately that the source of the controversy was Moore's hysteria rather than student misconduct.[87] The strong doubts UCLA students had about Moore's disciplinary action became evident the day after the suspensions, when over 3000 students participated in a spontaneous protest rally on campus. This was the largest political demonstration ever seen at UCLA.[88]

Like its counterpart at CCNY, the UCLA administration proved unwilling to permit students to hold peaceful campus demonstrations in protest against college policy. Barely a moment after the start of the rally on behalf of the suspended students, two police officers moved in, and attempted to disrupt the demonstration by evicting the student who was addressing the crowd. This move angered the demonstrators, who began chanting "Let him talk." The police found it impossible to remove the speaker because as they began forcing him off, they were tackled by several students and thrown in the bushes. After this scuffle, and facing a huge angry crowd, the police allowed the rally to proceed. Speakers demanded a fair hearing for the suspended students, and one condemned Moore's red baiting, arguing that under the terms which the provost had used against the suspended students, "if you are for freedom of speech then you are a communist too."[89]

Not all UCLA students opposed the suspensions and Moore's campaign against the student Left. The provost enjoyed considerable support from conservatives in traditional campus organizations, including the fraternities, athletic teams, and ROTC. Some of these students allied themselves with the police, scuffling with demonstrators at the anti-suspensions rally. These scuffles helped to provide the administration with a pretext for ordering in the riot squad, composed of some 200 officers, which cut the rally short. And at a Greek house meeting shortly after the suspensions were announced, representatives of UCLA fraternities and sororities voted to support the administration "100 percent in any action taken in their drive to oust the radical element from the UCLA campus."[90] The more extreme faction of this opposition soon formed the UCLA Americans, a self-proclaimed vigilante group with xenophobic tendencies, which pledged to prevent protesters from distributing literature on campus or doing any other organizing in support of the suspended students.[91]

Moore welcomed and encouraged this anti-radical organizing. In the wake of the anti-suspensions rally, Moore told the press that the demonstration proved how evil the student Left was and "that students should 'clean house' of the National Student League." The provost made a radio address calling upon UCLA undergraduates to "support the University and purge the Communists from their ranks." Going beyond the UCLA campus itself, Moore called upon conservative students in college fraternities and sororities across the nation to "become active helpers of the U.S. in its day of difficulty with radical agitation."[92]

It was not Moore, however, but the suspended students who attracted support from other campuses. At Stanford University the student newspaper accused Moore of denying undergraduates their fundamental political rights and working to ensure that "freedom of speech and thought no longer exist on the southern campus." The *Stanford Daily* went on to argue that Moore's refusal to allow students to hold an open forum to discuss the crucial gubernatorial race in California threatened to make "plain nincompoops" out of UCLA students. "While all the rest of the state of California is aflame with the keenest election in its history, are students of U.C.L.A. to practice argumentative celibacy?" At UC Berkeley student activists did more than criticize the suspensions; they organized a sympathy strike on November 5, 1934. Led jointly by the NSL and SLID, this one hour student strike was designed to press UC President Robert Sproul, who resided in Berkeley, to override Moore and reinstate the five UCLA students.[93]

The Berkeley strike proved a stormy affair. Sproul took a tough anti-strike position, denying students permission to demonstrate on campus, and issuing a "word of warning" that students who boycotted classes would "suffer the usual penalty." Monroe Deutsch, the provost of UC Berkeley, sent the faculty a memorandum ordering them to take the roll, report the names of any students who stayed out of classes during the strike, and do whatever was necessary to prevent students from making pro-strike speeches or announcements in class. "The whole tone of this "memo, complained Professor George Adams of the Berkeley Philosophy department, was "that of a high military officer in a state of siege and expecting attack." Adams was particularly alarmed that the administration's hard line position seemed "by clear implication" to encourage opponents of the strike "if not to use, at least to sanction the use of physical force against students."[94]

The most extreme form of administration opposition to the free speech strike did, as Adams implied, involve violence; it came from Berkeley Dean Louis O'Brien's collusion with undergraduate vigilantes. According to student affidavits, O'Brien held a planning meeting with conservative undergraduates from the Greek houses and the football team to organize the physical disruption of the strike.[95] As the strike rally began just outside the gates of the Berkeley campus on November 5, it became obvious that opponents of the strike were prepared to use violence to thwart the protesters. While a crowd of over 1000 students looked on, "self-appointed 'vigilantes' " ripped protest signs down and drowned out rally speakers with cries of "Red," and "Down With Everything." Soon the counter-demonstrators were hurling not only epithets, but rotten eggs and tomatoes at the strike leaders, who tried in vain to complete their speeches.[96]

Strike organizers had not anticipated this disruption, nor did they recognize until the rally began that the attacks had been premeditated and carefully coordinated. "I'm sure now that in looking back and being somewhat more knowledgeable in the ways and methods of suppression of free speech that it was something that had been organized," recalled Richard Criley, one of the speakers at the strike rally. "There was a truck load of ripe tomatoes in the middle of this crowd of over 5000 people outside of Sather Gate [obviously a sign that students opposed to the strike had come prepared for disruptive action]." Though speakers pleaded with the counter-demonstrators to respect their constitutional right to free speech, the vegetable and egg barrage continued, preventing the completion of any speeches. According to Criley, not even the American flag could stop the counter-demonstrators:

> These tomatoes began flying thick and fast, and I remember ducking them. I'd say "fellow students" and then I'd duck and a tomato would whiz over my head. And it was all very funny until one of our student strike committee members who happened to be a very good looking young women got up to speak and she didn't duck. And pretty soon these tomatoes that had been funny when watching the guys being hit or ducking became sort of cruel; they were lashing and hitting hard. Pretty soon she was just dripping with tomato juice, and she started to cry, but she wouldn't get down off the platform. At this point a Berkeley merchant, who had a store down the street, came running back with an American flag, and said "Look, you people stand for the American flag. Put it up next to the speaker." We did. And soon the flag was pelted with tomatoes and was running with tomato juice, which turned many of the patriotic people in the crowd towards us, and we ended up with somewhat of a consensus of sympathy of the majority of the crowd outside Sather Gate.[97]

The strike at Berkeley effectively placed the UCLA controversy on Sproul's doorstep. The Berkeley walkout demonstrated that Moore's offensive was not only causing turmoil at UCLA, but also spreading controversy and political embarrassment for the University beyond Los Angeles. The Bay Area press gave prominent coverage to the disruption of the Berkeley strike rally. Even the UC administration now recognized that this physical assault upon free speech demonstrators had hurt the University's image. Embarrassed by the wild melee it had inspired, the Sproul administration expressed "regret . . . that students of the University did not permit [the strike speakers] . . . to state their views freely." The tumult in Berkeley suggested that unless the UCLA controversy was resolved, protest and criticism of the UC administration would continue to grow.[98]

Two days after the Berkeley strike, protests over the UCLA suspensions spread to a third California campus: San Mateo Jr. College. At the invitation of San Mateo students, several leaders of the Berkeley strike addressed them and explained the UCLA situation, rallying support for the suspended students. Over four hundred students attended the demonstration, but as at Berkeley, an anti-radical group (of college athletes) threw eggs and tomatoes at the speakers, making it impossible for the free speech rally to be completed. The disruption of the rally made headlines and added to the furor over the suspensions.[99]

Besides the student protests, President Sproul came under pressure from numerous sources to intercede in the UCLA case. Four fathers of the suspended students had issued a joint statement condemning Provost Moore for "blasting their [sons'] reputations when they are on the threshold of life before giving them a hearing in which they could have disproved such charges." The parents hinted at a potential libel suit against the University, and urged President Sproul to overrule Moore and grant the students unconditional reinstatement.[100] Moore's political position was further weakened by a petition signed by over one hundred UCLA faculty members. The petition disputed the provost's claim that UCLA was a hotbed of communism and implied that Moore's inflammatory rhetoric and decision to suspend the students had damaged the University's reputation. Sensing that he was in trouble, Moore appealed to President Sproul to intervene and make a final decision in the case.[101] Sproul agreed to review the case.

Moore was not lacking, however, in influential supporters. Several of them sat on the University's highest policy making body, the UC Board of Regents. Even during ordinary times, the regents was a conservative body, composed primarily of business leaders. But in the fall of 1934 the board was in a particularly strong anti-radical mood because, like Moore, a number of its members had been badly frightened by the San Francisco General Strike and Upton Sinclair's campaign. According to Chester Rowell, one of the more liberal regents, several of his fellow board members had been "carried away by the prevailing [anti-radical] hysteria" by the time of the UCLA suspensions. In a confidential letter to Sproul, Rowell expressed his alarm at the political intolerance he had witnessed at the November Regents meeting during the discussion of the UCLA cases:

> In all my experience with the Regents, which, first and second hand, now covers over forty years, I never before saw or heard of a meeting which came so near to Upton Sinclair's otherwise unjust strictures in his "Goose Step" [where Sinclair depicted the Regents as an intolerant group of plutocrats warring with academic freedom]. If that is the way we are going to impose the personal opinions of the old and the rich on the education of the young and aspiring, by transforming the University into a propaganda bureau for economic orthodoxy, we shall only be playing into the hands of the most dangerous sect of radicals.[102]

Rowell's observation suggest that had Sproul chosen to back Moore, UC's president would have had considerable support from the regents. And, at first glance, it might seem as if Sproul would approve the UCLA suspensions, because he was a foe of radicalism, who had spied on Berkeley's student radicals, barred leftist rallies from campus, and publicly spoke of the need for universities to help prevent the spread of radicalism. But Sproul had never been one to invite unnecessary political controversy and therefore, unlike Moore, refused to engage in public redbaiting of his own university. Sproul understood that wild charges of subversion undermined the University's reputation. In the past he had responded to those who made such charges by asking them to either provide evidence or desist from their name calling. So though Sproul shared with Moore a desire to purge UC's Left "propagandists," he also believed that the battle against campus radicalism called for discretion, rather than the screaming headlines that Moore's abrupt actions and melodramatic rhetoric had generated.[103]

As Sproul investigated the UCLA suspensions, he discovered that Moore had not done his political homework. Sproul found that Moore had initiated the suspensions without evidence against those he disciplined. After reviewing the case, Sproul came to see that the major charges against the students were groundless. Sproul reinstated four of the five suspended students on November 14 and announced that

> having spent a week in careful investigation, having interviewed or read statements from everyone who claimed to have the facts, I cannot find any evidence, convincing to me, that the suspended students either directly or indirectly gave their approval to the work of the National Student League . . . traded votes for radical support, or . . . used their student offices "to assist the National Student League to destroy the University," or to destroy the University by handing it over to an organized group of communist students.[104]

Privately Sproul complained that the UCLA cases have "done serious injury to the University, whatever the outcome," and he confided to a friend that Moore had mishandled the entire affair. "How I wish," wrote Sproul, "I had never heard of these cases, or had been in on them from the beginning instead of being dragged in after they had been bungled."[105]

Despite Sproul's private misgivings about Moore's behavior and his dismissal of the major charges against the students, the president did all that he could under the circumstances to support his provost. While announcing the reinstatements, Sproul also stated that the initial decision to suspend the students had been proper because they had been guilty of insubordination: these undergraduates had wrongly defied Moore's orders by continuing to organize on behalf of an open forum at UCLA. Sproul concluded, however, that reinstatement of four of the suspended students was now appropriate because their temporary suspension had been punishment enough for their insubordination.[106] Like Moore, Sproul thought students too immature to be granted the political rights of adults. That is why Sproul, in his statement to the press following the reinstatements, joined Moore in condemning the idea of a student controlled open forum on campus; in addition, Sproul, like his colleagues at CCNY, maintained that it was intolerable for students ever to defy the orders of a University administrator. According to Sproul, "Whatever the merits of the students' position" in calling for an open forum, since they did so against the provost's orders " this is insubordination."[107] To Sproul, then, students lacked the freedom even to call for free speech, particularly if such advocacy contradicted the instructions of University authorities.

President Sproul stressed that he was not rebuking his provost and that he had interceded in the case only at Moore's request. There was, of course, an element of face-saving in Sproul's public statements regarding Moore. As at Columbia in the Reed Harris case, the UC administration seemed unable to acknowledge error even while revoking its previous disciplinary action. And the president wanted to do all that he could to avoid embarrassing a fellow administrator. But Sproul's support of Moore included more than face-saving; his support was also the product of shared ideology and values. Sproul shared Moore's belief that the University should free itself of radicalism and help American society fight communism, but Sproul was simply more perspicacious when it came to chosing methods to fight radicalism. This ideological link left Sproul unwilling to utter publicly a single word criticizing his redbaiting provost's goal of purging campus communists.

That Sproul shared with Moore a disrespect for student free speech rights and an intolerance of student radicalism was most evident in his handling of Celeste Strack's suspension. Strack was the only one of the five suspended students at UCLA who was a self-proclaimed radical and NSL organizer. Had Sproul not been a committed anti-radical, he would have treated Strack precisely as he treated the four non-communists, reinstating them together when he found that the charges against them were groundless. And, in fact, Sproul never had any evidence that Strack, despite her radicalism, was any less innocent of Moore's charges of seeking to destroy the university than were the suspended non-communists. Nonetheless, solely on the basis of her radical affiliations, Sproul divided Strack's case from the four others and refused to reinstate her with them.[108]

The influence of Sproul's anti-radical bias in the Strack case appears explicitly in a private letter he wrote in the midst of the controversy. Here Sproul contended that because Celeste Strack was a radical organizer her

> case is different [from the other four]. Miss Strack is not the *innocent* victim of a mistaken action, but she is a clever person against whom we have a very poor case. I have delayed my decision as to her in the hope that I might find some evidence to support the charge on which she was suspended," persistent and flagrant violation of University regulations in-

cluding the holding of Communist meetings on the campus." I have not found it as yet and Dean Laughlin, whom I have consulted has not been able to find it for me.[109]

Thus although Sproul, after a careful search, still lacked evidence of Strack's guilt, he refused to assume her innocent until proven guilty. Instead, he insisted that because she was radical it was unlikely that she could possibly be innocent. There was obviously a procedural double standard at work here, which held that a week of investigation without incriminating evidence was sufficient to acquit the four non-communists but insufficient to acquit Strack.

It took almost another full month after the reinstatements of the first four students for Sproul to agree to reinstate Strack. Had Strack not threatened to sue the University, moreover, it is likely that she would not have been reinstated at all. Sproul's decision to reinstate Strack came only after an independent counsel hired by the Regents examined all the evidence in the case and informed him that Strack's threatened legal suit could prove troublesome because "there does not exist sufficient proof to sustain the charges and . . . the administration is in no position to defend its action for want of any evidence of any tangible acts which could stand scrutiny in a court of law."[110] Sproul's private correspondence confirms that it was not concern for free speech, but fear of a potentially embarrassing lawsuit which brought about Strack's reinstatement.[111]

The five suspended students were fortunate in that their accuser, Provost Moore had been politically sloppy—making charges he could not support. The students also owed their reinstatement to their own good political sense. None of them had violated University regulations. Strack, herself, though a radical activist, had been careful to comply with the rules by holding her partisan political meetings off campus.

Even the grounds upon which the five were reinstated attest to the UC administration's disrespect for political freedom on campus. Had any of the UCLA students held NSL meetings on campus, used their offices to promote the NSL, formed an alliance with the NSL during the Student Council elections, or violated any UCLA regulations which virtually banned political organizing on campus, their suspensions would undoubtedly have been converted into permanent expulsions. Indeed, the very questions President Sproul asked the suspended students when he began his investigation of the case, suggest that he saw radical activism as a punishable offense on campus. The UC President sounded as if he were conducting a political interrogation and loyalty test, asking four of the suspended students:

> Have your actions on the Council been influenced in any way by N.S.L.? By Miss Strack? . . . Did you announce that you had a mandate to oppose the American Legion, the D.A.R., etc.? From where did it come? . . . Did you ignore Dr. Moore's warning that in backing [a] student con-

trolled open forum you were playing into the hands of the Communists
. . . ? Did you offer a written disavowal of communist or radical connections? . . . Did you talk with N.S.L. members after Council meetings and
give them material for anonymous attacks on the Council and Univ. officials?[112]

When the questioning had ended and Sproul opted for reinstatement, Moore was undoubtedly disappointed. But the reinstatements had
not chastened the UCLA provost. Moore continued his crusade against
campus radicalism—colluding with the police, spying on radicals, and
publicly denouncing the communist threat to education. Summarizing the
provost's activities following the end of the suspensions controversy, a
YMCA official at UCLA informed Sproul that

> we had hoped things would quiet down after the reinstatement of the
> four boys but Dr. Moore seems determined to keep things stirred up.
> One of his spies . . . abetted in the theft of the now famous L.I.D. letter
> [from national LID organizer Monroe Sweetland to Sidney Zsagri, one of
> the reinstated students at UCLA] . . . . Dr. Moore has had photostatic
> copies made of it. His conferences with Chief of Police Davis . . . are
> supposed to relate to an effort to have Mr. Zsagri arrested on a charge
> of criminal syndicalism. . . . The faculty feel more nervous than ever
> because of the general espionage that seems to prevail. An employe[e] of
> the telegraph company let out the fact that copies of telegrams having a
> bearing on University affairs are sent to Dr. Moore.[113]

By mid-November 1934, Moore had even begun moving his anti-radical
campaign to new fronts. The provost lobbied Frank Merriam, California's
newly elected Governor, to take a strong stand against campus radicalism.
Moore implored the Governor

> to prepare and sponsor a bill to make it a punishable offence (say with
> six months' imprisonment or a fine of $500, or both) for any outside
> organization, or the members of such organization outside the schools, to
> interfere with the work of any public school or university in the state of
> California. We must smash this thing or the dry rot it spreads will kill
> us.[114]

But Moore's attempt to legislate an end to radical influence on campus
proved just as ineffective as had his use of spies and suspensions.
    Moore's anti-radical offensive backfired politically at UCLA in a man-
ner almost identical to Robinson's offensive at CCNY. In both cases, administration acts of suppression built campus sympathy and support for
the student activists. The UCLA Left counted itself fortunate because
Moore's free speech violations provided it with an issue around which to
establish a broadly based protest movement on campus. The provost's arbitrary disciplinary action raised student concern about campus political

rights to a level that the NSL had never been able to reach in its prior campaign for an open forum. As Celeste Strack recalled, the suspensions

> radicalized the campus as nothing would have. Moore couldn't have done anything more calculated if he'd planned to radicalize that campus . . . . People to this day tell me how it opened their eyes . . . . Thousands of people that may never have noticed about the business of the open forum, or cared about it, cared very much when this thing [the suspensions] happened because it was an assault on the most elementary forms of student democracy. And people get angry in this country over things like that, and the students got upset over it.[115]

In the wake of this free speech controversy, the UCLA Left was able to organize political meetings and anti-war rallies far larger than any it had held prior to the suspensions.

Moore unwittingly contributed not only to the growth of the UCLA Left locally, but also to the rising national prominence of student activists from both UCLA and other West Coast campuses. The successful movement for reinstatement—arguably the most effective student free speech battle yet waged in Depression America—put UCLA and Berkeley on the political map, demonstrating to the eastern centered leadership of the NSL and SLID that a strong student movement was emerging on the West Coast. In the wake of this battle, Celeste Strack was elevated to a national leadership position in the NSL, and West Coast campuses received increasing attention from student movement organizers and publications.[116]

IV

While campus administrators played the most active role in the effort to suppress student radicalism from 1933 to 1935, some anti-radical pressure also came from outside the academic world. The flashiest of these off campus campaigns for the suppression of academic radicalism was waged by the Hearst press. Not confined by the ethics of professional journalism, this rightwing newspaper chain produced a series of sensationalized accounts of communist infiltration of the professoriate. Through distortions and outright fabrications, the Hearst press managed to make liberal professors sound like Bolsheviks and syndicated these wild stories from coast to coast. In one typical Hearst story, a pair of reporters from the *Syracuse Journal* posed as communist students and then visited a liberal Syracuse professor. After trying to coax the professor into making radical statements, the reporters distorted his words and depicted him as a dangerous syndicalist. Hearst reporters pulled this same stunt on professors at Columbia, New York University, and the University of Chicago.[117]

Hearst newspapers also attacked the student movement. Under such screaming headlines as "Communist Plot to Capture American Youth Revealed: Drive Pushed in Colleges," the Hearst press portrayed the antiwar movement as the product of a Moscow-based conspiracy. Among most students, however, these reports had little influence because of the Hearst newspapers' lack of credibility on campus. In fact, such reports and Hearst himself served as a rallying point for the student movement, which used them as a pretext for launching a highly popular campus boycott of Hearst newspapers and movie newsreels. Next to the ROTC, war and Depression, Hearst's redbaiting was the subject of more editorial criticism than any other topic in the college press during the mid-1930s.[118]

Much like the Hearst Press, anti-radical legislators on the warpath against the campus Left made a good deal of noise, but proved remarkably inept at curbing student radicalism. They simply did not understand student activism well enough to formulate realistic repressive actions. Victims of their own anti-intellectualism, these conservatives tended to assume that the evil geniuses behind the student movement were communist professors who propagandized their students. Working from this false assumption, the anti-radicals focused most of their legislative investigations and anti-radical bills against these allegedly subversive professors. They managed to impose new loyalty oaths on teachers in 14 states between 1931 and 1935. But in reality, these oaths—though a serious infringement upon academic freedom, and one which the student movement denounced vehemently—were aimed at people who played only a minor role in the student movement. There were few radical professors on American campuses during the first half of the Depression decade and fewer still who would align themselves with the student Left. Students, not professors, were the major source of radical activism on the American college campuses of the 1930s. This is why even as faculty oath requirements spread, the student movement could continue to grow at an unprecedented rate. Had the campus Left been dependent upon faculty, its activism would have been confined to only the few colleges and universities where radical professors taught, and there would never have been a mass student movement in the 1930s.[119]

For the faculty itself, moreover, during the first half of the Depression decade the greatest threat to political freedom came from intolerant college administrators rather than legislators. These administrators believed it improper and unprofessional for faculty to engage in political activism on campus. They therefore needed no outside pressure to purge radical faculty, but did so on their own initiative. Such administration intolerance resulted in the dismissal of most of those rare faculty members (usually young instructors rather than professors) who cooperated closely with the student movement. In short, the legislative offensive against faculty radicals was misdirected because academia had already done its own purging—leaving potential faculty activists convinced that if they wanted to keep their jobs and avoid falling victim to administration intolerance, they must not become openly involved in radical politics on campus.[120]

The biggest legislative threat to the student movement in the first half of the Depression decade emerged in New York, where conservative state legislators introduced a bill which would have imposed a loyalty oath upon college students. This oath legislation, the Nunan Bill, was an important test of strength for the student movement. The student activist community worked vigorously against the bill, fearing that this legislation would inhibit campus protest in the state where the movement had its strongest following. An NSL and SLID sponsored a delegation of over 500 collegians, led by women students from Vassar College, converged on Albany, lobbying the legislature against the bill. The editors of student newspapers throughout the state launched a coordinated editorial drive denouncing the proposed loyalty oath. Demonstrations demanding the defeat of the Nunan Bill were held in New York City. In the face of this energetic campaign, the Nunan Bill went down to defeat in March 1935, giving the student movement one of its most significant civil liberties victories.[121]

Attempts by anti-radicals to use legislative investigations as a weapon against the campus Left also ended in failure during the mid-1930s. In this period the two most ambitious legislative investigations of this type occurred in Illinois and Wisconsin. After charges of subversion were leveled against the faculty at the University of Chicago and the University of Wisconsin, conservative legislators in these states launched official investigations of professorial radicalism. But the investigations failed to uncover the alleged communist infiltration; they ended without purging a single faculty radical. Long after these investigations were over, the Universities of Chicago and Wisconsin remained among the most active campuses in the student anti-war movement.[122]

Though redbaiting news stories, loyalty oath campaigns, and legislative investigations failed to cause any significant damage to the student movement, they probably provided some assistance to the movement's enemies on campus. It is highly likely that this anti-radical clamor emboldened administrators such as Provost Moore of UCLA, mistakenly assuring them of overwhelming public support for their attempts to repress student radicalism. The presence of legislative anti-radicalism could also provide a convenient justification for administration assaults on the student Left, as college officials reasoned that the autonomy of the University could best be preserved if they preempted any anti-radical legislative action by taking a strong stand against campus radicalism.[123]

This anti-radical impact, however, was diluted substantially by countervailing pressure from advocates of civil liberty both on and off campus. College presidents who launched anti-radical crusades were likely to come under heavy criticism from the ACLU, the AAUP, the Left-liberal press, progressive alumni and faculty, and prominent liberals in Washington—including Eleanor Roosevelt, an influential friend of the student movement and critic of red probes and loyalty oaths.[124] Moreover, the larger political mood in the country was decidedly progressive, a consequence of the steamrolling reformism of the early New Deal years. The University, during the mid-1930s was not besieged by a public fearful of change and radicalism; it stood within a nation which because of the Depression was moving leftward itself and becoming more tolerant of radicalism. There was, therefore, nothing resembling a consensus—like that of the McCarthy era—supporting a purge of campus dissidents. This was a political environment which left anti-radicals without the support they needed for an effective national assault on faculty or student radicalism.[125]

The level of community political tolerance was such that student activists from 1933–1935 often found their free speech rights were safer not on, but off campus. This had been true, for instance, in the free speech fights at CCNY and UCLA. In both cases, student activists, after having their rallies banned from campus, avoided being silenced by simply holding their rallies just beyond the college gates. The photographs of student demonstrations during the first half of the Depression decade attest that this was not unusual. Students facing repressive administrators often rallied adjacent to campus, *on town or city property*. There were of course, exceptions to this rule, in more provincial regions of the South and Midwest, but in most of America, students were able to overcome political intolerance on campus by moving off.[126] For them, free soil and political liberty lay just outside the campus gates, beyond the reach of college officials. In other words, though students sometimes lost their First Amendment rights at the campus entrance, they picked them up again on the way out, and used these rights to build a mass movement.

The phenomenon of city property serving as a sanctuary for student protest indicated that off campus anti-radicals had been even less effective than campus officials in hurting the student movement from 1933–35. The major off campus anti-radical forces, such as the Hearst press and the American Legion, were unable to cause the expulsion or suspension of a single student radical. This was a sorry record indeed when compared with CCNY President Robinson's expulsion of 43 student radicals in 1933–1934, President Rightmire's suspension of 17 Ohio State drill resisters in 1934, President Butler's expulsion of six student anti-war activists in Columbia's medical school in 1935, or President Ruthven's expulsion of four anti-war leaders at the University of Michigan in this same period.[127] Nor could Hearst match the censorship, the banning of meetings and speakers which were routinely initiated against the anti-war movement by administrators throughout the nation from 1933–1935.

Though college administrators may have made Hearst look like an amateur in the art of political repression, ultimately even they were not able to turn back the rising tide of student activism in the early New Deal years. Despite the repressive incidents on dozens of campuses from 1933–1935, the anti-war movement grew at an increasingly rapid pace. The repression could be frightening or annoying, but it was just as often transformed—as at CCNY and UCLA—into an asset for the anti-war movement, enabling the student Left's skillful organizers to make repression an issue and thus gather support from their many classmates who believed in free speech. Moreover, the level of repression was significant, but not massive enough to do any lasting damage, which would have required thousands of expulsions in a coordinated national campaign. This kind of national campaign would have been beyond the pale of college administrators, whose interest in student politics did not usually extend beyond their own campuses and their *in loco parentis* responsibilities.

By 1936 the popularity of the student movement had risen to the point where even many college administrators realized that the old policies of repression and confrontation were futile and counterproductive. With about half of the undergraduate population mobilized and the anti-war movement beginning to draw support and praise from the Roosevelt administration, increasing numbers of college presidents switched to tactics of conciliation and cooptation. Where formerly strike rallies had been banned, now they were more likely to be permitted by administrators who tried to dilute their radicalism—renaming them "peace assemblies" and imposing speakers lists which included more moderates and conservatives. This attempt by administrators to push anti-war discussion rightward at times seemed manipulative, and on some campuses evoked resentment from student activists. Nonetheless, it represented far more administration-student dialogue than had occurred during the seasons of censorship and repression in the early 1930s. Through its own persistence and political strength, then, the student movement, by 1936, had taken the University a small step closer toward free speech.[128]

Chapter 6

The Popular Front on Campus

Gentlemen,

Until this week I have been an advocate of neutrality, and secretary of your organization. The startling rapidity of developments in Europe in the past few days has forced me to abandon the unrealistic policy of Isolation in favor of a more positive and practical peace program, namely . . . collective security as endorsed by the . . . [American] Student Union . . . . Nazi storm troopers lash Socialist workers in the factories—thousands of Jews flee . . . .—a wave of "suicides" hits the ranks of intellectuals in Vienna—Hitler sends 30,000 troops to Spain . . . .—Does isolation offer any solution to the Fascist aggression which is overwhelming Europe? . . . After thinking over all these factors, I find it necessary to resign from the Harvard Neutrality Council. I leave behind the shallow, impractical, dangerous policy of Isolation.

> Arthur Kinoy, Harvard '41, "An Open Letter to the Harvard Neutrality Council," *Harvard Progressive*, March 19, 1938.

The international threat posed by fascism became the central concern of the student movement during the second half of the Depression decade. For this generation of college students not a year passed without some ominous reminder of the rising strength, belligerence, and brutality of European fascism. There was Italy's invasion of Ethiopia in 1935, Hitler's and Mussolini's military support of the Spanish fascist revolt in 1936 and 1937, Germany's anti-Jewish pogrom and conquest of Austria in 1938, and the Nazi invasion of Czechoslovakia and Poland in 1939. These events, along with Japan's escalating war on China, prodded many student activists to rethink the isolationist assumptions their anti-war movement had popularized on campus in the early 1930s. The increasing aggression of the fascist powers led these activists to worry that the very neutrality that their movement had urged upon the United States to promote peace, instead, bred war by preventing America from orchestrating an international effort to thwart fascist expansionism. This mindset facilitated the rise of a major challenge to isolationism within the student movement, which by 1938 pushed the movement's largest organizations to abandon their isolationist policies and embrace collective security.

The first influential group within the student movement's leadership which sought to shift the movement away from isolationism was the communists. These radicals had the earliest and clearest vision of the student movement's need for a more explicitly anti-fascist foreign policy. Their thinking on this matter had been strongly influenced by deliberations of the Seventh World Congress of the Communist International (CI) in August 1935. The CI became concerned about the triumph of Nazism in Germany, its spreading influence in Europe, and the potential threat these developments posed to the U.S.S.R.'s security. The Seventh World Congress therefore urged the formation of broad national coalitions and international collective security arrangements on behalf of a Popular Front against fascism.[1] For communists in the American student movement, this implied the need to turn the movement's foreign policy away from American neutrality and toward the endorsement of collective efforts among the United States, the Soviet Union, and other anti-fascist states to prevent military aggression by Germany, Italy, and Japan.

In favoring this Popular Front position, communist students understood that they were sailing against the wind in the isolationist campus world of 1935. As key architects of the student peace movement, they knew from first hand experience the appeal of neutrality and anti-interventionism to college youth, who feared that their generation would be decimated by war just as the class of 1917 had been. It would not be easy to shake students out of their deeply isolationist mood. That mood had been created by disillusionment with the First World War, a pervasive feeling among students that United States intervention in 1917 had been a tragic blunder, and that any repetition of such interventionism would prove disastrous. The first two anti-war strikes and the Oxford Pledge movement had reinforced this collegiate isolationism, as had the Nye Committee revelations—concerning big business' complicity in pushing America into the First World War—and the victorious isolationist campaign for neutrality legislation on Capitol Hill.

Isolationism would also prove difficult to dislodge on campus because of its dedicated promoters within the student movement's leadership, particularly the socialists, Trotskyists and pacifists. For socialists and Trotskyists, United States neutrality was an ideological imperative, since these radicals believed that any form of interventionism by the government of capitalist America would be inherently imperialistic. They regarded anti-interventionism as a means of curbing United States imperialism. The student movement's absolute pacifists also clung to isolationism, but did so on moral rather than ideological grounds. Opposing all wars as inherently evil, these pacifists sought to avoid any departures from strict neutrality, which, in their eyes, threatened to move America into a war, just as they had in 1917.[2]

The strength of isolationist sentiment on campus prevented communist activists from orchestrating a quick rejection of anti-interventionism by the student movement; it compelled these young radicals to proceed cautiously on the road to collective security. Although communist students in 1935 aired their Popular Front positions, they did not seek to impose all of these upon the student movement overnight—recognizing that such an attempt would have been futile. With the mood on campus so strongly favorable to neutrality, the communists had to make compromises with isolationism, even though such compromises were inconsistent with the Comintern's Popular Front line.

The first such compromise occurred in November 1935, when students responded to Mussolini's invasion of Ethiopia. The communist-led NSL advocated League of Nations sanctions and a United States embargo against fascist Italy, to punish this aggression and help Ethiopia in its defensive war. Socialist students also condemned the invasion, but opposed League of Nations sanctions because they viewed the League as an imperialist tool. The socialists, along with the pacifists, feared that League sanctions and an American embargo against Italy could set a dangerous precedent that might ultimately draw the United States into an overseas war; they therefore urged official United States neutrality and an American embargo of *both* belligerents in the conflict. The socialists and pacifists then organized a national anti-Mussolini protest on campus, based on their rather contorted position of condemning fascist aggression while opposing sanctions designed to stop that aggression.

Though disagreeing with their position on League sanctions and American neutrality, the NSL joined with the socialists and pacifists in this demonstration against the Italian invasion. The NSL chose to be flexible here because its leaders realized that even if they could not agree on the specifics of United States policy regarding Italy, communists, socialists, and pacifists would be serving an important symbolic function in this demonstration by uniting students against Mussolini's aggression. In the isolationist campus world of 1935 such anti-fascist unity seemed a considerable achievement. From the NSL's perspective this demonstration represented the first step in an evolving process: students would now be mobilized against fascist aggression, and later be led to see the logic of collective security measures needed to curb that aggression. Communist willingness to compromise in this anti-Mussolini demonstration was undoubtedly strengthened by the fact that the neutrality policy for the United States advocated by the socialists and pacifists—embargoing both belligerents—would hurt Italy rather than Ethiopia, since only Mussolini's forces had the ability to import war-related goods from the United States.[3]

These responses to the invasion of Ethiopia suggested that the rise of fascist aggression was raising thorny new problems for the student movement. The question of whether to support League sanctions and United States embargoes against fascist aggressors was potentially divisive. Given the stark differences between the communist and socialist-pacifist positions on such questions, however, what was surprising in 1935 was how little discord these differences generated within the student movement. This was in part because the communist-led NSL, as had been clear in the Ethiopia demonstration, initially soft-pedalled the interventionist implications of Popular Frontism and searched for common ground with non-communists in the anti-war movement. Moreover, despite the tactical problems raised by the fascist threat, that threat actually helped to unify the American student movement in 1935 because the entire movement shared a revulsion for fascism. Indeed, the one part of the Popular Front that did have an immediate and wide appeal within the student movement was its stress on the need to unite activists from all sides of the political spectrum in opposing fascism. This general anti-fascist ethos promoted a solidarity among student activists that initially outweighed any disagreement over which specific foreign policies were best suited to thwarting war and fascism.[4]

The attraction of anti-fascist solidarity was particularly strong within the student Left. It was strong not merely because the communists, in line with their Popular Front goals, were bent on promoting unity, but also because non-communists too saw that disunity on the Left was dangerous at a time when fascism was on the rise. This fear of disunity was, as former SLID leader Joseph Lash pointed out, fostered by events in Germany:

> If there was one lesson out of Germany that we read, it was that the failure of the Socialists and Communists to work together against Hitler . . . had opened the way for Hitlerism in the crucial years. So that was an enormous pressure for us to think in terms of the unity of the American student movement.[5]

This type of thinking in 1935 would facilitate the greatest step toward unity ever taken by the student Left in Depression America: the amalgamation of the communist-led NSL and the socialist-led SLID into a single unified organization, the American Student Union.

The idea of amalgamation was not new. The NSL had proposed a merger with the SLID in December 1933 and again the following year.[6] During the early 1930s, the NSL's leadership had been much less prone than adult communist-led organizations to the extreme sectarianism of Third Period Communism. Owing to their youth, most NSLers did not have the bitter memories of communist-socialist feuding which so poisoned relations between their adult counterparts. A degree of comradery was also fostered by student status. As campus organizers NSLers and SLIDers shared common enemies, including repressive campus administrators and undergraduate apathy. These factors and the NSLers' realization that on most of the critical campus issues their positions paralleled those of the SLID, prodded the NSL to make overtures to the SLID concerning amalgamation. This occurred long before the Popular Front arose and brought such coalition politics to the adult CP.[7]

This does not mean, however, that the NSL and SLID loved each other in the early 1930s. The two organizations squabbled more than occasionally. The NSL's communist leaders tended to regard themselves as more genuinely revolutionary than the SLID, since they prided themselves on being affiliated with the one nation in which a proletarian revolution had occurred. The SLID's socialist leaders regarded themselves as more genuinely democratic than the NSL, because of their links to the electorally-minded Socialist Party; they were uncomfortable with the NSL's uncritical view of Stalin's dictatorship. Their different party affiliations and competition for members bred some friction, and left the SLID initially suspicious of the NSL's motives for proposing amalgamation. So in 1933 and 1934 the SLID leadership had turned down those proposals. But the SLID did agree to cooperate with the NSL wherever possible, and the two organizations in 1934–35 worked together on a series of increasingly large and successful campaigns on issues ranging from peace to student aid. The unprecedented size of the April 1935 anti-war strike made it evident that the closer their cooperation, the more effective the NSL and SLID could be in building the student movement. Such success eroded the mistrust between the two organizations, and this, along with the rising demand for anti-fascist unity, would help break the SLID leadership's resistance to amalgamation.[8]

Within the SLID, pressure for amalgamation came from the bottom up. SLID campus chapters functioned in a political environment more conducive to amalgamation than did the organization's national office in New York. SLID national officers had been influenced by the SLID's parent organization, the adult LID. These older leaders were wary of a merger with the communist-led NSL because the vicious attacks on them by the Communist Party during the 1920s and early 1930s had left them strongly anti-communist. But in SLID chapters outside New York's hothouse political atmosphere, few SLID activists had experienced such bitter feuding; most saw the compelling logic of merging with the NSL, since they were already cooperating with the League on most of their major political actions. The movement for amalgamation was particularly strong in the SLID's West Coast chapters, which, under the leadership of Berkeley SLID President Richard Criley, worked to push the organization's recalcitrant national leaders towards a merger with the NSL.[9]

Criley and his SLID comrades on the West Coast had become especially receptive to both amalgamation and anti-fascist unity because of the upsurge of political repression in their region. The Right had responded hysterically in 1934 to the upsurge of labor militancy on the West Coast's waterfront, the general strike in San Francisco, and Upton Sinclair's EPIC campaign. Redbaiting by the press and attacks on civil liberties by police and vigilantes were on the rise. Amidst such hysteria, western student activists had no way of knowing that this local red scare would prove short-lived; they feared that it might spread, and herald the advent of a home-grown fascist movement in the United States, much as Sinclair Lewis had predicted in *It Can't Happen Here* (1935). With his vision colored by anxieties concerning the rising strength of fascism in Europe, Criley viewed the arrests and harassment of West Coast radical organizers after the San Francisco general strike as a sign that California was "sliding into fascism very fast." Criley recalled that in the face of this "fascist" threat "it seemed to us—and I think this was true of both the National Student League members and the SLID members—that it was just insanity not to join the strength of the radical students who were the spearhead of the struggle for rights on campus."[10] Consequently, Criley worked first at Berkeley and then across the West Coast to promote a merger of the NSL and SLID.

By June 1935 the SLID's national leadership found it impossible to ignore this grass roots movement for amalgamation. That month the SLID's national executive committee met for three days to consider the question of amalgamation. Here the committee heard field reports attesting to the support of SLID chapters for a merger with the NSL. The committee learned that this support was so strong out West that the California chapters—under Criley's leadership—were planning a statewide amalgamation convention for the fall. There was clearly concern that unless the SLID national office moved toward amalgamation, a split with the West Coast chapters might occur. The committee also heard survey results of the new recruits at the SLID's summer school for student organizers, which revealed 100 percent favoring "future amalgamation."[11] All of this impressed Executive Secretary Joseph Lash, who recalled that though he and some of the other national officers had initially been "determined not to unite with the Communists, we found the pressure from our chapters, pressure within ourselves [for anti-fascist unity] was such that we felt we ought to give it a whirl."[12] The SLID national executive board agreed to establish a joint committee with its counterpart in the NSL to negotiate the terms for a merger. The negotiations went well, and in October 1935 the executive boards of both organizations recommended that their membership approve amalgamation into a new organization, the American Student Union (ASU), whose founding convention was scheduled for the coming Christmas break.[13]

Proponents of amalgamation in the NSL and SLID envisioned more, however, than simply a merger of their two organizations; they wanted the ASU to become a union of all progressive, anti-fascist students. The goal here was to overcome the key political weakness of both the NSL and SLID: their inability to become mass membership organizations. Although the NSL and SLID had mobilized an unprecedented 175,000 students in the 1935 peace strike, they were unable to convince even a substantial percentage of these demonstrators to join their organizations.

Indeed, at the time of the ASU's founding convention, the combined membership of the NSL and SLID was only about 5000.[14] The problem seemed to be that most students saw the NSL and SLID as campus appendages of the Communist and Socialist Parties and—despite NSL and SLID claims to the contrary—thought they had "to accept the whole of a revolutionary path when they signed membership cards."[15] These perceptions had apparently kept liberal students from joining the NSL and SLID, even though they would participate in demonstrations led by the two organizations. NSLers and SLIDers hoped that the ASU would prove more attractive to these students, since it was an amalgamated organization not tied to one radical party and was a self-proclaimed union of all campus progressives. With this in mind, the NSL and SLID invited students unaffiliated with either organization to join them in Columbus, Ohio as participants in the founding convention of the American Student Union.[16]

As the convention organizers prepared for the Columbus meeting, their first problem was securing a hall. Ohio State University had agreed to house the convention. But after the Hearst press redbaited the ASU's leftist sponsors, the Ohio State administration reneged on the agreement just a week before the convention. The administration claimed it lacked funds to light and heat the buildings for the convention, a shallow excuse exposed when the university refused the students' offers to pay these expenses. The convention site was then moved to the Columbus YWCA. This elicited complaints from the local American Legion, which tried to pressure the YWCA into cancelling. Because of this pressure, the convention delegates were uncertain, even after they arrived in Columbus, whether they were going to be evicted from their meeting hall. But the YWCA board, after convening a special session, confirmed that the students could use their hall.[17]

More than 400 delegates braved one of the worst snow storms of the year to attend the convention. Of these delegates 141 were NSLers, 116 LIDers, and the remaining 170 unaffiliated with either organization. These delegates represented 76 colleges and universities, 37 high schools, and 22 student councils. The delegates claimed to represent between 150,000 and 200,000 students. With the exception of the deep South, from which there were only a few delegates, every region of the country was well represented in what promised to be one of the most important student political meetings of the decade.[18]

Before the main ASU session could convene, however, the delegations of its two main constituent groups, the NSL and SLID, had to vote their final approval of the merger. The NSL delegation did so immediately after arriving in Columbus on December 28th. The SLID delegates met on the following day, but despite the SLID executive committee's prior approval of amalgamation, vocal opposition remained. Monroe Sweetland, a law student and one of the SLID's oldest national leaders, led the opposition to amalgamation. Sweetland feared that the merger would undermine the student movement's anti-war work because in contrast to the SLID, which remained opposed to United States entry into any war, the NSL was, in his view "prepared to support 'progressive' or 'anti-fascist' war." [19]

The SLID debate was long; it extended past the hour when the ASU session was supposed to convene on December 29. According to SLID delegate Nancy Bedford Jones, during the latter stages of this debate "the two hundred-odd unaffiliated students were clamoring in the halls, getting up committees to nag our leaders [to approve amalgamation] and getting more and more impatient with the delay." While the SLIDers continued to meet in closed session, the NSL delegation killed time and gave "the unaffiliated students something to sit-in on," by staying in session though it "had long since finished its business." Finally at 4 p.m. the SLID took a roll call vote. Despite the lengthy debate, the final SLID vote, reflecting chapter sentiment, went heavily in favor of amalgamation, 92 to 9, with 8 abstentions. When news of the vote reached the NSL session, which had been meeting upstairs, "for two minutes there was pandemonium, with the NSLers applauding, shouting hysterically, embracing each other."[20] All of the delegates proceeded immediately to meet in the first full session of the ASU, which lasted well into the night.

The main order of business at this meeting was the establishment of a platform for the ASU. Although the socialists and communists had been political rivals in the past, and though both were more radical than the unaffiliated liberal delegates, most of the platform discussion proceeded smoothly.[21] This was because almost all of the delegates were seeking common ground for their new organization. On most issues, moreover, agreement was easy because the students had cooperated in their prior campus activism.

The major planks of the ASU platform on domestic issues essentially codified the egalitarian demands that the student movement had championed since the early 1930s. The ASU plank on the "Right to Education and Security" demanded equal educational opportunity and economic security for all young Americans and urged social legislation to ensure that low income youth were not denied these "reasonable human rights"; it declared that "a society which cannot find places for its young people, except in work camps and on battlefields stands condemned." Carrying on the NSL's and SLID's strong commitment to racial equality, the ASU included in its platform a plank on "The Student and Minority Races," which began by citing "the evidences of racial discrimination which are alarmingly apparent in our educational institutions." The platform condemned the use of racial quotas to deny college admission to many Jewish and black students : "The ASU stands against . . . intolerance, Jim Crowism and segregation, whether these apply to Negro, Jewish, Chinese, Indian and other minority groups." The platform also reaffirmed the student movement's support for both the labor movement and the right of students and teachers to free political expression.[22]

Since the ASU was seeking to appeal to mainstream students, it avoided explicitly Marxist rhetoric in its platform. The document criticized the capitalists' greed and abuse of power, but did not condemn the capitalist system itself. Rather than speak in Marxist terms about class warfare between the workers and the bourgeoisie, the ASU platform used terms that, though more fuzzy, were indigenous to the American progressive tradition: describing a clash in the United States between "big business," "Tories," or the "inner oligarchy of high finance, industry and politics" and "the people." "A wide gulf separates this inner oligarchy . . . from the people. The latter wants peace; it foments war. The latter wants freedom; it inspires repression. The people demand jobs and social security, which the Tories block in order to secure their dividends and their rule."[23] Such language was not far from the iconoclastic liberal rhetoric used by FDR himself during the Second New Deal, and was clearly employed by the ASU with the liberal student in mind. The use of the term "Tories" to describe propertied conservatives also reflected the influence of the new Popular Front style of rhetoric of the Communist Party, in which the CP invoked patriotic themes—such as "Communism is Twentieth Century Americanism"—attempting to legitimate itself by laying claim to America's revolutionary heritage. This emphasis was also evident in the preamble to the ASU's platform, which declared that students had chosen to establish the ASU "because they, like their forefathers, are devoted to freedom and equality."[24]

Contrasting with the easy consensus on domestic issues, the discussion of foreign policy was tense and turbulent. This tension centered around the Oxford Pledge and the question of United States neutrality. Ever since the Seventh World Congress, socialist students had been skeptical over whether the communist-led NSL was still committed to the original anti-interventionist principles of the anti-war movement; they feared that NSLers would abandon those principles and support United States intervention in overseas war in the name of the Popular Front against fascism. Such fears had been fueled by the NSL's support of sanctions against Italy following the invasion of Ethiopia.[25]

SLID national leaders had become so concerned about this apparent NSL shift that in the month prior to the ASU convention they sent several letters quizzing NSL executive secretary Serril Gerber about his organization's stance regarding the Oxford Pledge. The first of these letters had asked whether the NSL still endorsed the Pledge "never to support the government of the United States in any war it may conduct." Gerber responded by reaffirming the NSL's support of the pledge; he explained that "We can conceive of no situation in which the government of the United States shall pursue other than imperialist [war] aims." Even this, however, had not stilled the doubts of the SLID leadership, which wrote back to Gerber, asking "would the NSL support a war against Japan conducted by the United States government in alliance with the Soviet Union?" Gerber again assured the SLID that the NSL would oppose war by the United States government "in all cases." Gerber's response was deemed sufficient by most of the SLID leadership.[26] But a vocal minority within the SLID remained unconvinced, and at Columbus they raised their doubts in a divisive fashion during the session devoted to establishing the ASU's peace plank.

The issue of the NSLers' attitude toward war was broached at this ASU session by socialist Hal Draper in almost precisely the same manner in which it had been raised in the SLID's letters to Gerber. Draper introduced a resolution pledging the ASU to oppose the United States government in its waging of wars in three different hypothetical international conflicts, including a war in which America allied itself with the Soviet Union. The Draper resolution brought to the surface the genuine difference which was already brewing between the pacifist/socialist bloc, which favored American neutrality and the communist/Popular Front liberal bloc, which leaned toward abandoning such neutrality. In this sense Draper's resolution represented a principled anti-war position. Such a position was, of course, consistent with the student movement's anti-interventionist tradition, which had aligned the movement with leading congressional isolationists.[27]

In introducing his resolution, Draper, a dogmatic socialist (en route to becoming an equally dogmatic Trotskyist), also had sectarian motivations. Draper had opposed the ASU's formation and had raised the war issue during the SLID caucus' debate to justify his stance against amalgamation. After losing this debate, when the SLID endorsed the merger with the NSL, he then carried the war issue into the ASU with his provocative resolutions. In effect, Draper, having failed to prevent the founding of the ASU, seized upon the war issue as a way of dividing the new organization. The resolution seemed particularly gratuitous in light of the fact that the ASU, including most of the delegates from the NSL, had already endorsed the Oxford Pledge, which specified non-support for the United States government in *any* war it might undertake. Indeed, in agreeing to continue supporting the Oxford Pledge the NSLers had already made a concession because the neutralist implication of the Pledge was at odds with their anti-fascism. Ignoring all this, Draper, who well understood the communists' devotion to the Soviet Union, was seeking to embarrass them by challenging them to take a public position distancing themselves from the U.S.S.R.[28]

The unaffiliated delegates held the swing vote in the ASU's consideration of the Draper resolution. Some of them opposed the resolution because it seemed awkward and abstract to discuss hypothetical war scenarios in the organization's platform; they also thought it unnecessary to include statements about any particular war since the platform already enunciated the general anti-war position of the Oxford Pledge. Other unaffiliated delegates opposed the resolution because they were beginning to question the strict neutrality position advocated by Draper, and were gravitating toward collective security. Their votes, along with the communists', defeated Draper's resolution. But the final vote was close, 193–

155, suggesting just how divisive the question of United States neutrality could be.[29] Indeed, the debate over the Draper resolution anticipated later conflicts in the ASU over the merits of both the Oxford Pledge and whether United States neutrality or collective security offered the most realistic solution to the growing international crisis.

The controversy over the Draper resolution was not the only indication in Columbus of the potential that communist-socialist tensions had to divide the ASU. The selection process for the new organization's leadership also evoked such tension. That process had been arrived at in October during the amalgamation negotiations between the NSL and SLID. The two organizations, in a kind of pre-nuptial agreement for their political marriage, had decided that the ASU's first national executive committee should include 11 SLIDers, 9 NSLers, and 10 students that had not been affiliated with either the NSL or SLID. It was agreed that the SLID and NSL representatives should be chosen in advance by their respective organizations. But in Columbus, after learning that the SLID had nominated Draper, the communists initially rebelled against his candidacy, since he had opposed amalgamation and played so divisive a role at the convention. The SLID delegates however, insisted that the NSLers live up to their agreement, and so the NSL delegates reluctantly dropped their opposition to Draper.[30]

With ASU leadership parcelled off in this prearranged manner among socialists, communists, and unaffiliated students, there was clearly a danger that the new organization would be polarized internally. Instead of becoming a true union of all progressive students, the ASU could erode into a battleground for competing blocs of communist and socialist members. At first glance the potential for this type of conflict might not seem strong, since the NSL and SLID leadership had agreed to disband these organizations as they merged to form the ASU. But in dissolving the NSL and SLID, the communist and socialist students had only given up their front groups, not the official party youth sections to which they belonged: the Young Communist League (YCL) and Young People's Socialist League (YPSL). These party organizations had both the power and the potential to factionalize the ASU. Indeed, through much of the ASU's life the communists and socialists who dominated its leadership would face a critical choice of priorities: Were their primary obligations to the ASU and promoting the growth of the student movement? Or, should the interests of the ASU and the student movement be subordinated to those of the Party youth organizations to which they belonged?

Fortunately for the ASU, during the critical early days of the organization, most of its national leaders were interested in mitigating socialist-communist factionalism, promoting unity within the ASU and building the student movement. Despite the tensions at the NSL-SLID wedding ceremony at Columbus, both partners came away in an upbeat mood and anxious for the ASU to enjoy a political honeymoon. This mood derived from the strong sense of pride that both NSL and SLID veterans took in their political achievement at Columbus; they had managed to overcome their differences and merge their organizations, a degree of unity which—notwithstanding the Draper controversy—far transcended anything achieved by the adult Left. At at time when the rise of fascism made unity on the Left seem imperative, these young radicals felt that they had risen to the occasion and avoided the tragic flaw of sectarianism that had left German radicals too divided to prevent Hitler's ascent. With this in mind, most of the ASU's socialist and communist activists came away from Columbus believing that the creation of this union of progressive students was, as James Wechsler put it, "a great landmark in leftwing political life. For that fleeting moment we really seemed to be making radical history."[31]

Most of the ASU's socialist and communist founders came away from Columbus delighted with their success in relating to liberal delegates. Since the ASU had been established by the Left in part to court liberal students, most socialist and communist delegates worked to establish a good relationship with them at the convention. In Columbus, socialists and communists had included liberals in writing the ASU platform and had persuaded ten of these unaffiliated students to serve on the ASU executive board. This spirit of cooperation between liberals and leftists was so strong that socialist delegate Nancy Bedford Jones boasted about it in the ASU convention report she sent to her comrades back in UCLA. Jones contrasted this cooperative atmosphere at Columbus with the southern

> California atmosphere, where the liberal abhors the radical. You all know it: The attitude that any matter, regardless of its own merit is undesirable because it comes from a radical. At the convention not a single vestige of this attitude existed. Liberals like Roger Chase of Columbia or Bruce Bliven of Harvard shared leadership with the known radicals, alternated chairmanship, worked harmoniously on committees together, felt and made it evident that this convention, this new-born organization was *theirs*, just as much as it was the LIDers and NSLers.[32]

Although liberal-leftist cooperation at the convention was impressive, the power relationship between these two groups was not nearly so equitable as Jones implied in her report. While liberals did chair convention sessions, serve on the ASU's executive board, and write platform planks, when it came to where the real power lay—the salaried national staff positions—the Left was firmly in the saddle. Not one of the six ASU staff positions was given to a liberal. Instead, these positions were divided equally between alumni of the socialist-led SLID and the communist-led NSL. This gave the Left disproportionate power within the ASU relative to the composition of both the convention, one third of whose delegates were liberals, and the national student body, in which liberals far outnumbered radicals. The liberals at the convention did not object to this situation, apparently because they thought that since the NSL and SLID were the two largest membership organizations responsible for creating the ASU, it was reasonable that their leaders should occupy the new organization's key offices. But even if it was not controversial, this Left monopoly of the officer positions attested to a certain shallowness among NSL and SLID veterans on the question of internal democracy. These leftists were seeking common ground with liberals, but not genuine power sharing—and later this would hurt the ASU because liberals would lack the power to stop the organization's radical officers from making major political mistakes.

The harm that this leftist monopoly on the ASU's paid leadership positions would do to the student movement was not, however, immediately apparent. This was due in part to the high caliber of the individuals elected to these positions in Columbus. Indeed, if one had to select only radicals for national leadership in the movement, the six activists chosen were probably the best possible candidates. They were all talented and experienced campus organizers. From the NSL came James Wechsler, ASU Director of Communications, whose primary responsibility would be editing the ASU's national magazine, the *Student Advocate*. He was a skillful writer and polemicist, who had served as editor-in-chief of Columbia University's student newspaper. Wechsler, an editor in the iconoclastic tradition of Reed Harris, made the ASU magazine the most lively and popular national student publication in Depression America. His talents would later carry him to the staff of the *Nation* and earn him the editorship of a major New York daily. Celeste Strack, ASU High School chair, was another former NSLer. A national debating champion, Strack had been the heroine of the UCLA free speech fight of 1934. Having organized amidst a conservative political environment in southern California, she was well suited for building the student movement in the even more inhospitable secondary school environment—where intolerant school principals tended to be even more repressive and paternalistic than their college counterparts.[33]

The other former NSLer among the ASU's first slate of officers was Serril Gerber, who served as ASU Field Organizer. Along with Strack, Gerber was a veteran of the Los Angeles area student movement. He was well qualified for the Field Organizer position because he had done extensive chapter building for the NSL while Executive Secretary of that organization. Gerber had also proven his political skill in organizing the second convention of the American Youth Congress, in summer 1935, which had been one of the largest national meetings ever held by student activists.[34]

The SLID veterans who served on this first slate of ASU national officers were every bit as impressive as their comrades from the NSL. The most politically experienced among them was ASU Executive Secretary Joseph P. Lash. As Executive Secretary of the SLID, Lash had played a key role in establishing the anti-war movement; it was Lash who had come up with the idea for a national student strike against war, which turned out to be the most effective protest tactic yet used by student organizers.

Lash had extensive editorial experience, producing the SLID's national magazine. He would become the ASU's most prolific author, associate editor of its *Student Advocate* and one of the movement's most effective pamphleteers—later in life his writing skills would win him a Pulitzer Prize.[35]

ASU National Chairman George Edwards was another talented SLID veteran. He had spearheaded one of the student movement's few successful southern campaigns, organizing an impressive anti-war strike at his undergraduate institution, Southern Methodist University. Edwards then served as an effective Field Organizer for the SLID, and became a leader of the student movement at Harvard during his graduate career there. And shortly after his tenure in the ASU, Edwards demonstrated that he could lead workers as well as students, becoming a prominent organizer in the United Auto Workers union, a role which would pave the way for his election to public office in Detroit and then to a federal judgeship.[36]

ASU Treasurer Molly Yard had also been an effective campus activist and national high school organizer for the SLID. As a Swarthmore undergraduate, Yard had led the campaign against racial discrimination in the college's Greek houses, which had culminated in the abolition of sororities on that campus. Decades later Yard would go on to become the most prominent social activist of all the ASU officers, emerging as a feminist leader and head of the National Organization for Women.[37]

With this talented leadership in place, the ASU quickly made its presence felt on campus. James Wechsler and Joseph Lash put together the first issue of the ASU national magazine, the *Student Advocate*, published in February 1936. The issue generated considerable excitement among students, selling out the full press run of 15,000, and going into a second printing. Wechsler and Lash struck an iconoclastic tone in the magazine, criticizing such traditional campus institutions as intercollegiate football, and exposing attempts at political suppression in both colleges and secondary schools. The magazine gave its biggest play, however, to the anti-war themes which had been central to the student movement; its main editorial, "American Storm Troops," offered a scathing indictment of the ROTC, and its lead story "Morgan: Wanted For Murder," featured an interview with isolationist Senator Gerald Nye, condemning big business for promoting war.[38]

Through the Wechsler-Lash editorship of the *Student Advocate* and Lash's supervision of the ASU's national office and chapter correspondence, they did more than any other officers in setting the tone of the new organization. This was particularly fortunate for the ASU because Lash, a socialist, and Wechsler, a communist, were both relatively independent-minded student leaders whose common interest in building the ASU and anti-fascist unity initially outweighed their different party loyalties. They came into the ASU determined to give higher priority to strengthening the student movement than to serving the narrow organizational interests of the YCL or YPSL. "Both of us," Lash observed, "felt that a mass student movement committed to a general militant program

. . . was more important than ideological purity."[39] Of his solidarity with Lash, Wechsler wrote in his memoirs that:

> The communists had stationed me in the ASU on the assumption that I would zealously carry on the communist line there. But I soon found myself far more interested in promoting the Popular Front idea than in performing factional communist assignments. I was sure Joe Lash and I could prove something to the world by working together harmoniously. He felt the same way about it.[40]

Wechsler's devotion to promoting a non-sectarian alliance against the Right went so far that in 1935 it led him into some trouble with the Young Communist League. The manuscript of Wechsler's forthcoming book on the student movement, *Revolt on the Campus* contained a two-page attack on the Hearst press for redbaiting Sidney Hook, a radical professor at New York University. This upset the YCL because Hook was an outspoken anti-Stalinist, who, according to the Communist Party, was a "Trotskyite agent of fascism." But though himself a YCL member, the free thinking Wechsler saw nothing wrong with defending Hook, and had in his own words "cavalierly forgot to submit a copy of the original manuscript" to Communist Party officials before bringing the book to the publisher. This led to criticism by YCL and CP leaders, "accompanied by clear admonitions not to go around publishing any more works without advance consultation on the highest level." The book went to press as written.[41]

Lash would prove as willing to stand up to his doctrinaire socialist comrades in the YPSL as Wechsler had been to defy communist sectarianism in the YCL. Lash's troubles with the YPSL began shortly before the the 1936 student strike against war. The conflict centered around an article YPSL leader Hal Draper published in the Socialist Party press attacking the ASU's approach toward this anti-war event. Draper accused communists in the student movement of "sapping the militancy of the ASU" by "*kowtowing*" to the sensibilities of "middle-class liberals." He charged that because communist ASUers were so intent on promoting anti-fascist unity with liberals—in accord with the Popular Front line of the Comintern—they were opportunistically abandoning any tactics which might seem too radical for liberals, including tactics that had been endorsed in the ASU's platform.[42]

As a case in point, Draper cited communist willingness to dilute the two most radical tactics used by student peace activists: the anti-war strike and the Oxford Pledge. Draper blamed the communists for the fact that at some campuses and high schools, students had agreed to substitute moderate peace assemblies (at which no classes were boycotted) for the more militant tactic of boycotting classes in the 1936 student strike against war. He also blamed the communists for the decision of high school ASUers to drop the controversial Oxford Pledge in their anti-war organizing. The communists' support of this dimunition of the student movement's militancy, in Draper's eyes, manifested the bad faith with which they had endorsed the ASU platform in the first place. Draper charged that the communists had approved the Oxford Pledge at the Columbus convention only because they had to in order to convince the SLID to merge with the NSL; the communists in actuality opposed the pledge because its anti-interventionist message was incompatible with the Popular Front and collective security. So their approach to the pledge, according to Draper, was "to leave it on paper as much as possible." Draper therefore characterized the ASU as "programmatically speaking, a 'shot-gun' wedding," between the genuinely anti-war socialists and the increasingly interventionist and pro-war communists.[43]

Indignant that Draper, an ASU national executive committee member, had issued this public attack on the ASU only a few months after the birth of the organization, Lash took to the pages of the Socialist Party press to rebut him. Lash insisted that the ASU had not lost its militancy. He accused Draper of being inflexible in his approach to student organizing, and thinking dogmatically rather than strategically: Draper had closed his eyes to the obvious fact that imposing radical tactics on students in the high school political environment would undermine the anti-war movement there. "The ASU," Lash explained,

> is weak in the high schools. Past experience with the SLID and NSL has shown that a weak high school chapter cannot by itself build the anti-war strike—that on the contrary, by calling a strike a weak chapter isolates itself from the student body and exposes to expulsion the most militant members in that chapter.[44]

According to Lash, then, it was this unfavorable political environment, not any change in the ASU outlook toward the Oxford Pledge, that had led the ASU to drop the pledge from its high school program.

Lash objected to Draper's hostile attitude toward communists in the ASU. He charged that Draper had been unfair in implying that communist ASUers had been insincere about the Oxford Pledge. Lash pointed out that the idea of removing the pledge from the high school program was "originally made" not by communists, as Draper had intimated, but "by socialists, and has the support of many leading Yipsels [YPSLs]. Draper's disagreement with them does not make them YCLers. And certainly it does not prove that the YCL is sapping the militancy of the ASU." As a YPSL member himself, Lash warned that if this organization was to play a constructive role in building the ASU and the student movement, it must not emulate Draper's divisive attacks on communist ASUers. He depicted the Draper article as representative of

> a dangerous tendency in some quarters to ignore the general needs of the student body and emphasize our differences with the YCL. Some of

us [YPSLs] seem to regard the ASU primarily as an enlarged forum for this purpose. The basis of a campaign against YCL theoretical errors becomes not a healthy one of hammering out a common approach, but of scoring debating points and winning the other fellow's following. If such becomes our primary purpose in the ASU, this splendid coalition of socialists, communists and liberals, which has swept the campus by storm will be rent asunder. One must believe that the program of the ASU will lead to actions that will dictate a common approach and solution to all the elements in the ASU.[45]

Lash's non-sectarian approach to student organizing was too unorthodox for the national YPSL leadership. Ben Fischer, YPSL national secretary, strongly criticized Lash's rebuttal to Draper. Fischer pronounced Lash "entirely incorrect" in emphasizing that

> YPSL criticism of the YCL has as its purpose the hammering out of a common approach [to student organizing] . . . . The differences between the YCL and YPSL today are of a basic nature and the YPSL cannot and will not submerge these differences or soft-pedal them in the interests of a "common approach."

The YPSL secretary felt that the type of unity Lash was advocating would not be possible until the YCL dropped its Popular Front "line of support of imperialist war." Fischer objected to Lash's priorities: his notion that the goal of building a united student movement was more important than the interests of the YPSL. For socialist students, "the central task," according to Fischer, "is the organization of students into the YPSL and the extension of the influence of the YPSL, organizationally and ideologically, among the students."[46] The implications of Fischer's strategy were strongly sectarian; for if recruiting students to YPSL was, as he claimed, the raison d'être for socialist student activists, then the differences between the YPSL and the YCL would have to be stressed. Otherwise it would not be possible to ensure that radicalized students were recruited into the socialist youth group instead of its communist competitor.

In this conflict with Draper and Fischer, Lash's non-sectarian position and willingness to defend the ASU showed that he was deeply committed, both politically and personally, to the new organization. Though still a YPSL member, Lash believed that socialists could be most effective in prodding the student body leftward if they stopped squabbling with the communists and focused on building a mass student movement championing peace and egalitarian social change. But Lash had become more than a socialist functionary; he took his new office and responsibilities as ASU executive secretary seriously, and thought that this obligated him to serve the broader interests of the student movement. As a founder of the ASU who had also spent several years leading the growing SLID, Lash felt he understood the interests of the student movement better than YPSL leaders like Fischer, who had never proven themselves effective campus organizers. Lash resented being told what to do by a YPSL hierarchy he regarded as politically inept and dogmatic, especially since their directives seemed both sectarian and ill suited to the task of strengthening the student movement.[47]

The significance of the dispute between these YPSL leaders and Lash lay as much in where it occurred as why it occurred. Both sides published their polemics not in the pages of the ASU's national magazine or any other ASU publication, but rather in the Socialist Party press. This might seem logical enough, since the debate was between socialists. Yet, it is striking that the ASU's publications did not even mention this dispute between the organization's executive secretary and two of the leading socialist youth leaders in the nation. This was not some aberration, but was part of a broader pattern, in which the ASU leadership sought to keep the doctrinal and tactical disputes as well as the sectarian conflicts of the Left out of the organization's publications and proceedings. The ASU leadership adopted this strategy in the hope of building a non-sectarian student movement that could attract liberals as well as radicals.[48]

As an organizing strategy this approach had considerable merit because it fostered student unity. But it also bred a style of ASU political organizing and political journalism that was less than honest in a way that typified the Popular Front. "Front" is indeed the operative word here because that was what the ASU and its magazine were offering: a facade of independent Left-liberalism from an organization whose leaders were never entirely independent of the Commumist Party, the Socialist Party and their official youth affiliates. Of course Lash, Wechsler, and the other more imaginative ASU leaders were striving to achieve a great degree of independence, but in so doing they had to battle with the radical party organizations, whose nominations had put them in office in the first place. Yet neither these struggles nor most of the conflicts within or between the YPSL and the YCL were dealt with openly in the ASU's publications or public proceedings. The ASU's convention reports said nothing about the negotiations and political horsetrading between the YPSL and YCL that helped to determine who would occupy the pivotal leadership positions on the ASU national committees and staff. The story of how power was really wielded within the ASU, then, was not one deemed fit for public consumption. The sanitized pages of the *Student Advocate* suggest that not even its talented editors, Wechsler and Lash, who rejected so much of the narrowness of the YPSL and YCL, could escape this duplicitous feature of the Old Left political style.[49]

The same lack of candor evident in the ASU's national magazine appeared at the campus level as well. Students unaffiliated with the YCL or YPSL were so often left in the dark about the conflicts and compromises between those two organizations that leftist students often referred to them as "innocents." On some campuses—especially in conservative regions— the submerging of Left conflicts and affiliations went so far that radical students were actually concealing their party membership from their fellow activists. At the University of Kentucky, for instance, YPSL organizer Joe Freeland reported that "the Communists are at present the dominant group in the [ASU] chapter . . . . They work absolutely under cover . . . and I am convinced that not more than two or three of the unaffiliated members of the ASU know that they are Communists." Similarly, Wechsler, in looking back upon *Revolt on the Campus,* (1935), the lengthy account of the student movement he had penned while a leader in that movement, noted that the "book is most disingenuous in its failure to identify" his "political commitments" as a YCL member. Nowhere in his otherwise illuminating narrative of over 450 pages had Wechsler even acknowledged that "most of those in the forefront of the . . . [student movement] were either YCL members or enrolled in the Young People's Socialist League."[50]

Although this lack of candor may be questioned on moral grounds, there is no arguing with the political effectiveness of the ASU, and its strategy of downplaying leftist doctrinal disputes. The ASU would prove more successful than any previous student organization in finding common ground for radical and liberal activists on campus. The results of the 1936 student strike against war suggested just how much potential this unified approach toward student organizing had for building the student movement. The strike represented the largest national mobilization of students in American history. Some 500,000 students, almost half the national undergraduate population, participated in the event, rallying against both war and compulsory ROTC.[51]

The 1936 strike day began with anti-war speeches by Joseph Lash and columnist Drew Pearson, broadcast over a national radio hook up. Lash urged students to support the strike and recognize that "the highest service to one's country today is to prevent it from going to war." Pearson praised the student strike as "a healthy and disillusioning protective" against war. Among the new endorsers of the strike was Albert Einstein, who issued a statement of support to student anti-war demonstrators at Princeton, terming it "the duty of enlightened youth to combat the politics of national egotism." Noting the strength of student anti-war sentiment, administrators on many campuses shifted away from their previous opposition to the strike; they either tolerated the demonstration or tried to dilute its radicalism by scheduling university-run peace assemblies. In some cases, classes were even called off to allow for strike participation. This occurred at Cornell University, for example, making it possible for more than 2000 students to join the anti-war protest. Even critics of the student movement were impressed by the size of the strike. Thus *Time* magazine quipped that the student anti-war strike was "turning into a full sized and characteristically noisy national institution, like Halloween."[52]

The 1936 strike was not only larger, but more colorful than the previous anti-war walkouts. Locals of a recently formed student organization, Veterans of Future Wars (VFW) added a touch of ironic humor to the strike. VFW chapters lampooned war and the military. Tongue in cheek, they had demanded that the government pay them a bonus now for military service before they were drafted and killed on the battlefield. Probably the largest ASU-sponsored demonstration integrating the VFW's political theatrics into strike day events occurred on Morningside Heights. A crowd of some 5000 line up along Broadway and 120th street to watch an anti-war parade of Columbia and Barnard students. Carrying signs which said "Spend your bonus here, not in the hereafter," two hundred members of the "William Randolph Hearst Post No. 1, Veterans of Future Wars," marched down Broadway, accompanied by twenty members of Columbia's band, and led by a drum major who twirled a crutch instead of a baton. They were followed by 150 Barnard college women, dressed as nurses and widows, carrying dolls representing "war orphans." At the conclusion of the march some 3000 Columbia, Barnard, Union Theological Seminary, Jewish Theological Seminary, and Teachers College students rallied against war and took the Oxford oath.[53]

In Lash's eyes the results of the 1936 student strike suggested that it was he, rather than Draper, who had been correct in their debate concerning the intentions of communist ASUers. Despite Draper's warnings that the abandonment of the Oxford Pledge in the high schools was part of a larger communist plot to purge the Pledge from its program, at the college level—where the ASU was strongest—the Pledge was generally retained. The strike call issued by the ASU had given the Pledge prominent play, and in fact there was only a single phrase, "Stop the Aggressor," which the YPSLs could object to as even vaguely interventionist in the entire call.[54] Observing the success of the strike and the phrasing of the strike call, Lash privately boasted of how wrong Draper had been in predicting that the communists would dilute the strike's anti-war content. Instead of trying to impose the Communist Party's collective security line on the student movement, communist ASUers had, Lash explained, subordinated that line for the sake of unity in the student movement.

> We have had differences with the Young Communist League on the question of how to fight war, but they have always accepted the position of the socialists when we have insisted upon it. For instance the national strike call urges support of mandatory neutrality. This is completely inconsistent with the Communist position on sanctions. I think it is a victory for the socialists when they can get the A.S.U. to adopt their position in this way. There is a good deal of confusion in the ranks of the Young Communist League on the subject of the Oxford Pledge, but it has not affected the work of the A.S.U.[55]

Lash's conclusions, however, proved premature. In the long run it was Draper who correctly perceived the direction in which the communists would push the ASU and the student movement. Lash erred in thinking the communists would always yield to the socialists as they had in April 1936, when they had allowed the Oxford Pledge and its anti-interventionist message to remain a central part of the campus strike against war. This communist accommodationism could not last because too much of a contradiction existed between the neutrality policies championed by the anti-war strike and the collective security policies increasingly favored by communist ASUers. Though for the sake of student unity, communist ASUers had obfuscated that contradiction during the 1936 strike, international events would make them less and less willing to continue making such concessions to anti-interventionism. And of all the international events propelling this break with anti-interventionism none was more important than the Spanish Civil War. The conflict in Spain from summer 1936–1939 would change the strategy of communist ASUers, as Draper had predicted, transforming the dominant foreign policy of the student movement so that it conformed entirely to the Popular Front line of the Communist International.

II

The Spanish Civil War served as the wake-up call for a generation of student activists who had been lost in isolationist slumber. Before the conflict in Spain, communist ASUers represented virtually the only force in the student movement critical of United States neutrality and supportive of international governmental action to prevent fascist aggression. During the early 1930s most American students had assumed that the United States could preserve peace by adhering to a policy of strict neutrality. But the news from Spain following the outbreak of the fascist insurgency in July 1936 exposed the naiveté of this assumption. The Spanish Civil War would begin to discredit United States neutrality in the eyes of many students, providing communist ASUers with a host of allies in their drive to convert the student movement from isolationism to collective security and anti-fascist interventionism.

This shift away from neutrality, initiated by Spain and orchestrated by communist ASUers, would not, however, come easily. The communists were, in effect, seeking to use the Spanish Civil War to alter the student movement's raison d'être by reversing the anti-interventionist policies that had launched the college peace movement in the first place. Intellectually, this effort boiled down to a battle between the present and the past—between the old lessons from World War I and the new lessons emerging from the Spanish Civil War. Through the first half of the Depression decade, the student movement's foreign policy had been shaped by disillusionment with World War I. Convinced that United States intervention in that conflict had been a tragic mistake, most American students and their anti-war movement supported neutrality legislation designed to prevent President Roosevelt from repeating that mistake. It had been comforting to think that Congress, heeding the lessons of the First World War, could simply legislate America out of any new world war. There was therefore considerable reluctance among students about parting with this happy illusion, even when events from Spain began to suggest that the lessons of 1917 were neither relevant to the international scene of the mid–1930s, nor a reliable guide to avoiding war.

It was equally difficult for students to part with the idealism of the Oxford Pledge. When they had transported the Oxford Pledge across the Atlantic in the early 1930s, American student activists had dared to dream of a warless world. For a generation scarred by the memory of World War I, the pledge had symbolized their hope that by refusing to fight, the youth of all nations could help prevent another world war.[56] Since this optimism had helped give birth to the anti-war movement on campus, student activists were understandably reluctant to surrender it. It was painful for the young to face up to the fact that their bright hopes and dreams were dying on the battlefields of Spain; that nonviolence and neutrality only encouraged fascist aggression and thereby heightened the prospects for the outbreak of a second world war.

It was with respect to United States neutrality legislation that events in Spain did the most to refute the simplistic lessons that students had drawn from World War I. The Spanish Civil War confronted American students with the harmful effects of the neutrality policy that their anti-war movement had once championed. When President Roosevelt and Congress, in the name of neutrality, imposed an embargo on the Spanish republic, the impact of this policy was anything but neutral. By withholding support from either side, the United States objectively aided General Francisco Franco's fascist forces; for with the fascists armed to the teeth by Hitler and Mussolini, it was only the republican side which, because of the embargo by America, Britain, and France, remained desperately short of military supplies. Supporters of the Loyalist cause worried that this United States policy was contributing to the starvation of the Spanish republic and facilitating a fascist victory there. Such a victory, Popular Fronters feared, would gratify Franco's German and Italian sponsors and breed further fascist aggression by suggesting that the western democracies would not act to halt such aggression. Spain would increasingly be seen on campus as an object lesson in anachronistic foreign policy: teaching that neutrality acts framed with Woodrow Wilson in mind were not appropriate for dealing with Hitler and Mussolini.[57]

The Spanish Civil War fostered this new realism in the American student movement because of not only the tragedy of the American neutrality policy, but also the courage of the anti-fascists in Spain. ASU activists watched in horror as Franco's cabal of fascist generals turned the Spanish army upon the Spanish people and their democratically elected government. Franco's insurgency seemed all the more sinister because its success hinged upon the support of thousands of troops from fascist Italy, bombers from Nazi Germany, and other military supplies from both Hitler and Mussolini. Despite the odds against holding off these well supplied fascist forces, Spaniards rushed to the defense of their republic, and through their determined military defense of Madrid in the fall of 1936 they prevented the expected rapid fascist victory in the war. The courage of this resistance, depicted so movingly by Ernest Hemingway and other leading American and European writers, captured the imagination of many students. Inspired by Spain, a new anti-fascist idealism was emerging on campus, whose partisans carried the slogan first heard in Spain, "No Pasaran!" ("they shall not pass"). In the American student movement, this new idealism, with its call for engagement in the international struggle against fascism, would first compete with and then prevail over the anti-interventionist idealism embodied in the Oxford Pledge.[58]

The Spanish Civil War was one of those rare historical events that have the power to change people's minds and prod them to reconsider their political assumptions. This process of change was emotional as well as intellectual; it was fueled by compassion for the Spanish republic, admiration for the Loyalists and their willingness to sacrifice their lives to battle fascism, as well as outrage at the brutality of Franco and his German and Italian fascist sponsors. The strength of such feelings, and their ability to alter the thinking of student activists, was evident, for instance, in a letter Tucker Dean sent to ASU leader Molly Yard. Dean, a student anti-war leader at Harvard, who previously had been a committed pacifist, confided to Yard that the Civil War in Spain had left him thinking in ways incompatible with his pacifist principles. Dean wrote that he had been seriously contemplating

> the possibility of volunteering [to fight] in Spain. Ordinarily I wouldnt consider such a thing, since I abhor war. But in the past months I've been thinking a good deal about Germany and Spain and their relationship to my old dream of pacifism. In fact I've been literally dreaming about myself fighting fascists, always to my own astonishment, since I'd hate to kill even a fascist.[59]

While Dean dreamed of fighting fascism in Spain, other American students were translating such dreams into reality. From 1936–1938 some 500 students and recent graduates slipped out of the United States and, in defiance of United States neutrality laws, made their way to Spain, where they served as soldiers for the Loyalists in the volunteer American unit, the Abraham Lincoln Battalion. Students constituted the largest white-collar group in the Lincoln Battalion of the International Brigade. Only the maritime industry, with its unionized seamen and their radical working-class tradition, provided more American volunteers in Spain than did the campuses. And within this substantial student delegation, the largest single contingent came directly out of the ranks of the student movement. Eighty-eight ASUers served in the Lincoln Battalion.[60]

This student participation in the Spanish Civil War would have a profound impact upon the American student movement. With students fighting in Spain, the struggle against fascism and the United States embargo of the Spanish republic ceased to be abstractions; they became matters of life and death. Students now felt that the embargo was jeopardizing the survival of not only the republic, but of American student movement veterans serving in the Lincoln Battalion, who were facing the much better armed fascist forces. This became an even more urgent matter as the Lincoln Battalion began suffering heavy casualties. The special intensity of this concern reflected the fact that the first American students to die for their political beliefs in the Depression decade were those who fell in battle during the Spanish Civil War.[61]

Nowhere was the Spanish anti-fascist cause felt with more immediacy than in the national leadership of the ASU during the early stages of the Civil War. All of the national staff members of the ASU had close friends serving in the Lincoln Battalion. Since their comrades stood on the front lines in Spain there was, as James Wechsler recalled, a strong feeling among ASU officers that "those who remained behind could not let them down." In his memoir Wechsler noted that as an ASUer he had felt inspired by the example set by David Cook, a fellow veteran of Columbia University's student Left, who fought in Spain. Despite the wounds Cook had suffered in battle, he sent Wechsler optimistic letters from a Madrid hospital, voicing his determination to fight on. "In the face of such communiqués," Wechsler explained, "one tried harder than ever to . . . serve selflessly in the movement which produced such men."[62]

In its first few months, the Spanish Civil War brought most of the national staff of the ASU closer together both personally and politically. Their strong desire to support the anti-fascists in Spain and to assist their friends on the front lines helped unite communists on the ASU staff with their socialist counterparts. These communist ASUers—the most prominent of whom were Wechsler and Strack—had from the outset been ardent boosters of the Loyalist cause, because of their own anti-fascism and because this was consistent with the Comintern's Popular Front line. Their enthusiasm had been buttressed in the fall of 1936 by the U.S.S.R.'s decision to provide military aid to the republic, and by the leading role that communists had played in organizing the Lincoln Battalion and volunteer units from other nations. But Spain also pushed several of the key socialist leaders in the ASU, including Lash, Yard, and ASU executive committee member Robert Spivack, away from United States neutrality and toward the collective security position advocated by the communists.[63] Their own unity over Spain encouraged these ASU leaders to believe that rank and file ASUers as well as the national student body would also eagerly embrace the Spanish anti-fascist cause. For these ASU leaders, the anticipation of such a united and effective crusade against fascism made the early stages of the Spanish Civil War, in Wechsler's words,

> a time of hope and excitement, of passions revived and faith rejuvenated. Earlier in the decade there had been the swift, crushing triumph of Hitler, and all the ensuing recriminations as to the blame for that disaster

. . . . Now the issue was drawn again and this time it would be different. As far as we could see at a distance, socialists, communists, anarchists and just freedom-loving men were united in the great stand of the century. "Make Madrid the tomb of Fascism" was the cry heard round the world, "*No Pasaran*" was to be the triumphant theme song of a generation. In Spain, at least, the air was clear and the battle lines plainly marked, so we believed, and there could be no doubt where every man of good will . . . must finally take his stand.[64]

This type of unity over Spain would, however, prove more difficult to duplicate in some quarters of the student anti-war movement. None of the ASU officers were pacifists, and so they did not experience the dilemma over Spain that pacifists confronted. The Spanish Civil War forced pacifists to chose between two evils that were almost equally loathsome to them: war and fascism. Some pacifists bent their neutralist principles in order to help the Spanish anti-fascists—by supporting humanitarian, non-military aid for the Loyalists; others, as was the case with Tucker Dean, abandoned neutrality and non-violence entirely by supporting anti-fascist military aid. But most pacifist students who remained affiliated with such organizations as the Fellow of Reconciliation and the War Resisters League could not bring themselves to back war or American aid for belligerents even if, as in Spain, that war was being waged against fascism. They continued to call for strict United States neutrality with respect to Spain. Since such absolute pacifists constituted only a small minority of the national student body, they could not prevent the student movement's shift toward collective security. Nonetheless, their stance made it impossible for the ASU to engineer that shift without alienating this small, yet vocal, group of activists.[65]

Nor were pacifists the only group of students reluctant to abandon United States neutrality during the Spanish Civil War. More mainstream students, brought up on isolationism, were in many cases initially uneasy about this change. At the University of Michigan, for example, the Spanish Civil War provoked much soul searching among students—some of whom just could not bring themselves to abandon isolationism. The issue of Spain was brought home to the Ann Arbor campus in March 1938 by the news that Ralph Neafus, of Michigan's class of '36, serving in the Lincoln Battalion, had been taken prisoner by the fascist forces. The State Department, citing the technicality that American volunteers in Spain had violated United States neutrality laws, refused to intercede on Neafus' behalf. Outraged by this stance and by the overall United States policy towards Spain, the Michigan ASU sought to rally the campus in protest against the State Department's unwillingness to aid Neafus.[66]

This campaign swayed the editors of Michigan student newspaper, the *Michigan Daily,* even though the paper had begun the academic year staunchly isolationist. The *Daily,* urged the State Department to work for Neafus' release, and praised him for "representing the finest elements in

Michigan tradition . . . risking his life for . . . democratic ideals. He offered his life to the Spanish Republic in the same way that Lafayette, von Steuben and Kosciusko offered their services that this republic might live." Not all of Michigan's isolationists, however, were this willing to change. Rigid isolationists viewed Neafus' service in Spain as a misguided intrusion into the internal affairs of another nation, and they felt that any intercession by Washington on his behalf would violate United States neutrality. This isolationist mind-set prevailed within Michigan's student council, which by a 14 to 13 vote refused to join the ASU in sending a telegram on Neafus' behalf to the State Department. The closeness of this vote on a campus once overwhelmingly isolationist suggested the ASU was making progress in using Spain to turn students against neutrality; but the loss on the vote also attested that collegiate isolationism was far from dead.[67]

There were also serious obstacles on the road to collective security within the ASU. Not all of the ASU's leadership was as united as the national staff on Spain. The ASU's national executive and administrative committees—which, along with the ASU national staff, implemented ASU policy—included leftwing socialists and Trotskyists who were die hard foes of collective security. These dissidents, most of whom were YPSLs, sympathized with the Loyalists, but would only support worker's (i.e. nongovernmental) aid to the Spanish anti-fascist cause; they opposed United States government involvement in either the Spanish conflict or any collective security alliances and international sanctions against fascism. They rejected all measures designed to give Washington a leading or even active role in thwarting fascism internationally. Clinging dogmatically to the socialist view of war inherited from 1917, the YPSL continued to insist that since the United States was inherently imperialistic, even ostensibly anti-fascist foreign policy initiatives only masked America's true expansionist war goals. Where collective security advocates saw in Spain proof that the United States must join with the U.S.S.R. and other anti-fascist nations in using state power to contain Hitler and Mussolini, the YPSLs refused to believe that the might of capitalist America could be employed for such benign ends. The YPSLs contended that America itself was so militaristic that it constituted as big a threat to world peace as did Nazi Germany or fascist Italy. Thus leading YPSLs in the ASU, including Hal Draper, Judah Drob, and Alvaine Hollister, refused to go along with the communists' attempt to focus the student movement's foreign policy exclusively on the fascist threat. They instead pushed for an ASU which, though anti-fascist, would emphasize the war danger emanating from the United States and the need to use the Oxford Pledge to resist American militarism.[68]

These doctrinaire YPSLs in the ASU not only refused to reconsider their own analysis of American foreign policy in light of the developments in Spain; they also attacked socialist students who dared to engage in such a reconsideration. Acting like cardinals in the church of the socialist Left, the YPSL leadership sought to purge its ranks of heretics who embraced collective security. One YPSL heretic who was the object of such an attack was Joseph Lash. The ASU Executive Secretary had angered the YPSL leadership in the fall of 1936 when he co-authored with James Wechsler, *War Our Heritage*, an anti-war book, narrating the history of the student movement. The first six chapters of the book had been completed before the outbreak of the Spanish Civil War; they were true to the anti-interventionist spirit of the early student movement, and as such were not offensive to the YPSL. But the book's final chapter was written during the Spanish Civil War; it upset the YPSL leadership because it reflected the authors' shift away from anti-interventionism. Here Lash and Wechsler, after criticizing Hitler and Mussolini for aiding "the Spanish fascist rebels in Spain in their war against a democratic government," warned that

> it would be folly for the American peace movement . . . to ignore this immediate crisis which fascist aggressiveness has precipitated . . . . America's absence from collective security may accentuate the peril of war in Europe. . . . Washington . . . could legitimately collaborate in an attempt to enforce peace and to halt recurrent menaces to peace.[69]

This support of collective security led the YPSL to attack Lash and challenge his leadership in the student movement.

The YPSL leadership's anger at both Lash and the general direction of the ASU became evident during the YPSL national executive committee meeting in November, 1936. This meeting had been convened to prepare YPSL strategy for the upcoming ASU convention. At this meeting YPSL leaders complained that Lash "will not fight aggressively" for socialist goals within the ASU "because basically he disagrees with many of the policies of the YPSL." Determined to battle "against the YCL effort to line up pacifists and liberals [in the ASU] for collective security," the YPSL leadership agreed that this could be done most effectively without Lash. YPSL's executive committee therefore voted unanimously to dump Lash from its slate of candidates for the ASU national staff, and ordered his removal from all student organizing. The committee also echoed Hal Draper's criticism that the ASU was not sufficiently radical. These YPSLs objected that "in order to placate liberals" the ASU had used such words as "Tories" in its platform instead of specifically naming and targeting the capitalist class. The YPSL executive committee planned to demand at the convention that the ASU become explicitly anti-capitalist. The committee ruled that if the ASU refused to move in this direction, then no YPSL should serve in the position of ASU Executive Secretary.[70]

Lash realized that by endorsing collective security in *War Our Heritage* he had opened himself to this type of attack by the YPSL. But he responded to the YPSL challenge by arguing that foreign policy was not at the heart of this dispute. He claimed that the real reason the YPSL leadership wanted him out of the ASU was that "the YPSL NEC [National Executive Committee] hates me because I would not utilize my post in the

ASU for an unjustifiable and sectarian attack upon the YCL—that I would not allow factional differences to disturb the whole of the ASU." Lash termed the YPSL's decisions regarding him and the ASU convention the "reductio absurdium of [sectarian] tendencies which have long been developing in the YPSL." Lash attributed this sectarianism to YPSL jealousy of him, the ASU, and Communist ASUers. The YPSL leaders felt such jealousy, according to Lash, because while the ASU and YCL had grown with the student movement, the YPSL had virtually stagnated. Lash observed that Socialist Party leader

> Norman Thomas has a tremendous following amongst youth. Gil Green of the YCL has sighed in my presence that if they had a man like Thomas they could build an organization of a hundred thousand. But the YPSL has not grown . . . because it never possessed a leadership with the ability and imagination to build a massive Socialist youth movement.[71]

The YPSL leadership's plan to impose its doctrinaire approach to politics upon the ASU was, in Lash's view, a recipe for political disaster: "Obviously if the ASU was to become a mass organization it could not utilize [the] Marxian terms [advocated by] . . . the YPSL. The YPSL has consistently paid lipservice to the need for mass work. Why doesn't it govern its action by this need?"[72]

There was, of course, a self-serving quality to some of Lash's counterattacks in his conflict with the YPSL. Aware that *War Our Heritage*'s collective security position made him politically vulnerable in socialist circles, Lash, in his contemporary discussions with socialist comrades, downplayed the extent of his dissent on this issue. He emphasized that most of *War Our Heritage* had been anti-interventionist and that his foes in the YPSL were focusing on the book's final chapter because they were out to get him.[73] What Lash conveniently ignored here was that with the YPSL preparing for the ASU convention, at which the debate over collective security promised to loom large, it was quite reasonable for the YPSL leadership to be concerned about his views on this issue—particularly since his last writings on foreign policy in *War Our Heritage* had endorsed the very collective security ideas that the YPSL opposed. Clearly the YPSL had reason to fear that Lash might use his pivotal position in the ASU's leadership to defeat YPSL foreign policy goals at the convention.

Lash was, however, on more solid ground in criticizing the YPSL leadership's penchant for sectarianism and ultra-radical posturing. It made little political sense for the ASU, after a successful year, to abandon its founding platform in favor of the explicitly anti-capitalist program favored by the YPSL. Such a move might have been more consistent with the YPSL's ideological line, but it was not compatible with the basic mission of the ASU, which was uniting liberal and radical students to build a mass student movement in America. It made even less sense for the YPSL national executive committee to insist that unless the ASU changed its program in this manner, YPSLs would not serve in the key ASU national staff position. This strategy seemed sure to leave the YPSL and the student movement weakened; it might, in Lash's words, "embroil the [ASU] convention in a polemic that could consolidate the liberals with the YCL, or completely disgust the non-YPSL-YCL elements and destroy the ASU."[74]

Fortunately for both Lash and the student movement, the YPSL executive committee decided at the last minute not to implement most of its initial strategy for the 1936 ASU convention. The YPSL plans to dump Lash and attack the ASU program were short circuited by Socialist Party leader Norman Thomas. Upon learning of these YPSL plans a few weeks before the ASU convention, Thomas voiced his disapproval to the YPSL leadership. Thomas thought it unrealistic for the YPSLs to insist on remaking the ASU platform into an explicitly socialist document. He cautioned the YPSL not to act as if it was functioning "in a closed circle with reference only to the YPSL vs the YCL." The Socialist Party leader thought it the height of sectarianism for the YPSL to bar its members from the ASU national staff simply because the ASU's program was not revolutionary. Chiding the YPSL executive committee, Thomas stressed that

> we cannot set a precedent for isolation. We have to seek a program and a psychology which will be effective . . . . We have to be guided somewhat by what is possible in dealing with youth . . . . Above all things we must avoid a tone resembling that of third period Communism. I do not think we can possibly maintain as a rule the position that socialists can be in a mass organization but cannot hold policy forming office within it.[75]

Thomas also noted that though he disagreed with the statements in Lash's book regarding collective security, this was not a dispute of sufficient magnitude to justify the YPSL's decision to remove Lash from his leadership position in the ASU.

Thanks to Thomas, Lash came out ahead in this conflict with the YPSL. At the ASU convention, held in Chicago over the 1936 Christmas break, the YPSL did not seek to change the ASU's platform. Nor did the League follow through on its plan to remove Lash from the ASU leadership. But Lash's conflict with the YPSL did have an impact upon both him and the convention. Having been criticized for his few pages of pro-collective security argumentation in *War Our Heritage,* Lash shied away from making an explicit endorsement of collective security in his convention speeches. Lash, being, as he recalled, "under Socialist discipline," actually spoke on behalf of an anti-collective security resolution at the convention, despite feeling very "uneasy" about this position. This YPSL-sponsored resolution, which would have had the ASU criticize collective security as incompatible with the Oxford Pledge, lost 136 to 99. This close vote and Lash's retreat from collective security convinced communist ASUers that any attempt to impose a full collective security position on the convention would be too divisive. They therefore supported Molly

Yard's conciliatory proposal, which, for the sake of unity, had the ASU not take any position on collective security. And it was her proposal which prevailed at the convention.[76]

Although the ASU convention was too divided to come out explicitly for collective security, there were indications in Chicago that the ASU was heading in this direction. The convention passed a resolution warning against the "danger of fascist aggression on democratic nations," which seemed to imply—as collective security advocates believed—that the key danger to international peace came from fascist Italy and Germany rather than from the United States. This change in tone was also discernible in Lash's keynote speech to the convention. Although Lash, under pressure from the YPSLs, had earlier supported their resolution championing the Oxford Pledge and criticizing collective security, his keynote speech suggested where his heart really lay on these issues. While careful not to mention the words "collective security" in this address, Lash maintained much of the tone of the Popular Front position he had taken in his controversial *War Our Heritage* chapter. In his discussion of the student peace movement, Lash urged the ASU delegates to make anti-fascism, support of the Loyalist cause, and opposition to the United States embargo of Spain their highest priorities. Lash conceded that "many absolute pacifists have been shocked because our Union" endorsed the Loyalists, who employed force in their anti-fascist struggle. He defended this position and argued that pacifists should endorse it too since the fate of Spanish anti-fascism and the student movement's goal of preventing a new world war were inextricably linked. "The victory of fascism in Spain," Lash prophesized, "would prolong and extend the conditions which bring war closer to the whole world."[77]

In this speech Lash came closest to repudiating the student movement's previous anti-interventionism when he discussed the Oxford Pledge. After denouncing United States neutrality for being unneutral and aiding Spanish fascism, Lash pointed out that the ASU's support for the Loyalist war effort was not inconsistent with the organization's endorsement of the Oxford Pledge. Lash reminded the ASU's pacifists that the Pledge did not oppose all military service, but only military service on behalf of an "imperialist war for the U.S. government." Treading on dangerous ground since both the YPSL and pacifists in the ASU gave unqualified support to the Oxford Pledge, Lash asserted that the "Oxford Pledge is not for the A.S.U. . . . . an ethical absolute."[78] By qualifying and implicitly challenging the very anti-war pledge that had helped give birth to the student peace movement, Lash was suggesting that it might be necessary to change the direction of the movement for the sake of the Popular Front against fascism.

Lash's veiled public challenge to the YPSL position on the Oxford Pledge was tame, however, compared to the challenge he mounted to YPSL authority in the convention's closed socialist caucuses. Upon arriving in Chicago, Lash obtained a YPSL memo revealing a YPSL plot against him.

The memo stated that though the YPSL executive committee would not challenge Lash at the ASU convention, YPSL leaders, including Ben Fischer, the organization's national secretary, had agreed that after the convention "a campaign must be organized to expel Lash" from the YPSL.[79] The memo indicated that the YPSL leaders had only heeded Thomas' advice not to seek Lash's ouster as ASU Executive Secretary at the convention out of strategic considerations; they had been afraid that such a challenge might prove divisive at the convention and that a last minute effort to oust Lash could well fail. Aware now that the YPSL leaders were only postponing their attack on him, Lash opted to force a showdown at Chicago, and did so in alliance with ASU national chairman, George Edwards.

The vehicle for Lash's confrontation with the YPSLs was Edwards' convention speech. By the time of the ASU convention, Edwards was on his way out of the student movement. He was devoting most of his time to organizing for the United Auto Workers union in Detroit, where he would play a prominent role in the sit-down strikes. But Edwards, a YPSL member himself, shared Lash's disdain for the dogmatism and sectarianism of the YPSL national leadership, and, as one of his last acts in the student movement, he gladly joined Lash in defying that leadership. Encouraged by Lash, Edwards, upon flying in from Detroit, refused to submit the text of his presidential address to a representative of the YPSL executive committee. He gave the speech to the convention without YPSL approval, in flagrant disregard of YPSL procedures. Edwards' defiance and Lash's support of it ignited a fiery debate in the YPSL caucus at the convention. The furious YPSL leadership wanted to organize a move to oust Lash from his ASU office. Only the intervention of several Socialist Party officers dissuaded them from doing so.[80]

Although the policy differences in the Lash-YPSL dispute could hardly have been larger, both sides proved remarkably similar in the way that they waged this fight. Lash had been rebellious enough to defy the YPSL leadership, but not enough to air these differences publicly in an ASU session. He chose instead to fight this battle within the confines of the Socialist Party and its YPSL caucus, as did his opponents. Both shared a loyalty to the Socialist Party, and that loyalty dictated a style of party politics that was in many respects as conventional as that of the Democratic or Republican party activists. This resemblance was most striking in the YPSL caucuses that decided whether or not to slate Lash for ASU office, and the private negotiations in which the YPSL and the YCL met to determine how many of their respective members would get to serve as ASU national leaders. There was an almost Tammany-like quality to these sessions, where young radicals in their private party sessions—the student Left's smoke filled rooms—played kingmakers for the ASU. The only difference between these parties of the Left and those in the mainstream was that the former sought to be more disciplined, and therefore had expulsion procedures for ridding themselves of dissenters. This would in fact be the path taken by Lash's foes in the YPSL.[81]

Recriminations from the Lash-YPSL dispute lingered long after the Chicago Convention. Several YPSL leaders followed through on their threats against Lash by filing formal charges against him in the Socialist Party, citing his collusion with Edwards at the convention, and his support of collective security in *War Our Heritage*. Lash fought back. He used the confrontation with the YPSL in Chicago to expose the Socialist Party leadership to his view that the YPSL executive committee had failed "to build a mass Socialist youth movement because their leadership is incompetent, unimaginative and afflicted with an anti-YCL phobia."[82] He effectively defended himself from the YPSL's charges and filed his own charges against the YPSL executive committee, criticizing its poor performance in student organizing. The YPSLs failed attempt to discipline Lash only further alienated him from the YPSL organization, and left him free to join with the communists in moving toward collective security. With Lash coming over to their side in the semester following the Chicago Convention, communists in the ASU national leadership could now afford to become increasingly explicit in their push for collective security.

It would, however, take another full year after the 1936 ASU convention before collective security would become official ASU policy. The Chicago Convention demonstrated that extensive organizing and educational work would be needed before the ASU and the national student body would embrace collective security. Here the ASU was a victim of its own success. Having been so effective in publicizing the Oxford Pledge and its anti-interventionist message, the ASU would have to find a way to convince students that this old message was now out of date. Even with Spain on their side, this was a formidable task. Hoping to avoid an outright split in the campus anti-war movement over collective security, the ASU officers in spring 1937 adopted a pluralistic style as they pushed to reorient the student movement's foreign policy.[83] That is, they stressed the primacy of the anti-fascist cause and de-emphasized the Oxford Pledge, but did not try to compel all student organizers to do the same. Their hope was that the force of international events would buttress their anti-fascist message and gradually win students over to collective security.

This pluralistic approach guided the ASU national office's work in the 1937 student strike against war. At the ASU's initiative, the strike was coordinated through the United Student Peace Committee (USPC), a recently formed umbrella organization of anti-war groups. Under USPC auspices the 1937 strike would be the most broadly sponsored national student demonstration of the decade. The walkout was endorsed by such USPC members as the pacifist War Resisters League and Fellowship of Reconciliation, religious student groups, including the National Council of Methodist Youth, the Joint Committee on United Christian Youth Movement, the National Councils of the Student YMCA and YWCA, the liberal National Student Federation, and the radically-led American Youth Congress and American Student Union. The USPC's strike call, reflecting the sentiments of the USPC's pacifist members, had an anti-interventionist emphasis, endorsing "strict neutrality legislation," and offering only a passing reference to the Spanish Civil War. To help support the strike the ASU agreed to sign the USPC strike call, which it termed "an intelligent and careful minimum for the united action of the overwhelming majority of the student body"; but the ASU also made clear its disapproval of the anti-interventionist message of that document.[84]

The ASU was walking a political tight rope, as it sought to both air its differences with the USPC and still maintain strike unity in spring 1937. This was evident in the ASU national magazine's strike editorial, "April 22: We Must Remember Spain." Here the ASU criticized as "the most profound shortcoming of the [USPC] strike call" its "treatment of the Spanish issue." The ASU charged that the USPC had understated the importance of the Spanish Civil War and had erred seriously in promoting United States neutrality legislation. "American neutrality is sham neutrality at best and overt aid to fascism at worst," explained the ASU magazine. "If while fascism throws all resources into Spain, the allies of the Spanish government remain inert, the simple and inevitable consequence will be world war." Yet for the sake of unity, the editorial advised ASUers to be tolerant of the type of sentiment expressed by the USPC strike call, even as they expressed their problems with the call and worked to sway students to the anti-fascist cause in the strike:

> Without seeking to impose our judgment upon other participants in the strike, the American Student Union must undertake the responsibility of clarifying the Spanish issue, of revealing its link to the war crisis, of winning sympathy and aid for the embattled Spanish people.[85]

As far as turnout was concerned, the ASU's strategy for the strike proved enormously successful. The 1937 student strike was by all accounts larger than even the previous year's massive walkout. The ASU claimed that about a million students had participated in the strike, and even the conservative *New York Times* conceded that at least 500,000 students had mobilized for the event. Exhilarated ASU leaders boasted of the strike's "astounding proportions," and termed this protest "the greatest student mobilization for peace in the history of the U.S."[86]

If judged by content instead of size, however, the 1937 student strike was far from a smashing success. The strike lacked a single coherent message; it was rather a babel of conflicting voices and opinions. On campuses where communist ASUers and Popular Front liberals dominated the strike, the Oxford Pledge and anti-interventionism were de-emphasized in favor of anti-fascism, aid to republican Spain, and collective security. Where YPSLs were in control, the prior strike's stress on the Oxford Pledge and opposition to United States militarism was retained. And in pacifist-controlled strike rallies support for tough United States neutrality legislation took center stage. So while the ASU officers were delighted with the turnout, they were, with good reason, concerned about the loss of coherence in the strike. ASU officers began to recognize that a political fight would be necessary to make international anti-fascist solidarity the student movement's top priority. They would soon insist upon collective security becoming the official line of both the ASU and the student strike—even though this meant alienating pacifists, YPSLs, and others favoring an isolationist United States foreign policy.[87]

It was, however, not only the results of the 1937 strike but events in Spain that were rendering the ASU officers willing to risk splitting the anti-war movement for the sake of collective security. Though Spain had initially been a unifying cause for much of the student Left, this changed dramatically in spring 1937. Begun as a broad republican coalition, the Spanish Loyalists forces were, by virtue of Soviet aid, becoming increasingly communist-dominated. The communists in Spain wanted to postpone revolutionary measures (such as land seizures), in order to unify all of the country's social classes against the fascists. But many anarchists, leftwing socialists, and Trotskyists in the Loyalist ranks disagreed with this strategy. They advocated an immediate social revolution, arguing that this would give the lower classes more of a stake in their battle against fascism. This dispute ended in bloodshed in May 1937 when, under communist orders, Spanish government troops attacked the anarchists and their leftist allies in Barcelona. Communist ASUers and liberal Popular Fronters responded to these events by rallying to the side of the Spanish government, while YPSLs and Trotskyists strongly criticized the government. This split drove a wedge through the student Left, which would encourage the ASU's increasingly communist-dominated leadership to break with the YPSLs, Trotskyists, and other foes of collective security.[88]

The impact that Spain had upon the ASU's communist-dominated leadership in 1937 can be seen clearly in the case of Joseph Lash. The cause of Spanish anti-fascism so moved Lash that in the summer of 1937 he made his way over to Spain, and began drilling with the Abraham Lincoln Battalion. At the time Lash departed for Spain, he was still a socialist, despite his running feud with the YPSL. But the journey to Spain finalized Lash's move out of the socialists' circles and into the communists'. Communists helped Lash get into Spain, and once there he became convinced that the communists were providing both the backbone and the most far sighted strategists of the anti-fascist resistance. To his wife Nancy, Lash wrote from Spain in July that

> the CP here has pursued a consistently fine policy which in the main accounts for the fact that it is now the dominant party in Spain. Its slogans have proven correct and have become the slogans of the nation. It was the first party to realize that everything must be subordinated to winning the war . . . .[89]

That month in his diary Lash noted feeling "more and more in sympathy with communist policy," and "ready to take out a C party card."[90]

Lash adopted much of the communist perspective on Spain's non-Stalinist Left. Though as an anti-war leader Lash had consistently criticized the political repression which gripped America during the First World War, he was willing to sanction even harsher repression against Trotskyists in Spain for the sake of the war effort. On this point, Lash, in a confidential letter from Spain, wrote that the Trotskyists'

> policy has been objectively harmful. So far as I am concerned the burden of proof rests with the Trotskyists that the govt. and not they were the provocators of the Barcelona events. This is an iron age and we are in a civil war. It's about time Norman [Thomas] discovered that there are more important things in the world than defending Trotskyists.[91]

Lash was not immune to doubts about the communists and the harsh suppression they inflicted upon their leftist critics. Lash confessed in his diary to feeling troubled when he "found out too much" from a friend who had come to Spain to investigate the disappearance of the son of an exiled Menshevik leader. But Lash felt it is his anti-fascist duty to stifle his doubts. Thus in his diary Lash notes a "long heart to heart talk" with a comrade about the need "to subordinate oneself, one's misgivings about some of the things that were going on in Spain and russia if we are going to win against the fascists." Lash was too intelligent, however, to adopt this position without misgivings, and wrote privately of "the danger of becoming political hacks, if one suppressed all critical feelings." [92] In the end, though, his anti-fascism overcame such misgivings, and he sent back to the ASU uncritical propaganda from Spain. Lash would personally help to promote such uncritical thinking in the student movement. The Lincoln Battalion and YCL leadership pressured Lash to halt his training with the International Brigade, urging him to return to America and the ASU in order to rally student support for the Loyalist cause. Though confessing that he felt "absolutely like a bastard" for leaving the Brigade, Lash finally gave in, returning to the United States and his duties as ASU Executive Secretary in October.[93]

Although Lash's case was distinctive because he had actually gone to Spain, his mind-set regarding the Spanish struggle was typical of the ASU's communist and Popular Front leadership. ASU communications director James Wechsler recalled that he too was troubled by the "discord behind the Spanish lines." But with Lash and other friends in Spain, Wechsler felt obligated "to stifle doubt" about communist behavior there—"trying to be a good homefront soldier" for the anti-fascist cause. For Wechsler part of being a "good homefront soldier" meant attacking those who had allegedly been responsible for disrupting anti-fascist unity in Spain: the Trotskyists.[94]

Looking back on the Trotsky baiting of the late 1930s, Wechsler observed that "nothing is more comparable to the intellectual overtones of McCarthyism than the Communist crusade against Trotskyists." While this crusade raged, any radical who disagreed with the Popular Front or any other communist position could be instantly dismissed and discredited by simply being branded "Trotskyist;" it was used, as Wechsler recalled, in an attempt "to crush any vestige of independent thought" on the Left. The crusade came to America via Russia and Spain. Reflecting the feud between Stalin and Trotsky, the communists in Spain had attacked left-wing insurgents (many of whom were not actually Trotskyists) as traitors to the Loyalist cause and Trotskyist agents of fascism.[95]

Wechsler and other communists in the student movement would hurl these same false charges at Trotskyist youth organizers in the United States, whenever they dared to criticize the communist-dominated government of Spain. They believed that such attacks served the Loyalist cause. In 1937, for example, Wechsler was selected to deliver an address on "The Danger of Trotskyism" at the student session of the YCL convention. Initially reluctant to address such a sectarian topic, Wechsler nonetheless did so, having "decided that I could face so small an ordeal while others were enduring far greater punishment on the Spanish front."[96] In Wechsler as well as Lash, then, passion for the Loyalist cause fostered the very type of sectarianism which they had so studiously avoided in launching the ASU—both seemed to forget for the moment that it had been non-sectarianism which had helped make the ASU America's largest and most influential Left-led student group.

The hostility of this communist-Trotskyist conflict flowed in both directions. The Trotskyists were on the offensive as much as their communist rivals. When, for instance, Lash returned from Spain, Trotskyist YPSLs greeted his fall 1937 campus tour with leaflets charging him with promoting a "counter-revolutionary line," "slandering the revolutionary workers of Spain," and serving as a political propagandist for the People's Front government which "directed their massacre."[97] Later, Trotskyist student leader Irving Howe would depict ASU activists as fascistic, making the unfounded charge that they were raising funds "for BOTH sides [in the Spanish Civil War], Loyalist and Franco."[98] The political atmosphere within the Left was becoming so poisoned that it was growing increasingly difficult for any genuine dialogue over the Popular Front policies to occur. Lash himself confessed in his diary to feeling stultified by this atmosphere, while on the midwestern leg of his national campus tour on behalf of the Loyalist cause. Lash noted his concern about a

> meeting at Minn. U. [which] ended in noise and confusion because of Trotskyists from town who came down to present "another point of view." . . . [The student chairing the meeting] refused to give them the floor for anything but questions and promised them a speech at the end of the meeting and then adjourned it without allowing the speech. One wonders at the effect of such a move on people. I was doubly disturbed because

there are no arguments of the Trotskyists that I fear and cutting off discussion this way created the impression that I didn't have an answer.[99]

Even when dialogue was not cut off in this manner, the Trotskyist and YPSL critics of the republican government had little impact upon campus opinion regarding Spain. The very complexity of these critics' position on the Civil War made it difficult to sell. Though their attacks on Spanish communist repression of the anti-Stalinist Left were brilliant and accurate, making such attacks placed them in an awkward position. In the midst of a war against fascism, they appeared to be contradicting themselves by simultaneously denouncing both the Spanish fascists and the republican government leading the fight against those fascists. Thus in explaining why she rejected the YPSL-Trotskyist position on Spain, socialist student activist Nancy Bedford Jones gibed "I am not a split personality, one of those who can both support and oppose [those working] . . . to defeat fascism in Spain . . . . Therefore my support [of the Loyalists] . . . is full."[100]

In contrast to the complexity and seeming ambiguity of the Trotskyist-YPSL position on Spain, the communist ASUers' message of unqualified support to Spain's beleaguered anti-fascists was simple, clear, and appealing to most student activists. Moreover, as Irving Howe recalled, he and his fellow Trotskyists in the ASU were at a disadvantage emotionally as well as politically in the debate on Spain. With fascism threatening to crush the Spanish republic, the Trotskyists were, as Howe put it,

> complicating the Spanish question in ways that seemed insufferable. That the loyalist Spain which so stirred hearts could be guilty of allowing the NKVD to kidnap and murder Andrés Nin, the POUM leader, was simply too much. People could not bear to hear that La Pasionaria, the flaming defender of Madrid, was also a ruthless Stalinist persecuting political opponents.[101]

As Spain and the rift with the Trotskyists fostered an all or nothing attitude toward collective security within the ASU, President Roosevelt also contributed to this trend. In October 1937 FDR mounted his first major challenge to isolationism, with his "Quarantine" speech. The speech reflected his anger over Japan's invasion of northern China and his concern about the growing threat to peace posed by Hitler and Mussolini. Speaking in Chicago, the heartland of American isolationism, the president warned that "mere isolation or neutrality" would not protect America from "the present reign of terror and international lawlessness." He implied the need for some form of collective security by "peace-loving nations, . . . a concerted effort in opposition to those" engaged in international aggression. The president suggested the need for a "quarantine of those spreading the epidemic of world lawlessness." Widely interpreted as a call for sanctions against aggressor nations, the Chicago speech drew angry denunciations from isolationists. In the face of these attacks Roosevelt retreated and did almost nothing to translate this speech into policy.[102] But FDR's brief challenge to isolationism helped provide an opening to collective security proponents in the ASU, who could now invoke the authority of the president for their position. This gave them hope that as they turned the ASU into an officially pro-collective security organization—a move which would obviously alienate the student movement's Trotskyist, leftwing YPSLs and pacifist minorities—the ASU and the student movement could retain support from liberals, who constituted a majority of the national student body.[103]

The final showdown over collective security within the ASU would occur during its 1937 national convention at Vassar College, two months after FDR's Quarantine speech. Both the pro- and anti-collective security factions within the ASU knew that the showdown was coming and began preparing for the fight well before the convention convened in December. The Oxford Pledge emerged as the key issue as the two sides geared up for the convention. There was no question that the communist ASUers and other proponents of collective security would seek to drop the Pledge from the ASU platform at the convention. For them the Pledge's anti-interventionist message was anachronistic, as was its implication that there was a serious war danger emanating from the United States. They were promoting a more benign image of the United States as a potential leader in the international effort to halt fascist aggression. The YPSLs, pacifists, and Trotskyists, on the other hand, were readying themselves for a vigorous defense of anti-interventionism and the Oxford Pledge at the convention. They also prepared for a possible split with the ASU in case the Pledge was dropped and collective security adopted at the convention. This preparation, which began in November, took the form of preliminary organizing to launch the Youth Committee for the Oxford Pledge (YCOP), a group designed to draw students away from the ASU and collective security.[104]

Tension over this imminent battle gripped the ASU's national leadership. Molly Yard, who was now ASU Organizational Secretary as well as Treasurer, noted in the month preceding the convention that the ASU staff—which more than doubled in size since 1935—had become so factionalized that it was limiting the efficiency of the national office. In a letter to Lash, Yard complained of a

> tendency for staff members to do other things—they come in looking haggard at 9:30 or later . . . . There is Brit[ton Harris] with the YCL and Alvaine [Hollister] with the YPSL and Robin [Myers] and Bob [Kelso] with the pacifists. I am getting God dam sick of all this. It is too much for me. I think it would be interesting to see what would happen to the ASU if everyone really concentrated on building it.[105]

Among the ASU's national staff and administrative committee, the personal relationships between pro- and anti-collective security advocates deteriorated as the convention drew closer. This deterioration accelerated after the YPSLs and pacifists began working on the YCOP, which to its foes clearly seemed an attempt to subvert the ASU through the creation of a rival organization. Lash, who by this time had resigned from the YPSL and Socialist Party because of their opposition to collective security, repeatedly fell into arguments with Oxford Pledge supporters in the ASU national leadership. YPSL leader Alvaine Hollister complained to a fellow YCOP activist in November that Lash "is getting very excitable these days, on almost any occasion. At the administration committee meeting Thursday night, he went off the handle completely—at one point called me a liar, and during the day he told Bob and Robin that they were just my 'stooges.' "[106]

The ASU leadership's meetings to prepare for the convention were particularly contentious. Since a majority of leaders in the ASU national office and administrative committee favored collective security, their opponents were quite concerned that they might structure the Vassar meetings unfairly, so that the collective security position could be railroaded through the convention. At one such meeting, Hal Draper, now a Trotskyist and ASU national Administrative Committee member, insisted that Oxford Pledge supporters be represented in every aspect of planning and conducting the convention. Yard was conciliatory, explaining that "we were not trying to keep out any point of view and had no intention of so doing." But the YCL members of the committee proved intolerant. According to Yard's account of the meeting,

> Celeste [Strack] and Brit were pretty terrible in my estimation . . . . They kept telling Draper he'd better leave if he didn't like things in very measured tones and were generally very antagonizing. If they act that way at the Convention I think they will lose all the liberal support. It is really disgusting.[107]

At the campus level similar conflicts occurred. As in the ASU national office, the majority of convention delegates elected by the chapters favored collective security, and their opponents charged that the majority was acting to preempt any dissent from the convention. "Some chapter elections which preceded" the ASU convention were, according to the YPSL,

> exemplary of what lack of democracy can mean in action. In New York, for example proportional representation in all chapters was prohibited . . . . In Philadelphia, all chapters were instructed by the District Committee that their delegates had to vote for collective security simply because the district convention had done so (72–30). In other chapters, speakers supporting the [old] ASU program [endorsing the Oxford Pledge] were refused the floor for no better reason than that the majority opposed the program.[108]

Although such complaints might sound rather hollow—the usual gripes from the losing side—the private correspondence of pro-collective security ASUers confirms that at least some of these complaints were justified. Thus Molly Yard in a letter to Lash reported on a Vassar College meeting, which in early November 1937 reversed its initial approval of the Oxford Pledge, thanks to the manipulative behavior of communist students, who packed the meeting. "The story," Yard gloated "is that the YCL pulled in a lot of delegates who never even registered to vote on it. Anyway the whole thing is very sweet."[109]

The ASU convention, which met at Vassar College over the 1937 Christmas vacation, revealed the degree to which collective security advocates had outorganized their rivals. Unlike some of the previous ASU chapter meetings, however, there was no attempt here to stifle criticism of collective security. An equal number of speeches were heard from supporters and opponents of collective security. The YPSLs were permitted to have Norman Thomas, the Socialist Party's most eloquent speaker, make their case against collective security at the convention. Thomas argued that the only form of aid to anti-fascists overseas that would promote peace would be that which workers provided "independently of their government." Any involvement by Washington in these conflicts would only serve the interests of American imperialism and militarism. "Collective sanctions," Thomas warned, "means probable war and certain militarization . . . . We are not anxious to join the collective suicide club as the proponents of collective action by governments would have us do." But Thomas swayed few delegates. The convention voted by an overwhelming 282 to 108 margin to drop the Oxford Pledge from the ASU program and embrace collective security.[110]

Though this lopsided vote for collective security had been facilitated by communist manipulation of the delegate selection process, even had such manipulation not occurred the collective security position would still have carried the convention. Indeed, collective security advocates at the convention were so confident that their views represented the ASU rank and file that they offered to hold a referendum on the new peace planks among the organization's general membership. That referendum found the ASU membership embracing collective security by an even more resounding majority vote than had the convention itself. Not even ASU opponents of collective security claimed that the communists' underhanded tactics had been the key cause of their defeat at Vassar. It was rather the threatening events overseas which did the most to defeat these Oxford Pledge supporters and render them a defensive minority within the ASU. Hitler's and Mussolini's intervention in Spain and Japan's invasion of China strongly suggested that something had to be done to halt fascist aggression. This sentiment on campus had been reinforced by the ASU's persistent anti-fascist agitation, the deaths of American students fighting in Spain, and by the president himself in his Quarantine speech. By the fall of 1937 most ASUers would not be attracted by the foreign policies advocated by

YPSLs, pacifists, and Trotskyists, who were insisting on retaining the Oxford Pledge and United States neutrality, because these isolationist groups
clearly lacked any realistic strategy for dealing with the fascist threat.[111]

The vote for collective security reflected a growing awareness among
ASUers that their anti-war movement had to adapt to this changing international scene, something which foes of collective security seemed unwilling to do as they urged the ASU to stand firm and retain the Oxford
Pledge. For most ASUers it no longer seemed enough to simply pledge
oneself against militarism at home, as students had done through the Oxford Pledge in the early 1930s; one now had to address the problem of
militarism overseas, which threatened to engulf the entire world in war.
Thus in justifying their decision to abandon the Oxford Pledge for collective security, ASU leaders stressed that recent international developments
had made the Pledge seem both outdated and provincial. Joseph Lash, in
the only convention address published by the ASU, told the delegates that
the Pledge was

> not only valueless in the present circumstances but actually a deterrent in
> the campaign for peace. Our concern is to keep America out of war; this
> demands a positive peace policy now. The Oxford Pledge talks fantasti-
> cally about what we will do when war comes. Our concern is with how to
> prevent war from spreading; how to maintain the peace we have; how to
> restore the peace that has been shattered by fascist aggression. The Ox-
> ford Pledge demobilizes this immediate struggle for peace. With the fas-
> cists madly brandishing their war torches, the Oxford Pledge assumes
> that the main instigator of war today is the United States. Directing itself
> solely against the United States it breeds the illusion that we can . . .
> keep the United States out of war, [without concern] . . . for what is
> going on in the rest of the world.[112]

Having rejected the Oxford Pledge, the convention endorsed specific
steps for the United States government to help halt fascist aggression.
The ASU urged "American leadership in naming aggressors and applying embargoes against aggressors through international collaboration." The
ASU took a strong stance against the neutrality policies which in the past
had guided both the ASU and American foreign policy. The convention
came out for "repeal or modification of the neutrality act so as to discriminate between aggressors and attacked and aiding those nations which are
attacked."[113]

While dispensing with the Pledge as a symbol of outdated isolationism, the delegates embraced new symbols which articulated their opposition to international aggression. The first of these symbols was the student
movement's own group of anti-fascist fighters and martyrs in Spain. Paying tribute to ASUers in the Abraham Lincoln Battalion, Lash told the
convention that

we are deeply proud of . . . the service records of our two N.E.C. members, George Watt and Paul MacEachron, and humble before those like Don Henry of the University of Kansas, Nate Schilling of Chicago University, Sam Levinger of Ohio State, Roy McQuarrie of Wayne and others who have been killed in action. What can we say to them save our pledge that the American Student Union will not forget them and will demonstrate its remembrance by its deeds. In an age which puts scorn upon the symbols of civilization—justice, freedom, democracy, humanity—these fellow students of ours have revitalized those values for our generation.[114]

Since the recent Japanese assaults on China had resulted in the deaths of many civilians, the convention also adopted a symbol of their solidarity with the victims of this aggression. After voting overwhelmingly to boycott Japanese goods in protest against the invasion of China, the delegates lit a bonfire and tossed silk stockings and neckties into the blaze. As the protesters fed the fire, they chanted "If you wear cotton, Japan gets nottin'."[115]

Throughout the convention, the ASU leaders championing collective security embraced an especially powerful symbol of their new position: President Roosevelt. Lash had solicited and received a letter of welcome to the delegates from the president, which was read at the convention and featured on the front page of the ASU's report on the Vassar proceedings. Though in October Roosevelt had quickly backed away from the anti-isolationist message of his Quarantine speech, this is no way diminished his usefulness as a symbol for ASUers promoting the new collective security policies. Their image of the president was of a leader who had urged the quarantining of aggressor nations. This was evident in Lash's convention speech, which attacked Oxford Pledge supporters for seeking "to resist President Roosevelt's moves toward international cooperation against fascist aggression." Lash warned that such opposition to the president "strengthen[s] the camp of isolation" and leads "inevitably into that world war which we all fear."[116] These pro-Roosevelt arguments proved helpful in attracting liberals to collective security at the ASU convention, and they would later have a similar impact on the national student body.

Although the ASU had made a dramatic break with its past in dumping the Oxford Pledge and endorsing collective security, there were also elements of continuity in the ASU's peace policy. The ASU continued to oppose United States "preparations for war," including "the skyrocketing military budget," and mandatory ROTC—positions the organization had held since its founding.[117] Though the pro-collective security ASUers at the Vassar Convention would have denied it at the time, there was an obvious contradiction between these old anti-preparedness policies and the new foreign policy adopted by the ASU. James Wechsler recalled that he harbored private doubts about the compatability of these two policies:

> If we were committed to the proposition that the free nations ought to band together with Russia to deter fascist aggression, much of the deterrent effect would depend on how strong they were. Neither Hitler nor Mussolini was likely to be impressed by a program of resistance based on unpreparedness. Any effective stand against aggression surely involved the risk of war; but we were now embracing a stand which called for the assumption of all the risks without any of the preparations.[118]

The reasons that the ASU convention left Vassar with such contradictory policies were both strategic and emotional. Obviously, it would be somewhat less traumatic for an organization making so fundamental a shift in its foreign policy if it avoided changing every aspect of its peace policy. By maintaining its opposition to preparedness, the ASU could continue to claim that it remained an anti-war organization and had merely changed its tactics for promoting peace. The retention of the anti-preparedness planks was also a sign of the ASU's reluctance to go all the way in surrendering the optimism that the student movement had previously cherished when it had embraced the Oxford Pledge. Even as it dropped that Pledge at Vassar, the ASU, as Lash recalled, "still . . . hoped that it would be possible to stop aggression without world war." The majority of ASUers came away from Vassar believing that if enacted, the foreign policy it was urging upon the American government—including the use of anti-fascist economic sanctions in conjunction with other western democracies and the U.S.S.R.—could help halt fascist aggression without dragging the United States into a new war.[119]

Such arguments did not sway the dissident minority within the ASU, which had lost the battle for the Oxford Pledge at Vassar. Most YPSLs, pacifists, and Trotskyists came away from the convention bitterly opposed to the ASU's new collective security policy. Leaders of this opposition, such as Alvaine Hollister, carried their criticism back to the campuses and into the leftwing and student press, warning that the ASU would now become a force for "Left jingoism on campus." Hollister told the *Socialist Call* that in the wake of the convention

> the ASU is no longer an organization devoted to the struggle against war . . . . Every working class or youth movement in Europe which had supported collective security has eventually come to the position of support of military programs and budgets of their countries. This must inevitably be true of the ASU. The American Student Union, when it dropped the Oxford Pledge and adopted a program of collective security deliberately aligned itself with the warmaking Roosevelt administration and gave the president a tacit pledge: "If you go to war against a fascist nation and call that war one for democracy, we will fill your armies and fire your guns."[120]

It was not merely such criticism, but the critics themselves that posed a serious problem for Lash and his allies as they worked to unite the ASU behind the new collective security policies. Several of these critics remained on the ASU national staff and were therefore in a strategic position to undermine the implementation of the new policies. Hollister, for example, who so scathingly indicted ASU "jingoism" in the press, had just been elected national high school secretary of the ASU. Robin Myers and Fay Bennett were also anti-collective security activists on the ASU national staff.

This situation had arisen because at Vassar the two sides had battled primarily over policy rather than personnel. Hollister and her allies had wanted to unseat Lash as ASU executive secretary, but lacked a candidate "willing and able to give Joe a real fight." They had also feared that such a challenge would anger the collective security majority at the convention, and result in all foes of collective security failing to be re-elected to national office in the ASU. For their part, Lash, and other pro-collective security leaders at the ASU convention blocked only one anti-collective security activist, Bob Kelso, from being elected to the ASU national staff. They had not tried to purge Hollister or most of her allies from the staff. This was apparently because Lash and his supporters already had their hands full orchestrating the ASU's programmatic change, and wanted to avoid a move that could further divide the convention. Moreover, since the collective security forces enjoyed a majority on the ASU's national staff, executive, and administrative committees, they initially thought they could afford to tolerate the presence of a few isolationists in the ASU's national leadership.[121]

Since the personnel conflict had not been fought out at the convention, it would rage within the national office itself, beginning immediately after the ASU leadership returned from Vassar. The anti-collective security staff members started working even more energetically than they had before the convention to promote the growth the Youth Committee for the Oxford Pledge (YCOP) and its successor in 1938, the Youth Committee Against War (YCAW). In effect, Hollister and her allies were seeking to use the contacts and resources of the ASU national office to subvert that organization, by launching the YCOP to compete with the ASU and its new foreign policy. This effort involved not only open competition, but factional plotting and spying. Only a few weeks after the Vassar Convention, Bob Kelso and another ASU staff member involved in organizing the YCOP slipped into the ASU national office late at night and began "reading through Joe's [Joseph Lash's] outgoing mail." Kelso reported to YPSL leader Al Hamilton on some of the instructions Lash's letters were giving to ASU opponents of the YCOP, gloating that he had "picked up some other good dope here last night in addition to copying some of the more interesting letters that Lash sent out."[122]

The anti-collective security faction seems to have had no monopoly on this type of political snoopery. In February 1938, for example, Joseph Lash obtained a copy of a confidential letter written by a YPSL leader. The letter, which apparently described a YPSL plan to remove Molly Yard from office, proved highly embarrassing to the YPSL leadership when

Lash showed the letter to Yard. The YPSL leaders were certain that the letter had reached Lash illicitly; it had, they thought, been given to Lash by YCL leader Gil Green, who himself allegedly obtained "it . . . thru a spy who went into Alvaine [Hollister]'s purse and personal folder and copied the carbon of the correspondence . . ."[123]

Such mistrust and deceit, even more than the Vassar Convention itself, attest that the Popular Front romance which had produced the communist-socialist marriage in the ASU was over: shattered by irreconcilable differences over foreign policy. Though the divorce between the ASU's pro- and anti-collective security forces had not yet been finalized, both sides knew that it was just a matter of time. Lash acknowledged this in a letter to Yard only a few weeks after the Vassar Convention, noting that "the YPSLs are just waiting for the opportune moment to break with the A.S.U . . . . Today they are not at all interested in building the A.S.U. but in criticizing it in such a way as to start a revolt."[124] The YPSL's internal reports and correspondence leave no doubt that Lash was correct in this estimation. The real question now was whether one party or the other in this divorce would carry off the family wealth: Would the ASU, with its collective security policies or the YCOP, with its advocacy of the Oxford Pledge, inherit the mass student anti-war movement which had been built when the two parties had been united? This question would be answered decisively by the American student body as it responded to the rival ASU and YCOP efforts to dominate the campus anti-war strike of 1938.

The struggle for control over the upcoming anti-war strike began shortly after the ASU convention; it was centered initially in the USPC's planning meetings for the strike. During the previous year, the ASU had been willing to cater to the pacifists and other anti-interventionists in the USPC by signing the organization's strike call, even though it promoted neutrality policies with which the ASU disagreed. The ASU had made that concession in 1937 for the sake of student unity in the strike. This time however, with the ASU having endorsed collective security and facing competition with the YCOP over the basic direction of the student anti-war movement, ASU leaders refused to make such major concessions. In the strike planning meetings of the USPC, ASU delegates took the position that they would under no circumstances agree to sign "an isolationist strike call."[125]

The ASU's collective security leadership did not, however, want to break up the USPC, since they realized that this broad coalition of leftist, liberal, and pacifist groups had played an important role in making the 1937 strike so large. Thus within the parameters of their collective security principles, the ASU representatives worked with the USPC on a strike call which might make some degree of unity possible. ASU leaders realized that they could not sell the USPC—with its pacifist affiliates—on a militantly anti-fascist strike call that urged such specific United States government steps as sanctions; instead, they pushed for a call which would be collective security in tone, but not so interventionist that it would alienate the pacifists. Joseph Lash proposed in February that the USPC strike call declare: "Whether America is at peace tomorrow depends upon whether American foreign policy is a force for peace today. We urge an American foreign policy which is based upon the distinction between the victim and aggressor." Lash thought that even for the pacifists such a statement would be

> a difficult one with which to take exception. Although the absolute pacifists think that it is worthless for the Spanish people to resist because they can gain nothing by violence, nevertheless they do not have the guts to say there is no distinction between aggressor and victim.[126]

Led by the YCOP, the socialist and pacifist student organizations attacked the language of Lash's proposed strike call. In a contentious USPC meeting held in mid-March, only a month before the national strike date, these supporters of the Oxford Pledge argued that the proposed call was too "weighted towards collective security." On this basis, the YCOP, the student sections of the Fellowship of Reconciliation, the National Council of Methodist Youth, and the War Resisters League announced at the USPC meeting that they would not sign the call. These groups wanted to drop Lash's language in favor of a strike call that presented the student walkout as "a dress rehearsal" for resistance to military service in any future war. This was, of course, the old anti-interventionist line of the first antiwar strikes, and was unacceptable to the ASU representatives, who depicted it as thoroughly outdated, arguing that "the time for a dress rehearsal is past. War exists."[127]

Unable to reach an agreement on the wording and message for its 1938 strike call, the USPC settled on a strike call without a text. The March meeting of the USPC decided to promote the strike through posters which said only, "Strike Against War," and listed the USPC's constituent groups, along with the date and time of the walkout. Instead of text, the USPC strike poster merely included a photograph of a shell-torn town. Since neither the ASU nor the YCOP had been able to incorporate its message into the USPC's strike call, the battle between them was on this level a draw. But in a sense the ASU won here because it removed the USPC, the strike's sponsoring organization, from the anti-collective security position it had taken in 1937, when its strike call had endorsed neutrality legislation and the Oxford Pledge. From a collective security standpoint the USPC's silence in 1938 was better than its anti-interventionist message in 1937.[128]

Since the battle between the ASU and the YCOP had not been settled decisively at the national level in the USPC, the critical test of strength would come on the campuses themselves. The YCOP, which in the spring changed its name to the Youth Committee Against War (YCAW) and affiliated with the Keep America Out of War Congress, began working frantically to prepare for the strike almost as soon as its leaders returned from the Vassar Convention.[129] But founding a new organization, rooting it in the campus communities, and preparing for a nationwide strike were large tasks, particularly since the April strike date meant that all of this had to be done in a hurry—and done in competition with the ASU. The YPSL, the key leftist organization behind the YCAW, had little experience in mass organizing; its activists were heavily concentrated in a few cities, particularly New York and Chicago. They had spent more time feuding with communists than mobilizing mainstream students, and it was unclear whether they could work effectively with such students. But the YCAW did have the benefit of the campus contacts of its pacifist students who, through their affiliation with such large national religious groups as the National Council of Methodist Youth, had more of a national student network than did the YPSLs.[130]

The YCAW had the advantage of promoting an anti-interventionist message which over the past few years had become both familiar and popular on campus. That message, after all, had mobilized hundreds of thousands of student anti-war strikers during the early and mid-1930s. Treating consistency as a virtue, YCAW organizers argued with great force that they rather than the ASU had been truer to the student movement's founding principles. YCAW leaflets quoted ASU leaders who had sung the Oxford Pledge's praises in 1936 and then repudiated the Pledge in 1937. YCAW organizers took this approach because they thought that students would continue to respond to those same isolationist appeals which had helped give birth to the campus peace movement.

A national poll taken by Brown University's student newspaper only a few weeks before the 1938 student peace strike suggested that the YCAW might be right. This poll of 31,515 students on 101 campuses found more support for United States neutrality than for collective security. Though the poll was not entirely reliable because of some poor wording on its questionnaire, its data left no doubt that isolationism remained a considerable force on campus. YCAW organizers understood that this student support of United States neutrality was rooted in collegiate disillusionment with World War I. They appealed to this disillusionment in much of their literature, and accused the ASU of following the Wilsonian path towards a new world war—only now anti-fascist rhetoric had replaced Wilsonian slogans to excuse the drift toward war.[131]

Given these advantages, the YCAW's performance in the 1938 strike was surprisingly weak. The YCAW had hoped that its separate strike rallies on behalf of the Oxford Pledge would match or exceed the turn-out at the ASU-led rallies for collective security. But by its own estimates, the YCAW mobilized only about 25,000 students in its strike actions, a turnout rate far below the YCAW's goals.[132] Frustration with this response pervaded many of the field reports by YCAW organizers. A pacifist YCAW activist from Berkeley, for instance, wrote with obvious disappointment that the effort to turn the local ASU chapter and strike against collective security had been voted down by a two to one margin.[133] Reports from the East were also discouraging, as YCAW executive secretary Alvaine Hollister noted:

> Philly has called off the Rayburn Plaza meeting—afraid they don't have enough strength for a demonstration—probably only too true . . . CCNY 23rd lost out . . . to c.s.[collective security] . . . Smith College . . . is overwhelmingly c.s., with a few faint traces of pacifist-socialist influence. The A.S.U.-communist strike [at Brooklyn College night school] had about 800 people and the best location; we had from 150–300, at a poorer location.[134]

There were only a few bright spots for the YCAW. The new organization did carry the day at the University of Chicago's anti-war strike in 1938. The Chicago campus witnessed a YCAW sponsored peace conference, which, according to one ASU report "was almost monopolized by the isolationists." Some 2000 students turned out on this campus to hear Norman Thomas' anti-interventionist speech. But the YCAW proved unable to duplicate this success in outorganizing the ASU on most campuses, even in the midwestern heartland of isolationism. Student response to YCAW organizers was often tepid. The YCAW field organizer in Ohio reported feeling "discouraged" about the student response to the strike.[135] A YCAW activist from the University of Illinois confessed to YPSL leader Judah Drob that the situation on that campus was "very discouraging," and that in his strike work he was making "no headway" against the ASU "political machine . . . . Ken Born (ASU organizer) was down here and clinched the hold that collective security has upon the . . . non-affiliated people."[136]

The YCAW's strike efforts seemed particularly ineffective in comparison with that of the ASU. Student participation in the ASU-led peace activities of the day of the strike was, according to ASU estimates, almost as high as the previous year. Even allowing for some exaggerating in the ASU reports, which claimed that 750,000–900,000 students were mobilized, the turnout was impressive. Though in this strike the ASU, for the first time in its history, faced competition from a hostile national student organization, the ASU had risen to the occasion with remarkable ease. Where the YCAW field reports had been grim, most ASU reports tended to be upbeat, reflecting the fact—confirmed by the press nationally—that at most major campuses the majority of demonstrators had joined the protests and rallies led by collective security advocates.[137]

The strike results reassured the ASU's leaders that their organization's shift to collective security would not threaten its position as the leading student activist organization in the United States. Indeed, in New York City alone, during the strike and the week following it, the ASU picked up 825 new student members. This was roughly comparable to the total national membership of the YCAW. Such successful recruiting, along with the national ASU membership figures, which stood at about 15,000, suggests just how effective the ASU had been in besting its new rival.[138]

The ASU's success against the YCAW in the 1938 mobilization was due in part to several key organizational advantages which the ASU carried into the strike. The ASU was by far the more established of the two groups. Since its founding in 1935, the ASU had constructed the nation's largest network of student activists. This network included not only the ASU and YCL chapters, but allied groups such as campus YW and YMCAs. At the national level, moreover, the ASU still had at its head the student movement's most experienced leaders, including Molly Yard and Joseph Lash, who had helped build the ASU and orchestrated the organization's effective national strike efforts in the past. All of this helped give the ASU a significant jump on its YCAW rivals.

The effectiveness of the ASU in the 1938 strike was facilitated by the organization's increasingly friendly relations with campus administrators. As part of its Popular Front approach to student organizing, the ASU had sought to enlist every element of the campus, including college officials in its anti-fascist coalition. For the sake of anti-fascist unity, ASU campus leaders were willing to negotiate with and even accommodate administrators over the format of strike day events on campus. When confronted by college officials who opposed the anti-war strike, ASU organizers would settle for peace assemblies, in which campus administrators helped shape, and in some cases even dominated the programs of these meetings. Relations between campus officials and the ASU also improved because the ASU's new foreign policy line made these activists no longer seem radical or threatening. It was not ASUers, but their rivals who were now promoting the Oxford Pledge, which administrators had tended to oppose as unpatriotic. This made it much easier for the ASU to gain some of level of administration support for their organizing, which in turn made the peace events seem more inviting to mainstream students.[139]

Its new rhetoric regarding President Roosevelt also aided the ASU peace mobilization. ASU activists invoked FDR and his Quarantine speech in their organizing for collective security, just as they had done in the Vassar convention.[140] This would, of course, appeal to the many liberal students who admired the president. It also would make it difficult for campus administrators to attack ASU-led events. Few college deans or presidents would see any need to suppress student organizers whose professed goal was rallying the campuses behind the foreign policy of the president of the United States.

These advantages notwithstanding, the ASU's success in outorganizing the YCAW was an impressive achievement. Indeed, though the ASUers in the 1938 strike had invoked the name of the Franklin Roosevelt for their cause, they had in fact proven much more daring and effective in challenging isolationism than had the president himself. FDR's challenge to isolation in his Chicago speech had been a brief foray, followed immediately by an almost complete retreat in the face of an isolationist criticism. Roosevelt had continued to defer to isolationists on Capitol Hill throughout the spring, and he remained too timid to remove the embargo on the Spanish republic. Unlike the president, the ASU, after openly embracing collective security in December 1937, refused to defer any longer to isolationists. The ASU not only challenged isolationism and proponents of United States neutrality, but defeated them both at the Vassar convention and at campuses across the nation in the spring anti-war mobilization.[141]

The inroads that the ASU made against collegiate isolationism owed much to the evolving international situation. The ASU's relentless criticism of the flaws and shallowness of isolationist thought was persuasive because it came at a time when the German and Italian sponsored fascists were on the march in Spain and while Japan brutalized China. These tragic events offered compelling evidence for the ASU's warnings about the evils of fascism and the need for international sanctions against aggressor nations. The collective security actions that the ASU proposed to halt such aggression may not have seemed ideal, since they could enmesh the United States in dangerous international conflicts; but no one was offering any better solutions—certainly not the YCAW with its calls for neutrality, which would have had the United States close its eyes to the crisis that was breeding a new world war. Recognizing this, and hoping that collective security might be able to prevent world war, students increasingly moved with the ASU away from isolationism.[142]

Although the dominance of the ASU and collective security in the 1938 strike suggests that isolationist forces were in a state of disarray on campus, the strike should not be read as signalling the death of collegiate isolationism. The fact that the isolationist YCAW mobilized far fewer students than expected was probably due more to poor organization (which is to be expected in a new student group) than to the lack of an isolationist student constituency. Moreover, the 25,000 student mobilization achieved by the YCAW seems small only in comparison to the ASU's. Placed into the broader context of the student movement's history in the Depression decade, the YCAW mobilization seems more substantial. Since this was the YCAW's first national strike effort, its 1938 mobilization—instead of being compared with the ASU's organization of this its third strike—might more properly be compared with that other first strike, the NSL-SLID sponsored peace strike of 1934. The YCAW in 1938, like the NSL and SLID in 1934, had rallied some 25,000 students. Given the persistent isolationist sentiment reflected in the student polls, the YCAW had considerable reason to hope that, like the NSL and SLID earlier in the decade, with experience its effectiveness in student strike mobilizations would grow. ASU leaders such as Lash were clearly worried about the YCAW. Indeed, in the wake of the 1938 strike, Lash warned a West Coast ASU organizer that because of the YCAW and the appeal of isolationism on campus "the

ASU is only beginning to experience hardship . . . . [The YCAW's] strikes and all its activities lead us to believe it will flower as a dual organization to the ASU, shortly."[143]

Such anxieties on the part of Lash and his fellow Popular Fronters in the student movement led them to intensify their efforts to promote collective security and battle isolationism. In August 1938 these efforts culminated in the largest single youth meeting of the decade, the second World Youth Congress (WYC). The WYC, which held its first meeting in Geneva in 1936 under the sponsorship of the League of Nations Association, had been founded to promote peace and international cooperation among the youth of the world. A broad coalition of student and youth organizations, which included the ASU, sought to turn the 1938 World Youth Congress, held in New York City and Poughkeepsie, into a major event on behalf of collective security. The idea was that if the strike against war had demonstrated American student support for the Popular Front against fascism, the WYC would demonstrate that such support among youth extended internationally.[144]

From the vantage point of the promoters of collective security, the World Youth Congress was an immense success. More than 500 delegates from 53 nations attended the Congress. This attendance lent credibility to the Congress' claims to speak for the world's youth. The WYC also demonstrated that the student movement's eagerness to align liberals and radicals into an anti-fascist front was winning it influential new friends. New York Mayor Fiorello La Guardia agreed to speak at the opening session of the Youth Congress, which helped attract a crowd of some 22,000 in Randall's Island Municipal Stadium in New York City. The WYC attracted additional attention nationally with First Lady Eleanor Roosevelt's address during the WYC sessions in Poughkeepsie, and with the radio broadcast on the gathering which was carried by the NBC radio network.[145]

The WYC's young organizers skillfully used all of this attention to publicize their Popular Front position. This was evident from the opening session of the Congress, which featured speakers from countries threatened by fascist aggression, such as Jiri Kasparek of Czechoslovakia, pleading for anti-fascist unity and collective security. F.Y. Young, of the Chinese delegation, told the crowd on Randall's Island that "Chinese youth wants more than sympathy from America. We want concrete action to help us halt the invasion of our homeland, and bring peace to the Far East." This same message prevailed as the Congress completed its working sessions on the Vassar College campus, culminating in the WYC's adoption of a strong collective security statement, the Vassar Peace Pact. Through this pact WYC delegates pledged

> to bring pressure to bear . . . upon our respective authorities to take the
> necessary concerted action to prevent aggression and bring it to an end,
> to give effective assistance to the victims of . . . aggression and to refrain

from participating in any aggression whether in the form of essential war material or other financial assistance.[146]

The Vassar Pact infuriated the YCAW. In the wake of the Vassar meeting, YCAW delegate Judah Drob charged that the communist-led collective security bloc at the WYC had railroaded the Pact through and had refused to allow discussion of the document on the floor of the Congress. Drob's complaint was not unjustified. Indeed, in responding to this complaint, the final published report of the WYC offered the feeble excuse that "limited time made impossible the discussion of the Vassar Peace Pact in a meeting of the United States delegation." Here, as was often the case within the anti-war movement during the late 1930s, when the communists faced an important vote, they displayed far more interest in winning than in playing by the rules of democratic process. Nor was this the only process abuse associated with the WYC. Prior to the Congress, the communist-dominated New York Planning Committee of the WYC had tried to exclude the YCAW from the WYC's American delegation. It was not until the YCAW and other peace organizations loudly demanded that all wings of the anti-war movement be represented at Vassar that the Planning Committee relented and admitted the YCAW.[147]

Despite these disputes, however, the WYC's adoption of the Vassar Pact represented a clear defeat for YCAW and its isolationist allies. After the YCAW had been admitted to the WYC, the American delegation did have representatives of all wings of the student anti-war movement. And despite the dissent of the YCAW minority, the American delegation voted overwhelmingly to endorse the Vassar Pact. Although the decision-making process would, of course, have been more judicious had the Pact been fully debated, the delegates did know what they were voting for, and they agreed to endorse a Pact that was unambiguous in its endorsement of collective security. Here, as in the 1938 strike against war, the YCAW proved unable to assemble majority student support for United States neutrality. But the failure of the YCAW at Vassar extended beyond the American peace movement.

The YCAW's socialist leaders found that they could not even attract the support of their socialist comrades from Europe who were representatives at the World Youth Congress. A frustrated Drob noted that at the WYC's caucus of the Socialist Youth International "the United States Socialists were the only members of the International who opposed collective security." Worried by the fascist menace on their continent, the young European socialists at the WYC "insisted that Hitler could only be defeated by the military strength of the United States." Drob and his fellow American socialists responded by "asserting that the workers of Germany were simply waiting for Hitler's entry into a war for a revolutionary uprising," which would topple the Nazi regime. But the Europeans, better acquainted with the strength of the Nazi threat, dismissed this argument as unrealistic. They accused the American YPSLs of being "romantic leftists," too absorbed in the "distant ideal of socialism" to recognize that the most important task at hand was uniting all anti-fascist nations to stop Hitler.[148]

The outcome of the WYC added to the sense of progress and momentum of student activists promoting collective security on campus. For them the Vassar Pact served as a symbol—much as the Oxford Pledge had been for the very different peace policies of the early 1930s—that American youth were part of an international anti-fascist movement. The WYC was, however, only one of the many ways in which the student movement used its international contacts to combat isolationism. Through much of the late 1930s the ASU sponsored collegiate speaking tours by activists recently back from Spain and China, who gave first hand accounts of fascist aggression, and who urged an American role in halting this aggression. Such reports on the international crisis and pleas for help from abroad placed collegiate isolationists on the defensive.[149]

The movement's most effective advocates of international solidarity against fascism may have been those unable to make such campus tours: the recent college alumni in the Lincoln Battalion, whose letters from Spain were circulated by the ASU and the student press. "Nothing must be left undone in stopping fascism; there is no sacrifice we can refuse to make" wrote Ralph Neafus of the University of Michigan, before being captured by Franco's forces. Sam Levinger, an Ohio State ASUer, agreed. Shortly before his death on the Aragon front, Levinger wrote: "the war is long . . . . Still let us climb the grey hill and charge the guns, . . . towards . . . A free bright country."[150] The emotional power of such appeals helped open the campuses to the Popular Front, and spread an internationalism that was more than rhetorical. They gave ASUers and many of their classmates a sense that fascism's triumphs abroad threatened freedom everywhere, including the United States. This internationalist sensibility left ASUers determined to battle isolationism no matter what the political risks— in stark contrast to the president himself; it enabled ASUers to march aggressively into the collegiate centers of isolationism and outorganize their isolationist rivals in the peace mobilizations of 1938.[151]

Internationalism of a more abstract, but no less influential, sort also steeled the ASU's resolve to battle isolationism. The ASU's communist leadership regarded the U.S.S.R. as a leftist utopia. They thought it their obligation as part of the international communist movement to defend the Soviet Union. This rigid loyalty left communist students determined to defy the strong winds of collegiate isolationism for the sake of collective security. They believed that collective security was critical for the protection of the Soviet Union because it would unite the world against the U.S.S.R.'s dangerous fascist enemies.[152]

The communists' pivotal role in challenging collegiate isolationism would give that challenge an ironic quality. Communists led the student body away from its dogmatically critical view of United States foreign policy, even though they previously had been among the most dogmatic crit-

ics of all. The movement had been born with communists, along with
socialists and pacifists, championing a litany of simplistic "lessons" from
the First World War: that all of United States foreign policy is inherently
imperialistic, as is any war involving capitalist states; that since the First
World War had been a bloody clash over imperialist spoils, so would any
new world war, and as such the public had no interest in fighting a war
between virtually indistinguishable rivals. Bound by such dogmas, the student movement in the early 1930s had been been lost in the world of
1917, endorsing neutrality legislation designed to halt a Woodrow Wilson,
and acting as if Wilsonianism rather than fascism posed the greatest threat
to peace. But in the mid-1930s, communist students rebelled against these
anachronistic views because the U.S.S.R. and the Popular Front had shown
them the way toward a more realistic appraisal of the fascist threat.

Communist ASUers would carry this realism to the student movement, as they pressed students to allow the crisis of the present—the tragic
events in Germany, Italy, Spain, China, and Japan—rather than the dogmas of the past to guide their outlook on United States foreign policy.
The student strike of 1938, with its emphasis on collective security, suggested that the ASU had been surprisingly successful in this effort, re-
placing dogmatism with political realism, and prodding students to see
that because of fascist aggression the international crisis of their own era
was different and more ominous than the crisis that had led to the First
World War. But this ASU realism would prove transient. The same communist ASUers who had freed much of the student movement of its isolationist dogma were afflicted by an equally dogmatic faith in Stalin and
his foreign policies—a faith which in the fall of 1939 would lead to the
destruction of the Popular Front on campus.

Chapter 7

Beyond the New Deal?
Egalitarian Dreams and
Communist Schemes

We are tired of waiting, Mrs. Roosevelt.

> Louis Burnham, an African American student leader in the
> ASU, responding to the First Lady's suggestion that young
> activists show some "patience" on the issue of racial equality.
> *Student Advocate* (March 1936), 16.

The student movement came to President Roosevelt's doorstep on February 20, 1937, when some 3000 young demonstrators marched on the White House. The protesters, representing student and youth organizations from across the nation, sought to dramatize the economic hardships of youth in Depression America. Marching down Pennsylvania Avenue, they waved banners and chanted their demands. "Pass the American Youth Act—We want jobs;" "Scholarships not Battleships;" "Homes not barracks." One group dressed in prison garb, carried a sign "We never had jobs." Others costumed as pilgrims, miners, and farmers made the same point. The California delegation rode in on a covered wagon bearing the battered sign "Go East Young Man." To the tune of Yankee Doodle, the protesters—carrying signs that identified their college, school, religious group, or trade union affiliation—sang "American youth is on the march for jobs and education." This was, as the *Washington Post* observed "a line of marchers such as Washington has never seen before."[1]

This march on the White House was part of a three day Youth Pilgrimage for Jobs and Education. The protesters did more than parade down Pennsylvania Avenue; they also lobbied Congress on behalf of greater federal assistance to the millions of young Americans hurt by the Great Depression. The pilgrimage attested that even though peace was the most popular cause on campus, the student movement of the 1930s was not merely an anti-war crusade. It was also a movement for social justice, whose leaders cared so much about the plight of low-income youth that they chose to make this, rather than war, the focus of the movement's first sizable national march on Washington.[2]

The pilgrimage symbolized the student movement leadership's commitment to building a more egalitarian America. The movement's leaders envisioned a society where education would be a right rather than a privilege; they thought Washington should ensure that no one would be—as millions of Depression era youth had already been—forced to drop out of school because of insufficient funds. The student movement sought to make America a nation free of unemployment, poverty, and racism. These were natural concerns for a movement led by leftists and born amidst the worst economic depression in American history.[3]

In pursuit of this egalitarian vision, the student movement's leaders had worked to broaden the base of their movement. These young leftists realized that the task of changing America and bringing educational and economic opportunity to their generation required more political muscle than could be found on the campuses alone. This was, after all, a time when inadequate financial and educational resources kept the vast majority of young Americans (almost 90 percent of the college age population) out of college. If the student movement was to have real credibility as a voice of Depression era youth, it would have to expand its constituency well beyond the small college elite. With this goal in mind, student activists in the mid-1930s began working to build a unified youth movement, which could link students and non-students in the quest for expanded federal aid to youth and egalitarian social change. The organization through which this was attempted was the same one which sponsored the Youth Pilgrimage for Jobs and Education: the American Youth Congress.[4]

Founded in 1934, the American Youth Congress (AYC) soon evolved into the most influential leftist-led youth group in Depression America. More than any other organization, the Youth Congress broke down the barriers between the college elite and non-student youth. The Youth Congress served as an advocate for millions of underprivileged young Americans—blue collar workers, blacks, the unemployed, and needy students—who traditionally had been ignored by the political process. Organized as a youth federation and lobby, the AYC assembled an amazingly broad group of affiliates, which included not only students, but labor, civil rights, religious, community and fraternal organizations. Among the Youth Congress' members were the National Student Federation, the YWCA, the National Intercollegiate Christian Council, the National Council of Methodist Youth, the Youth Committee Against War, the Young People's Socialist League, the Young Communist League, the Southern Negro Youth Congress, the Chinese Student League, Young Judea, the American Student Union, the Southern Tenant Farmers Union, youth divisions of the American Jewish Congress, the United Auto Workers, the United Electrical, Radio and Machine Workers, locals of the National Association for the Advancement of Colored People and many others. At its height in the late 1930s, the Youth Congress included dozens of national organizations and scores of local groups, claiming to represent 4.5 million American youths.[5]

If the number of affiliated organizations was impressive, so was the diversity of the delegates themselves, who participated in the national meetings of the Youth Congress. Thousands of delegates from different races, social classes, and occupations attended these meetings. Youths who participated in these gatherings for the first time often were moved by the experience. Most had never before attended meetings which so broadly cut across class, regional, and racial lines; they found it inspiring to meet fellow youths from such different backgrounds and to unite with them on behalf of a common political agenda. After returning from one such Youth Congress meeting in Washington, for example, Elliot Maraniss, editor of the University of Michigan student newspaper, wrote that the young activists at this gathering

> knew what problems were facing them . . . knew what they wanted and . . . knew how to get it. There were young Negro girls from the deep South who told us a tale of unbelievable misery and poverty; the Tom Joads and Rosasharons of the Grapes of Wrath Country who related the epic of the Oakies; the young men who will reap the corn on the Iowa plains; young auto workers, electricians, seamen and miners who told us the story of youth's part in the growth of trade unionism; young students expertly trained for some profession with no hope of employment; and there were the representatives of the four million of us who are without jobs; the kids who spent the . . . decade on box cars and highways . . . looking for work, who have known the hunger and frustration of enforced idleness. These young people were marching arm-in-arm to the future organized and determined to solve their problems, and inspired with the courage that comes with youthfulness, with strength and with a program that is based upon truth, fact and real need.[6]

By assembling this broad coalition of young Americans, the Youth Congress from 1934–1937 hoped to push the federal government beyond the New Deal. The Youth Congress advocated more sweeping and generous social legislation than had yet been provided by the Roosevelt administration. At the heart of this effort to surpass the New Deal was the Youth Congress' own aid package for youth, the American Youth Act (AYA). The AYA would have gone much further than the New Deal in providing federal aid to the young. It was in part to promote this legislation that the Youth Congress organized the 1937 Pilgrimage for Jobs and Education. During the pilgrimage, Youth Congress leaders brought their advocacy of this bill directly to President Roosevelt, presenting him with pro-AYA petitions, signed by close to a million Americans.[7]

The campaign for the American Youth Act was the culmination of an old dream on the part of student activists. Ever since the NSL's birth in 1931, leftist students had urged the government to assist youths who were unable to pay their way through school. Under FDR, the federal government finally became involved in rendering such assistance through the Federal Emergency Relief Administration (FERA) in 1934 and the National Youth Administration (NYA) in 1935. These New Deal agencies annually provided $15 a month jobs to some 110,000 undergraduates and graduate students—aiding about 12 percent of the students in American higher educational institutions. The NYA also gave jobs to over 200,000 secondary school students (at a maximum of $6 per month) and to about the same number of non-students.[8] Although applauding this new federal assistance as a welcome break from the do-nothing policy of the Hoover administration, the Youth Congress was quick to point out the NYA's shortcomings. The Youth Congress deemed the NYA far too limited and underfunded to provide a realistic solution to the economic problems confronting young Americans.[9]

Citing NYA director Aubrey Williams' own statistics, Youth Congress leaders pointed out that of the five to eight million unemployed and needy youths (between the ages of 16 and 25), only a half million would receive aid from the NYA. Youth Congress activists from many different campuses complained that demand for student NYA jobs far exceeded the supply; they charged that the more needy the student body, the more inadequate was the NYA's assistance because the aid program was limited to 12 percent of the total student population, irrespective of how much more needy one campus might be over another. Thus at North Dakota Agricultural College, where 661 out of a total—and hard hit—male student population of 991 applied for aid, only 154 were given jobs. At Howard University, a black institution whose students were also heavily burdened by the economic crisis, 1400 NYA applications were submitted, out of a student body of 1700, and only 153 students received NYA jobs.[10]

The Youth Congress also complained of the NYA's inadequate attention to youths who were not in college. Youth Congress activist Constance Dimock of Vassar College pointed out that in the NYA "32 million out of 50 million dollars was alloted for student relief, [which] indicates that the NYA has dealt more with the needs of students than with young workers." This seemed particularly inequitable, since the majority of the nation's unemployed and needy youths were non-students. The Youth Congress stressed the inadequacy of the six dollars monthly NYA wage allocated for secondary school students, since this amounted to only a minimal income supplement rather than a living wage.[11]

Youth Congress leaders took the NYA to task for its "complete lack of democratic administration." They charged that too little was being done to see that the NYA did not discriminate against blacks. Youth Congress activists were also disturbed that although the NYA's mission was to serve students and other low-income youth, these groups were excluded from the NYA's decision-making process. They complained that too many businessmen sat on the NYA's national advisory board, and that most of the local administrative boards "included no representative of youth or its natural ally organized labor." This was, in the Youth Congress' view, undesirable because it meant that "any appreciation which these members of the . . . [NYA administrative] committees have of the want, hunger and despair facing contemporary youth have been derived from theoretical rather than practical sources."[12]

Although many of its criticisms of the NYA were astute, the Youth Congress quickly grew dissatisfied with playing the role of critic. Rather than merely denouncing the flaws in the New Deal youth program, the Youth Congress in 1935 formulated the American Youth Act as an alternative to that program. Here the Youth Congress took its criticisms of the NYA and transformed them into a comprehensive legislative proposal. The Youth Congress then convinced Farm-Laborite Senator Elmer Benson of Minnesota and his counterpart in the House, Thomas Amlie of Wisconsin, to sponsor the bill.[13]

The American Youth Act was far more ambitious than the NYA; it mandated federal aid to *all* needy Americans between the ages of 16 and 25. Through massive public works projects, the American Youth Act would have provided federal employment to millions of jobless young Americans, rather than the few hundred thousand supported annually by the NYA. Where limited funds had led the NYA to turn down more job applicants than it accepted, the Youth Act would have granted aid to all youths who applied for it. Under the Youth Act the monthly student wage level would rise substantially—paying high school students $15 instead of the $6 NYA wage and college students $25 instead of the $15 NYA wage. The Youth Act provided for a more democratic means of administering aid than had the NYA; it would have established an advisory board in which representatives of youth organizations, labor unions, social service, and educational institutions supervised the program. The language of the Youth Act barred racial discrimination in the distribution of student aid. Funding for this aid program would have been structured in a progressive fashion, drawing upon corporate and inheritance taxes.[14]

The American Youth Act represented so radical an expansion of federal aid to youth that it stood little chance on Capitol Hill. Where the NYA's budget had been $50 million in 1935, the Youth Act would have required an allocation of at least $3.5 billion. Critics of the Youth Act charged that its final cost would approach $15 billion. Such criticism prevented the bill from getting out of committee in 1936 or any of the three other times that the legislation was re-introduced between 1937 and 1940. Nonetheless, the campaign that the Youth Congress waged on behalf of this legislation did much to publicize both the acute economic distress endured by millions of youths in Depression American and the inability of the NYA to relieve much of that distress. This agitation convinced the Senate Committee on Education and Labor to conduct hearings on the Youth Act. These hearings attracted national press attention, as the students produced witnesses from youth organizations, college faculties, social welfare and government agencies documenting the need for expansion of federal aid to youth.[15]

The campaign for the American Youth Act attracted attention not only in the press and on Capitol Hill, but also in the White House. Through this campaign, Youth Congress leaders established a relationship with influential New Dealers, including Eleanor Roosevelt. Through much of the second half of the Depression decade, the First Lady served as the key liaison between the Roosevelt administration and the student movement. Mrs. Roosevelt showed great interest in the problems of youth, an interest which was primarily humanitarian. Mrs. Roosevelt worried about the Depression's impact on the younger generation, fearing that joblessness would breed despair. "I have moments of real terror," she explained in spring 1934, "when I think we may be losing this generation. We have got to bring these young people into the active life of the community and make them feel that they are necessary."[16] The First Lady looked to the federal government to provide the job programs which could give hope and material aid to the young. Her vision was that of a younger generation rescued from poverty, and therefore able to lend its renewed energy and sense of idealism to the struggle for social reform—in alliance with the New Deal.[17]

Knowing of the First Lady's interest in youth problems, Youth Congress leaders sought and obtained a meeting with her to discuss the American Youth Act in January 1936. This meeting proved a stormy affair. The First Lady, accompanied by NYA director Aubrey Williams, told the Youth Congress' national council that she could not endorse the Youth Act, which she thought too expensive to stand any real chance of being enacted by Congress. The Youth Congress leaders confronted the First Lady with tough criticism of the NYA, implying that it had failed to "relieve the distress of from five to eight million unemployed youth." These young activists then spent a half-hour grilling the First Lady on the New Deal's other shortcomings.[18]

The tension at the meeting reflected the large gap between Mrs. Roosevelt's liberalism and the Youth Congress leaders' radicalism. On such key issues as the right of labor to organize, unemployment, and the fiscal crisis of educational institutions, Mrs. Roosevelt's young critics wanted quicker and more decisive federal intervention than she was willing to sanction. Joseph Lash, who was at this meeting, recalled being unimpressed with the First Lady's responses to their criticisms of the New Deal. The young radical found Mrs. Roosevelt a well intentioned but naive liberal "utterly lacking in knowledge of social forces," who "thinks she can reform capitalists . . . by inviting them to the White House for dinner and a good talking to."[19]

Despite her sharp policy differences with the Youth Congress leaders and the friction at this meeting, Mrs. Roosevelt reached out to them. She tried to defuse their hostility to the New Deal by acknowledging the NYA's shortcomings and conceding that more should be done to help youth. And she stressed the need for unity among people working to change America, advising that "it is wrong to be quite as divided as some of us are getting." Mrs. Roosevelt then invited the Youth Congress leaders to tea at the White House, assuring them that she understood their impatience at the pace of reform, since changes did seem to "take forever." "I used to be awfully impatient when I was your age."[20]

Mrs. Roosevelt's tolerance of dissent and her ongoing interest in the youth issue ensured that this first meeting would be the start of a long term relationship with the Youth Congress. She not only kept her lines of communication open to the Youth Congress leaders, but assisted them in gaining access to other prominent New Dealers. Mrs. Roosevelt was responsible for setting up the meeting between Youth Congress leaders and the president during the 1937 pilgrimage. At this meeting the president took the same position on the Youth Act that the First Lady had, refusing to endorse it on the grounds that it was too expensive. But here the president also made some sympathetic statements, telling the Youth Congress leaders that they "were on the right track in seeking federal aid for the nation's hard hit young population." President Roosevelt assured them "I am glad of what you are doing," and pledged to try to expand the NYA.[21]

President Roosevelt was not merely being polite in praising the youth delegation. The president was facing considerable Republican pressure to cut the NYA, and he and his administration perceived that the Youth Congress' campaign for greater federal aid could help offset this pressure. This same impulse toward converting the Youth Congress and the student movement into allies of the New Deal helped prod NYA Director Aubrey Williams to begin supporting and befriending the movement's national leadership. Indeed, on the day of the 1937 youth march on the White House, Williams congratulated the Youth Congress for helping to turn public opinion against cuts in federal aid to students. Williams told the protesters, "I know that your work has yielded some good results and will yield more. And I am in a good position to know whether it yields anything or whether it doesn't."[22]

This attention and praise from the president and NYA director suggested that the student movement was beginning to have some real impact in Washington. That impact was of course neither as dramatic nor complete as movement activists might have hoped, since the movement failed to enact its youth aid package. With the voting age 21, it was hardly surprising that a youth organization such as the AYC would lack the electoral power to win the Youth Act battle and push the New Deal leftward. Nonetheless, the Youth Congress' interaction with high ranking New Dealers attested that the movement was obtaining recognition as the leading advocate of youth's economic and political interests. Through the Youth

Congress, the student movement was helping to define youth's economic plight as a national issue and building a constituency for expanded federal aid to youth. These were considerable achievements for young activists simultaneously engaged in organizing a national student movement against war. If the national campus strikes showed America that students cared about peace, then the marches, hearings, and lobbying efforts of the Youth Congress in Washington showed that they also cared about educational and economic opportunity—and would fight to prevent the Depression from closing off those opportunities to youth.

II

While the Youth Congress brought the student movement's political agenda to Washington, student activists across the nation were engaged in similar efforts on their own campuses. Just as the Youth Congress from 1934–1937 sought to push the New Deal leftward, student activists first in the NSL, SLID and then in the ASU worked to push their classmates in this same direction. The student movement challenged the elitism, materialism, and conformity bred by traditional collegiate culture. Movement activists sought to convince the student body that its welfare and that of society would best be served by struggling to make both the campuses and the nation more egalitarian. They argued that the government could be pressed to ensure that the educational and economic opportunities of youth were not extinguished by the Depression only if students aligned themselves with other dispossessed groups—particularly blue-collar workers and their burgeoning labor movement.

Hoping to bring about an alliance between the student movement and the labor movement, campus activists made collegiate class prejudice one of their key targets. Student activists understood that college campuses had traditionally fed middle-class aspirations for upward mobility. These were institutions which readied students for competition in the corporate marketplace and left students placing a high value on individual wealth.[23] The flip side of this culture of aspiration had been a disdain for those without wealth, the working class. The nation's predominantly middle-class campuses had been so unfriendly toward workers and their unions that during many industrial disputes, college students had served as strikebreakers. In their struggle for a more egalitarian campus world, student activists in the 1930s sought to end such antagonism toward workers. This pro-labor orientation had been evident ever since the earliest days of the NSL, when students traveled down to Kentucky in 1932 to aid the striking coal miners; it had also been embodied in the Youth Congress, which united students and young trade unionists on behalf of federal job programs for youth. Throughout the mid-1930s, the student movement worked to perpetuate this type of unity. Thanks to the student movement, the sight of undergraduate delegations marching on the picket lines of organized labor would become common in many communities.[24]

The student movement's pro-labor actions were motivated in part by ideological considerations. As leftists, student movement leaders saw the working class as the primary agent of social change. "One of the basic tenets of the student movement was that it wasn't a movement in isolation from the rest of society" recalled NSL alumnus George Watt. "If anything, it was really auxiliary to what was going on outside, particularly in the working class and labor movement . . . [which we saw as] the moving force of history."[25] Thus campus radicals thought it critical that they awaken the student body to the historic class struggle beyond the college gates and align the campus with labor's battle to democratize American economic life.

The sense that labor represented the engine of egalitarian change grew especially strong with the upsurge of labor militancy during the mid-1930s, when general strikes and the CIO's organizing drive electrified the country. Moreover, the student Left thought that the publicity generated by its pro-labor actions could provide immediate assistance to unions and help attract much needed positive publicity to their strikes. Bringing students on to picket lines was also seen as a form of practical education which could help radicalize students, by exposing them to the poor conditions workers faced and the repression they confronted when they tried to protest those conditions.[26]

A strong humanitarian and personal element contributed to the movement's pro-labor work. Students recognized that working-class Americans suffered far more because of the Depression than had college graduates. There was a strong desire to ease the distress of the impoverished. Sometimes mixed in with this general humanitarian impulse to help labor were feelings of guilt, particularly among more affluent students at the elite private colleges—who thought it unjust that they lived in luxury while millions suffered. The activists "who came from wealthy backgrounds," explained James Wechsler, did have a tendency to be "excessively guilt ridden" because of "the ironies of their condition . . . , growing up [prosperous] in the Depression."[27] Guilt figured prominently, for example, in *Question Before the House,* a play about student-worker cooperation, co-authored by a Vassar undergraduate in 1935. This play, which was performed at Hallie Flanagan's Experimental Theatre at Vassar, glorified striking workers and the students who marched with them on picket lines protesting corporate greed. *Question Before the House* urged Vassar students to aid labor on the grounds that their own exclusive

> college is amazingly luxurious—luxury made possible by the unnecessarily low wages of the masses of people . . . . This college is . . . supported . . . by . . . corporations, many of which are guilty of very questionable labor practices . . . We have a definite responsibility to act in

this case. Why this college is . . . supported by profits squeezed out of . . . workers.[28]

Such guilt feelings may help explain why student activists on such relatively affluent campuses as Yale, Dartmouth, Harvard, Vassar, and Bryn Mawr conducted some of the student movement's more impressive pro-labor campaigns.

It was not only students from the more affluent campuses, however, who joined in labor protests. New York City's free municipal colleges were also centers of pro-labor activism. Many students in these colleges were themselves from working-class families with trade union backgrounds, who had learned to revere organized labor before they ever reached college. Recalling his experience, which was typical of many other City College radicals, literary critic Irving Howe explained how his parents' involvement in the garment workers' strike of 1933 had left him an avid supporter of the labor movement.

> Though they had never before shown any class militancy, my folks joined the picket lines . . . . Once the strike was won, life became easier: we could now have meat more often, my parents managed to squirrel away a few dollars in a savings account, and once my birthday came around my mother bought me a few "grownup" shirts. . . . The garment unions . . . [helped] ease . . . hardships . . . [and gave us] a fragment of dignity. In later years, whenever I heard intellectuals of the Right or Left attack unionism, I would be seized by an uncontrollable rage that then gave way to frustration: how to explain . . . what the strike of 1933 had meant, how to find words to tell of the small comforts the union had brought, the meat on the table and "grownup" shirts?[29]

Students in New York's municipal colleges who shared Howe's pro-labor perspective mounted the largest college labor support actions of the mid-1930s. Their involvement in the 1935 retail workers strike at Orbach's, one of Manhattan's more famous department stores, led to the largest mass arrest of students on a labor picket line. Police arrested more than 100 Hunter, City, and Brooklyn College students, while 10,000 spectators cheered these young picketers during the strike. The second largest arrest of students on a labor picket also occurred in the City system in 1935, when 39 Brooklyn College students were booked for their participation in a strike by food service workers.[30]

Employers in the neighborhoods of these city colleges found that if they became involved in labor disputes, they had to worry almost as much about large, well organized student pro-labor protests as they did about the striking unions. During a strike at Sorrell's, a popular cafeteria near Brooklyn College, in 1934, there were more students than workers on the picket lines. Describing this strike, the Brooklyn College newspaper reported that

At lunch hour, students gathered on the outside of the restaurant, forming long semi-circular lines, and booed all the students who entered the cafeteria. So long were the groups aligned in front of the food establishment that reserves from the 84th precinct were called and more than 10 patrolmen . . . [arrived]. Later three mounted policemen were called to supplement those dispersing the throngs of students.[31]

These protests and an increasingly effective student boycott of the cafeteria forced management to capitulate—raising wages and recognizing the union.

A similar result was obtained in the more turbulent student protests during a cafeteria strike in the CCNY campus neighborhood in 1935. Here the owner of a cafeteria on Broadway, incensed over student support of his striking workers, had the police arrest 27 CCNY undergraduates in a week of picketing. The students organized a boycott of the cafeteria, forcing management to settle with the union. The disorderly conduct charges against the students were soon dropped, with the judge admonishing them to "spend more time in school and let the strikers take care of their own affairs"—advice which went unheeded as CCNY students continued their labor support work.[32]

As with the Harlan delegation of 1932, some of the pro-labor campaigns were organized jointly by students from a number of different campuses. In a Hartford munitions strike in 1935, small groups of delegates came from colleges all over the Northeast to help the picketers. The colleges represented in this picket included Amherst, Barnard, Connecticut State College, Mount Holyoke, Smith, Trinity, Vassar, and Wesleyan.[33] The students hoped that by organizing such a broad intercollegiate group, they would convey the impression that there was great public support for the strikers, and thus put added pressure on management. This same approach was used by activists from Dartmouth, Bennington, Skidmore, Hunter, and the University of Vermont, who in 1936 jointly conducted a public hearing on the poor working conditions which had led to a strike by Vermont quarry workers.[34]

The issue of freedom of speech and assembly often became linked with pro-labor campaigns, after students observed police and management infringements on the constitutional rights of picketers. Protests against one such infringement caused the arrest of 21 Berkeley student activists in 1936, who had joined striking warehouse workers on the picket line in violation of Berkeley's anti-picketing ordinance—which made it unlawful "for persons to attempt to influence any person not to purchase goods at any business." Even after the strike was settled, the students continued their campaign against the ordinance, protesting directly to the Berkeley City Council.[35]

The student movement sought to end all collegiate involvement in strikebreaking activity. At the University of Southern California, for instance, NSL organizers heard rumors in 1934 that USC's employment office was recruiting strikebreakers for the longshoremen's strike. This elicited a quick response from campus NSL activists, including Celeste Strack, who

> called up to find out about this. And sure enough they were enlisting people to go down to the waterfront. And they had specifically gone after the football players from the fraternity houses. So we got out and visited the fraternity houses. And we also distributed a leaflet on campus about it. We made it very well known on campus and they stopped it. They actually stopped it. And we sent a delegation down to the waterfront to do some picketing with the longshoremen. That was our first direct connection with the labor movement from SC, and it was a very natural one because of the effort that was being made to send the scabs down.[36]

As part of such campaigns against strikebreaking, student organizers tried to educate their classmates on the evils of scabbing. When a few Columbia students were found strikebreaking in a 1936 building trades strike, they were admonished that scabs

> debase the living standards of American workmen . . . . The students have seized a chance to make money that in all likelihood they needed badly. It did not occur to them, perhaps, that their need is petty compared to that of the men who have been trying to raise families on $19 and less for a sixty hour week.[37]

Where education failed, movement activists tried to shame students out of strikebreaking, as at Berkeley, where the NSL newspaper included a scab list, naming all those collegians who served as strikebreakers.[38]

The student movement sought to uncover and halt any official university involvement in anti-labor work. A major controversy erupted over this issue at Berkeley in 1936, where student activists discovered that the campus ROTC class gave cadets an exam designed to groom them for an anti-labor military campaign. The exam question asked the cadets to contemplate a hypothetical waterfront strike in San Francisco, which resulted in a Bay Area general strike and the mobilization of the National Guard and ROTC to maintain order. In this strike, where a "considerable part of the population is sympathetic towards the strikers," the cadets were asked how the ROTC troops, equipped with tear gas and gas masks, could best be deployed to prevent pro-labor gangs from invading the campus and damaging University property. Once the students made public the use of this exam question, outraged local labor leaders complained, forcing the University to pledge not to allow such biased anti-labor materials to be used in the ROTC.[39]

Students aided labor in union recruitment efforts. Harvard radicals organized a Labor Committee which was in constant contact with the CIO; it provided student organizers who went into Boston's department stores to recruit members for the retail workers union. Harvard activists also established a special squad, consisting of 30 students, which in 1936 and 1937 worked with the United Rubber Workers of America in their attempts to organize in the New England region. Every day two members of this squad would travel with union organizers and speak to workers, encouraging them to join the union. University of Chicago students played a similar role in the CIO organizing drive in the packinghouses, as did Virginia Union University's students in the CIO's campaign in the tobacco industry.[40]

In addition to this pro-labor agitation, students participated in labor education and relief work. The student movement organized fundraising events and food drives for striking workers, and sent volunteers to the coal region of West Virginia, who assisted with Christmas parties and other events designed to brighten up the lives of the impoverished workers and their families. Students in the YWCA organized similar relief work and set up programs in which students could be educated to workers' problems both through factory visits and contact with young workers who belonged to the Y's industrial branches. Students, particularly from the women's colleges, served as volunteers in the labor schools at Bryn Mawr and Vineyard Shore, which provided workers with free educational opportunities.[41]

Sometimes unions found the support of students critical to the success of their local organizing drives. Stella Nowicki, a CIO packinghouse organizer in the Chicago stockyards recalled that at a crucial time in her local's history, University of Chicago student activists provided the union with much needed assistance

> in editing and getting funds. They would help us in writing material for leaflets and by distributing materials in the factory gates. They would get up real early and be there at 6:00 or 6:30 in the morning. (We would start work at 7:00.) They did this because we could not do so, for if we were caught giving out leaflets we would be fired.[42]

Labor leaders and publications acknowledged this pro-union work and welcomed the student movement as a valuable ally. In San Francisco, the maritime workers' union applauded student activists for opposing the use of their campuses as recruiting grounds for strikebreakers. The union also praised the students for bringing labor representatives to speak to campus audiences, from which they had been barred in the past. At the national level, CIO leader John L. Lewis in 1937 credited the student movement with helping to swing public opinion on to the side of organized labor:

> All of those who are associated with the United Mine Workers and the C.I.O., or, in other words, with the current movement for establishing industrial freedom and democracy in our mass-production industries

are fully conscious of the important bearing of the student movement upon our success.

Lewis maintained that the CIO, in attempting to bring a democratic revolution to American industry, realized that "no revolution in the history of the world has been successful unless it was supported from above," and that the student movement had been a "constant" source of such support.[43]

The student movement's most important contribution to organized labor, however, may not have been its campaigns, but rather its alumni. Former student activists became prominent in all levels of the labor movement, from national leaders such as Walter and Victor Reuther of the United Auto Workers to the hundreds of local union organizers—many of whom received their political baptism and their introduction to the labor movement through their work in the student movement. It was a relatively short and easy step for campus activists to move from their pro-labor work as students to careers as union organizers. The reverence for labor, which the student movement preached—and which was particularly strong among communist and socialist students, ideologically wedded to the ideal of a heroic proletariat—made a career in the labor movement seem very attractive. To join the labor movement meant serving on the front lines of the struggle for social change. This attraction proved so strong that, as former NSL activist George Watt recalled, it led some students to drop out of college, in order to work as union organizers:

> Some of the students who became young Communists left the student movement very early and went into the shops . . . . Once you became a Communist the highest status you could achieve was to become a factory worker. So they went into the factories. And some of them played a very important role in the early formation of the CIO. They went into factories; they went into the South; they went other places. Students did play that kind of role, but not as students; they became workers and tried to integrate themselves completely and submerge themselves into the working class.[44]

In entering the labor movement these alumni brought with them their college training, political experience, and idealism; they contributed to the labor upsurge which made the second half of the depression decade one of the great eras of union organizing in American history.

III

The student movement's attempt to build collegiate solidarity with labor extended to workers on campus as well as off. Among the key beneficiaries of these efforts were student workers. The movement championed the cause of low-income students not only with the Youth Act in Washington, but with a variety of organizing efforts at the local level. Promoting the idea that poverty was the product of the flawed economy rather than the fault of the individual, the student movement pressed the student body to stop ignoring the poor in its midst. Movement organizers and publications stressed that those who worked their way through college should not be snubbed because of their poverty, but admired because of their pursuit of knowledge and opportunity. The movement also encouraged working students to defend their interests, and sought to prod state and student governments to assist them.

Through regional and state Youth Congresses, students pushed for legislatures to deal with the problems of low-income students and unemployed youth. In Washington state, such agitation secured a boost in youth's share of the state welfare funds. Massachusetts student activists convinced the state legislature to conduct a survey of the economic problems of youth. In 1937 student organizers in California brought to Sacramento a youth aid package similar to the legislation being championed by the Youth Congress in Washington, D.C. This California Youth Act would have provided jobs for all needy college students. Advocates of this bill, like their counterparts in Washington, stressed that the New Deal had not gone far enough in assisting the young. Thus in calling on students to fight for the their state government to pick up where the New Deal had left off, these activists asked, "How many of us applied for NYA aid and didn't get it? How many of us are barely able to stay in school from week to week . . . . We need the California Youth Act."[45]

In addition to trying to find new sources of student aid, the movement pressed for more efficient and democratic administration of existing aid programs. The ASU was active in organizing student unions among NYA workers. At the Universities of North Carolina and Minnesota, these unions negotiated with NYA officials for increased job allotments and adapting jobs to the applicants' interests. The University of Chicago NSL organized a telephone barrage on the NYA office to complain about late paychecks, convincing NYA officials to place the University's payroll in the "rush order category." These protesters in Chicago also advocated a student majority on a University NYA Board, which they wanted to assume full responsibility for administering the campus aid program. After similar agitation at the University of Pennsylvania, the City College of New York, and Brooklyn College, NYA administrators allowed elected student NYA boards to share in administration of the program, and they agreed to negotiate with elected grievance committees.[46]

Organization of student employees was not confined to NYA workers. Student activists attempted to unionize undergraduates employed in the private sector, where many worked in restaurants, retail shops, and boarding houses in the campus area, and also served as "hashers"—food service workers in fraternities and sororities, who received meals for their labor. Such employees were ripe for exploitation because communities with large student populations had a ready supply of surplus labor, and many students were desperate for work during much of the Depression decade. Student unions also worked against the University itself when it appeared guilty of exploitative labor conditions, as at the University of Texas, where the Working Students Federation met with the dean to complain about overwork and other poor campus working conditions.[47]

Because unemployment was such a major problem on campuses, some student unions took almost as much interest in obtaining work for the unemployed as they did in improving conditions for those fortunate enough to have jobs. This unemployment problem was, for example, the theme of a "Keep the Student in School Week," sponsored by the University of Kansas' Self-Supporting Student Association in 1933. The Association appealed to the community, merchants, and professors to give work—even odd jobs—to as many unemployed students as possible.[48]

Prodded by the ASU, student governments became involved in protecting working students. One of the most creative and successful of these student government efforts on behalf of working students occurred at UC Berkeley. In 1936, the Welfare Council of the Associated Students of the University of California (the ASUC, Berkeley's student government) undertook an investigation of the working conditions of students employed in the campus area. The investigation revealed that these employees were often paid below prevailing wage standards and had to labor under "undesirable working conditions." The Council proposed, and the ASUC within a year established, a permanent Labor Board, whose purpose was the "maintenance of fair student working standards and conditions."[49]

The primary mechanism which the Board used to assist Berkeley student workers was the Fair Bear (the bear being the school symbol) program. The Labor Board established a set of minimum wage and working conditions, which it named Fair Bear Standards; it then notified local employers of these standards. Employers who complied with these standards received Fair Bear stickers from the ASUC. Those employers alleged to be violating the standards were denied a sticker and investigated; if they were found to be violating the standards they were placed on a list to be boycotted by the Berkeley student body—which was asked not to patronize stores and restaurants unless they had Fair Bear stickers in their windows.[50]

From the moment it was implemented, the Fair Bear program helped improve conditions for the most underpaid and overworked student employees at Berkeley. Because of the program's establishment eight employers immediately raised wages to the Fair Bear minimum of 40 cents per hour. In some stores and restaurants this amounted to a wage increase of over 30 percent—attesting to how poorly paid students had been in the past. The Fair Bear program's impact on the student labor market was so great that soon after the program began it generated public complaints from several local merchants. These employers claimed that the Fair Bear standards were too high and would cause them to hire fewer

students. But despite such grumbling, most campus area employers complied with the standards, since their businesses depended upon student
patronage and could not have afforded a possible student boycott.[51]

The Fair Bear program faced its biggest test in 1939, when Drake's,
a popular local restaurant, refused to comply with the ASUC's labor standards. Drake's paid low wages to its waitresses and required them to pay
for laundering their uniforms. The ASUC Labor Board responded to the
restaurant's persistent abuses by placing Drake's on its boycott list. The
incensed restaurant owner tried to go over the head of the ASUC by
complaining to UC President Robert Sproul. But the administration refused to overrule the Labor Board's decision. Indeed, Berkeley's dean of
undergraduates actually endorsed the Fair Bear standards as "worthy and
justifiable." Left with no one else to appeal to, and facing the prolonged
loss of student patronage, Drake's management agreed to comply with the
Fair Bear standards only a week after students began boycotting the restaurant. The Fair Bear program proved so effective that it attracted national attention, and was emulated on other campuses, such as Ohio State
University. Fair Bear drew praise from labor leaders, including James Carey,
the secretary of the CIO, who urged the adoption of similar programs at
campuses across the country.[52]

The success of the Fair Bear program was a testament to how effective the student movement had been in transforming the campus political
scene. A program such as this would have been unimaginable at Berkeley
at the start of the Depression decade, when the student Left was a small
minority under attack from the UC administration, the campus newspaper, and the fraternity-dominated student government. But with the growth
of the student movement, the ASU now had sufficient influence to get the
student government to implement the Fair Bear program and to attract
support for the program from the campus press, the UC administration,
and a majority of Berkeley undergraduates.[53]

IV

The Great Depression played a large, but not exclusive role in defin-
ing the student movement's domestic priorities. Because the Depression
gripped the nation and affected so many students, it gave a special urgency to issues concerning economic opportunity. This was why such causes
as aid to low-income youth received so much attention from student activists. The student movement's egalitarianism was not limited, however, to
economics; it also extended to race. The movement demonstrated a concern with both the new inequities created by the Depression and the old
inequities perpetuated by racism. The radicals who launched and led the
campus revolt of the 1930s criticized the racial discrimination of the North
and the Jim Crow system of the South. They envisioned an academic
community and a nation free of racial prejudice and discrimination.

Depression era student activists raised the banner of racial equality on more campuses than any previous generation of students in twentieth century America.[54]

Just how far removed the student activists of the 1930s were from mainstream American racial attitudes was made evident in the very first meeting between the Youth Congress' leaders and Eleanor Roosevelt. On the question of civil rights the First Lady symbolized the Roosevelt administration's most liberal wing. She was far more willing than the president himself to confront the problem of racial inequality. But in comparison to the student movement's leaders, Mrs. Roosevelt seemed timid and conservative on race—and this led to a strong difference of opinion in her January 1936 meeting with the Youth Congress' National Council. At that meeting, Elizabeth Scott, a black leader in the Youth Congress, confronted the First Lady with the New Deal's failure to challenge Jim Crow, and explained:

> I represent one-tenth of the citizens of this country. I refer to the Negro people. We are denied citizenship in the South. We do not have the right to vote in the Democratic primaries in the southern states. In this very city of Washington, my nation's capitol, I cannot get a meal in a restaurant, whether I am starving or not . . . . How do you think we should fight against Negro discrimination in this country and what are you going to do about it?

Mrs. Roosevelt, though mentioning her "great sympathy for the problems of the Negro people" and the "importance of equal education," counselled Scott to "have patience . . . these are not things that can be settled in a short time."[55]

The First Lady's gradualist argument swayed none of the young activists. They wanted the Roosevelt administration to stop evading the issue of discrimination, especially with regard to the racist southern court system. In fact, before Mrs. Roosevelt left the meeting, the Youth Congress leaders voted to send the president a telegram protesting "the lack of civil liberties in the South" and the use of "terror and intimidation against sharecroppers" in that region who sought to unionize. The telegram also expressed outrage at the attempt of Alabama law enforcement officials to frame the young African American defendants in the Scottsboro case; it called upon FDR to offer "federal protection of the Scottsboro boys," and demanded a "federal investigation of [racial] terror."[56] This was consistent with the Youth Congress' 1935 Declaration of Rights of American Youth, which contrasted Depression America's democratic pretensions with its racial practices:

> In song and legend America has been exalted as a land of the free, a haven for the oppressed. Yet on every hand we see this freedom limited

or destroyed . . . . The Negro people are subjected to constant abuse, discrimination and lynch law.[57]

Shortly after this meeting with the First Lady, student activists were again pressing the Roosevelt administration to do more on behalf of African Americans. The American Student Union supported immediate and complete desegregation of all New Deal programs. Thus in February 1936, ASU leader Joseph Lash called upon G.W. Studebaker, United States commissioner of education, to see to it that his department's community education forums should also be used to challenge Jim Crow—by being conducted on a racially integrated basis everywhere, including in the South. This was, however, too radical an idea for Studebaker, who in turning Lash down, claimed that it would be unwise "to dictate a vital change for the age-long and traditional social relations in the South . . . . Whether white and colored meet must depend upon the spirit and customs of the community."[58]

If the student movement's racial egalitarianism seemed bold in comparison to the Roosevelt administration, it was even more daring in comparison to the administrations that governed America's college campuses. Institutional racism pervaded the American college and university system of the 1930s. Throughout the South a rigid Jim Crow system barred African Americans from enrolling in white schools. In the North, discriminatory admissions practices made it almost impossible for blacks to attend many leading colleges and universities—which accepted either none or only a token number of black applicants. In 1933, for instance, such institutions as Stanford, Grinnell, and Bryn Mawr had only one African American undergraduate each; Smith, Rutgers, Tufts, Radcliffe, Wesleyan, and Dartmouth were among the schools which had just three blacks enrolled. Only nine campuses in the entire nation (excluding black colleges) enrolled more than 100 black collegians. Discriminatory admissions practices helped confine the vast majority of African American students to black colleges: In 1933 of the 23,038 black undergraduates, 20,296 were students on black campuses.[59]

The small minority of African American students (under 3000 in 1933) who did attend predominantly white colleges and universities in the North often found these schools and their surrounding communities quite racist. Jim Crow was almost as strong in many aspects of northern collegiate life as it was in the South. At such schools as the University of Minnesota, Ohio State, and the University of Chicago, segregation in dormitories and rooming houses prevented blacks from living on or even near campus. Campus communities regularly excluded blacks from restaurants, shops, recreational facilities, social clubs, and athletic competition.[60] Discrimination against black students was so severe at the University of Illinois, that the *Daily Illini* concluded in 1932 that

if you want to know what hell is, wake up colored some morning . . . .
Negro students are barred from all campus confectionaries and eating

establishments. The Home Economics Cafeteria is the only public place at which they may eat. They are segregated at shows and semi-public gatherings. Most of the public dance hall managers look upon them as pariahs.[61]

Most white college administrators either tolerated or actively promoted and defended such racial discrimination. A common administration attitude seemed to be that blacks were lucky to be enrolled in college and ought not complain about discrimination they encountered on campus. As one college official explained to a black theological student at Harvard in 1930,

> In admitting the Negro students to the opportunity for study we feel we have done our duty; he should respect our good-will by not causing such social problems as are bound to grow out of his attempt to participate in campus activities.[62]

College officials also argued that deferring to traditional racial practices—no matter how discriminatory—was the best way to avoid controversy and maintain racial harmony. This was the line of reasoning that the University of Minnesota Board of Trustees used when it ruled in 1935 that blacks would continue to be excluded from the men's dormitory. Discriminatory college administrators seemed to be motivated both by fear of offending the University's white alumni and benefactors and by their own racial prejudice.[63]

There seemed to be almost no campus community free of racial discrimination. Even at liberal Oberlin, which had been among the first colleges in the nation to admit black students, discriminatory patterns were visible. Esther Cooper Jackson, recalled that she and fellow black students at Oberlin during the 1930s had to contend with prejudiced college officials throughout their undergraduate years.

> There was racism at Oberlin despite its history. We had a very racist Dean of Men who used to discourage blacks and whites, for example, just going out on casual dates. And he had his spies. And he would write to the parents of a white girl or boy, and tell them "Did you know that your son or daughter went out, is going out with a black student?" And we burned him . . . in effigy on the campus.[64]

In the surrounding community, Oberlin's black students found themselves barred from recreational facilities and facing increased discrimination in local shops. The NAACP magazine had good reason, then, for expressing its regret in 1934 that "Oberlin O., of glorious Underground Railroad history, seems to be weakening after 100 years, and yielding to the intolerance which the city's stalwarts a century ago fought with unparalleled passion."[65]

Traditional student institutions, particularly fraternities and sororities, reinforced this discriminatory atmosphere on northern campuses. Greek houses almost universally barred blacks both from their membership and social events. Such discrimination was written into the constitutions of many of these houses through clauses limiting membership to students "without Negro blood." African Americans founded fraternities and sororities, but their organizations were not treated as equals by the white Greek Houses in the 1930s. At the University of Chicago, for instance, white fraternity leaders refused to admit the black fraternity Kappa Alpha Psi into the Interfraternity Council, thus barring the blacks from establishing their own house on the campus. This same pattern prevailed in athletic and honorary societies. Not even Jesse Owens, the most famous athlete in the history of Ohio State could cross this color line. In 1936 Owens was denied admission to Bucket and Dipper, the campus' athletic honor society.[66]

Racial discrimination was so widespread on campus that segregationist students felt no compunction about publicly endorsing the exclusion of African American students from local facilities, shops, and events. At Columbia University, for instance, conservative students in 1936 defended the right of barber shops in the campus area to refuse service to black students, on the grounds that the property rights of these shop owners entitled them to bar blacks. Similar views were expressed the following year at Ohio State University during a controversy concerning discrimination in the campus community. Bigoted Ohio State students wrote in to their campus newspaper that "in a country governed by the Nordic race it is impossible to put other races on a parity with that race . . . . Negroes . . . should not be allowed to eat where we of the white race do [n]or should they be allowed to go to our shows. If one starts it they all follow and soon take various places over completely." Such sentiments led to the formation of the Anti-Negro Guild, a short-lived group at Ohio State which sought to stop white and black student activists from integrating campus facilities.[67]

The persistent bigotry of white campuses discouraged many black students from even applying to them. Some thought it better to enroll in an underfunded black college than to expose themselves to the racism of white colleges. Such sentiments were expressed by black students in an article which appeared in a leading black magazine in 1934. Here one undergraduate, in explaining his decision to attend a black college rather than a predominantly white school, noted that the racism of the white campus was harmful to the black collegian in that it could

> crush him with an inferiority complex . . . . The negro college will be the saving grace of the negro race until the fundamental attitude of the white man towards the negro makes a radical change. The white college until that time can never prepare the young negro for life.[68]

There were virtually no African Americans on the faculties of northern colleges and universities during the Depression decade. Few blacks were admitted to northern graduate and professional schools. Even those within this small elite of black Ph.D.s coming out of top white graduate schools were expected to teach only in black colleges. Consequently, when psychologist Kenneth Clark received his Columbia doctorate in 1940, his professors told him: "Now you have your Ph.D., you can go back and serve your people." Clark, who would later become one of CCNY's first black faculty members, recalled that his response to their Jim Crow advice was "Well my people are in New York. I'm a New Yorker. I'd like to teach at City College or Princeton." Throughout the 1930s, then, top black academics in the nation were ghettoized—compelled to chose between teaching at black colleges or not teaching at all.[69]

With faculty, administrators, and traditional student groups perpetuating this pattern of discrimination, it may seem odd that the student movement of the 1930s condemned it. The movement's commitment to racial equality can be traced to its radical leadership, whose thinking on race was shaped not by the retrogressive practices of the academy but by progressive ideals of the adult Left. They followed the prevailing Left wisdom of the era, which held that racism had to be battled energetically because it was one of the most vile and effective means by which the capitalist class divided and ruled workers. This class analysis of racism appeared prominently in the student Left's publications, which stressed that race hatreds were inflamed to distract the nation from the failings of the capitalist system, and that interracial unity was the only effective weapon against this reactionary ploy. International events provided an added impetus to the fight against racism. By the mid-1930s, the student movement had begun to link the fight against racism with the broader international anti-fascist movement, and condemned Jim Crow as an American form of Hitlerism.[70]

The social composition of the student movement's leadership contributed to the movement's racial egalitarianism. The movement's national leadership included African American students, who saw racial discrimination as one of the most important targets for student protest. These black student leaders included Maurice Gates and James Jackson of the National Student League, Lyonel Florant of the Student League for Industrial Democracy, Louis Burnham, Frances Jones, and Le Marquis de Jarmen of the American Student Union, Edward Strong and Elizabeth Scott of the American Youth Congress. The heavy representation of Jews among the student movement leaders added to this anti-racist impulse. Young Jewish radicals such as Joseph Lash, James Wechsler, Joseph Clark, and Harry Magdoff had played a prominent role in launching the student movement and shaping the platforms of the student Left. They came to college aware, as were most Jewish students, that American colleges and universities in the 1930s often imposed quotas restricting Jewish enrollments. These Jewish radicals brought to the student movement a strong sensitivity toward the problem of racial discrimination, and an insistence that the movement adopt an uncompromising stance in support of racial equality.[71]

Even before they organized the first anti-war strikes, student movement leaders attempted to make a national issue of racial discrimination. In April 1933 the NSL held a Student Conference on Negro Student Problems in New York City. The NSL invited black students from all regions of the country. At this interracial conference, student delegates and prominent black social critics, including sociologist E. Franklin Frazier, denounced the Jim Crow system and the damage that racial discrimination did to education in both the South and the North.[72]

The content of this conference and the NSL's eagerness to promote racial equality impressed African American delegates. Lyonel Florant, a socialist student from Howard University, found the tone of the meeting far different from any interracial gathering he had experienced previously:

> It was not the old interracial get-together at which hands were shaken "for Jesus' sake," and after a few sessions of intellectual back-slapping, Negroes and whites returned to their isolated way of living. No, it was a fiery, militant conference that brought students and professors out of the deep South. The sugary spirit was absent; instead there was a common resolve to go back to the South and, for that matter, many areas of the North, and tackle shoulder to shoulder the problems of discrimination.[73]

James Jackson, editor of the *Panther,* Virginia Union's student newspaper during the 1930s, agreed, recalling the conference as "a very impressive event in my life." Here for the first time the black editor had a chance to participate in the formation of a student program to fight racism. Jackson found the NSL's racial militancy so unlike the attitude he had encountered among other whites that at one point he mistook one of the white NSL officers for a black:

> Joseph Clark, Executive Secretary of the National Student League [who addressed the conference] was a very dynamic speaker. And it's interesting. He in the summer was quite brown, and his hair was kind of frizzy. And I thought he was black and took great national pride that [he was] such a speaker who knew so much about the world.[74]

The student movement's leftist leaders not only preached racial equality, but practiced it in their national meetings. The NSL in 1933 held its annual convention on a black campus, Howard University, and defied the Jim Crow customs of the capital by having black and white delegates dine together in traditionally "whites only" restaurants on Connecticut Avenue. Similarly, the 1935 American Youth Congress in Detroit threatened to withdraw from the hotel in which it was headquartered unless management abided by its agreement to house the Congress' black delegates. The threatened exodus forced the segregated hotel to accommodate the black youths. This incident received prominent publicity in the

Youth Congress' publications. This scenario was repeated at the Youth Congress' 1936 convention in Cleveland, when delegates again encountered discrimination from a local hotel.[75]

Student radicals sought to spread this non-discriminatory ethos to student organizations outside the Left. In 1933 the NSL and SLID announced that they would picket the convention of the National Student Federation (NSF)—the mainstream association of student governments—because the federation had informed black students that they could not attend its dance in Washington's Mayflower Hotel. Afraid of the embarrassment from such a picket, the federation backed down, and black students were admitted to the dance. Not satisfied with this concession, the NSL, in its national magazine, ran an exposé by black activist Maurice Gates on the NSF's history of discrimination. Gates showed that the NSF had barred black students from its 1932 convention and warned that student activists would no longer tolerate such racism.[76]

The NSL worked to attract student interest in the Scottsboro case, which it saw as symbolic of all that was wrong with the Jim Crow system. The League promoted a national Scottsboro Week on campus, directing its chapters to hold forums on the case. The NSL magazine devoted several of its lead editorials to Scottsboro and drew connections between discrimination in the judicial and educational systems, urging "the student body" to "play a decisive part in the struggle against racial oppression. We must uproot it on the campus by fighting against Jim Crow clubs and schools." The NSL dispatched several student reporters to attend the Scottsboro trial, two of whom were arrested. They wrote accounts which vividly portrayed the racial injustice of the proceedings. One of these reporters was Muriel Rukeyser, who dispatched not only news stories, but also a poem, "The Trial," which would attract national attention as a searing indictment of southern racism—and start Rukeyser's career as a leading American poet.[77]

In northern campus communities, NSL and SLID chapters organized protests when racist incidents occurred. The SLID chapter at the University of Wisconsin picketed a local hotel when it refused to house a visiting black theater company in 1934. The SLID led the fight to have black students admitted to the Engineering School at the University of Cincinnati. NSL activists at the University of Michigan helped organize a meeting to protest the football coach's decision to bench black star end Willis Ward during a road game in the South. The NSL led protests against racial discrimination in UC Berkeley's campus barbershop, the hospital of the University of Chicago Medical School, the bowling alley near Oberlin College, and on the CCNY track team. The NSL also publicized the Phi Beta Kappa national organization's refusal to allow Howard University to establish a local chapter.[78]

The formation of the American Student Union helped the student movement in its civil rights work, just as it assisted it in other areas of agitation. The growth in both the number of activists and the influence of the student movement, which the ASU facilitated, allowed the movement to organize civil rights protests on more campuses than had the NSL and SLID. The ASU recommended that all its chapters proceed on an extensive civil rights agenda. Chapters were urged to support passage of federal anti-lynching legislation, equal allocation of educational dollars for black and white students, and abolition of the poll tax. There was an added emphasis on cultural and educational issues, with the ASU supporting "the inclusion of courses on Negro history and culture in the curriculum," and ASU participation in Negro History week. Most influential of all was the ASU's call for chapters to work with black students both in their own organizations and the ASU to challenge campus discrimination through "test cases."[79]

Under the influence of this civil rights program, campus ASU chapters established Negro Student Problems committees that worked with black students to uncover and protest racial discrimination in the campus community. ASU anti-discrimination battles were waged at such campuses as Berkeley, Butler, Chicago, CCNY, Columbia, Illinois, Missouri, Michigan, Minnesota, Northwestern, Ohio State, and Washington Universities. These battles, like those waged by the NSL and SLID in the early 1930s, were over basic rights for black students, including access to restaurants, dormitories, boarding houses, employment, shops, social clubs and events, athletic competition, and academic programs.[80]

This stance against racial discrimination made it difficult for the student movement to penetrate most campuses below the Mason Dixon line— where a strong regional consensus in support of segregation existed. Outside of the region's few larger and more cosmopolitan campuses, the southern student movement was quite weak. This was especially true in the deep South, where on such campuses as the University of Florida a majority of the students surveyed approved of lynching blacks accused of rape.[81]

Despite the unpopularity of racial egalitarianism in the South, however, scattered southern student radicals did challenge the Jim Crow system. In 1934 the University of Virginia's NSL chapter invited Richard Moore, a prominent black socialist, to speak on their Charlottesville campus. In inviting Moore to speak, these young radicals flouted the school's long standing tradition of racial exclusion. There had not been a militant black speaker at the University of Virginia since Reconstruction. The campus administration responded with outrage to the Moore invitation. Virginia NSL leader Palmer Weber recalled that the invitation "threw the Dean [Ivey Lewis] into a fit. He still believed in slavery. He forbade the use of any university building."[82] Weber and the NSL responded to the ban by obtaining space for Moore's speech in the Episcopal church across the street from the University. Weber, who was a writer for *College Topics*, Virginia's student newspaper, published a column blasting the University administration for violating the ancient and revered traditions of free speech and free thought. In doing so Virginia declares itself to be just another machine to hinder, even to destroy thought in the futile endeavor to support social mores, which can no longer be justified either in principle or as requisites for an ordered society.[83]

Weber also invoked the name of the University's founder, Thomas Jefferson, to indict the administration, accusing Virginia of initiating "a denial of Jeffersonian principles". "What manner of small-minded men have inherited Mr. Jefferson's University?"[84]

Much to the embarrassment of the Virginia administration, this free speech controversy attracted attention from the press all along the East Coast. John Newcomb, the University's president reacted by summoning Weber to his office. Pulling out a file of press clippings, Newcomb accused Weber of damaging the University's reputation. "My God, look what you've done to the University! This is the worst public relations in fifty years." Weber replied,

> President Newcomb, I didn't do it, Dean Lewis did it. I told him there was no way to keep it a secret that he'd forbade the use of any University building . . . . You know this is just impossible. Slavery is over. And these people are citizens of Virginia . . . and they have a right to be heard . . . . The man's been properly invited, he's qualified and he's going to speak at the Episcopal Church chapel.

Moore's speech went ahead as planned, and for the rest of the decade the Virginia administration—apparently chastened by the negative publicity from the Moore controversy—never tried to stop the NSL as it brought black speakers to campus.[85]

It was no accident that after Moore had been banned from speaking at the University, the one place the NSL could secure for their black speaker was a church. Among the few allies that the student Left found in the South were religious radicals—scattered and small groups of Christian Socialists or Left-leaning ministers and activists in the student YW and YMCAs. This is what an ASU field organizer was alluding to when he reported to Joseph Lash that "whatever there is of a student movement in the South is in the Y—you can get away with a great deal in the name of Christianity down here, which would not be listened to for a moment under any other auspices . . . ." Religious radicals were instrumental in promoting interracial meetings and work on behalf of racial equality; they were an indigenous southern group which controlled church buildings and could provide integrationists with at least limited accesss to the white student body.[86]

For these Christian allies the student Left owed a debt to Reinhold Niebuhr, Harry Ward, and Norman Thomas. As leading teachers at New York's Union Theological Seminary, Ward and Niebuhr were able to help propagate racial egalitarianism in the South because their students included southerners who would become ministers below the Mason-Dixon line. Among the students of these leftist teachers were Howard Kester and Myles Horton, who would help found two of the most radical interracial institutions in the South during the 1930s: the Southern Tenant Farmers Union, which organized sharecroppers, and the Highlander Folk School, which trained labor and civil rights organizers. Equally important were the clerics Norman Thomas had converted to socialism. Thomas, a former minister himself, frequently toured the South and managed to assemble a small network of ministers who were at least sympathetic to the goals of the student Left. Such ministers, as campus chaplains and heads of student Y's, were strategically placed to help bring an integrationist message to southern campuses.[87]

The influence of religious radicalism could be seen, for example, at Emory University in Georgia, where the student YMCA was headed by Emmet Johnson, a minister who was an avid integrationist. Johnson worked throughout the early 1930s to see that students in the YMCA from the (all-white) Emory campus met blacks on an equal basis. Without official permission from the University administration, Johnson set up small interracial student meetings in local churches and black campuses. One of the students who participated in these meetings was Jack McMichael, who would go on to become chair of the American Youth Congress. According to McMichael, these meetings—which were for their participants the first integrated and racially equal events they had ever attended—made a deep impression.

> The influence of Emmet Johnson [who led the interracial meetings] was very great on me. And these experiences made a big difference. You could read these things in a book, but when you know people who are black and you know that the taboos about them are not true you see you get this kind of deep feeling [against segregation].[88]

Johnson and McMichael sought to spread racial equality not only at Emory but through the entire religious network of the intercollegiate YM/YWCA. Aware that the local Y's, like all southern institutions, had succumbed to Jim Crowism in its regional meetings, the Emory University activists in the early 1930s, began "working together to make a sort of frontal assault on segregation in the YMCA and YWCA." This movement to reform the Y's, which united Protestant Left activists from a number of southern campuses, proved quite effective. According to McMichael,

> We went to Blue Ridge in the summers—to Blue Ridge, North Carolina, where there is a YMCA conference grounds. And they were accustomed to having all-white meetings. And we insisted on having blacks. And they said, you can have blacks, but they can't use the same toilets. And we took the position [for complete integration], largely through the

> influence of the YW's—because these meetings at Blue Ridge, though in
> YMCA territory, were Y and YW. The YW was much more progressive,
> and much more willing to stick its neck out on these things. And they
> were insisting that there be no segregation whatever, that they make no
> concession to it. And so we . . . finally broke down that barrier. That
> meant, of course, and we knew it, that we had to break the law, because
> the law often required segregation in public places.

Through the remainder of the 1930s, the Y's interracial committees would
bring black and white students together in southern conferences, and the
more liberal Y's would assist the student Left in airing integrationist ideas
which were otherwise locked out of many southern campus communities.[89]

Although able to win a few symbolic victories in the South, as with
the Moore speech at Charlottesville and the integration of the Y retreats
in North Carolina, southern student radicals lacked the numbers and influence to end or even seriously threaten the Jim Crow admissions polices
of their colleges and universities. This lack of influence was apparent, for
example, in connection with the Alice Jackson case in 1935. Jackson, a
black college graduate, had challenged the color line at the University of
Virginia by applying for admission to its graduate school. The University
promptly rejected her, in a move supported by most Virginia students.
The University of Virginia NSL was outraged; its officers sent a letter of
protest to the University's Board of Visitors, rebuking the University for
its violation

> of the right of equal opportunity for all people regardless of race, color
> or creed. In short, we criticise the Board's stand because it implies the
> desirabilty of continuing educational inequality. We are confident that
> every liberal, radical and christian thinker will concur with us in this pro-
> test.[90]

The NSL challenged not merely the Virginia administration's decision,
but the bigotry of the student body itself, filling the campus newspaper
with pro-integration letters and arranging debates with the leading student advocates of Jim Crow education.

The tone of the debate over Jackson's admission was angry. This reflected the fact that her application and the NSL's defense of it had for
the first time forced Virginia's elite white student body into the position
of having to defend its most deeply held racial prejudices. Thus one segregationist student, furious at his radical classmates' support of Jackson,
fumed that the "N.S.L will never convince me that they are not merely
talking through their hat . . . until they convince me that they would be
perfectly willing to see their sisters . . . married to negroes." Invoking
southern history, another segregationist student wrote the campus newspaper that:

In answer to the N.S.L. may I state if they were of a more analyzing nature they would realize that this is the South and not any other region of the country. From the time when the first Negro set foot in Virginia in 1619, that race has not been placed in the classroom with the whites so far as the public schools are concerned and they never will be.[91]

NSL activists at the University of Virginia infuriated these segregationists with well argued rebuttals to their Jim Crow arguments. They pointed out that the longevity of the educational color line had no bearing at all on the question of whether integration was desirable. Even if it was true that blacks and whites had not been educated together since 1619, "So What?," asked the NSL. "It says nothing of the desirability of placing Negroes and whites in the same classroom." The NSL charged that the segregationists had no proof for their claims that blacks were intellectually inferior to whites. These radicals argued that the University would be strengthened as an intellectual and cultural institution by the admission of blacks:

> The NSL stands for racial equality because it is just, and because it is culturally advantageous,—culturally advantageous because segregation deprives not only the Negro people of what whites have to offer, but also works the other way. The Negro people form an integral part of America. Their cultural tradition is an American heritage, to which the people as a whole, students especially have a right. Every genuine student in order to secure as broad an education as possible, must come into contact with all races and nationalities.[92]

The NSL also took issue with the emotional arguments about the alleged twin evils of integration and racial intermarriage. These activists found it "astonishing" that segregationist students had claimed they were upholding the South's tradition of racial purity in which "black is black and white is white and never the twain shall meet." Taunting one such segregationist, the NSL asked "Does the gentleman not know that nine million Negroes in the South have white blood in their veins? Surely he does not believe the stork story. Or does he?"[93]

Despite its eloquent arguments, the NSL throughout the Jackson controversy remained the only student group writing, debating, and organizing in behalf of Jackson's admission. This suggests that these civil rights advocates failed to sway many of their classmates. If *College Topics*, the campus newspaper, is a fair indicator of student sentiment, most Virginia students remained solidly segregationist. In its editorial on the Jackson case, entitled "But Not Here," the paper argued that Jackson's admission to UVA would be "disastrous" and inflame racial prejudice because the South was not yet ready for integration. The administration agreed, and refused to admit her.[94]

Four years later in Chapel Hill, the ASU waged a similar campaign in solidarity with Pauli Murray's attempt to cross the university's color line. Unlike the Virginia NSL during the Jackson case in 1935, the ASU at Chapel Hill was not totally alone its advocacy of desegregation in 1939. The ASU's integrationist efforts received support from Chapel Hill's campus YMCA, and two eloquent faculty liberals, historian Howard Beale and playwright Paul Green. Integrationist arguments seemed to have their greatest appeal among graduate students. A survey taken by the *Daily Tar Heel*, Chapel Hill's student newspaper, revealed that a majority of respondents in the University's law and graduate schools favored Murray's admission.[95]

The ASU sought to broaden student support for Murray by organizing a forum on black educational rights, which included speakers from several local black colleges. At one ASU sponsored meeting over 100 students and teachers voted their approval of the immediate integration of the University of North Carolina. The ASU's integrationist efforts received a significant boost from Murray herself. She wrote a brilliant open letter to President Graham, indicting Jim Crow education. This letter appeared in all the Chapel Hill area newspapers. These efforts failed, however, to win over the student body as a whole or the administration. There was no poll taken of the University's undergraduates, but the *Daily Tar Heel*, which itself opposed Murray's admission, claimed that majority sentiment at Chapel Hill was segregationist. A survey of other southern student newspapers also revealed majority opposition to desegregating the University. The southern student body remained solidly segregationist despite the best efforts of the ASU. Murray was not admitted to Chapel Hill, and it would take decades of legal battles before the NAACP could bring collegiate desegregation beyond the border states into the deep South. So though these student radicals had been daring in forcing upon their classmates unprecedented debates about segregation, the political climate in the South prevented them from winning those debates.[96]

If racial prejudice limited the impact of the student Left on white southern campuses, political repression played this same role on black campuses. The administrators of most black colleges were every bit as conservative as Ralph Ellison—a student at Tuskegee in the 1930s—described in his novel, *The Invisible Man*. Like Ellison's fictional Dr. Bledsoe, the administrators of black colleges were usually dependent on white philanthropy, wary of offending their schools' wealthy benefactors, and adherents of a gradualist approach to racial progress.[97] These characteristics left them intolerant of racial militancy and dissent, which they saw as a threat to the moderate image of their schools.

Social and political suppression were so severe on southern black campuses it shocked poet Langston Hughes, as he toured these campuses in 1934. Hughes protested the "astounding restrictions" and "lack of personal freedom that exists on most Negro campuses. To set foot on dozens of Negro campuses is like going back to mid-Victorian England, or Massachusetts in the days of the witch burning Puritans." Hughes found that administrators prohibited student smoking, dating, dancing, and even card playing; they required daily chapel meetings and enforced dozens of military-style regulations.[98]

During this tour, Hughes found college administrators on the black campuses even more eager to repress civil rights activism than they were to restrict student social life. At Hampton Institute, Hughes encountered a group of students outraged by both a white Birmingham mob's murder of a Hampton alumnus, and the death of a prominent black educator, who might have survived had the local white hospital not refused to treat her. These Hampton students organized a protest meeting and scheduled Hughes to speak there. But the meeting could not be held. Hampton's dean barred students from demonstrating, explaining "Hampton did not like the word 'protest.' That was not Hampton's way. He and Hampton believed in moving slowly and with dignity." Hughes was so appalled by this incident and similar experiences at other black colleges that he published an article, "Cowards From the Colleges," in the NAACP's *Crisis* magazine, bemoaning this collegiate "Uncle Tomism." The Hampton case was typical. Student radicals found that on almost every black campus during the early 1930s their organizing "had to be carried on underground. Membership in either organization [the NSL or SLID] was the basis for expulsion," reported SLID activist Lyonel Florant.[99]

Unlike student radicals above the Mason-Dixon line, their counterparts at southern black colleges had little opportunity to evade the political restrictions mandated by repressive college administrators during the early 1930s. If an NSL rally was banned from campus in the Midwest, Northeast, or far West, students could usually hold the rally on city property out of the jurisdiction of college officials. But in the South, black organizers barred from campus could count on an equally repressive response from the white segregationist officials off campus. Ishmael Flory, an African American NSL activist learned this lesson at Fisk University in 1934, when he tried to organize a protest against the lynching of Cordie Cheek, a black teenager, a few blocks from campus. Nashville's mayor and police chief refused him permission to hold an anti-lynching march off campus. Flory then held the demonstration on campus, but the mood of fear was so great that only fifteen students joined the march. That fear was well grounded because Thomas E. Jones, Fisk's white president, expelled Flory for organizing the march, and Fisk's faculty endorsed the expulsion.[100]

Although such repression inhibited student protest on black campuses, it could not kill it. Not even Flory's expulsion could completely silence Fisk students. Indeed, before the end of the year, dissent, expressed in a more moderate way, again emerged at Fisk. When President Roosevelt visited Fisk in 1934 to hear the Jubilee singers, he was presented with a petition signed by 250 Fisk students protesting the Scottsboro case and the lynching of a black in Florida. In addition, there were instances of interracial student protest in the South. The most well publicized of these actions in Virginia was the dispatching of an NSL-organized delegation of students from the University of Virginia and Virginia Union University to the state legislature. The delegation demanded increased expenditures on education and equal allocation of state educational monies between black and white students.[101]

In the hope of expanding such activism among African American students, the American Student Union chose Louis Burnham, a talented black organizer who had headed CCNY's militant Frederick Douglass Society, as its southern organizer. The combination of Burnham's skill and the ASU's autonomous image—the fact that its links with the Left were less explicit than the SLID and NSL and hence somewhat less likely to invite repression—allowed the organization to make more progress on the black campuses than had been made by the NSL and SLID in the early 1930s. Burnham established ASU chapters at eight or nine black colleges in the South, not a mass movement by any means, but at least a step in the direction of greater black student activism.[102]

African American student protest in the 1930s was strongest at Howard University, Black America's leading institution of higher education. The liberalism of Howard's faculty and the university's location in the nation's capital gave student activists at Howard an advantage over their counterparts on black campuses further south, since they fostered a freer political atmosphere at Howard. The Howard professoriate included some of Black America's most eloquent civil rights advocates, such as Ralph Bunche and Charles Houston, whose teaching, according to Kenneth B. Clark, a Howard undergraduate in the 1930s, encouraged "students to fight against the idiocy of American racism and segregationism."[103]

The critical role that liberal faculty played in protecting free speech and allowing room for dissent at Howard was evident in the controversy surrounding the demonstration by Howard students against segregation in the cafe of the United States House of Representatives in February 1934. After police arrested about 30 Howard students for demanding service in this segregated restaurant, Howard's President Mordecai Johnson began disciplinary proceedings against the protest leaders. Johnson feared that the protest had jeopardized the congressional funding upon which Howard was dependent, and it was on this basis that he summoned protest leader Kenneth Clark into his office and, in Clark's word's "gave me hell," and threatened him with expulsion. But as the disciplinary committee hearings began, Professor Bunche appeared and personally intervened on behalf of the students. Bunche told committee members that the protesters should not be disciplined, but rather they "should be given medals" for demonstrating against segregation, and he warned that he would fight any disciplinary action. Bunche swayed the committee, and none of the students were disciplined.[104]

Howard continued to produce some of the most memorable black student demonstrations of the decade, including one in which 150 Howardites rallied against the exclusion of lynching from the agenda of a national crime conference in December 1934. The protesters appeared outside the conference hall in Washington with hangmen's nooses around their necks and bearing signs indicating the numbers of blacks lynched in the South. Such activism made Howard the greatest source of national black leaders for the student movement of the 1930s.[105]

Black initiative played a pivotal role not merely in these Howard protests, but in many of the ASU's civil rights campaigns. It was often black student complaints about discrimination and segregation that brought civil rights matters to the attention of local ASU activists. The precise manner in which this interaction between black and white students occurred varied. Sometimes the black grievants were themselves ASU activists. This was the case, for instance with William Bell, a member of the ASU executive committee at Northwestern University, who sued the University for ejecting him from its campus beach. The ASU branch there followed up his suit with a broad investigation of racial discrimination on campus, and a meeting with the University president to demand change.[106]

On campuses where there were a sufficient number of blacks to form their own organizations, these groups helped bring discriminatory acts to the ASU's attention. Thus at CCNY, the Frederick Douglass Society and the ASU worked on a number of joint anti-discrimination projects. A third pattern emerged in which an unaffiliated black student, victimized by discrimination, made the ASU aware of this racism and joined or endorsed the ASU's subsequent campaign to eliminate the source of the discrimination. This occurred at Columbia University in 1936, where the ASU, acting on the report of an African American student, organized picket lines around two discriminatory barber shops in the campus area. In all three cases, black initiative and complaints, as well as interracial cooperation, paved the way for ASU civil rights protests.[107]

The same type of black initiative which the ASU encouraged and which facilitated the student movement's civil rights actions, led to the formation of the Southern Negro Youth Congress (SNYC), a black-led youth organization devoted to the pursuit of racial equality. SNYC emerged as the youth affiliate of the communist-led National Negro Congress. The African American students who founded SNYC in 1937, Louis Burnham, James Jackson, and Edward Strong were communists who had been national leaders in the American Student Union and the American Youth Congress. The student movement had served as a political training ground for these young black activists; it was the movement which first brought SNYC's founders together and showed them the potential of youth for political action. Given the student movement's commitment to racial equality, it is not surprising that it contributed to the birth of a youth and student-led civil rights organization.[108]

The founding of the Southern Negro Youth Congress did not mark a break, but rather a division of labor between white and black student activists. ASU and SNYC leaders would continue to work together in pushing for such goals as increased federal aid to youth; they met regularly as members of the American Youth Congress. SNYC's formation was, however, at least an implicit acknowledgement on the part of leaders like Burnham—who had tried recruiting black southern collegians as an ASU organizer—that the student movement had failed to mobilize many black southern youths. Those involved recognized that the ASU, which was simultaneously organizing a national movement against war and lobbying for student aid, lacked the resources to lead a large scale challenge to Jim Crow in the South. In essence, the problem of southern segregation was so massive it could only be battled effectively by a black-led southern organization, devoted exclusively to helping black people fight for equality.[109]

Organizationally, the SNYC was modeled after the American Youth Congress. As with the AYC, the Southern Negro Youth Congress started out as a federation of local youth and youth serving organizations—only in SNYC's case most of these constituent groups were black. SNYC also shared with the American Youth Congress a desire to reach beyond the campus, to join together student and non-student youth. Indeed, of all the organizations created by the student movement of the 1930s, SNYC's orientation toward off campus, non-student organizing was the strongest, and would very quickly lead SNYC to civil rights and labor mobilizations involving both old and young.[110]

SNYC's orientation toward community organizing derived from student idealism regarding the working class. SNYC organizers, like their ASU counterparts, saw workers as the ultimate agent of social change. This idealism about labor was fueled by both Marxist ideology and the new dynamism of the labor movement under the CIO. The oppressive southern political situation provided SNYC with an added incentive for moving beyond the campus, suggesting from the outset that students alone were too small a group within the black community to pose a threat to the social system which had left millions of blacks disenfranchised, impoverished, and segregated. SNYC was further impelled to move beyond the campus by the political vacuum which existed in the southern black community, where African Americans faced profound political and economic problems, but lacked militant organizations to address those problems.[111]

Headquartered initially in Richmond, Virginia, SNYC held its first convention, the All Southern Negro Youth Conference in that city in February 1937. The opening session was scheduled to coincide with the birthday of abolitionist Frederick Douglass. Over 500 delegates attended the conference, and the two largest delegations represented students and religious groups respectively. Delegates came from all classes and professions, ranging from sharecroppers and labor organizers to artists and teachers. The conference focused on the need for black economic and political opportunity. As SNYC leader Edward Strong told the delegates:

> We have come first of all, seeking the right to creative labor, to be gainfully employed with equal pay and employment opportunity—economic security . . . . The new Negro youth of the southland is rising to

manhood without the right to vote—for him we seek opportunity of political expression. And finally, we seek an existence free from the threat
of mob violence . . .[112]

From its office in Richmond, SNYC quickly reached out to one of the
poorest groups of blacks in the city: the workers in tobacco processing
plants. In the spring and summer of 1937, young SNYC organizers under
the leadership of James Jackson led a union organizing drive and a series
of walkouts among the city's tobacco workers. Jackson was responsible for
SNYC's decision to initiate this organizing drive. Having grown up in the
Richmond ghetto, Jackson Ward—or as it was commonly called "The Bottom"—Jackson had lived among the tobacco workers and known of the
oppressive conditions "in the sweatshops of the tobacco" industry. He had
resolved as a youth to "some day . . . strike a blow at this bloody system."[113]

The wages of these workers, most of whom were stemmers and thus
responsible for removing the stems of the tobacco leaves, were paid on a
piece rate basis. The wage was determined by the size of each stem, and
often this amounted to a paltry 10 cents hourly rate. Such wages left these
workers deeply in debt. A newspaper report from the strike scene described how "one women sobbed as she told how workers had to buy at
credit stores, could not make payment on the goods bought, and how
their wages were garnished time after time." Since these pay rates were
less than half the national minimum wage, securing that minimum of 25
cents an hour became a primary demand of the strikes.[114]

The SNYC-led strikes also focused on improving working conditions
in the tobacco plants. According to Jackson, the foremen in these plants
were whites who ran them "just like a plantation overseer," denying the
black work force ventilation (not allowing them to open the windows in
the steaming plants) and sanitation provisions. There were also no facilities for dining, causing the workers to "bring their food in newspapers
. . . and sit on the cement sidewalks outside the plant in all kinds of
weather to eat their food." The strikers therefore demanded that the
companies provide the workers with dining halls, restrooms, showers, a
place to changes clothes, cubby holds, fans, and a maintenance person
responsible for airing the factories.[115]

In one plant after another the strikes proved successful very quickly.
Wages rose to or slightly above the national minimum wage after brief
walkouts, and the changes demanded in working conditions were won for
most of Richmond's 5000 tobacco workers.[116] The victories in Richmond's
tobacco plants, as Jackson explained, helped prod other black factory
workers in the South to unionize and become part of the CIO's massive
organizing drive:

> We organized the tobacco industry in Virginia . . . that set off a
> kind of chain reaction for struggles in the Carolinas, especially in Winston-

> Salem, the R.J. Reynolds plants. And in the Virginia Carolina fertilizer
> chain that went all the way to Georgia. And DuPont Chemical-Nylon plants
> and so on . . . . On the success of the tobacco workers' strike . . . there
> was a general demand for organization. Workers on their own initiative
> wrote out on paper their names and so on and the words CIO, and ap-
> pealed to the tobacco workers to organize. And organization was . . .
> terribly easy really; it was a matter of issuing cards and making a speech.[117]

SNYC also sought to spread black community pride toward Black
America's history and culture. Much of SNYC's political discourse was
saturated with reminders that African Americans had a history of fighting
against racism and of achieving political and cultural progress in spite of
discrimination. In its Proclamation of Southern Negro Youth (1937), for
instance, which demanded racial equality, SNYC declared that

> From echoes of the past and from the deeds of the present we draw
> our inspiration and courage . . . . Uplifted by the bravery of Crispus
> Attucks; by his devotion to the cause of his people; by the courage of
> Frederick Douglass; by the high ideals and spiritual love of Sojurner Truth
> . . . . Mindful of the scientific contributions of Benjamin Banneker [and]
> . . . George Washington Carver; and stirred by the . . . high attainment
> in the arts of our own Marian Anderson and Paul Robeson . . . . Stim-
> ulated by the depth, the greatness, and creative genius of Langston Hughes,
> Richard Wright and Sterling Brown in the field of art and literature
> . . . . Proud in the stout hearts and strong fists of our champions of
> champions, Joe Louis and Henry Armstrong . . . . Striving to emulate
> the spirit of our heritage, pressing forward with pride in the past of our
> people and confidence in the future.[118]

SNYC did more than simply talk about black culture; it worked to
bring cultural events to both urban and rural blacks in the South. SNYC
established the Negro Community Theatre in Richmond, the People's
Community Theater in New Orleans, and a traveling dramatic group which
put on agit-prop puppet shows and Langston Hughes' one act play *Don't
You Want to Be Free?* in many parts of the rural South. According Esther
Cooper Jackson, who became a SNYC leader in 1938:

> We raised money and we purchased four model-T Fords. And we
> took puppet shows and drama groups with volunteers out to four south-
> ern states—Georgia, Alabama, Louisiana and I'm not sure of the fourth,
> where we put on shows with these puppets before groups of sharecrop-
> pers and in churches and in cities on how to register to vote, how to
> organize the sharecroppers, how to organize in the city, to take groups
> down to register to vote, how to train for it, how to study the Constitution
> . . . . Carrying the message of how to vote to small communities, rural
> areas. And people would come from all over; they had no movies; they
> had no theatres. Sometimes this was the first time they'd ever seen any
> kind of dramatic presentation.

In much of the rural South, where black outsiders were watched closely by police, such shows constituted the only way that SNYC could bring its egalitarian political message without harassment. Police were much less inclined to stop black organizers of a puppet show than they were to seize blacks organizing a political meeting.[119]

This cultural work was designed to assist SNYC in its expanding civil rights agitation. SNYC formed youth councils in over 20 communities in North Carolina, Virginia, Alabama, and Tennessee in 1937. These councils became involved in voting rights activity. Since the poll tax served as one of the key devices used to deny blacks the vote in these communities, it was a primary SNYC target. Recognizing that blacks lacked the power to bring about their ultimate goal of eliminating the poll tax, SNYC devised an immediate way that blacks could overcome this barrier to voting: forming poll tax clubs, which raised money so that blacks could pay the tax and thus vote. SNYC sought to make black disenfranchisement a national issue by organizing an anti-poll tax week, intended to place pressure on the House Judiciary Committee to pass the stalled anti-poll tax bill. The bill never made it out of committee, but this campaign, which included a mock election in New Orleans and public speeches and displays of anti-poll tax buttons, aired the demand for the franchise more boldly than it had ever been in the South during the Depression decade. SNYC investigated lynchings and police brutality, issuing reports designed to publicize this racial violence. The organization also promoted anti-lynching legislation and called for an end to racial discrimination in New Deal relief programs.[120]

V

The student activists in SNYC, the NSL, ASU, and AYC who fought against racial dicrimination lost far more battles than they won. Racism remained so deeply rooted in the society and campuses of America that movement organizers could not overthrow it. Despite SNYC's agitation, African Americans remained disenfranchised in the South. Despite the Fisk protests, lynching continued. Despite the campaigns waged at Charlotesville and Chapel Hill, the southern university system remained almost completely segregated in the 1930s.

Even with these defeats, however, the student movement had not lost completely because such battles highlighted the issue of racial inequality, creating its unprecedented visibility on campus. Though unable to knock out Jim Crow, the student activists of the 1930s were at least willing to step into the ring and fight it. Though these activists failed to end segregation, neither would they compromise with it. The student movement stood against racism even in the South, where doing so undermined the movement's popularity. In the North too, confronting racism was hardly expedient among a predominantly white student body, long accustomed to looking down on African Americans. At a time when the threat of war and the ravages of Depression were on everyone's mind, the movement could have ignored the issue of race entirely and focused on rallying students for peace and economic security. Yet rather than opting for this easy way out, the student movement's organizers stood by their egalitarian principles and insisted on raising the issue of racial inequality in their publications, meetings, and legislative campaigns.

The student movement pioneered a new form of campus activism, which stressed interracial cooperation and an ethic of absolute refusal to compromise with Jim Crow practices. Student activists repeatedly emphasized that a movement could not be truly committed to building a more egalitarian America unless it—in all of its elections, conventions, and campaigns—was free of racial discrimination. The movement rejected the traditional collegiate snobbishness which had almost exclusively elevated wealthy, white Protestants to leadership positions in the undergraduate peer culture. In effect, the movement turned collegiate elitism on its head, valuing diversity instead of homogeneity, revering the working class instead of the upper class.

Thanks in part to the student movement, the Depression decade marked an important turning point in the history of collegiate racism. For the first time in this century, segregation encountered vocal opposition on campus from not just African Americans, but also from white students on both sides of the Mason-Dixon line.[121] Academic racists began to be criticized for their discriminatory acts, and collegiate segregation started to become a national issue both on campus and in the courts. Student activists in the 1930s contributed to the campus civil rights ferment which was larger and more influential than the student movement itself. This ferment encompassed not only the political agitation of the students, but the legal activism of the NAACP and the scholarly work of pioneering social scientists. Before the end of the decade, the NAACP would win the *Gaines* and *Murray* decisions, desegregating professional schools in Missouri and Maryland and setting an important legal precedent in the struggle against Jim Crow on campus. Along with this progress in the Courts, came progress in the classroom, as iconoclastic academics such as Franz Boas published compelling criticisms of previously popular racist theories concerning culture and civilization.[122] The student movement represented a part of this insurgency in that it sought to popularize among students the racial egalitarianism for which the NAACP was litigating and Boas was publishing. These crucial first steps initiated a process that decades later would delegitimize both racism as an ideology and the segregationist system it had upheld.

VI

Throughout the 1930s the student movement's key activist organizations—the NSL, SLID, ASU, and AYC—promoted egalitarian social change. But was that change reformist or revolutionary? Was the student movement seeking to breed radicalism or merely liberalism as it involved collegians in struggles for educational opportunity, government aid to students, job programs for needy youth, racial equality, and collective bargaining rights for workers? The answers to these questions would change over the course of the decade. Where in the early 1930s, the leftist-led organizations that launched the student movement sought to radicalize their classmates, this goal faded later in the decade. The change was linked to the Popular and Democratic Front policies of the Communist Party and to the political realities of campus organizing—both of which encouraged the student movement's communist leaders to come to an accommodation with American liberalism.[123]

In their formative period during the early 1930s, the student movement's leading organizations exhibited considerable hostility toward both liberalism and capitalism. During these, the darkest days of the Great Depression, the NSL and SLID held that capitalism had fallen terminally ill. These radicals thought that such reformers as FDR were engaged in a futile attempt to prop up a doomed social system. In precisely the same manner as their adult Left counterparts, NSLers and SLIDers worried that the New Deal might be the entering wedge for fascism; they feared that the desperate capitalist class would resort to totalitarian methods to maintain its power and that FDR represented their class interests. This explains why in their publications during the early years of the Roosevelt administration the NSL, SLID, and AYC labeled as fascistic such New Deal programs as the Civilian Conservation Corps.[124]

Although they were radicals, when it came to campus organizing NSLers and SLIDers were also pragmatists who understood the campus political scene. They knew that a student body which as recently as 1932 had given a plurality to Herbert Hoover was not going to embrace socialism overnight. The student Left therefore did not insist that collegians who joined in its campaigns share its pessimism about capitalism or its preference for socialist alternatives. Instead, both the NSL and SLID sought to rally the campuses around causes—such as peace and student aid—whose appeal would reach beyond the Left. In effect, these were leftist organizations seeking to use reformist campaigns to first mobilize and then radicalize their classmates.[125]

NSL and SLID organizers believed that by involving students in struggles for specific and limited demands they could initiate a radicalization process. For example, the NSL thought that students who became active in protesting educational retrenchment would learn through this struggle that the cause of their hardships and the high cost of education was the capitalist system itself. These students would discover that they had to "fight capitalism because it stands opposed to the daily needs of the masses of students." At the end of this radicalization process, the NSL and SLID hoped that students would see the need "to commit oneself fully to bringing about [a] Socialist Society [because] . . . only under Socialism would you get full employment and only under Socialism would you end the threat of war and . . . . Fascism and create a situation in which there would be full rights given to minorities."[126]

With the advent of the Popular Front in 1935 the tone and rhetoric of the movement's leading organizations began to moderate. Where in the early 1930s the NSL and SLID had championed specific reforms in the hope of radicalizing students, the ASU (the Popular Front organization into which the NSL and SLID had merged) in the mid-1930s treated those reforms as ends in themselves. For the sake of anti-fascist unity, the ASU and the Youth Congress muted their anti-capitalist rhetoric. This shift was evident in the platforms of the Youth Congress. At the first Youth Congress, held in summer 1934, prior to the Comintern's adoption of the Popular Front, the young activists explicitly rejected American capitalism. In the preamble to the resolutions passed at this meeting the Youth Congress pledged "to work for the building of a new social order, based upon production for use rather than profit." The next Youth Congress occurred in summer 1935 just as the Communist Party—in preparation for the Comintern's Seventh World Congress—had begun to shift toward the Popular Front. Under the influence of its communist leadership, the Youth Congress avoided explicit anti-capitalist rhetoric in its resolutions. The second Youth Congress issued the "Declaration of Rights of American Youth," calling for the country to be "turned over to the working and farming people of America," without even implying that this would require a move away from capitalism.[127]

Even this vague reference to worker's control in the 1935 Declaration would seem revolutionary compared to the Youth Congress' rhetoric during the height of the Popular Front era. In their desire to foster national unity against fascism, the Youth Congress leadership sometimes fell into a saccharine brand of patriotic discourse. In August 1938, for example, when Youth Congress chairman Joseph Cadden addressed the opening session of the World Youth Congress he did not emphasize social problems and inequities, but rather the virtues of American democracy. In his speech to the delegates from 57 nations assembled at this session, Cadden sounded more like a boy scout than a young radical. He welcomed the delegates to

> an America you have never seen . . . . You know our land for its tall buildings, its great cities . . . . But there is another side of America which you have never seen on picture post cards, a side of America which the young people of our country cherish even more than the New York skyline. In the United States we have built . . . a civilization on the firm foundation of freedom and justice. And it is of this that we are most proud.[128]

In this same mind-set the Youth Congress in July 1939 adopted its "Creed of American Youth." The Creed, which served as the new organizing document of the Youth Congress, was saturated with patriotic language. Here each member of the Youth Congress pledged that he or she would

not permit class hatred to divide me from other young people. I will
work for the unity of my generation and place that strength at the service
of my country, which I will defend against all enemies. I pledge allegiance to the Flag of the United States of America and to the Republic
for which it stands, one Nation indivisible with liberty and justice for
all.[129]

As the movement dropped its criticism of capitalism, it also softened
its stance regarding President Roosevelt and the New Deal. Talk of the
New Deal's fascistic tendencies, which had been so prominent in the early
student movement, ceased in the mid-1930s. More temperate criticisms of
the limits of the New Deal's social programs continued through 1937. The
New Deal was now depicted as a well intentioned but inadequate social
program. But by the following year, when the CP had embraced FDR as
an ally in the international struggle against fascism—during the period of
CP history appropriately dubbed the Democratic Front—both the ASU
and the Youth Congress began singing Roosevelt's praises.[130]

ASU organizers in 1938 portrayed FDR as a key leader of the western anti-fascist forces and endorsed his New Deal as a bulwark against
American reaction. They began to speak of the ASU as a "New Deal
agency," which would mobilize youth behind the president. Typifying this
new position, in an article prepared for the 1938 ASU convention, Celeste
Strack, a national officer of both the ASU and the YCL, explained that
"the leadership of the ASU . . . plans at this convention" to see "that the
ASU can become a force for winning not only the student body to the
New Deal, but through them sections of the middle class." ASU leaders
discarded earlier descriptions of their organization as a coalition of radicals and liberals, and began to speak of the ASU as a pure and simple
liberal organization. "We are the liberal youth of the nation," explained
ASU chair Robert Lane in 1938. "We must identify ourselves with . . .
the New Deal."[131] With the ASU and the Youth Congress making this
shift, their influence in Washington grew. Both the ASU and Youth Congress proved adept in bringing the student movement into the New Deal
coalition and cultivating an extraordinarily fruitful relationship with key
figures in the Roosevelt administration. The closest of these relationships
was with Mrs. Roosevelt.

The First Lady warmed up to the Youth Congress and formed personal friendships and a political alliance with its national leaders as they
grew more receptive to the New Deal. Mrs. Roosevelt served as the keynote speaker at a regional meeting of the Youth Congress in January
1938. She joined with the Youth Congress in sponsoring the World Youth
Congress in August 1938 and attended its sessions at Vassar—answering
questions from the young delegates for more than an hour. Mrs. Roosevelt, along with NYA director Aubrey Williams, were featured speakers
at the Youth Congress' convention in July 1939. The First Lady raised
funds for the Youth Congress, repeatedly invited its leaders to the White

House, interceded with the president on their behalf, and defended both the Youth Congress and the student movement in her newspaper columns. She praised the Youth Congress for raising public awareness of the "problems of 21,000,000 young people," and expressed "great confidence in the wisdom, the idealism and the honesty of" these young activists. Such endorsements from the highly popular First Lady added significantly to the Youth Congress' reputation as the voice of the young in Depression America. No leftist-led student movement before or since has enjoyed such support from the White House.[132]

This improved relationship with the Roosevelt administration did more, however, than enhance the movement's public image. It also gave these young activists a chance to participate in the process by which the Roosevelt administration shaped its aid policies for the colleges and youth. ASU and Youth Congress representatives were consulted by the WPA as it designed programs to assist playwrights and theaters on campus. Youth Congress leaders began to serve on the NYA's national advisory committee in Washington. The NYA in turn assisted the Youth Congress by providing the organization with office staff.[133]

Not everyone within the student movement was happy about the ASU's and Youth Congress' liberalism and their budding romance with Roosevelt administration. This shift enraged a small but vocal group of Trotskyists and leftwing socialists in the YPSL. These leftists accused the ASU and Youth Congress of selling out to liberalism and abandoning their radical vision. They charged that the communist-dominated ASU and Youth Congress had corrupted the student movement through a "process of class collaborationism, patriotism and junior people's frontism." In their view, the communist leaders of the student movement were so eager to form a multi-class coalition in support of the Comintern's people's front against fascism that they were willing to dispense with serious social criticism and agitation. They charged that since the ASU and Youth Congress now thought class conflict and analysis were divisive, these were being shed in favor of a more bland and nationalistic program upon which all classes could unite. The ASU and Youth Congress now promoted, according to their leftist critics, the liberal illusion that there could be meaningful "social change without class struggle."[134]

Among the worst sins of the ASU and Youth Congress, in the eyes of these leftist critics, was their support of the New Deal. The YPSLs and Trotskyists claimed that the ASU and Youth Congress had reduced themselves to cheerleaders for the Roosevelt administration, surrendering their role as champion of the "locked out generation" of "five million unemployed young people in the United States." When in 1938 the ASU began preaching that "the New Deal is Youth's Deal" it was, the YPSL charged, ignoring the fact that "the Roosevelt administration had failed utterly to answer the plight of" these millions of jobless youths.[135]

These critics were correct in noting the shift in the student movement away from anti-capitalism and toward liberalism. But this searing indictment of the ASU and Youth Congress also reflected the partisanship of its authors. The YPSLs and Trotskyists who made these criticisms were already in the process of breaking with the larger student movement because of its abandonment of the Oxford Pledge. Bitter and angry, the YPSLs and Trotskyists were so eager to denounce the communist leadership of the ASU and Youth Congress, that they cast the changes in the student movement in the worst possible light. As leftwing ideologues, they saw any shift away from a strict revolutionary line as a sellout. But the relationship between radicalism and reform within the student movement remained more complex than these critics cared to admit. The student movement had always had a strong reformist side. The Popular Front policies represented less a sell out of the movement's principles than an extension of its pragmatic (some might say opportunistic) approach to student organizing.

The continuities within the student movement in the early and late 1930s are as striking as the changes. True, the early literature of the NSL and SLID spoke of the imminent demise of capitalism, while the ASU did not. But if one probed the *activities* of these organizations, crucial similarities emerge. All three devoted almost all of their time to campaigns on immediate issues. The bulk of their energy went into promoting peace, student welfare, civil rights, and solidarity between the student movement and the labor movement. The real difference here was that unlike the ASU, the NSL and SLID spoke of using such activities to radicalize students. But this difference in intent did not amount to much. For, although the NSL and SLID had hoped their campaigns would lead to widespread student radicalization, they learned differently. Students would rally with the NSL and SLID for peace or student aid, but only a small minority would become sufficiently radicalized to join either organization. Combatting the flaws in capitalism did not—as the NSL and SLID had naively expected—lead many students to embrace socialism. Indeed, as the New Deal began to restore America's faith in liberalism in the mid-1930s, students increasingly viewed reform as a viable option. This left both the NSL and SLID in a paradoxical situation. Much as they might thumb their noses at liberal reform, NSLers and SLIDers had the most influence on campus at those moments when they were leading their classmates in reformist campaigns.

As pragmatists, NSLers and SLIDers sensed that given the non-revolutionary environment on campus in the mid-1930s, their agitation could be most effective if channelled into a new organization—the ASU—that would not be associated in the student mind with revolutionary parties and dogmas. The idea was that if freed from the revolutionary rhetoric and image of the early student Left, the ASU could attract many more members than had the NSL and SLID. The ASU was designed by its founders from the NSL and SLID to continue their campaigns for peace and social justice, but to do so in a style which would enlarge them; and this was just what the ASU accomplished.

Even though the rhetoric was new, the concept behind the ASU remained consistent with the basic organizing strategy which had guided the student Left since the early 1930s. From the very beginning of the movement both socialists and communists had suspected that an official party youth organization with the "socialist" or "communist" label would seem too revolutionary for the American student body. That is why socialist students did not center their national campus organizing in the Socialist Party's YPSL, but instead used the SLID—an organization not officially affiliated with the Socialist Party—as their main membership organization on campus. The same was true of the communists, who focused their campus organizing in the NSL rather than the YCL. So though the ASU was the first official Popular Front organization on campus, its parent organizations had in a sense already been fronts for the more explicitly ideological and partisan communist and socialist organizations. The ASU extended this approach by going further in submerging its ties with leftist parties and ideologies than had the NSL and SLID.

These were not the only continuities between the student Left of the early and late 1930s. Indeed, during the early 30s, the NSL and SLID experimented with a form of coalition politics which the adult Left would embrace later in the decade—during the Popular Front era. The NSL was championing causes which appealed to liberal students at a time when the CP's revolutionary posturing—a byproduct of the Comintern's ultra-radical Third Period line—was still alienating liberal adults. The NSL and SLID also pioneered the type of non-sectarianism which would later become a main tenet of the Popular Front. For example, during the spring 1934 anti-war strike and in the summer 1934 Youth Congress, socialist and communist student organizers worked together in the name of peace and anti-fascism, while the SP and CP were still feuding. And in working to build the Youth Congress into a multi-class organization of progressive youth (while the CP was still focusing almost exclusively on workers) the movement anticipated another key element of the the Popular Front. Long before the Comintern in the summer of 1935 declared a Popular Front by advocating unity of the Left with all classes and political groups against fascism, the student movement was already promoting such unity.[136]

These continuities in the movement suggest that the Popular Front policies may not have been quite the dire change and sell out that its critics charged. But, of course, along with such continuity did come the stunning reversal on the New Deal. The founders of the NSL and SLID in the early 1930s could barely have dreamed that their successors would so warm up to Roosevelt. If viewed in strictly ideological terms, this warmth between student radicals and a liberal administration would seem to represent—as the Trotskyists and YPSLs claimed—an abandonment of principle.[137] Here again, however, the image of the movement selling out does not quite correspond with political reality. The interaction between the student movement and the Roosevelt administration was far less one sided than its critics imply.

Even as the ASU and Youth Congress linked themselves closer to the New Deal, they still retained much of their old desire for more sweeping social legislation than the Roosevelt administration was delivering. The tone of the demands for such legislation was different and softer than in the early 1930s, since now students spoke from inside rather than outside the New Deal coalition. But the basic dynamic was the same: student activists seeking to push the federal government leftward. This could be seen, for instance, in the evolving relationship between the Youth Congress and the NYA. In May 1937, NYA director Aubrey Williams told Youth Congress leaders that the NYA was in danger because of a conservative rebellion on Capitol Hill. Williams came to the Youth Congress "appealing for a campaign to keep the relief budget from being slashed to $1,000,000,000 which would probably mean ending the National Youth Administration." The Youth Congress worked to rally national support for the NYA in order to prevent thousands of youths from losing their jobs. But while seeking to help the NYA preserve existing jobs, the Youth Congress in 1937 continued to push for expansion of youth aid through its own much more generous aid package—the American Youth Act. The Youth Congress' assistance helped prevent the feared NYA cuts. Even after this campaign, however, the Youth Congress did not completely abandon its critical view of the Roosevelt youth program. In the fall of 1937, when President Roosevelt indicated his desire to spend less on the NYA than the $75 million authorized by Congress, the Youth Congress protested the president's policy.[138]

Publicly the Youth Congress' (and ASU's) leftwing critics condemned all such cooperation with New Dealers. But privately even some of these critics conceded the logic and pragmatism of the Youth Congress' position. For instance in a letter to a fellow YPSL organizer, Hy Weintraub confided his doubts about the arguments that they had been making against fighting for an expanded and better funded NYA. Weintraub expressed his "wish" that

> someone could make a clear statement on why the YPSL does not support the fight for better conditions on the NYA. I think the Communist position on this is correct—we fight for the AYA but we also participate in the immediate struggles of youth by asking for more for the NYA. The AYA is too far away and utopian for those people who need relief immediately.[139]

Although the Youth Congress continued its support of the American Youth Act in 1938, by the following year this crusade had fizzled and the Act was not even re-introduced on Capitol Hill. This was clearly because of the growing links between the Youth Congress and the NYA. The Youth Congress had become so closely enmeshed in the NYA that its leaders were no longer interested in pushing for the AYA. However, this work with the NYA had not rendered the Youth Congress leadership complacent regarding the New Deal program. This was evident in the behavior of Youth Congress chair Abbot Simon as a participant in the NYA advisory board's 1938 meeting with FDR. Where the members of the board used their conference with the president to trumpet the NYA's accomplishments, Simon chose instead to criticize the NYA's limitations. Simon told the president that the NYA should be expanded immediately and dramatically so that it would aid 1,500,000 youths instead of the mere 500,000 it had been assisting. Similarly, at its 1939 convention, the Youth Congress praised the NYA, but also pushed for a new loan program and more vocational training and apprenticeship programs for youth.[140]

This continuing willingness of student movement leaders to press the president for more generous social programs—especially for youth—did not go unnoticed in the White House. Ironically, it helped cement their relationship with Eleanor Roosevelt during the late 1930s. At a time when the New Deal was stalemated and its youth programs threatened by Congressional cutbacks, Mrs. Roosevelt saw these activists as allies in her effort to "win the president over to doing more for young people." As Joseph Lash explains, part of the reason she "enjoyed having them to dinner with the president" was because "unlike many of the people he saw the young people stood up to him."[141]

The president, on other other hand, sometimes was irritated by the student movement's demand for increased social spending. When, for instance, the First Lady sent him a copy of Lash's keynote speech from the ASU's convention, held in December 1938—which, though pro-FDR, also called for expansion of the NYA and other social programs—the president responded testily. He wrote a memorandum in January 1939 implying that the ASU's suggestions were fiscally irresponsible. FDR advised her:

> If you want to start a discussion among young people some day, get them to discuss and answer the following question: The government deficit today is $3,000,000,000 a year . . . . We could very easily and usefully spend another billion dollars a year on aids to and improvement of education . . . . We could very easily use another billion dollars a year in . . . youth training . . . . How can the . . . new deficit, if such projects are carried out be financed?[142]

FDR's sentiments in this 1939 memorandum recalled those of his wife's at her initial meeting with the Youth Congress leadership back in 1936. At that meeting Mrs. Roosevelt had criticized the young activists and their American Youth Act for demanding far more social spending than the nation could afford.[143] The president was criticizing the ASU on this same basis in 1939. Much had changed in the student movement during the years between the 1936 meeting and the 1939 memorandum. The student movement was now supporting the Roosevelt administration rather than denouncing it and calling itself liberal rather than revolutionary. But in spite of these changes, and in spite of its occasional flights into nationalistic gush, the student movement, as the president's irritation suggests, had not become a mere FDR fan club. The movement retained the ability and inclination to ask for more—more social spending than the Roosevelt administration provided, more educational and economic opportunity than America afforded, and more racial equality than either academia or Washington supported.

VII

Athough YPSL and Trotskyist critics exaggerated some of the student movement's flaws during the Popular Front era, these critics were nonetheless astute in at least one respect. They may have been wrong about the movement selling out to FDR, but they were right to raise the issue of political integrity. The behavior of communist leaders in the student movement during the Popular Front does raise troubling questions about both their personal and political integrity. It was not their policies—their accommodation with liberalism—but rather the process by which those polices were executed that raises the most unsettling questions. Irving Howe, an alumni of both the YPSL and the Trotskyist student Left of the 1930s, captured the essence of this problem when in a recent essay he referred to the Popular Front as a "brilliant masquerade."[144] Communist activists in the student movement brilliantly expanded the movement by merging radicalism with liberalism; they accomplished this, however, by masking their ideological loyalties and party affiliations in a way that deceived not only the public but even their political allies.

The Youth Congress embodied all these problems. This organization's external history was, as we have seen, dominated by campaigns to expand political and social democracy in the United States. The Youth Congress' internal history was, however, anything but democratic. Through a process of infiltration and tactical maneuvering, communists gradually took control of the organization's national leadership. Communist students and youth organizers packed the important committees with members and sympathizers. At the very top of the Youth Congress too, communist domination was assured as succeeding AYC officers were brought into the communist orbit. Former YCL leader Gil Green recalled that "one after another" the Youth Congress chairs were

> recruited into either the YCL or the Party. Waldo McNutt [the first AYC chair] was recruited into the Party. Bill Hinckley, who became the second [AYC chair] was recruited. Joe Cadden after him was recruited. And Jack McMichael [the last AYC chair] no; but he was very sympathetic. He was *very*, very close [to the CP]. And I could mention a whole number of others.[145]

The real problem with this recruitment and infiltration was not its scope, but its secrecy. Had the communists been open about their identity and influence they would have been operating within parameters of democratic process—since they, like all other members of such a federation, have the right to compete for power. Unfortunately, this was not done openly. Instead, Green secretly recruited the top Youth Congress officers; the YCL clandestinely stacked the Congress' key committees; and the Youth Congress secretly became a communist-dominated organization.[146] These Communist machinations led to political misrepresentation. At the very time when the Popular Front and its rhetoric made the Youth Congress seem more liberal and mainstream it was actually growing more communist-controlled.

The student who read Youth Congress literature in the Popular Front era would have thought it an organization influenced not by the Soviet but the American revolution. To help give credence to this association with 1776 the Youth Congress had begun in 1935 to move its annual national convention to July 4. Its Declaration of Rights of Youth at this 1935 convention was written to frame the Youth Congress' demands in a way that called to mind the Declaration of Independence. The Youth Congress also effectively combined its egalitarian message with other images from America's liberal heritage. When, for instance, the Youth Congress advertised its American Youth Act, it did so by invoking images of frontier democracy, comparing this legislation to the Homestead Act of 1862, and in fact calling it "the Homestead Act of 1937."[147]

In using such rhetoric and setting its slogans—as it did in its 1937 Youth Pilgrimage—to the tune of Yankee Doodle, the Youth Congress was trying to reach out to non-radicals. This effort to speak in the language of American liberalism was obviously a creative and important step on the road to broadening the movement. It was not the use of such rhetoric alone which is problematic, but rather the use of such rhetoric by an organization which hid its communist domination. People were being recruited into a liberal sounding organization, believing that it was run by liberals, when in fact it was run by communists. These recruits also had no way of knowing that the Youth Congress' increasingly moderate rhetoric and growing ties to the New Deal were changes linked to the influence of communists and their Popular Front line on the organization. In short, the movement's literature failed to clue students in to who ran the organization or how its policies were shaped ideologically.[148]

The deception employed by the communists in the Youth Congress was not always this subtle and implicit. Some of the leading and secret communists in the Youth Congress leadership did not simply fail to mention their Party affiliation; they publicly lied about their ties to the Communist Party and YCL. When rightwingers accused these individuals of being communists and charged that the Youth Congress was communist-dominated, these communists—including Youth Congress chairs—denied everything, misleading the press, the public, and the Youth Congress membership.[149]

Why the deception? Communists in the Youth Congress had good reason to hide their political affiliations. Even in an era as liberal as the 1930s, anti-communism remained a strong political force in America. Throughout the Depression decade state legislatures, superpatriot groups, and the Hearst press denounced and investigated red influence over youth and education. By 1938 Congress was funding its own brand of anti-communist crusading, led by Representative Martin Dies and the House Un-American Activities Committee, which he chaired. The Youth Congress would itself become the target of a red probe by Dies and his committee before the decade ended.[150] With such powerful and influential people seeking to deny civil liberties to communists, many felt that if they were to remain politically active and effective, they had to hide their party affiliations. The communists' deception here was, in part, a response to America's political intolerance—a way of evading redbaiters. This political context must be borne in mind, so as to avoid demonizing the communists or neglecting the connections between the maladies of the CP and those of the larger national polity. But this context does not excuse the communists, nor should it obscure the ways in which a political movement more concerned with ends than means compromised its integrity.

The tenor of the Popular and Democratic Fronts also provided a more positive rationale and inducement for communists in the Youth Congress to keep their Party loyalty to themselves. At the heart of the communist line in this era lay the notion that all other considerations should be secondary to the building of the broadest possible anti-fascist coalition. This meant that everyone should, as much as possible, ignore party differences and identifications in order to work together on the building of the anti-fascist front. In this sense, submerging one's CP affiliation could be seen as a virtuous act on behalf of anti-fascist unity. It was, in the student movement's case, a means of protecting the movement from the divisiveness and controversy which might have resulted had the Youth Congress' communist leadership gone public. During this era communists also felt that they shared so many foreign and social policy goals with liberals that party labels were becoming irrelevant. What mattered was not who you were or how you voted, but whether you were willing to join in the crusade to stop international fascism from exterminating democracy. This was what one of the secret communists at the top of Youth Congress leadership meant when he confided to a colleague that "it was all right for CPers in the democratic front to deny they were CPers by virtue of the fact that they were defending democracy."[151]

Although this communist secrecy represented an understandable response to intolerance and in the short run a practical step for building a broader movement, the long run consequences of it would prove disastrous for both the Youth Congress and the entire student movement. However they rationalized it, the fact was that communists in the student movement were, as ASU activist Junius Scales put it, "full of duplicity."[152] They were lying about their party ties not only to strangers, but even to their close political allies and friends. Among those so deceived was Eleanor Roosevelt. Though the First Lady did more than anyone in Washington to aid the Youth Congress and became personally close to some of the its leaders, they hid their communist ties from her. With Mrs. Roosevelt and other liberal allies of the student movement this deception would go undetected for several years. So long as the Popular Front lasted, and liberals and communists took compatible positions on key policy questions, the Party question was submerged. But when the communists, in the wake of the Nazi-Soviet Pact, began to destroy the Popular Front against fascism, their old lies would come back to haunt them. Suddenly liberals such as Mrs. Roosevelt found themselves under attack by student activists who had been their close friends. The communists flip-flopped on foreign and domestic policy questions in a manner so transparently dictated by the new Comintern line that liberals both on campus and in Washington discerned the deception. The feelings of betrayal and mistrust borne of that deception would poison the political atmosphere and contribute to the decline of both the Youth Congress and the entire student movement.[153]

Chapter 8

Activist Impulses

"How can I explain the position of organized labor to Father when you keep passing me the chocolate sauce?" The earnest college girl in the cartoon is arousing the social conscience of her well-off father while her embarrassed mother vainly tries to stanch the flow of ideology with rich food. Anne Cleveland, Vassar '36, drew the scene, and everyone who went to a liberal arts college in her time recognizes the mood of social protest.

We felt that the New Deal would never get to the bottom of the trouble. We felt that something basic was wrong with the setup and it was up to us to find out what was wrong and do something about it. We enjoyed a pleasurable sense of millenium. Things could not go on as they had. We felt injustice as personal guilt. "If you give your coat to the first man shivering on the street," we used to say, "then what are you going to do for the next one?" It worried us that we had a coat . . . . We were ashamed that our parents had sent us to snobby private schools. We imagined that the unemployed looked hungrily over our shoulders, just as we had imagined that the starving Chinese suffered when we refused to eat our spinach.

Caroline Bird, *The Invisible Scar* (New York, 1966), 138.

N o sooner had the student movement emerged than speculation began about the sources of campus activism. Since such large scale student protest was unprecedented in the nation's history, it was natural that a variety of theories would evolve as Depression America sought to explain this new phenomenon. An assortment of conservatives—which included superpatriots, redbaiting editors, and politicians—wrote the most and screamed the loudest about the causes of student radicalism during the 1930s; they did so because of their outrage at the growth of Left-led organizations and student anti-war demonstrations on campus. Their most frequent explanation for this unwelcome upsurge of student activism centered on the faculty, whom they blamed for corrupting and radicalizing youth.

The conservative press depicted college faculty as dangerously subversive. Professors emerged in these pages as a sort of academic branch of the Red Army. "There are few colleges or universities where parents may send their sons and daughters without their being contaminated with some phase of the vilest of Communistic and allied teaching," warned Roscoe J.C. Dorsey, in the *The National Republic,* a superpatriot magazine which crusaded against faculty and student radicalism. In this same journal E.D. Clark, president of the Indiana State Medical Association, diagnosed "Red Microbes in Our Colleges," evoking fears of political and sexual radicalism. The Hoosier doctor claimed that "under the guise of 'academic freedom' many professors . . . are not only teaching communism, socialism, anarchy . . . but are also endorsing 'free love' and unrestricted sex relations between unmarried people."[1]

This rightwing indictment of the faculty was not confined, however, to the college level. Conservatives hurled similar charges against teachers in secondary and even elementary schools. The Hearst press, which did so much to give such charges national circulation, claimed in 1935 that thanks to the work of subversives in the nation's school systems "two hundred thousand Soviet schoolbooks have been imported into America."[2] According to these rightwing critics, youths' support for radicalism in college derived from exposure to subversion by teachers at all levels of the American educational system. Typifying this faculty-bashing, the Hearst editorial "Red Teachers" concluded that

> the danger to the country of the growth of Communism in our seats of learning should not be blamed on our students. There is the element of youthful effervescence and the emotional hurrah of the novel that often pass away when the student begins the struggle for existence and finds that rugged individualism is his only asset. The danger lies in the teachers of communism in our colleges and schools. A student may outgrow his revolutionary effervescence. But it is hard for him to overcome the subtle and overt injections into him by persons he regards as authorities. The teaching of communism in our . . . institutions of learning is a breach of trust and a perversion of professional responsibility. A teacher is paid to expound and explain, not to indoctrinate.[3]

Although the sensationalism of such Hearst stories (which produced those mythological textbooks smuggled from Russia) makes it difficult to take the conservative view of student radicalism too seriously, that view did have serious consequences. It led anti-communists, seeking the elimination of student radicalism, to launch political attacks on the purported source of that radicalism: subversive faculty members. This was expressed through a movement, spearheaded by superpatriot groups, to impose loyalty oaths on teachers. By the end of the Depression decade, twenty-one states had adopted such oaths. The volatility of the faculty radicalism issue was also evident in such conservative assaults on faculty dissent as that which occurred at the University of Chicago in 1935. Here pharmacy magnate Charles R. Walgreen caused great upheaval by removing his niece from the University, and charging that he did so because she had been indoctrinated in communism and free love by Chicago faculty members. Though not even Walgreen's niece fully supported his charges, they were all the Illinois state legislature needed as a pretext for launching an investigation into subversion at the University of Chicago—an investigation which failed to turn up any Bolsheviks or free love advocates on the faculty.[4]

The loyalty oaths and the Chicago investigation attest that for conservatives such faculty-baiting was almost irresistable. It appealed to both the anti-radical and anti-intellectual currents in 1930s conservatism. For rightwing politicians and journalists, moreover, this seemed a cause tailor made for public approval—complete with emotionally charged images of adult "Commie" professors preying on innocent youths. The free love charge added incestuous overtones to an already explosive brew. But whatever its merits as a tool for demagoguery, such faculty scapegoating misrepresented the political situation in American educational institutions. Throughout the Depression decade, the Right exaggerated the dimensions of faculty radicalism and the role of teachers in both sparking student protest and building the student movement.

The best sources for assessing the role that faculty played in turning students to activism are the students themselves. The SLID in 1935 and the ASU in 1938 and 1939 held summer leadership institutes for student organizers, during which more than 70 activists completed essays about their politicization. Dozens of activists have written memoirs and given interviews in which they too discussed the roots of their activism. These sources suggest that faculty did not play a predominant role in the politicization of 1930s activists. Only 21.6 percent of the activists reported that a faculty member fostered their politicization, and most of these activists mentioned such faculty influence as only one of many factors which contributed to their politicization. This 21.6 percent figure looks even smaller, moreover, in light of the fact that another 20 percent of the student activists cited unpleasant experiences with reactionary faculty who had sought to stifle student dissent and non-conformity.[5] There were, in other words, almost as many student organizers who viewed faculty as an obstacle to Left-liberal activism as viewed faculty as facilitators of such activism.

Among the 20 percent recording negative encounters with conservative faculty were young men and women with painful classroom memories dating back to elementary school. One ASU activist recalled that his parents' organizing on behalf of Sacco and Vanzetti had made a "deep impression" on him. In grade school, however, his teacher lectured the class on "what kind of 'bad' men Sacco and Vanzetti were." This led to "my spontaneous outcry that she was a liar, and [a] subsequent talk with the public school principal about how the labor movement was a bad thing."

Another activist told of being frightened by an elementary school teacher, who had become "aghast . . . and furious" after she told the teacher—as her radical parents had told her—that in 1917 the United States "had *not* entered the war to avenge the *Lusitania* . . . that it had something to do with munitions makers and raw materials." Faculty intolerance sometimes had ethnic as well as ideological dimensions, judging by a Columbia student radical's memories of his kindergarten teacher, who in 1919 called him a "little enemy" and marched him off to see the principal because he had sung a German song taught him by his parents. A University of Wisconsin ASU organizer wrote of being scolded by a teacher and sent to his junior high school principal's office for expressing "opposition to larger armaments. This was my first experience with narrow-mindedness in the school system."[6]

Even some students who had not experienced such traumatic confrontations recalled their pre-college education as dull or deadening to dissident thought. A Vassar ASU leader looked back upon her prep school as a place whose classrooms and student body were pervaded by "narrowness and conservatism." The students there were a "group of girls of the typically Boston sub-deb[utant] variety . . . whose main interest seemed to be boys and parties." Another ASU activist noted that her only contact with politics in secondary school had been

> a course in social problems from a high school teacher, who was anti-New Deal, anti-labor, anti-progress. He was a militarist, a fatalist, and a pessimist. I came out of that course a completely defeated person. The state of the human race was hardly better than . . . 3,000 years ago, and there was not much use in our fretting and striving about to improve it.[7]

A Bryn Mawr ASU organizer termed as "disgraceful" the faculty at her Philadelphia High School. "Little or no independent thinking is encouraged. Students are expected to repeat parrot-like the opinions expressed to them . . . [by] reactionary or escapist" teachers.[8]

Youths who entered the student movement before graduation from such schools were not—as the Hearst press preached—following the direction of teachers; they were rebelling against the orthodoxy and conformity fostered by those teachers. And those daring enough to engage in this open rebellion often encountered strong hostility from faculty and school authorities. An ASU organizer from Cleveland noted that in her high school

> the faculty still used its power over scholarship awards to force two members out of the [ASU] chapter, and witnesses heard the principal announce that he would do everything in his power to block the award of scholarships to the leading members of the ASU regardless of the superior qualifications of the students.[9]

A New York City ASUer described how a repressive teacher monitored the radical students in his high school's Current Problems Club: "We were silenced by the faculty advisor whenever we tried to mention ASU . . . . At High School we protested consistent faculty censorship of the paper, of assemblies, of clubs, magazine and student council." Another New Yorker with similar high school experiences believed that he had come out of this intolerant milieu strengthened by adversity. His "long initiation of . . . arguing with teachers . . . . standing up against the discipline of Principal Boylan, the many threats of violence from the football team, as well as the threats of arrest for distributing literature must have been good training for leadership" in the student movement.[10]

Not only these individual memoirs, but also the student movement's publications refute the Right's equation of American educators with revolutionary subversion. In the ASU's national magazine, *Student Advocate*, teachers, professors, and educational administrators appear much more frequently as foes than friends of the student movement. The magazine's most extensive feature on American educators was a six part series on intolerant college presidents, indicting these "Academic Napoleons" for trying to stamp out dissent on their campuses. The magazine's other coverage of the American educational scene—with such headlines as "University Sweatshops," "Gagging High Schools," "Kansas Is A White Man's School," "ROTC Trains Strike Breakers," "How to Be A Censored [Student] Editor,"—paints an equally unflattering portrait of reactionary, narrow-minded and repressive educational leadership. The *Student Advocate* lampooned stodgy and conservative professors, depicting them as comically inept teachers, out of touch with recent political and cultural developments. In fact, the ASU magazine even invoked this image in an ad for new subscribers, which featured a professorial caricature, accompanied by the words:

> Hey You! Don't think this bearded gent knows all the answers. Sometimes he doesn't even know the questions! Ask him the story behind the NYA cuts [or] who controls his Board of Trustees—and see what happens. Ask him how we can keep out of war and where you can get a job when you graduate—or why you can't.[11]

Not all teachers, of course, were as uninformed or reactionary as these ASU stories implied. After all, 21.6 percent of the student activists surveyed did credit a faculty member with helping to politicize them and pave the way for their participation in the student movement. Who were these faculty? Here again the Right's revolutionary imagery of red teachers engaging in communist indoctrination was simplistic. More than a third of the students (in the 21.6 percent group) who reported that a faculty member helped politicize them referred not to radical instructors preaching revolution, but to liberal faculty teaching about reform.[12]

This considerable liberal role reflected the fact that the 1930s was the decade of the New Deal, an era in which liberalism prevailed in the White House and much of America. Nationally, faculty were more affected by this liberalism than they were by radicalism. An overwhelming 84 percent of social science professors supported New Deal liberalism, according to a 1937 national poll.[13] Some of this sentiment would, of course, be reflected in the classroom. The result was that at least some students would be exposed to liberal idealism and critical thought about American society. This would not make instant revolutionaries out of these students; but it exposed them to new political ideas, in a way that could leave them more receptive to the appeals of ASU organizers. This was particularly true during the Popular Front era, when the politics of the ASU and the New Deal were so similar.

There were a variety of ways in which liberal teachers prodded students to think about social problems and thereby helped to politicize them. These included teaching students about social science, political problems, and the need for reformist efforts to address those problems. One ASU activist recalled that several progressive teachers in the private high school she attended introduced her

> in an undoubtedly careful and scientific manner to the social sciences for the first time in my life . . . . I learned why workers organized, what a black list is, the techniques utilized by labor and capital, the value of social legislation, and the danger of thoughtless "conservatism." . . . By the time I was ready for college I considered myself a full fledged progressive, having travelled in those two years from a disinterested Republican to an avid New Dealer to theoretically more inspiring and revolutionary horizons.[14]

A midwestern ASU organizer observed that he too had become politically conscious after his exposure to critical thought in the social sciences. College "courses in economics, history and political science awakened me to local, national and international affairs . . ." So when Molly Yard and another ASU leader came to his campus, he helped organize an ASU chapter, seeing this activist group as a vehicle "to solidify and to integrate my many new interests."[15] In other cases, it was not social science methodology, but the idealism of liberal teachers that inspired students to become politically active. A North Carolina ASU organizer, for instance, found that "one of the greatest stimuli to liberal and intelligent thinking I have received came from my high school history teacher. She had a great deal of faith in and understanding of the common person and this she passed on to some of her pupils."[16]

The liberal teachers who helped inspire student activism came not only out of the New Deal tradition, but also out of other progressive strains in American political culture. ASU national officer Celeste Strack, for instance, recalled that her first steps toward political consciousness came before college, through the influence of a feminist teacher, who was the principal of her small private school in San Diego. This teacher had herself once been a student rebel, active at Vassar during the women's suffrage campaign. She taught Strack in a manner that reflected the critical sensibility of the women's movement, having, as Strack put it,

> the knack of teaching you how to think, to question . . . . And her way was not to try to convince you of a viewpoint but to get you to think critically about the world you were in, and given the Depression that wasn't hard to do. So that it was this which I brought to USC and this . . . enabled me to be responsive [to the student movement].[17]

African American student activist Kenneth Clark had a similar experience with Howard University faculty, whose critical teachings on race relations in the United States prodded him to engage in civil rights agitation. Other students headed in an activist direction after learning from teachers influenced by progressive education—particularly in the Ethical Culture schools—which emphasized liberal values and the importance of acting on them.[18]

By understanding the role played by liberal faculty as well as their conservative counterparts, it becomes possible to put faculty radicalism into perspective. Among the students in our sample activist group who cited some faculty role—either positive or negative—in their political evolution, more than twice as many mentioned liberal and conservative faculty as mentioned radical faculty. Out of the entire activist group sampled only 11.2 percent said that radical faculty contributed to their politicization. This low number suggests that though leftist teachers contributed to politicizing students and strengthening the student movement, that contribution was much less significant than Hearst and other rightwing critics of the faculty imagined.[19]

The relatively small contribution leftist faculty made to the movement was linked to the tenuous nature of such professorial radicalism. Faculty radicals constituted a small and insecure minority. Since college administrators usually believed it improper for faculty to engage in leftist agitation, they used their power to discourage such activity. This administration anti-radicalism meant that faculty members who chose to identify themselves closely with the student Left were risking their jobs. Among the faculty who took this risk (usually young instructors rather than professors) and lost were Oakley Johnson at CCNY, Donald Henderson at Columbia, Herbert Miller at Ohio State, and Jerome Davis at Yale. Their firings received extensive press attention and served as a strong deterrent to leftist faculty—who were not anxious to lose their jobs in a depressed era, when faculty positions were particularly hard to come by. In addition to fear of firing, a professorial ethical code sometimes inhibited faculty expression of radicalism. Some (though by no means all) leftist faculty thought it unprofessional to use the "classroom as an instrument of indoctrination." "We had," as one radical faculty member explained, "a lurking feeling that it wasn't quite good sportsmanship to try to influence young people [politically]—at least to make use of our position in the classroom to do this."[20]

Few students could expect to encounter an overtly radical faculty member in Depression America, when such faculty were small in number, insecure in their jobs, and divided themselves about the propriety of radical proselytizing in the classroom. About the rarest experience of all was encountering teachers who explicitly incorporated Marxist ideas into their lectures and other regular classroom activities. This did occur, however, in a few college courses in the social sciences and humanities, usually on campuses reputed to be among the most permissive. At Harvard, for instance, the Marxist economist Paul Sweezy, jointly offered a course with a more conservative colleague to give students both the pro- and anti-capitalist perspective.[21] Vassar College, with its unique feminist tradition, allowed several radical professors the freedom to give their courses a socialist slant. At a scattering of the more progressive private secondary and lower schools, it was also possible to run into a teacher who brought radical politics into the classroom. One student activist from Western Reserve University noted that a teacher in her Ethical Culture school, who "preached a sort of Utopian Socialism" helped to shape her politics.[22]

Since the atmosphere on most campuses was not free enough for such overt radical teaching, student encounters with faculty radicalism tended to occur outside the classroom. The vehicle for this encounter was sometimes the campus' Marxist study group, where small groups of leftist faculty, graduate students, and undergraduates assembled for informal discussions of radical theory. A socialist student organizer from the University of Louisville recalled that on arriving at college

> I thought about politics in terms of Republicans and Democrats, about economics not at all. Then came the dawn! . . . Two of my college friends invited me to attend a meeting at the house of my psychology professor . . . . It was a radical discussion group, meeting every week and known as the Pen and Hammer Club; radicals of every creed were there. The meeting was just a little over my head, but I was interested and went back again.[23]

The covert nature of these encounters sometimes gave them a special intensity, as students and teachers shared forbidden Marxist knowledge. This was evident in the memoirs of an ASU activist in a prominent eastern women's college. In linking her radicalization to "a fascinating series of Marxist" discussion group meetings with a leftist faculty member, she explained that "there was an exciting atmosphere of secrecy about each meeting. It was only as I got more involved in the actual analysis of Marxian theory that I realized how terribly important the class struggle was and how equally important my relationship to it could be."[24] An African American student radical from Fisk recalled that here too secrecy was necessary because the administration and town authorities were so anti-radical. The underground nature of her interaction with the few Communist professors on campus added to its allure:

> One professor had almost like an Anne Frank's room at the back of his house . . . packed with all kinds of radical literature. And when they got to know me I was free to visit there and just read. And there were things like the *Daily Worker* there and all kinds of books—books there would be no way of getting on the Fisk campus.[25]

She soon became involved in a radical discussion group with these leftist professors. Similarly, an ASU activist from Randolph-Macon College noted that the secret conversations she had with a young radical psychology professor were "the most important single influence in my intellectual growth." After taking a course with this professor and becoming her research assistant,

> I found out that she liked poetry, especially Auden and Spender. I was slightly suspicious of her extreme enthusiasm for them because I had read somewhere that they were Communists . . . . [We] discussed the state of Christianity. She denied that our democracy was based upon Christianity. In fact, she said it wasn't even democracy. When she explained herself, saying that there were a few people, who because they owned wealth could exploit many people, there was no equality of opportunity and therefore no democracy, I called her a Communist. She said "Sh." I was tremendously excited because I felt as if I were conspiring in a dark and dangerous discussion. In an incredibly short time I was turned into a socialist, partly because I was tired of being nothing and partly because I enjoyed the daring of being a socialist.[26]

Whether such learning was covert or overt its impact could be great on the individual student. Radical faculty willing to share their ideas with undergraduates were exposing them to criticism, authors, and a worldview that could seem new and exciting. This was particularly true for students from conservative families, such as Celeste Strack, who had never before been exposed to Marxist ideas. She first encountered Marxism in her class with a radical economics teacher at USC, and found it to be a "very different way of looking at the world, and it was a very critical way." Strack viewed Marxist concepts—dialectical materialism and class analysis—as a "scientific instrument" that enabled her to dig below the rhetoric of politicians and businessmen, revealing the economic interests and structures that had caused the Depression and shaped history. Strack looked back upon this introduction to radical ideas as "an enormously liberating experience," like " a light turning on in the room; it was literally the illumination of the world . . . a profound experience."[27] For her, the teachings of this radical professor were so memorable that even a half century later she still vividly recalled the course's final exam question which probed the "contradictions" of capitalism. At Harvard, Paul Sweezy made a similar impact on the young Leo Marx, who would later become one of America's leading cultural historians. Marx rated Sweezy "a strong teacher" who persuaded him

> to adopt a radical view of American society, to recognize that the great contradictions of American society are deeply systemic and structural and probably cannot be resolved by piecemeal reform. It's a view of the world that I've since modified in many ways, but I also think I have held onto it ever since.[28]

Not all students who encountered such faculty radicalism recall it with the same warm glow as Strack and Marx. Some viewed this political teaching as an abuse of authority and a form of indoctrination. In novelist Mary McCarthy's memoirs of her years at Vassar, she scorned

> Lockwood's press course (Contemporary Press), a junior year offering renowned for the unlearning she made girls in it do. According to the course description, the class was taught to read the press critically— doubtless a healthy thing. But it was not just the fine art of reading *behind* the news that the girls learned, sitting around a long table seminar style; they were getting indoctrinated with a potent counter-drug. The class, we heard (I never took it) was the scene, almost like a camp meeting, of many a compulsory transformation as hitherto dutiful Republican daughters turned into Socialists and went forth to spread the gospel. It was said that Miss Lockwood insisted that a girl completely break with her mother as the price of winning her favor. The effect on the girl was a kind of smug piety, typical of the born anew, that could last for years, long after the one-time converts, now alumnae (married, with 2.4 children), had turned back into Republicans.[29]

Even though such heavy-handed proselytizing was uncommon among leftist faculty, McCarthy's words confirm that it did go on. Sometimes, in fact, faculty went even further, actually recruiting students into communist or socialist-led organizations. The Fisk student discussed above was approached by a faculty member about joining the Communist Party, as was James Wechsler by a zoology instructor at Columbia. An economics instructor played this same role for the LID at the University of Louisville. But these were extremely rare cases, involving only 2.4 percent of the activists sampled. Moreover, such recruitment went on outside the classroom and was confined to students who had already participated in extensive political discussions or radical activities with the instructor.[30]

Viewed in the context of the total educational experience of the 1930s, the controversy over radical indoctrination seems not only overblown, but also representative of a political double standard.[31] The autobiographical essays, interviews, and published memoirs of the 125 activists sampled here indicate that students confronted all kinds of politics in the classroom: conservative, liberal, and radical. If bringing politics into the class-room is equated with indoctrination, then this was not merely a sin of the Miss Lockwoods of the Left. The teacher who scolded his student for opposing armaments and the principal who lectured the pro-Sacco and Vanzetti pupil on the evils of organized labor engaged in conservative indoctrination. Likewise, the instructor who preached to students about her Jacksonian faith in the common man and the professor who stumped for unions and reform engaged in liberal indoctrination. Those radical faculty who brought their politics into their classes were not guilty, then, of some uniquely sinister approach to teaching. Their only crime con-sisted of teaching an opposing point of view, too far out of the main-stream to be tolerated by the Right.

II

Hearst and his allies failed to understand that dissidence and activism were being taught far more effectively outside than inside the classroom. Nor did they comprehend that such instruction did not usually come from members of the teaching profession. Rightwing critics of the student movement were correct in one respect: the students' elders helped to pave the way for the campus insurgency; however, they were focusing on the wrong elders. It was not the school teachers and professors, but the moth-ers and fathers, the sisters and brothers of campus activists who did the most to incline them toward student protest. Of the student activists in our sampled group, 41.6 percent credited some family members or home influence with facilitating their politicization. Family was by far the most frequent factor the students cited as they discussed the people whose in-fluence fostered their emergence as campus activists.[32]

The fact that so many students credited family—and especially par-ents—for their dissident politics suggests that the campus activists of the 1930s were surprisingly free of youthful narcissism. Up until its final years, the student movement displayed little generational rage. These student rebels promoted political protest, but not a cultural rebellion or youth culture in revolt against the lifestyle of their elders. Snapshots of 1930s campus rebels show that this was not a movement of youthful bohemians. The protesters tended to wear suits and ties, skirts and dress coats, which resembled nothing so much as the attire of their parents. The entire style of politics was adult-like. In fact, movement organizers wanted to leave behind the juvenile modes of behavior that had characterized the fraternity-dominated youth culture inherited from the 1920s. Any violence or row-diness on college campuses in the 1930s was much more likely to be the work of fraternity men and their hazing than anti-war protesters and their much more sober protest activity.[33]

Though the Depression era student insurgency represented a move-ment of young people, it prided itself on its ties with parallel movements of adults. This reflected the Left ideological orientation of its leaders, who saw class rather than age as the most important dividing point in America. These activists viewed the student movement as an auxiliary—albeit an important one—to the labor movement and its struggle for a more egalitarian social order. This lack of generational rancor was made explicit, for instance, in the American Youth Congress' founding platform in 1934. In its preamble to this document the Youth Congress voted to

> reject the explanation which seeks to place the blame on the old as such for the evils which youth can repair just because they are young. We do not believe that the fundamental problems before us are special "youth problems," amenable to solution by special "youth demands" alone. We declare that they are the general problems of the masses of the people, who are subject to the same insecurity and the same danger, to be solved by all those whose interests drive them to seek a solution, young and old, youth from industry, farm and school.[34]

This rejection of generational politics was based on more than abstract theory; it was drawn from lessons that American student activists learned as they looked at Europe's reactionary youth movements. That is why the Youth Congress' preamble argued that stressing the special virtues of youth was dangerous and potentially fascistic:

> Emphasis upon a youth movement which glories in regimented ranks of young people, enthusiastically moving towards some goal—the goal itself being secondary—resembles the fascist movements of Germany and Italy where the sufferings and idealism of youth were perverted by the selfishly calculating guardians of a decaying economic order to bring oppression and terror to the masses of people.[35]

As in this public document, the autobiographical essays student activists wrote in the mid-1930s reflect far more generational solidarity and respect than hostility. In most of the activists' essays that mention their families, those references are positive. These activists seemed eager to link their own political activism to some legacy from their parents or siblings. Most seemed to take pride in citing this shared determination to better society.[36]

The types of positive connections the activists drew between themselves and their parents were as varied as the students themselves. In some cases, students gave much of the credit for their own politics to *activist* parents. ASU leader Molly Yard, for instance, expressed reverence for the activism and political integrity of her parents, both of whom had served as Methodist missionaries in China. Yard was especially proud of her father, a "belligerent idealist" and "radical" who "resigned from his position" in the missionary movement because "he did not see eye to eye with those in control." Here Yard was referring to her father's agitation against the missionary movement's racially segregationist practices. She also praised her father's subsequent work as religious director of Northwestern University, where his "decisive stand on all problems of race, economics and religion" again cost him his job. Yard concluded that thanks to "my parents' beliefs and their stands I have had quite a thorough education in the realm of social progress." And in fact, the link between Yard's own career as a student activist and her father's agitation is striking. Following in his footsteps, her first campaign—and one which would carry her into national leadership in the student movement—was against bigotry and discrimination in Swarthmore College's sorority system.[37]

Yard's political background was, of course, somewhat unusual. Among WASP student activists—raised in the politically conservative 1920s—only a few had so strong a radical role model as she. Radical parents were more common among student activists who were the sons and daughters of immigrants, especially Russian Jewish immigrants. Several of the essays by these students attest that they were not only second generation immigrants, but second generation student activists. "My father," wrote one ASU organizer

> was one of the student leaders in pre-revolutionary Russia [who] . . . carried on a great deal of educational work among the peasants. He left Russia because he did not believe in compulsory military training . . . . It is interesting to see that youth of a previous generation fought the same issues that we are fighting now.[38]

A Barnard ASU member described her Jewish immigrant parents attending "underground meetings" during Russia's 1905 revolution. In America her father, a dentist, became first a socialist and then a communist, active

> in the fight for socialized medicine, and more recently in arousing approval for the Wagner Health bill . . . . At home I was taught the meaning of racial and religious tolerance, and was told stories of pogroms in Russia, of the persecution of Negroes in the South . . .[39]

Another significant model for student activists came from parents and even grandparents who had been involved in liberal rather than radical organizing. Several of the young activists had parents who were veterans of the settlement house movement. A Vassar ASU organizer wrote with pride of her mother's role in "social work, she and a friend founding a summer camp for children from the slums, which is still in existence and cares for a thousand underprivileged youngsters annually." It was easy to see why she might be attracted to anti-war protest at Vassar, when her "parents were both opposed to war on principle . . . [and] neither my younger brother nor I was allowed to play with toy guns or soldiers."[40] A high school ASU organizer recalled that her grandmother had been an "active social worker in the Henry Street settlement." Over the summers her family housed young workers in their large country house to give them an escape from the slums. Through this family activism and "these contacts [with the underprivileged] I became conscious of some sort of social inequality based on wealth, which seemed puzzling and unjust. By the time I was ten, I had some vague ideas of a socialist society as an ideal."[41] A University of Chicago ASU member traced her politics to family ties with other phases of progressive era reform:

> My mother was . . . brought up in a stiffling bourgeois . . . society. Nevertheless, she had liberal tendencies . . . . Her first activities were anti-sweat shop labor agitation, visiting the sweat-shops to see for herself the actual conditions. Then she became an active suffragette. She remained a liberal throughout my youth and still is one. She started encouraging me to read the newspapers at an early age. I wasn't very interested . . . . Finally my mother shamed me into a real interest when, at an early age, she asked me who Mussolini was, and I didn't know. That settled my ignorance, and I didn't dare not read the papers.[42]

By her high school years she was an ardent pacifist, involved in the ASU and emulating her mother's activist career.

Several of the student movement's more prominent African American activists came from homes where parents had been involved in civil rights agitation. James Jackson, who organized on behalf of the NSL, the ASU, and the Southern Negro Youth Congress, recalled that his father was a loyal follower of W.E.B. DuBois. "We grew up with *Crisis* (the NAACP magazine edited by DuBois). As a matter of fact we learned to read on DuBois' column 'As the Crow Flies.' " His father was assaulted and arrested while participating in protests against Richmond's segregated trolley car system. The elder Jackson also took part in protests against racially restrictive housing covenants in the 1920s. With a role model like this, it was natural for the son to become a civil rights activist long before entering college. His activism began with a battle against segregation in the Boy Scouts of America, and a campaign to establish the first black Boy Scout troop in Virginia.[43]

More commonly, however, student movement organizers had parents who, though not active in the liberal or radical politics, were Left-liberal *sympathizers*. In many of these cases the students drew connections between their own activism and the liberal or radical values taught them by their parents. "My parents were liberal almost to the point of socialism," noted a Harvard ASU leader, who termed this "a determining factor" in his political development. A Vassar ASU organizer wrote that she owed her political orientation to her father, "a paper manufacturer . . . . Although his job . . . boosted the family social standing yet his own farm uprbringing has been to a large extent responsible for his liberal outlook and a sympathy toward labor that, one may safely say are unusual in a New England business man."[44] "The liberal tradition in my thinking I got mostly from my parents," explained an Amherst ASU activist.

> My father has a responsible position in a large leather corporation
> . . . . But instead of having any particular reverence or respect for busi-
> nessmen he has considered them a rather shallow group in any kind of
> intellectual accomplishment. Also a sympathy for labor has distinguished
> him from most of his associates. By talking with my parents I have grad-
> ually absorbed this same attitude of not having the business world as an
> idol as some middle class youths have.[45]

Parents also transmitted their political values indirectly, through formal educational institutions. Liberal or radical parents would commonly
send their children to progressive and experimental schools, which brought
them into contact with teachers who would help politicize them.[46] Academia's rightwing critics, in their rush to indict teachers and pose as defenders of the family, conveniently ignored the phenomenon of family involvement in *chosing* to send their sons and daughters to liberal educational
institutions. This phenomenon was evident, for example, in the case of
the parents of a Vassar ASU member. Although her father had been a
Hoover Republican, as the Depression intensified, he moved towards New
Deal liberalism and had no qualms about sending his oldest daughter to
liberal Vassar. This daughter returned from Vassar "and brought home
a great many liberal and radical ideas that were new to our family," explained her younger sister. "My father admits now that my sister made
him give much more serious thought to the political and economic problems of our day," a process which led him to embrace "democratic socialism . . . as the goal we must work for."[47] The father was more than
willing to pay for his younger daughter to attend Vassar, and she—influenced by her family's leftward shift—became a prominent ASU organizer
during her college years.

Even when parents did not try to teach their progressive political views
to their children, this could occur unintentionally. A socialist student from
Antioch College noted that though his parents were radicals "they themselves avoided discussing political questions with me, because they did not
want to influence my ideas." But "unhindered browsing in the family
bookcase" led him to his parents' politics anyway through a reading of
Edward Bellamy's utopian socialist novel *Looking Backwards:*

> When I found that mother could not explain . . . why Bellamy's
> beautiful system was not adopted, I turned to reading and lectures for
> the answer. I religiously attended the lecture series at the Labor Institute,
> becoming acquainted with socialist thought and gaining my first knowl-
> edge of the labor movement. My . . . belief in the necessity for change
> was intensified.[48]

Joseph Lash also grew up with socialist reading material in his home.
In his case it was the Yiddish socialist press, which opposed World War I,
giving Lash (even though this was not discussed with his parents) the
impression that "we must have been mildly anti-war." With Lash, how-

ever, the most memorable anti-war lesson he received as a child from his father occurred accidentally. While walking with his father down Amsterdam Avenue in Manhattan during World War I, the two were approached by federal agents searching for draft evaders. The agents demanded to see the draft card of Lash's father. "My Father," Lash recalled,

> who had fled Czarist Russia in 1905 and had an abiding fear of the arbitrariness of officials, especially police, in their dealings with Jews was very frightened even though as the father of five children, all under the age of eight . . . he was in a deferred status. The agent looked at his card and waved him on. But a small boy is very sensitive to his father's reactions. He had communicated his sense of fright to me. I can still feel it.[49]

The relationships between children and parents are, of course, too diverse to be fit into any one model. Not all the activists who mentioned their families in their autobiographies saw themselves as simply following in the footsteps of their parents. Sometimes the relationship was more complex than that, and the path from the parents' lives to the child's politics more winding and rocky. A CCNY communist wrote in his autobiographical essay of the painful experience of his parents. They had left Lithuania in pursuit of the American dream. "However, the land of 'golden streets' soon became a land of poverty," working in sweatshops and living in a "Lower-East-Side firetrap." Although the CCNY student's elder brother finally prospered and moved his parents out of the tenement, these ghetto years had left scars. "It was not very long ago," admitted the young communist, "that I looked upon this background with shame. I also felt ashamed of my 'greenhorn' parents." Through the radical movement, which made his working-class origins seem a virtue rather than a vice, this young activist believed he had overcome his feelings of shame and inferiority. Here radicalism seemed to offer a vehicle for both generational reconciliation and the child's redemption of the parent's American dream:

> If the working-class movement meant nothing more than the reestablishment of pride in my working-class parents, it was enough. I am proud of the struggles that my parents went through to feed me. I am proud of their true love for America, not the hypocritical flag waving of our professional patriots. Not only has the working-class movement meant this for me, but it also has given me an accomplishable vision of a new society, a society, which my parents thought they would find here.[50]

Only five out of the 125 student activists in our sample linked their politics to rebellion against their parents. Three of these five, however, indicated that during their student activist days they had gotten over this stage of youthful rebellion; they had become both reconciled with their parents and comfortable with their new politics, which was now based on political principle rather than generational hostility. But even these low figures do not fully capture the insignificance of generational rage in producing student radicalism. Almost half of this small group of five, it turns out, had in their stage of generational revolt, been rebelling against *radical* parents! These two included an SLID activist from Cleveland College, who confessed that her socialist father's "long tirades against 'the system' which he delivered with never diminishing gusto at each dinner-time, fell on unreceptive ears, resulting in my junior high school days, in a strongly negative attitude towards anything of social content . . ." A Wayne University student, whose father had been a socialist since his days in Yugoslavia's "student terrorist oganizations" wrote that he also "went through a period of adolescent revolt" against his father's politics. "Ever since I was a child I was almost religiously indoctrinated with Socialism and Atheism." During his period of rebellion, the son "became completely sceptical about Socialism in the same manner as one brought up in a religious environment becomes sceptical about God." But in both cases, these second generation radicals returned to the politics of their parents; the first because friends in the student movement re-connected her with her radical roots through their anti-war agitation, and the second because his own readings persuaded him that his overbearing father had been right about the merits of socialism.[51]

Of the three students who had rebelled against non-radical parents, one did not do so in a spiteful or purely emotional manner. The rebellion of this ASU activist evolved out of tensions which may naturally arise between first generation college students and their much less educated parents. In this case, the parents were southerners with "strong prejudices against foreigners, Jews, and Negroes," who, to their radical daughter, seemed hopelessly narrow-minded. She confessed in her 1938 autobiographical essay that she had developed a "superiority complex" toward her provincial parents. In defense of this attitude, the young activist noted that her "superiority feeling accomplished a good purpose. It kept me from adopting their prejudices." Having staked out her own political territory, this rebellious daughter, however, came to realize that she could respect her parents even as she rejected their prejudices. She wrote that her feelings of superiority had "now, I am glad to say, [been] supplanted by respect for them because they are really intelligent parents, and good parents, who have struggled hard to give us advantages they didn't have."[52]

No student movement is entirely free of at least a few youths whose embrace dissident politics as a way of antagonizing parents with whom they have been in conflict. This was clearly the case with an SLID activist, whose autobiographical essay reflected disdain for her family of Wyoming farmers. She noted that she had become active in the student LID "partly because I agreed with its aims, partly because I knew my family wouldn't like it." In his memoir, *Is Curly Jewish?*, Paul Jacobs made a similar connection between his radicalization and generational conflict. Jacobs had a tempestuous relationship with his middle-class Jewish parents, and felt "contempt for the values of the family." He termed his emergence as an active leftist at CCNY "an affirmation of my contempt for and impatience with the making of money, pursuits I identified with my parents . . . . The CCNY radical regarded businessmen as a very low form of life." Yet what is striking about these two cases, was their rarity; they were the only ones out of the 125 activists in our sampled group who traced their politics to an unresolved, open, and ongoing conflict with parents.[53]

The generally high level of respect of student activists for their parents was often reciprocated. Few of the activists in our sampled group reported that parents had tried to interfere with their political lives. The lack of such parental interference contrasted starkly with the much more frequent incidents of political suppression of students by teachers and educational administrators. Indeed, in most of the major free speech fights involving conflicts between student activists and administrators, parents sided with their children against school authorities. This occurred in 1932 at Columbia University, during the first major campus free speech fight of the decade, after the Columbia administration expelled student newspaper editor Reed Haris. The expelled editor's father, Tudor Harris boasted to the press: "My son and his associates have brought new vigor and life to the editorial page" of Columbia's student newspaper, "heretofore little more than a 'yes' organ"; he publicly condemned President Butler for expelling his son, and declared that he "would regard a diploma received at the hands of a college president who would sanction, let alone direct, such an action for such a cause as a stigma."[54]

At UCLA during the West Coast's biggest free speech fight in 1930s, parents again played a prominent role in opposing repressive administrators. Soon after the UCLA administration had suspended five students on charges of assisting in a communist plot "to destroy the University" in 1934, the parents of four of these students rushed to their defense. The parents issued a joint press release attacking UCLA's provost "for the injury he has done these young people for blasting their reputations when they are on the threshold of life before giving them a hearing in which they could have disproved such charges"; they demanded that UCLA quickly correct "this injustice." The same thing happened at the University of Michigan in 1935, when an expelled NSL activist's father publicly challenged President Ruthven's disciplinary action against his son. Similarly, Hunter College's president found that a delegation of parents were among the first to protest his decision to take a campus job away from a student because of her anti-war activity.[55]

Parental support for student dissent was especially prominent at CCNY during the longest and most turbulent campus free speech fight in Depression America. Here parents appeared at the disciplinary hearings for their sons, who had gotten into trouble with the administration for protesting the visit of an Italian fascist delegation at CCNY. At these hearings, one parent told the presiding CCNY administrators that "if his son should have been expelled for his anti-Fascist beliefs I would not stand for it . . .—anti-Fascist action I always support." "I think my boy has a right to a different opinion," explained another parent. In one very tense exchange with the dean, a protester's mother made it clear that she took a dim view of both the disciplinary hearings and the fascist invitation that had led to it. The dean told her "the point is whether the faculty [or the student body] is going to run the college . . ." She replied, "I suppose students have some rights." "It is the faculty who run the College," argued the dean. "For whose benefit?" asked the mother. "I know the faculty was placed in an embarrassing position, but they should have taken into consideration that the student body didn't wish to receive them [the fascist delegation]."[56]

Nor were such objections confined to a few dissident parents. When the hearings culminated in the expulsion of twenty-one CCNY students, one of the city's largest parents organization, the United Parents Association (UPA) protested. UPA delegates, representing 201 parents organizations voted in their January 1935 meeting to oppose the expulsions. The UPA president sent a letter to the CCNY administration charging "that the penalties which have been imposed on the expelled students are far more severe than the situation warranted."[57]

There were even occasions in which parents joined their activist sons and daughters on campus picket lines. This occurred, for example, during the 1936 anti-war strike at Brooklyn College. Here a delegation of thirteen mothers marched together to show parental solidarity with the student crusade against war. The parents at this strike rally attracted press attention with their picket signs, which proclaimed that they "preferred sons to gold stars," and warned that they "had not raised their sons to be cannon fodder."[58]

Parental support did, however, have its limits. Some parents encouraged their sons and daughter to exercise caution and discretion in their political activism. These parents feared that their children might jeopardize their careers if they gained too much notoriety from protest activity. This was the case with Celeste Strack. After her initial conflicts with the USC administration, Strack found that her family was

> scared to death. They were getting phone calls threatening me at home during the summer, when I came home from USC. All sorts of pressure was brought to bear on them. And while they would argue with me, they were never attempting to disown me or throw me out. They were mainly just scared to death. I have to say looking back on it they were very forebearing, considering how conservative they were and how scared . . . and worried they were.[59]

Such fear also afflicted the father of Youth Congress chairman Jack McMichael. The Youth Congress leader's father was a physician in southern Georgia, whose liberal idealism led him to crusade on behalf of low-cost medical care for the rural poor. This crusade by Dr. McMichael had played an important role in fostering his son's politicization. But he grew quite concerned about Jack shortly after the Youth Congress' break with the Roosevelt administration, when the organization was attacked for opposing conscription and charged with communist domination. Aware that his own activism had helped inspire his more radical son, Dr. McMichael advised Jack to be less headstrong and learn from his mistakes. "It has been my nature," Dr. McMichael wrote his son,

> to go ahead with a thing I thought was right, regardless of the consequences, social, financial or other wise. In doing this I have paid a big price . . . . In looking back I believe I should have been willing to go slower after my objective, and compromise more . . . . I realize you have your own life to live, and as you know I have never asked you to let me think in place for you. At the same time I would not allow you as a child to do anything I thought might hurt you. My love for you, my age and experience I think justifies me in asking you to avoid doing anything radical. Try . . . to take as much good from all isms and make it fit democracy. It is hard to believe that so many Commentators and such a large part of the Press would say so many hard things about the Youth Congress unless they had good reason for doing so . . . . Stop and try to believe that at least some of the criticism of these older and more experienced people have made is just. Personally I would be willing to follow Mr. and Mrs. Roosevelt all the way . . . . Please be cautious in what you say and always remember that you may have to justify this later in life. Remember too that your happiness & success mean more to me than anything else.[60]

The most extreme cases of parental criticism were those in which fathers of activists publicly denounced the radicalism of their children. This occurred at Berkeley in 1940, when Professor Samuel May announced he was disowning and disinheriting his son Kenneth because of his communist activism. The father implied that his son—a teaching fellow at Berkeley—had been lured into the communist movement by his new wife, a communist "woman much older than himself." Kenneth avoided any direct attack on his conservative father; but he did refute his father's claims about his wife, telling the press that:

> I first joined the Communist party as an undergraduate at the University because I found by actual experience in student activities that the Communists were consistent and uncompromising fighters for the interests of the students and against reaction within and without the university.[61]

The other major public dispute between activist and parent also involved a California student. This time, however, it was a female undergraduate at UCLA and her rightwing father. The father in this case was H. Bedford Jones, a writer, and his daughter Nancy. Here, as in the May case, the father added sexual overtones to the story of his child's radicalization. But Mr. Jones was even less subtle in this regard than Professor May had been. Jones' 1935 *Liberty* magazine article on his daughter's radicalization appeared under the lurid title "Will the Communists Get Our Girls in College?" The article told the story of three coeds who had been led to subversive activities by a wily "young Red [who] seduces girls." Nancy Bedford Jones, an SLID activist, publicly repudiated these and other charges made by her father. In her article, "My father Is a Liar!," which she published in the student press, Nancy revealed that the three coeds discussed by her father in his *Liberty* article were in reality a fictionalized version of her own experience. She charged that her father had completely distorted the story of her radicalization in order to slander and discredit the student movement.[62]

The May and Jones disputes attracted considerable press attention. This attention came, however, because public, hostile clashes between activists and parents were so rare. Through the entire decade of student activism, from 1931 to 1941, the May and Jones cases stand out as the only examples of conservative parents mounting public attacks on their activist children. The similar dynamic of these two conflicts is also significant because in both cases it was the parent rather than the student who had initiated the public conflict—again suggesting that student activists were neither seething with generational rage nor anxious to go on the attack against their parents. In fact, part of the reason Nancy Bedford Jones became so outraged by her father's veiled public attack on her political activism was because in the past her relationship with him had been so positive. "I had," Nancy wrote, "always loved my father as a pal and I was heartsick when I learned of this. I didn't believe a father could do this to a daughter and even more to the movement in which her ideals are bound."[63]

It is possible that the fiery type of conflicts that student activists like May and Jones had with their parents in public may have gone on more frequently in private. Parents would, after all, be far more likely to air such differences at the breakfast table than in the national media—where their children's reputations would be jeopardized. But judging by the autobiographical data, even private conflicts over student activism between parents and children were unusual and generally much less heated than in the May and Jones disputes. Irving Howe, for instance, recalled that though his parents disapproved of his Trotskyist politics, they "objected more to my late hours, a result of wandering the streets with cronies after meetings." A Vassar student reported a similar conflict with her parents, after extensive campaigning for Norman Thomas led her to neglect her studies. Finding her liberal mother more upset by her falling grades than by her politics, she observed that "my mother's chief objection to Norman Thomas is not on account of his views but because he was the principal cause of my flunking that history course. I was too busy making American history to study it."[64]

III

Both in the families that did witness generational conflict and many of those that did not, a common leftward trend was discernible. Student organizers were often more radical or more active politically than were their parents. This was obviously the case for students from conservative homes like Jones and May; but it was also true in liberal families. Though students from liberal homes proudly traced their dissidence to their parents, in many cases, the autobiographies reveal that even as they appreciated their parents' reformist politics, they were moving beyond it. This leftward shift was evident with such activists as Jack McMichael, son of a liberal physician, becoming a Christian socialist and ally of the Communist Party; James Jackson son of an NAACP-style liberal, becoming a communist; Irving Howe, son of trade unionists, becoming a Trotskyist; Alice Dodge, daughter of liberal Republicans, becoming a socialist. Even in families already on the Left this trend had a significant parallel, in that the children often tended to be more politically active and militant than their socialistic parents.[65]

When asked to account for this leftward trend, the NSL and SLID during the early 1930s pointed, above all, to economics. They viewed the Depression as the great radicalizing force of their time. Thus in its December 1932 editorial, "Why Students Are Turning to Socialism," the Student LID's magazine *Revolt* traced undergraduate radicalism to "the impact of the economic crisis."

> Family incomes have declined and student budgets have been curtailed. Working students have discovered the usual summer jobs are no longer available, while wages for part-time work have fallen. Tuition fees have been increased . . . [and] the sacrifices involved in securing a college education are now less handsomely rewarded . . . . Educated for jobs that do not materialize, students will grow resentful towards the existing order and will use the learning they have acquired to overthrow it.[66]

This economic theory of radicalization evolved out of both the personal experience and political ideology of NSL and SLID leaders during the early 1930s. By the end of the Hoover era, the Depression had (as seen in Chapter I) transformed the mood on campus. The economic crisis had made it possible for leftists to challenge the insularity, complacency, and elitism of traditional student culture. Seeing the contrast between the increasingly progressive student politics of their own era and the Republican campuses of the affluent 1920s, student radicals had good reason to see economics as the key to the student revolt of the early 1930s. Moreover, NSL and SLID leaders were predisposed toward this kind of interpretation, since they were influenced by Marxist ideology and its assumption that economics was the driving force in history.

This theory of radicalization mirrored the travails of students whose own incomes and home lives had been diminished by the Great Depression. Among these students was Junius Scales, an ASU organizer and young communist, who attended the University of North Carolina. Home for young Junius included a mansion and affluent lifestyle in a prominent southern family. But the real estate market crash brought "severe financial reverses" to his family, devastating his father, who suffered a nervous breakdown and heart attack. These events left Junius receptive to the anti-capitalist talk of leftist students who congregated in the radical bookstore near the Chapel Hill campus.[67] Economic hardship and family tragedy also caused the politicization of a Vassar ASU activist. When she was a young girl, her father lost his well paying job in the western Kentucky oil fields because of the Depression. Thrown out of work, her father then lost his house and

> tried everything desperately. We moved into a little town in Tennessee where it was somewhat cheaper to live. A small income from a part interest in an oil well supported us for a while. That ran out. We moved into a two-room apartment, had the electricity turned off, bought at each grocer's in town in turn as we used up our credit. Practically the only jobs open at this time were traveling salesman jobs on commission. My father worked in insurance, school supplies, refrigerators, gadgets for oil stoves. Perhaps we should not have been too surprised when after a desperate penniless Christmas at home, he went off in his second-hand Ford and did not come back. We understood why . . . . I was sixteen then. I knew that my father loved us, that my mother still loved him, and I knew too that when every door was closed, there was no other way.

Thanks to her "absolutely mad obsession to go to a good college," she studied hard and performed well enough to obtain a Vassar scholarship. She became "a member of the ASU at Vassar because knowing what I know, I must learn to act." Similarly, a midwestern student traced the roots of his activism to his father's hours being lengthened and wages being cut in half: "Watching him become dehumanized, my mother becoming more ill intensified my feelings, and I felt the necessity for becoming [politically] active."[68]

With wages being cut, students who paid for their education had to work longer and harder than previous generations of self-supporting undergraduates. Whether they tried to make ends meet by washing dishes, cleaning houses, or waiting tables, the hardships these students experienced at home and at school sometimes moved them leftward. A University of Iowa ASU activist was among this group of students. His father lost his farm, had to move to town, and "went to work as a day laborer, #[$]3.50 a day when he worked, and employment was unsteady." The son found that at high school affluent students shunned him because of his poverty. He realized that higher education would only be possible if he could join

> that growing crew of college students who "work their way through." I
> chose the University of Iowa because it was cheap and because bad jobs
> were plentiful. Far be it from me to question the truth of Horatio Alger
> and the great American tradition of working-your-way-up-from-the-bottom,
> but my first three years in college were a kind of ever conscious hell—
> three hours sleep, day-old meals, heavy eyes, trying to keep awake in
> classes, being too tired to try for debate, studying in odd minutes . . . .
> I combined the three—scholastic success, activities and work. It's not a
> pleasant combination.[69]

The memory of these hardships remained even after this student won a
scholarship to study in Europe; it prodded him to become critical of the
economic system that had victimized him, and it led him to a group of
young radical British intellectuals, with their Marxist perspective and calls
for a Popular Front against fascism.

For some student movement veterans, economic hardship was such
an important source of their activism that they looked back upon the entire movement as an outgrowth of such hardship. Film critic Pauline Kael,
for instance, viewed the student movement during her college days at
Berkeley in the 1930s as an insurgency produced by lower class youths.
She recalled very well defined class lines distinguishing movement activists
from the rest of the Berkeley student body; "there was a real division
between the poor who were trying to improve things on the campus and
the rich kids who didn't give a damn." Palmer Weber, an NSL leader
from the University of Virginia, observed a similar class division on his
campus in the 1930s. In both cases, the wealthiest students, belonged to
Greek houses and had nothing to do with the student movement. At Virginia, according to Weber, the most affluent students were "people who
came" to campus "in their Cadillac cars," and who were much more interested in holding golf clubs or hunting rifles than picket signs. During
Christmas vacations, while radicals hitched their way to leftist student conventions, the University of Virginia's "car crowd, hunting crowd, golfing
crowd . . . went off to Bermuda." Virginia's radicals came not from this
rich upper crust, but rather from the third or so of the student body that
was much too poor for Caribbean cruises. Since these students were feeling the pinch of hard times, they were, as Weber explained, "willing to
think, talk and entertain ideas of how to reorganize society."[70]

This class analysis of the student movement, offered by Kael and
Weber, accounts for some, but by no means all of the student activism of
the 1930s. The findings from our sampled activist group indicate, in fact,
though students hurt economically by the Depression constituted a significant minority, they were not a majority within the student activist community. In our sampled activist group, economic hardship was cited by
29.6 percent of the students as they explained their politicization. The
29.6 percent figure ought not be interpreted too rigidly. It is possible that
lower-class students may have been underrepresented in our sampled
group, since over half the sample was drawn from participants in SLID

and ASU summer leadership conferences—which some working students, due to time limitations, may have been unable to attend. But even if this was a significant distortion (and the presence of lower-class students at both conferences suggests that it was not), and if one builds in a huge 20 percent margin of error, this would still leave a majority of students whose activism was not linked to economic hardship or class interests.[71]

The limitations of class analysis as a mode of understanding student activism in the 1930s was also reflected in the memoirs of the student movement's national leaders. One such leader, Celeste Strack, entered the student movement at UCLA in 1934 with assumptions about the movement's social base identical with those of Kael and Weber. Strack's own family had been hard hit by the Depression, as were the families of many of her comrades in the UCLA student movement. She assumed that student activists across the nation came from families that had been hurt by the economic crisis. But when Strack went beyond her own campus, and became a national NSL leader with contacts at other colleges and universities, she found that her class analysis of the student movement had been simplistic. Strack came to this realization during her first visit to New York. She had recently made a name for herself as a leader in the free speech fight at UCLA and was in New York to assume her new national office in the NSL. Here Strack's comrades in the student movement put her up in the home of Helen Simon, a Barnard College NSL leader. Strack was startled to find that this Barnard radical's home was an

> apartment on Fifth Avenue or right off it . . . . There was a doorman. I go in with Helen. We go up on the elevator. We go walking through carpets ankle deep, and I'm ushered into my own private bedroom with its own private bath that belonged to her sister who was in Europe. The next morning I was woken by somebody knocking on the door, and it was the maid saying breakfast was ready. I said "Well just give me a minute and I'll be right out." "No," she said, "I have it here," and arrived with a tray with breakfast. I can still see it; there was a silver vase with a rose on it, and next to it was a folded copy of the *Daily Worker*. I could not believe my eyes. I, of course, was under the impression that I had come to New York to become associated with a left-wing revolutionary movement . . . . The initiation was a little more than I could bear. I didn't know whether to laugh or what to do, so I said nothing about it.[72]

Strack's encounter with this affluent Ivy League radical had parallels on other campuses. Theodore White observed a similar disjunction between economic hardship and student radicalism as a Harvard undergraduate during the 1930s. White recalled that he and his friends—lower-middle class commuter and scholarship students, who were poor by Harvard standards—found themselves visited

> regularly by Harvard's intellectual upper-class Communists, who felt that we were of the oppressed. Occasionally such well-bred, rich or elite Com-

munist youngsters . . . would bring a neat brown-paper-bag lunch and join us at the round tables to persuade us, as companions, of the inevitable proletarian revolution.[73]

But Harvard's affluent student radicals made few converts among White and his plebian classmates. This failure, White explains, derived from the fact that

> We were . . . middle class in the flesh—hungry and ambitious. Most of us, largely Boston Latin School graduates, knew more about poverty than anyone from Beacon Hill or the fashionable East Side of New York. We hated poverty; and meant to have no share in it. We had come to Harvard not to help the working classes, but to get out of the working classes. We were on the make. And in my own case, the approach to Harvard and its riches was that of a looter.[74]

At Columbia James Wechsler found that the class divisions his Marxism had led him to expect—with the more blue-collar students assuming leadership—in student politics did not materialize. Columbia's most proletarian students were football players, recruited from mining towns and other working-class communities. But according to Wechsler, "these same athletic battalions tended to produce the most violent opponents of radicalism . . . . The athletic proletarians were always warring against the champions of Marxism and any symptom thereof."[75]

The pattern that Strack, Wechsler, and White observed was by no means confined to the Ivy League. Joseph D. Martini, assessing the social base of the student Left at the University of Illinois, in the most thorough quantitative case study of a single campus in the 1930s, revealed that here too relatively affluent students played a prominent role in radical politics. The largest group of Illinois student radicals came from families whose fathers were employed in professional occupations. At the Illinois campus 45.8 percent of the student activists came from such families, as compared to the overall student body of which only 17.9 percent came from households headed by fathers in the professions. The proportion of working-class students was also lower in the Illinois student Left than it was in the student body as a whole—8.3 percent of the student radicals came from blue-collar homes as opposed to 15.2 percent in the overall student body.[76]

These contrasting images of student activists' class background derive from the diversity of the movement itself. The movement included *both* the type of lower-class rebels described by Kael and Weber and the more affluent radicals described by Strack, White, and Martini. The autobiographical essays of participants in the SLID and ASU leadership institutes leave no doubt at all that privileged and underpriviledged students were both well represented in the movement. The ability of the student movement to transcend class lines was also evident in the movement's political geography. The largest and most active ASU chapters included such working- and lower-middle class campuses as CCNY, Brooklyn, and Hunter Colleges, but also much more elite campuses, such as Harvard, Vassar, and Columbia.[77]

The movement's diverse social composition suggests that student activism involved much more than economic self-interest. Even a glance at the motivations of affluent student activists reveals that their activism had little or nothing to do with their class interests. The Depression moved them leftward by evoking guilt and compassion rather than economic insecurity. Such guilt was visible, for example, in the political autobiography of a Vassar ASU organizer. In explaining how she first became aware about social inequality in America, this activist recalled that as she grew up in her prosperous Boston household

> I began to realize that my family had more money and more things than the majority of the families in the country . . . . We moved into a larger house, unnecessarily large, which made the difference even more marked . . . . I began to feel quite guilty and ashamed at having really more things than I wanted, when so many had nowhere near enough. This feeling increased during the depression.[78]

Affluent student activists were more likely to experience the tragedy of the Depression vicariously, through less fortunate friends rather than through their own families. This was the case, for instance, with Kay Martineau, an ASU organizer whose father ran a successful New Hampshire newspaper. Her first personal encounter with the economic crisis came when the father of a blue-collar high school friend tried to commit suicide after he went broke during the Depression. This led to her first stumbling steps toward social criticism. "I wished they weren't so poor and I disliked the comfortable and selectman. But I didn't know just why." These early stirrings accelerated after a visit to another school friend, the daughter of an impoverished carpenter, whose family "ate meals of boiled potatoes from tin plates [and] . . . slept in meal bags." At college she "began to question" the undemocratic features of American life on campus and off, after encounters with the hardships and inequities confronting her friends. One of these encounters involved her college roommate,

> who was working her way through. She stayed in and I went out, she had no clothes, I had a lot, she got long letters from her family, telling her that her brother had no work and that her mother was thinking of illegally selling beer to make enough to eat. I joined a sorority. She didn't and I found her crying one night because she was called a "drip."

Outraged that her sorority denied membership to lower-class and Jewish women, she resigned and began to think of herself as "a kind of social outcast." She gravitated toward the ASU as the most egalitarian group on campus and the one most committed to combatting the social injustices which had victimized her friends.[79]

The presence of affluent activists such as Martineau in the student movement was one of many indications that the movement was not merely an economic phenomenon. Had economic hardship been the most important source of student activism, then the movement would likely have been strongest during the worst years of the Depression on campus, 1932–33. These were years when unemployment was at its peak, when Hoover was stumbling, the viability of the New Deal uncertain, and student enrollments slipping. As Theodore Draper recalled of his college days in this era,

> My generation was a hopeless one . . . utterly defeatist. There were no jobs; the place was coming down. Most boys I knew didn't prepare themselves for careers at college because there weren't any opportunities. There was a real sense of a society in total collapse.[80]

These economic hardships had facilitated the rise of the student movement in Draper's generation, prodding students to become critical of Hooverism and the failing capitalist system. Yet, in these hard times the movement would not grow nearly as fast as it did in 1936–1937, when economic conditions improved for the college middle class.

The contrast between 1936–37 and the early days of the student movement was striking. Where in the early 1930s the movement never mobilized more than 25,000 students, in the later period the movement's national demonstrations involved about 500,000 students. This astonishing growth had occurred while collegians were benefitting from the moderate economic gains achieved by the New Deal. Thanks to the NYA, some 10 percent of the national student body, which otherwise might have had to drop out of college for economic reasons, received federally funded part-time work. The NYA and the mild economic upswing ended the decline in college enrollments that had begun under Hoover. Where in the early 1930s the news from the job market for college graduates worsened steadily, during the mid-1930s employment opportunities became far more promising. College seniors about to graduate in 1936, felt encouraged by surveys, like that published in the *New York Times* showing that nationwide their "employment opportunities had doubled . . . compared with 1935 . . . and that salaries are higher by an average of $10 per month." Job recruiters, who had all but disappeared from campus in the early 1930s, returned in the mid-1930s. By the fall of 1936 even teachers—one of the groups hardest hit by the Depression—were again in demand.[81]

The economic climate improved so dramatically on campus in this period that much of the student Left muted its talk of a declining middle class and collapsing capitalist system. Student activists began to worry that classmates might be lulled into political lethargy by their improving economic situation. Thus in his keynote address to the ASU convention in

1936, Joseph Lash expressed his regret that the "glamor of tinsel, temporary prosperity has hit the campus. Students are deluding themselves into believing that the jazz twenties are returning. They want to convince themselves that the crisis which had descended upon the campus has passed." This same concern led the ASU in the fall of 1936 and 1937 to publish in its national magazine articles debunking the "new prosperity." These articles stressed the limited and temporary character of the economic recovery; they reminded students that mass unemployment continued. The ASU's warnings about the durability of the Depression proved well founded. The recovery faded during the 1937–1938 academic year. But the period of economic recovery on campus had shown that ASU leadership had erroneously thought that an improving economy would impede student activism. The growing anti-war strikes in these years attested that the student movement could enjoy good health whether or not the economy was in bad health.[82]

The student movement's expansion in this period of recovery does not mean that Depression or social class were unimportant to the movement. The Depression remained a standing invitation for student activism throughout the decade; it reminded both lower-class and affluent students that America had severe social problems that merited their attention. Students radicalized by personal economic hardships or insecure about their career prospects in Depression America were always a significant segment of the student activist community. But the growth of student activism in the improved economy of 1936–37 does indicate that student movement's strength and concerns extended beyond economics.

Even though this was the Depression decade, it was not this crisis, but rather the crisis in international relations which generated the largest student mobilizations in the United States: the annual student strikes against war. James Wechsler found this to be the case even at Columbia, one of the nation's most active campuses:

> When student fees were raised, we believed we had at last found an issue which touched the deepest economic nerve and which according to our dogma, should have stirred the largest indignation. But far more students attended anti-war rallies than ever gathered to decry this attack on their parents pocketbooks.[83]

Since the cause of peace and anti-fascism concerned the entire younger generation, it enabled the student movement of the 1930s to transcend class lines and to organize impressive protests irrespective of the state of the economy.

IV

The student movement existed as more than a compilation of causes; it also represented a community, composed of activists united by a shared egalitarian ethic. Some students were drawn to the movement as much by this sense of community as by any particular issue. This was the case with some of the more affluent student activists. By virtue of their privileged economic status in a nation beset by economic distress, Left-leaning students from affluent homes felt isolated. The movement helped break down these feelings of isolation; it offered such students a new community, enabling privileged to unite with underprivileged, upper class with middle and working class. This new sense of community was especially powerful because it not only offered friendship and warmth, but a common sense of purpose and political idealism rooted in a passionate commitment to social equality.

The student movement's ability to satisfy this longing for community was nowhere more evident than in the reports movement activists published on their labor solidarity work. One such report by Dartmouth ASU activist Budd Shulberg told the story of efforts by students in this very elite college to aid striking marble workers. Shulberg begins his account by describing the students' sense of isolation. When the Dartmouth ASU contingent first arrived at the local union hall to offer their support to the strikers, they were met by "a burly Irishman [who] did not seem glad that they had come." The workers, thinking that all college "kids did was have dances and good times," had seen little reason to welcome the students or put much stock in their pledges of support. Shulberg then notes, however, that after the students worked long and hard on fund raising and publicity for the strikers, a sense of political community between these upper-class students and the workers had been established. Proudly underscoring this change, Shulberg described the very different reception ASU activists received at the union hall.

> This time the burly, strong-jawed Irishman greeted them warmly . . . . Other strikers hurried over to smile and shake hands. In three months Dartmouth students had proven that liberalism does not have to be a philisophical apologetic for inaction. Between the first hesitant visit and the latest one they had demonstrated that the twain, worker and student, can meet.[84]

Affluent students were not the only Depression era activists whose attraction to the student movement was linked to a search for community. If these students embraced the student movement as a means of transcending their privileged backgrounds, others embraced the movement as a means of transcending their underprivileged background. Among this latter group were Jewish students for whom the movement functioned as an avenue out of their immigrant ghettoes. The movement enabled them to meet and work with students from all over the country, and, in the words of NSL leader George Watt,

> made us feel that as part of this movement we were really part of America. It was a way for many of us who were New York Jews to become

integrated into American society. I remember when I began to attend national meetings of the NSL and you have . . . real native southerners like Francis Franklin with the thickest southern accent . . . or Jim Jackson from Howard University, or . . . Boone Schirmer from Harvard, who was a direct descendant of Daniel Boone, or people from the Midwest. These were people who gave a flavor to those of us who were from New York, gave us a sense of the movement out there that was really part of the American tradition.[85]

The student movement conferred a measure of acceptance upon Jewish students which they had never before found on American college campuses. In the past Jews had been barred from many campus social organizations and from leadership in student life. By creating new and non-discriminatory institutions, the movement enabled Jewish students to obtain national leadership positions which they could not have achieved in traditional undergraduate institutions. Thus at a time when Jews could not even belong to many student fraternities, the student movement elevated Jewish students, such as Joseph Lash, to top national offices in the largest political organization on the campuses of Depression America: the American Student Union. Lash's case was by no means unusual. Jews were prominent at all levels of the student movement, both locally and nationally. This prominence reflected the fact that this was not only a non-discriminatory community, but also a community deeply committed to stopping fascism, a force which Jewish students in this age of Hitler, found especially abhorrent and threatening.[86]

For African American students too, part of the student movement's appeal lay in this new and non-discriminatory form of community. James Jackson recalled being struck by the contrast between the segregationism and hostility of whites he had encountered while growing up in Richmond, Virginia, and the racial egalitarianism of the student movement. In Richmond, whites came into the African American community "as invaders or policemen, but hardly ever a friendly face." It was in the student movement that Jackson attended his first interracial meetings, and here "for the first time . . . saw white people who acted like they were human beings. They were concerned and humane in all respects. It was quite an experience . . . a nodal point in my life." Jackson was drawn to this community of activists which would not only admit him, but recognize his talents, elevate him to a leadership position, and support his goal of freeing America of racism.[87]

The student movement's racial and ethnic diversity was part of its attraction for Left-leaning WASP students. In a society segmented by race, ethnicity, and class, the campus activist community afforded an unusual opportunity to transcend these divisions. For an activist like Celeste Strack, who came from white suburban San Diego, the movement seemed especially exciting in that it enabled her to befriend and work with students from backgrounds much different than hers. As she began to become politically active at USC, Strack encountered in the student Left a group of foreign students who were "very interesting . . . red politically . . . who brought a kind of intellectual sophistication that was very unusual." Similarly, when Strack transfered to UCLA she grew close to a number of Jewish student activists, who she felt "had a more sophisticated" background politically than she did because they came from radical families. All of this gave Strack a sense that she was moving beyond the provincialism of her past, toward a more cosmopolitan community and more penetrating view of the world.[88]

This impulse toward a more diverse and egalitarian community was perhaps strongest of all in that small circle of southern student radicals. This was not only true for black activists, as James Jackson described so eloquently, but also for their white counterparts. Junius Scales recalled that as a student at the University of North Carolina, part of the ASU's appeal was that it allowed him to leave behind a past of racial segregation and to move toward a genuinely equal interracial community. Scales joined the ASU after attending a North Carolina student-labor conference that had been organized on an interracial basis:

> The conference recessed for dinner . . . . I was seated next to a male Negro student from A&T College in Greensboro. We'd barely introduced ourselves when I was joined on my right by a breathtakingly beautiful Negro woman student from Bennett College . . . . She was as charming and gracious as she looked, and I was soon at ease and talking excitedly with my neighbors. I had never known a Negro, except as a servant, and yet there I was in utter delight, defying all the taboos, customs, rules and laws that kept the races apart, talking with complete naturalness as one student to another, one young *person* to another! . . . My companions must have noticed the impact of the meeting on me, because a day or two later I was asked by one of them to join the American Student Union.

Once in the ASU, Scales worked to duplicate this experience for other students. He arranged interracial student meetings in Greensboro. The first of these meetings began with "considerable social awkwardness" caused by the inexperience of most students with racially integrated gatherings, but it ended with the participants making "new friends" and gaining "new insight into their differently complexioned counterparts; and there was an atmosphere of unforgettable warmth."[89]

The egalitarian ethic of the activist community had a special appeal to female undergraduates. Refusing to sanction discrimination in its ranks, the student movement accorded women much more opportunity for political leadership than did most traditional undergraduate institutions, which tended to be male-dominated. It was not at all uncommon for women to head campus chapters of student movement organizations and to assume important roles in regional and national leadership of the movement. According to Hal Draper, during the early 1930s "in SLID, as in the YPSL student activities women were by and large MORE in the leadership than men. At one point, when I was acting as Student Director of the NY YPSL, working closely with SLID, almost the entire regional officers of the SLID were women."[90] When the ASU was founded in 1935, women occupied two of its six national officer positions. Three years later, as Molly Yard recalled,

> when the question came up as to who was going to become chair of the Student Union, it turned out that both Joe [Lash] and I decided that each one of us should have that role. I said to Joe . . . "You know, Joe, that in this world of ours, everyone will expect you to become the chair because you are the man. That's the way that society is. But I think I should become the chair. That makes some kind of a statement which I think is important." And Joe agreed. So I did become chair of the Student Union.[91]

This sensitivity to the issue of women's rights also found expression in some of the student movement's anti-fascist rhetoric. American student activists noted with alarm Hitler's reactionary policy toward German women, which would remove them from political life, relegating females to the home and "the three K's—Kinder, Küche, und Kirche." They expressed outrage when in 1934 the Nazis abolished coeducation in the higher schools of Prussia. "Feminists struggled for a century and a half to reach what little there is today of feminine emancipation," explained the *Columbia Spectator*. "In sixteen months German fascism has been able to wipe out the work of 150 years . . . . The women of Germany are to devote themselves exclusively to raising Nazi cannon fodder. They are to be mothers of a new generation of soldiers who must die for the mad schemes of fascist militarism." A Hunter College student leader warned that if the Nazis succeeded, women would be reduced to the status of "slave . . . as . . . [were] their forebears of the Middle Ages."[92]

Concern about discrimination against women also occasionally found its way into the speeches of student movement leaders. In his address before an international conference of socialist and communist students in Paris, Joseph Lash mentioned the ASU's interest in campaigns to "give greater freedom to the women students who suffer from all sorts of restrictions imposed by the university authorities" in the United States. This concern also appeared in Molly Yard's annual report to the ASU. She pointed out that "Co-eds constitute a special problem—they do not have as good athletic facilities. They live under many rules and regulations while men have none."[93]

Although such egalitarianism was both significant and radical in the context of 1930s America, it would be an exaggeration to say that the student movement gave high priority to feminist issues. Very few instances occurred where the student movement's position favoring gender equality translated into concrete action against sexual discrimination either in the schools or society.[94] The movement's leaders sought to be non-discriminatory in their own ranks, but did not have an extensive feminist agenda or push women's issues the way they pushed on issues of race, class, war, and peace. Thus in the Lash speech quoted above, he mentioned the issue of women's rights last: after first discussing racial discrimination and economic problems. Yard's speech was structured similarly. And in fact, after mentioning the issue of gender discrimination, Yard quickly indicated that this was not the most pressing of problems, since "women are not the worst treated group on campus. Racial groups—especially Negroes are discriminated against at every turn."[95]

Yard's words suggest that not even the movement's leading female activists thought of women's issues as paramount. Like their male counterparts, the political agendas of these young women were set by the twin crises of Depression and war and by the larger milieu of the American Left. Generations removed from the suffragettes, women activists on campuses in the 1930s did not possess a fully developed feminist language in which to analyze gender issues. According to Molly Yard, during the Depression decade "we never thought in those days in terms of feminism. It was not a common word." But Yard and other female student activists did display at least elements of a feminist sensibility—even if they did not have a name for it—and held some notion that women should have equal access to positions of power in the movement.[96] (This is what Yard meant when she noted that "I didn't use the word feminist at that time although I was then and have always been one.") They found their male comrades usually willing to engage in such power sharing. In short, the movement was about as open to sexual equality as the women were themselves.[97] This openness—although not in itself the main precipitant of their politicization—made the activist community more congenial for women and helped draw them into it.

The significance of the activist community's egalitarianism was not lost on the conservative critics of the student movement. They well understood that the movement had built a community that defied the discriminatory divisions prevalent in Depression America. These critics were as upset about the non-discriminatory manner in which the activist community functioned as they were about the movement's protest activities. This could be seen, for example, in the publications of Elizabeth Dilling, who ranks among the Right's most prolific critics of the student movement. In one of her redbaiting books, published in 1936, Dilling, after condemning the movement for promoting "closer race relations," suggested that the student activist community had sanctioned dangerous violations of the social taboo against interracial sex. Dilling quoted extensively from a right-wing minister, who had observed the second American Youth Congress and testified that

> the most shocking thing I saw in connection with the Detroit Youth Congress was the social mixing of boys and girls of the black and white races.

Fully one third of the audience at one session was Negro. This I suppose was to be expected but I solemnly affirm that it is not to be expected, irrespective of the type of gathering that black men shall be the escorts and companions of white women. Such a situation, however, seemed perfectly natural around the Youth Congress. . . . Not three seats removed from me a white girl clung to the arm and openly petted one of the blackest sons of Africa I have ever seen. This was not an isolated incident . . . [and threatens to] destroy respect for the natural laws governing the race, remove old standards of morals and decency and reduce the human race to the level of soulless animals.[98]

Similar to Dilling's racist attack on the student movement were the xenophobic and anti-Semitic indictments of the movement by her fellow conservatives. At UCLA for example, a rightwinger wrote that the campus administration's attempt to suppress student radicalism during the free speech fight of 1934 was necessary because

there was absolutely nothing of the American or Anglo-Saxon in the appearance of the "red" students. Every one of them appeared decidedly foreign; appeared as if just imported from Soviet Russia. You can't be too severe with these obnoxious foreign elements![99]

The same point was made by the Engineering College Dean at the University of Texas, who attributed the anti-war strike of 1935 to a "bunch of Russians from the East Side of New York." An administrator at DePauw University blamed student radicalism there on "a bunch of neurotic Hebrews," and a Berkeley official claimed that the student Left was composed of "Jews and Russians mostly." Dartmouth's president attributed the rise of student protest on his campus to "the unhappiness and destructive spirit of revolt . . . characteristic of the Jewish race at all times under all conditions . . . . The jaundiced mulling of that [Jewish] . . . portion of our student body which loves to line up against the wailing wall."[100]

These attacks had two different meanings. On one level, they were irrational ravings on the part of prejudiced observers. It is obviously a testament to the depth of academic anti-Semitism that administrators at campuses such as Dartmouth, whose discriminatory admissions policies kept Jewish enrollments to a minimum, could depict Jews as the source of all the radicalism at their schools.[101] And there was a similar element of unreason and prejudice on Dilling's pages, which made the movement sound like one big interracial orgy. But though colored by fear and prejudice, their indictments were also significant because they caught something of the diversity, the tolerance, the egalitarianism of the student activist community. The movement crossed racial boundaries rarely approached in Depression America, where blacks and whites seldom socialized or cooperated closely. In her own sensationalistic way, this was what Dilling was underscoring, as she brought interracial sex into her account to dramatize the dangers of such racial egalitarianism.

Dilling's repugnance for racial egalitarianism was more explicit but no less strong than that of the campus administrators who scapegoated Jews for the rise of student radicalism. Accustomed to a campus scene in which Jews were kept on the fringes of academic life—barred from most social clubs, faculty, and top administration posts—these conservative WASP academics had every reason to feel shocked about a student movement which elevated these outcasts to leadership positions.[102] Coming out of these WASP-dominated institutions, critics such as Dartmouth's president were unable to imagine a truly multi-ethnic movement, and therefore naturally (and incorrectly) assumed that any movement with Jews in its leadership was a Jewish movement. The student movement seemed alien and un-American to conservatives because it rejected the WASP elitism and exclusionism which had been hallmarks of American society and academia. By exposing these conservatives to a new, more open, meritocratic and cosmopolitan vision of the academic world, the student movement scared and infuriated these guardians of the old order.

V

For students in Depression America there were many routes leftward. The array of factors inducing students toward political activism—including economic hardship, middle-class guilt, fears of war and fascism, the search for an egalitarian community, and the influence of progressive parents and teachers—were so numerous that one might well expect broad majorities of college students to become dedicated activists. And yet the number of students who actually went all out and became members of either the ASU or its rivals on the student Left was not overwhelming. In no single year did this activist core ever go much beyond the 20,000 figure which the ASU claimed as its national student membership.[103] This represented only a small minority of America's national undergraduate population, which annually averaged slightly more than a million. Thus to understand student politics in Depression America, it is necessary to discern not only the factors which facilitated, but also those which impeded the activist impulse on campus.

Throughout the Depression decade, traditional collegiate culture remained the biggest obstacle confronting the student movement. Thanks to Hollywood, millions of youths had been brought up with the idea that college was supposed to be a fun place, dominated by socializing sororities, frats, and football. This idea weakened considerably after it was challenged by both the student movement and the sobering crises in the American economy and in international relations. But it would be a mistake to confuse this weakness with collapse, for the old collegiate culture did not die. On campus after campus there were significant student mi-

norities—and in some cases even majorities—which continued to see extracurricular college life in this traditional manner. Weakened as they were
by the Depression, fraternities and sororities remained the largest resi-
dential social organizations of American collegians and a source of institutional power for non-radicals. Though the political and economic turmoil of the 1930s had made their collegiate lifestyle seem archaic to student
activists, others thought differently. Anti-radicals in the Greek houses reasoned that with life after college looking so bleak, they should at least
have some fun while they had a chance during their fleeting college years.
In this view the Depression was grim enough without having to be reminded of it by those depressing radicals.[104]

Youthful anti-intellectualism that had long been a part of traditional
undergraduate culture bolstered this apolitical mind-set. Those collegians
who dominated the world of frats and football were usually unfriendly to
more intellectual students, whom they disparaged as "grinds." They criticized and ostracized such serious students for being too engrossed in their
studies and not showing the proper collegiate spirit (ie. not throwing
themselves into the time-consuming socializing and juvenile rituals of the
frats and football set). Some of this same hostility to "grinds" was applied
to radicals, who also were depicted as overly intellectual party poopers.
"The Communists we knew," Henry May explains, "were too serious, intense . . . for most middle class young Americans, and most . . . students came from the middle class."[105]

Radical students and "grinds" did, as their critics charged, share a
more serious outlook than the average student. Indeed, there was some
overlap between these two groups. The ranks of the campus Left included some of the most intellectually gifted members of their college
generation. An impressive number of movement alumni would go on to
become prominent academics, writers and journalists, including Leo Marx,
Muriel Rukeyser, Irving Howe, Daniel Bell, Saul Bellow, Richard Hof-
stadter, Theodore Draper, Seymour Martin Lipset, Joseph Lash, Leon
Wofsy, Leslie Fiedler, Irving Kristol, Henry May, Pauline Kael, Harry
Magdoff, Budd Shulberg, Merle Miller, Richard Rovere, Carl Schorske,
Eric Sevareid, and James Wechsler. This does not mean, however, that
the movement was always a magnet for intellectually intense or studious
students. Hard times often tended to make diligent students more studious rather than more political. The Depression motivated many of them
to work harder so as to assemble the strongest possible academic record
and improve their chances in the constricted job market. Such students,
as Harry Magdoff recalled, made City College "horrendously competitive,
terribly competitive in terms of class work" during the early 1930s. Radical political activism could thus seem too time-consuming and risky (especially on campuses where students were expelled) for this type of job
conscious student.[106]

Time also posed an obstacle to activism for students who had been
hurt economically by the Depression. Often when sociologists have ex-

plained the propensity of students for political activism, they point to the fact that undergraduates have more time for political thought and action than their elders. This was definitely not the case for working students— and during the Depression the majority did work their way through college. Those who labored long hours in low paying jobs, studied, and attended classes often did not have time for sustained political activism. This is not to say that combining employment and activism was impossible. The memoirs of CCNY night school student activists offer some remarkable examples of students who worked full time jobs by day, did their academic work at night, and somehow managed to squeeze in some political organizing. But such schedule juggling was difficult and discouraged all but the most politically conscious and energetic of students.[107]

The movement had to contend as well with a substantial degree of hereditary politics. Not all collegians came—as had the radical student organizers portrayed above—from liberal or leftist homes. Indeed, throughout the Depression decade substantial numbers of students came from conservative middle-class families and reflected the political values of their parents. It is true that the national straw polls showed that in 1936 FDR became the first Democratic presidential candidate in more than a decade to win a plurality (48.3 percent) of the national student body. But significant as that victory was, it should not be forgotten that 44 percent of American students went Republican that year. This meant that a very significant minority of undergraduates nationally would not be friendly to the egalitarian agenda of a student movement to the left of the New Deal. In the South, moreover, even though the the student majority voted Democratic, its politics followed the racially reactionary path of local white supremacist politicians and parents, and was generally cool toward the integrationist student movement.[108]

Although these obstacles to radicalization helped limit the size of the ASU, it must also be borne in mind that the ASU's influence on American campuses during the Depression decade far transcended the size of the organization. Small as the ASU might seem in comparison to the overall student population, in the context of American student politics, the ASU was a formidable presence. Its membership of 20,000 not only far exceeded previous student activist organizations, but was also much larger than any competing national student group in Depression America. This meant that on many individual campuses and in every region except the South, the ASU's vocal and dedicated activists lacked effective competition and could set the tone of American student politics.[109]

The significance of the ASU's membership level becomes even clearer when one turns from the Left to the Right. One can understand the direction of student politics in Depression America by noting the absence of any kind of effective national organization of conservative student activists. Where the Left had the 20,000 member ASU, the Right had nothing of even half this size. Although students in the fraternities and those with Republican backgrounds might seem to offer the Right a natural constituency to challenge the ASU, the fact was that no serious effort was made to mount such a challenge. In the reformist New Deal era, conservatives knew they were out of step with majority student opinion. Consequently, they were unwilling to make the time commitments and personal sacrifices necessary to build national activist organizations when the political field seemed so unpromising.

The ASU both facilitated and benefitted from a leftward shift on campus which was far broader than its own dues paying membership. This shift was reflected in surveys of student opinion throughout the 1930s, which found majority support for more equal distribution of wealth, greater government regulation of business, and an expanded welfare state. Roosevelt's victory in the 1936 student polls was a testament to how far the Depression had brought the campuses since the 1920s, when large student majorities had gone Republican. This was particularly good news for the ASU, which in the mid-1930s moved into a political alliance with the Roosevelt administration. But, of course, the most dramatic sign of change and of the ASU's dominance of student politics in this era came each spring, when the ASU spearheaded anti-war demonstrations which annually mobilized hundreds of thousands of students.[110]

The influence of the ASU-led student movement was by no means confined to these spring strikes. The movement was helping to change some of the central institutions of American student life. This occurred most decisively in the case of the student press. At the dawn of the Great Depression, collegiate newspapers were overwhelmingly apolitical, often reporting more on college social life and football than serious news. By the mid-1930s, much of the college press was not only focusing on politics, but commenting upon it from a Left-liberal perspective. The movement had accomplished this by dispatching activists to work in the student press and by exposing editors to leftist ideas and causes. A *Fortune* magazine national report on college youth confirmed the movement's success in this area, finding that

> college newspapers are often far to the left of the undergraduate bodies. This is particularly true at Columbia, Vassar and Dartmouth, where the radicals provide almost the whole vocal element. Much of the energy that went into art in the undergraduate days of F. Scott Fitzgerald . . . now goes into the fledging political writing of a Left tinge for the college papers.[111]

In helping to politicize the campus and prod collegians leftward, the student movement transformed the very ideal of student leadership. In the 1920s collegians awarded leadership not to the politically aware or intellectually developed student, but rather to the one who was socially adept and prominent in campus social clubs or athletics. However, this ideal of leadership came under steady fire from the student movement. A new and more political conception of student leadership was gradually taking hold on campus. This change was reflected in a 1936 *New York Times* student survey, which concluded:

> Nowhere is the new liberalism more apparent than in the 1936-style campus leader . . . . He is no longer the star athlete, [or] the "smooth" prom man . . . . His stigmata are more apt to be brains, a good grasp of student and national problems and frequently leadership in the peace movement.[112]

The effect of this change was especially visible in student government elections. Formerly little more than popularity contests, these elections on many campuses became serious political races in which substantive social issues were raised. This trend even affected the nationwide association of student governments—the National Student Federation—which under the influence of the student movement began to support Left-liberal causes, including the American Youth Act campaign in the mid-1930s.[113]

These changes in the student press and government indicate the far reaching impact that the student movement—and the activist impulses which created it—had on Depression America's college campuses. The movement had made impressive progress in its goal of transforming student life; its national anti-war strikes, marches on Washington, ties with the Roosevelt administration, politicization of student leadership demonstrated that students had become serious political actors. The campuses were no longer, as they had seemed in the 1920s, merely playgrounds for middle-class youth.[114]

Such changes suggest that had the ASU and the student movement lived long enough, they might have achieved a lasting revolution in American student life. But this was not to be. The apolitical culture of frats and football, socials and sororities would prove more enduring—living through the war years and obtaining unparalleled supremacy in the 1950s. The ASU's failure to achieve any lasting impact on student politics and culture came about because the organization at the age of four began began to self-destruct, due to the the influence of the communists in its leadership. From the fall of 1939–1941 the increasingly communist-dominated ASU so discredited itself that the student movement died, burying as well the politically active style of student life that it had pioneered.

Chapter 9

From Popular Front to Unpopular Sect

> 1. The Soviet [Union] has signed a strong alliance with *Fascist* Germany!
> 2. It has entered into an act of aggression against Poland.
> 3. Immediately the Ally-German conflict becomes an "imperialist war" to the Reds in America.
> 4. And all anti-Fascist ideals go out the window! . . .
>
> I venture to make this prognastication: if the ASU makes the turnabout in policy that the Communists have, it will die—a suicide.
>
> Quentin Young, a Chicago ASU activist, to Joseph P. Lash, October 2, 1939.

Students in the 1939–1940 academic year had more reason than ever to worry that they might soon be carrying rifles instead of textbooks. With the start of classes in September came news of Hitler's invasion of Poland, followed by the British and French declarations of war against Germany. Before the first month of classes had ended, the Nazi conquest of Poland was complete. The great European war, which American student activists had spent much of the decade trying to prevent, was at hand. There followed several tense months without hostilities, Europe's "phony war." But any hopes that this was more than a temporary lull were shattered during the spring semester when Hitler struck again, launching Blitzkriegs which defeated Denmark and Norway in April and the Low Countries in May. The most shocking blow of all came at graduation time, when American students learned that France had fallen to a Nazi invasion.[1]

Although this news from Europe was horrible, it should have strengthened the student movement in the United States. After all, the movement's most influential organizations—the ASU and Youth Congress—had spent years warning Americans of the threat that Nazi Germany posed to world peace. Hitler's aggression had borne out those warnings. America seemed on the verge of adopting the anti-fascist position long advocated by the student movement. Even Congress began to move away from strict neutrality and rigid isolationism by repealing the arms embargo so as to aid Great Britain. All of this could have enhanced the student movement's prestige, conferring upon its activists a prophetic cast. Hitler's march through Europe should also have boosted the American student movement because it gave students an added impetus for turning out at rallies, lectures, and other movement events to protest Nazi aggression. At a time of surging student anxiety about a potential United States entry into the war, the student movement might have expanded greatly by continuing to carry its hopeful message that America could stay out of war by supplying Hitler's foes in Europe.[2] But instead of growing in this new crisis atmosphere, the American student movement began to crumble.

The 1939–1940 academic year proved disastrous for the American student movement. During this period the movement's key organizations lost members and credibility, the anti-war strike shrunk, and student activists began wondering whether campus protest was heading for extinction. Responsibility for this turn of events rested largely with communist student leaders. They alienated thousands of activists and potential activists from the student movement by championing first the Nazi-Soviet Pact, Stalin's shocking abandonment of anti-fascism, and then his brutal invasion of Finland. Through political manipulation and intrigue, young communists worked to force the ASU, America's largest Popular Front student organization to drop its anti-fascist principles and serve as an apologist for both the Pact and all the other twists and turns in Soviet foreign policy. These communist maneuvers fatally wounded the ASU and shattered the liberal-radical coalition which had been the life blood of the American student movement.

These political disasters might never have befallen the ASU had the organization followed the advice of the non-communists in its national office. This group, which included ASU Chair Molly Yard and Organizational Secretary Agnes Reynolds, was headed by Joseph Lash, the ASU Executive Secretary. Lash had been close to the Communist Party during the Popular Front era, because he felt the Party stood in the vanguard of the international struggle against fascism. But in August 1939, when the Nazi-Soviet Pact brought the Popular Front to an end, Lash lost faith in the Communist Party. He viewed the Pact as a sell out to Hitler and was determined that the ASU should have no part in this communist abandonment of anti-fascism.[3]

Given his own strong distaste for the Pact, Lash's advice regarding the ASU's reaction to it was quite restrained. He began the 1939 fall semester arguing that the ASU should take no public position on the Pact. Lash took this stance in the hope of saving the ASU from a ruinous split.

He understood that if the ASU endorsed the Pact it would surrender its anti-fascist principles and thereby alienate liberals and independent radicals, and if the ASU condemned the Pact it would lose the support of its many communist activists. "I do not think the ASU should become a battleground over the policies of Russia," Lash explained.[4] This would, however, prove an unrealistic hope, because the communists in the ASU were so ardently and uncritically pro-Soviet that they could not sustain neutrality on any question regarding the Soviet Union.

The first signs of trouble surfaced in early September 1939 at the ASU Fall Planning Conference, where more than 100 ASU chapter leaders and the national executive committee met. Here the growing tensions between the ASU's communists and non-communists became evident. YCL leader Bert Witt, who was also the ASU's New York district secretary, served as the key spokesman for the communist ASUers. Witt launched into a strident defense of the Nazi-Soviet Pact, provoking a heated debate with Lash. The communists and non-communists argued about not only the Pact, however, but also what foreign policy the ASU should promote for the United States. Lash and the non-communists continued to uphold the anti-fascist policies which the ASU had supported throughout the Popular Front era: opposing isolationism, calling for sanctions against Nazi Germany, and an end to the arms embargo on the victims of Nazi aggression. Communist ASUers, who had supported these policies for years, now—because of the Pact and Moscow's shifting foreign policy—criticized them and began to sound increasingly isolationist. Following Stalin's path of de-emphasizing the dangers of Hitlerism, a communist delegate from MIT explained that he "disagrees with [the] proposal to embargo Germany and aid the victim of aggression. [We] [c]annot see who is the aggressor in the present conflict."[5]

Although the debates at the Fall Planning Conference were contentious, the ASU's non-communist leaders came away from the meeting feeling that an important victory for unity had been won. The conference voted that the ASU should take no position on the Nazi-Soviet Pact. The willingness of communist ASUers to go along with this decision—in spite of their own sympathy for the Pact—left Lash optimistic that Stalin's new foreign policy would not lead to a divorce between the ASU's communist and non-communist activists. This communist-non-communist understanding would, Lash confided to a friend, strengthen the entire student movement, since "there are too many things we agree on that are urgent to allow ourselves to be divided on this issue. I say this as one of those who bitterly criticized the non-aggression pact at the NEC." Equally encouraging to the non-communist ASUers was the fact that the Fall Conference had reaffirmed the ASU's Popular Front positions, including support for amending the Neutrality Act "to permit the nation to give aid to the forces opposing Germany." This seemed to suggest that communist ASUers would respect the will of the ASU majority by not trying to force the organization to abandon its anti-fascist principles simply because Stalin had.[6]

This optimism, however, proved premature. Communist ASUers could not sustain the cooperative posture they had displayed in giving ground on the Nazi-Soviet Pact at the Fall Planning Conference. The ideological and organizational imperatives of the YCL would not allow communist ASUers again to show such independence and flexibility. The concessions communist ASUers made to non-communists at the Fall Planning Conference were unacceptable to the YCL's national leadership—which felt that in making such concessions communist ASUers had erroneously placed the interests of the American student movement ahead of the interests of the Soviet Union. This was why during the communist caucus at the ASU Fall Planning Conference, YCL leader Gil Green rebuked communist ASUers for not insisting that the ASU support the Pact; he accused them of "not defending the USSR," a cardinal sin within the communist movement.[7]

The concessions made at the Fall Planning Conference would probably not have been possible had the American Communist Party and YCL not been in a temporary state of disarray. The CP and YCL hierarchy had been shocked by the Pact and were not yet completely clear on the implications of the Pact for United States foreign policy. The American CP leadership had not yet understood that with the Nazi-Soviet Pact Stalin signalled a complete abandonment of anti-fascist collective security. Because of this confusion, the YCL hierarchy had not been able to orchestrate a disciplined factional assault on the ASU and its Popular Front policies at the ASU's Fall Planning Conference. It would, in fact, not be until the week following this conference that communist leader Earl Browder, with prodding from Moscow, announced the new isolationist CP/YCL line—in an interview published in the *Daily Worker*.[8]

This new clarity enabled the YCL to tighten the leash upon its members in the ASU, invoking Party discipline to prevent any repetition of the type of concessions that had been made at the Fall Planning Conference. From now on, the YCL hierarchy would require that all communist students defend the Pact, express relative indifference to Nazi aggression, and endorse strict United States neutrality in the European war. This would be done on the grounds that the war was simply a clash of rival imperialists. With this new line solidified, communist ASUers in mid-September 1939 began a sustained drive to rid the ASU of its Popular Front policies. Out went the anti-Hitler rhetoric and the calls for collective anti-fascist action, replaced by such isolationist slogans as "The Yanks aren't coming," and absurd claims that the Nazis were no more aggressive than their western enemies.[9]

It was, of course, more than simple Party discipline which made it possible for the young communists in the ASU to support the Pact and the new isolationist line. Communists were able to make this switch quickly because of their absolute faith in the Soviet Union; they saw it as the one nation which had completed a successful socialist revolution, which to them meant that it was the leading force of the international working-class movement and therefore, virtually infallible. The YCL faithful automatically assumed, consequently, that because the USSR had changed its line, this must represent the proper path toward peace. Embodying this mindset, shortly after the Pact, one communist student wrote Lash that it was "outright silly" for anyone to be

> amazed that [Communist loyalty to the USSR] has not wavered though Soviet foreign policy has . . . . I would consider a man a jackass if he didn't have faith in the law of gravity until it was proven to him by a physicist. A few objects falling would convince me, at least until I saw something fall upwards. The situation is similar here. Though the American CP may not fully understand every action of the USSR immediately, they have had no reason during the past 20 years to lose faith in the USSR, and until such time as there is proof of betrayal of Communist principle I see no reason why the Party shouldn't stick together.[10]

The Pact and the new isolationism had an additional appeal to young communists because it allowed them to express their most revolutionary sentiments. During the Popular Front era, when the emphasis had been on coalition building, communists were required first to mute and then to eliminate criticism of potential anti-fascist allies, including the Roosevelt administration, Britain, and France. With the ending of the Popular Front era and this need for unity gone, communists were again free to engage in anti-capitalist polemics. They could now depict the war in classic Leninist terms as a capitalist rivalry for imperialist spoils. For at least some of the young militants this was a liberating change, allowing them to feel again like true revolutionaries.[11]

Young communists also welcomed the Pact and the new line because in their eyes these seemed fitting Soviet revenge for the irresponsible foreign policies of the capitalist West. They saw the refusal of Britain and France to forge an anti-fascist alliance with the U.S.S.R. as well as Chamberlain's appeasement policy—particularly his deal with Hitler at Munich—as having been designed to isolate the Soviet Union. There was among communists therefore, as Lash put it, a desire "for venegance against [the] bourgeois world which by path of appeasement asked for its destruction."[12] The Pact also seemed to these young communists a necessary means of Soviet self-preservation, since in the wake of Munich it appeared to them too risky for the Soviet Union to remain Europe's only major anti-fascist power. As one young communist explained in defending the Pact, "I see no reason for the USSR . . . committing suicide for the Fascist groups in England or France who have created this mess and those in America who quite willingly let it be created."[13]

The zealous support that communist ASUers gave to the Pact and the new Party line angered non-communist ASU leaders. Having worked long and hard with the communists in opposing isolationism and promoting an anti-fascist foreign policy, non-communist ASUers could barely believe that their comrades would embrace isolationism and abandon the anti-fascist cause. "One went around with a terrible sense of betrayal," Lash recalled.

> It is clear now that our surprise was a sign of our political naiveté, but it was a stunning blow . . . . [What was] disheartening was the way in which young people with whom one had worked for years accepted the new [CP] policy, a policy in contradiction with the one they had been voicing, a policy they had no influence in deciding. I had assumed as we built the . . . Student Union and other organizations together that our methods of evaluation of political events were so similar, that if a new situation arose our response to that situation would be a similar one. Now, instead, person after person [within the ASU's communist ranks] began to echo the new slogans, which just didn't make intellectual sense.[14]

Non-communist ASUers were shocked as much by the suddenness of the communists' flip-flop as they were by the new party line itself. They saw their communist classmates, who in mid-August had ardently championed revision of the United States neutrality acts—to help halt Nazi aggression—opposing revision by mid-September. The communist ASUers were not only carrying new isolationist slogans, but denouncing those who would not go along with them as "warmongers." "All the independents in the ASU," Lash observed in late September, "wonder where the hell the change is coming from. They resent people who three weeks ago held one position coming around with another today and demanding that chapters obediently swing with them." Nor did most non-communist ASUers find persuasive the communists' arguments in defense of the Pact and isolationism. It seemed simple common sense that if it was important to stop Hitler last month it was no less important this month. In fact, it was the very weakness of the communists' defense of the Pact (and the transparent fact that their uncritical view of Stalin was at the root of that defense) which so concerned Lash and his followers. They recognized that if the ASU followed this line, ASUers would lose all credibility on campus—being "indelibly stamped as CP stooges."[15]

This split damaged not only communist-non-communist political alliances but also longstanding friendships within the ASU. Lash found that communist ASUers and YCL leaders, who only a few weeks earlier had been his friends, now did not hesitate to employ "character assassination and the shabbiest kind of political maneuvering" against him. Lash's personal diary from this era, reflected his anguish over these tactics and the harm they were doing. In his September 12 entry, Lash noted that one communist ASU leader "attacked me for individualism" and another accused him of being "viciously anti-Soviet" because he had urged that the

ASU avoid endorsing the Nazi-Soviet Pact.[16] The communists would also denounce Lash as a "warmonger," even though he had spent most of the decade leading the student movement against war. What hurt even more was that Lash's friend, YCL leader Gil Green, with whom he had worked closely in the student movement for almost four years, began hurling reactionary epithets at him in this dispute. Green charged that Lash had been " 'Hearst'like" in criticizing the Pact. Shocked that Green would compare him to this rightwing editor, Lash walked out of his meeting with the YCL leader, observing in his diary that "I thought I would break down and weep because the breach is widening."[17]

The communist attempt to maneuver the ASU into making the same foreign policy flip-flop as Stalin also aroused strong opposition because it brazenly violated democratic process within the ASU. Less than a week after the Fall Planning Conference, at which communists had gone along with the ASU decision to take no position on the Nazi-Soviet Pact, communist ASUers broke that agreement; they flouted majority rule in the ASU by using the organization's resources to agitate on behalf of both the Pact and an isolationist United States foreign policy. The process problem was particularly striking with respect to the ASU's communist staff members, who, by following the CP line rather than the will of the ASU membership, subverted the anti-fascist policies they were being paid to promote—policies that had been endorsed by large ASU majorities at the last national convention. Lash observed this breach of faith first hand at Harvard shortly after the Fall Planning Conference, while attending a New England ASU district meeting. Lash noted that this meeting

> was opened by the district secretary, a paid official of the American Student Union, whose speech was an outright apologia for the Nazi-Soviet Pact and defense of the [CP's] new isolationist line. It was quickly evident to me that the . . . [meeting] was packed. The same thing happened in other districts. Our district secretaries had two decent alternatives: either express the policy of the American Student Union or keep quiet. Instead, they went to town for the new [CP] line. What happened on the district scale was also going on in the chapters. The nuclei of the Young Communist League mobilized to establish the new position.[18]

Lash's bitterness toward the ASU's four district secretaries derived from the critical role that these officials played in the communist effort to rid the ASU of its Popular Front policies. All of the district secretaries were communists, who in mid-September 1939 spearheaded the YCL attempt to deprive the ASU's national officers—the non-communists Lash, Yard, and Reynolds—of their administrative authority and political influence. The idea was that because these influential national officers were critical of both the Nazi-Soviet Pact and the YCL's new isolationism, the communist district secretaries would seek to usurp their authority: pushing the new Party line on the districts and chapters, while keeping the national office, which formerly coordinated ASU affairs, as much in the dark as possible.[19]

Lash quickly recognized that something was wrong. He suspected that the YCL was plotting against him and the other non-communists in the ASU national office, noting in his diary on September 21, 1939 that at least one ASU "district [was] not coming to me with problems on war situation and ycl establishing its new position in asu by infiltration." Lash's worst fears were confirmed two weeks later, when he obtained the minutes of the ASU New England district staff meeting, which "disclosed a nat'l [YCL] drive to isolate [the ASU's] national office by having work head up in districts and having districts coordinated outside [the] n.o." Though fully aware of what he, Yard, and Reynolds were up against, and ready to fight back, Lash confessed in his diary that this confirmation of the YCL plot left him "very despondent." Lash sensed that the divisive and potentially fatal showdown between the ASU's communist and non-communist leaders, which he had tried so hard to prevent, was now inevitable.[20]

At first glance it might seem that because of the student political environment in 1939 Lash and his allies in the ASU leadership should have found it easy to turn back the communist challenge. After all, the vast majority of the ASU's 20,000 members were not communists, and that majority had solidly backed the foreign policy positions that Lash was seeking to defend against the communists. Moreover, the Nazi-Soviet Pact was extremely unpopular both on campus and off, leaving the communists in the very difficult position of having to explain why after years of promoting anti-fascism they were now forsaking it for isolationism. This would hardly seem an opportune moment for communists to mount a successful challenge to the ASU's experienced and popular non-communist leadership.

But these factors favoring the ASU's non-communists were more than offset by the communists' organizational advantages. The communists were the only faction within the ASU which in the fall of 1939 had a tight national political network in place. This network of campus YCL units was by mid-September 1939 already coordinating a national effort to reverse the ASU's foreign policies and drive non-communists out of the leadership of the student movement. This gave the communists a big headstart over their non-communist rivals in the ASU, who had to try to create their own national network almost overnight to compete with the communists at the upcoming ASU convention over the Christmas break. Lash worked frantically, attempting to assemble this network, but it was, as he explained to a friend in late September, a formidable task: "I am leading a one man struggle to galvanize the ASU into action . . . . I have never written so many letters—exhorting, demanding, threatening, philosophising—but I feel that the time spent is worth it, for a false move now and the ASU is finished."[21]

The task of building this non-communist network was made even more difficult by the reluctance of Lash and his allies to attack the communist issue head on in public during much of the fall 1939 semester. Though Lash publicly campaigned to retain the ASU's anti-fascist peace policy, he would not come right out and tell the ASU's membership that more was at stake than this: that he was struggling to prevent a complete communist takeover of their organization. Only in his private correspondence did Lash acknowledge the centrality of this issue. Here Lash wrote that stopping the communists from imposing their new isolationist foreign policy on the ASU was essential because "if the YCL succeeds in changing the ASU line . . . the ASU is finished as a united organization—it will then become nothing but a communist front in truth."[22] Had Lash gone public with this message early in the fall, it might have imparted a sense of urgency to the membership and helped mobilize them against the communists. This Lash refused to do, however, because of his sense of morality, his tactical sense, and his Old Left political style.

Having been frequently redbaited himself, Lash could not rid himself of the idea that a direct public attack on communist ASUers would smack of demagoguery and political persecution. Lash was especially sensitive to this problem because at the very moment he was preparing for his showdown with communist ASUers, the nation's most prominent redbaiting group, the House Un-American Activities Committee, was on the offensive against both the ASU and the entire student movement. The Committee, headed by Texas Congressman Martin Dies, threatened throughout the fall of 1939 to probe the ASU's communist connections, and would subpoena ASU leaders—including Lash—before the end of the year.[23]

Like most ASUers, Lash viewed the work of Dies' committee as part of a rightwing assault on both the American Left and liberalism. He therefore avoided public discussion of his battle against communist domination in the ASU so as not to aid that committee. A Lash diary entry in the late fall of 1939 confirms that these congressional anti-communists were simply making it more difficult for communist domination to be battled in the ASU: "Should one pr[e]cipitate open break with ycl—since cp means to narrow asu down to ycl. org on campus? opposed to such a break . . . [because] it plays into hands of dies committee." Lash's approach here was guided by not only moral but also tactical considerations. Lash knew that if he even gave the appearance of raising the communist issue while Dies was red hunting, he could lose the support of many non-communist ASUers, who would have seen him as giving aid and comfort to the student movement's enemies in Congress. This would have strengthened the communists by enabling them to villify Lash and his political allies as traitors to the movement.[24]

This unwillingess to discuss the communist issue openly was also an outgrowth of the vanguard mentality—the elitist political style common to Lash and virtually the entire ASU leadership. For much of the ASU's history, the YCL had existed as an organized faction within the Union. While the ASU grew in the mid-1930s this faction, along with its socialist counterpart, played a preeminent role in selecting the ASU's slate of national officers, including Lash himself. But these were facts that the leadership had not shared with either the public or the ASU rank and file, since it was thought that doing so would earn the ASU a red label and frighten off potential recruits.[25]

Most ASU leaders had, in fact, always denied that the ASU was a communist front organization. Lash himself told the *New York Times* on the eve of the Dies inquiry that the ASU was "not dominated by communists."[26] This was, however, at best a half-truth. Communists had never *unilaterally* dominated the ASU, but they had dominated the ASU in alliance with like-minded activist groups. In the early days of the ASU, the communists together with the socialists had dominated the ASU's leadership. Later, during the height of the Popular Front era, communists and Popular Front liberals had dominated that leadership. Now in the fall of 1939, communist ASUers were angling to take unilateral control of the ASU in order to dump the Popular Front.

Having kept silent about these machinations at the top of the ASU for the four years when they had agreed with the communists' anti-fascist foreign policy, Lash and his political allies in the ASU were in no position to go public with the communist issue now. Had they dealt frankly and openly with the problem of communist domination in 1939, they would almost have had to acknowledge their own complicity in the similar pattern of communist domination and elite manipulation within the ASU in the past. This would undoubtedly have damaged their credibility and hampered their efforts to organize a bloc to counter communist influence in the ASU at the upcoming convention. Such considerations helped lead Lash and his supporters to try to keep their battle against communist domination of the ASU out of the headlines.

The battle between the ASU's communist and non-communist leaders began to heat up as the ASU national office prepared for campus Armistice Day demonstrations. These were scheduled to be the first major anti-war protests of the fall 1939 semester. The literature that the ASU national office began preparing for these protests was strongly anti-fascist. As part of this mobilization effort, Lash, on September 25, sent an open letter to President Roosevelt, endorsing his attempt to revise the Neutrality Act. The letter also condemned isolationism and stressed "that a victory for Hitler will menace *our* security, *our* well being, *our* democratic institutions."[27] Though this letter was consistent with ASU policy, as set in the ASU's Fall Planning Conference and last convention, it elicited an angry response from communist leaders in the ASU. On the day that Lash wrote the FDR letter, Bert Witt, the ASU's most vocal communist leader, personally rebuked Lash over the contents of the letter. Witt argued that the letter ran contrary to the current sentiment of the ASU National Executive Committee and warned that if Lash sent out the letter the committee might force him to "issue [a] retraction."[28]

Less than a week after this angry confrontation, Lash's letter to FDR became the focus of a stormy meeting of the ASU National Executive Committee. Witt told his fellow committee members that Lash's letter distorted both the international situation and ASU policy. Witt found especially objectionable the portion of Lash's letter which stated that "the victory of Hitlerism in Europe . . . would have disastrous effects on American democratic institutions." Witt argued that this was "not a correct analysis" because "the defeat of Hitler does not necessarily mean the defeat of Chamberlain and Daladier, nor does aid to Daladier defeat Hitler, as was implied in the letter." Witt charged that the entire idea of revising the Neutrality Act to aid France and Britain, which Lash so strongly urged in the letter, was misguided and inconsistent with the ASU's peace policy. "Chamberlain and Daladier are not to be depended on and therefor[e]," Witt concluded, "this is not a war against Hitler—and the peoples must make the peace." Witt's supporters at the meeting joined him in promoting the new communist line, arguing that Britain and France were as imperialist as Germany and just as much a danger to peace.[29]

The non-communists at the meeting quickly and forcefully repudiated the communist line. Agnes Reynolds pointed out the inconsistency between what the communists were saying now and the anti-fascist foreign policies that they (and the rest of the ASU) supported in the past. "We have always said that equating British imperialism with German fascism is an aid to appeasement and this is still true." Molly Yard told the communists that their new line would prove unpopular on campus and that the ASU would lose all credibility with students if it adopted that line. Yard warned "those wanting to change the ASU position" that though

> there is confusion on the campus about peace . . . the feeling on the whole is that the situation is the same today as it was a few weeks ago. Poland has been invaded, and England and France are defending Poland. We still stand for aid to victims of aggression and their allies. If we deny this, students will say the ASU is communist-dominated and is doing this only because of the Soviet Union . . . . We must remember that to most people there is a distinction between Chamberlain and Hitler.[30]

This debate brought out the resentment Lash felt over the methods the communists were using in their campaign to reverse the ASU's peace policies. Lash confronted the district secretaries at the meeting with reports that they were agitating for the new CP line rather than the ASU's anti-fascist policies; he "expressed the hope that this matter could be cleared up, with honest discussion." Lash also refuted Witt's claim that his letter to FDR had violated the ASU peace program. Suggesting that Witt's attacks had been made in an unethical manner, Lash

> charged that there was a certain amount of evasiveness being shown at the meeting, and that it consisted in this: that there are certain people who have changed their position since the NEC meeting. But, he said, we

are not discussing here the validity of the change of opinion; we are discussing the ASU position as determined by the convention and the NEC. It is not decent to charge now that those who do continue to believe in the ASU program as adopted at the Fall Planning Conference have changed their position, and that those who in reality have changed their opinion have not. There are, of course, people who say that the victory of Hitlerism makes no difference. But this is not the position of the ASU. If you have lost your confidence in me, and no longer trust my interpretation of the ASU program, I will have to resign . . . . I cannot agree to Bert's statement as the present position of the ASU. It does not mean what I mean.[31]

After all this acrimonious discusssion, the Executive Committee made one last stab at compromise. Lash's letter to the president was allowed to stand, as was the ASU national office's attempt to make revision of the Neutrality Act a key theme in the Armistice Day mobilization. But to conciliate the communists, some of their anti-imperialist rhetoric was incorporated into the ASU's official Armistice Day Statement. The preamble of that statement, came close to echoing the CP line equating German and British imperialism:

> War has broken out. It is the war everyone has feared. It is a war which mankind enters with few illusions and a heavy heart. Hitler made this war, but the judgment of history will be equally severe on the Chamberlains who made Hitler, and on the system of greed and empire which has produced them both.[32]

The compromise proved ineffective. The ASU was a house dividing, with communists and non-communists moving in opposite directions on fundamental questions of war and peace. This internal strife left the ASU in no position to organize an effective national mobilization on Armistice Day. Equally damaging was the spreading anger among non-ASUers over the communist ASUers' support of the Nazi-Soviet Pact and sudden abandonment of anti-fascism. Across the nation—even at campuses where the ASU had formerly been strongest—there came word of poor turn-out and complaints that the "Armistice Day [mobilization] was a disastrous failure." At campuses where communists dominated the ASU chapters came reports of "a breakdown of confidence in the leadership of the ASU . . . [because local] officers of the ASU changed their position rapidly."[33]

Making matters worse for the ASU, the socialist-led YCAW—still bitter at the communists for pushing the ASU away from the Oxford Pledge—pounced upon the ASU in its moment of weakness. The YCAW did all that it could to publicize the communist students' flip-flop on anti-fascism. In its Armistice Day literature, the YCAW asked how anyone could

> have any faith in the ability of the ASU to fight totalitarianism when it is controlled by people giving allegiance to a government which gives sup-

port to Hitler . . . . So long as the A.S.U. is dominated by the Y.C.L., and so long as American Communism remains the blind instrument of a foreign dictator, we cannot look forward to any cooperation.[34]

Such attacks contributed to the Armistice Day fiasco because students were becoming disgusted with the feuding in the anti-war movement. According to the ASU's national report on the Armistice Day mobilization, many students reacted to the ASU-YCAW polemics by withdrawing and saying "a plague on both your houses."[35]

The low turn-out and dissension at the Armistice Day protests worried Lash. He warned the ASU executive committee that this poor showing suggested that "the ASU is in the most serious crisis it has ever faced." But the communists on the committee were not listening. Convinced that the party line was correct, they thought the campuses just needed a little time to adjust to the ASU's new analysis of the world situation. There was, the communists believed, no need to panic, but rather a need to educate students about the struggle in Europe and the strength of the isolationist case. "Everybody is saying keep America out of war," a communist ASUer explained to the executive committee. "[The] ASU must give reasons why we should stay out. Most people are saying England and France are fighting a just war. We must make them understand that this is an imperialistic war."[36]

It was Lash, however, and not the communists who had correctly diagnosed the implications of the Armistice Day fiasco. This failed mobilization was, as he claimed, a clear sign that the ASU was losing its following and sinking into the most serious crisis in its history. Within a few weeks, moreover, the crisis would grow much worse. If the response of communist ASUers to the Nazi-Soviet Pact damaged the ASU's credibility on campus, their response to the Soviet invasion of Finland virtually eliminated that credibility.

Stalin's invasion of Finland on November 30, 1939 elicited an angry American response. President Roosevelt condemned the Soviets' "dreadful rape of Finland," and suggested that 98 percent of the American public agreed with him. The invasion seemed a clear case of naked aggression and the bullying of a small country by one of the world's largest nations. Before the war had ended a half million Soviet troops marched into Finland; Russian planes bombed Finnish towns and cities. American sympathy for the victims of this aggression was compounded by the fact that the Finns defended themselves so valiantly. The Kremlin and much of the world had expected the defeat of the badly outnumbered Finnish forces in a matter of days or weeks, but they held out for more than two months. The wave of American sympathy for Finland proved so strong that President Roosevelt was able to overcome the resistance of Congressional isolationists and secure some financial aid to Finland. FDR also called for a "moral embargo" against Russia, discouraging American manufacturers from supplying airplanes or equipment to "nations obviously guilty of such unprovoked bombings." [37]

At the very moment when American sympathy for Finland was surging, communist ASUers, along with their counterparts in the adult CP, rushed to the defense of the Soviet Union. Knowing that the non-communists in the ASU national office would be unsympathetic, communist ASUers used their authority at the district level to place the ASU on record in support of the invasion. These communist efforts resulted in the convening of an irregular meeting of New York City ASU chapters, which on December 9, 1939, cheered the Soviet attack on Finland. The resolution endorsed by this gathering portrayed the Soviet attack as a justifiable act of self-defense, claiming that "Finland existed . . . as . . . a puppet state created and maintained by imperial powers from abroad, a threat to and base against Russia." These ASUers charged that Americans who embraced the cause of Finland were the victims of "propaganda" and "atrocity tales." They claimed that Wall Street was seeking to use Finland to whip up an anti-Soviet war hysteria in the United States in order to draw America into the conflict, so as "to make profits from blood, to make the world safe for British and American imperialism." This communist-led group concluded by urging the student movement to adopt the isolationist slogan "NOT TO FINLAND OR TO FRANCE—THIS YANK AIN'T COMING." [38]

Non-communist ASU activists reacted with outrage and disgust to this pro-invasion stance. They were appalled that members of the ASU, an organization dedicated to opposing aggression and preserving peace, would applaud this massive act of Soviet aggression. Expressing the sentiment of these students, Robert Klein, an ASUer and vice president of the Student Council at the CCNY, fumed: "the suggestion that Finland provoked or invaded the mighty U.S.S.R. (1/6 of the earth's surface, greatest standing army, greatest natural resources, etc.) is almost too preposterous to consider if it were not seriously advanced" by communist ASUers. "The U. S. S. R. has followed the fascist nations in adopting a policy of aggression as a means of settling international disputes that they fabricate themselves." Klein noted that the "vast majority of students . . . are on the side of Finland," and that by backing the invasion the New York ASU leadership was alienating thousands of students. The CCNY leader reported that on his own campus, formerly a key ASU stronghold, the local ASU chapter's backing of both the invasion of Finland and the Nazi-Soviet Pact had seriously wounded the ASU. "Never before," Klein observed, "has the City College Chapter been held in such low esteem by the student body; never before has the active membership, and consequently the activity, of the Chapter been so low." [39]

In the national office of the ASU, the non-communists immediately acted to repudiate the New York district's statements. Lash issued a press statement criticizing the Soviet invasion and asserting that the New York

district's endorsement of the invasion was not representative of the majority of ASUers. He was angry that communist ASUers had tried to give
the impression that they, rather than the ASU national office, spoke for
the ASU. Though still refusing to raise the issue of communist domination directly, Lash was now willing at least to be more explicit and public
about the growing communist-non-communist split within the ASU. Lash
told the press that his attack on New York district's statement attested to
the division in the ASU between

> those who are prepared to justify any policy of the Soviet Union and the
> rest of us who are concerned with a movement based on the needs of the
> American people. The best way to build up contempt for everything pro-
> gressive in this country is to identify it with the policies of Soviet Russia.[40]

This public split over the Finnish invasion intensified the communist-
non-communist rivalry within the ASU. It was now clear to all that the
two sides were heading for a final showdown at the ASU convention over
the Christmas break. As the convention approached, the communists accelerated their campaign of vituperation against Lash. News of this campaign reached Lash from non-communist ASUers in all regions. Chicago
ASU activist Quentin Young, for instance, wrote to warn Lash:

> Intrigue! I don't comprehend exactly what goes on. When you were
> in Chicago last things made sense. But now . . . I know you do not fol-
> low the Party Line—which . . . displeases the Reds and so out of the
> Chicago [ASU] District Office comes wierd sounds. You are guilty of . . .
> (according to them) Red Baiting at an NEC meeting . . . [and] Being
> generally dictatorial. The reason for this, they say is that you are 'losing
> power' and trying to retain it.[41]

Lash thanked Young for the warning, but told him that the stories afloat
in Chicago were only a small part of the communist ASUers' effort to
turn the ASU against him; they had circulated so many negative stories
about him that Lash could barely keep up with them. "One day I am
splitting the ASU in cahoots with FDR, the next day, I am splitting the
ASU in cahoots with the Trotskyites. One rumor has it that I am running
out on the ASU because I insist on leaving this January, the next that I
am 'trying to retain power' as your letter cites." Lash concluded that the
communists' campaign against him was designed to discredit him before
the convention even met so "they will not have to answer with arguments"
his criticisms of the Pact and the Finnish invasion.[42]

With both sides positioning themselves for the convention battle, the
ASU executive committee meetings became increasingly acrimonious. The
two sides feuded about everything from the location of the upcoming
convention to the resolutions to be considered there. The most heated
exchange at the NEC occurred after the communists repeatedly accused

Lash of promoting factionalism and discord in the ASU. The communists raised this charge of factionalism in response to Lash's request that before the Convention ASU delegates be briefed about the policy disputes between the ASU's non-communist and communist leaders. Lash wanted the ASU executive committee to mail the delegates position papers representing both sides in the dispute. The communists initially opposed this move, on the grounds that it would promote factionalism within the ASU. Lash found this communist position "incredible" and "hypocritical." "Here were the spokesmen for an organized faction opposing our efforts to organize on the grounds that factionalism would split the American Student Union."[43]

During this argument a member of the anti-Lash bloc barbed that "he was not interested" in paying "the salary of a national secretary to organize factionalism." This was, as Lash later explained, too much to bear, "since my salary has not been paid for several months, since all through my period of national secretaryship I have had to borrow, sponge off friends, etc." A furious Lash called his accuser "a swine," and though he later wrote a letter of apology for this remark, the exchange was indicative of just how deep the bad feelings went.[44]

In the aftermath of this bitter argument, the communists did, however, agree to Lash's demand for the mailing. The two position papers sent to the chapters defined the lines of argument which would prevail at the convention. While the communists' position paper merely reiterated the Party line, the non-communists' polemic, "Save the American Student Union" was a far more original political manifesto. Written by Yard, Reynolds, and Lash, this position paper spoke of the critical need for independent thought on the part of American liberal and radical student activists. A student movement working for peace and egalitarian change in America needed to develop its own policies, based upon "the needs and traditions of the American people," instead of mindlessly echoing "the policies of the Soviet government." The statement warned against "the viewpoint that any genuine program for peace and democracy must start with a defense of Soviet policy in Finland." Such a program would "transform the character of the ASU," so that the organization would "not be the broad ASU founded at Columbus to unite our student generation in the interests of the American people." Instead the ASU would shrink "into a narrow sect."[45]

Although critical of the communists' line and their attempt to impose it upon the ASU, the authors of "Save the American Student Union" took pains not to treat communists as pariahs. Lash, Yard, and Reynolds were careful to distinguish between their own position and those of anticommunists who wanted to deny communists a place in the American political process:

> We want to make it perfectly clear that we believe Communists have a place in the ASU. We are mindful of the great services they have ren-

dered the ASU. We have no sympathy for the various efforts headed by
Mr. Dies to outlaw the Communists. Their program, however, does not
express the interests of progressive and liberal student opinion.[46]

These ASU leaders were, then, not at all the redbaiters that their communist rivals had claimed. They were seeking to allow the ASU's communist minority to remain in the ASU while simultaneously retaining an
ASU program representative of the non-communist majority. In this sense,
"Save the American Student Union" was more of a non-communist than
an anti-communist document.

Unfortunately for Lash's bloc, however, the fate of the ASU would
be settled not by logic, merit, or rank and file sentiment, but by simple
political arithmetic. The bloc with the most delegates to the 1939 ASU
convention in Madison, Wisconsin would win the argument. Although the
non-communists tried to remain hopeful as they entered the final stages
of their mobilization effort for the convention, they knew their campaign
confronted some major problems. One of their biggest problems was, as
Lash, Yard and Reynolds acknowledged in "Save the American Student
Union," that "increasingly good ASU'ers, genuine progressives have
dropped into inactivity because of actions and policies of which the New
York resolution is only a symptom."[47] The danger was that the non-
communists would lose the delegate race because the ASU's rank and file,
disillusioned with the organization because of the behavior of communist
ASUers, had already voted with their feet—dropping out of the ASU before the convention.

Reports came in from campus chapters of just such desertions. Right
up to the eve of the convention, Lash was receiving letters from disillusioned ASUers, who were leaving the organization. One such ASUer wrote
Lash to express "hearty approval" of the ASU Executive Secretary's stance
on the Soviet invasion of Finland; he wished Lash luck in his upcoming
convention battle, but said he could not in good conscience retain his
membership in the ASU so long as his local chapter continued to support
the communist line on Finland and the Nazi-Soviet Pact. Lash replied by
urging these ASUers to defend rather than desert their organization.
"Frankly," Lash wrote to one of these drop-outs,

> while I appreciate your good wishes, what I, and the hundreds of other
> ASU leaders who agree with me, need, is your active support . . . . If
> you wait while others elect delegates then ASU policy will reflect their
> point of view . . . . We need . . . students . . . who will go into the
> ASU and fight to save it, fight for delegates and fight for support of
> progressive policies. Unless this fight is carried to the membership, unless
> the broad masses of students . . . enter the fray by becoming active in
> pre-convention discussions, etc. the fight at Madison will be difficult indeed
> . . . . Liberals who are critical of communist policy . . . [have] a special
> responsibility to come into the ASU and fight for their policies. The ASU
> has become a testing ground for progressivism: do non-communists have

> a program? do they have the capacity for unity? do they have the . . .
> courage to carry their program through?[48]

This drop-out problem was, however, only one of many indications that in gearing up for the Convention ASU non-communist rank and filers were far less motivated than their communist counterparts. As highly committed political activists, communists had always been generally more willing than non-communists, "to do the difficult and unrewarding . . . work of organization" in the ASU—writing flyers, attending meetings, arranging demonstrations. The communists' reward for this labor had been that they were traditionally overrepresented (relative to their numbers in the overall ASU membership) in ASU convention delegations and "important posts in the Union's district apparatus."[49] This problem of communist overrepresentation was compounded in the weeks before the 1939 convention because the international situation left the communists even more highly motivated politically than in the past. Communist ASUers believed that in the wake of the invasion of Finland, an anti-Soviet war hysteria was taking hold of America. Rallying to the Soviet side in what they saw as the communist motherland's hour of political crisis, communist ASUers worked themselves into a frenzy of activity. They organized intensively to ensure communist control of the convention. They were determined to prevent the ASU from attacking the U.S.S.R.

Such tireless organizing by the ASU's communists left informed observers convinced that it would be they rather than the non-communists who would dominate the Convention. James Wechsler, the former ASU leader and ex-communist, predicted in a penetrating *Nation* article that because the communists acted "as a unified bloc in the election of delegates," this "disciplined minority" would dominate the Convention, even though most of the ASU's membership was unsympathetic to the new communist line. The communists, Wechsler explained, were willing to make "limitless sacrifices to attend conventions when lukewarm members are content to celebrate Christmas."[50] In the socialist press, Daniel Bell offered an even more sarcastic, but equally prescient prediction:

> There is no doubt that the YCL will dominate the convention. Its machine is well-oiled, and all vital manipulative posts are in its hands. Joe Stalin's boys are well trained in these arts . . . . [This] communist control means destruction and decay, and the subordination of students' interests and needs to the propaganda tasks of the communist movement seeking to whitewash a bloody Russian totalitarian state.[51]

In their eagerness to control the delegation selection process, communist ASUers often behaved, as Bell implied, like machine politicians. They did not hesitate to use ASU rump meetings, packed with fellow communists, or to employ other underhanded tactics in order to elect pro-Soviet delegates. Here communist activists showed no concern about

whether their campus delegations to the convention were actually representative of majority opinion in their chapters. The president of MIT's
ASU chapter, for instance, wrote Lash on the eve of the Convention that
because of such communist tactics "our pre-convention meeting was *not*
representative."[52] An ASU chapter leader in New York reported that at
her school the communists had abused democratic process brazenly and
repeatedly ever since the invasion of Finland, when

> the N.Y. district called a "Leaders" meeting [the communist-dominated
> ASU gathering that defended the invasion of Finland]. Only two people
> [YCLers] from our chapter knew about this meeting, [and these two com-
> munists voted for the pro-invasion resolution, sponsored by YCL leader
> Bert Witt]. The elected delegate was not informed that there was to be a
> meeting and so was not there. At the next meeting of . . . [the school's]
> A.S.U. [the chapter] went on record as being against the Bert Witt reso-
> lution . . . . [The YCL leader in the chapter] then answered that in spite
> of this vote, if he were elected delegate, he would vote for it at the con-
> vention. It was then that the real "fun" began. Thursday there was an
> [ASU chapter] executive committee meeting. I asked for the a[d]dress.
> One of the exec. members refused point blank to give it to me. The girl
> in whose house it was held gave me the wrong a[d]dress. It was only by
> accident that I eventually got to the meeting . . . . At Monday's chapter
> meeting there were 28 people . . . [to vote on the] candidates for the
> delegate to the convention . . . . One girl abstained and the chairman
> cannot vote, so that the vote was 13–13 [between the communist and
> non-communist candidates. The YCL leader then] . . . came forward
> with three proxy votes [that elected the pro-Soviet candidate] . . . . Be-
> fore the actual counting [of] the votes took place, no one knew that proxy
> voting could be used. In fact, never before in the history of . . . [the
> school's] ASU had proxy voting been used.[53]

With the deck stacked so heavily against them, Lash and his political
allies at the ASU's 1939 convention in Madison never had a chance. The
key moment in the convention came when Lash's bloc introduced a resolution which would have placed the ASU on record as opposed to the
Soviet invasion of Finland. The convention rejected the resolution by a
lop-sided margin of 322 to 49. The convention then refused requests from
the floor that the ASU hold a general membership referendum on this
resolution. The communist-dominated gathering whole-heartedly embraced the CP's isolationist "Yanks are not coming" foreign policy. The
convention also chose YCLer Bert Witt to replace Lash as the ASU's executive secretary.[54]

Though the communists won all the key votes at Madison, this quickly
proved to be a hollow victory. The convention's refusal to criticize the
invasion of Finland did irreparable harm to the ASU's reputation. Former
admirers of the ASU now felt that the organization had been converted
into a puppet of the Communist Party, thereby losing all claim to speak
for the campuses. The national Left-liberal press, which had welcomed

the student movement in the early 1930s and consistently supported the ASU, expressed outrage over the outcome at Madison. The *Nation* termed the ASU Convention's decision on Finland "a precious New Year's gift to Martin Dies."[55] The *New Republic* fretted: "What has happened to the American Student Union?" Running a story suggesting that at Madison communist ASUers had all but destroyed the credibility of America's most influential student activist organization, The *New Republic* concluded: "the Communists can congratulate themselves that they have done maximum harm to the whole student movement."[56] Events on campus would quickly bear out this pessimistic conclusion.

As word made its way back to the campuses about the decisions at Madison, the ASU's reputation among undergraduates sank far and fast. The news was all the more devastating when it was carried back personally to the student body by disillusioned convention delegates. One such delegate, Vic Stone, a non-communist activist from Oberlin, reported to his campus that the Madison convention attested that a communist "minority [was] dominating the student movement . . . . By demonstrating blind faith in a . . . leader [Stalin] and in a political doctrine, the delegates made it practically impossible for the ASU to lead the free thinking students of America in our fight for peace and security."[57]

Reports came in from campuses across the nation that "since the convention all hell has broken loose in the [ASU] chapters." By early January key ASU chapters, including Harvard, Reed, and Wisconsin had begun to discuss disaffiliation, and this kind of talk was spreading. It was heard, for instance, at the University of Iowa, where Merle Miller, a convention delegate and columnist in his student newspaper, wrote that "here in Iowa City, . . . the life of the ASU ended . . . on the day the convention closed." He argued that student activists at his university could now be most "effective by withdrawing from the national organization and building a local, campus organization." Similar feelings of anger and disillusionment led Grinnell College delegate Lee McIntosh to conclude that "from the looks of things the ASU will dissolve and leave only a skeleton which should rightly be called the ACU [American Communists' Union]."[58]

Much as McIntosh predicted, the ASU declined rapidly following the fiasco in Madison. Not even the work of Lash's successors in the ASU's non-communist bloc—now calling themselves the Union's Liberal Caucus—could halt this deterioration. These non-communists, led by Alan Gottlieb of the Harvard ASU, hoped they could reverse the convention's decision on Finland by sending a referendum on the Soviet invasion to the ASU general membership. The referendum, however, could not save the ASU; it was too late. Referendum organizers found that most of their potential supporters felt that the ASU was a lost cause. Chad Walsh, for instance, an ASU activist from the University of Michigan, wrote to one of these organizers that

the sincerity and conviction of your letter almost won me over, but not quite. I admire the fight you are making, but I'm afraid that by the time the organization has fought the question out it will be pretty well wrecked by internal dissension, and will be in no position to accomplish anything . . . . So my resignation still stands.[59]

Like Walsh, some two thirds of the ASU's members, in the months following the Madison convention, dropped out of the ASU—making a meaningful referendum impossible. The remaining, shrunken ASU chapters were quickly losing their political influence on campus. The ASU was becoming, as Lash had warned, "a narrow sect" and a carbon copy of the Young Communist League; it would prove incapable of orchestrating anything approaching the successful campus mobilizations that the organization had led during the Popular Front era.[60]

Unfortunately for the student movement, the communists learned nothing from the ASU debacle. Though their apologetics for Soviet aggression had left the ASU in shambles, communist activists repeated those apologetics in the American Youth Congress. Communists worked to impose upon the Youth Congress the same unpopular party line that had wrecked the ASU. As in the ASU, communist Youth Congress leaders disregarded democratic process in their rush to align the movement with Stalin's new foreign policy. Without consulting the Youth Congress' constituent groups, communist and communist sympathizing AYC officers reversed the direction of the Youth Congress' peace policy; they used AYC resources to promote strict United States neutrality, ignoring the fact that at its last national Congress in July the AYC had endorsed Popular Front policies favoring American aid to victims of Nazi aggression. Communists in the AYC also sought in the winter of 1940 to create the public impression that the Youth Congress opposed United States aid to Finland, even though the Youth Congress' rank and file had never approved this policy.[61]

These communist machinations led to a political fiasco as damaging to the Youth Congress as the Madison Convention had been to the ASU. This was the Youth Congress Citizenship Institute, held in Washington, D.C. on February 9–11, 1940. No single event did more to drive liberal students away from the student movement than did the Citizenship Institute. The difference between the initial concept and actual convening of this Institute convinced many liberal students that the Youth Congress was nothing but a communist-front, run in a deceptive manner by Party hacks who could not be trusted. The Institute had been planned—prior to the Nazi-Soviet Pact—as a political and educational event in which the Youth Congress would bring young men and women to Washington to learn how government works, and to lobby for federal jobs and student aid programs. This was supposed to be done in cooperation with the Roosevelt administration, which in the late 1930s had shared with the Youth Congress a strong desire to prevent conservatives on Capitol Hill from cutting New Deal social programs. But at the last minute communist organizers in the Youth Congress transformed the political character of the

Citizenship Institute, making its primary message not jobs but isolationism and opposition to United States aid for Finland. Since President Roosevelt had favored just such aid, this meant that the Institute was being changed from a pro- to an anti-administration event.[62]

This communist posturing over Finland not only alienated liberal students, but also turned the Citizenship Institute into a public relations disaster for the Youth Congress by provoking an open confrontation with President Roosevelt. The president had agreed to address a crowd of participants in the Citizenship Institute at the request of his wife. FDR, however, had become increasingly annoyed with the student movement's leadership ever since the ASU Convention had refused to criticize Stalin's invasion of Finland. At Hyde Park two weeks after that convention, Youth Congress leaders got their first hint of the president's anger about the movement's handling of the Finland issue. Here, in the presence of student movement leaders who were guests of his wife, FDR had "spoken scoffingly of the ASU and referred with pointed sarcasm to the 'young liberals' of the ASU." The president further signalled his mistrust of the movement's leadership on the eve of the Citizenship Institute, when he informed Youth Congress leaders he "did not want any AYC officials on [the White House] portico with him [when he addressed Institute activists and a national radio audience] or speaking over [the] air with him."[63] FDR's anger at the student movement's leaders surged when he learned that enroute to the Citizenship Institute, the New York Council of the Youth Congress had passed a resolution attacking his plan to provide Finland with economic aid.

The president vented this anger at the Youth Congress in his address to its Citizenship Institute on February 10. Roosevelt stunned the 4466 Youth Congress activists assembled on the White House lawn by delivering a tough speech, in which he denounced the Youth Congress' position on Finland. Referring to the Finland resolution passed by its New York branch, the president issued a "word of warning," to the Youth Congress not to pass resolutions on subjects "which you have not thought through and on which you cannot possibly have complete knowledge." The president dismissed as "unadulterated twaddle" the charge made by New York Youth Congress leaders that a United States loan to Finland represented "an attempt to force America into an imperialistic war." FDR argued "that the Soviet Union would because of this [loan] declare war on the United States is about the silliest thought that I ever heard advanced in the fifty-eight years of my life, and that we are going to war ourselves with the Soviet Union is an equally silly thought." Roosevelt defended the loan as an expression of the sympathy the American people felt for a "small republic" that had been invaded by the large Soviet state—"a dictatorship as absolute as any . . . in the world."[64]

The president understood that communists in the Youth Congress had played a leading role in shaping the organization's stance on Finland. In his speech to the Citizenship Institute, he therefore discussed the issue

of Communism in the Youth Congress. FDR, in contrast to the Dies Committee, defended the "constitutional right" of radicals "to call yourselves
communists and to peacefully and openly advocate certain ideals of theoretical communism." But he also lectured the young radicals on their
responsibility as citizens to confine their political advocacy "to the methods prescribed by the Constitution of the United States," warning that
"you have no American right by act or deed of any kind to subvert the
government and the Constitution of this nation."[65]

If Roosevelt's words seemed designed to cast the Citizenship Institute
and its communist leaders in a negative light, the young activists' response
to the speech assisted him. The crowd not only booed the president, but
did so in a selective fashion which contributed to the growing public
impression that the Institute and its Youth Congress sponsors were
communist-dominated. The young activists stood silently in the rain while
FDR offered a provocative defense of the New Deal—a defense in which
he cited economic statistics comparing America in 1932 and 1939, which
actually proved nothing except that the Hoover Depression was even worse
than the Roosevelt Depression. Nor did they react to FDR's curt dismissal
of radical solutions to the Depression or to to his condescending warning
not "to seek or expect Utopia overnight." Instead, the young communists
raised their voices against the president only when he broached Soviet
topics, booing him when he criticized the Youth Congress' position on
Finland and when he termed the U.S.S.R. an absolute dictatorship. Though
this jeering only served to strengthen FDR's hand by ensuring that the
press would focus on the parts of his speech most unfavorable to the
AYC, the young communists could not help themselves; for it was the
Soviet Union which most concerned them and Roosevelt's criticisms of it
which most offended them.[66]

This confontation with the president brought the Youth Congress
and the student movement a flood of negative publicity. Before a national
radio audience and the entire Washington press corps, FDR had humili-
ated the Youth Congress leadership and signalled the break between his
administration and the student movement. It was this speech more than
any of the dozens of sessions of the Citizenship Institute which captured
headlines and shaped the national image of the gathering. *Life* magazine,
for instance, reported that the "highlight" of the meeting of Youth Congress activists in Washington "was the spanking given them by President
Roosevelt for their antagonism towards U.S. aid to Finland, for their par-
tiality to the Soviet system." Leading columnists denounced the Youth
Congress, charging that "either those kids are phonies or they're idiots."
Youth Congress activists also drew criticism for booing the president, an
act which was widely condemned as a sign of politicial immaturity and
disrespect for the office of the president.[67]

The Citizenship Institute fiasco suggested just how much the new
communist line impaired the student movement's ability to communicate
its egalitarian ideals to the student body and the nation. At the Citizenship

Institute, static from the communists' propaganda on the Finland issue drowned out the young activists' criticism of the Roosevelt administration's social programs. The Institute had a strong case to make in Washington on behalf of jobs and aid for impoverished youths. The New Deal had been stalled ever since FDR's failed court packing scheme. Roosevelt had not managed to end the Depression. Some four millions youths remained unemployed. The Institute had gathered white and black youth from America's farms, factories, and campuses to dramatize these problems; it had the additional asset of John L. Lewis, the fiery labor leader who, having recently broken with FDR, delivered a passionate speech to the Institute indicting the New Deal's record on youth unemployment. But because of the the flap over Finland, it was Soviet foreign policy— and Youth Congress support of that policy—rather than Roosevelt's domestic policy which attracted public criticism in the wake of the Citizenship Institute.[68]

The Citizenship Institute further damaged the Youth Congress because it undermined the important relationship between the AYC's leaders and Eleanor Roosevelt. The First Lady had been the Youth Congress' most steadfast and influential ally in the Roosevelt administration. Mrs. Roosevelt had worked to ensure that key New Dealers, including the president, paid attention to the Youth Congress' concerns. She helped raise funds for the Youth Congress and played a powerful role in legitimating the Congress with both liberal students and the general public.[69]

Mrs. Roosevelt had proven an especially valuable ally to the Youth Congress and the ASU when those organizations came under attack by the Dies Committee in the fall of 1939. The First Lady loathed the Dies Committee and what she termed its "Gestapo methods." The committee had recklessly redbaited hundreds of innocent individuals—engaging in trial by headline and refusing to accord most of the accused any opportunity to respond to the charges. Indeed, within a few days of its founding in 1938, the Committee had already produced witnesses accusing 640 organizations, 483 newspapers, and 280 labor unions of being communistic. When the committee turned its guns on the young activists with whom she had worked ever since the World Youth Congress in 1938, Mrs. Roosevelt made a principled stand in defense of civil liberty. Here the First Lady stood up to the Dies Commitee, defending free speech and due process, and resisting congressional red probers more boldly than any other occupant of the White House in this century.[70]

The First Lady used her syndicated newspaper column and her personal prestige to fend off Dies' attack on the youth leaders in the fall of 1939. Her column praised the Youth Congress and ASU. She further demonstrated her solidarity with the subpoenaed youth leaders by accompanying them to the Dies Committee hearing and inviting them to the White House. Mrs. Roosevelt spoke to the press about the value of political tolerance and suggested that rather than seeking to ban radicalism, the nation should concern itself with eliminating the social problems that bred radicalism. The First Lady then published a column calling into question the fairness of the Dies proceedings, charging that the committee had not given the youth leaders sufficient time to prepare for the hearing. She criticized the way that J.B. Matthews, the Dies Committee's chief investigator, treated the youth leaders at the hearings: "His whole attitude, tone of voice and phraseology made one feel that a prisoner, considered guilty, was being tried at the bar." This assistance from the highly popular First Lady helped arouse sympathy for the youth leaders and support for their free speech rights; it prevented Dies from damaging the Youth Congress.[71]

Mrs. Roosevelt's defense of these young activists had been based not only upon political principle, but also personal friendship. Having cooperated with the Youth Congress on behalf of several causes—especially on their common goal of expanded federal aid to needy youth—the First Lady had befriended that organization's national leaders. She trusted them. Some of those leaders, however, would prove unworthy of that trust. The Youth Congress officers who were either in or close to the Communist Party, hid their Party ties from Mrs. Roosevelt. James Wechsler, himself a former communist comrade of these Youth Congress leaders, recalled this as one of the most shameful deceptions in the student movement's history. "Mrs. Roosevelt," Wechsler explained, "gave warm and generous help to the Youth Congress in the years preceding the debacle of 1939. The communists who held strategic posts in it responded to her benevolence by lying to her about themselves and seeming to enjoy the hoax."[72]

This deception initially went undetected by Mrs. Roosevelt. As the Dies Committee accusations began, she met with Youth Congress officers at the White House and

> told them that since I was actively helping them, I must know exactly where they stood politically. . . . I told the young people in the group that if any of them were communists I would quite understand, for I felt they had grown up at a time of such difficulty as to explain their being attracted to almost any ideas that promised them better conditions. However, I felt it essential that I should know the truth. If we were going to work together, I must know where we really agreed and where we differed. I asked each one in turn to tell me honestly what he believed. In every case they said they had no connection with the communists, had never belonged to any communist organizations, and had no interest in communist ideas. I decided to accept their word . . .[73]

Having been so misled, Mrs. Roosevelt unknowingly became a party to this political masquerade of the communists and communist sympathizers in the Youth Congress' leadership. She made front page news by rebutting the Dies Committee witnesses who charged that Youth Congress leaders Joseph Cadden and William Hinckley were part of a communist delegation which had dined with her. Mrs. Roosevelt told the *New York*

Times that Cadden and Hinckley, with whom she was "well acquainted," had no ties with the Communist Party. The First Lady had no idea at the time that her two young friends had misled her. She had admired them for their youthful idealism and social consciousness and saw no reason to doubt their honesty. Mrs. Roosevelt's boldness in challenging Dies, then, was coupled with a naiveté in trusting these Youth Congress leaders.[74]

These Youth Congress leaders kept Mrs. Roosevelt in the dark about their Party loyalty apparently because this made it easier for them to influence her decisions regarding the student movement. By concealing their communist ties, they could give the First Lady the impression that they were non-partisan and objective in advising her about the movement—when in fact they were profoundly partisan. The initial effectiveness of this ruse was evident in the discussions between Mrs. Roosevelt and these Youth Congress leaders regarding the 1939 ASU Convention. They told her that the convention's refusal to criticize the Soviet invasion of Finland derived not from communist domination of that convention, but from "fear of war" on the part of "liberal" delegates and the American student body. Unaware that she was hearing a biased communist interpretation of the convention, Mrs. Roosevelt trusted the assessment of her young friends. The First Lady proceeded to echo this interpretation of the ASU Convention in her newspaper column, implying that the press attacks on the ASU Convention over the Finland issue were unjustified. The ASU's communist-dominated leadership liked the column so much that they included it in their publication of the convention's proceedings. This support from the First Lady was, of course, a great asset, and communist Youth Congress leaders were unwilling to jeopardize this by disclosing to her their Party affiliations.[75]

It was not until the Citizenship Institute fiasco that Mrs. Roosevelt began to realize that some of her friends in the Youth Congress leadership had deceived her. The Institute exposed the First Lady to the shabby side of the Old Left political style. Mrs. Roosevelt had been misled by the Youth Congress' leaders concerning the purposes of the Citizenship Institute. They had led her to believe that the Insititute would be a pro-administration event, as it had been originally planned the previous summer. Thus Mrs. Roosevelt had gone all out to assist the Institute, doing everything from finding free housing for participants to seeing to it that high ranking officials, including the attorney general and the president himself, addressed the gathering. Though the Youth Congress' communist-dominated leadership had spent the weeks preceeding the Institute preparing to turn the event into an anti-administration pilgrimage, most Youth Congress leaders tried to keep the First Lady unaware of this change.[76]

This deception left Mrs. Roosevelt in the uncomfortable position of playing hostess to a political event hostile to her husband. And if this was not humilating enough, the First Lady, who addressed the Citizenship Institute the day after her husband, was booed when she implied that the Youth Congress' position on Finland reflected a poor understanding of the world situation. These events shook Mrs. Roosevelt's faith in the Youth Congress leadership and opened her eyes to the problem of communist domination of this organization; they led her first to loosen and then break all her ties to the Youth Congress. The loss of Mrs. Roosevelt's support would prove extremely costly to the Youth Congress. Without her, the Youth Congress lacked a means of gaining access to high ranking administration officials. Having been attacked by the president and abandoned by the First Lady, the Youth Congress lost the support of leading liberals both in the capital and on campus.[77]

The decline of the Youth Congress was a terrible blow to the student movement because the Congress had played such a critical role in giving the movement a presence and youth lobby in Washington. The Congress was increasingly perceived as a narrow communist sect rather than as a broadly based organization and voice of young America. The crisis in the Youth Congress was all the more devastating to the student movement because of its timing. Just as the ASU was losing its ability to rally students, the Youth Congress lost its influence with the Roosevelt administration. With the ASU moribund and the Youth Congress failing, the student movement sank into a crisis which would prove irreversible.

Although the Youth Congress' crisis began more dramatically than that of the ASU—because it came in the form of an open confrontation with the president and First Lady in Washington—the decline of both organizations emanated from the same source. That source was the Russia-centered mind-set of the Youth Congress' and ASU's communist leaders during the 1939–1940 academic year. "The problem for the YCLer . . . was," as Lash noted in his diary, "that on one side he saw the status quo and on the other the USSR."[78] These young radicals so revered the Soviet Union as the international communist vanguard and inspiration for progressive social change that they elevated Soviet interests over those of the American student movement. Communist activists were determined to shackle the student movement to Stalin's increasingly unpopular foreign policy, even if this meant shrinking or destroying that movement and its key organizations. From their perspective it was better to have no movement at all than to have one which criticized Stalin.

This communist willingness to subordinate the student movement's interests to those of the U.S.S.R. had been evident ever since the ASU's 1939 Fall Planning Conference. Here YCL leader Gil Green had told a caucus of communist ASUers that "faith in the [Communist] Party's position on the [Nazi-Soviet] Pact means that party people will fight to establish that position in ASU *irrespective of [the] consequences for [the] ASU.*" (emphasis added).[79] This attitude had also been articulated by communist ASUers as they pushed to mobilize the student movement against an American loan to Finland. Thelma Grafstein reported that as she tried to convince her ASU chapter in New York to condemn the Soviet invasion of Finland, a communist ASUer told her that "rather than see that (meaning my) program adopted, she'd rather not see any A.S.U. on the campus." She was shocked to find that "this sentiment was expressed by some other [communist] A.S.U.ers," and that when she pointed out the impossibility of building "a united progressive student movement on the" basis of the new CP line on Finland, "they answered 'I don't give a damn about the A.S.U.' "[80]

These fights within the student movement during the 1939–40 academic year revealed that though communists had labored long and hard to build the ASU and the Youth Congress, their loyalty to those organizations was quite limited. Lash came to this painful realization as he observed the communists' attempt to sabotage the ASU national office following the Nazi-Soviet Pact. Communists in the ASU had, in Lash's words, displayed a "dual loyalty," to the student movement and the Communist Party: that "when the loyalty to the ASU conflicts with the loyalty to the YCL, the former is disregarded . . . . Their loyalty . . . [is] first and foremost to the YCL, even when they are leaders of the ASU."[81]

This problem of dual loyalty deeply troubled Lash as his tenure as ASU executive secretary drew to a close. Although before the Dies Committee Lash had defended the right of communists to participate in the student movement's leadership, privately he began to have doubts. Lash came to suspect that the divided loyalty of the communists left them unfit to lead a democratic protest movement. The behavior of communist ASU national staffers after the Pact led Lash to see that they had no qualms about defying policy decisions made by the ASU's membership and elected leadership when these conflicted with YCL policy. They would "advance the communist line, irrespective of the" decisions made democratically by ASU "conventions, and other organizational bodies that determine policy." This threatened to yield political disaster, Lash concluded, because of the impossibility of maintaining "a broad student movement supported by the masses of American students if the YCL has a veto power over our policy, and that veto places the Soviet Union beyond criticism."[82]

It may seem odd that it took Popular Front liberals so long to begin grappling with the problems posed by communist participation in the student movement's leadership. But there was a good reason for this. These problems only took center stage in the eleventh hour of the ASU's life because they did not start to damage the student movement until this very late point in its history. It was, in fact, because communists had served the student movement so faithfully prior to the Nazi-Soviet Pact that their behavior after that Pact came as such a shock to many non-communists in the movement. After years of unity and cooperation with communists, it was difficult to believe that they would sabotage a student movement that they had been so instrumental in creating.

The Popular Front experience had left liberals in the student movement ill prepared to deal with communist machinations in the post-Pact era. That experience had rendered them too trusting of the communists. This trust had evolved because communists and Popular Front liberals in the student movement from 1935 to August 1939 had become so closely aligned in promoting anti-fascism and social reform. The differences between these groups had become submerged. Communists in this era worked hard to promote this process of submergence by sounding more like liberals than radicals—supporting FDR and the New Deal with great enthusiasm.[83]

The prospect of the YCL working as a disciplined faction to disrupt the ASU had also seemed remote in the Popular Front period. At this time, communists—as part of their strategy for promoting unity—were, as Lash put it, discussing "in their publications . . . the abolition of fractions in mass organizations such as the ASU." Indeed, Lash claims that at the height of the Popular Front era, "so great was the agreement within the ASU that the communists dropped their work as an organized group within the ASU." There had seemed little reason to ponder the problem of communist "dual loyalty." The notion that communist ASUers would work to reverse the ASU's anti-fascist policies would also have seemed farfetched in the mid-1930s, when communists stood in the vanguard of international anti-fascism, risking their lives fighting against fascists on the battlefields of Spain.[84] Given their background in this happier period of the student movement, then, non-communists can hardly be blamed for being naive about their communist allies.

The shock which Lash and his supporters felt as they confronted communist machinations following the Pact underscores the startling discontinuity in communist behavior. Through most of the Depression decade communist students had acted as creative and constructive political organizers. By responding to the needs, anxieties and idealism of a generation troubled by Depression, war and fascism, young communists had helped build the first mass student movement in American history. The movement was at its best in the pre-Pact years as communists pioneered tactics contrary to the sectarianism and proletarianism which had weakened the adult Left. Their effective student mobilizations against war and fascism proved that liberals and radicals could work together, and that the university could be as much a source of progressive activism as the factory. But the behavior of communist students after the Nazi-Soviet Pact revealed that their virtues as political organizers were transient; they could only endure so long as the interests of Soviet foreign policy and American student politics coincided. When the two interests clashed in 1939, communist students began to act in a sectarian fashion, dedicated not to sustaining a broadly based student movement but rather to serving the narrow organizational interests of the YCL and the U.S.S.R. Blinded by their loyalty to the Sovet Union, the communists failed to see the disastrous consequences of forcing the movement's key organizations to defend a Soviet deal with Hitler and invasion of Finland that most students found indefensible.[85]

The ASU and Youth Congress could not long endure once student disllusionment with the communists' flip-flops on foreign policy, their abandonment of anti-fascism, and their defense of Soviet aggression, had set in. But although the largest wounds of the ASU and Youth Congress were self-inflicted, the decline of both organizations was accelerated by external repression. Rightwingers well understood that the Nazi-Soviet Pact had alienated American communists from liberals and left these radicals unpopular and vulnerable to attack. Seizing the moment, conservatives along with some liberal anti-communists launched a series of legislative red probes, loyalty oath campaigns, and moves to restrict free speech rights for communists—which threatened to evolve into a national red scare.[86]

On campus the relatively free political space that had been created by the ASU during the Popular Front began to constrict. Free speech violations became more common, beginning with the disruption of Communist Party leader Earl Browder's campus tour in the fall of 1939. The ban began at Harvard. The Conant administration claimed that Browder's indictment for a passport violation raised the possibility that he was a lawbreaker and therefore unqualified to speak at Harvard. Critics pointed out that the ban was unprecedented, and that in 1855 Harvard had opened its doors to an abolitionist speaker under indictment for violating the Fugitive Slave Act. But the ban stood; it was emulated by such other institutions as Oberlin College, Brooklyn College, and the University of Chicago. The weakened ASU could not mobilize sufficient support to win any of these free speech fights.[87]

The ASU's decline became even more evident in April 1940, the time of the annual student strike against war. The ASU's fall in membership meant that the organization had far fewer strike organizers than in previous years. Due to the ASU's defense of Soviet aggression, the YCAW and other anti-war organizations—though sharing with the ASU support of an isolationist foreign policy for the United States—denied that the ASU was a genuine peace group and refused to cooperate with the communist-led organization in the strike. Instead, the YCAW held its own isolationist strike rallies. If this split in the isolationist camp weakened the strike, so did international events. At the time of the strike, news had just come in of the Nazi invasion of Norway and Denmark. This rendered many students more fearful of fascist aggression and unreceptive to an ASU which had abandoned the idea of a Popular Front against fascism. Thus even at some of the ASU's traditional strongholds, the strike—featuring the CP's "Yanks are not coming" slogan—was the smallest since the first campus peace strike of 1934. At Columbia University, where as many as three thousand students had turned out for past strikes, the student newspaper noted that for the 1940 walkout "a disappointing crowd of less than a thousand" rallied against war. Brooklyn College's strike drew less than half the students than had attended strike rallies during the Popular Front years. At Berkeley the student movement was in such disarray that for the first time in years no strike rally was held.[88] These strike results left no doubt that the ASU had lost its ability to lead the student movement effectively. Though once the leader of a mass Popular Front movement on campus, the ASU was deteriorating into an unpopular sect.

II

The loss of the ASU's leadership wounded but did not immediately kill the anti-war movement on campus. Although nationally the student protests against war in 1940 mobilized far fewer students than they had in the 1930s, these protests did continue. Indeed, despite their much less impressive size, the student anti-war actions of 1940 attracted almost as much attention from the press and politicians as had their counterparts during the previous decade. This was because with the war crisis growing more acute and the nation wrapped up in its great debate about United States intervention, campus opinion took on a whole new importance. Everyone, it seemed, wanted to know how the young men who might soon have to fight the coming war felt about it. Interventionists in 1940 repeatedly published articles in the press expressing alarm that isolationism was running rampant among college youth.[89]

This concern about collegiate isolationism arose in response to the new phase which the student movement entered with its peace strike of 1940. That strike differed from its Popular Front predecessors not only in size, but in content. During the peace strikes of the late 1930s, ASUers had given voice to anti-isolationist sentiment and showed the nation that students cared passionately about stopping fascism. But with the dying ASU now in the isolationist camp and no other national student organization ready to carry on the pro-Allies work that the ASU had abandoned, the peace strike of 1940 was largely an isolationist event. For the moment at least, isolationism had no organized national student competition on American college campuses. This monopoly would prove temporary; but it enabled isolationists to dominate student protest activity while it lasted.

President Roosevelt was among the first to learn about this increased prominence of collegiate isolationism. During the Nazi invasion of the Low Countries in May 1940, FDR received petitions signed by 1486 Yale students urging that the United States "stay out of the European war . . . give no credits, supplies, or manpower but should direct its effort toward making democracy safe at home." The President received similar petitions from Harvard, Dartmouth, and Cornell students.[90] Roosevelt, who by now was moving toward preparedness and aid for the Allies, found such student sentiment disturbing. In fact, as Interior Secretary Harold Ickes noted in his diary, the President, after making an anti-isolationist speech in May 1940, told the Cabinet he "was struck by the fact that most of" the telegrams critical of his speech

> came from youth organizations and college students. This is most significant and alarming. Not only for what they said but what they implied, the senders of these telegrams made it clear that they were more interested in jobs than in wars that might make a few people richer but many people poorer.[91]

The persistence of collegiate isolationism was a product of both fear and disillusionment. The fear was, of course, fear of war—fueled by the Nazi military advances and a sinking feeling that the United States was moving inexorably toward war. Several sources contributed to the disillusionment. Disdain for World War I remained strong among undergraduates. A poll of Columbia students in the spring of 1940 revealed that by an almost five to one margin they saw United States entry into war in 1917 as "the result of propaganda and selfish interests"; and most thought that if the United States went to war again its motivation would be equally sordid.[92] By 1940, moreover, new sources of disillusionment had been added to this old one. The Allies had stood by while Spain fell to fascism; Chamberlain had bowed to Hitler at Munich; the Soviets, who had championed an international movement for collective security against fascism had abandoned that cause by signing their pact with Hitler. All of this left a vocal segment of the student population feeling cynical about the Allies and their anti-fascist slogans. Reflecting this mind-set, the editor of Vassar College's student newspaper explained her reason for moving from collective security to isolationism.

> Hitler's barbarism and aggression have always filled us with revulsion. We urged, before it was too late, a policy of collective security for peace. Chamberlain and Daladier, however, preferred "appeasement;" they fattened the Nazi government on Spain and Austria and Czechoslavakia . . . . [War did not begin until] Chamberlain and Daladier saw their imperial interests at stake in the fight of the Poles and came in. We, in the United States can see the dirty hands on both sides and must not be drawn in.[93]

With neither the ASU nor any other national student group disposed to combat such isolationism, that task in the spring of 1940 fell out of student hands. The most prominent foes of collegiate isolationism in this period were college and university presidents and faculty. When Yale students sent their isolationist petition to FDR in May, they drew a sharp public rebuke from Arnold Whitridge, Yale English professor and ardent interventionist. Whitridge told the *New York Times* that the student petition represented "muddled thinking. If we wish to stay out of war . . . we must do everything possible to furnish such aid to the Allies as will enable them to win the war." Dartmouth's president Ernest Hopkins offered an even more scalding rebuke to the signers of the isolationist petition at his college, telling a Dartmouth student assembly that there "was basis for questioning the extent that college breeds discriminating intelligence when hundreds of men sign petitions to the president that they see nothing of a struggle against the forces of evil." Hopkins imputed cowardice to isolationist students, whom he ridiculed for fearing to offend "the protaganists of force and brutality, race extinction and mass murder." A similar approach was taken at Harvard by Professor Roger Merriman, who derided isolationist students as "shrimps." FDR, who was grateful for this stance by his old Harvard teacher, wrote Merriman in May 1940 agreeing that "the best thing for the moment is to call them shrimps publicly and privately . . . . Most of them will get in line, if things should become worse."[94]

Such conflicts over collegiate isolationism introduced a new generational element into American student politics. Isolationist students, finding that their harshest critics were their elders, began to discuss the foreign policy debate as a clash of young and old. "The old men do the talking, but the young men do the fighting," UCLA's *Daily Bruin* complained in the spring of 1940. Another isolationist student editor denounced Nicholas Murray Butler, Columbia's interventionist president, as "one of a few old men who are urging youth to war. We think it is time we urged the old men to go put on their uniforms." At the University of Kansas, an interventionist professor who had questioned the courage of isolationist students was told by the *Daily Kansan* that "you'd be afraid yourself if you weren't past the shooting age . . . . Anyone who isn't afraid of getting blown to bits is on the red side of the psychological ledger." At Dartmouth, where angry exchanges between interventionist faculty and isolationist students had filled the campus press all year, the student newspaper ran a bitter editorial, "Fathers and Sons," accusing their professorial elders of hypocrisy: "The same teachers who told us we should avoid involvement in a European war at any cost are now telling us that we are cowards or pro-Nazis because we listened to what they taught us . . ."[95]

This generational conflict at times spilled off campus, pitting isolationist students against alumni of their colleges who had fought in the First World War. One of the most emotional of these clashes occurred at Harvard in May 1940; it began when the *Harvard Crimson* published a petition signed by hundreds of students, pledging their determination "never under any circumstances to follow in the footsteps of the students of 1917." The petition implied that the students who served in the First World War had been duped by President Wilson's democratic rhetoric into fighting an imperialist war. This elicited an angry response from 35 members of Harvard's class of 1917, whose joint letter to the *Crimson* denied that they had been misled by Wilson or that the war had been imperialistic. These alumni called upon students to abandon isolationism and get prepared for war; they argued that the new generation of college youth had an "even bigger job to do" for the defense of democracy than had the class of 1917.[96]

Such appeals from alumni did not go over well with Harvard's isolationists. This became evident during the 1940 commencement season. At the Harvard class day ceremonies, David Sigourney, another of Harvard's World War I veterans, delivered a passionate interventionist speech, and told the graduates "we would be proud to see our boys go out there and do the job again." As Sigourney went on with his speech "each sentence was met with a round of boos and hisses, making it almost impossible to hear the speaker. There were cries of 'throw him out.' Several times he pleaded for consideration."[97]

With the Nazis on the march in Europe, it was natural for interventionists to be upset when they encountered such isolationist sentiment among students, particularly students of their alma maters. The international tensions of the time fed fears—and criticism, expressed even by such usually astute observers as Archibald MacLeish—that the younger generation was being lost to isolationism.[98] But most of those who so criticized youth, amidst the hothouse political atmosphere of America in the spring of 1940, overreacted. The tensions of the moment, which made these critics so sensitive to any expression of isolationism, led them to exaggerate the depth of isolationism among youth. None of these critics seemed to notice, for instance, that on most college campuses the student peace strike of 1940 had signalled isolationist weakness rather than strength—that in comparison to prior student peace strikes the 1940 walkout was a small affair. Nor did they notice the national polls that showed students endorsing several key positions at odds with isolationist orthodoxy, including support for FDR's cash and carry policy, lifting the arms embargo, and offering aid to the Allies short of war.[99] Students in the spring of 1940 still wanted the United States to stay out of war, but so did most Americans. The difference was only one of degree. Collegians, knowing the lives of their generation hung in the balance, were especially exuberant in their anti-war expressions and especially reluctant to substitute United States troops for less costly forms of aid to the Allies.

The limits of collegiate isolationism were also evident on the issues of conscription and preparedness. Over the summer of 1940 both the YCAW and the Youth Congress sought to rally the nation's youth against the Burke-Wadsworth conscription bill. These Left-led isolationist groups depicted conscription as a loathsome means of militarizing youth and dragging America into war. Even allowing for the fact that such summertime youth mobilizations are difficult for student groups (because school is out of session), the campaign swayed few students. The largest youth rally of this anti-draft campaign, a YCAW event featuring such prominent speakers as Norman Thomas and Senators Nye, Wheeler, and Holt—drew barely a thousand people.[100] The Burke-Wadsworth amendment made its way through Congress and in September established America's first peacetime draft.

Passage of the conscription act did not, however, bring a surrender on the part of its young isolationist critics. Now that classes were back in session, the YCAW hoped it would be better able to generate student protest against the draft. The YCAW sought to launch a large national student protest urging repeal of the new draft law. The mobilization was planned as a national "Day of Mourning," scheduled to occur on October 16, 1940, the day that thousands of students—in accord with the new law—would be registering for the draft. But on almost every campus in the nation this anti-draft mobilization failed. Only a handful of campuses had any demonstration at all, and even here participants usually numbered in the dozens rather than the hundreds or thousands. The anti-draft event was such an embarrassing failure that the YCAW newsletter, after having headlined the preparations for this "Day of Mourning" in its October issue, did not even mention the mobilization in its November issue.[101]

The anti-conscription demonstration failed because most students did not share the YCAW's views on either the draft or the entire issue of preparedness. National student polls dating back to December 1939 showed that over 70 percent of the student body favored increases in American armaments and extension of the United States military. The polls in 1940 and 1941 also reflected majority student support for conscription. At Oberlin, for instance, some 70 percent of the student body endorsed the new draft law. The vast gulf between this pro-preparedness majority and the YCAW was one of the major reasons why this isolationist organization remained so small—with a student membership never exceeding a thousand.[102]

The student body's support for the draft and military preparedness did not, however, signal a case of war fever on campus. Students still opposed war, but also wanted America to be prepared if such a war was forced upon the nation. The *Michigan Daily* explained that students supported "conscription as a weapon only for defense," and hoped that the president could "abandon conscription as soon as America's safety permits." Ohio State's student paper termed conscription "distasteful" yet "necessary for defense," and urged that it only be maintained as a temporary emergency measure. "A *permanent* system of drafting young men who have a right to live their own lives while their nation is at peace violates both democratic privilege and sound reasoning."[103] This restrained support of the draft was reflected in collegiate commentary on the issue of exemptions. There was almost universal endorsement on campus for draft deferrals to allow undergraduates to complete their studies—so that while supporting the draft in principle, few in the 1940–41 academic year were eager for service. Linking this lack of military enthusiasm to economics, one Ohio State student explained that the class of '41 was in the

> same situation as the college graduates of 1929, the year of the depression. Then there were no jobs available and the unlucky graduates were called the "lost generation." Our own graduates who have jobs awaiting them but can't take advantage of them because of the draft law, could very aptly be termed the "lost generation" also for their situation is just about as discouraging.[104]

The poor performance of the YCAW in the October conscription mobilization revealed that the student Left had fallen to a new low in its influence on most campuses. Having in the past academic year suffered the decline of the ASU and the loss of its ability to mobilize a majority of students, the Left—including its non-communist segment represented by the YCAW—was now losing its ability to dominate even the isolationist forces on campus. The tone of collegiate isolationism, as the conscription issue made clear, was now being set by more conservative anti-interventionists. These were students with a "Fortress America" position, who preached that the United States should stay out of the war overseas but build an impregnable home defense force so that the United States could fend off any threat to its hemisphere. The main organizational representative of this new tendency was the America First Committee. And though this organization's focus would be off campus, its roots sprang from East Coast collegiate isolationism. A group of Yale isolationists headed by Kingman Brewster, editor of the *Yale Daily News* (and future Yale president), and several law students at New Haven initiated the formation of America First in the fall of 1940.[105]

The fall of 1940 also witnessed a continuation of the clashes between isolationist students and their interventionist elders. The opening salvo came just as classes began with the appearance of "Where Do You Stand? An Open Letter to American Undergraduates," in *Atlantic Monthly,* in which Yale Professor Arnold Whitridge accused isolationist students of "hysterical timidity." The Yale professor's article quickly drew a polemical response, "We Stand Here," by Kingman Brewster and *Harvard Crimson* editor Spencer Klaw, which also appeared in the *Atlantic.* Brewster and Klaw held that it was unfair for interventionists to single collegians out for special condemnation when a majority of all Americans opposed war; they offered the standard America First arguments that the United States was not ready for a European war and that such a crusade would constitute "a transoceanic war of aggression with no end in sight"—which would scuttle "democracy and freedom" in America. Americans must "take our stand here on this side of the Atlantic . . . because at least it offers a chance for the maintenance of all the things we care about in America, while war abroad would mean their certain extinction."[106]

At Harvard this intergenerational clash moved from polemic to theater. For almost a year Harvard's isolationist students had been feuding with President James Conant, one of the nation's most vocal interventionists. The *Harvard Crimson* found it appalling that Conant's agitation was helping to bring America closer to a war which "may soon send to destruction the lives" of his own students. The *Lampoon* and the *Crimson*—both dominated by isolationists—used the occasion of the 1940 Harvard-Yale football game to take a swipe at Conant, burlesquing Harvard's president in the halftime show at the Yale Bowl.

A student with a big "1941" on his back lay down on the field reading a book when a figure appeared in cap, gown and mortarboard and wearing the sign "Conant." He began to annoy the student by parading around him with a wooden bayoneted rifle. After a short interval, the student reluctantly took the gun but then turned to prodding "Conant" with the bayonet and chasing him around the field. Finally "Conant" was presented with a large retort and removed from the scene on a cart, presumably back to the laboratory.[107]

Before the fall semester of 1940 was over, however, isolationist students would have more to contend with than middle aged critics. The isolationist monopoly on student organizing came to an end. Inspired by England's courage in the Battle of Britain and worried by the fall of France, interventionist students on scores of campuses began to organize. Joseph Lash, who participated in this anti-isolationist resurgence, saw it as "a heartening sign" that the "condition of shell shock or paralysis among liberal young people" that had lasted for "a long time after the Nazi-Soviet Pact" was finally ending.[108] As Lash's words suggest, the timing of this anti-isolationist resurgence was in part linked to organizational factors. Lash and other foes of isolationism had been tied down the previous year first by the futile battle to free the ASU and Youth Congress of communist domination, and then by the demoralization and disorganization which followed the failure of those efforts. Now, however, with their own organizations, they were able to focus on the task of influencing the campuses.

International events also made the fall of 1940 a good moment for such an anti-isolationist offensive. The German conquests the previous spring had demonstrated that America could no longer hope that a stalemate in Europe would curb Nazi aggression. And the Battle of Britain, waged over the summer, had suggested that with the English determined to fight on, it might be possible for the United States—through aid to Britain—to play a role in stopping Hitler without actually entering the war. This was the time of Winston Churchill's stirring calls for an unending fight against Hitler; and simultaneously came Edward R. Murrow's moving radio broadcasts from London documenting the brutal Nazi bombings of civilians.[109] Such events enabled student foes of isolationism to reconstruct some of the anti-fascist idealism which had been so powerful and appealing to collegians during the Popular Front era.

Lacking any central organization—like the old ASU—to mobilize anti-isolationist sentiment, a variety of different student groups emerged over the fall semester. By December, twenty college chapters of William Allen White's Committee to Defend America by Aiding the Allies were functioning. Agnes Reynolds, a former ASU leader, presided over the creation of Student Defenders of Democracy, a group urging war preparations and aid to Britain. This group attracted endorsements from student leaders on more than 100 campuses. Joseph Lash took over the leadership of the International Student Service (ISS), and converted it from a refugee aid group into an aid the Allies organization. The ISS managed to sponsor some high profile events for the interventionist cause, thanks in part to the fund raising, contacts, and sponsorship of Eleanor Roosevelt, who was by now a good friend of Lash's. The ISS also attracted the National Student Federation, the organization of American student governments, as an affiliate, after the NSF broke with the isolationist and communist-dominated American Youth Congress.[110]

This return of anti-isolationist activism put an end to the myth of invulnerable collegiate isolationism. The stream of hysterical articles bemoaning the cowardice of youth soon diminished. As the academic year progressed, opinion polls found undergraduate isolationism declining. Students proved increasingly willing to back FDR's escalating efforts to aid England. Nationally, student endorsement of the president's Lend-Lease plan came in at an overwhelming 67 percent. At Berkeley, which in the fall had organized the only sizable anti-draft rally in the nation, a poll in February 1941 found the isolationist position opposing aid to Britain had attracted the support of only a miniscule 6.8 percent of the student body.[111]

Although their fortunes were clearly dwindling, isolationists remained a vocal group on campus. Isolationism still had on its side, for instance, much of the college press. This reflected the fact that student editors—most of whom were chosen on an annual basis—had been elected the past spring, during the high tide of collegiate isolationism in this decade. The American Youth Congress, though steadily losing affiliates and strength, could still manage to bring a few thousand students to Washington to protest against Lend-Lease in February 1941. Isolationists in the 1940–1941 academic year could also take some solace in the continuing absence of war fever on campus. Most students—even the majority of the organizers urging expanded aid to Britain—still wanted the United States to avoid going to war. Indeed, one of the main arguments anti-isolationist students used for supporting aid to Britain was that such aid might stop the Nazis and make American entry into the war unnecessary.[112]

The last national campus mobilization effort on the part of Depression era leftists and isolationists came with the eighth annual student strike against war in April 1941. Since student support for Lend-Lease and material aid to Great Britain was so overwhelming, the isolationist strike organizers avoided that whole issue. Instead, they focused on the more volatile issue of the use of armed American convoys for supply ships bound for Britain—which risked involving Americans in hostilities with the German Navy. The convoy issue seemed promising; it evoked memories of the U-boat attacks that had helped to lead the United States into World War I and might appeal to the widespread student desire to avoid a shooting war.[113]

Not even the convoy issue, however, could revitalize collegiate isolationism. Isolationist strike rallies on most campuses were the smallest since the birth of the student movement. At Yale even the prominent speaker, Senator Nye—appearing at a YCAW sponsored strike rally—could not draw an impressive crowd. Only 600 Yale students turned out to hear him, a stark contrast to the 3000 who had packed Woolsey Hall to hear

Lindbergh the previous fall. Nor would communist sponsored rallies fare any better. The communists were in no position to orchestrate an effective national strike effort. The ASU was at this point a virtual paper organization on most campuses outside New York City. The communists therefore shifted responsibility for the strike to the Youth Congress. Since the Youth Congress was a federation of affiliated groups rather than a membership organization, it had been able to stay active a bit longer than the ASU. But the Youth Congress too was dying; it had been losing affiliates ever since the Nazi-Soviet Pact and fared poorly in the strike. At UCLA, for instance, a Youth Congress led strike rally drew only 250 students, the smallest strike in years. At Vassar, once the most active womens' college in the student movement, the Youth Congress proved unable to organize any rally.[114]

Even in New York, long the capital city of American student activism, the anti-interventionist strike mobilizations went poorly. The Youth Congress organized nothing at Hunter College, and the YCAW rally there turned out only a dozen students. The group of 500 to 800 students who turned out at Columbia University was more substantial, but slim in comparison to strikes in the previous decade. On only one campus in the entire city, CCNY, were the anti-interventionists able to draw a crowd of more than a thousand. But even this CCNY rally, attended by some 2500 students, was not purely an anti-interventionist event; it was actually more of a free speech demonstration, in which students rallied to hear Morris Schappes, one of the communist instructors at the College, who had been fired as a consequence of the Rapp-Coudert red probe. That probe had hounded communist students as well as faculty, generating a repressive atmosphere which hampered Youth Congress activism; it contributed to the organization's poor showing in the strike efforts at most of the city's campuses.[115]

Making matters worse for the strike's organizers was the student opposition they encountered. Unlike the 1940 walkout, the 1941 anti-war strike found anti-isolationist students organized and vocal. The interventionist Student Defenders of Democracy used the strike day as the occasion to launch a national student petition drive in support of convoys. The SDD proved most effective at Brooklyn College. Here, with the support of the campus administration, the SDD organized a strike day rally endorsing convoys, which drew some 2000 students. This rally was about five times the size of the anti-convoy rally sponsored by Brooklyn's Youth Congress organizers.[116] ISS leader Joseph Lash was also vocal in denouncing strike agitation against convoys. Anti-isolationist activists on campus made use of literature distributed by Lash and the ISS to oppose isolationist strike events. At Dartmouth, for instance, the student newspaper greeted strike day speaker, New Hampshire's Senator Charles Tobey—sponsor of a Congressional resolution against convoys—by lambasting him and his student supporters: "We don't like the strike, any little bit of it," the *Dartmouth* explained in its strike day editorial "Not on Strike."

The reason is simple . . . . More than we're opposed to war, we're opposed to the domination of the world by Fascism . . . . Of the "peace strike" Joseph P. Lash, a former ASU member and originator of the "strike" plan in the early 1930s said last week: "No sophistry can mitigate the basic fact that to strike against American aid to England, Greece, Yugoslavia, is to help a victory for Hitler . . . . To oppose the Lend Lease policy, to oppose the transfer of destroyers, to oppose every policy this government has undertaken against Hitler is to betray the youth of Europe."[117]

Weak as the strike had been, even this level of anti-war activism would not be matched the following semester. Isolationist demonstrations were almost unheard of during the first few months of the fall 1941 semester— a time when naval conflicts between the United States and Germany were heating up in the north Atlantic and the country geared up for war. Student support for supplying the allies against Hitler and Japan soared to 93 percent by early November. Isolationism also lost its last major stronghold on campus: the student press. President Conant would no longer have to worry about attacks from the *Crimson;* its editors were as opposed to isolationism as he. The *Yale Daily News,* which had helped give birth to America First, elected an interventionist editor. The turnarounds were equally dramatic in the traditionally isolationist Midwest, where the student newspapers at Northwestern University and the Universities of Iowa, Minnesota, and Kansas abandoned isolationism.[118]

Communist students also returned to campus in the fall of 1941 with a different attitude toward isolationism. Now that the Nazis had invaded the Soviet Union, communists in the Youth Congress dropped their isolationist slogans and became the most interventionist students in the nation. But by this point it really did not matter. The communists had already so discredited themselves by their previous foreign policy flip-flops that their new position barely attracted any attention on campus—except as a source of ridicule by classmates bemused by their willingess to constantly march in step with Stalin's zig-zagging policies. The communists had long since lost their ability to influence American student politics.[119]

The student movement was dead. But in one respect at least, its spirit lingered on right up until the eve of Pearl Harbor. The movement had been born denouncing war and pledging students against it. And despite the demise of isolationist activism on campus in the fall of 1941, students remained among the most anti-war groups in the nation. Even as America fell into naval clashes with Germany in the North Atlantic, students were still less willing than the general public to support measures that might escalate that conflict. A November 1941 national poll found America as a whole—by a 46 to 40 percent margin—favoring revision of the neutrality act to allow the arming of British-bound American ships; but college students opposed the plan 52 to 41 percent. Only 14 percent of the national student body at this point favored a declaration of war against Germany and Japan.[120] The student body would not accept war as a solution to the international crisis until the Japanese attack at Pearl Harbor foreclosed all other options.

III

After the U.S. entered the war, former peace protesters often became soldiers, sailors, and pilots. Neal Anderson Scott, the commencement day orator who preached the isolationist gospel to his graduating class at Davidson College in 1940, died in battle as a navy ensign in the Pacific War less than two years later. There were many like Scott. Few students who had been peace activists during the Depression decade became conscientious objectors during the war. The ranks of conscientious objectors were so thin and their influence so slight that they barely attracted public attention in wartime America.[121] Similarly, the nation's immersion in total war following Pearl Harbor quickly dimmed its memories of the student movement which had tried so persistently and vainly to prevent that war. The onset of this mammoth conflict with fascism suddenly made the history of collegiate isolationism seem small and irrelevant.

The collapse of the anti-war movement appears as inevitable as the war itself. No student peace movement could have survived in a nation as threatened by war and fascism as America became during the early 1940s. In retrospect, then, it was not the movement's collapse but rather the *way* that it collapsed that was so memorable. The ill will generated by the conflicts between communists and non-communists during this process of dissolution would have consequences that lasted long after the final shots had been fired in World War II. In these campus conflicts of the late 1930s and early 1940s one hears early expression of the bitter debates and restrictive philosophies that would yield so much political bloodletting and repression in Cold War America. Liberals, who had entered the Popular Front era of the student movement willing to work with communists, came away from the post-Nazi-Soviet Pact period embittered; they began to articulate an anti-communist language of exclusion.

Fundamental to this exclusionary mind-set was the notion that communists represented not a normal political party, but rather a conspiratorial group. Communists, in this view, could not be counted on to be honest about either their goals or affiliations. Since they often hid their motives and identifications, they might one minute be cooperative and tireless workers for the student movement, and the next minute—because of a shift in the Soviet and American CP's line—reverse gears, sabotaging the movement and using secret communist factions to take over the movement's organizations.[122]

This hostile view of the communists led exclusionists to the conclusion that communists had to be banned from non-communist political organizations in order to ensure the integrity of those organizations. This was precisely what happened in the anti-isolationist student organizations after the collapse of the ASU-AYC Popular Front. As the Students For Defense of Democracy, the student Committee to Defend America By Aiding the Allies, the ISS, and other anti-isolationist student groups met in 1941 to discuss a possible merger,

> the problem of communist infiltration was discussed . . . and it was agreed that there should be no cooperation with communist or communist front groups, that we should be very careful to exclude them . . . and should not work with them on the campus . . . . any cooperation might too easily result in their gaining control of our groups, and if the line shifted, using us for their own undesirable ends.[123]

There was no mystery about why such exclusion came into vogue. It arose in response to the hijacking of the ASU and Youth Congress out of the Popular Front by the communist factions within those organizations. The packing of meetings, the breaking of agreements, the numerous violations of democratic process which communists used following the Nazi-Soviet Pact won them control of the ASU and Youth Congress but made them pariahs in the eyes of many liberals.[124]

This shift toward exclusion was illustrated most dramatically in the case of Joseph Lash. As late as November 1939, when the ASU's internal communist-non-communist struggle was escalating, Lash had stood for an inclusive student movement. Called before the red probing Dies Committee, Lash praised communists for helping to build the student movement and defended their right to participate in the ASU—arguing that a democratic organization must be open to all. In the midst of his hearing before the Dies Committee, Lash ridiculed the red hunters, bursting into song: "If you see an un-American lurking far or near / Just alkalize with Martin Dies and he will disappear." Yet within two years Lash abandoned the principles which had led him to advocate an inclusive ASU and was defending an exclusive ISS.[125]

As ISS General Secretary, Lash opposed the admission of communists into the organization. Nor would he allow ISS cooperation with the communists, even after the German invasion of Russia when the communists' new interventionist position placed them in agreement with ISS foreign policy. Explaining this position in 1941, Lash cited his experience in the Youth Congress and ASU. The "inescapable conclusion from the events of the past two years" was that communists were "unreliable allies in the march towards a more democratic America and a better world." The communists "paraded as liberals" and anti-fascists then as "isolationists," leaving non-communists who had worked with them wondering why "the slogans and loyalties of one month became the anathemas and heresies of the next." Lash observed that the communist slogans used for public consumption, whether interventionist or isolationist, masked their true goal of serving Soviet foreign policy interests. In the Youth Congress, the communist faction would "not frankly espouse its fundamental conviction that defense of the Soviet Union must be the over-arching" goal of the student movement. "Hence the aroma of conspiracy and duplicity about it . . . ." In the ISS Lash would stress the need to develop a non-communist student leadership, capable of preventing communists from controlling campus politics. "Joe taught me," recalled former ISS member Louis Harris, "how to out-think, out-maneuver, and to out-sit the communists whom we were struggling against in the student movement."[126]

A large share of the responsibility for breeding such anti-communism rested with the communists themselves. Their behavior in taking control of the ASU and Youth Congress after the Nazi-Soviet Pact was every bit as manipulative as Lash had suggested. As if that was not enough to alienate non-communists—and drive them toward exclusionism—communists in the student movement during their final isolationist period embraced a sectarian style of agitation that did even more to poison their relations with liberals. Perhaps reflecting the frustrations common to declining organizations, the Youth Congress' communist-dominated leadership hurled wild and scurrilous charges at their former allies. Worst among these were the accusations that the YCL and Youth Congress leader Joseph Cadden made against Eleanor Roosevelt. They charged that the First Lady was involved in "a Fascist or Nazi scheme" to "force all young men and women into Nazified labor camps." In fact, all that Mrs. Roosevelt had done was support an ISS program in which youth would provide voluntary public service for a year. Lash looked back upon the communist distortion of this program as "propaganda worthy of Goebbels."[127] Such behavior suggests that the communists, though indeed victims of an anti-communist ban, were not innocent victims. They had helped create the harsh political atmosphere which made it impossible to preserve a working—or even a civil—relationship between communists and liberals.

The shift away from inclusionary politics had more repressive implications than Lash and the other liberal student leaders in the early 1940s realized. Lash and his allies continued to oppose anti-radical witch hunts and red probing committees. Unlike such reactionary politicians as Dies, these student movement veterans did not support the outlawing of communist organizations, or other draconian restrictions on the civil liberties of communists.[128] And yet, in banning communists from their own student organizations and in promoting hostile anti-communist rhetoric and images of communism as a conspiracy, these liberal youths inadvertently helped lay part of the intellectual foundation for the post-war attacks on communists' political rights. Liberals who preached that communists were sinister and beyond the pale of democratic organizations—that they therefore had to be banned from those organizations—helped to popularize the idea that communists were pariahs in a democratic society. If communists were too untrustworthy to be allowed into the organizations of liberals, why were they any less dangerous in their own organizations? And should not those communist organizations too be banned as nests of sinister conspirators? Once this process of banning had begun it would prove difficult to stop, especially when the tensions of the Cold War era fostered ever greater distrust and fear of communism as an international conspiracy.[129]

The bitterness and exclusionary politics which grew out of the campus battles of the Depression era endured even into the 1960s. They shaped the way that leading liberal anti-communist alumni of the old student movement initially responded to the new generation of student rebels who had begun to protest the Vietnam War. James Wechsler, for example, had written many editorials for the ASU magazine during the 1930s promoting student anti-war activism. But Wechsler would scorn such activism in the 1960s, as editor of the *New York Post*—at that time one of America's leading liberal newspapers. When Students for a Democratic Society (SDS) organized the first national anti-war march on Washington in 1965, Wechsler turned a deaf ear to their compelling critique of the Vietnam War. He had been disturbed that SDS had refused to exclude communists from the march, and his virulent anti-communism left him disinclined to support such protests against America's war on communism in Indochina. Wechsler thererefore used the pages of the *Post* to mock the protest as a "pro-communist production" and a "frenzied, one-sided, anti-American show." Such bitter words said more about Wechsler and the scars from the 1930s than they did about this SDS-led demonstration. They were the aftermath of the student movement of the Depression era—a movement which in its heyday had promoted political tolerance, but which died in a fit of intolerance.[130]

Appendix: The FBI Goes to College: A List of Informants and Information They Gave the FBI on American Student Union Activists[1]

The surviving—or at least the released—FBI documents on the ASU indicate that the Bureau did its most extensive investigation of the student movement beginning in the fall of 1940 and extending into the early years of World War II. The timing of this investigation was linked to the war mobilization. Since the ASU in 1940 was an anti-interventionist, communist-led organization, the FBI deemed it necessary to gather intelligence on the ASU's strength, anti-war agitation, and potential resistance to the recently adopted conscription act.

In the context of the student movement's own history, however, there is an ironic quality to the timing of this secret FBI probe. The FBI's most sweeping national investigation of the ASU (and the American Youth Congress) did not occur when the ASU was influential and leading a mass student movement, but rather when the ASU was discredited, weak, dying, and finally dead. Thus the FBI probe could not document any sizable ASU-led movement to violate the conscription act, nor any other violation of law which might make the investigation even remotely justifiable from a law enforcement standpoint.[2] The fact that the investigation continued after Hitler's invasion of the U.S.S.R. in 1941, when the communist-led ASU fully supported America's mobilization for war (and that the FBI probe lasted through 1943, when young communists strongly endorsed the United States war effort), suggests that the probe had more to do with FBI director J. Edgar Hoover's anti-radicalism than any genuine need to police a security threat.

The timing of this probe is important to bear in mind because it gave the FBI reports from the investigation a special quality, revealing the ideological underpinning of the informing done by university administrators (and other FBI informants). These campus officials knew that the ASU was dead or dying and posed a threat to no one. Indeed, the most common scenario in the FBI reports on Bureau interaction with campus administrators began with the college or university official telling the FBI

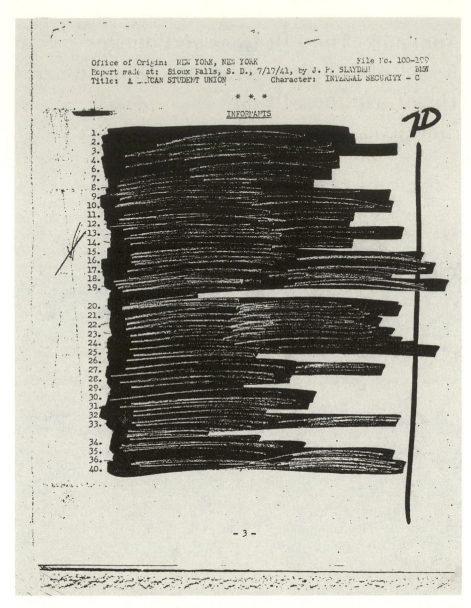

A sample of FBI censorship of its reports on the American Student Union. Such censorship makes it impossible to gauge the full extent of FBI surveillance and campus informing on student protesters during the 1930s and early 1940s.

agents about the surge of student protest that had occurred during the 1930s and narrating the recent decline or death of the ASU. The campus official then often noted that he or she saw no threat of a resurgence of radicalism on campus. Nonetheless, because of their loathing for radicalism and their sense that such dissent was not a legitimate part of university life, these campus administrators—after expressing scorn for these radical troublemakers—matter of factly opened their files on ASUers to the Bureau and freely turned over their students' names to the FBI.[3]

This list of FBI informant activity is offered as a window onto the important—but hidden—underside of academic freedom in America.[4] A full accounting of this policing of dissent will not be possible, however, until the FBI stops censoring its campus reports (many of which are more than a half-century old).

COLLEGE/UNIV.	INFORMANT	TYPE OF DATA GIVEN TO FBI
Brown University	1) American Legion "Americanization man"	Names leading ASU organizer.
	2) Confidential Informant RIDC-1	Names ASU members and sympathizers.
California, University of at Berkeley	1) Confidential Informant SF–12	Names ASU and YCL leaders and reports on ASU meetings.
	2) Confidential informant SF–59	Gives names of ASU and YCL leaders as well as reports on ASU meetings.
Chicago, University of	1) Dean's office—name deleted by FBI censors	Gives names and phone numbers of ASU leaders and ASU membership list.
Cincinnati, University of	1) Informant's name deleted by FBI censors	Names ASU leaders.
Cleveland College	1) Name deleted by FBI censors	Names leading ASUers and details their political actions.
	2) J.M. Woods, Faculty advisor to student organizations	Names student who attempted to found an ASU chapter.
Columbia University	1) John J. Swan, Comptroller	Calls attention to the "Communistic . . . control" of the Columbia ASU. Gives ASU leaflets.

COLLEGE/UNIV.	INFORMANT	TYPE OF DATA GIVEN TO FBI
Connecticut, University of	1) University administrator, name deleted by FBI censors	Names leading ASUers "inclined toward communism."
	2) Professor Andre S[rest of last name illegible]	Describes rise of ASU chapter and anti-ROTC agitation. Names ASU leaders. "Stated that he had watched the organization rather closely due to his connection with the American Legion and that he had sent information on the organization to MID [the Military Intelligence Division?] at Boston, Mass."
Cornell University	1) Charles Manning, Proctor	Names leading ASUers.
	2) Student, name deleted by FBI censors	Names ASUers, describes radical books in the room of ASU leader.
	3) Informant, name deleted by FBI censors	Gives names, local and home addresses, phone numbers, academic fields of ASU leaders.
DePauw University	1) G. Herbert Smith, Dean of Administration	Gives correspondence between ASU and DePauw administration, and ASU petition for campus recognition, which includes names of 45 students. Points out which of the ASU members have been the most active and mentions the recent collapse of the ASU chapter.
Earlham College	1) William C. Dennis, President	Names founders of campus ASU chapter. Gives political background of ASU leaders, including their ideological tendencies. Describes ASU peace strike agitation, and gives copy of ASU constitution.

COLLEGE/UNIV.	INFORMANT	TYPE OF DATA GIVEN TO FBI
George Washington University	1) Myra Sedwick, Secretary to the President	Gives files on campus radicals dating back to 1929.
Hawaii, University of	1) E.C. Webster, Dean of Men	Gives names of ASU officers at Hawaii.
	2) Walter Chun, student govt. president	Gives names of ASU organizers, list of 36 ASU members.
Howard University	1) Confidential Informant T–1	Report deleted by FBI censors.
	2) Confidential Informant T–2	Names student radicals, faculty sympathizers.
Hunter College	1) William C. Martin, State Senator, New York	Gives the names of 46 Hunter students who signed a petition protesting his bill to ban the ASU from New York's municipal colleges.
Illinois, University of at Champaign-Urbana	1) Campus official? name deleted by FBI censors	Gives local ASU membership list with names, local and home addresses of 32 student ASUers.
	2) Dean, name deleted by FBI censors	Gives literature of local ASU with names of 31 ASUers. "Advised that he was keeping a close watch on the activities" of local ASU. Describes its sponsorship of "PEACE" meetings.
	3) Fred H. Turner, Dean of Men	Names campus ASU leaders, agrees to provide ASU membership list. Describes ASU agitation.
	4) U. Ill. official (probably Dean Turner)	Provides ASU membership list, with 18 names.
	5) Ronald Nystrom, editor *Daily Illini*	Gives name and address of ASU chapter president.
Indiana State Teachers College	1) Sara Bence, Secretary to the Dean	Names student organizer of ASU and faculty supporter.

COLLEGE/UNIV.	INFORMANT	TYPE OF DATA GIVEN TO FBI
	2) Informant name deleted by FBI censors	Names ASU activists, faculty supporters, local minister who assisted ASU.
Indiana University	1) Informant name deleted by FBI censors	Gives petition for recognition of ASU chapter, listing 45 members and officers. Names two faculty supporters of ASU.
	2) Registrar's Office	Provides information on ASU officers.
Indiana University Extension	1) Dorothy McMahon, Clerk at the Registrar's Office	Names ASU leaders.
Michigan, University of	1) Confidential Informant T–1	Names 3 ASUers.
	2) Confidential Informant F–1	Names ASUers expelled from U. of Michigan.
	3) Sergeant Eugene Gehringer, Ann Arbor Police Dept.	Submits report "fully covering" ASU protest meeting in 1940, listing 12 speakers at the meeting.
	4) Professor More	Gives pamphlets published by local ASU chapter, names the activist who distributed this literature.
	5) Norman E. Cook, Chief of Police, Ann Arbor	Reports on ASU meeting, names speakers at this meeting.
	6) Eleanor H. Scanlan, Secretary to the Dean of Students	Gives a list of ASU officers, 1939–1941.
	7) Dr. Alexander Ruthven, President	Describes conflicts between his administration and the ASU. Gives off campus location where the ASU met after being barred from campus. Attests that the ASU in 1942 was no longer active. Agrees to notify of any future agitation by ASU "trouble makers."

COLLEGE/UNIV.	INFORMANT	TYPE OF DATA GIVEN TO FBI
	8) Informant name deleted by FBI censors (but clearly a University administrator)	"They watched very closely the activities of any students that were . . . radical." Summarizes the roles played by ASU leaders in campus protests. Gives personal information on one ASU leader, his academic problems and the manner in which the father of this student reacted to these problems (during the father's conference with campus officials).
Middlebury College	1) Dr. E.B. Womach, Dean of Men	Names leading ASU organizers, describes ASU chapter and its conflict with campus administrators.
	2) Paul D. Moody, President	Names college ASU's leader. Describes ASU-sponsored meeting. "Happy to observe" demise of ASU in 1941. "Feels the wave of patriotism" has "swept" the student body "clean in all unhealthy influence in this respect."
Minnesota, University of	1) Dean Nicholson	Names the head of ASU chapter.
Missouri, University of, at Columbia	1) Darwin Hindman, Dean of Men	Names leading ASU activists.
	2) University official, name deleted by FBI censors	Gives records with names and addresses of ASU activists.
	3) Confidential Informant KC-C-31	Names ASU leader.
	4) Confidential Informant KC-C-34	Names ASU leaders. Names radical professor at William Jewell College, agrees to obtain names of those who distributed ASU literature.

COLLEGE/UNIV.	INFORMANT	TYPE OF DATA GIVEN TO FBI
	5) Professor Stephens, Dean of Arts and Sciences	Describes anti-ROTC agitation of ASU chapter. Terms ASU efforts to win student exemptions from ROTC training "a constant source of annoyance." Names a local pastor who aided the ASU in this anti-ROTC work.
	6) Harlan Byrne, student editor of the *Missourian*	Names ASU chapter leaders.
	7) American Legion member, name deleted by FBI censors	Has a fellow Legion member "discreetly attend" ASU meetings. He provides notes on these meetings, names of speakers.
Montana State University	1) Confidential Informant A	Names students and librarian who tried to organize ASU chapter in April 1939.
	2) J.E. Miller, Dean of Students	Names student who led the attempt to organize an ASU chapter. Assesses the "apparent radicalism" of this student and its decline since graduation.
New Jersey College for Women	1) Dean Leah Boddie	Gives names, addresses of ASU officers, 1939–1941.
North Carolina, University of, at Chapel Hill	1) Confidential Informant 50	Names leading ASU activists. Provides biographical data on the academic and family background of ASU leaders. The detailed nature of this and other data provided by this informant (who even reported on the number of chairs requested in 17 separate ASU meetings) indicates that in-

COLLEGE/UNIV.	INFORMANT	TYPE OF DATA GIVEN TO FBI
		formant was a campus official or faculty member with access to University files.
Oberlin College	1) Dean Carl Wittke	Names two local ASU leaders as communists. Describes the size, influence, focus of Oberlin's ASU from its heyday in the mid-1930s to its decline in 1940–41. His official aids FBI in ascertaining that 18 protesters who had sent a petition against an anti-ASU bill in New York state legislature has been Oberlin students.
	2) D.M. Love, College Secretary	Describes the rise and fall of the local ASU.
Ohio State University	1) J.A. Park, Dean of Men	Gives names, addresses of student leaders of anti-war and free speech protests. Provides ASU branch literature with names of leading activists. Describes rise and fall of the campus ASU chapter.
	2) J.F. Stecker, Assistant Dean of Men	Names communist student organizer.
Ohio University at Athens	1) Irene Delvin, Assistant to the President	Describes ideological tendencies and goals of campus protesters. Refers reporting FBI agent to Dean of
	2) Dean of Women	women, who apparently provides officer list for the now defunct ASU chapter.
	3) B.T. Grover, Public Relations Director	Names radical leaders on campus.
	4) Informant, name deleted by FBI censors	Names a student with "Socialist tendencies."

COLLEGE/UNIV.	INFORMANT	TYPE OF DATA GIVEN TO FBI
Pennsylvania, University of	1) Dr. Arnold Henry, Dean of Student Affairs 2) William DuBarry, Vice President	Henry and DuBarry name students who led ASU chapter and those involved in the campus-area "Communist bookstore." They describe recent ASU anti-war activity. Dean Henry later supplies an update on the ASU at Penn, noting latest list of ASU officers. Dean Henry contacts FBI a third time, naming a student he suspected of communist activity.
Purdue University	1) F.I. Goldsmith, Dean of Men	Gives a 1936 petition for campus recognition of the ASU chapter, signed by 31 students.
Smith College	1) Informant name deleted by FBI censors (but clearly a member of Smith College administration)	"[P]roduced the records of her office" on ASU leaders at Smith.
	2) Mrs. C. Eaton Miller, Assistant to the Registrar	"Produced the records of her office" on four ASU leaders.
	3) Former member of Smith ASU, whose name was deleted by the FBI	Names Smith student activists "who advocated the Communist form of government for this Country."
	4) Mrs. J.F. Duffey, Secretary, Alumnae Association	Provides current addresses and employment information on four ASU alumnae of Smith.
	5) M.A. Thannhauser, Smith student and former ASU member	Names six Smith ASU activists.
Southern Illinois State Teachers College	1) Robert Calless, Secretary to the Dean	Gives ASU membership list.
	2) L.B. Sherretz, head of campus police	Names the college's most prominent radical student activist.

COLLEGE/UNIV.	INFORMANT	TYPE OF DATA GIVEN TO FBI
Swarthmore College	1) Swarthmore student, name deleted by FBI censors	Names three communist students.
Syracuse University	1) Frank Piskor, Dean's Office	Names the campus' leading anti-fascist student organizers.
Temple University	1) Conrad Siegars, Dean of Men	Names nine former members of the ASU at Temple. Describes their ideological tendencies, personal backgrounds, and roles in the local student movement. Names the most influential ASU leader at Temple and terms him a "Red." Describes the rise and fall of the ASU chapter. Claims that the ASU leaders at Temple were "planted by Communists organizations in this country."
	2) Name of informant deleted by FBI censors	Names the leader of the Temple ASU.
Texas, University of	1) Informant's name deleted by FBI censors	Describes ASU agitation against ROTC and ASU organizing of a strike by student waiters. Names six student activists and a radical instructor.
	2) Former resident of Campus Guild, the Univ. of Texas men's co-op dormitory. Informant's name was deleted by FBI censors	Advises that this co-op was a " 'hot bed' for Communists." Names twenty "ringleaders of communistic activity at the Campus Guild."
Tulane University	1) Kendall Cram, Graduate Manager of Student Activities	Provides documents naming student leaders of the Tulane SLID and organizers of local student group seeking affiliation with national ASU.

COLLEGE/UNIV.	INFORMANT	TYPE OF DATA GIVEN TO FBI
Washington, University of	1) Herbert T. Condon, Dean	Names radical student leaders and a leftist minister. Describes rise of anti-war agitation on campus and conflicts between protesters and University officials. Names a minister who allowed ASU to meet in his church after the ASU had been banned from campus.
	2) University official, whose name was deleted by the FBI censors	Gives names, addresses, dates, places of birth, and next of kin of 22 student activists.
	3) Confidential Informant SE–1	Names 7 University of Washington students active in both the ASU and the Communist Party
	4) Colonel Edward Kimmel, ROTC commander	Gives files with names of anti-war leaders, reports of student protest meetings.
	5) Albert Seeman, Professor and faculty advisor to student activities groups	Provides copies of student anti-war flyers and correspondence between protesters and administration concerning the banning of a controversial anti-ROTC rally. Describes the process by which student radicals "infiltrated" mainstream campus groups.
Wayne University	1) Confidential Informant T–3	Names ASU leader at Wayne.
	2) Informant name deleted by FBI censors	Names student who initiated the formation of the Wayne ASU chapter.
Wesleyan University	1) Associate Dean Butterworth	Names ASU leaders.
	2) Elmer Schattschneider, Professor of Government	Names ASU leader.

COLLEGE/UNIV.	INFORMANT	TYPE OF DATA GIVEN TO FBI
Western Reserve University: Adelbert College and Flora Stone Mather College	1) Robert E. Bates, Dean of Students 2) H.F. Doolittle, Assistant Registrar	Bates advises FBI that Doolittle has information on campus ASU chapter. Dolittle names ASU leaders.
	3) Dr. M. Ogle, Professor, Political Science, Adelbert	Tells FBI that the campus' ASU members were "maladjusted little Jew boys." Ogle names two ASU leaders and explains that some ASUers were "militant Communists," but most were "theoretical Marxists, socialists or leftwing Democrats." Describes ASU meetings.
	4) Informant, whose name was deleted by FBI censors	Names 9 ASUers. Describes their ideological tendencies.
	5) Kenneth Deacon, former student at Western Reserve	Names 3 ASU leaders.
	6) Elinor R. Wells, Registrar, Flora Stone Mather College	Names top ASU leader at Flora Stone Mather. Assesses the activities, degree of influence of local ASU chapter.
Wilson Teachers College	1) Dr. Clyde M. Huber, Dean	Gives file on ASU leaders, including documents on suspension of students for distributing radical literature.
Yale University	1) William DeVane, Dean, Yale College	Names the Yale ASU chapter president. Advises FBI agent that this ASU leader "had been examined by Dr. Fry, the school Psychiatrist . . . but that Dr. Fry had found nothing wrong with him. He advised that perhaps Dr. Fry would be able to give a better picture of . . . [the ASU leader's] attitude." De-

COLLEGE/UNIV.	INFORMANT	TYPE OF DATA GIVEN TO FBI
		Vane furnished the official membership list of the ASU to H.B. Fisher, who in turn made it available to the FBI.
	2) Harry Fisher, Liasion Officer of Yale, and who with the knowledge of the Yale administration, served as official liaison between Yale and the FBI (apparently paid by both institutions)	Reports on ASU meetings and membership. Works with an agent in the FBI field office in New Haven, interviewing a Smith College student who named ASU activists at Smith.
	3) Professor Mommsen	Names ASU leader.

Notes

[1] This list of informants is by no means exhaustive. Hundreds of pages and probably more than a thousand informant names were deleted from the FBI files by FBI censors. There were no documents at all included by the FBI from many of the campuses with the most active ASU chapters, but it is very likely that extensive informing for the FBI occurred on these campuses. Moreover, my list only summarizes the most personal data given by these individuals to the FBI; it does not (because of space constraints) detail all of the political intelligence given to the Bureau by the listed informants. This list only covers the ASU and not the other significant student and youth protest organizations in Depression America (such as the American Youth Congress and the Southern Negro Youth Congress, which were subject to extensive FBI surveillance). The list also does not cover high schools, where there was—according to the FBI documents—a significant amount of informing against the ASU.

Note that all Confidential Informant numbers specified in the list were assigned by the FBI, as were all other deletions of informant names. In employing the word "informant" in this list I am using the dictionary definition of informant as "one who gives information," and I am not implying a paid or continuous informant relationship with the FBI.

[2] Even during the American Student Union's most isolationist phase on the eve of World War II, the ASU position on the draft—which was public information, known to the FBI—did not sanction violation of the law. In 1940, the sixth annual ASU convention took the moderate position of urging "every legal and constitutional means" to convince Congress to repeal conscription, while simultaneously pledging that so long as conscription remained the law of the land ASUers would "comply with the Selective Service act . . ." (FBI File # illegible, Report on the American Student Union February 7, 1941).

[3] The college administrators who gave the FBI their files and political intelligence on ASU activists were under no legal obligation to do so. But if the federal statutes did not compel them to cooperate with the FBI, neither did the law obli-

gate these college officials to keep student files confidential. Given the undeveloped state of the laws of privacy and student rights in America during the late 1930s and early 1940s, the question of whether or not to turn over the names of student radicals to the FBI was strictly an ethical and political question, which for this conservative generation of administrators meant that it was not a question at all (Robert B. Meigs, "The Confidential Nature of Student Records," *National Association of College and University Attorneys* (June 1962), 14–15).

Not until the 1960s would this type of collusion between academic administrators and federal red probers encounter major opposition within the educational establishment. In 1967 the American Council on Education (ACE) urged universities not to comply with the House Un-American Activities Committee's attempts to subpoena the membership lists of student anti-war groups. In the Council's view, college officials had an obligation to "protect students from unwarranted intrusions into their lives and from hurtful or threatening interference in the exploration of ideas and their consequences that education entails." Such language attests to a much more liberal reading of academic freedom than existed in Depression America. The position the ACE took in 1967 also contrasted with that of the informing administrators of the 1930s and 40s in that it acknowledged student privacy rights—affirming that "maintenance of student records, especially those bearing on personal belief and organizational affiliation, creates a personal and confidential relationship" ("Statement of Confidentiality of Student Records by the American Council on Education," Washington, D.C., July 7, 1967; William T. O'Hara, John G. Hill Jr., *The Student/The College/The Law* (New York, 1972), 53–54; On other restrictions on the release of information from student records, see the discussion of the Buckley Amendment (1974) in William A. Kaplin, *The Law of Higher Education* (San Francisco, 1985), 358–361; On restriction of police surveillance on campus, see the 1975 decision *White v. Davis* 13 Cal 3d 757, 120 Cal Rept. 94   533 P.2d).

[4]Copies of the FBI documents cited below as the sources for this list are in the author's possession and were obtained from the FBI through a Freedom of Information Act request. The informant list has been compiled from the FBI files reporting on the American Student Union at the campus level. On informing at Brown Univ., see FBI file # 100–160, Dec. 5, 1941, Report made by Norman Hanson, Providence; on UC Berkeley, see FBI file # 100–2071, Sept. 16, 1943, Report made by Theodore S. Cruise, San Francisco; on the Univ. of Chicago, see FBI file # 61–327, Dec. 6, 1941, Report made by J.F. Desmond, Chicago; on the Univ. of Cincinnati, see FBI file # 100–365, Feb. 1, 1941, Report made by S.H. Horton, Cincinnati; on Cleveland College, see FBI file # 100–608, Sept. 3, 1941 Report made by S.E. Hobbs, Cleveland; FBI file # 100–608, Feb. 12, 1942, Report made by G.E. Irwin, Cleveland; on Columbia Univ., see John J. Swan note to FBI, May 5, 1941, FBI file # 61–7491–1; on the Univ. of Connecticut, see FBI file # 100–589, 1941 [month and day illegible, reporting agent name illegible] New Haven; on Cornell Univ., see FBI file # 100–483, Nov. 4, 1941, Report made by P.D. Beachum, Albany, N.Y.; on DePauw Univ., see FBI file # 100–475, Feb. 20 [?], 1941, Report made by Richard C. Godfrey, Indianapolis; on Earlham College, see FBI file # 100–475, Jan. 23, 1943, Report made by George A. Brouillard, Indianapolis; on George Washington Univ., see FBI file # 100–920, Sept. 14, 1942, Report made by M.J. Connolly, Washington, D.C.; on the Univ. of Hawaii, see FBI file # 100–1241, June 28, 1941, Report made by John I. Condon, Honolulu; on Howard Univ., see FBI file # 100–920, Sept. 14, 1942, Report

made by M.J. Connolly, Washington, D.C.; on Hunter College, see FBI file # 100–483, May 28, 1941, Report made by J.V. Beale, Albany, N.Y.; on the Univ. of Illinois, see FBI file # 100–191, Jan. 10, 1941, Report made by W.A. Temple, Springfield; FBI file # 100–191, Feb. 1, Aug. 27, Oct. 30, 1941, Reports made by J.J. Racan, Springfield; FBI file # 100–191, Nov. 14, 1941, Report made by Arthur R. Day, Springfield; FBI file # 100–191, April 21, 1942, Report made by Charles F. Douglas, Springfield; on Indiana State Teachers College, see FBI file # 100–475, Feb. 20 [?], 1941, Report made by Richard C. Godfrey, Indianapolis; on Indiana Univ., see FBI file # 100–475, Feb. 20 [?], 1941, Report made by Richard C. Godfrey, Indianapolis; on Indiana Univ. Extension, see FBI file # 100–475, Jan. 23, 1943, Report made by George A. Brouillard, Indianapolis; on Univ. of Michigan, see FBI file# 100–1217, Nov. 29, 1941, Report made by Maurice E. Goudge, Detroit; FBI file # 100–1217, Feb. 8, 1943, Report made by John C. Hall, Detroit; on Middlebury College, see FBI file # 100–483, Feb. 6, 1942, Report made by Frank C. Wood, Albany, N.Y.; on Univ. of Minnesota, see [FBI file # illegible], Feb. 1, 1941, Report made by R.T. Noonan, St. Paul, Minnesota; on Univ. of Missouri, see FBI file # 100–1193, June 11, 1941, Report made by M.B. Rhodes, Kansas City; FBI file # 100–1193, Oct. 10, 1941, Report made by R.E. Sherk, Kansas City; FBI file # 100–1193, Dec. 5, 1941, Report made by W.C. Fuller, Kansas City; FBI file # 100–1193, March 21, 1942, Report made by R.B. Ayers, Kansas City; on Montana State Univ., see FBI file # 61–195, August 12, 1941, Report made by Elmer W. Parrish, Butte; on New Jersey College for Women, see FBI file # 100–1453, June 19, 1941, Report made by V. Walser Prospere, Newark; FBI file # 100–1453, April 19, 1943, Report made by Clement L. McGowan Jr., Newark; on Univ. of North Carolina at Chapel Hill, see FBI file # 100–419, March 5, 1941, Report made by B.F. Wiand, Charlotte; on Oberlin College, see FBI file # 100–608, Sept. 3, 1941, Report made by S.E. Hobbs, Cleveland; on Ohio State Univ., see FBI file # 100–365, March 20, 1941, Report made by Edward S. Sanders, Cincinnati; FBI file # 100–365, June 18, 1941, Report made by D.G. Jenkins, Cincinnati; on Ohio Univ. at Athens, see FBI file # 100–365, May 27, 1941, Report made by A.W. Richardson, Cincinnati; FBI file # 100–365, March 9, 1942, Report made by J.T. Delaney, Cincinnati; on Univ. of Pennsylvania, see FBI file # 61–136, Sept. 28, 1942, Report made by Harry C. Leslie Jr., Philadelphia; FBI file # 61–136, Nov. 24, 1942, Report made by Harry C. Leslie Jr., Philadelphia; on Purdue University, see FBI file # 100–475, Nov. 12, 1942, Report made by Douglas J. Williams, Indianapolis; on Smith College, see FBI file # 100–279, Feb. 20, 1943, Report made by James A. Hanley, Boston; FBI file # 100–589, Oct. 7, 1942, Report made by Charles E. Stine, New Haven; on Southern Illinois State Teachers College, see FBI file # 100–191, Feb. 1, 1941, Report made by W.A. Temple, Springfield; on Swarthmore College, see FBI file # 100–432, Dec. 5, 1941, Report made by C.H. King, Philadelphia; on Syracuse Univ., see FBI file # 100–483, Jan. 23, 1942, Report made by P.B. Beachum, Albany, N.Y.; on Temple Univ., see FBI file # 61–136, Sept. 28, 1942, Report made by Harry C. Leslie Jr., Philadelphia; on Univ. of Texas, see FBI file # 61–121, Jan. 25, 1940, Report made by J.O. Peyronnin [?, last name only partially legible], New Orleans: FBI file # 61–188, May 27, 1941, Report made by Alan H. Mayer, San Antonio; on Tulane Univ., see FBI file # 100–311, May 22, 1941, Report made by S.W. Reynolds, New Orleans; on the Univ. of Washington, see FBI file # 100–942, July 3, 1941, Report made by R.D. Auerbach, Seattle; File # [illegible], Sept. 19, 1941, Report made by R.D. Auerbach, Seattle; on Wayne University, see FBI file # 100–1217, Feb. 8, 1943, Report made by John C. Hall, Detroit; on Wesleyan Univ., see FBI file # 100–589, 1941 [month and day illegible, reporting agent name illegible] New Haven; on Western Reserve Univ.-Adelbert College-Flora Stone Mather College, see FBI file # 100–608, Sept. 3, 1941, S.E. Hobbs, Cleveland; FBI file # 100–608, Feb. 12, 1942, Report made by G.E. Irwin, Cleveland; on Wilson Teachers College, see FBI file # 100–920, Sept. 14, 1942, Report made by M.J. Connolly, Washington, D.C.; on Yale Univ., see FBI file # 100–589, [day and month illegible], 1941, [Reporting FBI agent's name illegible], New Haven; FBI file # 100–589, [month illegible], 21, 1941, and July 17, 1942, Reports made by G. J. McDonough, New Haven; FBI file # 100–589, Oct. 7, 1942, Report made by Charles E. Stine, New Haven; Sigmund Diamond, "Surveillance in the Academy: Harry B. Fisher and Yale University, 1927–1952," *American Quarterly* (Spring 1984), 7–43; Robin W. Winks, *Cloak and Gown: Scholars in the Secret War, 1939–1961* (New York, 1987), 32–35.

Abbreviations

ACLU   American Civil Liberties Union Archives, Mudd Manuscript Library, Princeton University

BC   Brooklyn College Archives, Gideonse Library

CCNY   City College of New York Archives, Cohen Library

CUC   Columbiana Collection, Butler Library, Columbia University

ECM   Ernest C. Moore Papers, Department of Special Collections, UCLA Research Library

ER   Eleanor Roosevelt Papers, Franklin D. Roosevelt Library, Hyde Park, N.Y.

FU   Fisk University Archives, Fisk University Library

HARV   Harvard University Archives, Pusey Library

JM   Jack McMichael Papers, Woodruff Library, Emory University

JPL   Joseph P. Lash Papers, Franklin D. Roosevelt Library, Hyde Park, N.Y.

NNC   National Negro Congress Papers, Schomburg Center for Research in Black Culture, New York Public Library

NT   Norman Thomas Papers, New York Public Library

NYT   *New York Times*

NYU   Tamiment Institute Library, New York University

RH   Reed Harris files, Low Library, Columbia University

SCPC   Swarthmore College Peace Collection, McCabe Library

SP   Young People's Socialist League files, Socialist Party of America Papers, Duke University (used on microfilm at the Tamiment Library, NYU; and at Carlson Library, University of Toledo)

UC   Special Collections Department, Regenstein Library, University of Chicago

UCB   University of California Archives, Bancroft Library, UC Berkeley

UM   Michigan Historical Collections, Bentley Historical Library, University of Michigan

UT   University of Toledo Archives, Carlson Library

UTEX   University of Texas Archives, Lyndon B. Johnson Library

UVA   University of Virginia Library, Manuscripts Department

UW   University of Washington Archives, Seattle

UWISC University of Wisconsin Archives, Memorial Library, Madison

VC   Vassar College Archives, Thompson Memorial Library

YCAW   Youth Committee Against War files, Keep America Out of War Congress Papers, Swarthmore College Peace Collection

YWCA   Young Women's Christian Association National Board Archives, New York

Notes

Introduction

1. John P. Roche, *Shadow and Substance: Essays on the Theory and Structure of Power* (New York, 1964), 436. From the outset radical student activists in Depression America expressed disdain for Europe's fascist youth movements. Indeed, one of the justifications these radicals used for organizing students in the U.S. was to preempt any possible rightist youth movement here (*Hunter Bulletin*, March 27, 1933; Theodore Draper, "American Youth Rejects Fascism," *New Masses* (Aug. 23, 1934), 11–13; *Columbia Spectator*, May 7, 1934; "Should the American Student Go the Way of the German? A Student Conference Against Fascism," leaflet, N.Y., May 1934, JPL).

2. The best account of Depression-era violations of academic freedom among the faculty in the U.S. is Ellen Schrecker, *No Ivory Tower: McCarthyism and the Universities* (New York, 1986), 63–83.

3. On *Tinker v. Des Moines,* see William G. Millington, *The Law and the College Student: Justice in Evolution* (St. Paul. Minn., 1979), 160–213.

4. The secret political dossiers that the FBI—with the help of college officials—assembled on Depression-era student activists will be discussed in Chapter 5 of this study; also see Appendix. Athan G. Theoharis has uncovered unlawful behavior by the FBI in its political surveillance of these activists. FBI agents burglarized the New York office of the American Youth Congress and photocopied correspondence between the Youth Congress and Eleanor Roosevelt. See Athan G. Theoharis, "J. Edgar, Eleanor - and Herbert Too?: The F.D.R. File," *Nation* (Feb. 20, 1982), 200–201. On the FBI break-in at the offices of the International Student Service, a leading student activist organization during the last stages of the Depression era student movement, see Athan G. Theoharis and John Stuart Cox, *The Boss: J. Edgar Hoover and the Great American Inquisition* (Philadelphia, 1988), 191. Campus administrators also demonstrated a disregard for students' civil liberties by initiating some of their own political surveillance on student protesters. This will be discussed in Chapter 5.

5. Theodore Draper, *American Communism and Soviet Russia* (New York, 1986), 5, 445–82; Theodore Draper, *The Roots of American Communism* (New York, 1957), 395; Maurice Isserman, *Which Side Were You On?: The American Communist Party During the Second World War* (Middletown, Conn., 1982), vii-xiv, 1–31; Maurice Isserman, "Communist Caricature," *In These Times* (April 4–10, 1984), 18, 22.

6. Joseph P. Lash, "Do the Thirties Have Anything to Tell the Sixties?" (New York, 1968), Introduction to Greenwood Press reprint of *Student Advocate*, 2.

7. William E. Leuchtenburg, *Franklin D. Roosevelt and the New Deal* (New York,

1963), 290; Arthur Schlesinger, Jr., *The Politics of Upheaval* (Boston, 1966), 199; Robert S. McElvaine, *The Great Depression* (New York, 1984). The published historical monographs on the student movement of the 1930s are Eileen Eagan, *Class, Culture and the Classroom* (Philadelphia, 1981); Ralph Brax, *The First Student Movement* (Port Washington, N.Y., 1981). Also see Winifred Wandersee, "ER and American Youth: Politics and Personality in a Bureaucratic Age," in Joan Hoff-Wilson and Marjorie Lightman, eds., *Without Precedent: The Life and Career of Eleanor Roosevelt* (Bloomington, 1984), 63–87; George Rawick,"The New Deal and Youth: The Civilian Conservation Corps, the National Youth Administration and the American Youth Congress" (Ph.D. diss., Univ. of Wisconsin, 1957).

8. The Fund for the Republic study with the chapter on Depression-era student radicalism is Robert W. Iversen, *The Communists and the Schools* (New York, 1959), 119–47. The repressive political atmosphere of the McCarthy era left publishers under pressure not to publish memoirs that were at all sympathetic to the radical movements of the 1930s. For example, in 1953 playwright Arthur Miller wrote an article for *Holiday Magazine* on Michigan student life, which briefly but warmly recalled Depression era student radicals and their support of the militant auto strikes (his article is quoted at the beginning of this Introduction). Miller later learned that the "advertising department of the Pontiac division of General Motors had warned [*Holiday* publisher Ted] Patrick that Pontiac would cancel all its advertising in *Holiday* if they ever published another piece by Arthur Miller" (Arthur Miller, *Timebends: A Life* (New York, 1987), 96).

9. Jack McMichael interview with author, Athens, W.Va., Aug. 22, 1982.

10. Among the best of this memoir literature by Depression era student activists is James Wechsler, *The Age of Suspicion* (New York, 1981), 3–132; Irving Howe, *A Margin of Hope: An Intellectual Autobiography* (New York, 1982), 1–89; Joseph P. Lash, *Eleanor: A Friend's Memoir* (Garden City, N.Y., 1964), 1–254; Henry F. May, *Coming to Terms: A Study in Memory and History* (Berkeley, 1987), 185–266; Junius Irving Scales and Richard Nickson, *Cause at Heart: A Former Communist Remembers* (Athens, Ga., 1987), 53–88; Roche, *Shadow and Substance*, 432–41; Paul Jacobs, *Is Curly Jewish?* (New York, 1965), 3–110; Eric Sevareid, *Not So Wild a Dream* (New York, 1965), 48–73; Hal Draper, "The Student Movement of the Thirties: A Political History," in Rita Simon, ed., *As We Saw the Thirties* (Urbana, 1967), 153–89; Pauli Murray, *Song in a Weary Throat* (New York, 1987), 82–129.

11. *NYT*, Feb. 11, 1940.

12. May, *Coming to Terms*, 207.

13. Joseph P. Lash, "Memorial to Spain" (April 13, 1980), an address on the occasion of the dedication of a memorial to the City College of New York students who fought and died in the Spanish Civil War, JPL.

Chapter 1. Dancing on the Edge of a Volcano

1. Irving Bernstein, *The Lean Years: A History of the American Worker, 1920–1933* (Baltimore, 1960), 254–57; *NYT*, Aug. 13, 1931; "The Hoover Happiness Boys," *Nation* (June 18, 1930), 692.

2. *Daily Californian*, Aug. 13, 1931.

3. *San Francisco Chronicle*, Aug. 12, 1931.

4. William Harlan Hale, "A Dirge for College Liberalism," *New Republic* (May 13, 1931), 349; Reed Harris, *King Football: The Vulgarization of the American College*

(New York, 1932), 195; *Michigan Daily,* May 7, 1932; *Intercollegian* (Jan. 1932), 130.

5. *Daily Cardinal,* Oct. 23, 1931. On the large number of campus parties, also see *University Daily Kansan,* March 22, 30, 1931, April 12, 1931; *Intersorority Council Minutes, Toledo University, book I, 1927–1943,* 37, UT; Univ. of Buffalo *Bee,* May 15, 1931. The student press treated such partying as a central undergraduate interest. See, for instance, the enormous banner headline accorded the "Prom King" election at the Univ. of Wisconsin in *Daily Cardinal,* Oct. 13, 1931.

6. *Michigan Daily,* Nov. 28, 1931; *Daily Cardinal,* Feb. 16, 1930.

7. *NYT,* May 8, 1930. To contrast this juvenile collegiate violence with the political violence which accompanied the hunger marches, see *NYT,* March 7, 1930.

8. *NYT,* Feb. 13, May 2, 1930, Jan. 6, Feb. 15, 1931, and March 9–11, 1930; *Daily Cardinal,* Oct. 15, 1931.

9. *Columbia Spectator,* April 15, and May 2, 1930. At Columbia and other campuses raiding class dinners was an annual campus ritual. See "Springs of Student Rioting : Psychology and Tradition Play Parts in the Occasional Collegiate Outbursts," *NYT Magazine* (Feb. 1, 1931), 16.

10. "Springs of Student Rioting," 16. Though student riots brought injuries, arrests and extensive property damage, some nostalgic alumni claimed that the riots in the early 1930s were not as impressive as those in their own college days during the 1920s. How much trouble one made in such disturbances was apparently a matter of generational pride. See *Daily Cardinal,* Oct. 17, 1931. Participants often defended these apolitical college riots on the grounds that they promoted a laudable "unifying spirit" among undergraduates. See *Michigan Daily,* Nov. 15, 1929; and see the reprint of the *Ohio State Lantern*'s editorial in *Daily Cardinal,* May 25, 1930.

11. Harris, *King Football* (New York, 1932), passim; *Daily Californian,* Nov. 18, 1983; *Michigan Daily,* Oct. 8, 1930; James Wechsler, *Revolt on the Campus* (1935; reprint, Seattle, 1973), 42–43. *Hunter Bulletin,* Dec. 5, 1933. College football's great popularity in the 1920s led to an awesome expansion of the game's physical presence on campus. One report covering 135 campuses found that seating capacity in college football stadiums had more than doubled from 929,521 in 1920 to 2,307,850 in 1930 (almost twice the size of the national undergraduate population). Attendance at college football games had soared by 119 percent in this same era. At many colleges the stadium was the largest or among the largest structures on campus. See *University Daily Kansan,* Jan. 19, 1933.

12. *University Daily Kansan,* Nov. 18, 1930.

13. A.M. Sperber, *Murrow: His Life and Times* (New York, 1986), 29–30, 34–44; E.R. Murrow, "National Student Federation," *American Association of University Professors Bulletin* (April 1931), 240.

14. *NYT,* Dec. 28, 1931.

15. Harold J. Laski, "Why Don't Your Young Men Care?: The Political Indifference of the American Undergraduate," *Harper's Magazine* (July 1931), 129. On the apolitical mindset of American undergraduates, also see "Collegiate Sheep," *The De Pauw* editorial reprinted in *Daily Illini,* Nov. 26, 1931; "Our Attitude Towards Politics," *Daily Iowan* editorial reprinted in *Daily Illini,* Oct. 4, 1931; *Columbia Spectator,* March 10, 24, 1931. On how disillusionment with reformers and their failures during the Progressive era left students jaded about liberalism, and fostered political apathy on campus during the early Depression years, see Robert Paul Cohen, "The Revolt of the Depression Generation: America's First

Mass Student Protest Movement, 1929–1940" (Ph.D. diss., UC Berkeley, 1987), 28–30.

16. Laski, "Why Don't Your Young Men Care?," 130, 135.

17. *LID News Bulletin,* Jan. 1926; Norman Thomas, "Youth and the American Colleges," *Nation* (Aug. 1, 1923), 106.

18. Thomas, "Youth and the American Colleges," 106.

19. *NYT,* Dec. 21, 1930; On the middle-class background of college students, see U.S. Office of Education, *Economic Status of College Alumni* (Washington, D.C., 1939), 23–25; O. Edgar Reynolds, *The Social and Economic Status of College Students* (New York, 1927), 14–21.

20. Arthur Schlesinger, Jr.'s classic *The Crisis of the Older Order, 1919–1933* (Cambridge, 1957) exemplifies the tendency of historians to ignore class distinctions in their accounts of America's response to the onset of the Great Depression. Schlesinger writes that by the spring of 1930 the Depression had bred a "contagion of fear . . . [whose] shadow fell over the cities and towns; it fell as heavily over the countryside. . . . In country and city alike anger [provoked by the economic crisis] was spreading" (*The Crisis of the Older Order,* 166, 174, 176). The problem here is that Schlesinger, whose account details the suffering of the unemployed and farmers, generalizes from these specific groups to all of society. Schlesinger erroneously assumes, without evidence, that the suffering wrought by the Depression immediately produced anger and a sense of crisis throughout society. But the facts from the campus world in 1930 and 1931 contradict Schlesinger's assumptions, and we see not fear but frivolity, not anger but apathy, among the nation's predominantly middle-class undergraduate population. On American student culture in the 1920s, see Paula Fass, *The Damned and the Beautiful: American Youth in the 1920s* (New York, 1970), passim.

21. U.S. Office of Education, *Biennial Survey of Education in the United States, 1930–1932* (Washington, D.C., 1935), 13; Malcolm Wiley, ed., *Depression, Recovery and Higher Education: A Report of the X Committee of the American Association of University Professors* (New York, 1939), 23; *NYT,* Dec. 21, 1930. The one significant exception to the rule concerning undergraduate enrollments was that of college women. While male enrollments rose in 1930 and 1931, female enrollments dipped slightly—about 1.6 percent. This reflected the sexual double standard common among parents of college students in this era concerning who needed a college education: for a son that education was viewed as a necessity because he would be the breadwinner, whereas for a daughter, who supposedly would become a housewife, that education was seen as a luxury that could be dispensed with during a depression. See *NYT,* Dec. 21, 1930, and June 3, 1931; Raymond Walters, "Statistics of Registration in American Universities and Colleges," *School and Society* (Dec. 12, 1931), 783. What is striking, however, is how little student discussion there was of this trend, and how the declining female enrollment failed to change the mood on campus. Perhaps the drop in female enrollments was not sharp enough to cause alarm. And since it was at co-educational institutions rather than at women's colleges where the early female enrollment drop was concentrated, the change occurred amidst a male-dominated student culture—which did not even seem to notice.

22. *NYT,* Feb. 17, Oct. 12, 1930.

23. Robert Angell, "The Influence of the Economic Depression on Student Life at the University of Michigan," *School and Society* (Nov. 14, 1931), 650, 653. Note, however, that elsewhere in this article Angell (649) argues for more rapid

economic decline at the Univ. of Michigan than I have found on campus nationally. For good correctives to Angell on this point, and for discussion of how "cloistered" and "pleasantly remote" students initially felt from the Depression, see *Daily
Cardinal*, Sept. 23, 1931; "Yale in Depression," *Harkness Hoot* (Nov. 23, 1931), 3–
4; *Intercollegian* (Jan. 1931), 130; *Michigan Daily*, June 3, 1932.

24. *Vassar Miscellany News*, Nov. 27, 1929.

25. *Daily Californian*, Nov. 19, 21, 1929. On this enduring faith in Hoover
and the economy, see *Michigan Daily*, Oct. 11, 1931; *University Daily Kansan*, May
4, 1930. On student support for Republicans in the 1920s, see Fass, *The Damned
and the Beautiful*, 343–44.

26. U.S. Office of Education, *Biennial Survey of Education in the United States,
1936–1938* (Washington, D.C., 1942), 8.

27. James Wechsler, *The Age of Suspicion* (New York, 1981), 20; also see *Columbia Spectator*, March 18, 1931.

28. *Columbia Spectator*, Dec. 3, 1930. Other unrealistically optimistic statements and stories concerning the employment prospects for college graduates during
the early Depression years can be found in *NYT*, July 20, 1930; "Employment of
Cornell Graduates," *School and Society* (Aug. 22, 1931), 264. There were a few
more negative reports, which, of course, turned out to be more accurate. See *NYT*,
May 3, 1931.

29. *Barnard Bulletin*, June 6, 1930.

30. Walter Greenleaf, *Self-Help for College Students* (Washington, D.C., 1929),
60–61; *NYT*, Feb. 17, 1930, Oct. 17, Nov. 3, 1931. On other campuses where
students had difficulty securing part-time jobs, see *Michigan Daily*, October 8, 1930;
Daily Cardinal, Oct. 4, 1931. Of the college employment statistics, those showing
that 20 percent male and 11 percent female students being entirely self-supporting
are the least ambiguous. These were students who had to have employment in
order to put themselves through college. But once one moves to the larger group
of employed students, the significance of job-holding is less clear. Some students
who were not fully self-supporting worked part-time jobs—even though they were
already comfortable economically—to pay for the added luxuries of an active collegiate social life. We know this because as the part-time job market tightened in
campus communities, college administrators urged students who did not absolutely need jobs to avoid seeking employment—so as to make way for those students whose ability to stay in college depended upon securing jobs. In other words,
while fully self-supporting students were thrown into economic crisis, some portion of students who worked were at worst only inconvenienced by the job crunch,
because they did not truly need the money from that employment. See *University
Daily Kansan*, Sept. 17, 1930.

The Hoover administration's response to the growing crisis in the market for
part-time jobs among college students was belated and ineffective. Refusing to use
federal funds to create new jobs for college students, the administration instead
sought to eliminate foreign job-seekers. In September 1932, Hoover's Secretary
of Labor, William Doak barred foreign college students from holding part-time
jobs. Since foreign students accounted for only a tiny fraction of the students
seeking employment, the ruling had virtually no impact on the job crisis, but it
did hurt foreign students and was condemned by college administrators. See *NYT*,
Sept. 27, 1932.

31. Angell, "The Influence of the Economic Depression on Student Life,"
653.

32. *University Daily Kansan,* Jan. 22, 1930.

33. Studs Terkel, *Hard Times: An Oral History of the Great Depression* (New York, 1970), 398. Also see "A Letter from an Unemployed Student," *The Spark,* June 1932, UTEX.

34. *Harvard Crimson,* May 2, May 22, 1933; Theodore White, *In Search of History: A Personal Adventure* (New York, 1978), 42–43.

35. *University Daily Kansan,* Oct. 10, 1930; Berkeley *Student Outpost,* Feb. 15, 1933, UCB; on the "real class warfare" between rich and poor students at the University of Virginia, see Terkel, *Hard Times,* 400.

36. *Time* (Nov. 24, 1930), 46; *University Daily Kansan,* Dec. 8, 1931.

37. For other occasions in which students organized to protest adult policing of their social life, see "Barnard Girls Revolt Against 'No Stockings' Edict at Meals," in Wisconsin *Daily Cardinal,* March 14, 1930; the report on the University of Chicago student riot protesting "dry snooping" (spying by the campus police to determine if the prohibition laws were being violated by undergraduates), in Wisconsin *Daily Cardinal,* May 25, 1930.

38. How important lifestyle issues, and in particular the freedom to consume liquor, could be to college students was suggested by an editorial in the Michigan student newspaper. More than two years after the stock market crash, and with the American economy collapsing, this editor could still claim that "of all the major problems before the American public today, prohibition is . . . [by] far the most important" (*Michigan Daily,* Nov. 3, 1931). Such sentiment was based at least in part on self-interest. According to a poll taken of eastern and midwestern undergraduates the previous year, a majority of students—15,000 out of the 24,000 students polled—violated the prohibition laws by drinking liquor. Since this made them subject to arrest, students had good reason to favor a change in the liquor laws. This problem was not merely theoretical. One of largest collegiate scandals in 1931 occurred when Michigan's fraternity houses were raided for violating the prohibition laws, and 79 students were arrested (*NYT,* March 27, 1930, Feb. 12, 13, 1931; *Michigan Daily,* Dec. 9, 1931, Jan. 13, 1932).

39. On the tradition of collegiate cultural liberalism inherited from the student peer culture of the 1920s, see Fass, *The Damned and the Beautiful,* 327–70.

40. *NYT,* May 11, 1932; William Harlan Hale, "A Dirge for College Liberalism," *New Republic* (May 13, 1931), 349.

41. Hale, "A Dirge for College Liberalism," 349–50. The editor of the Univ. of Michigan student newspaper agreed with Hale's conclusions, adding that "college liberalism" was fading not only in the East, but in the Midwest as well (*Michigan Daily,* May 6, 1931; also see Univ. of Buffalo *Bee,* Nov. 6, 1931).

42. *NYT,* Oct. 3, 1932; Wiley, *Depression, Recovery and Higher Education,* 473. On the hardships of students forced to drop out of college because of the economic crisis, and on their parents' personal grief over this, see Kenneth L. McGooden to Robert M. Hutchins, Aug. 16, 1933, and Rachel Mickolas to Robert M. Hutchins, Aug. 21, 1933 in President's Papers, *UC.* On the financial sacrifices parents made attempting to keep their children in college, see *NYT,* Oct. 23, 1932.

43. Wiley, *Depression, Recovery and Higher Education,* 170–75.

44. *Ibid.*

45. *NYT,* Oct. 3, 1932; *Daily Californian,* Oct. 6, 1932.

46. *NYT,* Oct. 3, 1932. On this new, more serious campus mood, see Robert Angell, "The Trend Toward Greater Maturity Among Undergraduates Due to the Depression," *School and Society* (Sept. 23, 1933), 391–96.

47. *Michigan Daily,* Dec. 8, 10, 1932. Also see "Privation & Co-operation," *Time* (Jan. 9, 1933), 46; *Daily Cardinal,* Jan. 11, 1933.

48. *Daily Cardinal,* Feb. 25, March 11, 1932. Other expressions of sympathy for working students can be found in *Daily Illini,* Jan. 3, 1932; *Daily Texan,* Dec. 17, 1932.

49. *Why SWF?* (Ann Arbor, n.d.); *Daily Illini,* Dec. 20, 23, 1931.

50. Berkeley *Student Outpost,* Feb. 15, 1933.

51. *Michigan Daily,* March 29, 1933.

52. *Daily Illini,* Jan. 17, 1932. The increasingly somber tone of college employment officers was evident in Christian Gauss' article, "The Lost Generation: What Chance for the College Graduate of 1931?," *Forum* (Sept. 1931), 190. On this job crisis, also see R.T. Sharpe, "The Present Problem of Student Employment," *AAUP Bulletin* (Nov. 1932), 503–4; Charles A. Maney, "College Graduates Face the Future," *Journal of Higher Education* (Oct. 1935), 371–75; University of Toledo *Collegian,* March 24, 1933; *Daily Cardinal,* Nov. 17, 1933; Bedulah Amidon, "After College-What?," *Survey Graphic* (June 1933), 320–23.

53. *Columbia Spectator,* Nov. 25, 1931; *Collegian,* Oct. 1, 1932; *Revolt* (Dec. 1932), cover graphic.

54. *Vassar Miscellany News,* Nov. 2, 1932.

55. *Ibid.*

56. *Ibid.,* Nov. 2, 5, 12, Dec. 10, 1932.

57. *Ibid.,* Nov. 2, 1932.

Chapter 2. Cafeteria Commies

1. Lionel Abel, *The Intellectual Follies* (New York, 1984), 55. On New York City radicalism during the Depression, also see Malcolm Cowley, *The Dream of the Golden Mountains* (New York, 1980), 46–62, 106–26; Irving Howe, *A Margin of Hope* (New York, 1982), 1–86; Harvey Klehr, *The Heyday of American Communism: The Depression Decade* (New York, 1984), 32–34, 265–69; Alexander Bloom, *Prodigal Sons: The New York Intellectuals and Their World* (New York, 1986), 11–120.

2. James Wechsler, *The Age of Suspicion* (New York, 1981), 42–49; Robert Hall interview with author, Willsboro, N.Y., Dec. 17, 1982; Larry Rogin interview with author, Washington, D.C., June 4, 1982.

3. Council of Christian Associations, *Towards a New Economic Society: A Program for Students* (New York, 1931), passim; Donald B. Meyer, *The Protestant Search For Political Realism* (Berkeley, 1960), 173–74; F. Palmer Weber, interview with author, Manhattan, N.Y., Jan. 25, 28, 1982; Anthony Dunbar, *Against the Grain: Southern Radicals and Prophets* (Charlottesville, 1981), 1–125.

4. Max Gordon, "Seeds of Conflict: A Memoir of 50 Years Ago," *City College Alumnus* (Oct. 1981), 10–11; Oakley Johnson, "Campus Battles for Freedom in the Thirties," *Centennial Review* (Summer 1970), 341–67; Howe, *A Margin of Hope,* 60–64.

5. David Boroff, "A Kind of Proletarian Harvard," *NYT Magazine* (March 28, 1965), 19, 106–9; Harry Magdoff interview with author, Manhattan, N.Y., March 19, 1982; Max Gordon interview with author, Manhattan, N.Y., Feb. 2, 1982; Max Weiss interview with author, Manhattan, N.Y., May 5, 1982.

6. Harry Magdoff interview with author.

7. Arthur Liebman, *The Jews and the Left* (New York, 1979), 26–37, 77–365.

8. Alfred Kazin, *Starting Out in the Thirties* (Boston, 1965), 4.

9. Harry Magdoff interview with author; Max Gordon interview with author; Max Weiss interview with author; Joseph Clark interview with author, Manhattan, N.Y., May 4, 1982.

10. George Watt interview with author, Northport, N.Y., Sept. 16, 1982.

11. *Ibid.*

12. *Ibid.*

13. *Ibid.*

14. Harry Magdoff interview with author.

15. *Ibid.*

16. *Ibid.* Note that even in New York's City Colleges the activist group was initially a small minority of the student body. At the time of the NSL's birth most of the City College's low-income students responded to the Depression not by embracing radicalism, but by buckling down in their academic work, hoping that by performing impeccably at college they would improve their chances for employment in the dismal job market. Moreover, though growing up in New York ghettoes fostered greater toleration of radicalism—which facilitated the quick growth of the student Left in the City colleges—many of these students came to college with little grounding in radical ideas. While the student body was sympathetic to the Left, the majority nonetheless did not come to college with the political sophistication of either young radical intellectuals like Magdoff or experienced activists like Weiss. Underscoring this point, Magdoff recalls that in his speech class at CCNY "I gave a talk on the need for unemployment insurance. Now you have to remember that this is a period when 20 percent, 25 percent of the population was unemployed. A lot of these kids at school, their parents were unemployed. . . . And the guys in class were . . . astounded at this crazy idea. Now you look at City College, a hotbed of revolution—of communism, of socialism—but this is as much the reality" (Harry Magdoff interview with author).

17. Howe, *A Margin of Hope*, 11. For a brilliant analysis of the ways in which such outsider status sustained a vibrant tradition of dissident thought on the Jewish Left, see Issac Deutscher, *The Non-Jewish Jew and Other Essays*, ed. Tamara Deutscher (New York, 1968), 25–41.

18. Harry Magdoff interview with author.

19. *Ibid.*; Theodore Draper, "City College's Rebel Generation," *New Masses* (Nov. 27, 1934), 15; Theodore Draper interview with author, Princeton, N.J., June 17, 1982; Max Weiss interview with author; Joseph P. Lash interview with author, Manhattan, N.Y., Nov. 23, 1982. Several vivid descriptions of the political debates in the alcoves have been published by alumni, but most of these were by CCNY students in the late 1930s—a time when the Left at City College was larger and more polarized than in the early 1930s. See Irving Kristol, "Memoirs of a Trotskyist," *NYT Magazine* (Jan. 23, 1977), 51, 54–56; Howe, *A Margin of Hope*, 64–69. It is the importance of the cafeteria as a center of radical politics and debate at CCNY that E. L. Doctorow apparently alluded to when he used the term "cafeteria Commie" to invoke the youthful radicalism of the 1930s in his novel *The Book of Daniel* (quoted at the beginning of this chapter). The allusion was especially appropriate in a novel about the Rosenberg case, since Julius Rosenberg had been a young Communist at CCNY in the 1930s. On Rosenberg's political activism at CCNY, see Morton Sobell, *On Doing Time* (New York, 1974), 30–33; Ronald Radosh and Joyce Milton, *The Rosenberg File: A Search for the Truth* (New York, 1983), 51–52.

20. *Frontiers* (Feb. 1931), 1, CCNY.

21. Harry Magdoff interview with author; *Frontiers* (Feb. 1931), 2.

22. *Frontiers* (Feb. 1931), 1.

23. Max Gordon interview with author; Max Weiss interview with author; Judah Drob interview with author, Washington, D.C., Jan. 22, 1982; Harold Goldstein interview with author, Washington, D.C., Jan. 22, 1982; Sol Becker and Archie Deno, "Seven Years of Suppression," *Frontiers* (April 1933), 6–7, CCNY.

24. *NYT*, Oct. 30, 1932; Barbara J. Dunlap, "From the Pen of President Robinson," *The City College Alumnus* (April 1981), 6.

25. CCNY *Campus*, Feb. 27, 1931, March 2, 4, 6, 10, 13, 17, 1931; Max Gordon interview with author. "The Case for the Social Problems Club," leaflet [1931], CCNY.

26. CCNY *Campus*, Feb. 27, 1931, and March 2, 4, 6, 10, 13 and 17, 1931; Max Gordon interview with author.

27. Max Gordon interview with author; Max Weiss interview with author; Gordon, "Seeds of Conflict," 10–11; *Building a Militant Student Movement: Program and Constitution of the National Student League* [n.d.].

28. Max Gordon interview with author; Max Weiss interview with author; Gordon, "Seeds of Conflict," 10–11; *Building a Militant Student Movement*; "Role of the Student—1931," *Student Review* (Dec. 1931), 2; "For a National Student Movement: A Suggested Basis," *ibid.* (Jan.-Feb. 1932), 3.

29. Max Gordon interview with author; Max Weiss interview with author; Gordon, "Seeds of Conflict," 10–11; *Building a Militant Student Movement*; "The National Conference," *Student Review* (March 1932), 16. "The National Conference Report," *Student Review* (May 1932), 19; *Daily Worker*, March 29, 1932; "Building a Student Movement: On the Second National Student League Convention," *Student Review* (Dec. 1932), 5.

30. On the history of the ISS and LID, see Max Horn, *The Intercollegiate Socialist Society: Origins of the Modern American Student Movement* (Boulder, 1982), passim; Harry Laidler, *Twenty Years of Social Pioneering : The League for Industrial Democracy Celebrates Its 20th Anniversary* (New York, 1926), 3–21. Harold Lewack, *Campus Rebels: A Brief History of the Student League for Industrial Democracy* (New York, 1953), 8–10.

31. Even the LID's tiny non-student membership outnumbered its student membership. According to the LID files, at the end of 1929 students did not constitute a majority of the League's total of 2,058 campus and community members. See Minutes, "LID Board of Directors Meeting," Dec. 4, 1929, LID Papers, NYU

32. For an example of the academic tone set by the LID's adult leadership, see Norman Thomas's professorial introduction to the study by Kenneth Meiklejohn and Peter Nehemkis, *Southern Labor in Revolt* (New York, 1930), 3–4. Here Thomas does not ask students to become active in the labor movement, requesting only that they conduct dispassionate studies of labor problems.

33. Riva Stocker, "The I.S.C. Program," *LID Monthly* (Nov. 1931), 8. Not only Stocker, but other students in the LID conceded that that the LID's intercollegiate council had been poorly organized and "somewhat inactive" (Paul Porter, "The League on Campus," *LID Monthly* (Feb. 1931), 11). Observing that it was older figures, such as Laidler and Thomas, who set the tone for the LID, the NSL, criticized the LID for being "dominated by a . . . non-student leadership which

is completely out of touch with students and their problems . . ." ("Program of the National Student League," *Student Review* (May 1932), 17).

34. F. O. Matthiessen, "The Education of a Socialist," *Monthly Review* (Oct. 1950), 175.

35. *The League for Industrial Democracy* (New York, 1921), 3, 10–11; Horn, *The Intercollegiate Socialist Society*, passim; Laidler, *Twenty Years of Social Pioneering*, 17.

36. "Liberalism in the Middle West," *LID News Bulletin* (May 1923), 3; *New Student*, June 17, 1922; Stanley Mallach, "Red Kate O'Hare Comes to Madison: The Politics of Free Speech," *Wisconsin Magazine of History* (Spring 1970), 204–22.

37. "Our Annual Student Conference," *LID News Bulletin* (Jan. 1923), 2.

38. *Ibid.*, 3. There was, however, a radical minority in the LID during the 1920s—a few militant campus chapters—which sought to get the organization to drop its educational orientation in favor of a more militant agitational approach to student organizing. But such calls for greater militancy aroused little support nationally in the LID. See "Our Intercollegiate Conference," *LID News Bulletin* (Feb. 1927), 2.

39. Joseph Clark, introduction to Greenwood Press reprint of *Student Review* (New York, 1968), 2.

40. "For a National Student Movement: A Suggested Basis," 3–4. This program contrasted starkly with that of the LID's national leadership. For example, even while noting the unemployment "crisis of tragic proportions" wrought by the Depression, LID leader Paul Porter, in issuing "A Call for Student Action," lacked a concrete program for student protest. Indeed, rather than calling for the creation of a student protest movement, Porter clung to the academic ideal. His key suggestion to students was that they "engage in vigorous education toward a new society" by arranging lectures and distributing LID educational materials (Paul Porter, "A Call for Student Action," *LID Monthly* (June 1931), 7–8). The only act of the national student LID that went beyond education was the rather tepid national petition drive against compulsory ROTC (Nathaniel Weyl, "The Student Fight Against Militarism," *LID Monthly* (March 1931), 11). This does not mean, however, that at the campus level all LID members shared the educational emphasis of the organization's national leadership. As in the 1920s, the LID had some action-oriented campus chapters. And due to the Depression this militant minority had grown—as had its impulse for anti-militarism and pro-labor agitation. What the challenge of the NSL and its agitational approach did was prod the LID in 1932 to elevate this militancy from minority status into the official program of the student LID's leadership. The volume of the debate was undoubtedly louder by this time because the Left had expanded greatly since the early days of the student movement (On these militant chapters and the move of the student LID from education to agitation, see "Among the Colleges," *LID Monthly* (Feb. 1930), 6–7; Frank Braun, "Detroit's Fighting Pacifists," *LID Monthly* (Jan. 1932), 13; Paul Porter, "Yours for the Revolution," *LID Monthly* (Feb. 1932), 11. "Blueprints of Action: A Handbook for Student Revolutionists," *Revolt* (Oct. 1932), 2).

41. "For a National Student Movement: A Suggested Basis," 3–4.

42. Martin Abern, "The Young Worker and the Student," *New Student* (Nov. 17, 1923), 6.

43. Max Weiss interview with author.

44. Max Gordon interview with author; Theodore Draper interview with author. When the Communist Party leadership spoke about youth in 1931 it was always about the need to organize young workers. See, for instance, the Commu-

nist Party Central Committee's statement on youth, made in its 13th Plenum, *Daily Worker,* Sept. 17, 1931; also see William Z. Foster, "Build the Youth Movement," *ibid.,* Sept. 29, 1931.

45. Harry Magdoff interview with author.

46. Joseph Clark interview with author.

47. *Ibid.*

48. *Ibid.*; Max Weiss interview with author; Max Gordon interview with author. That during the period of the NSL's emergence the YCL national leadership gave blue-collar youth priority over students can be seen in YCL events" such as its national Youth Day in 1931. Here working-class youth were urged to take up the "class struggle," and college youth were not even mentioned (*Daily Worker,* Sept. 2, 1931; also see *Daily Worker,* Jan. 23, 29, 1932; *Young Worker,* May 25, 1931 and Jan. 18, 1932). This does not mean, however, that in 1931 and 1932 the YCL leadership was "cold" towards the NSL, as Hal Draper erroneously suggested in his otherwise illuminating article on the student movement. Interviews with NSL founders and YCL leaders as well as contemporary YCL commentary reflect a supportive attitude towards the NSL from the time of the student movement's first major actions (*Young Worker,* April 11, 18, 1932; Joseph Clark interview with author; Max Gordon interview with author; Hal Draper, "The Student Movement of the Thirties: A Political History," in Rita Simon, ed., *As We Saw the Thirties* (Urbana, 1967), 165.) Though Draper was incorrect about the YCL leadership, his point does have validity for some of the more sectarian rank and filers in the YCL. A vocal group of them did carry to extremes their reverence for blue-collar organizing—contending that the only place for the true revolutionary was among the working class, and that students were so petty bourgeois that communists should not waste their time doing campus organizing. But in contrast to the 1920s, such explicitly anti-student sentiment was rejected by the YCL national leadership in the early 30s and publicly condemned by that leadership in the mid-1930s (Max Gordon interview with author; Max Weiss interview with author; Gil Green, *Young Communists and the Unity of Youth* (New York, 1935), 19; Otto Kuusinen, *The Youth Movement and the Fight Against Fascism* (Moscow, 1935), 18; Gil Green interview with author, Manhattan, N.Y., Sept. 29, 1982).

49. Harry Magdoff interview with author. Magdoff's use of the term "guys" in discussing the NSL's founders should not be taken literally. Women, particularly from Hunter College, played a significant role in this founding group—as Magdoff himself indicated, later in the interview.

50. Max Gordon interview with author.

51. Harry Magdoff interview with author.

52. Joseph Clark interview with author.

53. George Watt interview with author.

54. Theodore Draper interview with author.

55. *Ibid.*

56. In a 1934 essay, SLID leader Joseph P. Lash condemned the Communist Party's policy of instilling "among its members a hatred of rival working class organizations," and blamed this for the general failure of the Party's united fronts. However, he excepted from this generalization the NSL. According to Lash, "The only place they have succeeded is in the student field, where the National Student League has not followed the Party line with respect to the Student L.I.D" (Joseph P. Lash, "Why I Am a Socialist," *The Clionian* (Sept. 1934), 4, CCNY). The NSL was not completely immune to sectarianism, but it was far less pronounced than

in adult and non-student communist and communist-dominated groups. This can be seen, for instance, in the pages of the NSL's national magazine, *Student Review*. There were occasional sectarian attacks on socialists and the LID, but not the stream of vitriol which ran on an almost daily basis in the Communist Party's *Daily Worker* and the YCL's *Young Worker*. According to Theodore Draper, a former editor of the *Student Review*, because the NSL focused primarily on concrete student problems and was well removed from the Party leadership, "we could avoid ideological issues which caused divisions. We were left out of these controversies, which was all to the best because we wouldn't have been interested in them. . . . For example you'd never [in the *Student Review*] have an attack on Trotskyism. . . . The NSL had Manny Geltman, an outright Trotskyist. He came to meetings and was permitted to have his say. In the Party this would have been unspeakable. . . . The NSL, then, had a loyal opposition. We had Trotskyists, Lovestoneites. In fact, in Party organizations you actually didn't talk to Trotskyists; in the NSL you got away with it" (Theodore Draper interview with author).

Trotskyists remained in the NSL throughout the organization's life, as Draper suggests. However, there were some NSL chapters—particularly in Chicago—where YCLers did not display the same degree of tolerance as the NSL's national leadership. The Trotskyist youth newspaper complained that sectarian YCLers had expelled Trotskyists students from the Chicago NSL chapters (*Young Spartacus*, Oct. 1932, Jan. 1933; Emanuel Geltman interview with author, Manhattan, N.Y., Feb. 22, 1982). But since this was the only time anti-Trotskyist expulsions from the NSL were reported in the Trotskyist press, such extreme intolerance does appear to have been the exception rather than the rule in the student organization. This was especially notable because on many occasions the Trotskyist NSLers were strong critics of NSL policy. That criticism usually derived from the Trotskyist's own sectarian spirit. The Trotskyists urged ultra-radical tactics on the NSL, which the League's leader rejected as unrealistic. The NSL leaders correctly sensed that if the League went in the direction advocated by the Trotskyists by always adopting the most revolutionary positions and refusing to compromise with pacifists and other reform-minded students, the League would never be able to mobilize mainstream students, and would remain—like the Trotskyists themselves— a small and isolated group (on Trotskyist criticism of the NSL for its coalition politics, see M. Garrett [Geltman], "The Student Review," *Young Spartacus*, Sept. 1932; "Student Notes," *ibid.*, April 1934). It was this less sectarian mindset which enabled the NSL to pioneer a Popular Front style of coalition politics long before the Communist Party adopted such tactics. Later in the decade, however, a harsh anti-Trotskyist mindset would be carried into the student movement by communist activists (which will be discussed in Chapter 6).

57. "Role of the Student—1931," 2.

58. Theodore Draper interview with author.

59. "For a National Student Movement: A Suggested Basis," 3.

60. *Ibid.*

61. Celeste Strack Kaplan interview with author, Beverly Hills, Jan. 6, 1982; Harry Magdoff interview with author.

62. Joseph Clark, introduction to reprint of *Student Review*, 1; R. F. Hale, "The Tragedy of a Liberal," *Student Review* (Dec. 1931), 13.

63. Wechsler, *The Age of Suspicion*, 36.

64. There are no documents indicating the precise number of students in the NSL at the peak of the organization's strength in Dec. 1935. However, 13 months

earlier the NSL's combined college and high school membership stood at 2,660, according to a fairly detailed listing given out at the League's fourth convention. Since the NSL continued to grow in the coming year it seems safe to estimate the membership at somewhere between 2,660 and 3000 members. Harvey Klehr puts the NSL total at 600–700 members, but this figure is not documented convincingly and was apparently drawn from testimony given to the House Committee on Un-American Activities by Joseph P. Lash. Lash was not an NSLer, and he offered no documentation for this estimate. Since Lash was speaking before this anti-communist committee, he obviously had an interest in minimizing communist influence in the student movement—and particularly in the American Student Union, the group formed when the communist-led NSL merged with the socialist-led SLID (*Bulletin of the Fourth National Convention, National Student League* (St. Louis, 1934), 8–9, President's Papers, UCB; Klehr, *The Heyday of American Communism*, 317, 467).

65. Joseph Clark interview with author.

66. Donald Henderson, "League for Industrial Democracy: What Does It Offer?," *Student Review* (July 1932), 15.

Chapter 3. Springtime of Revolt

1. Harry Laidler, "Across the Country," *LID Monthly* (April 1932), 7.

2. *Student Outpost*, March 22, 1932; Robt. F. Hall, "Kentucky Makes Radicals," *Student Review* (May 1932), 7–8; "Columbia University Strikes," *ibid.* (May 1932), 12–14. Though the major protests, which attracted national attention occurred primarily in the Northeast, this section of the country did not have a monopoly on student activism. At campuses in the Mid- and Far West, small NSL and LID chapters were beginning to stir too at this time. Their actions were less dramatic than their counterparts on the East Coast, but nonetheless, they suggested that the trend toward active protest demonstrated most graphically in the East had the potential to become a national phenomenon. At UC Berkeley, for instance, NSLers in the spring semester of 1932 began agitating against the student government activities fees, which discriminated against low income students. NSLers at the University of Wisconsin began organizing a labor union to protect student employees. NSL activists in Chicago and Washington joined in picket lines with organized labor. The LID chapter at Detroit City College organized a protest against establishing a campus ROTC unit (*Student Outpost*, March 25, 1932. "On the Student Front," *Student Review* (May 1932), 15; Frank Braun, "Detroit's Fighting Pacifists," *LID Monthly* (Jan. 1932), 13).

3. Theodore Draper interview with author; Robert Hall interview with author, Willsboro, N.Y., Dec. 17, 1982.

4. Hall, "Kentucky Makes Radicals," 7–8.

5. Bert Cochran, *Labor and Communism: The Conflict that Shaped American Unions* (Princeton, 1977), 53–54; Malcolm Cowley, *The Dream of the Golden Mountains: Remembering the 1930s* (New York, 1980), 59–60.

6. Cochran, *Labor and Communism*, 53–56; Cowley, *The Dream of the Golden Mountains*. 59–76.

7. Cochran, *Labor and Communism*, 53–56; Cowley, *The Dream of the Golden Mountains*, 59–76.

8. Cowley, *The Dream of the Golden Mountains*, 59–76.

9. See editor's notes introducing article by John Dos Passos "Free Speech Speakin's," *Student Review* (Jan.–Feb. 1932), 5.

10. Dos Passos, "Free Speech Speakin's," 5.

11. CCNY *Campus,* March 4, 1932.

12. Robert Hall to author, Dec. 10, 1982.

13. *Columbia Spectator,* March 22, 1932; *NYT,* March 25, 1932. On other threats made in Kentucky against the students, see *Pineville Sun,* March 17, 1932.

14. Lewis Feuer, *Conflict of Generations: The Character and Significance of Student Movements* (New York, 1969), 354. Though there is some useful information on the Kentucky expedition in Feuer's history of student protest, his psychological interpretation of the expedition (as well as the entire student movement of the 1930s) is narrowly polemical and unconvincing. Feuer tries to fit the Kentucky expedition into his monocausal generational interpretation of all student movements—which holds that student protest is simply the expression of the oedipal rage of youth against their fathers. For a discussion of why Feuer's generational interpretation is inaccurate regarding the Kentucky expedition, see Robert Cohen, "Revolt of the Depression Generation: America's First Mass Student Movement, 1929–1940" (Ph.D. diss., UC Berkeley, 1987), 128–30; on the relative absence of generational rhetoric and rage in the larger student movement of the 1930s, see Chapter 8 of this book.

15. *Columbia Spectator,* March 23, 1932.

16. Letter of one delegation member "to a friend," March 18, 1932, cited in Feuer, *Conflict of Generations,* 354. Feuer apparently inserted the "X" to protect the privacy of the correspondents.

17. Robert Hall to author, Dec. 10, 1982; also see, *Knoxville News-Sentinel,* March 25, 1932.

18. *Harlan Daily Enterprise,* March 27, 1932.

19. Joseph P. Lash, "Students in Kentucky," *New Republic* (April 20, 1932), 267.

20. There is no complete list of the student delegation to Kentucky. All of the participants interviewed by the author stressed that the majority of delegation members were from New York City campuses, but that there was a sprinkling of students from campuses outside the metropolitan area. See Robert Hall interview with the author. From the combined newspaper reports on the delegation, which list about half the students on the trip, the campus breakdown was as follows : 12 students from Hunter College; 9 from Columbia University; 5 from the City College of New York; 3 from New York University; 2 from the University of Cincinnati and 7 others from Ohio; 2 from Harvard, 1 from the Union Theological Seminary; 1 from the University of Tennessee; 1 from the University of Wisconsin; and 1 from Colby College. The group seems to have been diverse in its economic background, ranging from the low-income students in New York's municipal colleges to students from elite private schools, including Margaret Bailey, the daughter of a prominent attorney and director of the American Civil Liberties Union.

21. Feuer, *Conflict of Generations,* 354. In opting for a non-sectarian approach to organizing the Kentucky expedition, the NSL demonstrated substantial initiative and independence from the Comintern's sectarian Third Period line, contradicting Harvey Klehr's claim that communist-led organizations were always totally subservient to the Comintern. When Klehr speaks of the Communist Party's "need to control with an iron fist any organization associated with it," he is speaking in

terms that are simply not relevant to the NSL and the student movement in 1932 (Harvey Klehr, *The Heyday of American Communism: The Depression Decade* (New York, 1984), 83). During this period neither the Comintern nor the adult Party elite understood the potential for building a mass student movement in the United States; they did not demonstrate a desire to control the NSL "with an iron fist."

In an appendix to the most recent edition of his classic history of the American Communist Party, Theodore Draper contends that the story of cooperation between socialist and communist students in 1932 was "largely an apochryphal tale," and "largely imaginary" (*American Communism and Soviet Russia* (New York, 1986), 467). Draper erred here. There was nothing "imaginary" about communist-socialist cooperation in the 1932 student expedition to Kentucky. Socialist expedition members attested to that cooperation (both in 1932 and in retrospect). See the letter cited in Feuer, *Conflict of Generations,* 354; Joseph P. Lash interview with author, Manhattan, N.Y., Nov. 23, 1982; and socialist Student LID leader Joseph P. Lash's glowing review of the communist-led Harlan expedition, "Students in Kentucky," *New Republic* (April 20, 1932), 267–69.

22. Hall, "Kentucky Makes Radicals," 7; Lash, "Students in Kentucky," 269.

23. Gabriel Carritt, "American Students and Kentucky Gunmen," *New Statesmen and Nation* (May 28, 1932), 703; U.S. Congress, Senate Committee on Manufactures, *Hearings on Conditions in the Coal Fields of Harlan and Bell Counties, Kentucky,* 72nd Congress, 1st Session, May 12, 13, 19, 1932, pp. 22–23.

24. Charles Croix, "The Students Invade Kentucky," *New Masses* (May 1932), 9; *Middlesboro, [Ky.] Daily News,* March 26, 1932; U.S. Senate. *Hearings on Conditions in the Coal Fields,* 23; CCNY *Frontiers,* April 1932.

25. Carritt, "American Students and Kentucky Gunmen," 703; *Middlesboro Daily News,* March 26, 1932.

26. Croix, "The Students Invade Kentucky," 10. Jewish representation in the Kentucky expedition was played up not only by the county prosecutor, but by the press in the coal region—apparently exploiting anti-Semitism—to whip up local hostility toward the students. See *Middlesboro Daily News,* March 26, 1932. On the local Jewish community's response to this, see *Middlesboro Daily News,* March 28, 1932; *Pineville Sun,* March 31, 1932.

27. *Middlesboro Daily News,* March 26, 1932; Carritt, "American Students and Kentucky Gunmen," 703; Croix, "Students Invade Kentucky," 10; U.S. Senate, *Hearings on Conditions in the Coal Fields,* 24.

28. Croix, "Students Invade Kentucky"; *Harlan Daily Enterprise,* March 27, 1932.

29. Lash, "Students in Kentucky," 267–68; Carritt, "American Students and Kentucky Gunmen," 703.

30. Croix, "Students Invade Kentucky," 10; U.S. Senate, *Hearings on Conditions in the Coal Fields,* 24.

31. Lash, "Students in Kentucky," 268.

32. *NYT,* March 27, 28, 1932; Hall, "Kentucky Makes Radicals," 7–8.

33. *NYT,* March 29, 1932; *Harlan Daily Enterprise,* March 29, 1932; Hall, "Kentucky Makes Radicals," 7.

34. U.S. Senate, *Hearings on Conditions in the Coal Fields,* 25.

35. *New York Herald-Tribune* editorial reprinted in the *Middlesboro Daily News,* March 27, 1932.

36. Hall, "Kentucky Makes Radicals," 8; Univ. of *Cincinnati Bearcat,* March 30, 1932; Univ. of Toledo *Collegian,* April 14, 1932.

37. On Southern support for the delegation, see Senator Costigan's remarks in U.S. Senate, *Hearings on Conditions in the Coal Fields,* 27.

38. *Columbia Spectator,* March 29, 1932.

39. James Wechsler, *Revolt on the Campus* (New York, 1935), 105–8.

40. *Ibid.,* 107–8.

41. *Ibid.,* 108; Carritt, "American Students and Kentucky Gunmen," 703.

42. Hall, "Kentucky Makes Radicals," 7–9; Lash, "Students in Kentucky," 269; George Glasgow, Charles Schrank, Walter Relis, Morris A. Shapiro, "I Am the Law," *Frontiers* (April 1932), 1; *Middlesboro Daily News,* March 26, 1932.

43. Joseph Clark interview with author.

44. U.S. Senate, *Hearings on Conditions in the Coal Fields,* 21.

45. Lash, "Students in Kentucky," 267–69.

46. Joseph P. Lash interview with author.

47. *Nation* (April 6, 1932), 383.

48. *Middlesboro Daily News,* March 27, 1932.

49. James C. Katz, "The Legacy of Reed Harris '32," *Columbia College Today* (Spring 1983), 34–35; U.S. Congress, Senate Permanent Subcommittee on Investigations of the Committee on Government Operations," Testimony of Reed Harris," 83rd Congress, 1st Session, March 3, 1953, pp. 363–64; Reed Harris, "College Fraternities-Obstacles to Social Change," *Revolt* (Dec. 1932), 7; Reed Harris, "Campus Tammany," *Student Outlook* (May 1933), 15.

50. U.S. Senate, "Testimony of Reed Harris," 375.

51. A good summary of Harris' innovative editorial work can be found in Wechsler, *The Age of Suspicion,* 22–26. Also see *Columbia Spectator,* Sept. 19, Nov. 12, 15, 1931, March 23, 29, 1932. Harris would pay a high price for his editorial radicalism, not only during the 1930s, when he was expelled from Columbia, but also during the Cold War era, when he was hounded by Senator Joseph McCarthy. As deputy chief of the Voice of America, Harris was called to testify in the Wisconsin Senator's inquiry into subversion in the federal government in 1953. Lacking evidence that Harris had been disloyal while serving in the government, McCarthy tried to discredit him by reading radical passages he had written in his youth as a student editor. This reliance on twenty-one year-old evidence made McCarthy's depiction of Harris as a dangerous radical—which Harris in his days of government service was certainly not—seem ludicrous. The "words he had published in a volume called *King Football* more than two decades ago were being hurled at him [by McCarthy] as if they were the text of a subversive directive he had just issued from a strategic government outpost," observed James Wechsler. But Harris stood up to McCarthy and paid for it by losing his job. In the end, however, Harris triumphed over the Wisconsin Senator. His defiant testimony was shown as part of Edward R. Murrow's historic "See it Now" broadcast on CBS, in March 1954, which helped to discredit McCarthy. And in 1961, when Murrow became the head of the U.S. Information Agency he brought Harris back into government service (see James C. Katz, "The Legacy of Reed Harris, Part Two : Confrontation with McCarthy," *Columbia College Today* (Fall 1983), 17–21; Wechsler, *The Age of Suspicion,* 4–5).

52. *Columbia Spectator,* Nov. 10, 1931; Wechsler, *The Age of Suspicion,* 23.

53. *Columbia Spectator,* Nov. 12, 1931

54. Wechsler, *Revolt on the Campus,* 109; Robert Hall, "Student Publications," *Varsity Review* (March 1931), 25.

55. *Columbia Spectator,* Nov. 12, 1931.

56. *Ibid.*

57. *Ibid.*

58. *Columbia Spectator,* March 23, 29, 1932.

59. Wechsler, *Revolt on the Campus,* 112–13; Reed Harris, *King Football: The Vulgarization of the American College* (New York, 1932), 188–92; *NYT,* April 2, 3, 1932.

60. Reed Harris to Dean [Herbert] Hawkes, April 1, 1932, RH; American Civil Liberties Union, *The Case of Reed Harris, Student Editor at Columbia University: His Expulsion for Criticism of College Affairs, and Subsequent Reinstatement* (New York, 1932), 1–2.

61. Harris to Hawkes, April 1, 1932, RH.

62. *NYT,* April 3, 1932.

63. ACLU, "The Case of Reed Harris," 1–10; *Daily Worker,* April 5, 1932. On the violations of academic freedom at Columbia during World War I, see Walter Metzger, *Academic Freedom in the Age of the University* (New York, 1955), 225. Political intolerance on campus in the early 1930s seemed to grow as the economic crisis did. The cases of reported violations of academic freedom almost quadrupled during the first three years of the Depression, according to the American Association of University Professors (see *Student Review* (Feb. 1933), 3). On the persistence of such political intolerance throughout the first half of the Depression decade, see James Wechsler, *Revolt on the Campus* 185–325; Harris, *King Football,* 146–58.

64. *NYT,* April 3, 1932.

65. *Ibid.,* May 12, 1935; Nicholas Murray Butler, "University Freedom," *School and Society* (Jan. 18, 1936), 99–100; Nicholas M. Butler to John Godfrey Saxe, April 9, 1932, RH.

66. Harris, *King Football,* 195.

67. *Ibid.,* 192–93.

68. *Ibid.,* 196.

69. "Private Government on the Campus—Judicial Review of University Expulsions," *Yale Law Journal* (1963), 1367.

70. *Anthony v. Syracuse Univ.,* 224 App. Div. 487, 489, 231 N.Y.S. 435, 438 (1928); William G. Millington, *The Law and the College Student: Justice in Evolution* (St. Paul, Minn., 1979), 10–11.

71. *Barker v. Bryn Mawr College,* 278 Pa., 121, 122 Atl. 220 (1923); John B. Stetson Univ., 88 Fla. 510, 516, 102 So. 637, 649 (1924); *Koblitz v. Western Reserve Univ.,* 21 Ohio C.C.R. 144 (Cuyahoga Co.), 11 Ohio C.C. Dec 515 (1901); State *ex rel. Ingersoll v. Clapp,* 81 Mont. 200, 263, 263 Pac. 443, *cert. denied,* 277 U.S. 591 *error dismissed,* 278 U.S. 661 (1928); "Private Government on the Campus," 1373.

72. *Samson v. Trustees of Columbia Univ.,* 101 Misc. 146, 167 N.Y. Supp. 202 (1917); *People ex rel. Goldenkoff v. Albany Law School,* 198 App. Div. 460, 191 N.Y. Supp. 349 (1921); *Hamilton v. Regents of the Univ. of California,* 293 U.S. 245 (1934); David W. Lousiell, "A Statement on the Legal Issues," Seymour Martin Lipset and Sheldon S. Wolin, eds., *The Berkeley Student Revolt: Facts and Interpretations* (Garden City, N.Y., 1965), 281. These legal limitations on student political rights were not lifted until the 1960s. See Millington, *The Law and the College Student,* 16–70, 160–226.

73. "For a National Student Movement: A Suggested Basis," *Student Review* (Jan.–Feb. 1932), 4.

74. *NYT,* April 4, 5, 1932.

75. *Ibid.*; *Columbia Spectator*, April 5, 1932; ACLU, "The Case of Reed Harris," 2–12.

76. *Columbia Spectator*, April 4, 1932.

77. CCNY *Campus*, April 6, 8, 12, 1932; *NYT*, April 4, 1932; Univ. of Buffalo *Bee*, April 8, 1932.

78. *New York World-Telegram*, April 6, 1932; *Nation* (April 13, 1932), 411; *New Republic* (April 13, 1932), 219.

79. *NYT*, April 5, 1932; Wechsler, *The Age of Suspicion*, 27–28.

80. *NYT*, April 5, 1932; Wechsler, *The Age of Suspicion*, 27.

81. *NYT*, April 7, 1932; "Strike Today," leaflet, CUC.

82. *NYT*, April 7, 1932.

83. *Ibid.*

84. Wechsler, *The Age of Suspicion*, 29–30.

85. *New York World-Telegram*, April 7, 1932.

86. James Wechsler, *The Age of Suspicion*, 25.

87. *NYT*, April 10, 1932.

88. *NYT*, April 21, 1932; John Godfrey Saxe to Nicholas Murray Butler, April 19, 1932, RH; N.M. McKnight telegram to H.E. Hawkes, May 2, 1932, RH.

89. Nicholas Murray Butler to John Godfrey Saxe, April 21, 1932, RH.

90. John Godfrey Saxe memorandum to President Butler, Dean Hawkes et al., April 22, 1932, RH.

91. John Godfrey Saxe to Nicholas Murray Butler, April 25, 1932; John Godfrey Saxe, "Confidential Interim Report" on the Reed Harris case, sent to President Butler et al., April 15, 1932; John Godfrey Saxe memorandum to President Butler et al., April 14, 1932. All in RH.

92. John Godfrey Saxe to Nicholas Murray Butler, April 19, 1932, RH.

93. *NYT*, April 21, 1932.

94. *Ibid.*

95. *Ibid.*

96. *Columbia Spectator*, April 21, 1932.

97. *Ibid.*;"Columbia University Strikes," *Student Review* (May 1932), 12–14. This was to be the first, but not the last time Harris would be unable to obtain a Columbia degree. During the final years of Harris' life, his admirers at Columbia, including Columbia Professor Fred Friendly, who had helped produce the Murrow exposé on McCarthy, fought in vain to have the University grant the ailing former editor a Columbia degree ("Reed Harris' Death: Columbia's Disgrace," *Columbia Spectator*, Oct. 22, 1982). The year after his death, however, Columbia finally honored Harris by endowing the Reed Harris Memorial Lecture on Free Speech and the First Amendment (Katz, "The Legacy of Reed Harris, Part Two," 21).

98. Wechsler, *The Age of Suspicion*, 25.

99. *Ibid.*, 30–31.

100. *Ibid.*

101. Hilda Rubin, "The Students Fight Fees," *Student Review* (July 1932), 11–13. Nathan Solomon interview with author, Pound Ridge, N.Y., May 13, 1982; Ted Draper, "What About Fees?," *Frontiers* (Nov. 1932), 6.

102. *Ibid.*; Thomas Coulton, *A City College in Action: Struggles and Achievement at Brooklyn College, 1930–1955* (New York, 1955), 104–5. The NSL questionnaire on fees is reprinted in Oakley Johnson, "Campus Battles for Freedom in the Thirties," *Centennial Review* (Summer 1970), 350–51.

103. *NYT*, May 24, 1932: Nathan Solomon interview with author.

104. CCNY *Campus,* April 29, 1932; *NYT,* May 25–26, 1932; Coulton, *A City College in Action,* 105; *Hunter Bulletin,* May 9, 1932.

105. Rubin, "Students Fight Fees," 13; *NYT,* May 28, 1932.

106. Rubin, "Students Fight Fees," 13; *NYT,* June 11, 1932.

107. *Ibid.*

108. *NYT,* March 26, 1932; Rubin, "Students Fight Fees," 13.

109. *NYT,* June 4, 1932; Draper, "What About Fees?," 6.

110. *NYT,* Oct. 16, 24, Nov. 3, 1932.

111. *Student Review* (May 1932), 6, 15; *Young Worker,* April 18, 1932; *Young Spartacus,* June 1932.

112. Beluah Amidon, "After College—What?," *Survey Graphic* (June 1933), 320; *NYT,* June 21, 24, 1932; *Student Outpost,* March 25, 1932.

113. *NYT,* June 6, 1932.

114. *Student Review* (July 1932), 3.

Chapter 4. The Making of a Mass Movement

1. *Daily Tar Heel,* Nov. 3, 1932; *Harvard Crimson,* Oct. 31, 1932; James Wechsler, *The Age of Suspicion* (New York, 1981), 40; *Vassar Miscellany News,* Oct. 29, Nov. 15, 1932; "Why Students Are Turning to Socialism," *Revolt* (Dec. 1932), 3. Because most undergraduates were not of voting age (which was 21) in 1932, the college straw polls are the best guide to student political opinion of the Presidential race that year, which is why the discussion of student views of those elections in this chapter draws upon those polls.

2. "Coolidge Carries Colleges," *New Student* (Nov. 1, 1924), 1–4; *NYT,* Oct. 29, 1928; *Daily Californian,* Nov. 1, 1928; Norman Thomas, "Conservatism Is Jarred—Push on to Socialism," *Revolt* (Dec. 1932), 13; *Harvard Crimson,* Oct. 21, 1932.

3. *Daily Californian,* Oct. 19, 1932.

4. *Ibid.,* Oct. 14, 1932.

5. *Columbia Spectator,* Dec. 1, 1932; *Barnard Bulletin,* Oct. 18, 1932; William Leuchtenburg, *Franklin D. Roosevelt and the New Deal* (New York, 1963), 10.

6. "Coolidge Carries Colleges," 1–4; *NYT,* Oct. 29, 1928; *Daily Californian,* Nov. 1, 1928.

7. *Columbia Spectator,* Oct. 28, 1932; Robert S. McElvaine, *The Great Depression* (New York, 1984), 133.

8. "Why Students Are Turning to Socialism," 17.

9. Wechsler, *The Age of Suspicion,* 40–41.

10. "Why Students Are Turning to Socialism," 3, 17; Joseph P. Lash interview with author.

11. On the more militant, action-oriented style of the LID in fall 1932, see "Blueprints of Action: A Handbook for Student Revolutionists," *Revolt* (Oct. 1932), 2. Here the LID began to sound like the NSL, in calling for the building of a *student* movement with an agenda for protest on a series of campus related issues ranging from opposition to ROTC to support for academic freedom. Responding to the NSL's charge that they had been merely an appendage of the adult LID, student LIDers became more autonomous—founding their own magazine in 1932 (modeled after the NSL's *Student Review*) and calling their organization the *Student* League for Industrial Democracy (SLID) in 1933.

12. *Michigan Daily,* Nov. 4, 1932.

13. *Daily Tar Heel,* Oct. 28, 1932; *NYT,* Oct. 28, 1932.

14. The NSL's lack of enthusiasm for electoral politics was reflected in the pages of its national magazine in fall 1932. The League ran only one story on the election. The story was of course pro-CP, but stopped short of endorsing any ticket (to preserve its official non-partisan status). The NSL also buried the letter from Communist Party candidates William Z. Foster and James W. Ford near the end of the Oct. 1932 issue of *Student Review.*

15. On the political distinctions between the YPSLs and the SLIDers, see Hal Draper, "The Student Movement of the 1930s: A Political History," in Rita Simon, ed., *As We Saw the Thirties* (Urbana, 1969), 158–59. Note, however, that Draper's account, though generally quite incisive, at points becomes inaccurate because of his pro-YPSL bias. Draper, a former national leader of the YPSL, exaggerates the importance of the YPSLs and overlooks their weaknesses. For instance, he writes that the student YPSLs were "numerically more important than the 'LID types.' " This would have been true only in a few metropolitan centers, such as New York and Chicago. In most of the country, the SLID was a much larger student organization than the YPSL and had chapters where there were no YPSLs (see Monroe Sweetland interview with author, San Mateo, Calif., March 6, 1982). Moreover, though the YPSLs brought their energy and militance to the student movement, as doctrinaire socialists they also tended to be somewhat sectarian, a problem whose negative impact on the student movement will discussed in Chapter 6. For examples of complaints about YPSL sectarianism, see Jeffrey Campbell to Al Hamilton et al., June 2, 1938; Harry Laidler to Al Hamilton, March 3, 1937; Al Hamilton to Harry Kingman, March 20, 1937. All in YPSL files, SP.

16. *Columbia Spectator,* Oct. 28, 1932.

17. Joseph P. Lash interview with the author.

18. *Ibid.*

19. *Michigan Daily,* April 20, 1933; *Daily Californian,* March 14, 1933.

20. *Daily Californian,* March 22, 28, 1933; *Columbia Spectator,* April 18, 1933.

21. *The* [London] *Times,* Feb. 11, 1933; *NYT,* March 18, 1933.

22. *The* [London] *Times,* Feb. 13, 17, 18, 1933; *NYT,* March 17, 1933.

23. *NYT,* March 18, 1933; *The* [London] *Times,* March 3, 1933.

24. "Refuse to Fight!," *Student Outlook* (May 1933), 3; Harold Seidman, "The Colleges Renounce War," *Nation* (May 17, 1933), 554; *NYT,* May 25, 1933; Univ. of Toledo *Collegian,* April 7, 1933.

25. *NYT,* May 25, 1933.

26. *NYT,* March 28, 1933; *Daily Californian,* March 9, 15, 1933.

27. F.M. Hardie, "Political Tendencies at Oxford," *New Statesman and Nation* (Feb. 18, 1933), 182.

28. *Brown Daily Herald,* March 22, 1933; Joseph P. Lash, *The Campus Strikes Against War* (New York, 1935), 27.

29. Joseph P. Lash and James A. Wechsler, *War Our Heritage* (New York, 1936), 43. For examples of the great influence that the First World War had on student anti-war thought during the early and mid-1930s, see *Barnard Bulletin,* Oct. 20, 1933; *Columbia Spectator,* Oct. 16, 17, 1933; *Daily Texan,* Dec. 11, 1934; *Vassar Miscellany News,* Nov. 13, 1935; *Ohio State Lantern,* Nov. 8, 1935; *Daily Tar Heel,* Nov. 8, 1935.

30. Al Hamilton, *Students Against War* (Chicago, 1937), 30–31; Warren Cohen,

The American Revisionists: The Lessons of Intervention in World War I (Chicago, 1967), 50–51, 113, 132–33, 144.

31. Charles Chatfield, *For Peace and Justice: Pacifism in America, 1914–1941* (Knoxville, 1971), 168. For examples of the popularity of this economic interpretation of war among students, see *Program and Resolutions of the Student Congress Against War* (Chicago, 1932), 2; "The Student and War," Univ. of Wisconsin *New Student* (Dec. 1933), 4–6; Buffalo *Bee*, Nov. 16, 1934; Univ. of West Virginia *Daily Athenaeum*, Dec. 7, 1934; *Emory Wheel*, Dec. 7, 1934; UCLA *Anti-war Bulletin*, March 11, 1935; *Dartmouth*, Jan. 10, 1936; *Daily Tar Heel*, May 5, 1936.

32. Eric Sevareid, *Not So Wild a Dream* (New York, 1956), 61.

33. Lash and Wechsler, *War Our Heritage*, 49.

34. "Refuse to Fight!," 3.

35. Sevareid, *Not So Wild a Dream*, 62.

36. *Ibid.*, 61; *Columbia Spectator*, March 6, April 3, 1935; Lash, *The Campus Strikes Against War*, 21; James Wechsler, *Revolt on the Campus* (1935: reprint Seattle, 1973), 11–21.

37. Al Hamilton, *Students Against War* (Chicago, 1937), 28.

38. Lash and Wechsler, *War Our Heritage*, 42–43.

39. Wechsler, *Revolt on the Campus*, 120.

40. Lash and Wechsler, *War Our Heritage*, 36.

41. Leuchtenburg, *Franklin D. Roosevelt and the New Deal*, 197.

42. Lash and Wechsler, *War Our Heritage*, 101.

43. *Daily Worker*, Jan. 17, 1933; Colonel J.E. Woodward to the Adjutant General, Jan. 11, 1933, "Estimate of the Subversive Situation for the Month of December 1932," 18 *U.S. Military Intelligence Reports: Surveillance of Radicals in the US, 1917–1941* (Frederick, Md., 1984), reel 24.

44. Joseph Cohen, "We Are International," *Student Review* (Oct. 1932), 11–12; also see call to Chicago Congress on p. 13 of the same issue. Note that Joseph Cohen changed his surname to Clark, and it appears (with the exception of one quotation) as Clark in the text.

45. The student LID leadership came close to splitting the college antiwar movement in 1932, when it organized its own peace conference in New York a month prior to the Chicago Congress and seemed bent on refusing to participate in the Chicago Congress. But at the LID's anti-war conference, the delegates—after a sustained floor fight—opted for a more cooperative stance and agreed to send representatives to the Chicago Congress (see *Young Spartacus*, Jan. 1933; "An Open Letter"; Arthur J. Bartlett, "An Antiwar Conference," *Student Review* (Dec. 1932), 12–13; Ben Fischer, "Realism in Anti-War Discussions," *Student Outlook* (Feb. 1933), 5).

46. Fischer, "Realism in Anti-War Discussions," 5. On the controversy surrounding the resolution about the Socialist International's role in supporting the First World War, see Woodward to the Adjutant General, Jan. 11, 1933, "Estimate of the Subversive Situation for the Month of December 1932," 18.

47. Harry Magdoff interview with author.

48. *Daily Worker*, Jan. 17, 1933; "Carry on the Work," *Student Review* (Feb. 1933), 13.

49. Fischer, "Realism in Anti-War Discussions," 5; *Program and Resolutions of the Student Congress Against War* (Chicago, 1932), 2; *Columbia Spectator*, Jan. 4, 1933.

50. Chatfield, *For Peace and Justice*, 155; Hamilton, *Students Against War*, 25;

Wechsler, *Revolt on the Campus,* 146; Fischer, "Realism in Anti-War Discussions," 5; *Breaking the War Habit,* Feb. 15, 1933; *I Resign* (New York, 1932), passim.

51. Buffalo *Bee,* Jan. 13, 1933; Fischer, "Realism in Anti-War Discussions," 5.

52. Howard Stone, "After the Student Congress?" *Student Review* (Feb. 1933), 13; *Daily Worker,* Jan. 17, 1933.

53. Wechsler, *Revolt on the Campus,* 136; *Columbia Spectator,* Jan. 4, 1933.

54. Joseph P. Lash, Untitled typescript of a lecture on the student movement of the 1930s, 18, JPL

55. Hamilton, *Students Against War,* 9; Wechsler, *Revolt on the Campus,* 141.

56. Joseph Clark interview with author; Hal Draper, "The Student Movement of the 1930s," 169–70.

57. Joseph Clark interview with author. Though acknowledging that he and the other NSL leaders took the initiative on the Oxford Pledge without CP approval, Clark also emphasized that if the Communist Party had been inflexible and come out against the Pledge—which it did not—the NSL would have complied by dropping the Pledge. Clark's point in the interview was that political creativity and autonomy of the communist student activists were always capable of being nullified by CP leaders because these young communists were subject to Party discipline.

58. NSL National Executive Committee, "An Open Letter," *Student Review* (Dec. 1933), 5–6; "One Big Student Movement?," *Student Outlook* (Feb. 1934), 3, 22.

59. On the origins of the student strike against war, see Lash, *The Campus Strikes Against War,* 31. Cooperation between communist and socialist students was not an infrequent occurrence during these pre-Popular Front years, as student activists repeatedly proved themselves less sectarian than their adult counterparts (see *Daily Cardinal,* April 30, 1933; CCNY *Campus,* April 28, May 12, 1933; *Columbia Spectator,* Oct. 17, Nov. 17, 1933; Richard Criley interview with author, Carmel, Calif., June 17, 1982).

60. "April 13th—Strike Against War," *Student Outlook* (March 1934), 4; Lash, *The Campus Strikes Against War,* 34.

61. Transcript of Joseph P. Lash interview with Joel Chernoff, April 2, 1978, p. 18, JPL; Joseph P. Lash, untitled typescript of a lecture on the student movement of the 1930s, 19, JPL; "Why a Strike," *Student Outlook* (April 1935), 3–4.

62. *NYT,* April 14, 1934; "Students Strike Against War," *Student Outlook* (May 1934), 12–16. Not all students, however, welcomed the antiwar strike. As was the case in the Reed Harris strike, conservative students—centered in the fraternities, athletic teams and ROTC—opposed the strike, and in several cases expressed their opposition through violence. These foes of the antiwar strike acted on the belief that the strikes were unpatriotic and uncollegiate. Their outbursts did not lead to any institutionalized conservative student resistance to the antiwar movement at the national level; and they virtually died out by the time of the third antiwar strike (see Wechsler, *Revolt on the Campus,* 347–63; Heywood Broun, "Harvard Indifference," Heywood Hale Broun, ed., *Collected Edition of Heywood Broun* (New York, 1941), 332–34; Robert Cohen, "Revolt of the Depression Generation: America's First Mass Student Movement, 1929–41" (Ph.D. diss., UC Berkeley, 1987), 346–52.

63. Eunice Barnard, "Students Lay a Barrage Against War," *NYT Magazine* (April 19, 1934), 5.

64. Joseph P. Lash interview with author.

65. Leuchtenburg, *Franklin D. Roosevelt and the New Deal*, 218.

66. On the influence that the Nye Committee investigation had upon students, see Ernest R. Bryan, "Munition Makers on the Spot," *National Student Mirror* (Nov. 1934), 25–27; Univ. of Wisconsin *New Student*, Dec. 1934; *Barnard Bulletin*, April 9, 1935; *Daily Tar Heel*, Dec. 3, 1935; *Brooklyn College Pioneer*, April 10, 1935; *The Dartmouth*, April 12, 1936; Joseph P. Lash, "Morgan: Wanted for Murder," *Student Advocate* (Feb. 1936), 10–11.

67. Major G. W. Lester to Assistant Chief of Staff, "Internal Report Reference on the Subversive Situation," Nov. 26, 1935, p. 12, *U.S. Military Intelligence Reports: Surveillance of Radicals in the US, 1917–1941*, reel 24; *Oberlin Review*, April 11, 1935; "Why a Strike," 4.

68. Joseph P. Lash to Hayes Beall, Feb. 28, 1935; Rix Pierce Butler to Joseph P. Lash, March 5, 1935, both in JPL.

69. Wechsler, *Revolt on the Campus*, 179–80; *NYT*, April 13, 1935.

70. *Ibid.*

71. Hamilton, *Students Against War*, 19.

72. *Barnard Bulletin*, April 16, 1935. A similar political message was articulated on campuses across the nation. See *NYT*, April 13, 1935; *Daily Texan*, April 13, 1935; *Harvard Crimson*, April 14, 1935; Univ. of Virginia *College Topics*, April 12, 1935; *Oberlin Review*, April 11, 1935; *Challenge of Youth*, April 1935; Lash, *The Campus Strikes Against War*, 34.

73. Chatfield, *For Peace and Justice*, 259–60; *Ohio State Lantern*, Nov. 18, 1935.

74. Joseph Clark interview with author.

75. "Refuse to Fight!," 3.

76. *Ibid.*; "War is Now an Immediate Probability," *Student Outlook* (Oct. 1935), 4.

77. Jean Ford, "The CCC Stands Ready," *Student Outlook* (March 1934), 8–9; Selig Adler, *The Isolationist Impulse* (New York, 1961), 219–49; Hamilton, *Students Against War*, 32. Though the student movement depicted the U.S. as an aggressive war machine, the American standing army in 1934 was composed of only 118,750 men ("A Student Strike Against War," *Literary Digest* (March 23, 1935), 17).

78. Adler, *The Isolationist Impulse*, 238–43.

79. *Daily Californian*, April 14, 1933; Ruth Rubin, "I Heckled Luther," *Student Review* (Jan. 1934), 7–8; Edwin Alexander, "Guttersnipes at City," *Student Review* (Dec. 1934), 11–12; *Harvard Crimson*, May 22, 1934.

80. *NYT*, May 10, 11, 1933; Philip Metcalfe, *1933* (New York, 1988), 122; *Harvard Crimson*, May 7, 16, 18, 1934.

Chapter 5. Spies, Suppression, and Free Speech on Campus

1. Celeste Strack interview with author. The most thorough published account of the repression of student free speech rights on campus during the first half of the Depression decade is James Wechsler, *Revolt on the Campus* (1935: reprint, Seattle, 1973), 185–435. This was the first book-length account of the student movement of the 1930s, written by a leader of that movement. The fact that Wechsler, then a NSL and YCL activist, devoted more than half of the book to political repression and free speech suggests that the issue of student political rights was of critical importance to the student movement. Wechsler's account is also valuable in that it provides a wealth of information about collegiate free speech

battles in this era. But as a young communist, Wechsler proved unable to keep his partisanship out of the narrative, and the result is an interpretation of the national campus scene which tends to overdramatize and exaggerate the threat from the American Right in the 1930s.

Wechsler viewed the rise of political repression on college campuses in the U.S. during the first half of the Depression decade as evidence that America was experiencing a full scale red scare, which he saw as an ominous sign of the nation's potential to drift toward fascism (197, 223). What Wechsler failed to see here—in part because he was writing during the height of this repression in 1935—was that the repression would fade, and that it would prove unsuccessful in either hindering the growth of the student movement or producing an effective red scare. Indeed, Wechsler was so anxious to trumpet the danger from the Right and to apply the term "red scare" to the national campus political scene in the 1930s that he became much too loose in his use of that term. When a red scare sweeps the nation, as it did in 1919 and in the early 1950s, an almost hysterical anti-radicalism becomes popularized, leading to massive intolerance of the Left and the smashing or radical organizations both on campus and off. Though anti-radicals hoped to launch such a red scare in the early Depression years—and fostered the suppression of radicalism on campus wherever they could—they failed miserably, and the student Left therefore was able in the mid-1930s to experience one of its greatest periods of growth and influence in twentieth-century America.

2. FBI Office Memorandum, Clyde Tolson and the Executive Conference to The Director [of the FBI], March 28, 1949. Copies of this and all the FBI documents cited below are in the author's possession and were obtained under the Freedom of Information Act; they are also available in FBI headquarters in Washington, D.C. Though the documents provide a valuable glimpse of the informing against student protesters of the 1930s and early 1940s, they are not complete. The FBI censored the documents by frequently deleting the names of its informants, and at some points deleting entire pages of the documents.

3. In more than 3000 pages of FBI documents covering the student movement of the Depression decade, I did not find a single case in which a college or university administrator refused to cooperate with the FBI. None expressed any concern that informing on students might constitute a violation of their rights.

4. On the Univ. of Pennsylvania, see FBI file #61–136, Sept. 28, 1942, Report made by Harry C. Leslie Jr., Philadelphia; on Ohio State Univ., see FBI file # 100–365, June 18, 1941, Report made by D.G. Jenkins, Cincinnati; on Montana State Univ., see FBI file # 61–195, Aug. 12, 1941, Report made by Elmer W. Parrish, Butte; on Temple Univ., see FBI file #61–136, Sept. 28, 1942, Report made by Harry C. Leslie Jr., Philadelphia; on Purdue Univ., see FBI file #100–475, Nov. 12, 1942, Report made by Douglas J. Williams, Indianapolis; on the Univ. of Illinois, see FBI file# 100–191, Jan. 10, 1941, Report made by W.A. Temple, Springfield; FBI file #100–191, Feb. 1, Aug. 27, Oct. 30, 1941, Reports made by J.J. Racan, Springfield; FBI file #100–191, Nov. 14, 1941, Report made by Arthur R. Day, Springfield; FBI file# 100–191, April 21, 1942, Report made by Charles F. Douglas, Springfield; on the Univ. of Missouri, see FBI file # 100–1193, Oct. 10, 1941, Report made by R.E. Sherk, Kansas City; FBI file# 100–1193, Dec. 5, 1941, Report made by W.C. Fuller, Kansas City; FBI file #100–1193, March 21, 1942, Report made by R.B. Ayers, Kansas City; on Middlebury College, see FBI file #100–483, Feb. 6, 1942, Report made by Frank C. Wood, Albany, N.Y.; on DePauw Univ., see FBI file #100–475, Feb. 20 [?], 1941, Report

made by Richard C. Godfrey, Indianapolis; on the Univ. of Minnesota, see [FBI file# illegible], Feb. 1, 1941, Report made by R.T. Noonan, St. Paul, Minn.; on the Univ. of Hawaii, see FBI file #100–1241, June 28, 1941, Report made by John I. Condon, Honolulu; on the Univ. of Washington, see FBI file # 100–942, July 3, 1941, Report made by R.D. Auerbach, Seattle; on Yale Univ., see [day and month illegible], 1941, [Reporting FBI agent's name illegible], New Haven; FBI file #100–589, [month illegible], 21, 1941, and July 17, 1942, Reports made by G. J. McDonough, New Haven; FBI file #100–589, Oct. 7, 1942, Report made by Charles E. Stine, New Haven; Sigmund Diamond, "Surveillance in the Academy: Harry B. Fisher and Yale University, 1927–1952," *American Quarterly* (Spring 1984), 7–43; on Wesleyan Univ., see FBI file #100–589, 1941 [month and day illegible, reporting agent name illegible] New Haven; on Oberlin College, see FBI file # 100–608, Sept. 3, 1941, Report made by S.E. Hobbs, Cleveland; on Wilson Teachers College, see FBI file# 100–920, Sept. 14, 1942, Report made by M.J. Connolly, Washington D.C.; on George Washington Univ., see FBI file# 100–920, Sept. 14, 1942, Report made by M. J. Connolly, Washington, D.C.; on Indiana State Teachers College, see FBI file #100–475, Feb. 20 [?], 1941, Report made by Richard C. Godfrey, Indianapolis; on the Univ. of Chicago, see FBI file # 61–327, Dec. 6, 1941, Report made by J.F. Desmond, Chicago; On the Univ. of Michigan, see FBI file #100–1217, Feb. 8, 1943, Report made by John C. Hall, Detroit; on Ohio Univ. at Athens, see FBI file # 100–365, May 27, 1941, Report made by A.W. Richardson, Cincinnati; FBI file #100–365, March 9, 1942, Report made by J.T. Delaney, Cincinnati; On Earlham College, see FBI file #100–475, Jan. 23, 1943, Report made by George A. Brouillard, Indianapolis.

5. There is evidence of similar political intelligence work at several other campuses. See Confidential Report on American Student Union meeting held in the Michigan Union on Nov. 11, [1940]; City of Ann Arbor Police Report, Nov. 18, 1940, both in Dean of Students Papers, UM; Colonel Edward Kimmel to Commanding General Ninth Corps Area, May 21, 1938, Presidents' Papers, UW. Political surveillance of UCLA student activists will be discussed later in this chapter.

6. Monroe Deutsch to Earl Warren, M.B. Driver, Sheriff of Alameda County, Hollis Thompson, Berkeley City Manager, J.F. Hassler, Oakland City Manager, Ralph Bryant, Alameda City Manager, J.A. Greening, Berkeley Chief of Police, B.A. Wallman, Oakland Chief of Police, Vern Smith, Alameda Chief of Police, Fred Heere, Piedmont Chief of Police, James F. Hooey, District Attorney, Contra Costa County, R. R. Veale, Sheriff of Contra Costa County, J.A. McVittie, Richmond City Manager, David P. Barrows, General, California National Guard, Joseph P. Sanches, Adjutant, Berkeley Post No.7, American Legion, L.C. Thumen, Oakland Post No. 5, American Legion, James K. Fisk, Department Adjutant of the California American Legion, July 23, 1934, President's Files, UCB; Earl Warren to Provost Monroe Deutsch, July 24, 1934, President's Files, UCB. In this letter to Deutsch, Warren alludes to a May 1934 meeting he had with UC Comptroller Luther Nichols and another UC administrator, during which he had urged the University to take a strong stand against campus radicalism. He also agreed to provide the UC police and administration with any intelligence information that his office gathered on campus radicals at Berkeley.

7. Monroe Deutsch to Earl Warren [et al.], July 23, 1934, President's Files, UCB.

8. Albert E. Boynton to Robert G. Sproul, Aug. 22, 1934; Robert G. Sproul

to Albert E. Boynton Aug. 24, 1934; Monroe Deutsch Memorandum to the President, Aug. 9, 1934, President's Files, UCB.

9. Harry Noland, Monterey County District Attorney to President Sproul, Nov. 1, 1934; Robert G. Sproul to E.A. Hugill, UC Berkeley Grounds and Buildings, Nov. 3, 1934, both in President's Files, UCB; Sproul also responded to Noland's report on Criley's political affiliation by thanking him, writing Noland that it was "most helpful to know the background of these persons with whom one must deal" (Sproul to Noland, Nov. 3, 1934, President's Files, UCB). Sproul's letter to Hugill, asking him to obtain further information on Criley is revealing in that it shows that the president's office used Hugill's department—Building and Grounds—in conjunction with the campus police to gather intelligence on the student Left at UC Berkeley (see E.A. Hugill to Robert G. Sproul, Aug. 23, 1934; Monroe Deutsch to Robert G. Sproul, Aug. 22, 1934; Harold Ellis Memorandum for President Sproul, Oct. 31, 1934 (which suggests that Hugill's department photographed radicals and student protest meetings as part of its political surveillance work). All in President's Files, UCB).

10. Monroe Deutsch to Robert G. Sproul, Nov. 8, 1934, President's Files, UCB.

11. *Ibid.*

12. David P. Barrows to Monroe Deutsch, Aug. 1, 1934; David P. Barrows to Monroe Deutsch, Aug. 22, 1934, President's Files, UCB.

13. David P. Barrows to Monroe Deutsch, Aug. 22, 1934.

14. *Ibid.*; David P. Barrows to Monroe Deutsch, Aug. 1, 1934.

15. *NYT*, May 19, 1935. For an incisive discussion of this notion—widespread among campus administrators—that radical activism was antithetical to the intellectual mission of the university, see Marianne Ruth Phelps, "The Response of Higher Education to Student Activism, 1933–1938" (Ph.D. diss., George Washington Univ., 1980), 74–75.

16. Charles Wesley Flint, "Academic Freedom," *Educational Record* (Oct. 1935), 442.

17. Robert Gordon Sproul, "Problems of an American University," *School and Society* (May 30, 1936), 723–24.

18. L.D. Goffman, "The Exploitation of Youth," *Educational Record* (Jan. 1936), 95–96.

19. Wechsler, *Revolt on the Campus,* 208.

20. *Daily Californian,* Oct. 30, 1934.

21. Wechsler, *Revolt on the Campus,* 190; Ruthven proved true to his word, expelling four University of Michigan students in 1935 because of their antiwar organizing. See Wechsler, *Revolt on the Campus,* 191; Nicholas Olds to President Ruthven, Oct. 8, 1935; Ruthven to Olds, Oct. 9, 1935; both in ACLU.

22. Flint, "Academic Freedom," 433, 439.

23. On this notion that student speech was not protected by the right of academic freedom, see Chapter 3 of this study, and see *NYT*, May 12, 1935.

24. Sproul, "Problems of an American University," 723.

25. James L. McConaughy, "Education in a Democracy," *School and Society* (Sept. 25, 1937), 389.

26. Sproul, "Problems of an American University," 724.

27. McConaughy, "Education in a Democracy," 387.

28. Wechsler's *Revolt on the Campus* documents abrogations of student political rights at Berea (218–22); UC Berkeley (279–83); CCNY and the CCNY Busi-

ness School (383–96); the Univ. of Colorado (187); Columbia Univ.(406–16); Commonwealth College (245–57); Connecticut State College (310–24); Harvard, (347–54); Hunter College (396–402); UCLA (274–79); Los Angeles Jr. College, (192–93); MIT(336–44), Univ. of Michigan (190–92); Michigan State Univ. (299–310); Univ. of Missouri (438); Oregon State Univ. (344–45); Univ. of Pittsburgh (198–206); San Jose State College (275); Santa Clara Univ. (189–190); Syracuse Univ. (207–12); Univ. of Virginia (346); George Washington Univ.(189); Univ. of Washington (187–188); Univ. of Wisconsin (331–33).

For campus free speech violations not covered by Wechsler, see Case Technical College, Alexander Buchman, "Smashing the Campus Revolt," *Student Review* (April 1933), 8; and *Cleveland Student*, March 8, 1933, ACLU; the Univ. of Chicago, *NYT*, April 13, 1935; Fisk Univ., *The Crisis* (April 1934), 111; Hartwick College, *Time* (June 5, 1933), 44; Howard Univ., Rayford Logan, *Howard University: The First Hundred Years, 1867–1967* (New York, 1968), 392; Johns Hopkins Univ., *NYT*, April 14, 1934; Hunter College Bronx Extension, *Hunter Bulletin*, Oct. 24, 1933; the Univ. of Idaho, Merwin R. Sawnson, "Student Radicals at the Southern Branch: Campus Protest in the 1930s," *Idaho Yesterdays* (Fall 1976), 21–26 ; Louisiana State Univ. "Strike of Students of Journalism at the State University of Louisiana," *School and Society* (Dec. 8, 1934), 766; MacMurray College, Monroe Sweetland to American Civil Liberties Union, April 29, 1935, ACLU; Marietta College, "Campus Notes," *Student Review* (April 1935), 13; the Univ. of Maryland, *National Student Mirror* (Oct. 1934), 12; Medill Jr. College, Jean Horie, "The War-Makers Strike Back," *Student Review* (June 1935), 9; the Univ. of Minnesota, Richard M. Scammon and Lester Breslow, "Booting Out ROTC." *Student Outlook* (Oct. 1934), 13; Breslow and Scammon, "One Front in Minnesota," *Student Review* (Nov. 1934), 14 ; Sevareid, *Not So Wild a Dream*, 61; the Univ. of Nebraska, "Pacifists 39 percent," *Time* (June 5, 1933), 44 ; New York Univ., "Striking for Students' Rights," *Student Review* (March 1933), 12–13; the Univ. of Oklahoma, *Student Outlook* (May 1934), 14–15; Univ. of Oregon, "Regimentation in the Colleges," *New Republic* (Nov. 1934), 6; Ohio State Univ., *The Ohio State University Peace News*, Jan. 30, 1934; Pasadena Jr. College, *Student Outlook* (May 1934), 16; San Mateo Jr. College, *Student Outlook* (Nov.–Dec. 1934), 36; USC, Celeste Strack Kaplan interview with author; the Univ. of Tennessee, *Student Outlook* (March 1934), 21; the Univ. Texas, *National Student Mirror* (Jan. 1936), 24–25; the Univ. of West Virginia, Monroe Sweetland interview with author, San Mateo, Calif., March 6, 1982; Western Reserve Univ., Monroe Sweetland interview; Wright Jr. College, Horie, "The War-Makers Strike Back," 9; Univ. of Wyoming, *Student Outlook* (Nov.–Dec. 1934), 37.

Such widespread repression leaves the impression that all administrators thought alike on the question of student political rights during the early 1930s. But there were some distinctions in how administrators viewed this question. The most self-consciously repressive administrators were the absolute paternalists, who, like President W. Coleman Nevills of Georgetown University, thought it proper to "exclude all political activities among student bodies." These administrators tended to be political conservatives. A second group were more moderate paternalists, such as President Robert M. Hutchins of the University of Chicago. They tended to be liberals, who preferred to at least give the appearance that they were tolerant of dissent. This group argued that "campus political activity is to be tolerated *under careful supervision*" (emphasis added). The supervision turned to suppression, however, when student politics became too militant to suit the administration. For example, the Hutchins administration, which presented itself as liberal, was not above banning NSL meetings and requiring prior approval of all socialist leaflets distributed in the campus area. Since both types of paternalists engaged in repressive conduct towards students, it is easy to overlook the distinction between them. But at the very least, their rhetoric was different. See *NYT,* May 19, 1935; William E Scott to Mr. Hauser, Feb. 6, 1933, President's Papers, UC; Univ. of Chicago *Upsurge,* Feb. 6, 1935, UC.

Out of the mainstream were the few college presidents who took a principled civil liberties stance, making a point of respecting the free speech rights of their students. This was the case, for instance, with President Samuel P. Capen of the University of Buffalo—who not only wrote in defense of academic freedom, but also lived up to his rhetoric during the early 1930s (Univ. of Buffalo *Bee,* Oct. 21, 1932; Samuel P. Capen, "The Obligation of the University to American Democracy," *School and Society* (June 22, 1935), 819–22). A similar pattern of tolerance prevailed at the few colleges which had special liberal, feminist, or pacifist traditions. See, for example, the support for student civil liberties within the administration of Swarthmore College—a school founded by Quakers (Harold B. Speight to Norman Thomas, May 14, 1935, NT).

29. *Time* (April 22, 1935), 30.

30. Wechsler, *Revolt on the Campus,* 275.

31. *Ibid.,* 306.

32. *Ibid.,* 308.

33. UC Berkeley *Student Rights Association Bulletin* Nov. 27, 1934, UCB; C. Michael Otten, *University Authority and the Student* (Berkeley, 1970), 111.

34. *NYT,* June 5, 1933.

35. *NYT,* April 14, 1934, April 13, 1935; Wechsler, *Revolt on the Campus,* 299–310, 324–36 336–44, 405–6; *University Daily Kansan,* April 23, 1936.

36. This ranking is based upon the repressive incidents on 53 campuses. The 14 campuses which witnessed violent attacks on student activists between 1933 and 1935 were UC Berkeley, the Univ. of Chicago, CCNY, Columbia Univ., Connecticut State College, Harvard, UCLA, Los Angeles Jr. College, MIT, Michigan State Univ., Oregon State Univ., San Jose State College, Univ. of Washington, and University of Wisconsin. University authorities denied students the right to hold anti-war meetings, or banned student movement rallies on 17 campuses from 1933 to 1935 : Berea College, UC Berkeley, CCNY, the Univ. of Colorado, Connecticut State College, Howard Univ., Hunter College and Hunter's Bronx extension, Los Angeles Jr. College, UCLA, Univ. of Michigan, Univ. of Minnesota, Univ. of Missouri, Ohio State Univ., Univ. of Pittsburgh, George Washington Univ., Univ. of Washington.

Anti-war and radical student organizations were banned—at least temporarily—at 8 campuses between 1933 and 1935: Berea College, the Univ. of Chicago, CCNY, the Univ. of Pittsburgh, Syracuse Univ., George Washington Univ., Univ. of Washington, Univ. of Wisconsin.

University administrators expelled or suspended (or threatened disciplinary action against) student activists engaged in lawful protest activity at 16 campuses between 1933 and 1935: Case Technical College, CCNY, Connecticut State College, Columbia Univ., Fisk Univ., Howard Univ., Hunter College, UCLA, Louisiana State Univ., Univ. of Maryland, Univ. of Michigan, Ohio State Univ., the Univ. of Pittsburgh, Santa Clara Univ., USC, George Washington Univ., Univ. of West Virginia.

Censorship of antiwar literature, movement publications and campus newspaper editorials occurred on 16 campuses between 1933 and 1935: UC Berkeley, Case Technical College, CCNY, CCNY Business School, Columbia Univ., Hartwick College, Louisiana State Univ., Univ. of Michigan, Michigan State Univ., Univ. of Nebraska, New York Univ., Oregon State Univ., the Univ. of Oregon, Santa Clara Univ., Syracuse Univ., the Univ. of Texas.

All these free speech violations are covered in the sources cited in note 28 and in the following sources: Univ. of Virginia *College Topics,* May 21, 1935; *Hunter Bulletin,* Oct. 23, 1934, and March 18, 1935; Theresa Levin, "Academic Napoleon No. 5 , Dr. Colligan: Tammany's Aloysius," *Student Advocate* (Oct. 1937), 9–10; Univ. of Wisconsin *Daily Cardinal,* Jan. 8, 1936; "Academic Freedom in the U of C," Univ. of Chicago *Upsurge* (Aug. 1935), 1; Theodore Draper, "The Expulsions at Ohio State," *Student Review* (Feb. 1934), 14–15; *University of Washington Daily,* Feb. 17, Nov. 14, 1934; "At Columbia," *School and Society* (June 8, 1935), 778; *Columbia Spectator,* May 2, June 4, Oct. 18, 22, 1935; "Strike of Students of Journalism at the State University of Louisiana," *School and Society* (Dec. 8, 1934), 766; Univ. of West Virginia *Daily Athenaeum,* Feb. 23, Oct. 30, 1935; Marianne Ruth Phelps, "The Response of Higher Education to Student Activism," 92–125; Clifford McVeagh, "Academic Napoleons No. 1 : Ruthven of Michigan," *Student Advocate* (Feb. 1936), 13–15; Arthur Wilson, "Academic Napoleons No. IV: Chancellor Bowman of Pittsburgh," *Student Advocate* (Feb. 1937), 21–22.

37. Kenneth Walser, "What the Supreme Court Decided," *Intercollegian* (Jan.–Feb. 1935), 95–97; Joseph Lash, *The Campus Strikes Against War* (New York, 1935), 24.

38. Judah Drob interview with author, Washington, D.C., Jan. 22, 1982.

39. For a fuller discussion of the Johnson case, see Robert P. Cohen, "Revolt of the Depression Generation: America's First Mass Student Movement, 1929–1940" (Ph.D. diss., UC Berkeley, 1987), 180–96; Oakley Johnson, "Campus Battles for Freedom in the Thirties," *Centennial Review* (Summer 1970), 350–64.

40. *NYT,* Oct. 31, 1932; CCNY *Campus,* Nov. 1, 1932; Johnson, "Campus Battles For Freedom," 363–64; Harry Magdoff interview with author; S. Willis Rudy, *The College of the City of New York, 1847–1947* (New York, 1949), 416–17. Note, however, that though outrage over the Johnson firing and the suspensions helped fuel the growth of the CCNY Left, the protests failed to force the CCNY administration to reinstate Johnson. This would prove the case repeatedly at CCNY: administration repression hurt individual activists and disrupted their careers, while simultaneously igniting further protests which strengthened the student movement.

41. CCNY *Student,* May 26, 1933.

42. *NYT,* May 30, 1933.

43. *Ibid.;* *City College and War: Why Were 21 Students Expelled?* (New York, 1933), 5–9, CCNY.

44. *NYT,* May 30, 1933.

45. *Ibid.*

46. The statement disputing Robinson's version of the umbrella incident is by Florina Lasker, chair of the New York Committee of the ACLU, in *City College and War,* 10.

47. *Ibid.,* 8–9; Judah Drob and Harold Goldstein interview with author, Washington, D.C., June 22, 1982.

48. CCNY *Advance,* May 31, 1933.

49. *NYT,* June 1, 1933.

50. *NYT* June 3, 7, 1933.

51. *New Republic* (June 21, 1933), 138.

52. *NYT*, June 2, 1933.

53. *NYT*, June 5, 1933

54. *NYT*, May 31, 1933.

55. *Testimony in the Matter of the Field Day Disturbance of May 29, 1933*, 240, CCNY.

56. *Ibid.*, 459.

57. *Ibid.*, 117

58. *Ibid.*, 42

59. *Ibid.*, 23.

60. *Ibid.*, 401.

61. *Ibid.*, 55; at women's colleges a similar ideal was invoked by administrators and other critics of the student movement. They charged that radical activism was "unladylike" (see *Hunter Bulletin*, April 1, May 6, 1935; "Stop Playing with Dolls," *Vassar Alumnae Magazine* (Oct. 1, 1935), 9–10).

62. *Testimony . . . Field Day Disturbance*, 342, 395.

63. *Ibid.*, 110, 116–18.

64. *Ibid.*

65. *Ibid.*, 241; "Report of the Special Committee Appointed by the Faculty, June 12, 1933, CCNY"; *City College and War: Why Were 21 Students Expelled?*, 13.

66. CCNY *Campus*, April 17, 1934.

67. CCNY *Student*, Oct. 26, 1934; CCNY *Campus*, Oct. 8, 1934. In requesting that CCNY not hold a reception for the Italian fascist students, the Student Council had argued that the college should not allow them to come to campus to promote fascist propaganda. This argument is not very different from that which administrators used to ban Left activists—whom they derided as "propagandists," and it underscores the fact that student radicals advocated political liberty on campus for themselves but were far from absolute civil libertarians where the Right was concerned (see the perceptive discussion of this limited view of civil liberty in Eileen Eagan, *Class, Culture and the Classroom: The Student Peace Movement of the 1930s* (Philadelphia, 1981), 73–79). However, at CCNY in 1934 the question was less one of allowing the fascists to speak on campus than it was of the administration honoring them with a special reception, barring any counter demonstration in proximity to that reception, and confiscating the placards and leaflets of students who tried to organize such a counter demonstration. See CCNY Alumni Association, *Final Report of the Special Committee* (New York, 1936), 30–31, JPL.

68. CCNY *Office of the Dean, Hearings, October 10–November 7, 1934*, vol. I, 10–11, CCNY; Edwin Alexander, "Guttersnipes at City," *Student Review* (Dec. 1934), 11–12.

69. CCNY *Office of the Dean, Hearings, Oct. 10–Nov. 7, 1934*, vols. I and II, passim; CCNY *Student*, Oct. 10, 15, 26, 1934; CCNY *Campus*, Oct. 16, 19, 1934.

70. CCNY *Campus*, Oct, 23, 26, 29, 1934, Nov. 14, 16, 23; CCNY *Student*, Oct. 15, 26, 1934, Nov. 2, 9, 19, 23, 1934.

71. CCNY *Student*, Nov. 23, 1934.

72. *City College Alumnus* (Oct. 1934), 127–28; Rudy, *The College of the City of New York*, 427–32.

73. *NYT*, Oct. 30, 1932.

74. Barbara J. Dunlap, "From the Pen of President Robinson," *The City College Alumnus* (April 1981), 6.

75. Ernest C. Moore to Frederick B. Robinson, Dec. 7, 1934, ECM.

76. Wechsler, *Revolt on the Campus*, 276–77.

77. UCLA *Daily Bruin*, Oct. 30, 31, 1934, *Los Angeles Times*, Oct. 30, 31, 1934; UCLA Student Council Minutes, Oct. 3, 24, 26, 19, 1934, President's Papers, UCB; Earl Sacks, "A Student Observation of the UCLA Situation," ECM; Anna Wallace, "Fascism Comes to the Campus: The University of California as a Case in Point," *New Republic* (Jan. 9, 1935), 238–41; Celeste Strack Kaplan interview with author.

78. Claudie Little, "Vigilantism at U.C.L.A.," *Student Outlook* (Nov.- Dec. 1934), 20–21; Celeste Strack Kaplan interview with author.

79. *Ernest Carroll Moore Diary, Jan. 1933–Sept. 1937*, reel 3, July 15, 1934, ECM.

80. Norman Lee Ridker, "Ernest Carroll Moore and the Red Scare" (unpublished paper, UCLA, 1961), 16–17, 23, UCLA Archives.

81. Ernest C. Moore to Robert G. Sproul, May 10, 1934, President's Files, UCB.

82. *Ibid*; *Moore Diary*, Aug. 31, 1934, *ECM*.

83. *Moore Diary*, Aug. 31, 1934.

84. J. Finlinson, acting chief of police of Los Angeles, to E.C. Moore, Sept. 7, 1934; Luke Lane, detective lieutenant, commanding Intelligence Bureau of the Los Angeles Police Department to Ernest C. Moore, April 17, 1935; *Moore Diary*, Nov. 22, 1934. All in ECM.

85. *Moore Diary*, Oct. 20, 22, 1934, ECM.

86. Roberta Monks to President Sproul, Oct. 31, 1934, President's Files, UCB.

87. *Ibid.*; *Report on the Investigating Committee on the Five Suspended Students*, President's Files, UCB.

88. UCLA *Daily Bruin*, Oct. 31, 1934; *Los Angeles Times*, Oct. 31, 1934.

89. *Ibid.*

90. *Daily Bruin*, Oct. 30, 31, 1934; Wechsler, *Revolt on the Campus*, 277; Sacks, "A Student Observation of the UCLA Situation," 4–5.

91. *Daily Bruin*, Nov. 5, 1934.

92. *Los Angeles Times*, Oct. 31, 1934; Anna Wallace, "Fascism Comes to the Campus," 238–41.

93. *Daily Bruin*, Nov. 1, 1934; John Rockwell, "The Strike at Berkeley," *Student Outlook* (Nov.–Dec. 1934), 23–24.

94. "Statement of the Central Strike Committee, events of November 5, 1934," President's Files, UCB; Rockwell, "The Strike at Berkeley," 23–24; Richard Criley interview with author. Sproul's anti-strike statement was reprinted in the *San Francisco Chronicle*, Nov. 6, 1934; Provost Monroe Deutsch "Memo to Members of the Faculty," Nov. 3, 1934; Professor George Adams to President Robert G. Sproul, Nov. 6, 1934, both in President's Files, UCB.

95. UC Berkeley *Student Rights Association Bulletin*, Nov. 27, 1934, UCB; Otten, *University Authority and the Student*, 111.

96. *Daily Californian*, Nov. 6, 1934; Richard Criley interview with author.

97. Richard Criley interview with author.

98. Monroe Deutsch Statement, Nov. 5, 1934, President's Files, UCB

99. *Daily Californian*, Nov. 7, 1934.

100. *Daily Bruin*, Oct. 30, 31, 1934.

101. *Ibid.*; *Daily Californian*, Nov. 7, 1934.

102. Chester Rowell to President Robert Sproul, Nov. 5, 1934, President's Files, UCB. Moore also enjoyed the support of two of Los Angeles' leading newspapers, both of which were right-wing. Indeed, the local Hearst paper had gone

so far as to endorse the use of vigilante tactics by anti-radical students at UCLA (*Los Angeles Herald Examiner,* Nov. 9, 1934; *Los Angeles Times,* Oct. 31, 1934).

103. *Oakland Tribune,* Aug. 31, 1934; Robert G. Sproul, "Universities Face Radicalism, *Rotarian* (Oct. 1934), 22–23. Robert Sproul to Glenn Chadwick, Nov. 28, 1934, President's Files, UCB.

104. President Sproul, preliminary draft statement, [n.d] President's Files, UCB.

105. President Sproul to Mr. Dickson, Nov. 17, 1934, President's Files, UCB.

106. *Daily Bruin,* Nov. 15, 1934.

107. *Daily Californian,* Nov. 14, 1934.

108. Sproul to Dickson, Nov. 17, 1934; Sproul's bias against Strack apparently grew after he read the intelligence reports produced by the political surveillance network that he and Moore had helped construct. At Moore's request, the San Diego police chief had provided him with a detailed report—which Moore then gave to Sproul—on Strack's leadership role in off campus communist meetings. See Geo. M. Sears, San Diego chief of police, to Ernest C. Moore, "Re: Celeste Strack," Nov. 19, 1934, President's Files, UCB.

109. Sproul to Dickson, Nov. 17, 1934.

110. Minutes of the Univ. of California Board of Regents meeting, San Francisco, Dec. 14, 1934, President's Files, UCB.

111. Sproul to Dickson, Nov. 17, 1934.

112. President Sproul's handwritten notes used in his questioning of the suspended students [n.d.], President's Files, UCB.

113. H. Rodison to President Robert G. Sproul, Dec. 1, 1934, President's Files, UCB. The story of this intercepted LID letter was one in which Provost Moore was once again playing political policeman. After having apparently obtained this letter through one of his spies, Moore tried unsuccessfully to use the letter as proof that he had been correct all along about the suspensions and the communist plot to destroy UCLA. (Waldemar Westergaard telegram to President Robert Sproul, Nov. 29, 1934; Monroe Sweetland to Sidney Zagri [Zsagri], Oct. 31, 1934, President's Files, UCB.) Moore's diary confirms that the provost did try to prod Chief Davis of the Los Angeles Police Department to arrest Sweetland (*Moore Diary,* Nov. 22, 1934, ECM). Contrary to Moore's claim, the Sweetland letter contained nothing implicating the LID organizer in any communist plot to destroy UCLA. Indeed, Sweetland was not even a communist, but was rather a socialist.

114. Ernest C. Moore to Governor Frank F. Merriam, Nov. 17, 1934, ECM.

115. Celeste Strack Kaplan interview with author; UCLA *College News,* Dec. 1934.

116. Celeste Strack Kaplan interview with author.

117. Wechsler, *Revolt on the Campus,* 226–32.

118. *San Francisco Examiner,* Feb. 25, 1934. For another example of Hearst's redbaiting, see *New York American* article "Rid Our College of Reds," reprinted in *School and Society* (March 14, 1936), 373–74; also see "Yellow Newspapers See Red," *ibid.* (Jan. 19, 1935), 100. Student editorial attacks on the Hearst press include *Vassar Miscellany News,* March 2, 1935, Oct. 30, 1935; *Daily Texan,* Nov. 6, 1936; *University Daily Kansan,* Jan. 22, 1935; Univ. of West Virginia *Daily Athenaeum,* Oct. 11, 23, 1935; reprints of editorials from Williams, Amherst, and Princeton, in *Daily Athenaeum,* Oct. 18, 1935; *Oberlin Review,* Dec. 1, 1936. On the anti-Hearst boycott, which caused the cancellation of contracts for Hearst's Metrotone news at theaters in Princeton, Amherst, Williams, and other campus com-

munities, see *Time* (May 27, 1935), 59; Univ. of Wisconsin *Daily Cardinal*, June 2, 1935; *New Republic* (May 22, 1935), 31; Ruth to Joe [Lash], Oct. 12, 1936, JPL.

119. On the loyalty oath bills, see Wiley, *Depression, Recovery and Higher Education*, 441–48; Cohen, "Revolt of the Depression Generation," 379–80; "Teachers' Oaths," *School and Society* (Nov. 1935), 604–5; *NYT*, Oct. 8, 13, 1935; "First Casualties," *Time* (Jan. 27, 1936), 57; *Daily Athenaeum*, Oct. 16, 1935.

On the scarcity of faculty radicals, see Statement of Quentin Orgen [to the Illinois State Investigating Committee], June 6, 1935, President's Papers, UC; Univ. of Chicago Socialist Club, "An Open Letter to the Legislative Investigating Committee," Univ. of Chicago *Soapbox* (May 1935), 3, UC; *Hunter Bulletin*, May 29, 1933; Univ. of West Virginia *Daily Athenaeum*, Oct. 17, 1935; Harry Magdoff interview with author; Morris Schappes interview with author, Manhattan, N.Y., May 7, 1982; Robert Iversen, *The Communists and the Schools* (New York, 1959), 141–42; Budd Shulberg. "The Disenchanted," in *A Dartmouth Reader*, ed., Francis Brown (Hanover, 1969), 325. Even at Brooklyn College—one of the nation's leading centers of Left student activity—there was, according to former NSL organizer Theodore Draper, "not a single Communist professor in the school" during the early 1930s. It was not until later in the decade, long after the movement had become a powerful force on campus, that the Brooklyn College faculty came to include Communists (Theodore Draper, "The Class Struggle: The Myth of the Communist Professor," *New Republic* (Jan. 26, 1987), 29). The relationship between leftist faculty and student radicalism will be explored more fully in Chapter 8 of this study.

120. Ellen Schrecker, *No Ivory Tower: McCarthyism and the Universities* (New York, 1986), 68.

121. *NYT*, March 13, 1935. Actually the worst oaths and pledges imposed upon students came from within the University itself. Well before the legislative investigations and other outside anti-radical pressures had emerged in the mid-1930s, the University of Pittsburgh had already imposed a loyalty oath upon its students, in an effort to purge the campus of student radicals. This oath was initiated by Chancellor John Bowman, who had a long record of violating the academic freedom of liberal professors at Pittsburgh (*Pittsburgh Press*, Sept. 23, 25, 1932; Leonard Grumet to Chancellor John Bowman, Sept. 26. 1932, ACLU; Wechsler, *Revolt on the Campus*, 198–206).

122. Schrecker, *No Ivory Tower*, 69–70; even when opposing legislative red probes, university administrators—including some of the more tolerant college presidents, such as Robert Hutchins of the University of Chicago—displayed their intolerance of radicalism. Instead of making a strong stand on principle for the academic freedom of all academics whether radical or not, these administrators often defended the University on the grounds that there were few radicals on the faculty. In offering this type of defense, the administrators, were, as James Wechsler has put it, "retreating, by granting the essential premise of the investigation," which was that radicals had no place on a university faculty (Wechsler, *Revolt on the Campus*, 265; *Daily Athenaeum*, Oct. 17, 1935; CCNY *Campus*, Oct. 11, 1935; "Teachers' Oaths," *AAUP Bulletin* (Nov. 1935), 605).

123. This preemptive strategy was hinted at in Earl Warren to Monroe Deutsch, July 24, 1934, President's Files, UCB.

124. In the UCLA expulsion case, for instance, President Sproul received numerous letters from free speech advocates both on and off campus, which may

have helped sway him toward reinstating the students (Chester S. Williams [Organizing Director, ACLU of Northern California] to President Sproul, Nov. 16, 1934; Professor T. K. Whipple to President Sproul, Nov. 3, 1934, Rev. Theodore R. Leen to President Sproul, Nov. 4, 1934, President's Files, UCB). It was strong pressure from Left-liberal alumni and the progressive LaGuardia administration which finally drove the repressive President Robinson from CCNY (Rudy, *The College of the City of New York*, 427–32; also see *Hunter Bulletin*, April 1, 1935).

Nationally, both the American Civil Liberties Union and the American Association of University Professors took strong positions in support of student political rights (Committee on Academic Freedom of the American Civil Liberties Union,"The Principles of Academic Freedom," 4, ACLU. On the AAUP's position, see "The Right to Agitate," *AAUP Bulletin* (Oct. 1934), 1). On Eleanor Roosevelt's opposition to loyalty oaths, see *Vassar Miscellany News*, March 7, 1936. Harold Ickes took a similar position in his speech "The Need for Academic Freedom" (*AAUP Bulletin* (Nov. 1935), 562–65. For other endorsements of free speech on campus by prominent political leaders, see Cong. Maury Maverick to Dr. Robert Hutchins, President of the Univ. of Chicago, June 7, 1935, President's Files, UC; Pennsylvania Governor Pinchot's attack on the repressive Univ. of Pittsburgh administration, *School and Society* (July 28, 1934), 128).

125. Joseph P, Lash, typescript on student movement of the 1930s, 16–17, JPL.

126. Though nationally the reformist atmosphere severely limited the Right's effectiveness in attacking campus radicalism during the 1930s, the Right was not totally impotent. In isolated communities without a strong progressive presence or tradition, right wing groups—particularly the American Legion—could and did stop student radical meetings. See Monroe Sweetland to American Civil Liberties Union, April 29, 1935, ACLU.

127. Wechsler, *Revolt on the Campus*, 190–92, 387–95, 411–16; *Ohio State University Peace News*, Jan. 30, 1934.

128. On the decline in free speech violations as the antiwar movement grew, and on the shift of campus administrations to a more tolerant policy towards the antiwar strikes, see Minutes ASU National Executive Committee, June 22, 1936, JPL; *New Republic* (April 22, 1936), 298; (May 6, 1936), 254; (May 5, 1937), 371; *Harvard Crimson*, March 27, 1936. On one of the student movement's greatest free speech victories in the mid-1930s—the passage of the McGoldrick amendment authorizing student political organizations in New York's municipal colleges—see "Back of the Student Front," *Broeklyndian* (1938), 134, BC.

Note, however, that while nationally campus administration attacks on student political liberty declined dramatically, they did not completely cease in 1936. See *NYT*, April 21, 1936; Joseph Lash and James Wechsler, *War Our Heritage* (New York, 1937), 120; Bob to Ben [Fischer], April 2, 1936, YPSL files, SP; *The Dismissal of Bob Burke: Heidelberg Comes to Columbia* [1936], CUC. There would be a revival of such suppression when the student movement began to collapse following the Nazi-Soviet Pact, which will be discussed in Chapter 9.

Chapter 6. The Popular Front on Campus

1. Joseph Clark interview with author; Harvey Klehr, *The Heyday of American Communism* (New York, 1984), 167–85. This is not to say, however, that commu-

nist students embraced anti-fascist Popular Front policies simply because the Comintern had. These young communists were already heading in a Popular Front direction well before the Seventh World Congress, because of their growing awareness of the fascist menace and their sense that broad coalitions of leftists and liberals would be needed to defeat fascism. Thus communist students worked with their socialist counterparts to form an anti-fascist front (the American Youth Congress) in July 1934, a whole year prior to the Seventh World Congress. What the Comintern's adoption of the Popular Front did was to validate and accelerate the turn towards such policies already under way in the student movement (Gil Green interview with author; Robert Cohen, "Revolt of the Depression Generation: America's First Mass Student Movement, 1929–41" (Ph.D. diss., UC Berkeley, 1987), 389–99; Fraser Ottanelli, *The Communist Party of the United States: From the Depression to World War II* (New Brunswick, 1991), 62–63).

2. "A Symposium on Peace," *Student Advocate* (Dec. 1936), 29; Hal Draper, "The Case Against Sanctions and 'Neutrality Legislation,' " *Socialist Appeal,* June 1936; *Socialist Call,* Dec. 27, 1937. I use the term "isolationist" here and throughout the book to denote those who, in the words of historian Manfred Jonas, advocated for the U.S. "the avoidance of political and military commitments to or alliances with foreign powers, particularly those of Europe (Manfred Jonas, "Isolationism," *Encyclopedia of American Foreign Policy,* Alexander DeConde, ed. (New York, 1978), 496). I term "interventionists" those who wanted the U.S. to make such commitments or alliances, and in this case did so in the name of anti-fascism—which is the collective security position.

3. *NSL Organizer,* Oct. 1935. Also see Joseph P. Lash, "Veterans of Future Sanctions," *Challenge of Youth* (July 1936), 7; Harold Preece, "Sanctions Against War," *National Student Mirror* (Feb. 1936), 44–45; Joseph P. Lash to Jef Rens, May 7, 1936, JPL; Robert A. Divine, *The Illusion of Neutrality* (Chicago, 1962), 123.

4. Richard Criley interview with author.

5. Joseph P. Lash interview with author.

6. "An Open Letter," *Student Review* (Dec. 1933), 5–6; "One Big Student Movement?," *Student Outlook* (Feb. 1934), 3; Jean Symes, "The Student LID Convention," *ibid.* (Feb. 1935), 17.

7. On NSL-SLID cooperation in this era, see "Meaning of April 13," *Student Review* (Summer 1934), 4–5; Harold Draper, "The First American Youth Congress," *Student Outlook* (Oct. 1934), 15–16; Theodore Draper, "American Youth Rejects Fascism," *New Masses* (Aug. 28, 1934), 11–13; Joseph P. Lash, "Why I Am a Socialist," *Clionian* (Sept. 1934), 4; *Columbia Spectator,* Oct. 17, Nov. 2, 1933, May 7, 1934; CCNY *Campus,* April 28, May 12, 1933; *Daily Cardinal,* April 30, 1933.

8. "The American Student Union: A Recommendation from the National Executive Committee," *Student Outlook* (Oct. 1935), 3. Harry Magdoff interview with author; Monroe Sweetland interview with author.

9. Minutes of the SLID National Executive Committee, June 28–29–30 [1935], SDS Papers, NYU; Joseph P. Lash interview with author; Richard Criley interview with author; "Free for All," *Student Outlook* (Feb. 1935), 31. The chapter pressure for amalgamation did not come exclusively from the west coast. See U.S. Congress, Special House Subcommittee on Un-American Activities, "Testimony of Joseph P. Lash," 76th Congress, 1st Session, 7075.

10. Richard Criley interview with author.

11. Minutes of the [SLID] National Executive Committee, June 28–29–30 [1935].

12. Joseph P. Lash interview with author.

13. Minutes of the [SLID] National Executive Committee, June 28–29–30 [1935]; Joint Statement of the NSL-Student LID Subcommittee, SDS Papers, NYU.

14. SLID membership mailing [Oct.] 1935, 1, SDS Papers; Special Subcommittee on Un-American Activities, "Testimony of Joseph P. Lash," 7075; *Bulletin of the Fourth National Convention of the National Student League* (St. Louis, Dec. 1934), 8.

15. SLID membership mailing [October] 1935, SDS Papers, NYU; "Three Views on the ASU," *Student Review* (Oct. 1935), 16–17.

16. *Ibid.*

17. *Student Union Bulletin,* Jan. 7, 1936; *Columbus Citizen,* Dec. 23, 27, 1935; *Ohio State Journal,* Dec. 28, 30, 31, 1935; *Columbus Citizen,* Dec. 30, 1935; *Columbus Sunday Dispatch,* Dec. 29, 1935; Nancy Bedford Jones to Herman, Jan. 1, 1936, JPL; Celeste Strack, "The American Students Unite," *New Masses* (Jan. 14, 1936), 19–20; minutes Saturday session ASU convention, JPL.

18. Minutes of Dec. 29, 1935, ASU session, 10, Helen Schmock, "ASU Convention" minutes, 1–2, JPL; Nancy Bedford Jones to Herman, Jan. 1, 1936.

19. Nancy Bedford Jones to Herman, Jan. 1, 1936; on Sweetland's opposition to amalgamation, see SLID membership mailing [October] 1935, SDS Papers, NYU.

20. Jones to Herman, Jan. 1, 1936.

21. Strack, "The American Students Unite," 20.

22. *Student Union Bulletin,* Jan. 7, 1936.

23. *Ibid.*

24. *Ibid.*; Malcolm Sylvers, "Popular Front," in Mary Jo Buhle et al., eds., *The Encyclopedia of the American Left* (New York, 1990), 591–94.

25. Minutes of ASU Convention, Dec. 29, pp. 4–9, JPL.

26. Serril Gerber to Joseph P. Lash, Nov. 13, 1935; Lash to Gerber, Nov. 15, 1935; Gerber to Lash, Nov. 20, 1935. All in JPL. Resistance to amalgamation within the left wing of the socialist student groups was also linked to doctrinaire thinking about the nature of student movements. Much like the Communist Party during the Comintern's ultra-radical Third Period, some of the revolutionary socialists in the YPSL saw the student movement as at best an auxiliary of the labor movement (since the proletariat was assumed to be the main agent of radical social change). These YPSLs therefore reasoned that students should follow labor's lead rather than innovate on their own. Applied to the NSL-SLID amalgamation question, this meant that such a merger was inappropriate because communist and socialist-led labor organizations had never so merged. Thus at the 1934 SLID convention, the YPSLs presented an anti-amalgamation resolution, which concluded that "until the labor movement is unified, amalgamation of student groups with very different political orientations is impractical and utopian" (Ruth Oxman, "The Student LID Convention," *Young Socialist Review* (Spring 1935), 3, Daniel Bell Papers, NYU).

27. Minutes ASU Convention, Dec. 29, pp. 4–9; Strack, "The American Students Unite," 20.

28. Minutes ASU Convention, Dec. 29, pp. 4–9; YPSL report on the ASU convention, 2, JPL.

29. Hal Draper. "The Student Movement of the Thirties: A Political History," in Rita Simon, ed., *As We Saw the Thirties* (Urbana, 1967), 175; ballot for the [ASU] National Executive Committee, JPL.

30. Draper, "The Student Movement of the Thirties," 175.

31. James Wechsler, *The Age of Suspicion* (New York, 1981), 85.

32. Nancy Bedford Jones to Herman, Jan. 1, 1936, JPL. The NSL and SLID leadership worked so hard to hammer out a platform acceptable to liberals that this angered a dissident ultra-left minority at the convention, most of whom were Trotskyists. The Trotskyists, who had opposed the NSL-SLID merger from the beginning because of their mistrust of the Communists, viewed the ASU convention as a sell out to liberalism and an "opportunistic catastrophe" (Georg Mann, "Mistakes at Columbus," *Socialist Appeal* (Jan.-Feb. 1936), 5–6).

33. Wechsler, *The Age of Suspicion,* i-vii, 1–84; Celeste Strack interview with author.

34. Serril Gerber interview with author, Long Beach Calif., April 5, 1986.

35. Joseph Lash interview with author.

36. George Edwards, *Pioneer at Law* (New York, 1974), 122–56; U.S. Congress, Senate Subcommittee of the Committee on the Judiciary, "Nomination Hearings of George Clifton Edwards, Jr.," 88th Congress First Session, Oct. 1 and Nov. 21, 1963, pp. 12–21.

37. Molly Yard interview with author, Washington, D.C., March 21, 1983.

38. *Student Advocate* (Feb. 1936), 3–8, 10–11, 13–14; "An Apology," *Student Advocate* (March 1936), 5.

39. Joseph P. Lash interview with the author.

40. Wechsler, *The Age of Suspicion,* 85. Considering the limits on internal criticism in the Party-bound Old Left, Lash and Wechsler were—during the ASU's early days—remarkably iconoclastic in their thinking about the Communist and Socialist parties. Thus Lash noted in his diary that Wechsler was "contemptuous of the intellectual cravenness and mediocrity of the Communists, yet . . . even more against the sectarian line of the socialists." Echoing Wechsler's criticism of the adult Left, Lash noted that "I feel very much an outcast these days. The Socialists don't trust or like me because I champion cooperation with the CP, and my intellectual integrity makes me rebel against the mediocre application of the CI line to the US . . ."(Lash diary, Oct. 21, 1936, JPL).

41. Wechsler, *The Age of Suspicion,* 81–82.

42. Harold Draper, "The American Student Union Faces the Anti-War Strike," *American Socialist Monthly* (April 1936), 7.

43. *Ibid.,* 7–10.

44. Joseph P. Lash, "Another View of the A.S.U.," *American Socialist Monthly* (May 1936), 28–29. Lash's description of the situation in the high schools was accurate. See Celeste Strack to Dorothy Shoemaker, March 5, 1937, Committee on Militarism in Education Papers, SCPC; Osmond K. Fraenkel to Lewis J. Valentine, Dec. 12, 1935, ACLU.

45. Lash, "Another View of the A.S.U.," 28–29.

46. Ben Fischer, "YPSL position," *American Socialist Monthly* (May 1936), 30–31. On this self-serving YPSL view of its role in the ASU, also see Lewis M. Cohen to Joseph P. Lash, Oct. 6, 1936, JPL.

47. On Lash's low regard for the YPSL leadership, see his "Comments on the November 29, 1936, meeting of the YPSL national executive committee," 2–5, JPL. The YPSL controversy helped cement Lash's ties with Wechsler in the ASU leadership. Both increasingly saw themselves as allies in the struggle to eliminate dogmatism and destructive communist-socialist feuding in the student movement. Lash recalled: "The thing that . . . made Jimmy Wechsler and myself very sympathetic was he was having the same problem with the YCL . . . Well I guess we

never wore intellectual harnesses very easily" (Joseph Lash interview with author). Lash's willingness to take a stance against YPSL dogmatism also enhanced his stature with less sectarian socialist students—including some YPSL regional leaders and rank and filers—who were "sick and tired of the splitting tactics" of the YPSL national leadership in the student movement. See Jeff Campbell to Joseph Lash, April 2, 1936, JPL; (Bob [Newman] to Joseph Lash [n.d.], JPL).

48. Joseph P. Lash interview with author; Joseph P. Lash, "500,000 Strike for Peace: An Appraisal," *Student Advocate* (May 1936), 3–5, 21.

49. Typifying this lack of candor was the ASU's official account of its 1936 convention, which made it sound as if all the decisions at this convention were made openly by the full ASU membership. (See "One Year of Student Unionism: A Report of the Second Annual A.S.U. Convention," *Student Advocate* (Feb. 1937), 11–13.) But contrast this sanitized public account of the convention with the account recorded in the YPSL's internal bulletin, which detailed the private political horsetrading between the ASU's communist and socialist factions over the composition of ASU national executive committee at the convention. The YPSL "Student Bulletin" reported that "the YCL proposed a 5–5–20 (YCL, YPSL, and liberal) ratio. We proposed a 10–10–15 ratio which would have meant the addition of 5 members. . . . There was a sharp cleavage in outlook on the ASU here which was not resolved by the compromise of 8–8–14 finally agreed upon"("YPSL Student Bulletin," Jan. 10, 1937, p. 3, JPL). On similar private YPSL-YCL deal-making in the ASU, see [YPSL] National Student Committee Minutes, Nov. 4, 1936, JPL. On the ASU magazine's lack of candor on such questions, see Joseph P, Lash, introduction to Greenwood reprint of *Student Advocate,* "Do the Thirties Have Anything to Tell the Sixties?" (New York, 1968), 2.

50. Joe Freeland to Alvaine Hollister, Jan. 25, 1938, YPSL files, SP; James Wechsler, *Revolt on the Campus* (1935: reprint, Seattle, 1973), viii.

51. Lash, "500,000 Strike for Peace," 3–5, 21; Minutes of the American Student Union National Executive Committee, June 22, 1936, JPL.

52. *NYT*, April 23, 1936; *New York Herald-Tribune*, April 23, 1936; "Peace Day," *Time* (May 4, 1936), 53.

53. *Ibid.* Veterans of Future Wars was founded by two affluent Princeton undergraduates early in the spring semester of 1936. Within a little over a month it had chapters on some fifty campuses, and was, in the words of a *Time* reporter, "rampaging over the campuses." A female auxiliary, the "Association of Gold Star Mothers of Future Veterans," quickly arose at Vassar and spread to other campuses. Although VFW proved a transient phenomenon, and an exercise in political humor, it did indicate how popular opposition to war and the military had become on campus. This was a genuine grass roots movement, in which rank and file students organized themselves against war with little prodding from any national organization. Indeed, there was a huge gap between what the VFW's conservative Democratic founders had intended and what the VFW chapters were doing. The Princeton students had established the VFW as a parody of veterans' demands for a bonus—and conservatives initially welcomed the organization's clever attack on "extravagant" social spending. These Princeton organizers had not intended to link up with the antiwar movement, and had in fact refused to support the 1936 antiwar strike. Students out on the campuses where the VFW spread, however, changed the emphasis of the VFW from an attack on social spending to an attack on war and militarism, and many VFW chapters joined in the antiwar strike. Thus the VFW, which had initially been praised by the Right, now drew

vitriolic criticism from conservatives ("Future Veterans," *Time* (March 30, 1936), 38; Joseph P. Lash and James Wechsler, *War Our Heritage* (New York, 1936), 135–42; *Harvard Crimson,* March 18, April 21, 1936).

54. YPSL National Student Office, "Strike Bulletin," April 1936.

55. Joseph P. Lash to Elizabeth Gilman, April 20, 1936, JPL.

56. *Daily Californian,* Oct. 7, 1937.

57. "April 22nd: We Must Remember Spain," *Student Advocate* (April 1937), 3–4.

58. Wechsler, *The Age of Suspicion,* 100–101.

59. Tucker Dean to Molly Yard, May 10, 1937, JPL. On other abandonments of pacifism because of Spain, see Monroe Sweetland interview with author; David S. Burgess, "I'm No Longer a Pacifist Because," *Intercollegian and Far Horizons* (Oct. 1939), 17–18.

60. George Watt essay in *50th and 25th Anniversary ASU-SDS National Reunion* (Long Beach, Calif., 1986), 2; Robert A Rosenstone, *Crusade on the Left* (New York, 1969), 104; Arthur Landis, *The Abraham Lincoln Brigade* (New York, 1968), 249–55; Murray Kempton, *Part of Our Time: Some Monuments and Ruins of the Thirties* (New York, 1955), 310–18.

61. Wechsler, *The Age of Suspicion,* 100–101.

62. *Ibid.*; Celeste Strack Kaplan interview with author; Ruth to Joe [Lash] March 3, 1937, JPL; Molly Yard to Leonard J. Grumet, July 12, 1937, JPL.

63. E. H. Carr, *The Comintern and the Spanish Civil War* (London, 1984), 19–44; Robert G. Spivack, "A Letter to Norman Thomas," *New Masses* (Feb. 23, 1937), 21; Lash and Wechsler, *War Our Heritage,* 147.

64. Wechsler, *The Age of Suspicion,* 100.

65. Jeff Campbell to Joseph P. Lash, May 11, 1937, JPL; James Alter, "Why I Am Still a Pacifist," *Intercollegian and Far Horizons* (Nov. 1939), 39–40; *Socialist Call,* Late-Feb. 1937; Norman Thomas, "The Pacifist's Dilemma," *Nation* (Jan. 16, 1937), 66–68.

66. *Michigan Daily,* March 22, 24, 1938. The State Department's refusal to intercede on behalf of Neafus and the three other volunteers who had been captured with him had tragic consequences. Neafus and his comrades were murdered—shot without trial—by their fascist captors. The historian of these prisoners makes a convincing case that pressure from Washington would almost certainly have saved their lives. See Carl Geiser, *Prisoners of the Good Fight: The Spanish Civil War 1936–1939* (Westport, 1986), 59.

67. *Michigan Daily,* March 22, 24, 30, 1938. Also see George Watt letter from Spain, *Vassar Miscellany News,* Oct. 16, 1937.

68. Hal Draper, "The Student Movement of the Thirties: A Political History," 178–79; Al Hamilton and Alvaine Hollister, "Left Jingoism on the Campus," *Socialist Review* (Jan.-Feb. 1938), 9–10, 19; Judah Drob, "Thoughts on the ASU-SDS Anniversary" [1986], (unpublished paper, distributed at the 50th Anniversary Reunion of the ASU, Long Beach, Calif., 1986).

69. Lash and Wechsler, *War Our Heritage,* 147, 149. Gus Tyler, "We're for Peace, But . . .," *Socialist Call,* Dec. 26, 1936.

70. Joseph P. Lash, Notes on the YPSL national executive committee meeting, Nov. 29, 1936, 1–2, JPL; *Socialist Call,* Dec. 26, 1936.

71. Joseph P. Lash, Notes on the YPSL national executive committee meeting, Nov. 29, 1936, 2–5, JPL.

72. *Ibid.*

73. Statement by Joseph P. Lash to the Grievance Committee of the Y.P.S.L. [1937]; [YPSL] Hearing on Joe Lash [1937], 3, both in JPL.

74. Joseph P. Lash, Notes on the YPSL national executive committee meeting, Nov. 29, 1936, p. 3, JPL.

75. Norman Thomas, Memorandum on the YPSL-ASU Situation, Dec. 4, 1936, JPL.

76. Transcript, Joseph P. Lash interview with Joel Chernoff, 16–17, JPL; "Ten-minute remarks of Joseph Lash in support of resolution stating that support of the Oxford Pledge was incompatible with support of collective security," JPL; Minutes Second National Convention, American Student Union, Chicago, Dec. 27–30, 1936, JPL; YPSL (Fourth Internationalists, "Compromise?" [Trotskyist leaflet distributed at the 1936 ASU Convention], JPL). The beginnings of Lash's shift towards collective security had brought him into conflict with YPSL and other Socialist Party officials as early as Oct. 1936. Lash noted in his diary that month that on the collective security issue: "We've had several long sessions of various party committees in which patient attempts were made to argue me out of my heresy. Now I am not allowed to advocate the position publicly on the ground that it is incompatible with the party position" (Lash diary, Oct. 21, 1936, JPL). Note that Lash and his socialist comrades were here being insensitive to democratic process within the ASU. Rank and file ASUers, not privy to the deliberations of this Left elite, would have no idea that their organization's national executive secretary was barred from fully expressing his views on the crucial question of collective security because of his Socialist Party allegiance.

77. Minutes Second National Convention, American Student Union, Chicago, December 27–30, 1936, JPL; Joseph P. Lash, *Toward a Closed Shop on Campus* (New York, 1937), 24.

78. Lash, *Toward a Closed Shop*, 25.

79. [YPSL] NEC Motion by Ben Fischer, Dec. 15, 1936, JPL; Joseph P. Lash to Norman Thomas, Jan. 5, 1937, JPL.

80. George Edwards to Joe [Lash], Dec. 6, 1936, JPL; Joseph Lash to George [Edwards], Dec. 14, 1936, JPL; National Student Department, "Student Bulletin," Jan. 10, 1937, JPL ; Roy E. Burt to Norman Thomas, Dec. 30, 1936, NT; Frank Trager to Norman Thomas, Dec. 30, 1936, NT. Roy Burt, the Socialist Party's Executive Secretary, and Frank Trager, the party's Labor and Organization Secretary were the adult Socialist Party leaders who persuaded the YPSL leadership at the convention not to bring their dispute with Lash to the convention floor, and not to try to get back at him for his collusion with Edwards by seeking his immediate ouster from the ASU leadership. Note that the YPSL procedure (involving socialist and Trotskyist YPSLs) of screening speeches by socialist ASUers was another example of factional control, at odds with the ideal of the ASU as an open and democratically led organization.

81. On the confrontation with Lash at the YPSL caucus, see Roy E. Burt to Norman Thomas, Dec. 30, 1936; Frank Trager to Norman Thomas, Dec. 30, 1936, NT; YPSL "Student Bulletin," Jan. 10, 1937, p. 4.

82. Joseph P. Lash to Norman Thomas, Jan. 5, 1937; Judah Drob to Milt Friedman, Feb. 1, 1937; "The Case Against Joe Lash," [1937]; "Report on the Special Grievance Committee to the NEC on the Charges by Ben Fischer and Alvaine Hollister Against Joe Lash" [1937]; "Statement by Joseph P. Lash to the

Grievance Committee of the Y.P.S.L."; [YPSL] Hearing on Joe Lash; Ben Fischer and Alvaine Hollister, "A Reply to Joseph P. Lash"; Harold Draper, "A Reply to Comrade Lash" [1937]; Roy E. Burt to Joe Lash, Jan. 25, 1937; Joseph P. Lash to George Edwards, Feb. 2, 1937; George Edwards and Joseph P. Lash to Roy Burt, Jan. 29, 1937. All in JPL.

83. Joseph P. Lash to John Morris, Feb. 5, 1937, JPL.

84. "April 22nd: We Must Remember Spain," *Student Advocate* (April 1937), 3.

85. *Ibid.*, 4. On this flexible approach to strike organizing in 1937, also see *Chapter Guide First Bulletin on the Student Strike Against War for April 22, 1937-11 A.M. American Student Union* (March 3, 1937), 3–5, United Student Peace Committee Papers, SCPC.

86. *NYT*, April 23, 1937; "The Great 1937 Strike in Review," *Student Advocate* (May 1937), 4.

87. "The Great 1937 Strike in Review," 4–5.

88. John Gates, *The Story of an American Communist* (New York, 1958), 52–55; Irving Howe, *A Margin of Hope* (New York, 1982), 74–76; Wechsler, *The Age of Suspicion*, 102; Allen Guttmann, *The Wound in the Heart: America and the Spanish Civil War* (New York, 1962), 150–51; Burnett Bolloten, *The Spanish Civil War: Revolution and Counterrevolution* (Chapel Hill, 1991), 429–531; Gabriel Jackson, *A Concise History of the Spanish Civil War* (New York, 1980), 118–21; *Vision on Fire: Emma Goldman on the Spanish Civil War*, David Porter, ed. (New Paltz, N.Y., 1983) 132–71.

89. Joseph Lash to Nancy [Bedford Jones], July 20, [1937]; on Lash's resignation from the Socialist Party, see Joseph P. Lash to Norman Thomas, Oct. 2, 1937; both in JPL.

90. Joseph Lash Diary, July 11, 17, 1937, JPL. There is no indication in Lash's writings that he actually followed through on his intention (as stated in his Spanish diary) of joining the Communist Party. In subsequent interviews Lash maintained that although he considered himself very close to the Communist Party during the Popular Front era, he never actually joined the Party—terming himself a "non-Party Bolshevik" in that era (transcript of Joseph Lash interview with Joel Chernoff, April 2, 1978, p. 5, JPL; Joseph Lash interview with author). However, Gil Green, who headed the YCL during the Popular Front years, recalled that though "Joe Lash may not admit it today, he joined the CP" while a leader of the student movement (Gil Green interview with author, Manhattan, N.Y., Sept. 29, 1982). Whether Lash or Green is correct about Lash's membership in the CP cannot be determined with absolute certainty (since by definition secret membership is covert and therefore not documented). However, Lash's correspondence tends to support his claim of non-membership (see William Sussman to Joseph P. Lash [n.d.]; Joseph P. Lash to Avram [Goldstein], May 19, 1939; Joseph P. Lash to Bill [Sussman], Sept. 30, 1939. All in JPL). This disagreement over the question of formal party membership should not, however, obscure the more essential point upon which Lash and Green agree: that Lash as ASU executive secretary—the most influential national leader in the student movement—was firmly in the communist camp on all key policy questions from 1937 to summer 1939. Just how close Lash's identification was with the CP in this era can be seen in his unpublished memoir, which indicates that until the end of the Popular Front era, Lash "conferred with young c.l [Communist League] leaders on problems of the youth

movement and expected after leaving the ASU to become a full-fledged dues-paying card-carrying member of the communist party" (Joseph P. Lash, "My Political Position Before the Fall of 1939," JPL).

91. Joseph P. Lash to Nancy [Bedford Jones], July 20, [1937], JPL.

92. Joseph P. Lash Diary, July 17, 1937, JPL.

93. Joseph P. Lash to Nancy [Bedford Jones], July 20, 1937; Lash Diary, June 18 and 21, 1937, JPL. Lash was dismissive of leftwing critics and what he termed their "bogy-man tales of maneuvering, terrorism and opportunism" in republican Spain (Joseph P. Lash, "Time Works for Us—Spain 1937," *New Masses* (Oct. 19, 1937), 6–8). During this period, Lash was not only uncritical of communists in Spain, but was also also unwilling to criticize the Moscow trials publicly. In fact, he wrote a letter to one of his former colleagues in the Socialist Party, criticizing the adult LID for "cast[ing] doubt on the integrity of Soviet justice." See Joseph P. Lash to Harry Laidler, March 4, 1938, JPL. Privately and to close associates, however, Lash was more critical of the trials. See Lash Diary, March 3, 6, 1938, JPL.

94. Wechsler, *The Age of Suspicion,* 101–3.

95. *Ibid.,* 88–89, 102–3; Leo Rifkin, "900,000 Strike," 23; Ruth Watt, "Struggle Against Trotskyism in the Student Movement" [n.d.], JPL; *Daily Worker,* April 24, Oct. 23, 1937; *Communist Campanile,* Summer 1937, UCB. On the Soviet roots of this Trotsky-bashing, see Issac Deutscher, *The Prophet Outcast: Trotsky 1929–1940* (New York, 1963), 1–6, 125–26, 413–19.

96. Wechsler, *The Age of Suspicion,* 103. Despite his earlier non-sectarian approach to campus organizing, Lash too became so influenced by communist rhetoric—and so angered by the Trotskyists' divisive tactics in the student movement—that by 1939 he had become engaged in some nasty Trotsky-bashing. During the 1939 ASU summer leadership institute, Lash gave a lecture on the Trotskyists in which he referred to them as "the syphilis of the working class." See "Lash Lectures on Student Movement," *ASU Summer Leadership Institute Newsletter,* July 2, 1939, JPL.

97. "A Letter to Joe Lash" [leaflet, n.d.], JPL.

98. Irving Howe, "An Open Letter to Joe Lash on the 1938 A.S.U. Convention," *Challenge of Youth,* Jan. 1939, p. 3. Describing the extreme sectarianism of the Trotskyists in this era, two socialist student activists wrote, " Many Trotzkyists openly advocate the policy of splitting and liquidating the [American] Student Union on the grounds that it is a 'students people's front.' Just as the Communists are obsessed with a 'people's-front mania,' the Trotzkyites are afflicted with 'anti-people's front phobia.' They are constantly on a witch hunt for people's front tendencies. Every statement, decision, or action by anybody is immediately examined for 'people's frontism.' Any participation in joint activities with non-Socialists is condemned on that basis" (Hyman Bookbinder and Melvino Willbach, "An Appeal for the Preservation of a Young Socialist [Movement]" [n.d.], Daniel Bell Papers, NYU.

99. Lash Diary, Nov. 4, 1937.

100. Nancy Bedford Jones to Al Hamilton [Aug. 1937], JPL.

101. Howe, *A Margin of Hope,* 75–76.

102. Dorothy Borg, "Notes on Roosevelt's 'Quarantine' Speech," *Political Science Quarterly* (Sept. 1957), 405–33.

103. One of the most striking aspects of the debate within the student move-

ment over collective security was the way President Roosevelt was viewed. Even though FDR had quickly retreated from the pro-collective security implications of the Chicago speech, *both* the foes and supporters of collective security within the ASU continued, long after this speech, to act as if the President was a firm supporter of collective security. It was, of course, natural for supporters of collective security in the ASU to view FDR as a champion of collective security, since this enabled them to use Roosevelt's name to bid for liberal student support. It may seem puzzling, however, that opponents of collective security within the ASU failed to challenge this view of Roosevelt. Had they wished to do so, they could have pointed to FDR's statements opposing sanctions and his retreat from the "quarantine" idea to show that FDR had not in fact endorsed collective security. This would certainly have helped them in competing for liberal support on campus. But here ideology got in the way of political expediency. The anti-collective security forces were led by YPSLs, who as socialists loathed Roosevelt and regarded him as a warmonger. In their eyes, by associating itself with FDR, the pro-collective security bloc in the ASU was selling out, diluting its radicalism, and discrediting itself within the antiwar movement by becoming part of the "Roosevelt war machine." The YPSLs seemed out of touch with liberal student opinion and failed to grasp how useful FDR's name would be in helping to sway it. Thus they gave FDR away as a political symbol, setting themselves up for losses to the ASU's collective security bloc because they cared more about leftwing ideological purity than winning the hearts and minds of the American student body (*Socialist Call*, Dec. 25, 1937, Jan. 15, 1938; Joseph P. Lash, *The Campus: A Fortress of Democracy* (New York, 1938), 22–23).

104. Molly Yard to Joseph [Lash], Nov. 9, 1937, JPL; "For a Left Wing in the ASU," *Challenge of Youth*, Nov. 1937; Alvaine Hollister to Fay Bennett, Nov. 27, 1937, YPSL files, SP; Lewis Conn to ASU Administrative Committee, Nov. 12, 1937, JPL; Joseph Lash to Lewis Conn, Nov. 24, 1937, JPL; "A Proposal for a Youth Committee for the Oxford Pledge," YPSL files, SP.

105. Yard to Lash, Nov. 9, 1937. Also see Alvaine Hollister to Fay Bennett, Nov. 27, 1937.

106. Alvaine Hollister to Fay Bennett, Nov. 19, 1937, YPSL files, SP.

107. Molly Yard to Joseph [Lash], Oct. [1937], JPL.

108. *Socialist Call*, Dec. 25, 1937; "The ASU at the Crossroads," *The CCNY Redbook* (1937–38), 5–6, YPSL files, SP.

109. Yard to Lash, Nov. 9, 1937.

110. Al Hamilton to Jeff Campbell, Nov. 24, 1937, YPSL files SP; *Socialist Call*, Jan. 15, 1938.

111. *Socialist Call*, Jan. 15, 1938; Joseph Starobin, "The Students Reject Isolation," *New Masses* (Jan. 11, 1938), 13–15. In the ASU membership referendum, collective security positions won by more than a four to one margin. See *Unite the Campus to Save Peace* (1938), 12–13, JPL.

112. Lash, *The Campus: A Fortress of Democracy*, 22.

113. ASU, *The Vassar Convention of the A.S.U Convention* [n.d.], 2, JPL.

114. Lash, *The Campus: A Fortress of Democracy*, 11.

115. *Daily Worker*, Dec. 31, 1937; Bob Kahn, "Conventional Stuff," in ASU, Brooklyn College Chapter, *Convention Guide* (Feb. 1938), 7. Joseph Lash, who had shown his penchant for tactical innovation in the early stages of the student movement by coming up with the idea of a national student strike against war, was also

responsible for the idea of a bonfire protesting Japanese imperialism. See *American Student Union Chapter Guide* (Oct. 23, 1937), 4, JPL. This protest drew considerable press attention. See *Time* (Jan. 10, 1938), 42.

116. Lash, *The Campus: A Fortress of Democracy*, 23.

117. ASU, *The Vassar Convention* [n.d.], 2.

118. Wechsler, *The Age of Suspicion*, 91.

119. Joseph Lash, "Fascism Means War," JPL. The ASU convention also approved two other measures suggesting that while embracing collective security, it was still unwilling to surrender its opposition to the U.S. military and unwilling to trust in Washington's intentions to preserve peace. These measures were: (1) ASU support for "the withdrawal of United States military forces from all foreign countries" (a move obviously intended to prevent a U.S.-Japanese clash in Asia, where there had been American troops); (2) ASU endorsement of the Ludlow amendment "that war should be declared only after a national referendum" (ASU, *The Vassar Convention*, 2). These positions were obviously inconsistent with the interventionist thrust of the ASU's new collective security policy, and would therefore be dropped by the time of the next ASU Convention. The Ludlow amendment position was so at odds with the mood of the anti-isolationist rank and file that in the 1938 referendum on the ASU's peace platform it was rejected by 60 percent of the membership (and then dropped immediately from the ASU program). See *Unite the Campus to Save Peace* (1938), 13, JPL.

120. *Socialist Call*, Jan. 15, 1938.

121. Fay Bennett to Alvaine Hollister, Nov. 27, 1937, YPSL files, SP; Al Hamilton to Norman Thomas, Nov. 20, 1937, NT.

122. Bob [Kelso] to Al Hamilton, Jan. 14, 1938, YPSL files, SP.

123. Lewis [Conn] to Al[Hamilton], Feb. 18, 1938, YPSL files, SP.

124. Joseph P. Lash to Molly Yard, Jan. 19, 1938, JPL. Another sign of this deterioration in socialist-communist relations within the student movement was the use of some new hardball anti-communist tactics by the socialists at the campus level. On this point, the correspondence from Joseph Freeland, a socialist student organizer at the University of Kentucky ASU chapter, is particularly revealing. At Kentucky, for reasons of political expediency, communist student activists in the ASU had not been candid about their Party affiliation. Liberals in the University of Kentucky ASU were not told that the students who dominated the chapter were communists. During the early stages of the ASU's development at the University of Kentucky, socialists in this ASU chapter had, in Freeland's words, "respected the incognito which the communists have chosen to assume" because "in the ASU we had a common program and a common interest." But now in early 1938, with the split over collective security, it was "no longer true" that the ASU's communists and socialists shared the same goals. Thus Freeland wrote to the YPSL national office, asking whether in light of this split, he and other socialists should expose the red affiliations of the communists in his ASU chapter. YPSL national secretary Al Hamilton responded affirmatively, instructing Freeland "absolutely that you should point out to your ASU members the source of the new policy in the American Student Union. In the past you may have been correct in preserving the incognito of the YCL members. But this will have to be sacrificed if necessary to point out the source of the new pro-war policy of the American Student Union. . . . On the question of your local chapter you should attack the [national] leadership of the YCL for forcing down the throats not only of the ASU but of the [Univer-

sity of Kentucky] YCL their policy" (Joe Freeland to Alvaine Hollister, Jan. 25, 1938; Al Hamilton to Joe Freeland, Feb. 11, 1938, both in YPSL files, SP.

125. Joseph P. Lash to Howard Lee, Feb. 16, 1938, JPL.

126. *Ibid.*

127. Minutes United Student Peace Committee meeting, March 15, 1938, JPL.

128. *Ibid., NYT,* April 24, 1938.

129. On the the YCAW's early preparations for the 1938 strike, see "Report of the Executive Secretary to the Opening Youth Session of the National Anti-war Congress," YPSL files, SP.

130. Youth Committee for the Oxford Pledge, "An Open Letter to American Youth," YPSL files, SP. During the mid-1930s there were many complaints—from within the YPSL and among the organization's allies—of the YPSL tendency to spend more time feuding with the YCL and engaging in doctrinal hair splitting than recruiting new activists into the student movement (see Flora McClain to YPSL national office, June 20, 1936, YPSL files, SP; Harry Laidler to Al Hamilton, March 3, 1937; Al Hamilton to Harry Kingman, March 20, 1937, YPSL files, SP; Jeff Campbell to Joseph P. Lash, Dec. 1, 1936, JPL; Ed Bond to Joseph P. Lash, Dec. 2, 1936, JPL). On one level this penchant for factionalism can be seen and even defended as a natural response to the manipulative political behavior of the communists—that since the YPSL confronted a well-organized YCL faction in the ASU it had to embrace factionalism to survive in the movement. But such factionalism was more than an expedient for the YPSL; it was also a *preferred* style of politics which was fundamental to most YPSL organizing. The way YPSLs often expressed their passion for socialism and their loyalty to the policies of the Socialist Party was by promoting their organization's influence over all movement policy and personnel decisions, no matter who this alienated. Thus even in the YCAW, where there was no communist faction for the YPSL to contend with, YPSL leaders still engaged in self-interested factional maneuvering in defiance of democratic process. This led Jeffrey Campbell, a socialist and New England YMCA leader, to complain bitterly to the YPSL leadership about its manipulative and undemocratic behavior in the YCAW. Shortly after returning from an early YCAW national meeting, Campbell told these leaders that he was "burning up" over "the method in which offices and representative positions were elected at the Youth Committee Against War. I saw again the same tendency which so thoroughly disgusted me with the YPSL role in the Chicago convention of the ASU. At the time I laid it to Trotskyite presence in the movement plus the need of opposing the C.P. To find its identical techniques emerging at the start of a newly organized cooperatively united and friendly body drives me to express myself as strongly as I am capable. In my opinion to enter . . . the Youth Committee Against War with a small highly organized and disciplined wedge and to start assigning offices and election on the basis of prearranged agreements from which the mass is automatically excluded threatens everything fine and worthwhile accomplished by the Congress" (Jeffrey Campbell to Al Hamilton, Alvaine Hollister, Judah Drob, June 2, 1938, YPSL files, SP).

131. Youth Committee for the Oxford Pledge, "An Open Letter to American Youth." On both the poll results and the problems with the poor wording of the questionnaire, see "Brown Daily Herald Student Survey on Peace," April 15, 1938, United Student Peace Committee Papers, SCPC; Antone Singsen to Joseph P. Lash, April 8, 1938, JPL.

132. *Socialist Call,* May 7, 1938.

133. William Meyer to Al [Hamilton], Feb. 21, 1938, YPSL files, SP. A similar situation existed in southern California. See Fay Bennett to Alvaine Hollister, April 13, 1938, YPSL files, SP.

134. Alvaine Hollister to Al [Hamilton], April 20, 25, 1938. YPSL files, SP.

135. Alvaine Hollister to Al [Hamilton], April 20, 1938. On the "awful" defeat of the YCAW position in the Ohio State University antiwar rally, see Robin Myers to Alvaine Hollister, April 26, 1938, YPSL files, SP. Also see *YPSL Affairs,* May 4, 1938. On isolationist strength at the Univ. of Chicago strike, see Bud James to Joseph Lash, April 25, 1938, JPL.

136. Harold [Goldstein] to Judah [Drob], March 31, 1938, YPSL files, SP. The YCAW also flopped in its attempt to prevent the student YM and YWCAs— probably the most influential Christian student organizations in the U.S.—from moving with the ASU towards collective security. See "Report of the [YCAW] Executive Secretary to the Opening Session of the National Anti-war Congress" [1938]. On the weakness of the YCAW in New England on the eve of the 1938 student strike against war, see Helen James to Al Hamilton, March 31, 1938. All in YPSL files, SP.

137. Minutes, United Student Peace Committee meeting, May 12, 1938, p. 2, JPL; *NYT,* April 28, 1938; Garland Embrey to Joe [Lash], April 18, 1938, JPL; Sidney Koblenz to Joe [Lash], March 1, 1938, JPL.

138. Joseph P. Lash to Garland Embrey, May 12, 1938, JPL. The YCAW's total membership in 1938 and 1939 never exceeded 400. See Patti McGill Peterson, "The Young Socialist Movement in America from 1905–1940: A Study of the Young People's Socialist League" (Ph.d. diss., Univ. of Wisconsin, 1974), 199. The ASU membership would peak at about 20,000. See transcript of Joseph Lash's retrospective speech on the student movement of the 1930s [n.d.], 22–23, JPL.

139. YCAW, *Youth Challenge the War Makers* (New York, [1938]), 19, YCAW; Hal Draper, "The Student Movement of the Thirties: A Political History," 179–81; Garland Embrey to Joe [Lash], April 18, 1938, JPL.

140. *Student Advocate* (March 1938), 4–6.

141. In one respect, however, the president was ahead of the ASU on the road to interventionism in that he supported expanding the military while the ASU had not yet adopted this position. It was not until its Dec. 1938 convention that the ASU changed its position on defense in favor of preparedness, endorsing an ROTC program for fighter pilots. See *Wisconsin Soapbox,* April 1939, JPL; *ASU Chapter Guide* (Jan. 1939), ACLU. Also see FDR's lecture to movement leaders criticizing their ignorance of military matters, Lash Diary, Jan. 16, 1940, JPL.

142. *Socialist Call,* Feb. 19, 1938; Arthur Kinoy, "An Open Letter to the Harvard Neutrality Council," *Harvard Progressive,* March 19, 1938, HARV.

143. Joseph P. Lash to Garland Embrey, May 12, 1938, JPL. On Communist fears concerning the YCAW, also see Mac Weiss to Carl [Ross?], Nov. 21, 1938, JPL.

144. Dave Grant, "World Youth Speaks For Peace," *Young Communist Review* (Sept. 1938), 3–4, 27.

145. *Ibid.; Daily Worker,* Aug. 17, 1938.

146. *Daily Worker,* Aug. 24, 1938.

147. Judah Drob, "The World Youth Congress," *Socialist Review* (Sept.-Oct. 1938), 13–15; George Rawick, "The New Deal and Youth: The Civilian Conservation Corps, the National Youth Administration and the American Youth Con-

gress" (Ph.D. diss., Univ. Of Wisconsin, 1957), 343; Alvaine Hollister to Action Committee Member, Aug. 6, 1938; Minutes, YPSL exec. committee, Aug. 10, 1938, both in YPSL files, SP; Alvaine Hollister to Governing Committee Member, Aug. 11, 1938, YCAW.

148. Drob, "The World Youth Congress," 15.

149. *Vassar Miscellany News,* Jan. 11, 1939; *Oberlin Review,* Sept. 22, 1937; *Michigan Daily,* March 24, Dec. 2, 1938, Jan. 4, 1939; *Unite the Campus to Save Peace* [n.d], 8, 10, 11, JPL; Ruth to Joe [Lash], March 3, 1937, JPL.

150. *Michigan Daily,* March 24, 1938; Samuel Levinger, "The War Is Long," *Student Advocate* (Dec. 1937), 7; "Oppressed and Invaded Spain," Univ. of Chicago *Student Partisan* (Dec. 1937), 1, UC; Avram Goldstein, "Forging a New Tradition," *Harvard Progressive* (Sept. 1939), 8; CCNY *Campus,* April 9, 1937; George Watt, letter from Spain, *Vassar Miscellany News,* Oct. 16, 1937; "Two Letters from Spain," *Brooklyn College Observer* (April 1938), 8, 25, BC; *Michigan Daily,* Jan. 4, 1939.

151. Wechsler, *The Age of Suspicion,* 100–101; CCNY *Campus,* Oct. 15, 1937; *Daily Worker,* Nov. 10, 1938; Celeste Strack Kaplan interview with author.

152. William Sussman to Joseph P. Lash [Fall 1939], JPL.

Chapter 7. Beyond the New Deal? Egalitarian Dreams and Communist Schemes

1. *Washington Post,* Feb. 21, 1937; "After the Pilgrimage," *Student Advocate* (April 1937), 5; *NYT,* Feb. 21, 1937; Joseph P. Lash, *Eleanor and Franklin* (New York, 1971), 712.

2. Leslie A. Gould, *American Youth Today* (New York, 1940), 63–84. Although the Youth Pilgrimage was the student movement's first sizable national march on Washington, movement organizers held two previous, much smaller protests at the White House during the Roosevelt era. The first of these was a demonstration by thirty unemployed college graduates. In May 1933, they marched to the White House to call for federal grants for education and aid to the unemployed. Led by Joseph Lash, this delegation was part of a short-lived organization, the Association of Unemployed College Alumni. A delegation of these protesters met with Roosevelt aide Louis Howe, who greeted them warmly. A second youth demonstration occurred in Dec. 1933, when about 300 NSL and SLID activists, in town for a political conference, held an anti-ROTC demonstration outside the White House (*Washington News,* May 4, 1933; *NYT,* May 4, Dec. 19, 1933; Joseph P. Lash memoir typescript, 2A, JPL; *What Is the "A.U.C.A."?* (New York, 1933), JPL.

3. *Declaration of Rights of American Youth* (New York, 1935), 1–5; William Hinckley, *Youth Seeks Peace, Freedom and Progress* (New York, 1936), 3–22.

4. Jack McMichael interview with author, Athens, W. Va., Aug. 22, 1982; Gould, *American Youth Today,* passim.

5. *Proceedings Third American Youth Congress* (Cleveland, 1936), 5–47; Gould, *American Youth Today,* 113, 299–300; *Proceedings Congress of Youth* (New York, 1939), 50–51. On the founding and early activities of the AYC, see Robert Cohen, "Revolt of the Depression Generation: America's First Mass Student Movement, 1929–1941" (Ph.D. diss., UC Berkeley, 1987), 390–402; William Hinckley, *American Youth Acts: The Story of the American Youth Congress* (New York [1936]), 3–13.

6. *Michigan Daily,* Feb. 18, 1940; George Watt interview with author.

7. *Student Review* (Oct. 1935), 10; *Daily Worker,* Feb. 22, 1937.

8. "For a National Student Movement: A Suggested Basis," *Student Review* (Jan.-Feb. 1932), 4; George Rawick, "The New Deal and Youth: The Civilian Conservation Corps, the National Youth Administration and the American Youth Congress" (Ph.D. diss., Univ. Wisconsin, 1957), 206.

9. *Student Review* (Oct. 1935), 11.

10. U.S. Congress, Senate Committee on Education and Labor, *American Youth Act Hearings* 74th Congress, 2nd Session, 13, 19, 119, 138, 182, 224. Williams estimated that despite the NYA's efforts, some 3.5 million youths could not afford to attend high school. See *NYT,* March 12, 1938.

11. *American Youth Act Hearings,* 197, 276; *Student Review* (Oct. 1935), 11.

12. *American Youth Act Hearings,* 14–15, 198, 231.

13. Gould, *American Youth Today,* 71–72.

14. *Student Review* (Oct. 1935), 10; *American Youth Act Manual* (New York, 1936); " 'Suffer Little Children . . . ,'—The Unmentionables of American Education," *Student Advocate* (Feb. 1936), 16–17.

15. *NYT,* March 21, 1936; transcript of Address by Rep. Thomas R. Amlie over the Columbia Broadcasting System, Jan. 29, 1936, JPL; Charles Beard, Francis Gorman, Celeste Strack, "Save the Lost Generation! Three Pleas to Congress for Passage of the Youth Act," *Student Advocate* (April 1936), 17–18; *Challenge of Youth,* March 5, 1940.

16. *NYT,* May 7, 1934.

17. "Address by Mrs. Eleanor Roosevelt," in *Proceedings Congress of Youth,* 34–37.

18. "A Summary of the Proceedings of the National Council of the American Youth Congress Held in Washington, D.C., on January 25–26, 1936," 1–3, JPL; Lash, *Eleanor and Franklin,* 708–10; Joseph P. Lash, *Eleanor: A Friend's Memoir* (Garden City, N.Y., 1964), 3–4.

19. Lash, *Eleanor and Franklin,* 709.

20. Lash, *Eleanor: A Friend's Memoir,* 3–4.

21. Lash, *Eleanor and Franklin,* 711; *Daily Worker,* Feb. 22, 1937.

22. Lash, *Eleanor and Franklin,* 712–13: William Hinckley to Friend, March 8, 1937, JPL.

23. David O. Levine, *The American College and the Culture of Aspiration* (Ithaca, N.Y., 1986), 113–35. I borrow the phrase "culture of aspiration" from Levine, who offers a penetrating analysis of this phenomenon.

24. Robert E. Lane, *The Student and Labor* (ASU pamphlet, n.d.), 1–7, NYU; Joseph P. Lash, *The Campus: A Fortress of Democracy* (New York, 1938), 34–35; Wechsler, *Revolt on the Campus* (1935: reprint, Seattle, 1973), 149–66.

25. George Watt interview with author.

26. *Ibid.*

27. James Wechsler interview with author.

28. Doris Yankauer and Herbert Mayer, *Question Before the House* (New York, 1935), 16–17, VC. Vassar student support work for striking factory workers in Beacon, N.Y., may well have inspired the authors of this play. See *Vassar Miscellany News,* Oct. 4, 26, 1935.

29. Irving Howe, *A Margin of Hope: An Intellectual Autobiography* (New York, 1982), 8.

30. Brooklyn College *Pioneer,* Feb. 14, 20, 25, 1935; *NYT,* Feb. 17, 1935.

31. Brooklyn College *Pioneer,* Oct. 31, 1934. This strike support work was led jointly by the campus NSL and SLID branches.

32. CCNY *Campus,* Feb. 15, 18, 1935.

33. *Barnard Bulletin,* May 10, 1935. Students did support work for rural labor and farm strikes. See *Daily Cardinal,* Nov. 4, 5, 8, 1933, Jan. 13, 1934; Visalia *Times Delta,* Oct. 19, 1933; Berkeley *Student Outpost,* Nov. 13, 1933, UCB.

34. Budd Shulberg, "Dartmouth Rejects the Academic Mind," *Student Advocate* (April 1936), 13, 30.

35. *Daily Californian,* Sept. 10, 11, 16, 17, 22 23, Oct. 19, 28, 1936; *Berkeley Daily Gazette,* Sept. 21, 1936; *Oakland Tribune,* Sept. 25, 1936.

36. Celeste Strack Kaplan interview with author. Also see *Young Spartacus,* June 1934.

37. *Columbia Spectator,* March 6, 1936.

38. *Student Outpost,* Aug. 23, Sept. 26, 1934.

39. *Daily Californian,* Oct. 14, 1936; "The ROTC Trains Strikebreakers," *Student Advocate* (Oct.-Nov. 1936), 6; *Voice of the Federation,* Oct. 8, 1936.

40. *The Harvard Student Union: A Record and a Promise,* 5; *Harvard Crimson,* May 10, 1933; Alice and Staughton Lynd, eds., *Rank and File: Personal Histories by Working Class Organizers* (Boston, 1973), 76.; James E. Jackson interview with author, Manhattan, N.Y., Aug. 31, Nov. 17, 1982.

41. Dorothy Thompson, "Of Mines and Men," *The Intercollegian and Far Horizons* (April-May 1938), 135–36; "Students in Industry," *Intercollegian* (April 1931), 235–36; *Barnard Bulletin,* Dec. 3, 1937; *Vassar Miscellany News,* Oct. 8, 1932, April 29, 1933, Oct. 13, 1934; Anna Caples, "The Union Is Santa Claus," *Student Outlook* (Feb. 1933), 9.

42. A. and S. Lynd, eds., *Rank and File,* 76.

43. *Voice of the Federation,* Oct. 24, 1935, Oct. 22, 1936; John L. Lewis, "CIO: A Challenge to the Campus," *Student Advocate* (Feb. 1937), 14.

44. George Watt interview with author; on the role that alumni of the student movement played in the labor movement, see Nathan Solomon interview with author, Pound Ridge, N.Y., May 13, 1982; Larry Rogin interview with author, Washington, D.C., June 4, 1982; James E. Jackson interview with author; Celeste Strack Kaplan interview with author; Kay Cline Burton essay in *ASU 50th Anniversary Reunion* (Long Beach, Cal., 1986), 6.

45. Gould, *American Youth Today,* 121–22; Campus Committee for the California Youth Act, leaflet (n.d.), "A Call: Northern California Assembly of Youth to Draft A California Youth Act" (Jan. 9–10, 1937), both in pamphlet collection of Henry May.

46. Lash, *Toward a Closed Shop on Campus* (New York, 1937), 6; Univ. of Chicago *Upsurge,* Nov. 14, 21, 1935, UC.

47. Student Workers Federation of the Univ. of Michigan, *Why SWF?* (Ann Arbor, 1936), 1; Agnes Reynolds to Molly Yard, Aug. 22, 1937, JPL. *Daily Texan,* May 17, 1934; Radical activists at the Univ. of Texas also organized a strike by students who worked in campus area restaurants, and they attempted to unionize all student waiters in Austin. See FBI file # 61–121, Jan. 25, 1940, Report by J.O Peyronnin [? last name only partially legible], New Orleans.

48. *University Daily Kansan,* Oct. 11, 15, 1935; on the LID's role in founding this student union in Kansas, see Paul Porter interview with author, Reston, Va., June 4, 1982.

49. *Daily Californian,* Oct. 16, 1940.

50. *Ibid.,* Jan. 14, 24, 1938.

51. *Ibid.,* and Jan. 20, 1938; Lawrence A. Maes, "Development and Applica-

tion of Fair Bear Standards at the University of California," unpublished paper, UC Berkeley, 1948, Institute of Industrial Relations Library, UC Berkeley.

52. *Daily Californian,* Sept. 6, 1939; M. R. White to Robert G. Sproul, March 22, 1939, President's Files, UCB; *Daily Californian,* Oct. 5, 1939. On the similar Labor Board which ASU activists helped establish at Ohio State University, see *Ohio State Lantern,* Oct. 19, 1939, Jan. 10, Feb. 28, Oct. 7, 8, 10, 1940.

53. *Daily Californian,* May 1, 1936. Also see Reynold Cohn, "Labor Board," *Occident* (Oct. 1937), 14–15, UCB; Henry May interview with author, Berkeley, June 22, 1982.

54. "For a National Student Movement," 4; *Program of American Youth Congress* (New York, 1934), 8, 11, 14; *Student Union Bulletin,* Jan. 7, 1936; Jack Mc-Michael to author, July 24, 1982.

55. "A Summary of the Proceedings of the Meeting of the National Council of the American Youth Congress held in Washington, D.C. on January 25–26, 1936," 3, JPL.

56. *Ibid.*

57. *Declaration of the Rights of American Youth,* 1.

58. G. W. Studebaker to Joseph P. Lash, Feb. 17, 1936, JPL.

59. "The American Negro in College, 1932–1933," *Crisis* (Aug. 1933), 181–82.

60. Univ. of Wisconsin *Daily Cardinal,* Oct. 26, 1935; *Ohio State Lantern,* May 17, 1937; Univ. of Chicago *Student Partisan* (Dec. 1937), 16–17, *UC.* On the barring of blacks from intercollegiate athletics, see *University Daily Kansan,* Feb. 14, 1935, Oct. 17, 1939, and May 3, 1940; *Daily Bruin,* Oct. 29, 1940; on racial discrimination in the ROTC, see *Ohio State Lantern,* Dec. 5, 1939.

61. *Daily Illini,* Jan. 10, 1932. Racism was by no means confined to the extra-curricular part of campus life. Bigoted professors could make life miserable for African American students inside the classroom. See Everett W. Johnson to Henry J. Doermann, Feb. 9, 1929, President's Papers, UT; Randolph Edmonds, "Education in Self-Contempt," *Crisis* (Aug. 1938), 262–63, 266.

62. "Lights and Shadows of Being a Negro: A Symposium," *Intercollegian* (Dec. 1930), 71.

63. *Columbia Spectator,* Oct. 15, 1935; " 'Kansas Is a White Man's School,' " *Student Advocate* (March 1936), 23.

64. Esther Cooper Jackson interview with author, Manhattan, N.Y., Sept. 17, 1982.

65. Caroline Wasson Thomason, "Will Prejudice Capture Oberlin?" *Crisis* (Dec. 1934), 360–61.

66. Sigma Nu constitution cited in Thomas J. Cunningham to Dean Arleigh Williams, Aug. 15, 1960, President's Files, UCB; Alfred Lee, *Fraternities Without Brotherhood* (Boston, 1955), passim; R. Cohen, "Greeks Ignore Racist Past," *Daily Californian,* Oct. 16, 1986; Harold Kaplan and Alec Morin, "Jim Crow on Campus," Univ. of Chicago *Student Partisan* (Dec. 1937), 17.; Univ. of Chicago *Phoenix* (March 1937), 1, UC; *Ohio State Lantern,* May 17, 1937; Wechsler, *Revolt on the Campus,* 366–67; Univ. of Toledo *Collegian,* Feb. 25, 1938.

67. *Columbia Spectator,* April 14, 15, 1936; *Ohio State Lantern,* May 14, June 1, 1937.

68. William McClendon, "Which College—White or Negro?" *Crisis* (Sept. 1934), 264. The reputation of elite white campuses in the North for racial discrimination was so strong within the black community that it discouraged blacks not only from

attending such colleges, but even from going to conferences on these campuses. On the eve of the ASU's 1937 convention, for instance, Sarah Murphy, a black activist from South Carolinia, wrote the ASU's national leadership expressing concern over whether she would be welcome at this convention, since "I understand that Vassar frankly is not desirous of having colored students in its student body." ASU leader Molly Yard's response to Murphy cited the ASU's "no discrimination" policy. Yard assured her that at all ASU conventions there "could be absolutely no question as to whether Negro delegates would be welcome," and that "we are very glad that you will be coming to the convention" (Sarah Murphy to Joseph P. Lash, Nov. 8, 1937; Molly Yard to Sarah Murphy, Nov. 11, 1937, JPL).

69. Kenneth B. Clark interview with author, Manhattan, N.Y., Aug. 3, 1982. Mordecai Johnson, "The Day of Reckoning for the College Bred," *Intercollegian* (Dec. 1930), 70, 74. Michael R. Winston. "Through the Back Door: Academic Racism and the Negro Scholar in Historical Perspective," *Daedalus* (Summer 1971), 678, 695.

70. "They Shall Not Die!," *Student Review* (Oct. 1932), 3; James Wechsler, *Revolt on the Campus,* 354–73. The student movement's racial egalitarianism was also strengthened by the access its leftist leaders had to communist historiography, which was free of many of the racist myths which distorted American history textbooks in this period. At the ASU's summer leadership institute, for example, student organizers studied and praised communist historian James Allen's revisionist work *Reconstruction,* with its positive interpretation of Radical Reconstuction and interracial democracy ("ASU Newsletter, Thyra Edwards Group," July 24, 1939, JPL).

71. Max Gordon interview with author; the student movement's African American leaders frequently raised civil rights issues and other black student concerns in articles published in the student movement's national magazines. See Maurice Gates, "Howard Must Answer!," *Student Review* (Feb. 1934), 4–5; Maurice Gates, "South Revisited," *ibid.* (March 1935), 15; Maurice Gates,"Inciting to Riot," *ibid.* (Oct. 1935), 9; James Jackson, "We Tell the Congressmen," *Student Review* (June 1935), 5–6; Lyonel Florant, "Negro Education and Status," *Student Outlook* (Oct. 1935), 10–11; Louis Burnham, "We Are Tired of Waiting, Mrs. Roosevelt," *Student Advocate* (March 1936), 16.

72. Muriel Rukeyser, "Starting the Ball Rolling, the Student Conference on Negro Student Problems," *Student Review* (May 1933), 17–18; "A Guide to Action-Proposed Resolutions of Student Conference on Negro Student Problems," *ibid.,* 19–20.

73. Lyonel Florant, "Youth Exhibits a New Spirit," *Crisis* (Aug. 1936), 237.

74. James E. Jackson interview with author.

75. "Three Conventions," *Student Review* (Feb. 1934), 5; Gould, *American Youth Today,* 64–65, 77; Nick Aaron Ford, "Oklahoma Youth Legislature Hits Jim Crow," *Crisis* (April 1938), 116.

76. "Three Conventions," *Student Review* (Feb. 1934), 5; Gates, "Howard Must Answer!," 4–5.

77. "They Shall Not Die!," 3–4; *Student Review* (Dec. 1932), 3; (May 1932), 4; Muriel Rukeyser, "The Trial," *ibid.* (Jan. 1934), 20; Muriel Rukeyser, "From Scottsboro to Decatur," *ibid.* (April 1933), 12–15.

78. "Agitate! Educate! Organize," *Student Outlook* (March 1934), 23; Hilia Laine, "The Michigan Color-Line," *Student Review* (Dec. 1934), 12; Berkeley *Student Outpost,* March 11, 1935; CCNY *Campus,* Sept. 19, 1935; Univ. of Chicago *Upsurge,*

Feb. 20, 1935; "A Communication on Phi Beta Kappa from Howard," *Student Review* (Nov. 1934), 19; *Bulletin of the Fourth National Convention of the National Student League* (St. Louis, Dec. 1934), 3. On student protests against racial discrimination in a campus employment agency, see CCNY *Campus,* March 13, 1936; a hall hosting a student dance, see CCNY *Campus,* Dec. 20, 1936; the hiring of faculty, see CCNY *Campus,* Sept. 19, 1935; college admissions policies, see *Vassar Miscellany News,* Nov. 8, 1939.

79. James E. Jackson interview with author; Lash, *The Campus: A Fortress of Democracy,* 45–47.

80. *Ibid.*; Harvard Sitkoff, *A New Deal for Blacks* (New York, 1978), 265; Univ. of Chicago *Soapbox,* Jan. 1937, UC; Univ. of Chicago *Student Partisan* (Dec. 1937), 16–17; *Ohio State Lantern,* May 3, 17, June 3, 1937; *Columbia Spectator,* April 17, May 1, 1936; CCNY *Campus,* Dec. 20, March 13, 1936, April 27, 1937.

81. Dan T. Carter, *Scottsboro: A Tragedy of the American South* (Baton Rouge, 1969), 114; on this support of lynching, see *Daily Texan,* March 4, 1934. A survey of college students in North Carolina found that 87.1 percent thought blacks should remain segregated and 47.8 percent believed that the lynching of blacks for rape was justifiable. See K. C. Garrison and Viola S. Burch, "A Study of Racial Attitudes of College Students," *Journal of Social Psychology* (May 1933), 232; on the student movement's difficulty in penetrating the segregationist South, see Jack McMichael interview with author; Monroe Sweetland interview with author.

82. F. Palmer Weber interview with author, Manhattan. N.Y., Jan. 25, 1982.

83. Univ. of Virginia *College Topics,* May 18, 1934.

84. Studs Terkel, *Hard Times: An Oral History of the Great Depression* (New York, 1970), 401. The subject of this interview, though appearing under the pseudonym Chance Stoner, was in fact F. Palmer Weber. See Weber interview with author.

85. Transcript of F. Palmer Weber interview with Charles Moran, 16, UVA; Weber interview with author; *College Topics,* Nov. 26, 1935. The Univ. of Virginia NSL also joined with African American students from Virgina Union University in protesting the state legislature's inferior funding of black schools in 1933. See James E. Jackson, "The Youth Movement," *Souvenir Bulletin* [of the Southern Negro Youth Congress], Feb. 13–14, 1937, NNC; James E. Jackson interview with author.

86. Dave to Joe [Lash], April 21 [1937?], JPL.

87. On this Christian radicalism and civil rights work in the South, see Jack McMichael interview with author; F. Palmer Weber interview with author. Anthony Dunbar, *Against the Grain: Southern Radicals and Prophets 1929–1959* (Charlottesville, 1981), 1–135; "An Action Story," *Intercollegian* (Dec. 1930), 86–89; "Interracial Tour," *ibid.* (Jan. 1931), 127; "What Is the 'Race' Problem?," *ibid.* (May 1936), 195–96; "South Carolina's First Interracial Student Conference," *ibid.* (May–June 1934), 23.

88. Jack McMichael interview with author; *Emory Wheel,* Jan. 12, 26, 1933. Emory's mainstream student leaders strongly criticized the campus YMCA chapter for sponsoring these interracial meetings. See *Emory Wheel,* Oct. 3, 1935.

89. Jack McMichael interview with author; *Southern Regional Council Minutes,* vol. II, June, 1936, *YWCA.* McMichael also took the fight against segregation beyond the South in 1935, when he was elected chair of a committee charged with setting the racial policy for the national council of the student YM/YWCAs. Through this committee, McMichael committed the Y's to "direct our united efforts towards the establishment of a student Christian movement and a social order which pro-

vides for every individual regardless of race, all opportunities to participate and share alike all the relationships of life"—working towards the "elimination of all segregation and discrimination" (*Moving into a New Century: An Historical Overview of the National Student YWCA* (Princeton, 1974), 3).

90. Univ. of Virginia National Student League to Univ. of Virginia Board of Visitors, Oct. 4, 1935, President's Papers, UVA.

91. Univ. of Virginia *College Topics,* Oct. 10, 17, 1935.

92. *Ibid.,* Oct. 12, 22, 1935.

93. *Ibid.,* Oct. 12, 1935.

94. *Ibid.,* Oct. 24, 1935.

95. Univ. of North Carolina *Daily Tar Heel,* Jan. 7, 8, 10, 11, 13–16, 1939; Pauli Murray, *Song in a Weary Throat* (New York, 1987), 114–29.

96. *Daily Tar Heel,* Jan. 7, 8, 10, 11, 13–16, 1939; on the early stages of this legal battle, see Richard Kluger, *Simple Justice* (New York, 1975), 173–213.

97. Ralph Ellison, *The Invisible Man* (New York, 1952), 34–148.

98. Langston Hughes, "Cowards from the Colleges," *Crisis* (Aug. 1934), 226. Also see Howard Univ. *Hilltop,* May 13, 1936. These conditions provoked black student strikes in the 1920s. See Raymond Wolters, *The New Negro on Campus: The Black College Rebellions of the 1920s* (Princeton, 1975), passim.

99. Hughes, "Cowards from the Colleges," 226; Lyonel Florant, "Youth Exhibits a New Spirit," *Crisis* (Aug. 1936), 237.

100. Ishmael Flory interview with author, Chicago, Oct. 29, 1982; Joe M. Richardson, *A History of Fisk University* (Birmingham, 1980), 128–30; "Fisk and Flory," *Crisis* (April 1934), 111; Thomas E. Jones, "Some Fisk Ideals," *Fisk News* (March-April 1934), 6; President's Trustees Series, No. 3; Thomas E. Jones to [L.] Hollingsworth [Wood], Feb. 26, 1934, both in Thomas E. Jones Papers, 1926–1946, FU; Andrew J. Allison, "The Flory Decision," *Fisk News* (March-April 1934), 5.

101. "Excerpts from the Address of John Hope Franklin, President of the Student Council, 1934–35," *Fisk News* (May-June, 1935) 12; *College Topics,* Nov. 26, 1935; James E. Jackson interview with author; Maurice Gates, "Negro Students Challenge Social Forces," *Crisis* (Aug. 1935), 232.

102. James E. Jackson interview with author.

103. Kenneth B. Clark interview with author, Manhattan, N.Y., Aug. 3, 1982.

104. *Ibid.; Baltimore Afro-American,* March 24, 1934. Unlike the typical accommodationist black college president, Johnson was a contradicatory figure. He often engaged in civil rights advocacy himself, and allowed faculty to do so as well, but he also worried about Howard's financial health and would lash out at any protests—particularly by students—that he thought might threaten Howard's funding. Johnson's egaliltarian sympathies and institutional responsibilties as a college president often clashed, and from one event to another one never knew which Johnson would appear: Johnson the civil rights advocate or Johnson the cautious college president (see Howard Univ. *Hilltop,* March 26, 1940; Rayford Logan, *Howard University: The First Hundred Years* (New York, 1969), 279–93; Augusta Strong, "Southern Youth's Proud Heritage," *Freedomways* (Winter 1964), 39; Sitkoff, *A New Deal for Youth,* 156).

105. *Hilltop,* Dec. 22. 1934.

106. Richard Collins, "Liberalism and Negroes," *Student Advocate* (Feb. 1937), 8.

107. CCNY *Campus,* Dec. 20, 1936; *Columbia Spectator,* April 15, 17, 1936.

108. James E. Jackson, "The Youth Movement"; James E. Jackson interview

with author; Dorothy Burnham interview with author, Brooklyn, N.Y., March 16, 1983. Robin D. G. Kelley offers an excellent summary of SNYC's activities in his *Hammer and Hoe, Alabama Communists during the Great Depression* (Chapel Hill, 1990), 200–219.

109. James E. Jackson interview with author.

110. *Ibid.*

111. *Ibid.*

112. Strong, "Southern Youth's Proud Heritage," 38.

113. James E. Jackson interview with author.

114. *Ibid.*; Norfolk *Journal and Guide,* April 24, 1937.

115. James E. Jackson interview with author.

116. *Norfolk Journal and Guide,* April 24, May 15, 1937.

117. James E. Jackson interview with author.

118. *Proclamation of Southern Negro Youth* (Birmingham, 1938), 1, NNC.

119. Esther Cooper Jackson interview with author.

120. *Official Proceedings of the Second All Southern Negro Youth Conference,* April 1938, NNC; Henry Winston, "Freedom, Equality and Opportunity: Southern Negro Youth Congress Charts Road to Progress," *The New South* (May 1938), 10–11. Augusta Strong, "Youth Meets in Birmingham," *Crisis* (June 1939), 178–80; Augusta Strong, "Southern Youth's Proud Heritage," 44–45; James E. Jackson, Jr., "Our Battle for the Ballot" (Birmingham, 1940), passim, NYU. James Jackson interview with author; Strong, "Southern Youth's Proud Heritage," 50; *Cavalcade,* April and May, 1941, NNC.

121. Though collegiate racism emerged as a national issue in the 1930s, during the preceding decade racism and white paternalism sparked protests at several northern campuses and black colleges. See Wolters, *The New Negro on Campus,* 316–39.

122. Sitkoff, *A New Deal for Blacks,* 190–243; ASU, *Students Serve Democracy* (New York, 1939), 20; "The Inevitable Mr. Gaines," *Missouri Student* editorial, reprinted in North Carolina *Daily Tar Heel,* Jan. 10, 1939; George Cech, "Spotlight on Missouri," *The Intercollegian and Far Horizons* (March 1939), 111–12; "Why Not Negroes?," Univ. of West Virginia *Daily Athenaeum* editorial, reprinted in *Ohio State Lantern,* May 11, 1937; *Daily Texan,* Dec. 19, 1937; Charles Houston, "Don't Shout Too Soon," *Crisis* (March 1936), 79, 91; "University of Missouri Case Won," *Crisis* (Jan. 1939), 10–11; Kluger, *Simple Justice,* 155–213.

123. Note, however, that though the largest organizations in the student movement—the ASU and the Youth Congress—spearheaded this shift towards liberalism not every movement organization was supportive of this. The small but vocal left wing of the student movement, which included the YPSLs and the Trotskyists, clung to a revolutionary line (YPSL memo, "Youth and the New Deal," Oct. 10, 1938, YPSL files, SP). Although the YPSLs and Trotskyists were increasingly isolated and steadily lost influence in the student movement of the late 1930s, they did offer some cogent criticism of the shifts in ASU and Youth Congress policy, which will be discussed below.

124. *Program of the American Youth Congress,* 6, 7, 13.

125. Joseph Clark interview with author; Richard Criley interview with author.

126. *Student Review* (Dec. 1934), 8; Joseph P. Lash, typescript speech, "Student Movement of the 1930s" [n.d.], 13, JPL.

127. *Program of the American Youth Congress,* 5; *Declaration of the Rights of American Youth,* 3.

128. *Daily Worker,* Aug. 13, 1938.

129. "The Creed of the American Youth Congress," *Young Communist Review* (Aug. 1939), 7.

130. *Program of the American Youth Congress,* 6–7, 13. ASU Staff Meeting Minutes, March 15, 1937, JPL; William W. Hinckley to Joseph P. Lash, Nov. 19, 1937, JPL; Celeste Strack, "The ASU Convention," *Young Communist Review* (Dec. 1938), 28.

131. Ruth Watt, "On the Campus," *Young Communist Review* (April 1939), 18; Strack, "The ASU Convention," 28; "The National Chairman Speaks," *Student Advocate* (March 1938), 20.

132. *NYT,* Jan. 29, 1938; Eleanor Roosevelt, "My Day," reprinted in *Proceedings, Congress of Youth* (New York, 1939), 43; Lash, *Eleanor and Franklin,* 713–15; Jack McMichael interview with author.

133. Rawick, "The New Deal and Youth," 323–24.

134. "Resolution on the American Youth Congress passed by the YPSL NEC at meeting at Philadelphia, May 29 to 30, 1937," YPSL files, SP.

135. YPSL memo, "Youth and the New Deal," Oct. 10, 1938, YPSL files, SP.

136. Joseph Clark interview with author; Joseph P. Lash interview with author; Gil Green interview with author; Richard Criley interview with author; Harold Draper, "The First American Youth Congress," *Student Outlook* (Oct. 1934), 15–16; Theodore Draper, "American Youth Rejects Fascism," *New Masses* (Aug. 28, 1934), 11–13.

137. YPSL memo, "Youth and the New Deal."

138. Minutes of Resident Board [of the American Youth Congress], March 13, 1937, JPL; Gould, *American Youth Today,* 86; *NYT,* Oct. 10, 15, 1937, Dec. 7, 1937.

139. Hy Weintraub to Maxwell Haraway, Aug. 5, 1936, YPSL files, SP.

140. Minutes of Resident Board, Feb. 17, 1938, JPL; *Proceedings, Congress of Youth* (New York, 1939), 9.

141. Lash, *Eleanor and Franklin,* 716; Joseph P. Lash, *Love Eleanor: Eleanor Roosevelt and Her Friends* (Garden City, N.Y., 1982), 281.

142. Franklin D. Roosevelt memorandum, Jan. 17, 1939, reprinted in Lash, *Eleanor and Franklin,* 717.

143. "Proceedings of the National Council of the American Youth Congress, January 25–26, 1936," JPL; Lash, *Eleanor and Franklin,* 709.

144. Irving Howe, *Socialism and America* (New York, 1985), 87–104.

145. Gil Green interview with author.

146. Rawick, "The New Deal and Youth," 295–97; the leaders of the Youth Congress always publicly denied that it was communist-dominated. See Gould, *American Youth Today,* 137–64. But these denials were disingenuous. See Gil Green interview with author; Lash Diary, April 26, 1938, March 22, 1940, JPL; David Dubinsky to Eleanor Roosevelt June 20, 1940, ER.

147. Arthur Clifford, *The Truth About the American Youth Congress* (Detroit, 1935), passim; Gould, *American Youth Today,* 293; Brooklyn College *Vanguard,* Feb. 8, 1937.

148. *American Youth Today,* the official history of the Youth Congress by Leslie A. Gould is a case study in such disingenuousness and is typical of the literature

put out by the Youth Congress. This account of the Youth Congress is 300 pages long, but devotes only two pages (162–63) to the Young Communist League. In these two pages we are told that it was "patently absurd" to suppose that the mere "handful" of communists in the Youth Congress could dominate that organization. Gould also claimed that communists in the Youth Congress "always abided by the rules of democratic procedure." Both of these claims were false. On communist domination of key Youth Congress committees and staff positions, see Rawick, "The New Deal and Youth," 295–97, and see Resolution on the American Youth Congress passed by the Y.P.S.L. N.E.C. at Meeting at Philadelphia, May 20 to 30, 1937, JPL; on the secrecy involved in this domination, see Gil Green interview with author; Wechsler, *The Age of Suspicion,* 70–73; on YCL abuse of democratic process in achieving this domination, see Report of the First Meeting of the Permanent Council of the Hennerin County Youth Conference, June 12, 1936; and see Minutes of the YPSL District Executive Commitee, Aug. 10, 1938; both in YPSL files, SP.

149. Gould, *American Youth Today,* 137–64; Gil Green interview with author; Lash Diary, March 22, 1940; David Dubinsky to Eleanor Roosevelt, June 20, 1940, ER. Such disingenuousness was as pronounced in the ASU as it was in the Youth Congress. Thus in Lash's address to the 1938 ASU convention, the ASU leader asserted that "We are not a leftist or anti-capitalist organization. . . . I am sure that no one in the American Student Union would advocate the socialization of toothbrushes" (Joseph P. Lash, "Students in the Service of Democracy," in *Keep Democracy Working by Making It Serve Human Needs: Proceedings Fourth National Convention of the American Student Union* (New York, Dec. 1938), 37). Although Lash was correct in saying the ASU was not an explicitly anti-capitalist organization, its leadership was then and had always been dominated by leftists. Indeed, Lash himself, the ASU's highest ranking officer, was, at the time he gave this speech, a committed socialist, closely allied with the YCL, the CP, and their Popular Front policies—so that his denial that the "leftist" label applied to the ASU was at best a half-truth. Also see *NYT,* Nov. 28, 1939.

150. Joseph P. Lash, *Eleanor, a Friend's Memoir,* 1–2, 7–15; Schrecker, *No Ivory Tower,* 63–83.

151. Lash Diary, March 22, 1940, JPL; Joseph P. Lash interview with author.

152. Junius Irving Scales and Richard Nickson, *Cause at Heart: A Former Communist Remembers,* (Athens, Ga., 1983), 67. Mark Greenly, a Philadelphia ASUer, recalled that at his very first ASU meeting he encountered this same type of disingenuousness about the relationship between the ASU and the Communist Party. See Paul Lyons, *Philadelphia Communists, 1936–1956* (Philadelphia, 1982), 37.

153. Wechsler, *The Age of Suspicion,* 72; David Dubinsky to Eleanor Roosevelt June 20, 1940, ER; Eleanor Roosevelt, *This I Remember* (New York, 1949), 200; Don Fabun, "Is the ASU a Communist Front?," *Daily Californian,* Feb. 7, 1941. Since they played a decisive role in shaping movement policy, I have focused here on communists and their leadership role. But it should also be kept in mind that the ASU's history during the Popular Front era was also influenced by liberals— who came into the movement in response to its Popular Front policies and whose support helped encourage and expedite the movement's shift toward the New Deal. The "influx of a vast number of students who were neither socialist or communist . . . but believed in a wider utilization of the resources of government to meet human needs" added to the ASU's new liberal tone. In the Cold War era these liberals would have been termed dupes, but such terms are simplistic. Lib-

eral students wanted an organization which would work for progressive social change in alliance with the New Deal, and the ASU was responsive to them—at least temporarily (Joseph P. Lash to Rhea Whitley, May 16, 1939, JPL; Bruce Bliven Jr., "Citizens of Tomorrow," *New Republic* (Jan. 11, 1939), 283; Joseph P. Lash to Avram, May 19, 1939, JPL).

Chapter 8. Activist Impulses

1. Roscoe J.C. Dorsey, "The Future of Our Youth," *National Republic* (May 1939), 3; E. D. Clark, "Red Microbes in Our Colleges," *National Republic* (Jan. 1937), 1. Also see "Yellow Newspapers See Red," *School and Society* (Jan. 19, 1935), 100.

2. *New York American* editorial "Red Teachers," reprinted in *National Republic* (July/Aug. 1935), 28.

3. *Ibid.*

4. *NYT,* April 12, May 14, 1935; *Chicago Tribune,* April 13–15, 18, 1935; "W.R. Hearst Baits College 'Reds'," *The Social Frontier* (Jan. 1935), 3–4; Ellen Schrecker, *No Ivory Tower* (New York, 1986), 68–70; "Liberty in U.S.A," *The Social Frontier* (Nov. 1936), 63.

5. These statistics and all of the figures in this chapter on the sources of student activism are drawn from a sample group of 125 Depression-era student activists. Data on these activists come from the following sources: 55 autobiographical essays, written by student activists during the ASU's 1938 and 1939 summer training institute and 16 autobiographical essays written by student activists during the SLID's 1935 summer training institute, both in JPL; 24 interviews of student activists with the author; memoirs of six 1930s campus activists in *Political Activism and the Academic Conscience: The Harvard Experience 1936–41,* John Lyndenberg, ed. (Hobart and William Smith Colleges, 1977), 2–54, 67–73; three interviews in Vivian Gornick, *The Romance of American Communism* (New York, 1977), 101–4, 126–30, 140–45; five interviews in John Gerassi, *The Premature Anti-Fascists* (New York, 1986), 44–45, 48–49, 63–64, 69–70, 74–75; one interview in Studs Terkel, *Hard Times: An Oral History of the Great Depression* (New York, 1970), 398–99; additional memoirs of student activists in Irving Howe, *A Margin of Hope* (New York, 1982), 1–89; Junius Irving Scales and Richard Nickson, *Cause at Heart* (Athens, Ga., 1987), 29–87; James Wechsler, *The Age of Suspicion* (New York, 1981), 3–132; Henry F. May, *Coming to Terms* (Berkeley, 1987), 169–266; Pauli Murray, *Song in a Weary Throat* (New York, 1987), 59–91; John Gates, *The Story of an American Communist* (New York, 1958), 7–27; Eric Sevareid, *Not So Wild a Dream* (New York, 1956), 48–73; Richard Rovere, *Arrivals and Departures* (New York, 1976), 41–60; Paul Jacobs, *Is Curly Jewish?* (New York, 1965), 3–110; Leslie Fiedler, *Being Busted* (New York, 1969), 13–27; Thomas Merton, *The Seven Storey Mountain* (New York, 1948), 3–4, 131–65; John P. Roche, *Shadow and Substance* (New York, 1964), 432–41; Morton Sobell, *On Doing Time* (New York, 1974), 3–38; Victor G. Reuther, *The Brothers Reuther* (Boston, 1976), 1–69; Nancy Bedford Jones, "My Father Is a Liar," *Student Review* (Oct. 1935), 13–15; Jack McMichael, autobiographical essay, JM; Joseph P. Lash, memoir typescript, JPL; Daniel Boone Schirmer interview with Bill Schecter, Oral History of the American Left, NYU.

6. Anonymous, "My Autobiography"; Florence Dubroff autobiographical essay; Morton Jackson autobiographical essay; all in JPL. Carl Schorske, "A New

Yorker's Map of Cambridge: Ethnic Marginality and Political Ambivalence," in Lyndenberg, ed., *Political Activism,* 10.

Survey research on teachers in the 1930s suggests that the anecdotal evidence in these interviews concerning the narrow-mindedness and intolerance of conservative faculty reflected a very significant phenomenon in America education. One such survey found that 35 percent of the teachers polled "would deliberately omit from textbooks facts that might lead to criticism of the social order on the part of the young" (Manly H. Harper, "Social Attitudes of Educators," *The Social Frontier* (Feb. 1937), 146). Another survey found 48 percent of teachers favored the deportation of aliens who criticized the Constitution. See William H. Kirkpatrick, ed., *The Teacher and Society* (New York, 1937), 194.

7. Nancy Phillips autobiographical essay; also see Betsy Pifer autobiographical essay; both in JPL.

8. Anonymous autobiographical essay [of Bryn Mawr student], JPL.

9. Maxine Ture autobiographical essay, JPL.

10. Alice Berman autobiographical essay; Bernard Wolf autobiographical essay, both in JPL.

11. Clifford McVeagh, "Academic Napoleons #1: Ruthven of Michigan," *Student Advocate* (Feb. 1936), 13; Nancy Bedford Jones, "Academic Napoleons No. II: Provost Moore of UCLA," *ibid.* (March 1936), 19–20, 30; Roger Chase, "Academic Napoleons No. III: Nicholas Murray Butler," *ibid.* (April 1936), 20–21; Arthur Wilson, "Academic Napoleon No. IV: Chancellor Bowman of Pittsburgh," *ibid.* (Feb. 1937), 21–23; Theresa Levin, "Dr. Colligan: Tammany's Aloysius, Academic Napoleon No. 5," *ibid.* (Oct. 1937), 9–10, 26; Alberta Reid, "Academic Napoleon No. 6: Marvin of George Washington U.," *ibid.* (Dec. 37), 13–14, 18; "University Sweatshops," *ibid.* (Feb. 1936), 4; "Gagging the High Schools," *ibid.,* 20; "Kansas Is a White Man's School," *ibid* (March 1936), 23; "ROTC Trains Strikebreakers," *ibid.* (Oct.-Nov. 1936), 6; Robert N. Kelso, Jr., "How To Be a Censored Editor," *ibid.* (Oct. 1937), 16–17, 31; Jack Pollack, "Dr. Broadbent," *ibid.* (Feb. 1937), 18; Robert Rhinestone, "Gentleman and Scholar," *ibid.* (May 1936), 9; "Hey You!," *ibid.* (Oct. 1937), 2. Also see *Harvard Communist* (Nov. 1937), 19–20, HARV.

In the ASU's *Student Advocate,* the most widely circulated magazine put out by any 1930s American student activist organization, there were only six articles by or about radical faculty members during the entire three-year run of the magazine. Three of these six concerned academic freedom cases. None of the articles even remotely suggests that the student movement was dependent on leftist faculty. See D. E. Martin, "Still Sweetness and Light," *Student Advocate* (Feb. 1936), 24–25, 30; "Professors Speak Out," *ibid.* (March 1936), 5; Calvin J. Sutherlin, "For God, for Country—for the Yale Corporation," *ibid.* (Dec. 1936), 6–7; Reinhold Niebuhr, " 'Is Education a Private Industry'?," *ibid.* (Feb. 1937), 19–20, 29; Robert Kaltenborn, "Why Men Leave Harvard," *ibid.* (May 1937), 7–8; Dr. Leonard Lawson, "Peace on the Curriculum," *ibid.* (Dec. 1937), 21–22. On the limited relationship between radical faculty and students, see Leon Wofsy interview with author, Berkeley, April 29, 1986.

12. In our sample group of 125 activists, 10 of the 27 students who said that a faculty member fostered their politicization indictated that this faculty member was a liberal—while 14 named a radical faculty member and three did not specify whether the teacher was liberal or radical. For examples of this liberal role, see Virginia Sanford and Jeanette Schaeffer autobiographical essays, JPL.

13. Everett Ladd and Seymour Martin Lipset, *The Divided Academy* (New York, 1975), 27. On this growth of faculty liberalism, also see Harper, "Social Attitudes of Educators," 145–47; Kirkpartick, *The Teacher and Society,* 196, 223–24.

14. Jeanette Schaefer autobiographical essay, JPL.

15. Rembert Stokes autobiographical essay, JPL.

16. Virginia Sanford autobiographical essay, JPL.

17. Celeste Strack interview with author.

18. Kenneth B. Clark interview with author; Emily Shield autobiographical essay; Anonymous [Bryn Mawr] student autobiographical essay; both in JPL.

19. The exact figures were 25 mentioning conservative teachers, 10 liberal, 14 radical, and 3 not specified.

20. Schrecker, *No Ivory Tower,* 43, 68; Lyndenberg, ed., *Political Activism,* 19. Student activists, especially during the first half of the decade, complained about the relative lack of radical faculty at their colleges and universities. See *Soapbox,* May 1935; *Hunter Bulletin,* May 29, 1932; "Hearst at Harvard," *New Republic* (June 30, 1935), 335.

21. John Ise, "Shackles on Professors," *The Social Frontier* (May 1937), 242–45; Leo Marx, "The Harvard Retrospect and the Arrested Development of American Radicalism," in Lyndenberg, ed., *Political Activism,* 33; Kaltenborn, "Why Men Leave Harvard," 7–8.

22. Ernestine Freidl autobiographical essay, JPL.

23. Lewis Morton Cohen autobiographical essay, JPL.

24. B. Walker autobiographical essay, JPL.

25. Esther Cooper Jackson interview with author.

26. Nancy Philips autobiographical essay, JPL.

27. Celeste Strack Kaplan interview with author.

28. Marx, "The Harvard Retrospect," 33.

29. Mary McCarthy, *How I Grew* (New York, 1987), 205. Also see Alfred Kazin, *Starting Out in the the Thirties* (New York, 1965), 138.

30. For the only activists in our sampled group to be recruited directly into radical organizations by faculty members, see Esther Cooper Jackson interview with author; Lewis Morton Cohen autobiographical essay, JPL; Wechsler, *The Age of Suspicion,* 62.

31. Historians of American communism have failed to recognize the existence of this political double standard. Their oversight has left them in a historical vacuum as they debate the behavior of communist professors. Thus the anticommunist historian Theodore Draper attacks communist professors for failing to maintain scholarly neutrality and worshiping the Soviet Union, while anti-anticommunist historian Ellen Schrecker defends these communists by arguing that they displayed "fairness and lack of bias" in their teaching. Both sides of this debate seem to assume that the presence of any bias in the teaching of communist faculty would constitute both a terrible indictment of them and a unique departure from professional standards. This is a naive assumption that reflects a lack of familiarity with what was going on in the classrooms of Depression America. The problem with both Schrecker and Draper is that since they only study communist teachers and not conservatives or liberals, they do not understand that these non-radical teachers were every bit as biased in their classroom work as their radical counterparts. However one judges radical teachers in Depression America, their instructional work cannot be set into historical context unless it is recognized that during this turbulent era bias entered the classroom from all positions on the

political spectrum—right, left, and center. Unless this context is understood, we will never move beyond the unreality of this debate which casts communist teachers as either apolitical saints or indoctrinating sinners. On this debate see, Schrecker, *No Ivory Tower,* 43–44; Theodore Draper, "The Class Struggle: The Myth of the Communist Professors," *New Republic* (Jan. 26, 1987), 29–36.

32. Fifty-two of the 125 activists credited their family with facilitating their politicization. This pattern was remarkably similar to that found in studies of 1960s student activists. See Richard Flacks, "The Liberated Generation: An Exploration of the Roots of Student Protest," *Journal of Social Issues* (1967), 66–74; Kenneth Kenniston, *Young Radicals: Notes on Committed Youth* (New York, 1968), 51–76.

33. Joseph P. Lash interview with author; Celeste Strack Kaplan interview with author; Richard Criley interview with author. For photos attesting to the most non-bohemian style of dress among radical student organizers, see James Wechsler, "The Education of Bob Burke," *Student Advocate* (Oct.-Nov. 1936), 13; Joseph P. Lash, "Awakening at Oxford," *ibid.,* 23; "Striking for Students' Rights," *Student Review* (March 1933), 12–13; James Jackson, "We Tell the Congressmen," *Student Review* (June 1935), 5. The one major exception to the rule concerning generational conflict in the student movement occurred when the movement was declining in 1940. Here there was some generational conflict—or at least generational rhetoric was used by isolationist students to attack interventionists. Even in 1940, however, generational attacks (which proved quite transient) were directed neither at parents nor the older generation in general, but at teachers and administrators who had taken a strong anti-isolationist stance. This conflict will be discussed in Chapter 9.

34. *Program of the American Youth Congress* (New York, 1934), 5.

35. *Ibid.*; also on this rejection of generational rhetoric, see Gil Green, "A Communist Reply," *The Social Frontier* (May 1935), 22.

36. Former SLID activist Victor Reuther, for instance, devoted the first chapters in his memoirs to what was for him the inspiring story of his father's immigration to America and emergence as a labor militant and trade union organizer. See Reuther, *The Brothers Reuther,* 1–31.

37. Molly Yard autobiographical essay, JPL; Molly Yard interview with author.

38. Esther Feldman autobiographical essay, JPL.

39. Florence Dubroff autobiographical essay, JPL.

40. Mary Ann Loeser autobiographical essay, JPL.

41. Claire Lippman autobiographical essay, JPL.

42. Emily Shield autobiographical essay, JPL.

43. James E. Jackson interview with author.

44. Robert Lane and Betsy Pifer autobiographical essays, both in JPL.

45. P.A. Kitchell autobiographical essay, JPL.

46. Emily Shield autobiographical essay, JPL.

47. Betsy Pifer autobiographical essay, JPL.

48. Grace Smelo autobiographical essay, JPL.

49. Joseph P. Lash memoir typescript, Oct. 14, 1986, p. 7, JPL.

50. Bernard Wolf autobiographical essay, JPL.

51. Maxine Ture autobiographical essay; Stoyan Menton autobiographical essay, both in JPL.

52. Nancy Phillips autobiographical essay, JPL.

53. Jean Scott autobiographical essay, JPL; Paul Jacobs, *Is Curly Jewish?*, 17,

19. Generational conflict of a quieter, more ambiguous and subtle type than that impelling Jacobs's radicalism contributed to the radicalization of Arthur Miller. In his autobiography Miller notes that "I never raised my voice against my father." But the Depression's bite on the family income created tension between father and son. Miller recalled that "I knew perfectly well, it was not he who angered me, only his failure to cope with his fortune's collapse. Thus I had two fathers, the real one and the metaphoric, and the latter I resented because he did not know how to win out over the general collapse." Was the young Miller's radicalism a way of revolting against his father and the failing bourgeois role model he represented? In Miller's view the meaning of his radicalism was more complex than that: "If Marxism was on the metaphorical plane, a rational for parricide, I think that to me it was at the same time a way of forgiving my father, for it showed him as a digit in a kind of cosmic catastrophe that was beyond his powers to avoid" (Arthur Miller, *Timebends: A Life* (New York, 1987), 112, 114).

54. *NYT,* April 3, 1932.

55. UCLA *Daily Bruin,* Oct. 30, 1934; Philip Feldman to President Alexander Ruthven, Aug. 26, 1935, reprinted in Martin Anderson, "Interfering with Students," *Student Review* (Oct. 1935), 12–13; *Hunter Bulletin,* April 1, 1935.

56. *CCNY Office of the Dean Hearings, Oct. 10–Nov. 7, 1934,* vol. I, 63, 68, 70, 71, CCNY.

57. Mrs. Robert V. Russell to Frederick Robinson, Jan. 11, 1935, *CCNY Hearings,* vol. II.

58. *NYT,* April 23, 1936.

59. Celeste Strack Kaplan interview with author.

60. J.R. McMichael to Jack McMichael [n.d.], JM.

61. *Daily Californian,* Sept. 27, 1940.

62. Nancy Bedford Jones, "My Father Is a Liar!," *Student Review* (Oct. 1935), 13–15.

63. *Ibid.,* 13.

64. Howe, *A Margin of Hope,* 14; Alice Dodge autobiographical essay, JPL. In several cases students in our sampled group sought to avoid conflicts with conservative parents over their radical activism by keeping their leftist affiliations from them. (See Mary Ann Loeser autobiographical essay, JPL; Gerassi, *The Premature Anti-fascists,* 70.)

65. Howe, *A Margin of Hope,* 1–89; Jack McMichael, autobiographical essay, JM; James E. Jackson interview with author; Alice Dodge autobiographical essay, JPL.

66. *Revolt* (Dec. 1932), 3.

67. Scales and Nickson, *Cause at Heart,* 32–46.

68. UT Miller autobiographical essay; Ralph Meinking autobiographical essay; both in JPL.

69. Anonymous autobiographical essay, "A Rebel Is Born," JPL.

70. Terkel, *Hard Times,* 398, 400; F. Palmer Weber interview with author. Univ. of Michigan President Ruthven told the FBI that the campus ASU's membership had tended to come "from what has been characterized as the underprivileged group." See FBI Report #100–1217, Detroit, Feb. 8, 1943.

71. This was also the reason student organizers by the mid-1930s had come to recognize that economic campaigns alone would not be enough to mobilize their predominantly middle-class constituency. See Hal Draper interview with author, Albany, Calif., Oct. 26, 1981; Wechsler, *The Age of Suspicion,* 74.

72. Celeste Strack Kaplan interview with author. On affluent student radicals, also see Merton, *The Seven Storey Mountain,* 147; *Columbia Spectator,* Dec. 11, 1933.

73. White, *In Search of History,* 66

74. *Ibid.*

75. Wechsler, *The Age of Suspicion,* 28

76. Joseph R. De Martini, "Student Activists of the 1930s and 1960s: A Comparison of the Social Bases of the Two Student Movements," *Youth and Society* (June 1975), 408.

77. Celeste Strack Kaplan interview with author; Joseph Lash interview with author; Joseph P. Lash, "Action Notes," *Student Advocate* (April 1937), 25; "Action Notes," *ibid.* (Feb. 1937), 28.

78. Alice Dodge autobiographical essay, JPL. For other examples of such guilt feelings, see Leah Levinger, "We Shall Not Be Moved," *Student Advocate* (May, 1936), 15; Doris Yankauer and Herbert Mayer, *Question Before the House* (New York, 1935), 16–17, VC; James Wechsler interview with author.

79. Kay Martineau autobiographical essay, JPL.

80. Theodore Draper interview with author.

81. *NYT,* May 31, Sept. 6, 1936. By 1937, college placement officers, in an exuberant mood after months of economic progress, began to speak about the Depression in the past tense. See *NYT,* Jan. 10, July 4, 1937. Also see "To the Class of 1936," *Student Advocate* (Oct.-Nov. 1936), 14.

82. Lash, *Toward a Closed Shop on Campus,* 7. Lewis Corey, "Debunking the New Prosperity," *Student Advocate* (Oct.-Nov. 1936), 19–20, 27; "Pilgrimage to Washington," *ibid.* (Feb. 1937), 5; "Class of 1941;" *ibid.* (Oct. 1937), 3. On the returning crisis in the job market for graduates, see *NYT,* Oct. 2, 1938; Univ. of Toledo *Collegian,* Feb. 18, May 6, 1938.

83. Wechlser, *The Age of Suspicion,* 74.

84. Budd Shulberg, "Dartmouth Rejects the Academic Mind," *Student Advocate* (April 1936), 13, 30.

85. George Watt interview with author. Leslie Fiedler also recalled being attracted to the student movement because it offered a means of transcending his lower-class Jewish roots. See Fiedler, *Being Busted,* 20.

86. Paul Jacobs, *Is Curly Jewish?,* 18–19.

87. James E. Jackson interview with author.

88. Celeste Strack Kaplan interview with author; Toni Locke interview with author, Oakland, Calif., April 14, 1983.

89. Scales and Nickson, *Cause at Heart,* 60, 77.

90. Hal Draper to author, Dec. 10, 1981.

91. Molly Yard, memorial tribute to Joseph Lash in *Joseph P. Lash* (New York, 1987), 40, JPL. Lash's diary suggests that his support for women's rights was closely linked to his socialist idealism. He noted here that "socialism [was] much more than a materialisic creed. It had an ethos—stopped you from smoking, obliged you to treat women as . . . p[e]rsonalities not adjuncts . . ." Lash discovered, however, during a trip to Europe for a socialist student conference, that socialism did not lead all of its followers to support women's rights. He recalled being "surprised by the attitude of the young [European] Socialists towards women . They were not as good as men, they stoutly argued, [and] had special functions . . ." (Lash Diary, Dec. 4, 1934; Joseph P. Lash typescript memoirs, "A Trip," 26; both in JPL).

The earliest statement of support for women's rights within the American student movement came soon after the first stirrings of student activism in the Hoover era. The NSL's founding platform included a plank demanding "for women educational and professional opportunities equal to those of men" ("For a National Student Movement," *Student Review* (Jan.-Feb. 1932), 4).

92. *Columbia Spectator,* April 13, 1934; *Hunter Bulletin,* Dec. 12, 1933. Students also offered criticism of the treatment of women in fascist Italy. See *Hunter Bulletin,* Oct. 16, 1934.

93. Joseph Lash speech, minutes of the International Unification Conference of Socialist and Communist Students, Paris, July 15–18 [1937]; Report of Molly Yard, *Summary of N.E.C. Meeting September 11, 12, 13 [1937],* 4; both in JPL.

94. The one impressive feminist campaign of the ASU occurred not nationally, but locally, when the Chapel Hill ASU chapter petitioned for the admission of women to the University of North Carolina (*Daily Tar Heel,* Feb. 2, 11, 16, 1937). In contrast to this Chapel Hill chapter, the Harvard ASU ran an article in its magazine which—though urging "closer academic cooperation between Harvard men and Radcliffe women"—opposed the admission of women to Harvard on the grounds that "to suggest coeducation for Harvard would be as rash as advocating the admission of nuns into Franciscan monasteries" (G. Robert Stange, "The Harvard Women: A Study of Radcliffe Repression," *Harvard Progressive* (April 1940), 18). Here the contrast between race and gender is striking. No ASU chapter would have published such an anti-integration article on the race question— since racial discrimination was so vehemently and repeatedly denounced in ASU platforms and meetings.

95. Minutes of the International Unification Conference; Report of Molly Yard, *Summary of N.E.C. Meeting September 11, 12, 13 [1937],* 4.

96. Yard, memorial tribute to Joseph Lash, 40. Also see Howe, *A Margin of Hope,* 43–45.

97. Yard, memorial tribute to Joseph Lash, 40; the limits on feminist consciousness among both men and women in the student movement can be seen in "The Zest to Nest: Man-hunt at Vassar," published in the ASU's national magazine (*Student Advocate* (Dec. 1936), 10–11); Howe, *A Margin of Hope,* 44; Celeste Strack Kaplan interview with author; also see the *Student Advocate* story on the pioneers of women's education, America's "first co-eds" at Oberlin. The article paid tribute to these early female collegians for promoting "freedom and power," but the male author of this article also suggested that "Cupid" and husband hunting may have been responsible for "the first move of the female sex into the male-hallowed halls" (Ian McCreal, "Coeds-Model 1837 Four Females Invade Gentlemen's Sanctuary," *Student Advocate* (Dec. 1937), 19–20; also see "4.2 Husbands," *ibid.* (April 1937), 19; Bill Murrish, "Decline of American Womanhood," *ibid.* (Dec. 1937), 26; on Lash's suggestion that the Youth Congress chose "a Miss Young America to ride at the front" of its second march in Washington, see Joseph Lash to William Hinckley, March 3, 1938, JPL). Note that it took three years for the ASU to elect a women chair. Moreover, though women were elected to their national offices and committees, neither the NSL, the SLID nor the Youth Congress ever had a woman in their top executive post. This was also the case with the ASU national magazine, which throughout its life was edited by men.

Limited as it was, feminist consciousness in the student Left of the 1930s compares favorably with the sexism which prevailed during the early stages of the New Left student movement of the 1960s. When women in the Student Nonviolent Coordinating Committee (SNCC) and Students for a Democratic Society (SDS) first raised feminist issues in the 1960s, they encountered hostility and ridicule from their male comrades. But on those few occasions where such issues were raised by female student activists in the 1930s, they were given a respectful hearing. This was the case not only in the incident Yard discussed above with respect to Joseph Lash and the ASU chair, but also in the ASU's founding convention.

Helen Levy, an NSL delegate from Barnard College, objected on the floor of this first ASU convention that in the draft of the ASU's platform "no reference has been made to discrimination against women." The delegates reponded to Levy by indicating that they would "favor inclusion" of a plank against sexual discrimination, and referring her proposal to the ASU "program committee to include when they saw fit." No minutes from this committee have survived to indicate what discussions it held concerning the Levy proposal. The final ASU platform, which had an entire section on racial discrimination, did not have a specific plank against sexual discrimination. However, the program's one mention of gender was premised on the feminist assumption of equality between men and women. This came in the platform's section on "The Right to Education and Security," which declared, "we are not a lost generation. Unemployment is not inevitable. The continued progress of our nation requires the service of all its young men and *women.* It requires especially an increasing number of doctors, engineers teachers, and other professional groups [emphasis added]." ("American Student Union Program," *American Student Union Bulletin,* Jan. 6, 1936; ASU Convention Minutes, Saturday afternoon Session, 4., JPL; on the student Left of the 1960s and SNCC and SDS antipathy towards feminist demands, see Sarah Evans, *Personal Politics* (New York, 1979), 83–89; Todd Gitlin, *The Sixties: Years of Hope, Days of Rage* (New York, 1987), 362–76). In the Depression decade women also played an important leadership role in the Southern Negro Youth Congress. See Esther Cooper Jackson interview with author.

The Youth Committee Against War, the ASU's main rival on the student Left in the late 1930s, was slightly ahead of the ASU in empowering women. The first two students elected to the YCAW's top position (the national executive secretary) were females—Alvaine Hollister and Fay Bennett. And yet even in the YCAW, traditional sexist imagery appears in the organization's publications. For example, the YCAW's guide to its 1939 convention introduced Fay Bennett to the delegates as "the beauteous blond who charms people into cooperation and donation." Of the YCAW New England organizer, the guide notes that "a certain Yale man complained that it was unfair sending such a pretty girl to organize for the YCAW." None of the men listed in the guide had their physical attributes discussed (*National Youth Antiwar Congress* (Dec. 27–30, 1939), YCAW).

98. Elizabeth Dilling, *The Roosevelt Red Record and Its Background* (Chicago, 1936), 253. Echoing Dilling, the "business people of Urbana . . . complained to Sheriff Walker [of Urbana] because this organization [the Univ. of Illinois ASU branch] advocated allowing colored and white students to associate together and to eat at the same restaurants . . ." (FBI file #100–191, Feb. 1, 1941, Report made by W.A. Temple, Springfield).

99. Anon. student letter signed "100 percent for the Administration Students," to Provost E.C. Moore, Oct. 30, 1934, ECM.

100. Wechsler, *Revolt on the Campus,* 189, 361; Jim to Lute, Office of the Comptroller, April 7, 1933, President's Files, UCB; David O. Levine, *The American College and the Culture of Aspiration* (Ithaca, 1986), 156–57. Also, see "Red School-

houses: Young Jewish Reds in Control of American Student Union," *Social Justice* (Nov. 20, 1939), 9–10. This article, by an anti-Semitic Coughlinite, seeking to depict the ASU as the product of a Jewish radical conspiracy, was peppered with inaccuracies. Thus ASU National chair Molly Yard, a Protestant whose parents had both served as missionaries in China, and whose father was the Northwestern University chaplain, was labeled a "Jewess."

101. On Dartmouth's discrimination against Jewish applicants and on the anti-Semitism of Dartmouth's president in the 1930s and the 1940s, see Tamar Buschbaum, "A Note on Anti-Semitism in Admissions at Dartmouth," *Jewish Social Studies* (Winter 1987), 79–84.

102. On this ethnic dimension of the conflicts between radical students and conservative administrators, see Carl Schorske, "A New Yorker's Map of Cambridge," 11–20; Joseph P. Lash, "College—O Quae Mutatio Rerum," 40, JPL.

103. Molly Yard, "Action Notes," *Student Advocate* (Oct. 1937), 27.

104. John Kenneth Galbraith essay, in Irving Stone, ed., *There Was Light: Autobiography of a University, Berkeley, 1868–1968* (Berkeley, 1968), 28; *Columbia Spectator,* March 15, 1933; Monroe Sweetland interview with author; Wechsler, *The Age of Suspicion* (New York, 1981), 18–23; Dwight Croessman, "Fraternities Are Anti-Educational and Anti-Democratic," *Intercollegian and Far Horizons* (April 1940), 139–40. There is considerable evidence that college and university administrators saw the fraternity system as a political ally and strove to involve the Greek houses in anti-radical activism (Robert G. Sproul to Clifford Swan, June 5, 1941, President's Files, UCB; *University of Washington Daily,* Nov. 6, 1934).

105. May, *Coming to Terms,* 202

106. Harry Magdoff interview with author.

107. Nathan Solomon interview with author.

108. *Barnard College Bulletin,* Oct. 30, 1936.

109. Hal Draper, "The Student Movement of the Thirties: A Political History," in Rita Simon, ed. *As We Saw the Thirties* (Urbana, 1967), 182–89.

110. W. J. Boldt and J.B. Stroud, "Changes in the Attitudes of College Students," *Journal of Educational Psychology* (Nov. 1934), 616–19; Theodore R. Bramfeld, "College Students React to Social Issues," *Frontiers of Democracy* (Nov. 1934), 21–26; Walter Buck, "A Measurement of Changes in Attitudes and Interests of University Students in a Ten-Year Period," *Journal of Abnormal and Social Psychology* (April 1936), 12–19; H. H. Remmers and C. L. Morgan, "Changes in Liberalism and Conservatism of College Students Since the Depression," *Journal of Social Psychology* (1941), 99–107. When the radical party candidates are taken into account, the 1936 presidential race—as tracked in the college straw polls—reflects an even stronger student shift away from Republicanism. With Norman Thomas carrying 3.1 percent, Earl Browder 2.6 percent, the non-Republican vote (added with FDR's) was 54 percent on campus. See *Vassar Miscellany News,* Oct. 31, 1936. As the decade progressed, straw polls showed an even further erosion of Republican support nationally among college students. By December 1938 President Roosevelt's approval rating among collegians had soared to 62.8 percent, which was more than 7 percent higher than FDR's standing with the general electorate. A year later the President's approval rating among college students remained an impressive 61.9 percent. A May 1940 poll showed that only 39 percent of college students nationally said they favored the Republican party. See *Michigan Daily,* Dec. 15, 1939; Univ. of Toledo *Collegian,* May 10, 1940.

111. "Youth in College," *Fortune* (June 1936), 158.

112. Eunice Fuller Barnard, "The Class of '36 into a Baffling World," *NYT Magazine* (June 21, 1936), 20.

113. *National Student Mirror* (March 1935), 83; *ibid.* (April 1935), 116; *ibid.* (Feb. 1936), 41. In strongholds of student activism, such as the New York municipal colleges, the Left managed to dominate student government elections during the heyday of the student movement. See CCNY *Campus*, Feb. 18, 20, and 25, 1935; Brooklyn College *Vanguard*, March 20, May 15, 1936, Jan. 28, 1938.

114. *Vassar Miscellany News*, Dec. 6, 1939.

Chapter 9. From Popular Front to Unpopular Sect

1. On the general public response in the U.S. to these events the most comprehensive work is William L. Langer and S. Everett Gleason, *The Challenge to Isolation* (New York, 1952), vols. I and II.

2. The dominant trend in student opinion following the invasion of Poland was growing support for aid to England (and France until its fall), coupled with a passionate desire to keep the U.S. out of war. The students' hope was that such aid might stop Hitler and thereby make U.S. military intervention unnecessary. See *Michigan Daily*, Nov. 1, 11, 1939; Marshall Univ. *Parthenon*, Nov. 11, 1939; Olcutt [Saunders] to Robin [Myers], Oct. 18, 1940, YPSL files, SP; *Oberlin Review*, Nov. 12, 1940; *Columbia Spectator*, Oct. 24, 1940, Jan. 7, 1941; *NYT*, Feb. 8, 1941.

3. Joseph Lash, typescript memoir of ASU's collapse [n.d.], 1–3; Joseph Lash to Merle [Miller], Jan. 25, 1940; Joseph Lash to Monroe [Sweetland], Jan. 25, 1940; Joseph Lash to Max [Lerner], Sept. 6, 1939. All in JPL.

4. Joseph Lash to Lenore Carothers, Sept. 18, 1939, JPL.

5. *Fall Planning Conference, September 8–9, 1939* (New York, 1939), 4–5; Lash Diary, Sept. 12, 1939, both in JPL; *NYT*, Sept. 10, 1939.

6. Lash to Carothers, Sept. 18, 1939; *Fall Planning Conference, September 8–9, 1939*, 6.

7. Lash Diary, Sept. 12, 1939, JPL.

8. *Daily Worker*, Sept. 13, 1939. For useful summaries of the Communist Party leadership's confusion regarding the foreign policy implications of the Nazi-Soviet Pact from late Aug. through early Sept. 1939, see Harvey Klehr, *The Heyday of American Communism* (New York, 1986), 386–91; Joseph Lash, "The Pattern of Communist Action," JPL; "And the Communists Follow," *New Republic* (Sept. 13, 1939), 143.

9. *Ibid.*; The fullest student statement of this new isolationist position would later be published in *Student America Organizes for Peace: Proceedings of the Fifth Annual Convention, American Student Union* (New York, 1940), 1–4; James Wechsler, "Stalin and Union Square," *Nation* (Sept. 30, 1939), 342.

10. William Sussman to Joseph Lash [Sept.? 1939], JPL.

11. *Ibid.*; Lash Diary, Nov. 4, 1939, JPL.

12. Lash Diary, Nov. 4, 1939.

13. Lenore Carothers to Joseph Lash, Sept. 18, 1939, JPL.

14. Lash, typescript memoir of ASU's collapse, p. 3.

15. Joseph Lash to Bill [Sussman], Sept. 28, 1939; Lash Diary, Sept. 19, 1939, both in JPL. Also see, CCNY *Campus*, Sept. 29, 1939. On some campuses the

discord generated by the pact proved fatal to the ASU. See FBI file # 100–175, Jan. 24, 1941, Report made by William E. Moran Jr., Buffalo, N.Y.

16. Lash, ASU's collapse, 3; Lash Diary, Sept. 12, 1939, Oct. 8, 1939. "Individualism" was used by communist students as a pejorative, denoting excessive egotism and selfishness. They thought it profoundly egotistical for an individual such as Lash to assume that he knew better than the CP, the Comintern, and the USSR. Thus one of Lash's communist associates charged that he and other non-communists in the student movement were guilty of becoming "so infatuated with the idea . . . of thinking the way no one else does, of being able to change their minds with every passing fancy that they are now in the process of 'freeing' everyone from serious thought" (William Sussman to Joseph Lash [n.d.], JPL). Lash rejected this accusation and charged that it derived from the communist "tendency toward anti-intellectualism" (Lash to Lew Zuckerman, Oct. 12, 1939, JPL).

17. Lash, ASU's collapse, 3; Lash Diary, Sept. 12, Oct. 8, 11, 1939. Feelings of regret over this split within the movement affected not only Lash but also some of his communist critics. Among Lash's best friends in the movement at least one communist responded to his dissent by describing her own alarm over the decline of unity in the ASU. She privately pleaded with him to do all in his power to preserve that unity, and wrote that because of their friendship "I'd hate like Hell to see you on the other side of the barricade!"(Lenore [Carothers] to Joseph Lash, Nov. 24 [1939], JPL).

18. Lash, ASU's collapse, 3; also see, "Statement of Kenneth Born, Executive Secretary of the Chicago District of the American Student Union," press release, Dec. 18, 1939, JPL.

19. Daniel Bell, "Y.C.L. Puts Skids Under Joe Lash As Student Union Leader Deviates" [n.d.], JPL.

20. Lash Diary, Sept. 21, Oct. 8, 1939.

21. Joseph Lash to Bill [Sussman], Sept. 28, 1939, JPL.

22. *Ibid.*

23. Joseph P. Lash, *Eleanor Roosevelt: A Friend's Memoir* (Garden City, N.Y., 1964), 7–15.

24. Lash Diary, Nov. 4, 1939.

25. Hal Draper, "The Student Movement of the Thirties," in Rita Simon, ed. *As We Saw the Thirties* (Urbana, 1967) 175; National Student Department, Young People's Socialist League, "Bulletin #11," Chicago, Jan. 10, 1937, JPL.

26. *NYT*, Nov. 28, 1939.

27. Joseph P. Lash to Franklin D. Roosevelt, Sept. 25, 1939, reprinted in *Fall Planning Conference, September 8–9, 1939*.

28. Lash Diary, Sept. 25, 1939.

29. Minutes Administrative Committee of ASU National Executive Committee, Sept. 29, 1939, pp. 2–4, JPL.

30. *Ibid.*

31. *Ibid.*, 2–3.

32. "Armistice Day Statement Approved by the Administrative Committee—ASU," appendix to Oct. 5, 1939, NEC packet, JPL.

33. "Discussion on Armistice Day," ASU Administrative Committee Meeting Minutes, Nov. 17, 1939, 2–3, JPL.

34. *Youth Congress Against War News Bulletin*, Nov. 1939, YCAW.

35. "Discussion on Armistice Day," 2.

36. *Ibid.,* 3.

37. Langer and Gleason, *The Challenge to Isolation,* vol. I, 329–31; Ralph Ketchum, *The Borrowed Years, 1938–1941: America on the Road to War* (New York, 1989), 295–99. Majority opinion on campus was solidly behind Finland. A national campus poll, taken during the Soviet invasion, found 62 percent of American undergraduates favoring a U.S. loan to assist Finland—even though this would break with the longstanding policy of American neutrality (Univ. of Toledo *Collegian,* Feb. 4, 1940; "Soviet Aggression: A Condemnation," *Harvard Progressive* (Feb. 1940), 7, 11–12; *Michigan Daily,* Dec. 6, 1939). The communists' position on Finland had isolationist implications, since it opposed U.S. aid to Finland. But there was an important distinction between the communist and non-communist isolationist stance on Finland. Where the communists defended the Soviet invasion, non-communist isolationists—even though opposing a U.S. loan for Finland because this would violate their anti-interventionist policy—tended to view the invasion as an act of brutal aggression. Thus even the communists' potential allies in the isolationist camp were almost as angry about communist support of the invasion as the interventionists had been. See *Parthenon,* Feb. 6, 1940; *Dartmouth,* Feb. 27, 1940; *Daily Bruin,* March 19, 1940; *Oberlin Review,* Jan. 19, 1940; *Michigan Daily,* Jan. 11, 1940.

38. "Not to Finland or to France—This Yank Ain't Coming," Resolution passed by Enlarged Conference of College and High School Leaders of the New York District of the ASU, Dec. 9, 1939, JPL.

39. Robert L. Klein to Joseph Lash, Dec. 23, 1939, JPL. For a similar reaction at other key ASU strongholds, see *Harvard Crimson,* Dec. 12, 1939; *Columbia Spectator,* Nov. 29, 1939; *Michigan Daily,* Dec. 3, 1939. At the Univ. of Connecticut, the ASU chapter "broke up on the issue of the Russian invasion of Finland" (FBI Report on ASU [file number and reporting agent's name illegible], New Haven, Aug. 22, 1941).

40. *NYT,* Dec. 10, 1939. Lash was, however, careful to couple his criticisms of the invasion with opposition to reactionaries, who sought to use the Finnish events as the pretext for whipping up anti-communist hysteria in the U.S. Nonetheless, the invasion deepened Lash's disillusionment with the Soviet Union and the CP. Lash found it painful to "grapple honestly with the problems created by Russian aggression in Finland. For one of the terrible results of that aggression is that socialism . . . no longer in the minds of common men everywhere means . . . a warless world. . . . The Russian invasion of Finland [and] the CP apologies for it here have become so nauseating that one wants to get away to where people are plain rather than machiavellian. . . . It seems to me that the communist movement now has reached a point where it has made so many compromises which it has called tactical changes, resorted to so many ruthless and horrible means in the name of socialist objectives, that it has lost all significance as a movement of principle and justice" (Joseph Lash to Ed [Newman], March 13, 1940; Joseph Lash to Monroe Sweetland, Jan. 25, 1940; both in JPL).

41. Quentin Young to Joseph Lash, Dec. 2, 1939, JPL.

42. Joseph Lash to Quentin Young, Dec. 8, 1939, JPL.

43. Lash, ASU's collapse, 4; "Important! Memo on Place of Convention," Nov. 29, 1939; Executive Committee of the MIT ASU Chapter, "Don't Split the American Student Union"; Open letter from Vassar College chapter, American Student Union, Dec. 14, 1939. All in JPL.

44. Lash to Young, Dec. 8, 1939.

45. Molly Yard, Agnes Reynolds, Joseph P. Lash, "Save the American Student Union" [Dec. 1939], JPL.

46. *Ibid.*

47. *Ibid.*

48. Alan Otten to Joseph Lash, Dec. 10, 1939; Lash to Otten, Dec. 11, 1939. Also on the problem of non-communists dropping out of the ASU "because of intransigent YCL tactics," see Ray Mildernberger to Joseph Lash, Dec. 18, 1939. All in JPL.

49. James Wechsler, "Politics on the Campus," *Nation* (Dec. 30, 1939), 732.

50. *Ibid.*, 732–33.

51. Daniel Bell, "Y.C.L. Puts Skids Under Joe Lash."

52. Joe Havens to Joseph Lash, Dec. 18, 1939, JPL.

53. Thelma Grafstein to Joseph Lash [Dec. 1939], JPL. On other examples of communist maneuvers to keep their critics out of the ASU convention, see *Wisconsin Soapbox*. Dec. 1939, JPL.

54. Irwin Ross, "The Student Union and the Future," *New Republic* (Jan. 8, 1940), 48; *Student America Organizes for Peace*, 1–3.

55. *Nation* (Jan. 6, 1940), 3.

56. "The Meeting of the ASU," *New Republic* (Jan. 8, 1940), 37. The official communist interpretation of the Madison convention was, of course, much more upbeat. The ASU, in the communists' view, had taken a principled and popular anti-war position at Madison. The ASU's isolationist line and the convention's stance against those using Finland to whip up anti-Soviet war hysteria would, according to the communists, prove highly popular with American undergraduates. From communist accounts of the convention one would never guess that the ASU was in crisis and that it was on the verge of losing its campus base. See Milton Meltzer, "Collegians Reject War Racket," *New Masses* (Jan. 9, 1940), 12–13; "Students United Against War," *ibid.* (Jan. 16, 1940), 31.

57. *Oberlin Review,* Jan. 16, 1940. Attacks on the ASU for its refusal to criticize Soviet aggression pervaded the student press following the 1939 ASU convention. The *Ohio State Lantern* termed the convention's decision on this issue "incredibly stupid," and an act of "harikari"—taken because of the organization's "slavish devotion" to the USSR (*Ohio State Lantern*, Jan. 5, 1940; for similar criticism, see *Dartmouth*, Jan. 10, 1940; *University Daily Kansan*, Jan. 5, 1940; *Parthenon*, Jan. 16, 1940).

58. Joseph Lash to Max [Lerner], Jan. 8, 1940; Merle Miller to Joseph Lash, Jan. 19 [1940]; Lee McIntosh to Joseph Lash [n.d.]; Herbert B. Ross to Joseph Lash, Jan. 2, 1939 [1940]; Joseph Lash to Chad Walsh, Jan. 10, 1940. All in JPL. Even after the communist triumph at Madison, Lash, now an ASU alumnus, tried (but usually failed) to persuade non-communists to stay in the ASU and attempt to reverse its policies instead of dropping out of the organization (see Joseph Lash to Ed Newman, Feb. 14, 1940, JPL). On the collapse of the Pittsburgh ASU following the convention, see FBI report on ASU [file number illegible] by E. L. Boyle, April 1, 1941.

59. Chad Walsh to Joseph Lash, Jan. 12, 1940; American Student Union Addenda on National Referendum, March 1940, both in JPL.

60. Alan K. Gottlieb to Joseph Lash, May 5, 1940, Lash to Alan Gottlieb, March 13, 1940; John Sterling Stillman to American Student Union, Jan. 2, 1940. All in JPL. ASU membership in the spring of 1940 had, according to Gottlieb,

fallen to under 5,000, "about half of whom are in New York City." Only 3,000 ASUers would vote on the Finland referendum—evidence of how quickly the ASU (which once boasted some 20,000 members) was dissolving. It is, however, striking that even in this shrunken and communist-dominated ASU the vote was not nearly so pro-Soviet as the Madison convention had been. Where the Convention had by a 6–1 margin rejected the resolution criticizing of the Soviet invasion of Finland, the ASU membership in the March referendum rejected that resolution by only a 2–1 margin. This only hints, however, at how unrepresentative the 1939 ASU convention had been; for had the 15,000 or so non-communists not already left the ASU, this resolution would surely have won a resounding victory in the referendum (Gottlieb to Lash, May 5, 1940)). On the decline of the ASU, also see [Jack] Sessions Supplementary Statement, March 1940; [Robin Myers] to Al Lewis, Oct. 21, 1940; both in YPSL files, SP. By the time of the next ASU convention, the organization's national membership had sunk below 2,000 (Robert G. Spivack, "Youth Reorganizes," *Nation* (Jan. 18, 1941), 72; the FBI reports at the campus level confirm this picture of a collapsing membership. See FBI file # 100–476, Jan. 31, 1941, Report made by H. A. King, Portland, Ore.; FBI [file number illegible], Feb. 7, 1941, Report made by F.C. Dorwart, San Diego; FBI file # 61–327, Feb. 1, 1941, Report made by F. Schmidt, Chicago, which found that even in Chicago—the ASU's most active Midwestern city—membership no longer exceeded 100).

61. *NYT,* Feb. 4, 1940; on the manipulative tactics used by communist Youth Congress leaders to reverse the AYC's peace policy—without a vote from the full Youth Congress—see Josiah R. Bartlett's letter of resignation from the Youth Congress, Oct. 16, 1939; similar criticism and communist response to it can be found in Minutes of American Youth Congress Cabinet Meeting, Feb. 21, 1940; both in JPL.

62. Minutes of the American Youth Congress Cabinet Meeting, Feb. 21, 1940; "Draft Proceedings of the Citizenship Institute," Feb. 9–12, 1940, JPL.

63. Lash Diary, Jan. 14, Feb. 9, 1940, JPL.

64. *NYT,* Feb. 11, 1940.

65. *Ibid.*

66. *Ibid.*; Lash, *Eleanor Roosevelt: A Friend's Memoirs,* 57–58.

67. "Youth Congress in Washington Hears President Roosevelt Tell Them They're All Wet," *Life* (Feb. 26, 1940), 17; Joseph P. Lash, *Eleanor and Franklin* (New York, 1971), 596–611. In the aftermath of the confrontation with the president at the Citizenship Institute, the Youth Congress got such bad press that its leadership had to devote considerable energy to rebutting these press attacks (see "All the News That Misfits They Print," *Citizenship in Action: A Report of the American Youth Congress Institute—Washington, D.C., February 9–12, 1940,* 5–10; Abbot Simon to Eleanor Roosevelt, Feb. 20, 1940, JM). The one eloquent defense of the young activists came not from such pamphlets, but from folksinger Woody Guthrie, a supporter of the new CP line, who responded to FDR's speech by writing one of his better known anti-war songs, "Why Do You Stand There in the Rain?" (Joe Klein, *Woody Guthrie* (New York, 1980), 144–45). The Institute also drew criticism because its leaders sought to stifle dissent from participants—barring consideration of resolutions criticizing the invasion of Finland (see "Supplementary Memo on Undemocratic Practices Within the A.Y.C." (Spring 1940), YPSL files, SP).

68. *Michigan Daily,* Feb. 20, 1940; *Nation* (Feb. 17, 1940), 236–37; "All the

News That Misfits They Print," 5–10; Morris Milgram, "Behind the News of the A.Y.C.," draft article for *Socialist Call* [1940], YPSL files, SP.

69. Eleanor Roosevelt, *This I Remember* (New York, 1948), 199–205; Winifred Wandersee, "ER and American Youth: Politics and Personality in a Bureaucratic Age," in Joan Hoff-Wilson and Marjorie Lightman, eds., *Without Precedent: The Life and Career of Eleanor Roosevelt* (Bloomington, 1984), 73–78.

70. *NYT*, Dec. 3, 1939; Roosevelt, *This I Remember*, 202; William Leuchtenburg, *Franklin D. Roosevelt and the New Deal* (New York, 1963), 280.

71. *NYT*, Dec. 3, 1939; Freda Kirchwey, "Taming Mr. Dies," *Nation* (Dec. 16, 1939), 669–70.

72. James Wechsler, *The Age of Suspicion* (New York, 1981), 72.

73. Roosevelt, *This I Remember*, 200.

74. For Mrs. Roosevelt's public statement denying any links between Cadden, Hinckley, and the Communist Party, see *NYT*, Oct. 11, 1939. On at least eight separate occasions Mrs. Roosevelt, between fall 1939 and June 1940, denied that communists had any special influence over the Youth Congress. For these statements, see *NYT*, Oct. 11, Nov. 22, Dec. 5, 1939, Feb. 6, March 22, June 12, July 6, 1940; Eleanor Roosevelt typescript of article on the American Youth Congress for *Liberty* magazine, JPL. That the First Lady erred on the question of communist influence over the Youth Congress—and that these two Youth Congress leaders were secret communists—was later confirmed by several key organizers in the movement. Gil Green, who headed the YCL in this era and helped coordinate communist strategy among the Youth Congress national leadership, told me that both Cadden and Hinckley were recruited into the communist ranks as Youth Congress leaders, along with most of the other Youth Congress chairmen. (On Cadden's Communist Party ties, see Gil Green interview with author; David Dubinsky to Eleanor Roosevelt, June 20, 1940, ER; "An Analysis of the American Youth Congress Convention at Lake Geneva, Wisconsin, July 3–7, 1940," YPSL files, SP; Daniel Bell, "Liberals Shun A.Y.C. Parley as Communist Front," July 13, 1940, JPL; Harvey Klehr, *The Heyday of American Communism* (New York, 1984), 321, 468; Lewis Conn, "The American Youth Congress," *YPSL Organizer*, March 7, 1940. Note, however, that in his correspondence with Mrs. Roosevelt and other New Dealers, Cadden denied that he was a communist and claimed that the Youth Congress was no closer to the Communist Party than it was to the Democratic or Republican parties. See Joseph Cadden to Eleanor Roosevelt, July 1, 1940, ER; Joseph Cadden to Charles Taussig, Nov. 20, 1939, and Memorandum Re: letters to the Communist Party [n.d], Charles Taussig Papers, FDR Library, Hyde Park, N.Y.)

Although I find Green's memoir and the other evidence convincing, technically they do not "prove" that Cadden and Hinckley were YCL or CP members. One can only be definitive about such membership for those who were open about their CP affiliations at the time—such as Celeste Strack—or those who have since acknowledged those affiliations—such as James Wechsler. Those who kept their Party affiliation secret did so intentionally to obscure the record, and to an extent succeeded. While the actual Party *membership* of these Youth Congress leaders cannot be incontrovertibly proven, there is no question at all about their partisan *behavior;* they helped lead the pro-CP faction in the Youth Congress and hid this from Mrs. Roosevelt. (On Cadden, see Josiah R. Bartlett to member organizations, American Youth Congress, Oct. 16, 1939; Bob to Louise Meyerowtiz, April 9, 1940; both in JPL; Morris Milgram, "Behind the News of the AYC" [Feb. 1940],

YPSL files, SP; Minutes American Youth Congress Cabinet meeting, Jan. 18, Feb. 21, May 4, 1940, JPL; Joseph Lash diary, March 6, May 15, 1938, Sept. 14, 1939, Feb. 19, 22, March 21 and 22, Oct. 6, 1940; Joseph Lash to Joseph Cadden, March 16, 1940, JPL. Joseph Cadden to Eleanor Roosevelt, May 16, 1940, JM; minutes of confidential conversation between Joseph P. Lash and Max Weiss [n.d], JPL; M.J. [McKay] to Joe [Lash], April 5, 1940, in JPL; Report of meeting between Joseph Lash and Joseph Cadden, Sept. 11, 1941, JPL; Joseph Cadden to Eleanor Roosevelt, May 5, 1941, JM; Lorena Hickok to Eleanor Roosevelt, in Joseph P. Lash, *Love Eleanor: Eleanor Roosevelt and Her Friends* (Garden City, N.Y., 1982), 306; on Hinckley, see Al Hamilton to Norman Thomas, June 30, 1937, NT; George Rawick, "The New Deal and Youth," 336–37; Bill Hinckley to Joe [Lash], March 13, 1937, JPL; Klehr, *The Heyday of American Communism,* 321.)

75. *NYT,* Oct. 11, 1939; Lash Diary, Jan. 14, 16, 1940; Eleanor Roosevelt, "Students Union Attitude Reflects that of Elders," "My Day" column, Jan. 17, 1940, reprinted in *Student America Organizes for Peace,* appendix.

76. Vivian Liebman, "Cabinet Wives Contribute Housing for Youth Congress Leadership," American Youth Congress press release [Feb. 1940], JPL; Lash, *Eleanor Roosevelt: A Friend's Memoirs,* 74; Minutes, American Youth Congress Cabinet meeting, Feb. 21, 1940, JPL

77. Roosevelt, *This I Remember,* 200–204. In the months following the Citizenship Institute about two-thirds of the large youth groups that had been affiliated with the Youth Congress withdrew from the AYC (Spivack, "Youth Reorganizes," 72; *NYT,* April 13, May 14, July 3, Sept. 1, Nov. 18, 1940; also on the decline of the Youth Congress, see "The AYC and the Youth Movement" [Spring 1940]; YPSL Eastern NEC Meeting Minutes, Feb. 25, 1940; "Socialists Leave the Youth Congress" [YPSL pamphlet], July 1, 1940; Lewis Conn to Eleanor Roosevelt, July 5, 1940. All in YPSL files, SP; *NYT,* Dec. 31, 1940, and Jan. 31, 1941); Associated College Press report in *Parthenon,* March 1, 1940.

78. Lash, *Love Eleanor,* 286.

79. Joseph Lash Diary, Sept. 12, 1939, JPL.

80. Thelma Grafstein to Joseph Lash [Dec. 1939], JPL.

81. Joseph Lash to Lenore [Carothers], Oct. 19, 1939; Joseph Lash to Lee, Jan. 6, 1940, both in JPL.

82. *Ibid.*

83. Joseph Lash to Betty Sammons, Feb. 14, 1940, JPL.

84. Lash to Lenore [Carothers], Oct. 19, 1939; Lash to Lee, Jan. 6, 1940; Lash to Sammons, Feb. 14, 1940. All in JPL. For a valuable summary of this discontinuity in Communist behavior in the student movement before and after the Pact, see Connie Driusch to Bob [Jan. ? 1940], JPL. Lash does, however, seem to have overstated the degree to which communists abandoned their role as an organized faction within the ASU in the year prior to the Pact. At the Chapel Hill ASU chapter, for instance, the YCL at this time still served as a "wheel within a wheel," running the local ASU, according to a leading member of this chapter. Because Lash in this era was so close to Gil Green and trusted by the YCL, there was no need for the YCL to exert any pressure on him or to conduct active factional struggles at the ASU national office—giving Lash the mistaken impression that the YCL on campus had abandoned its role as an organized faction within the ASU (Joseph P. Lash interview with author; Scales and Nickson, *Cause at Heart,* 61).

85. [Robin Myers] to Hazel [Whitman], Oct. 29, 1940, YPSL files, SP.

86. On the resurgence of redbaiting following the Nazi-Soviet Pact, see *No Lights Out Here* (New York, 1939), 1–4; Ellen Schrecker, *No Ivory Tower* (New York, 1986), 71–83.

87. *Dartmouth,* Nov. 13, 1939; *Oberlin Review,* April 12, 1940; *No Lights Out Here,* 6; minutes of the Fourth National Youth Anti-War Congress, Dec. 27, 1940, YCAW; Deans of the College of the University of Wisconsin to Local Branch, Youth Committee Against War, Oct. 1940, President Clarence A. Dykstra Papers, UWISC.

88. *Columbia Spectator,* April 22, 1940; *NYT,* April 20, 1940. *Daily Californian,* April 29, 1940. The YPSL reported at this time that "outside of New York City, the ASU practically doesn't exist except where the YCL has a unit which calls itself the ASU" (*YPSL Organizer,* March 20, 1940).

89. Archibald MacLeish, "Post War Writers and Pre-war Readers," *New Republic* (June 10, 1940), 789–90; Charles Seymour, "War's Impact on the Campus," *NYT Magazine* (Sept. 29, 1940), 3, 15; Arnold Whitridge, "Where Do You Stand? An Open Letter to American Undergraduates," *Atlantic Monthly* (Aug. 1940), 133–37; Paul P. Cram, "Undergraduates and the War," *Atlantic Monthly* (Oct. 1940), 410–21.

90. *NYT,* May 26, 1940; Whitridge, "Where Do You Stand?," 133.

91. Harold Ickes, *The Secret Diary of Harold Ickes—Vol. III The Lowering Clouds* (New York, 1954), 179.

92. *Columbia Spectator,* April 18, 1940.

93. *Vassar Miscellany News,* Sept. 30, 1939.

94. *NYT,* May 26, 1940; *Dartmouth,* June 16, 1940; Franklin D. Roosevelt to Roger B. Merriman, May 20, 1940, in *Franklin D. Roosevelt: His Personal Papers,* vol. II, Elliot Roosevelt, ed. (New York, 1950), 1028.

95. UCLA *Daily Bruin,* May 14, 1940; *Dartmouth,* Dec. 29, 1939, May 24, 1940; *University Daily Kansan,* May 22, 1940; Irwin Ross, "College Students and the War," *New Republic* (July 15, 1940), 80.

96. James B. Conant, *My Several Lives* (New York, 1970), 217–18; *Dartmouth,* May 27, 1940.

97. *NYT,* June 20, 1940. Harvard's clash between interventionist alumni and isolationist students had reverberations that extended well beyond Harvard Yard. Only a day after Sigourney had been almost booed off the stage, a group of Harvard alumni used the gathering of their fellow graduates in Cambridge as the occasion for announcing the formation of a movement to prepare the nation for military conflict. This movement, under the auspices of the National Emergency Committee of the Military Training Camp Association, agitated for the introduction of conscription legislation in Congress—which in fall 1940 culminated in the establishment of the first peacetime military draft in American history. See *NYT,* June 21, 1940; J. Garry Clifford and Samuel R. Spencer Jr., *The First Peacetime Draft* (Lawrence, Kan., 1986), 1–130.

98. MacLeish, "Post War Writers and Pre-war Readers," 789–90.

99. *YCAW Bulletin,* Dec. 1939, YCAW; Ross, "College Students and the War," 80.

100. Clifford and Spencer, *The First Peacetime Draft,* 132. On the YCAW's rationale for opposing the draft, see *Conscription and Liberty* (New York, 1940), passim, YCAW.

101. *Michigan Daily,* Oct. 17, 1940; *Columbia Spectator,* Oct. 17, 1940; *YCAW News Bulletin* Oct., Nov.-Dec. 1940.

102. *YCAW News Bulletin,* Dec. 1939; *Oberlin Review,* Nov. 12, 1940; *Columbia Spectator,* Oct. 24, 1940; *NYT,* Feb. 8, 1941; *Parthenon,* Oct. 25, 1940; The YCAW's national leadership—aware that isolationism still had considerable support on campus—found their organization's inability to attract members and financial contributions "shocking" (Minutes of Special All Day Action Committee Meeting, May 4, 1940, YCAW; also on the YCAW'S inability to mobilize students, see [field report] to Jack Sessions, Oct. 1, 1940, YPSL files, SP).

103. *Michigan Daily,* Nov. 7, 1940; *Ohio State Lantern,* Oct. 15, 1940, and Jan. 7, 1941.

104. *Ohio State Lantern,* April 21, 1941. On student support for draft exemptions for undergraduates, see Univ. of Toledo *Collegian,* Sept. 27, Oct. 11, 1940; UCLA *Daily Bruin,* Feb. 21, 1941; *Ohio State Lantern,* April 7, 1941.

105. Wayne S. Cole, *America First: The Battle Against American Intervention in World War II* (Madison, 1953), 10–16.

106. Whitridge, "Where Do You Stand?," 133–37; Kingman Brewster, Jr., and Spencer Klaw, "We Stand Here," *Atlantic Monthly* (Sept. 1940), 277–79.

107. Whitridge, "Where Do You Stand?," 134; Conant, *My Several Lives,* 222.

108. Joseph P. Lash, "ISS and the Youth Movement," *ISS Bulletin,* Feb. 1941, JPL.

109. Ketchum, *The Borrowed Years,* 468.

110. Spivack, "Youth Reorganizes," 71–73; Joseph Lash, "ISS and the Youth Movement"; Lash, *Eleanor: A Friend's Memoir,* 220–26; "International Student Service and National Student Federation Agree to Pool Efforts," press release [n.d.], JPL.

111. *Dartmouth,* Nov. 31, 1940; UCLA *Daily Bruin,* Feb. 17, 1941; *Columbia Spectator,* Oct. 24, 1940; Univ. of Toledo *Collegian,* Feb. 14, 1941; *Daily Calfornian,* Feb. 10, 1941.

112. *Dartmouth,* Nov. 8, 1940; memorandum from Irwin Ross to Joseph P. Lash on trip to Cambridge Dec. 15–18 [1940], JPL; *NYT,* Feb. 9, 1941.

113. Special Bulletin on the Youth Strike Against War, April 3, 1941, YCAW.

114. *NYT,* April 24, 1941; Ketchum, *The Borrowed Years,* 512; UCLA *Daily Bruin,* April 28, 1941; *YPSL Organizer,* March 20, 1940; on the Youth Congress's decline in affiliates, see FBI Report # 100–358–7127, Feb. 14–21, 1941. Another sign of the movement's decline could be seen in the wild exaggerations its organizers made about strike turnout in order to save face. Nationally, strike organizers told the press that more than 500,000 students struck—a claim that was not and could not have been backed by any evidence, since the strike turnout was actually minuscule. Similar exaggerations went on at the local level. At Berkeley, for instance, strike organizers claimed that 3500 students rallied on behalf of an isolationist U.S. policy. But in fact fewer than a thousand students attended this strike rally, and more than two-thirds of those present opposed the isolationist resolutions proposed by the Youth Congress leaders. (See *Daily Californian,* April 24, 1941; Hurford E. Stone to President Sproul, April 30, 1941, Student Activities Office files, Sproul Hall, UC Berkeley.)

115. *NYT,* April 24, 1941; *New York Herald-Tribune,* April 24, 1941. On the chilling effect of Rapp-Coudert on student politics, see *Brooklyn College Vanguard,* Dec. 20, 1940, Jan. 7, 1941. With hostility towards the CP growing in the wake of the the Nazi-Soviet Pact, some New York students opposed the strike not only because it was isolationist, but also because it was communist-led (see *New York Herald-Tribune,* April 24, 1941). This surge of anti-communism also hurt the stu-

dent movement at Berkeley, where concern about the ASU's secret links to the Communist Party led the student government to revoke the ASU's campus recognition shortly before the 1941 student strike (see *Daily Californian* April 9, 1941). Similarly, at Ohio State Univ., the student government investigated and reprimanded the ASU chapter shortly after the strike (*Ohio State Lantern,* April 25, 29, 1941).

116. *NYT,* April 24, 1941; *New York Herald-Tribune,* April 24, 1941.

117. *Dartmouth,* April 23, 1941. Interventionist student activists also challenged their isolationist counterparts on the radio. See Agnes Reynolds, Joseph P. Lash, and William Bundy's transcribed remarks in "Shall We Convoy War Materials to Great Britain?," *The American Forum of the Air* (April 13, 1941), 1–6, JPL. The size and organizational skill of the anti-isolationist student groups should not, however, be exaggerated. The SDD, ISS, and other student aid to Britain groups never built their organizations up to anything approaching the level of the Popular Front era ASU. They managed to put their isolationist rivals on the defensive thanks largely to the fact that such events as the fall of France and the Battle of Britain had already weakened isolationism as a political force both on campus and off. Relative to the student movement in the previous decade, one would say of the early 1940s that student activism was dying out: small interventionist groups on campus were prevailing over a deteriorating isolationist movement (see Lash Diary, March 8, June 8, 1941, JPL).

Anti-isolationist student groups did not become mass organizations because to generate mass protest, students must have a strong incentive—a sense that their activism is really necessary. But such incentive was lacking by 1941. With isolationism declining and the President heading toward intervention, students who supported an expanded U.S. role in the fight against fascism had little to protest about since the policies they preferred were already in ascendance.

118. *Dartmouth,* Nov. 3, 1941; "Switch," *Time* (Oct. 13, 1941), 68–69.

119. For examples of collegiate ridiculing of the Communists for their flip-flops and subservience to Moscow's foreign policy, see *Ohio State Lantern,* Oct. 24, 30, 1941; UCLA *Daily Bruin,* Oct. 13, 1941; *YCAW News Bulletin* Aug. 1, 1941.

120. *Dartmouth,* Nov. 3, 1941.

121. Clifford and Spencer, *The First Peacetime Draft,* 138; Murray Kempton, *Part of Our Time: Some Monuments and Ruins of the Thirties* (New York, 1955), 303.

122. Joseph P. Lash, "New Directions for Youth," *Threshold* (Oct. 1941), 13.

123. Memorandum to the Executive Committee of the ISS Concerning a Proposed Merger of Several Student Action Groups [1941], JPL. Nor was such thinking confined to liberal interventionists. Throughout the final years of the student movement, the YCAW, led by socialists and pacifists, also had an exclusionary policy—refusing to cooperate with communist-led organizations. See *YPSL Torch,* Feb. 16 and March 12, 1940, YPSL files, SP.

124. Lash, "New Directions for Youth," 13.

125. *Ibid.,* 13–15, 34; the most vivid account of Lash's encounter with the Dies committee is John Oakes's tribute in *Joseph P. Lash* (New York, 1987), 36–37, JPL.

126. Joseph P. Lash, "ISS and the Youth Movement," *ISS Bulletin,* Feb. 1941; Lash, "New Directions for Youth," *Threshold* (Oct. 1941), 13. Louis Harris tribute to Lash, *Joseph P. Lash,* 24.

127. Young Communist *Review* (Dec. 23, 1940), 1; Joseph Cadden to Eleanor Roosevelt, May 5, 1941, JM; Lash, *Eleanor Roosevelt—A Friend's Memoir,* 230.

128. See Lash Diary, Dec. 19, 1940, on his refusal to cooperate with the Rapp-Coudert red probe, JPL.

129. Some of the leading figures in Lash's and the socialist wings of the student movement were led by this exclusionist mindset to play leading roles in promoting anti-communist politics during the Cold War era. They became founders of the Cold War liberal group, Americans for Democratic Action (ADA). One of the hallmarks of ADA liberalism was non-cooperation with communist-led organizations. By the early 1950s, the ADA was supporting President Truman's anti-communist loyalty oath program. On the role of former 1930s student activists in founding the ADA, see Monroe Sweetland interview with author; Wechsler, *The Age of Suspicion,* 211–12. On the ADA's grim record on civil liberties during the Cold War era, see Athan Theoharis, "The Politics of Scholarship: Liberals, Anti-Communism and McCarthyism," in Robert Griffith and Athan Theoharis, eds., *The Specter: Original Essays on the Cold War and the Origins of McCarthyism* (New York, 1974), 268–70.

130. Todd Gitlin, *The Sixties: Years of Hope, Days of Rage* (New York, 1987), 177, 183. Not all veterans of the Depression era student movement took so hostile a view of the anti-war movement of the 1960s. A small but vocal segement of 1930s movement veterans retained their radical or pacifist principles, and they supported the new student movement as well as the protests against the Vietnam War. Pacifist leader David Dellinger was the most prominent in this group. Dellinger, who had been a pacifist organizer at Yale in his student days before World War II, was so major a figure in the anti-war movement of the 1960s that the government chose to indict him—making him one of the defendants in the Chicago Seven conspiracy trial. See Charles DeBenedetti, *An American Ordeal: The Anti-War Movement of the Vietnam Era* (Syracuse, 1990), 24, 117, 189, 224–25, 282.

The most direct and unfortunate link between the student movement of the 1930s and the Vietnam War was provided by Dean Rusk. As a Rhodes scholar, Rusk was at Oxford University when the students took their pacifist oath not to fight for King and Country. Rusk later looked back on such anti-interventionism as not just wrong headed, but tragic in that it allowed the Nazis to feel that they could proceed with their aggression undeterred by the Western democracies. As Lyndon Johnson's Secretary of State, Rusk applied this lesson from the 1930s to Indochina in the 1960s, acting in Vietnam on the assumption that aggression had to be stopped immediately if another World War II-style cataclysm was to be avoided. But like the students in the early 1930s, who misunderstood the coming war by mechanistically applying "lessons" learned from the previous world war, Rusk did the same thing in Vietnam—mistakenly casting Ho Chi Minh as Hitler, misreading a civil war as a war of foreign aggression, and responding to the regional power of Vietnam as if it represented some Axis-style global threat. On Rusk's Oxford experience and its impact on his thinking about Vietnam, see Stanley Karnow, *Vietnam: A History* (New York, 1983), 179.

Index